The Dead Sea Scrolls Translated

FLORENTINO GARCÍA MARTÍNEZ

The Dead Sea Scrolls Translated

The Qumran Texts in English

Wilfred G. E. Watson   Translator

E. J. Brill   Leiden   New York   Cologne

Cover illustration: 11QTemple Scroll[a], cols 15-16 (translation on pages 156-157)
Copyright Bruce and Kenneth Zuckerman, West Semitic Research
Rolling Hills Estates, California, USA

Original title: *Textos de Qumrán*
Copyright © 1992 by Editorial Trotta SA, Madrid, Spain

English Edition (with corrections and additions)
Copyright © 1994 by E. J. Brill, Leiden, the Netherlands

Printed in the Netherlands

Library of Congress Cataloging-in-Publication Data

Dead Sea scrolls. English
The Dead Sea scrolls translated: the Qumran texts in English /
by Florentino García Martínez.
p. cm.
Includes bibliographical references and index.

ISBN 90 04 10048 2 (pbk.). –ISBN 90 04 10088 1 (cloth)

I García Martínez. Florentino II Title.
BM487.A3 1994
296. 1'55–dc20

94-17429 CIP

Die Deutsche Bibliothek – CIP-Einheitsaufname

The Dead Sea scrolls translated : The Qumran texts in English /
by Florentino García Martínez. – Leiden ; New York ; Köln : Brill, 1994

ISBN 90-04-10088-1 Gewebe   ISBN 90-04-10048-2 kart.
NE: García Martínez, Florentino [Bearb.]

WG: 12;13 /5221   DBN: 94.090756.9 /WT   94.04.14

Contents

Preface to the English Translation & Translator's Note

Between the publication of the first Spanish edition of *Textos de Qumrán* in November 1992 and the appearance of this English translation, research on the manuscripts from Qumran has proceeded at a faster pace and its fruits can be found collected here.

Of particular importance has been the publication of four works, very different in character. Each in its own way has contributed to the preparation of this volume and they account for the obvious differences which this English translation displays in respect of the first Spanish edition.

First and of most importance was the publication in the summer of 1993 of the complete edition on microfiche of all the manuscripts from the Dead Sea: *The Dead Sea Scrolls on Microfiche. A Comprehensive Facsimile Edition of the Texts from the Judaean Desert*, edited by Emanuel Tov with the collaboration of Stephen Pfann (E. J. Brill–IDC, Leiden 1993) which for the first time has placed at the disposal of all researchers the entire collection of material available. The second was the publication of the first two fascicles of *A Preliminary Edition of the Unpublished Dead Sea Scrolls*, reconstructed and edited by Ben Zion Wacholder and Martin G. Abegg (Biblical Archaeological Society, Washington 1991 and 1992) in which the text of the various copies of 4QD, 4QMishmarot, a series of Wisdom Texts and Sectarian Scriptures have been reconstructed with the aid of a computer using *A Preliminary Concordance to the Hebrew and Aramaic Fragments from Qumrân Caves II-X*. They have also made the reading of some badly preserved fragments much easier for me. The third was the publication by R. Eisenman and M. O. Wise of *The Dead Sea Scrolls Uncovered* (Element, Shaftesbury 1992), a book which contains the transcription and English translation of several previously unpublished texts. The quality of these transcriptions and translations sometimes leaves much to be desired (as shown in my review article 'Notas al margen de *The Dead Sea Scrolls Uncovered*', *Revue de Qumrân* 61 [1993] 123-150). Also, a large part of the texts they publish was already included in the Spanish edition. Even so, using this book helped me to read and translate several new texts now accessible in the microfiche edition. The fourth was the publication of the supplement to Klaus Beyer, *Die aramäischen Texte vom Toten Meer. Ergänzungsband* (Vandenhoeck & Ruprecht, Göttingen 1994) which completes the edition of the Aramaic texts from Qumran with the publication of some previously unpublished.

Thanks to these works and to continual study of the originals, this book claims to offer the reader a translation of the 270 most important manuscripts from Qumran. In other words, it is a virtually complete translation of the non-biblical manuscripts found there. Of course the 'List of Manuscripts from Qumran' has been brought completely up to date, taking new publications into account.

Like the Spanish edition, this English translation omits any kind of note or explanation, since everything needed to understand these difficult texts is in-

cluded in my *Introduction to the Literature from Qumran*, a forthcoming companion volume to this book. While awaiting its publication and as an aid to the
reader, I have added a short list of books in English to the Introduction.

I wish to thank Dr. W. Watson for the immense work carried out in trans-
forming the Spanish text into idiomatic and fluent English, for his patience in
including the changes I asked him to make as a result of checking the originals
again and for his readiness to sacrifice even some of his elegant solutions to my
desire for a more literal translation. I thank Hans van der Meij, Acquisitions
Editor of Brill Publishers, for the interest and care with which he has directed
the publication process of this book at each and every stage.

FLORENTINO GARCÍA MARTÍNEZ

Qumrân Instituut – University of Groningen
June 1994

The present comprehensive translation of the non-biblical texts from the Qumran library was prepared from the Spanish version by Florentino García Martínez in close collaboration with him and the publisher. The only liberties I have taken have been with the alphabetic acrostic poems, in an attempt to reflect the initial letters within these patterns. Professor García Martínez was patient enough to work through my drafts and solve the many translation problems that inevitably arose. To him and to Hans van der Meij, of Brill, I extend my thanks for their hospitality during my brief stay in Groningen and for their help over the past year.

WILFRED G. E. WATSON

Department of Religious Studies
The University
Newcastle upon Tyne UK

Foreword

This book comprises an English translation of the Hebrew and Aramaic texts commonly known as *The Dead Sea Scrolls*. To be more precise, it offers the reader a translation of the non-biblical manuscripts found in the various caves in the region round Qumran since, as explained in the Introduction, the prevalent terms *Dead Sea Scrolls* or *Manuscripts from the Judaean Desert* in fact denote a range of manuscript collections from very different periods, varying widely in content and origin.

The decision by the Huntington Library, on September 22nd 1991, to place copies of the photographs of the manuscripts in its possession at the disposal of research scholars and, above all the decision by the Israel Antiquities Authority, on October 21st 1991, to cancel all existing restrictions on the use of photographs of unpublished manuscripts, created a completely new situation. For the first time it was possible to envisage a *complete* edition of all the manuscripts recovered from the caves. Several months of frenzied work on the many hundreds of as yet unpublished manuscripts of Cave 4 persuaded me that fulfilling such a dream was neither necessary nor possible. A large part of the unpublished manuscripts – like a good part of the manuscripts published already, comprises such fragmentary remains that to translate them would be of absolutely no value to the reader.

This translation then is not a translation of *all* the non-biblical manuscripts recovered from the vicinity of Qumran. However, it does claim to include all the most important ones. The total number of manuscripts recovered comes to about 800. Of these manuscripts, 225 are copies of various biblical books, and a translation of them would be out of place here. Of another 275 or 300 manuscripts, so little of the text has been preserved that translating them would make no sense. These are minute remains of unidentified manuscripts and of fragments which mostly contain traces of a few complete words. Also, fragments with traces of several lines of text, but in such condition that it is not possible either to make sense of them or decide what work they contained. And, in addition, fragments, the content of which or even the work to which they belong can be determined with a degree of certainty, but the text is so short its translation would be of no use to the reader. This is not to imply that such minute fragments cannot be interesting, as shown by the intensive debates concerning the minute Greek fragments from Cave 7, as yet unidentified, or the dust storm of November 1991 in *The New York Times* concerning the five broken lines of 4Q285, a text related to the *War Scroll*. Of the other 300 or so manuscripts, the 200 longest and most important have been included in this translation. (The most complete translation so far, the third edition of the English translation by Geza Vermes, published in 1987, contains only the better preserved sections of 62 manuscripts). Although the number of the remaining manuscripts, between 100 and 150, might still seem large, the amount of text which can be recovered from them is comparatively small, since all of them comprise very small fragments. A rough calculation shows that the contents of them all could not be expected to be 5 percent of the text of the manuscripts included here. To give a concrete example: the five copies of the *Hymns* of Cave 4 (4Q427-431), which have not been included in the present translation, together comprise a shorter text than a single one of the 25 columns of 1QH^a.

The purpose of the translation offered here is to allow the interested reader, without any knowledge of the original languages of the manuscripts, to be able to enjoy the riches of a vast library, accumulated over several centuries by a sectarian group and stored in caves in the Desert of Judah in the year 68 of the first century CE, part of which has survived to our own time. This aim has shaped the final translation: as literal, as neutral and as close to the Hebrew and Aramaic text as possible, even if the outcome lacks both finesse and fluency. It is only in the texts which are evidently poetry that I have allowed myself some freedom, such as occasionally omitting the ubiquitous conjunction or using synonyms.

This same purpose has induced me to translate different surviving copies of a single work with special attention to minute variations between them, so as not to prejudge whether they are actual copies of the same text, different editions, re-use of the same material in another context, etc. I have only attempted to restore parallel passages when the layout of a text so restored, in the particular script of each manuscript, seems to allow this.

This same purpose has determined the presentation of the translations which attempt to reflect the actual state of preservation of the various manuscripts. Hence the indications of spaces left blank (*Blank*), intralinear insertions, corrections or erasure of certain words, etc. Hence the sparse restorations. Only when the presence of parallel passages, the repetitiousness of the formulas used or other equally persuasive factors permit, have I allowed myself to restore (in square brackets) the text actually preserved. In any case, these restorations are no more than suggestions and are intended simply to make the text easier to read. The symbols used in the translation are as given on the following page.

For the same practical purpose, and as an aid to the reader, each work is provided with a title which will make identification much easier to remember than the serial number of the official publication. A large number of the manuscripts already published has been provided with titles of this kind by the editors. In fact, at least three MSS have preserved the original title on the back. A manuscript fragment from Cave 1, which contained all three compositions known as the *Rule of the Community* (1QS), *Rule of the Congregation* (1QSa) and the *Rule of the Blessings*, has on the outside, in large letters, '[Ru]le of the community and of [...]'. Fragment 8 of 4Q504 has the title of the composition on the back: 'Words of the Luminaries'. And the manuscript 4Q250 is, in fact, the reverse of one of the papyrus fragments of 4Q249 (not included here), a cryptographic

[xxx]

text restoration

xxx[xxx] [xxx]xxx

partially preserved text

[…]

lacuna of unspecified length in the manuscript

] … [

traces of illegible words or letters in the manuscript

{xxx}   {…}

legible or illegible text erased by the copyist

⟨xxx⟩

text inadvertently omitted (or repeated) by the copyist

/xxx/ /…/

legible or illegible text inserted between the lines by the copyist

Blank

space left blank in the manuscript, either intentionally (new paragraph) or by mistake

(?)

uncertain reading or translation

(xxx)

explanation required for the meaning of the English text

****

four dots in the manuscript to represent the tetragrammaton text which has the title of the work in clearly legible square characters: 'Midrash on the Book of Moses'. In order to avoid confusion, the titles given by the editors have been retained, even when they are clearly unsuitable. In most cases the title assigned describes in some way the contents of the manuscript.

All the translations have been made with photographs of the originals in front of me. The text used for the translation of most of the Aramaic texts and of the biblical interpretations is the one I was able to prepare in Jerusalem, between 1974 and 1979, thanks to a grant from the Fundación Juan March. In the case of other manuscripts already published, the *edito princeps* or the preliminary edition, as well as later translations and studies, have been taken into consideration. However, this does not imply that the reading or interpretation adopted here is always that proposed by editors or other scholars. In the case of the texts from Caves 4 and 11, here translated for the first time, the translation is based on my own transcription of these same texts.

The book is arranged in the following way: a short introduction presents the reader with a history of the discoveries and of their publication, and offers him the basic elements to be able to place the manuscripts in their actual historical context. The material has been set out systematically, which enables the internal relationships among the different manuscripts to be perceived and highlights the homogeneity of content of the Qumran library.

The first chapter contains the main *Rules* of the sect. These documents provide us with the most information concerning the organisation, way of life, customs and thought of the community or communities for which they were intended. Chapter two is a collection of texts which are equally normative, the halakhic texts, which show us in practice the characteristic application of Old Testament law current within the group. The third chapter is an assortment of compositions, though all of them share the same theme dominant in the concerns of the Qumran community: the exploration of the truths of 'the last days'. Chapter four collects the exegetical output of the community, compositions directly concerned with showing us how the biblical text was interpreted, translated and even altered. Chapter five assembles a long series of 'Para-biblical literature'. Some of these are compositions parallel to the biblical text, approximating the original text in different degrees. Others represent independent traditions developed around biblical personages. Others again reveal to us literary creations of the same type as the biblical narratives which by chance were not included in the bible, although a few of them, such as the *Book of Jubilees*, seem to have enjoyed truly biblical authority within the community. Chapter six gathers together poetic compositions which may or may not have been used in the liturgy, aprocryphal psalms, wisdom poems, etc. Chapter seven contains those works probably intended for liturgical use or which are remains of rituals. In chapter eight, astronomical compositions, calendars and horoscopes found in the caves, are represented, all works of fundamental religious importance for the Qumran community. The ninth chapter contains a single document: the *Copper Scroll*, a unique text the meaning of which continues to be mystifying.

A closing appendix contains a complete list of all the manuscripts found in the caves in the area around Qumran. This *List* has two functions. First, it gives the reader an exact idea of all the texts recovered. Accordingly, it contains biblical manuscripts as well as non-biblical manuscripts, and includes manuscripts already published as well as those which remain, as yet, unpublished. The second function is to provide the requisite bibliographical references in order to locate the editions of the texts already published and those studies which provide information concerning texts still unpublished.

Every translation presupposes some degree of interpretation, all the more so when it is a question of texts which can be read in several ways. In the case of unvocalised texts, like ours, and when in the scripts of the different manuscripts some consonants are identical in form, very frequently translation implies a prior decision concerning both reading and interpretation. The scientific explanation and justification of these decisions would require space not available here and would be of no interest to the reader unfamiliar with the original languages.

In spite of the fragmentary and incomplete condition of the manuscripts, these texts have completely transformed the way we understand the formation and development of the Old Testament books. They have increased our knowledge concerning the origins of Christianity and Judaism. They have opened unsuspected viewpoints in our understanding of the history, culture, religion and language of Palestine in the centuries prior to the destruction of the Temple. Without them, the study of the bible, of Judaism and of Christianity as historical events is unthinkable today. However, in spite of their riches, these texts, like most ancient religious texts, yield their secrets reluctantly. Their contents can only be absorbed after deep study. The limitations of a literal translation devoid of footnotes, which I freely accepted, have prevented me from noting the literary, historical and theological problems they present, the contributions of every kind which they contain, the influences they reflect, the avenues they open up, etc. All these aspects, as well as the results of forty years of research on the first manuscripts to be published, are to be found in my forthcoming *An Introduction to the Literature from Qumran*

One of the more pleasant privileges of an author at the close of his task is to acknowledge publicly the debts incurred during the preparation of a book and express his gratitude to all those who have contributed to its gestation. However, when it is a matter of a work which has developed gradually over the years, this privilege becomes an impossible task. There are too many names and too many influences, there is too much material making up the scaffolding which enabled its construction. Of course, I cannot go without mentioning some of the people who throughout these years have sustained my enthusiasm for these texts. In first place come the members of the first generation of editors of these manuscripts, in particular Professor John Strugnell and Professor Josef T. Milik. Without their pioneering work it would not have been possible to understand most of these texts. Then, Professor L. Alonso Schökel, who in those far off years of study in Rome encouraged me to relinquish studying the tannaitic *midrashim* (a field as esoteric as my own specialty) in order to devote myself entirely to Qumran. The colleagues of the Instituto Español Bíblico y Arqueológico of Jerusalem, our 'Casa de Santiago' and especially Professor Julio Trebolle Barrera, of the Department of Hebrew and Aramaic in the Universidad Complutense, who knew and know how to make every hour of joyful meetings an hour of reflexion. The colleagues of the 'École Biblique' in Jerusalem, especially Professor Émile Puech, who shared with me the responsibility of editing the Revue de Qumran, for the hours we spent together over the photographs of fragments. The colleagues of the Department of Biblical Studies of the University of Groningen, especially Professor A. S. van der Woude, who was able to establish in his 'Qumrân Instituut' the ideal conditions for free development of research. The Spanish Ministry of Education and Science which, in 1991, funded my stay for a sabbatical semester in the Instituto de Filología Bíblica y Oriental of the Consejo Superior de Investigacciones Cientificas, during which I was able to produce the first draft of this book. The director of that Institute, Professor Natalio Fernández Marcos, as well as Professor Emilia Fernández Tejero and Professor M. Victoria Spottorno Díez-Caro, close colleagues who turned this stay into an unforgettable experience. Above all, my own family, Annie, Julián and Jean-Baptiste. Annie was able to share with pleasure my enthusiasm for the 'Teacher of Righteousness' and 'the sons of light'; Julián and Jean-Baptiste have grown up surrounded by cryptic texts and a father not always accessible on account of those texts; she and the children have patiently endured my periods of absence over these months. To them I dedicate this book, for it is the product of time stolen from them.

FLORENTINO GARCÍA MARTÍNEZ

Introduction

1 The Dead Sea Scrolls

Over the course of the last forty years, chance finds and the systematic exploration of the ruins and caves of the various Wadis of the Judaean Desert have
supplied a large number of manuscripts from different periods and of various
types. All these are known as 'the Dead Sea Scrolls' and they have all been, or
are to be published in the series *Discoveries in the Judaean Desert* of the
Clarendon Press, Oxford, or in the series devoted to manuscripts found in
Israeli excavations, prepared by the Shrine of the Book and the Israel Museum.
All these manuscripts have been classified into collections according to find-
spot, whether they were found on the site by archaeologists or whether they
were acquired on the flourishing antiquities market. The collections are as
follows (in the sequence of the palaeographic dating of the preserved material:)

Papyri from Wâdi Daliyeh or *Samaria Papyri*: a collection of papyri from the 4th
century BCE, discovered in 1962 in several caves about 15 kilometres North of
Jericho.[1] Although archaeological exploration of the caves in 1963 and 1964[2]
also uncovered remains of human occupation from the Bronze Age and the
period of revolt by Bar Kokhba, most of the material comprised remains from
the Persian Period. This included nearly 200 human skeletons of all ages together with a large quantity of pottery, coins, jewels, foodstuffs and the most
important collection of papyri ever discovered in Palestine. These documents,
which were legal in character and written in Aramaic, are dated between 375
and 335 BCE and made up part of the possessions of a group of persons in flight
before the destruction of Samaria by the soldiers of Alexander the Great in 331
BCE Caught by surprise in the caves by the Macedonian soldiers, it seems that
they died from suffocation from a fire lit by the soldiers at the entrance to the
caves. At present only one of the twenty best preserved papyri has been published in its entirety.[3]

The Manuscripts of Qumran: comprise Hebrew, Aramaic and Greek manuscripts
stemming from 11 caves in the area around Khirbet Qumran, either those discovered during the various campaigns of archaeological exploration of the caves
or those purchased on the antiquities market.[4]

The Masada Manuscripts: comprise the texts discovered during excavation of the
fortress of Masada. Together with a series of Hebrew and Aramaic ostraca and
fragments of papyri in Latin, the collection includes several biblical texts,[5] a
Hebrew manuscript of Ben Sira[6] and a copy of *Songs of the Sabbath Sacrifice*,[7]
a composition of which there are several copies in the manuscripts from
Qumran, as well as many fragments in Hebrew, Aramaic, Greek and Latin.[8]
The actual collection has not yet been published in full,[9] but its contents are
known thanks to the description given by the excavator, Y. Yadin.[10]

The Manuscripts of Murabbaᶜat: comprise the manuscripts found in various caves of Wadi Murabbaᶜat. Besides a 7th century BCE palimpsest, some remains from the 1st century CE and a limited number of Arabic texts, this collection comprises documents in Hebrew, Aramaic, Greek and Latin of the period of Bar Kokhba's revolt, among which contracts and letters signed by Bar Kokhba himself stand out. The complete collection has been published in *Discoveries in the Judaean Desert* II.[11]

The Manuscripts of Nahal Hever: comprise the manuscripts discovered during archaeological campaigns by the Israelis in 1960 and 1961 in two caves of Nahal Hever:[12] the 'Cave of the Letters' and the 'Cave of Horror'. In the 'Cave of the Letters' were found a couple of biblical fragments (a fragment of Num 20 : 7-8 and a fragment with traces of Pss 15 and 16) and a large quantity of Hebrew, Aramaic, Nabataean and Greek papyri, arranged in two large units: the family archive of Babata and documents concerning Bar Kokhba.

   The family archive of Babata, which tells us about all the facets of a rich Jewish family from En-Gedi and south of the Dead Sea CE, comprises 35 documents: 17 written in Greek, 9 in Greek with signatures in Aramaic, Nabataean or both, 6 written in Nabataean and 3 in Aramaic. They are all papyri and contain contracts or deeds of different types. The Nabataean and Aramaic documents have been described by Y. Yadin,[13] those in Greek by H. J. Polotsky[14] and four of the Greek texts have been published in preliminary form.[15] All the Greek texts from the archive of Babata, now given the label *P. Yadin*, have been published recently.[16]

   Even more significant are the many documents connected with Bar Kokhba. These are a bundle of 14 Hebrew, Greek and Aramaic papyri and a wooden tablet written in Aramaic found during the excavations of 1960[17] and another bundle of six papyri, in Hebrew and Aramaic, written in En-Gedi, discovered during the 1961 excavations.[18] All these manuscripts, letters, contracts etc., together with the texts connected with Bar Kokhba from Murabbaᶜat, provide information of inestimable value for an understanding of the Second Jewish Revolt.[19]

   The material which comes from the 'Cave of Horror'[20] is much less abundant; a few *ostraca*, a fragment in Hebrew, remains of unidentified Hebrew and Greek papyri and the remains of a Greek manuscript of the Twelve Prophets. Together with one of the fragments of a Nabataean papyrus from the 'Cave of the Letters', these Greek fragments show the real origin of some of the material in the collection from Wadi Seiyâl, and the strong resemblance between both collections.

The Manuscripts from Wâdi Seiyâl: the collection of manuscripts coming from Wadi Seiyâl is divided into two groups, kept in the Rockefeller Museum and in the Shrine of the Book, respectively. The first group contains manuscripts acquired between 1952 and 1954 by the erstwhile 'Palestine Archaeological Museum' as coming from Wâdi Seiyâl (biblical manuscripts and legal documents in Greek, Hebrew, Aramaic and Nabataean). The exact source of several of these texts is dubious even though in some cases it is known for certain that material submitted as found in Wadi Seiyal actually comes from clandestine excavations in Nahal Hever.[21] The Greek manuscript of the Twelve Prophets has recently been published as the first volume of the Seiyâl Collection[22] in *Discoveries in the Judaean Desert* VIII, and the remainder of the collection will appear in another volume of the same series, edited by J. T. Milik, E. Puech and J. Schwarz.[23] The group kept in the Shrine of the Book comprises manuscripts discovered during Israeli archaeological excavations in 1960 and will be published separately from the earlier manuscripts.[24]

The Manuscripts from Nahal Mishmar: the caves of Nahal Mishmar are remarkably rich in artifacts from the chalcolithic period (4500–3000 BCE) but provide hardly any documents. In actual fact the collection amounts to no more than a couple of papyri found during exploration of the caves in 1961.[25]

The Manuscripts from Khirbet Mird: the collection comprises Greek, Christian Palestinian Aramaic and Arabic manuscripts from the ruins of the ancient monastery of Castellion, both those acquired from the Bedouin as well as those discovered by the Belgian expedition in 1953. It contains fragments of the New Testament, both in Greek and in Christian Palestinian Aramaic as well as other documents in Greek, Christian Palestinian Aramaic and Arabic, all of them from the Byzantine and Arab periods.[26]

These collections as a whole are known as 'the Dead Sea Scrolls'. Undoubtedly, each of these collections has a character of its own and the texts they contain come from different periods. The Samaria papyri, official documents, most of them dated, all come from the 4th century BCE. The manuscripts from Qumran and Masada are from the period before the destruction of both sites during the great war against Rome in the first century CE. Although dating by palaeography and the content of the material which comes from both these collections is compatible, and although both equally include such a typical work as the *Songs for the Sabbath Sacrifice*, the exact archaeological and historical context of both discoveries compels us to consider them as two separate collections. Although the manuscripts from Murabba°at, Nahal Hever, Wadi Seiyal and Nahal Mishmar contain incidental remains of earlier periods, they are placed by most scholars as belonging to the revolt by Bar Kokhba, in the second century CE, and they are related to it directly. They can be considered as a single collection in terms of content – mainly autographs, contracts, letters, etc.–and in terms of their origin in connection with the Bar Kokhba revolt and of the dating of the manuscripts to the second century CE. As for the manuscripts from Khirbet Mird, their Christian character, their late date and their origin clearly mark this collection as different from the preceding.

The subject of this book consists exclusively of those manuscripts found in the various caves in the area around Khirbet Qumran, the longest, most varied and undoubtedly the most interesting of the 'Dead Sea Scrolls'.

II History of the Qumran Finds and their publication

1 *1947-1956: The First Manuscripts*

Each of the main actors in the discovery of the manuscripts coming from the various caves in the area around Khirbet Qumran has conveyed to us his own account of how and when the manuscripts were discovered, acquired, acknowledged as authentic and identified.[27] The details of these accounts are, of course, conflicting; however they can be summarised in outline as follows:[28]

Everything begins with the Bedouin of the Taᶜâmireh tribe. They were the chance discoverers at the start and the passionate prospectors later on, of most of the manuscripts originating from the area of Qumran. In one version of the events it is a shepherd of the tribe, Mohammed ed-Dhib, who in search of a stray goat came across the first of the caves with manuscripts. In another account there are three shepherds, Khalil Musa, Jumᶜa Mohammed and Mohammed ed-Dhib who get into the cave and retrieve a number of jars, some empty, some filled with manuscripts. The precise date of the first discovery cannot be determined for certain: either towards the end of 1946 or at the beginning of 1947. What is certain is that in the spring of 1947, seven manuscripts originating from Cave 1 pass into the hands of two 'dealers in antiquities' in Bethlehem: Jalil Iskandar Shalim, the famous Kando, and Faidi Salahi. Kando was later to become the indispensable middleman between the Bedouin who made the discoveries and the authorities of the Palestine Archaeological Museum.

Four of these seven manuscripts (i.e. 1QIs^a, 1QpHab, 1QS and 1QapGen) were acquired by Athanasius Yeshue Samuel, the archimandrite of the Syrian-Orthodox monastery of Saint Mark in Jerusalem, in the hope of making some profit from their sale. The other three (1QIs^b, 1QH and 1QM) were offered to Professor E. L. Sukenik of the Hebrew University, Jerusalem. In November 1947, on the very day the State of Israel was proclaimed, apparently, Professor Sukenik understood these manuscripts to be of interest and perhaps to be ancient. He acquired them for the Hebrew University, together with two of the jars in which the manuscripts had been stored. Mar Athanasius, on the other hand, after a lengthy and unsuccessful round of various individuals and institutions in Jerusalem, from whom he requested information concerning the manuscripts, ended up by offering the four manuscripts in his possession to the American School of Oriental Research (ASOR) in Jerusalem towards the end of February 1948. In the absence of the director, Millar Burrows, one of the research students, John C. Trever, luckily also a very good photographer, was to examine the manuscripts. He identified one of them as a copy of Isaiah, recognized it to be ancient and significant, and obtained from Mar Athanasius permission to photograph three of them (1QIs^a, 1QpHab and 1QS) in their entirety, with a view to publishing them on behalf of the American School of Oriental

Research. The fourth manuscript (1QapGen), in Aramaic, for a short time
called the 'Lamekh Scroll' because of the contents of one of the outer fragments, was to remain rolled up due to its bad state of preservation and Mar
Athanasius' conviction that this fact would make the whole lot more valuable.
In view of the political uncertainty of the country and the problems caused by
the setting up of the State of Israel, Mar Athanasius decided to transfer the
manuscripts in his possession to the United States with the prospect of selling
them. The excessive price he was to demand, in conjunction with the embit-
tered discussion concerning their authenticity, resulted in the sale taking place
as late as 1954. Through intermediaries, Yigael Yadin, Sukenik's son, managed
to acquire the four manuscripts belonging to Mar Athanasius for the Hebrew
University of Jerusalem. In this way the seven manuscripts found in 1947 were
together once more, and to house them a special museum was built in Jerusalem: the Shrine of the Book.

The official edition of 1QIs^a and of 1QpHab was published in 1950 by the
American School of Oriental Research,[29] and in 1951 the official edition of 1QS
came out.[30] The three manuscripts of the Hebrew University (1QIs^b, 1QH and
1QM) were published (posthumously) by Sukenik in 1955.[31] The following year,
there appeared an edition of the best preserved parts of the 'Lamech Scroll'
with the title *Genesis Apocryphon* (1QapGen),[32] the publication of which completed this initial phase.

2 1949-1955: Excavation of Cave 1 and publication of the material

The first news of the discovery of the manuscripts, a press release from the
American School of Oriental Resarch, followed by another from Sukenik, both
in April 1948, aroused enormous interest. This was to increase even more with
the publication of the first scientific descriptions of the manuscripts and their
contents that same year and in 1949.[33] It became obvious that in order to establish the authenticity and antiquity of the manuscripts without a shadow of
doubt, a 'scientifically controlled' excavation of the cave in which they had
been found was necessary. For completely understandable reasons the bedouin
refused to indicate from which cave, among the thousands to be seen in the
gorges of the Judaean desert, their treasures had come. Thanks to the intervention of the Arab Legion of Jordan, the cave was finally located by January 1949.
An archaeological expedition, under the direction of Lancaster Harding, director of the Department of Antiquities of Jordan, and of Roland de Vaux, director of the 'Ecole Biblique et Archéologique Française', a controlled excavation
of the cave could take place between February 15th and March 5th, 1949. The
archaeologists were dismayed to find that the cave had already been 'excavated'
previously, both by the bedouin and by the monks of the Syrian monastery of

St Mark, which meant that it was impossible to determine its stratigraphy. Of course, painstaking work on the material removed by the clandestine 'excavators', as well as on the half-metre of earth deposited within the cave, enabled them to retrieve much material. This included about 600 fragments deriving from 70 different manuscripts, together with plenty of pottery fragments from about 50 jars and other vessels. Also, fragments of the cloths in which the manuscripts had been wrapped, including a fragment of a jar inside which was stuck a lump of cloth with the remains of a scroll. Luckily, some of the fragments of manuscripts found by the archaeologists helped to complete the manuscripts discovered by the bedouin. This fact and analysis of the pottery found, led to the conclusion that the first seven manuscripts were original and truly ancient and established their importance with no shadow of doubt. The archaeological excavation of Cave 1 was published in 1955, in a volume which also included all the fragments from that cave and some of the fragments retrieved from clandestine 'excavations' (1Q8, 1Q19bis, 1Q20, 1Q28, 1Q34bis, 1Q70bis, 1Q71 and 1Q72).[34]

3 1951-1962: Excavation of Khirbet Qumran and of the 'Small Caves'

The same archaeological team decided to commence systematic excavation of the ruins known as Khirbet Qumran, in order to establish whether or not there was any connection between what appeared to be the remains of a fortress belonging to the Roman period and the manuscripts found in Cave 1. Under the joint direction of Harding and de Vaux, five consecutive archaeological campaigns were carried out. Right from the first of these, in 1951, a close connection between the ruins and the manuscript caves became obvious. What is more, the identical pottery could only be explained by a common origin. Succeeding campaigns between 1953 and 1956 were gradually uncovering the various phases of the building. They revealed the history of the group of humans who had lived there and to whom the manuscripts found in Cave 1 belonged.

Although the final publication of the finds from these excavations has not yet appeared, the most important material is already known. This is due to the preliminary descriptions of the results of each campaign which appeared regularly in *Revue Biblique*,[35] and especially to the overall view provided by de Vaux in the Schweich Lectures of the British Academy in 1959.[36]

To summarise, the results of the archaeological excavations show us that the same group of humans, labelled 'The Qumran Community', occupied the buildings excavated for a period of 200 years after having set up house in what was left standing of a fortress built in the 7th or 8th century BCE, and later abandoned for several centuries.

The archaeologists differentiated three phases during this period of occupation.

In the first phase (de Vaux's Period I*a*) which was very short, a small group of people occupied and re-used the abandoned buildings of an ancient fortress. This was a rectangular building with a number of rooms built against the inner part of one of the walls and a large circular cistern. The new residents did no more than adapt the existing buildings and add two new rectangular cisterns and two potter's ovens. Neither the exact beginning nor the close of this first phase is known for certain.[37] De Vaux conjectures that this occupation could have begun during the reign of Jonathan (161-143/142 BCE).

However, this conjecture contradicts the actual facts provided by archaeology and the very arguments used by de Vaux and is determined by a particular interpretation of the statements in the *Pesharim*.[38] The only absolutely certain facts are as follows. The initial occupation by the sect occurred *shortly* before the reign of John Hyrcanus or during his long reign (135/134-104 BCE), i.e., well into the second half of the second century BCE,[39] and this occupation lasted for a very short time since the remains attributable to it are very sparse.

During the reign of Alexander Jannaeus (103-76 BCE) or perhaps during the reign of his predecessor, John Hyrcanus, this initial occupation increased quite considerably and the buildings took on the form they were to retain, more or less, until their destruction (Period I*b* of de Vaux). The most noteworthy change to the existing buildings involved the construction of a complex arrangement for trapping the water of the nearby wadi by means of an aqueduct, and retaining it in large cisterns within the complex, three of them of enormous size. This is proof of a significant increase in the number of people. Just as typical are the addition of a massive square tower to guard the entrance and the building of storehouses and workshops. Also, several large-sized rooms, one of which in particular was clearly intended for the assembly of many people and at the side of which was found a room in which hundreds of plates, cups, jars and other objects needed for the table were found stored. In contrast, the number of rooms which could have been intended as bedrooms turns out to be very small compared to the buildings for common use. De Vaux's conclusion is firm and utterly convincing: the constructions excavated are the remains of buildings in which a large group of humans, living in tents or huts (or in the surrounding caves) would congregate for activities in common: assemblies, common meals, acts of cleansing, jobs in the various workshops, etc. This phase lasted a long time (until the reign of Herod the Great, 37-4 BCE) and ended suddenly through earthquake or fire, or from the effect of both, as can clearly be seen in the ruins.

The following phase (de Vaux's Period II) comes after a short interval when the ruins were abandoned as a result of the fire and the destruction which happened before that – there remains archaeological evidence for the period of abandonment – and began during the reign of Archelaus (4 BCE to 6 CE). This period of occupation is marked by the rebuilding and re-use of one part of the earlier buildings, which continue in communal use as before. A certain number of changes is clearly visible in the ruins without altering the appearance of the buildings to any extent. The most important room in terms of what was retrieved is, perhaps, the large room of the first floor which collapsed during the violent destruction which terminated this period. However, from the debris it was possible to salvage three long tables covered with plaster, and several inkwells. These show that it was a place intended for the preparation and copying of the manuscripts discovered in the caves. Thanks especially to the abundance of coins found, including a treasure comprising 560 coins in Tyrian silver buried in three little pots, it has been possible to establish the beginnings of this phase as between 4 BCE and 1 BCE, and its close in the year 68 of the first century CE. The ample remains of ashes resulting from the burnt ceilings, and the arrowheads that were found, are convincing proof that the end of this phase was caused by a battle. The remains found in the following phase make it just as evident that the destruction was the work of the Roman army in the course of the first Jewish War.

With Period II occupation of Qumran by the community ended. The next phase (de Vaux's Period III) presents us with a building totally different in shape and features. Only a small part of the ruined buildings is cleared and rebuilt: the large tower and adjoining buildings, strengthened with rough ramparts. In this way the whole complex takes on the form of a small Roman fortress, which it was to retain right until the excavations. The beginning of this phase is established from coins as the year 68, when the coins found from Period II end, and when the coins connected with the remains from Period III begin. Its close is very uncertain. The lack of coins later than the year 72/73 make it very likely that the occupation of the place by a small Roman garrison ended at the time of the capture of Fortress Masada, the last bastion of resistance in the area, in the year 73.

The results of these excavations have succeeded in providing an exact historical background to the manuscripts found in the caves. They have proved that these manuscripts originate from people who lived for two centuries in what are today the ruins of Qumran, and that at least some of them were copied there. They have also provided the definitive latest date when the manuscripts were stored in the caves: the year 68 of the 1st century. The implication is that all the manuscripts were copied before this date. In addition, the results have proved that the owners of these manuscripts lived in accordance with a particular type of community organization. Corroboration comes from the excavation of the large cemeteries in the vicinity of the ruins and the later excavation of ᶜAin Feshka, a construction next to a sweet water spring on the shore of the Dead Sea, belonging to the same period and occupied by the same people as were in the ruins of Qumran.[40]

This view was almost universally accepted when first proposed and went

unchallenged for some forty years. In recent years, however, alternative interpretations of the archaeological finds have been proposed. N. Gold argued that
Qumran was a desert fortress and P. Doncel maintained that Qumran was an
agricultural villa where balsam was produced. J. B. Humbert, who is in charge
of the publication of the final report on the excavations of de Vaux, suggests
that the Essenes built a place of worship at Qumran on the site of a
Hasmonaean pleasure villa at the end of the first century BCE.[41]

The hypotheses of Gold and of Doncel, which eliminate any connection
between the ruins of Qumran and the caves of the manuscripts, seem incom-
patible with the sum total of the evidence preserved. The restriction of the
period of 'sectarian' occupation of the ruins to de Vaux's Period II as proposed
by Humbert seems more plausible to me. However, until the definitive publication of the archaeological material, it is impossible to evaluate in detail the respective merits of these new hypotheses.

In 1952, in view of rumours that once again the Taᶜâmireh bedouin had found
another cave containing manuscripts in the Qumran area, the 'École Biblique
et Archéologique Française', the American School of Oriental Research and the
Palestine Archaeological Museum decided to arrange a systematic exploration
of the whole of the rocky wall of the region. Their aims were to locate the new
cave and to determine whether or not there were other hiding-places for manuscripts in the area. Between the 10th and the 29th March, seven teams were to
search each cavity, for a stretch of about 8 kilometres. It was possible, in fact,
to locate Cave 2, and the archaeologists managed to find a couple of tiny fragments among the remains of the bedouin's clandestine dig. The archaeologists
carried out 230 sondages without success, but in 40 caves they did find pottery
and other traces of human occupation. In 26 of these caves the pottery found
was of the same kind as found in Cave 1 and in the first archaeological campaign of Khirbet Qumran. Only one of the caves excavated provided a certain
number of manuscripts. This was Cave 3, in which the archaeologists found,
in addition, two 'Copper Scrolls'. In September the same year, the bedouin
found a new cave with manuscripts in the rocky wall. This is Cave 6, which
was excavated at once by the archaeologists, who were able to retrieve only a
few fragments of papyrus and leather.

Following the discovery of Cave 4 by the bedouin, which we will treat separately, in September 1952 the archaeologists also searched the ravines at the
foot of the ruins of Qumran and they located and excavated Cave 5. Later on,
during the archaeological campaigns of February and March 1955, they decided to make a systematic excavation of the slopes of the terrace on which the
ruins were situated, to ascertain whether a natural or man-made cave might
have remained hidden by later falls. This enormous task was successful. It
provided confirmation that no further treasure comparable to Cave 4 had re-

mained hidden, and also led to the finding and excavation of Caves 7-10, which contained remains of manuscripts. All the material of these 'small caves' together with the results of their excavation were published in 1962.[42]

4 1952: Cave 4

The ruins of Qumran are situated above a marl terrace, halfway between the rocky edge of the Judaean Desert and the deep rift of the Jordan and the Dead Sea. It comprises sedimentary rock and the combined effect of rain and of wadi Qumran have carved deep gullies in its sides. During the excavation of the ruins, the archaeologists had noticed several cavities in these precipices, but had considered them to be holes caused by the water and 'archaeologically barren' and so did not search them.

A mistake which was to be enormously expensive. As de Vaux relates in the official report of the excavation which came out straight after the discovery,[43] this was not due to chance but was the result of careful search. Commenting one evening, in his camp, on the results gained from the search and sale of the manuscripts, an old Tacâmireh man remembered that in the far off days of his youth, while hunting in the Qumran region, he had wounded a partridge which had found safety in a crevice in the wall of the wadi, not far from the ruins of Qumran. Not wishing to relinquish his prey, with difficulty he managed to slither in until he found it in a room full of rubbish, amongst which he made out fragments of pottery, from which he retrieved a clay lamp. Following his directions, several youths from the tribe managed to climb down to reach the small opening. In this way they hit on what turned out to be the principal hiding-place for manuscripts: the remains of the central library of the Qumran community. Word of this quickly spread, and after that the archaeologists arrived, preceded by a squad of police from Jericho, who succeeded in halting the clandestine excavation, by now well under way. The archaeological team excavated the lower levels of the cave which had been built as a dwelling-place, just like the other caves on the edges of the marl terrace and they discovered a small subterranean dwelling which the bedouin had not touched. In this way they were able to retrieve a thousand fragments stemming from about a hundred texts, a tiny fraction of the material contained in Cave 4. Luckily, though, most of these belonged to the same manuscripts excavated by the bedouin, thus providing a check that the material which they offered for sale was genuine. The gradual sale of the manuscripts was to continue until 1958.

The material is enormous: about 15,000 fragments which come from about 550 different manuscripts. The Jordanian Government immediately granted the sum of 15,000 pounds in order to assist acquisition by the Palestine Archaeological Museum. However, owing to the large amount of material, the Museum was forced to turn to foreign institutions in order to pay for its acquisition. The help of McGill University of Montreal, the Vatican Library, the University of Manchester, the University of Heidelberg and the McCormick Theological Seminary of Chicago, the All Souls Church of New York and of the University of Oxford made it possible to purchase the fragments, and in return they were granted the right to publish part of them.

Publication was entrusted to an international and interconfessional team which included representatives named by these institutions, united in Jerusalem under the direction of de Vaux. The biblical manuscripts were entrusted to P. Skehan and F. M. Cross. The non-biblical manuscripts were shared among J. M. Allegro, M. Baillet, J. T. Milik, J. Strugnell and J. Starcky.[44] The team completed the unbelievable task of arranging the jigsaw puzzle of thousands of fragments into groups of manuscripts. They also provided preliminary reports of their contents, prepared a complete transcription of all the fragments and even compiled a concordance of all the words that could be read in them. Yet, at the present time the only allocations of manuscripts published in their entirety are those which were assigned to John M. Allegro[45] and M. Baillet.[46] A large number of the other texts from Cave 4 have been published in preliminary form,[47] but the definitive edition in the series *Discoveries in the Judaean Desert* has not yet been finished.[48] With the aim of speeding up its publication, both Cross and Strugnell have joined with other scholars over the last few years in the task of preparing the final edition of their respective allocations. Also, the Israel Antiquities Authority has decided to entrust other scholars with part of the share allocated to Milik.

5 *1956–1977: Cave 11*

The significant profit received from the sale of the manuscripts from Cave 4 whetted the appetite of the untiring Taʿâmireh bedouin to such an extent, that in January 1956 they succeeded in finding another new cave with manuscripts: Cave 11. The entrance to the cave, located very near to Cave 3, had fallen in, so it could not be seen, which is why it had gone unnoticed in earlier searches. As in Cave 1, a certain number of manuscripts were recovered in a good state of preservation. This only resulted in complicating the haggling with Kando needed to acquire them, as well as increasing the price which the Palestine Archaeological Museum was forced to pay to acquire them. In the end, acquisition was possible thanks to the contributions from the American School of Oriental Research (ASOR) and the 'Koninlijke Nederlandse Akademie van Wetenschappen' (KNAW, the Royal Dutch Academy of Sciences). Both institutions received in return the right to publish the texts acquired. In this way the American School of Oriental Research obtained three biblical manuscripts: a copy of the psalms,[49] a copy of Leviticus in palaeo-Hebrew script,[50] and a scroll in such bad condition that it was not possible to retrieve from it more than a few fragments with traces of a copy of Ezekiel.[51] The KNAW were awarded three other scrolls (an Aramaic translation of the Book of Job,[52] a scroll with apocryphal psalms [11QsAp^a] and another scroll with a description of the 'New Jerusalem' in such bad condition that it has been possible to rescue only a few fragments from an outside protuberance[53]). They were also awarded another series of fragments originating from different manuscripts, most of which have already been published.[54] But for the Temple Scroll, the longest and best preserved of all the manuscripts found in this cave, the price demanded was so high that acquisition proved impossible. The situation changed drastically with the Israeli occupation of Jerusalem and of Bethlehem in 1967. The day after the occupation, Y. Yadin, who had previously wanted to buy the manuscript through middlemen, proceeded to confiscate it. The Government of Israel confiscated the manuscript without further ado, although after the war it ended up granting to the antiquary payment of more than $100,000 for the scroll. Ten years later there appeared the superb edition of this important text[55] which was over 8 metres long, the longest of any found in the Qumran caves.

III The dispute over authenticity and antiquity

The interest aroused by the discoveries of the Qumran manuscripts was immense, right from the start. This interest was provoked for reasons which are easy to understand. The mere fact that they were biblical texts or connected with the bible, that they were actually found on biblical soil and were not less than two thousand years old, placed them in a unique position. Since the discoveries included many biblical manuscripts copied at a time prior to the formation of the canon and the standardization of the biblical text, and before the work of the Masoretes, to study them would allow the process of development and fixing of the biblical text to be known It would also assist in checking or correcting the great mediaeval codices which are the foundation of our Hebrew bibles.

Given, too, that the manuscripts included a large number of extra-biblical compositions, they would fill a huge gap in our knowledge of pre-Christian Jewish literature. It is true that part of this literature was known, owing to translations preserved in a wide range of languages, but there were no original manuscripts. A cursory look at the material which provides the foundation for the historical dictionary of the Academy of the Hebrew Language for the years 100 BCE to 70 CE,[56] shows that almost all the literary texts in Hebrew for this period derive from the Qumran finds. The same applies to Aramaic texts, also.[57] The new discoveries, in providing us with part of pre-Christian Jewish literature in Hebrew and Aramaic, promised to close the existing gap between Biblical and Mishnaic Hebrew and between the Aramaic of Elephantine and Targumic Aramaic.

In addition, and for the first time, we would own a whole range of religious compositions which had reached us directly, absolutely devoid of any later interference. Since the texts had been preserved at the fringes of conventional life, they reached us free from the restraints of censorship. To a large extent Jewish censorship had suppressed religious literature which did not comply with rabbinic orthodoxy; Christian censorship would have assimilated some of these works, but after modifying them for their own purposes.

Since the new manuscripts stem from Palestine and are earlier in date than the destruction of Jerusalem, study of them promises to resolve the complex history of the country at this critical time. Also, since this time is a period of development both for Christianity and for Rabbinic Judaism, the new texts will make the background, origins and development of these two important religions intelligible.

However, this very intrinsic interest of the new texts immediately unleashed a bitter conflict over whether they were genuine. Although today this conflict is no more than a curiosity of the past, it is useful to rehearse briefly the attitudes which marked the history of research into these manuscripts in the first decades after their discovery.

It was natural, of course, that the apparition of the first manuscripts was received with a degree of mistrust over whether they were genuine and really old. The preservation of manuscripts as old as these was not believed possible, and there have been a great number of forgeries throughout history. The very secrecy and uncertainties shrouding the discoveries could only increase misgivings.

Although most of the scholarly community assumed an enthusiastic attitude, already by 1949 there was no lack of opinion stating emphatically that they were recent forgeries. According to S. Zeitlin, the manuscripts had been written by the Karaites in the Middle Ages, in an attempt to assume distinguished forbears. They came from the Karaite synagogue in Cairo and had been hidden in the caves shortly before they were discovered.[58] Archaeological excavation under scientifically controlled conditions of the caves in which they were found, and fragments of manuscripts which belonged to the same texts acquired from the bedouin, provided a formal refutation of the accusations of forgery and fraud. Likewise, analysis of the pottery excavated provided proof of the antiquity of the texts connected with them, since it was difficult for this pottery to be later than the first century. The conclusive proof concerning date was given by analysis using the method known as Carbon 14. The cloths which had been used to wrap the manuscripts were analysed in this way in 1950, and the result given was a date up to the year 33 of the 1st century CE.[59] In 1956 a charred palm-tree balk found during excavation of the Khirbet underwent the same analysis, providing a date of up to 16 CE.[60] It is true that the margins of error available by this method in the fifties were still large (about 200 years in the first instance and some 80 years in the second). However it did establish the date of the cloths between 168 BCE and 233 CE, eliminating conclusively the likelihood of recent forgeries.

The analytical method by progressive shrinkage of the parchment fibres according to their antiquity was applied to uninscribed fragments from both Qumran and Murabba‘at. It proved that the first were relatively older than the second. Since the latter were dated to the 2nd century CE, the dating of the former to the 1st century CE was established.[61]

The same date in the first century (CE) was established by analysis of the biblical texts found in the caves and from their divergences from the biblical texts found in Murabba‘at and Nahal Hever. The second group presented a biblical text virtually identical with the Masoretic text. The biblical texts from Qumran, however, still reflect in a very clear manner the textual fluidity prior to the final fixed form and for that very reason were earlier.

This first century CE date for the manuscripts, however, still did not completely exclude their origin to be either the Zealots or Judaeo-Christian.

The first theory was maintained by C. Roth,[62] G. R. Driver[63] and others. In essence, both Roth and Driver equated the leading figures in the history of the

Qumran community with the leading figures of the Jewish revolt against Rome. They suggested dating the manuscripts to the second half of the first century CE and in the first half of the second century CE, the same period as the New Testament writings.

The second theory was maintained in the fifties by J. L. Teicher[64] and has been revived quite recently by B. E. Thiering[65] and R. Eisenman.[66] The discrepancies in detail between these writers are remarkable, and so are the individuals with whom they identify the principal characters. (The Teacher of Righteousness would be Jesus and the Wicked Priest, Paul; or the Teacher of Righteousness would be John the Baptist, the Wicked Priest, Jesus of Nazareth; the Teacher of Righteousness would be the apostle James, the Wicked Priest Ananias, and the Man of Lies, Paul). However, common to all these theories is denial of the conclusions reached by archaeological investigation, which infers that all the manuscripts were deposited in the caves (and by the same token, were written) prior to the destruction of Khirbet Qumran in 68 CE. Above all, these theories deny the conclusions from palaeographic analysis of the manuscripts. This shows that they were all copied between the third century BCE and the final quarter of the 1st century CE. In particular, the proof from palaeography used in dating the manuscripts has been the target of attack and disagreement.

At the start of analysis of the Qumran manuscripts, Hebrew palaeography for ancient times had not advanced very much, for lack of comparative material. In actual fact, it amounted to no more than W. F. Albright's detailed analysis of the Nash Papyrus in 1937.[67] His analysis had succeeded in dating this text by means of comparing its script with the forms of letters in inscriptions on stone of the period, and it had caused Trever to acknowledge as ancient the first manuscripts which the American School was offered. The avalanche of new material, some of which, like the Samaria papyri and the contracts and letters from Murabbaᶜat were actually dated, enabled a typology of the evolution of the different kinds of script between the 4th C BCE and the 3rd CE to be drawn up for the first time. This work was undertaken initially by S. A. Birnbaum,[68] and much more comprehensively and exactly by N. Avigad[69] and F. M. Cross.[70] The results led to establishing the date on which a manuscript was copied with margins of error of about 25 years. However, it was a new field of research, with results which were difficult to check objectively. (In order to make an analysis by means of the Carbon 14 method it was necessary to use between 1 and 3 grams of carbon. This entailed destroying a significant part of each manuscript). Accordingly, the attacks by Thiering and by Eisenman in particular focused on the dates suggested for the different manuscripts, since these totally exclude their interpretation. Luckily, the discovery of a new technique in 1987[71] (Accelerator Mass Spectrometry) reduced the amount of material needed to be destroyed for analysis using the Carbon 14 method to 0.5-1.0

milligrams of carbon. The method could now be applied directly to the manu-scripts to establish whether the dates put forward by the palaeographers were correct or not. In 1990, this new technique was used on 14 manuscripts. Four contained dates (a papyrus from Samaria, a contract from Wadi Seiyal, a deed of sale from Murabbaᶜat and an Arabic letter from Khirbet Mird), eight manu-scripts came from Qumran which the palaeographers had dated between the second half of the 2nd century BCE and the first half of the 1st century CE, and two others stemmed from Masada.[72] The results of this analysis have com-pletely substantiated the method of dating by palaeography.[73] This new analysis has shown that not one of the manuscripts from Qumran and Masada was cop-ied after 68 CE. It has also shown that the much earlier dates ascribed to some manuscripts by the palaeographers were completely vindicated. In all the sam-ples analysed, the palaeographic date falls within the date margins reached by the analytical methods.[74] These latest analytical techniques eliminate once and for all the theories of a Zealot or Jewish-Christian origin for the manuscripts. The manuscripts found in the Qumran caves can now be regarded as ancient and genuine beyond any kind of doubt.

IV A sectarian library

If the reader scans attentively the 'List of Qumran manuscripts', located at the end of this book, he cannot fail to realize that in spite of the high number of compositions it reflects, the contents as a whole are surprisingly uniform. If you append a separate section in which to place all the manuscripts which are copies of the various biblical books, all the remaining texts could easily be contained in any one of the chapters making up this book. It comprises only religious literature, with no room for 'secular' literature. The reader will find there neither purely historical works nor scientific works. The compositions closest to this category, such as the calendars or the astronomical works included in chapter 8, (as well as *4QBrontologion*), are pervaded by clear religious purposes and have been written and preserved for liturgical reasons, or for the ordering of religious life. Even when within some works 'scientific' details are included (such as the list of trees in *4QEnoch*, or the explanation for the circulation of the blood in one copy of *4QD*) the religious purpose of these details is always to be found in the foreground. It is not, in fact, a library in the modern meaning of the term, i.e., a store for all the knowledge of a period, but is instead a specifically religious library. And since, among the works it contains, a significant number can be classified as representing sectarian theology and customs, we can describe this library as a sectarian library.

All the manuscripts found in the caves belong to the same library, as becomes evident from the following facts. The collection of topics found in each cave (to the extent that the texts could be salvaged) has the same general outline:[75] biblical works, associated religious literature, sectarian works. The *very same* apocryphal and sectarian compositions have been retrieved from different caves. Several manuscripts found in different caves were copied by the same scribe.

It is not a private library, as is apparent from the high number of works it contains and also because (at least in Caves 1, 2, 4 and 11) different copies of the same composition, whether biblical or extra-biblical texts, have been found.

This library belonged to a group of people with their central community in the ruins of Qumran, as has been adequately established by archaeological excavations. These show the pottery found both in the caves and in the ruins to be identical, differing completely from other Palestinian pottery of the period.

The proof that this group of people was a sect comes from the subject matter of certain works widely represented in the library. These compositions exhibit a *halakhah* which differs from the rest of Judaism. They also follow a calendar which is different from the current calendar[76] and include new theological approaches. In addition they exhibit clearly a tightly structured community with a hierarchical organization, the members of which considered themselves to be different from others, to have *isolated* themselves from the rest of contemporary

Judaism. What is even more significant, it is a community forbidding and avoiding any contact with non-members.

It is obvious that not all the manuscripts found in the caves originate from Qumran. Although many of the biblical manuscripts seem to have been copied in the *scriptorium* of the community, and some have even been copied by the same scribes who also copied other sectarian works, no-one has ever thought of ascribing a Qumranic origin to any of the biblical texts. The same applies to specific non-biblical works, the oldest copies of which are much earlier than the settlement of the group in Qumran. In fact the same is true of some sectarian works, known in a 'Qumranic' edition but with a long history of development that seems to demand for some of its elements an origin prior to the existence of the community as such. Several other compositions offer no typical features which enable their origin to be determined with certainty. However, due to the separatist nature of the community, the mere fact of belonging to the group library convinces us that the community considered them to be basically in agreement with its principles, with its halakhah and even with its tenets. The spectrum of ideas reflected in these works seems to have caused no more problems than the variety of ideas present within the books of the bible.

In view of the exclusive nature of the community and the reiterated ban on relations with 'the others' it is hardly surprising that among the abundance of compositions preserved, not one has been found which could be judged as epitomising the thought, the halakhah or the traditions of a *counter*-group, even for the purposes of argument or rebuttal. Clearly, a group that persisted for centuries could not have maintained a monolithic uniformity throughout its whole history. It must have undergone intense development in its theology, its halakhah and in its very organization. And, indeed, in the different texts or in the various editions of a single work, there are numerous hints of this development. However, perusal of all the manuscripts recovered has not succeeded in bringing to light any composition which dissents from the basic principles, the calendar or the halakhah of the group. The wide variety that can be observed is always kept within specified limits. This allows us to conclude that all the works which were retrieved belong to the longer history of the sect. Or else they were kept because the sect saw in them confirmation of their prehistory, of the religious movements which influenced their development and nourished their origins, forming part of the legacy within which, as in the various biblical books, the sect identifies itself.

This global view of the discoveries has recently been questioned in various studies by N. Golb.[77] In his view it is apparently implausible that Jewish literature of the period could have been irretrievably lost, while the library of a sectarian group could have fallen into our hands. Wishing to recover vanished treasure, Golb is resolved to suppress any connection between the manuscripts from the caves and the group which lived in the area around the ruins. He claims that these manuscripts stem from various libraries in Jerusalem and therefore represent the rich literary activity of Judaism at that time.[78] However, such conjectures do not take into account the solid data gained from archaeological excavation, nor do they explain the uniform content of the texts found. They do not explain, either, the typical lack of any work which could represent halakhah or the ideas of the Pharisees, ideas which were to be prevalent in Judaism after 70 CE It achieves no more than shift to Jerusalem and make even more difficult the resolution of the problems which the manuscripts display.

Since I have given a detailed rebuttal of the Golb's arguments in other publications,[79] there is no need to emphasize the matter. It might appear to be an irony of history that we possess a very great deal more information concerning a small group of fanatical separatists, who lived in seclusion in the middle of the desert than we do concerning the many well-stocked libraries which there must undoubtedly have been in Jerusalem. However, at heart this irony is no more astounding than the fact that we possess more documentary data concerning the tiny Jewish colony set up in Elephantine than we do of Western learning which at one time was housed in the library of Alexandria. The luck of discovery has no regard for the logic of our own interests. Yet the fortuitous nature of the discovery of the manuscripts does not undermine the conclusion that what we have retrieved comprises the remains of the former library of the Qumran community.

v Identity and origins of the Qumran community

Granted that the manuscripts retrieved stem from the library of a sectarian group, the first requirement in providing them with a specific historic background is to establish which group in particular they came from. This group (or groups) is denoted by various names in the manuscripts: *yaḥad* (community), *ʿedah* (assembly), etc. Its members are called 'sons of Zadok', 'sons of light', 'members of the New Covenant', 'poor', 'simple', 'devout', 'the Many', etc. In other words, the epithets to be found in the actual manuscripts do not provide us with the opportunity of identifying easily the group to which the library belonged with any one of the sectarian groups which, as far as we know, existed. It follows that the method which all scholars have been obliged to adopt, is to compare all the data known through other sources concerning the existing groups within the Judaism of the period, with the profile of the group that can be extrapolated from the various manuscripts. This task is not without risks. It is easy to favour one or other of the elements found, considered, perhaps, as central, making secondary all other aspects which are difficult to fit, and so distort the picture to emerge. However, the procedure has had positive results which can be regarded as well established.

In the first place, it has shown that the Qumran community cannot possibly be identified with the Zealots of the Jewish-Christian community since neither the chronological outline nor the resulting profile fits.

Second, it has determined that of the three best-known groups of Judaism in the mid-second century BCE until the time of the destruction of Qumran in 68 CE (the Sadducees, the Pharisees and the Essenes), the group most closely resembling the Qumran group is indeed the Essenes. Furthermore, the similarities between what classical sources tell us about the Essenes[80] and the information provided by the manuscripts are so close, that it would be impossible to deny a strong connection between the Qumran group and the Essenes.[81]

This connection is usually understood as a simple equation between the elements in question: Essenes = Qumran group. However, this equation is impossible.[82] The genuine parallels do require a connection between the two entities, but there are differences between them of such a nature as to preclude them being identical. The information on the Essenes provided by classical sources is correct in describing the Essene movement as very extensive, even nationwide. Its members did not live segregated from the rest of Judaism but instead were found distributed in every city of the land. To reduce Essenism to a peripheral oddity such as Qumran would be to leave unexplained non-Qumranic Essenism, a wider and more significant phenomenon than the phenomenon of Qumran.

It is possible to account for the undeniable similarities and the differences, which are just as valid, by invoking another form of connection between the two groups.[83] The Qumran manuscripts make constant reference to a split, a fundamental division, which occurred in the initial stages of the group. They even tell us that the founder of the Qumran community, the Teacher of Righteousness, as well as the Man of Lies, his rival in this clash, had previously belonged to the same community. They also tell us that in the conflict between them both, only a tiny minority sided with the Teacher of Righteousness. The best way to make sense of the undeniable connection that existed between the Essene movement and the Qumran community, is to accept that the Qumran community arose specifically on account of a rift caused within the Essene movement to which the founder-members belonged. This proposal comprises one of the essential elements of the 'Groningen Hypothesis',[84] which best explains the known facts in their entirety, both in respect of the Essenes and in respect of the Qumran community.

In this hypothesis, the origins of the Essene movement and the origins of the Qumran community are quite separate. Essenism, in the form that can be inferred from classical information concerning the Essenes, and from Essene compositions preserved in the Qumran library, is a Palestinian affair, which has its ideological roots within apocalyptic tradition.[85] This tradition flourished in Palestine towards the end of the 3rd century and during the 2nd century BCE, and would continue its own development up to the period of the revolt against Rome. (Flavius Josephus, for example, mentions Judas the Essene who taught in the Temple at the time of Aristobulos [115-104 BCE] and Menahem who worked in the court of Herod the Great [37-4 BCE]. Also, Simon the Essene who prophesied at the close of Archaelaus' reign [4 BCE to 6 CE]. He also mentions John the Essene, who was entrusted with the governorship of the province of Zama during the war against Rome, led the first attack on Ashkelon, and died in that battle in 66 CE.) From the works written during the period of development prior to establishment in Qumran, from documents of this period belonging to patently sectarian works, and from later works which refer expressly to the founding period, it can be deduced that the Qumran community, instead, has its origins in a rift which occurred within the Essene movement. This rift was to cause those siding with the Teacher of Righteousness to set themselves up with him in the desert, until 130 BCE.

Study of these documents enables us to conclude that the key controversies within the Essene movement during the period of formation of the Qumran sect, and which eventually caused the rift, focused on the matter of the calendar and the resulting organization of the cycle of feasts. Of particular concern was a certain way of interpreting biblical legislation concerning the temple, worship, and the purity of persons and of objects.[86] This special halakhah is based on the Teacher of Righteousness being aware of having received through divine revelation the correct interpretation of the biblical text. It is also based on his followers seeing this interpretation as revealed and binding.[87] This awareness of having received revelation would induce the Teacher of Righteousness to proclaim the end of time as imminent, the awareness of divine selection and predestination, the inadequacy of the temple and current worship, etc., In addition he was led to suggest a whole string of special halakhot conditioning daily life, and attempt to force the practice of this interpretation on all the members of the Essene movement. The rejection of these pretensions by the majority of the members of the Essene movement, and their disapproval of this halakhah, were to end in forcing the group of the Teacher of Righteousness and his disciples to retreat to the isolation of the wilderness.

vi The history of the Qumran community

The texts that have been found enable us to sketch with relative certainty the ideological reasons for the rift which gave rise to the Qumran community. They are much more sparing when it comes to providing us with exact details of the actual circumstances in which the break occurred, and of later developments over the 200 years that the community existed. From the manuscripts, little more can be ascertained than a broad historical outline. It establishes the time for God's 'visitation' at about 390 years from the exile, and the advent of the Teacher of Righteousness as twenty years later. Further, particular enemies can be equated with the Pharisees and Sadducees There is an enigmatic allusion to Alexander Jannaeus and his execution of 800 Pharisees who had sought the intervention of Demetrius III Eucarios. The external enemy (the Kittim) can be identified as the Romans. The most frequent references, which also provide the best hope for making a connection between the history of the community and official history, are to the 'Wicked Priest' in the *Habakkuk Pesher*. He is said to be the highest power in the land and at one stage he would persecute the Teacher of Righteousness and his community in their desert retreat. These references, though, continue to be useless, since the mass of features attributed to this person could not fit any of the High Priests of the 2nd century BCE.

On this topic, too, the 'Groningen Hypothesis' has succeeded in providing a solution. This solution is in agreement with all the details of the texts, fits in with the time-limits demanded by the excavations of the Khirbet, and establishes the chronology for the development of the initial stages of the history of the community. In essence, this part of the hypothesis[88] surmises that the title 'Wicked Priest' is not a nickname assigned to the High Priest. Instead, it is a honorary title applied to the various Hasmonean High Priests, from Judas Maccabaeus to Alexander Jannaeus, following an exact chronological sequence. This obviates the need for assigning to a single person all the different and contradictory features asserted of the 'Wicked Priest'. It also provides a historical framework within which can be fitted the earliest history of the community. The hypothesis allows us to understand the positive estimation of Judas Maccabaeus, when he first took up office and his later condemnation, once he was installed. It enables us to reject identifying the movement from which the Qumran group originates with the Hasidim of the Maccabaean revolt because of Alcimo's condemnation. We can determine that the formative period of the community covers, at least, the high priesthood of both Jonathan and Simeon, two of the 'Wicked Priests' with whom the Teacher of Righteousness was in dispute. Also, we can determine that this formative period is distinguished not only by the development of belief within the Essene movement, already referred to, but equally by the confrontations with the political and religious power of Jerusalem. In addition, that the first group of supporters of the Teacher of Righteousness comprised priests from circles close to power. This hypothesis shows us that the rift within the Essenian movement and the retreat to the wilderness of the group faithful to the Teacher of Righteousness, took place during the long high priesthood of John Hyrcanus, who tracked down the Teacher of Righteousness to his retreat. It dates the death of the Teacher of Righteousness during the same pontificate of John Hyrcanus, since no connection is made between him and the following 'Wicked Priest', Alexander Jannaeus. This hypothesis, in conclusion, allows us to place the first edition of *1QpHab* in the final years of the life of Alexander Jannaeus. We can see how the community succeeded in solving the problem of the delay in the onset of the 'end of time' and the destruction of all the wicked, expected some 40 years after the death of the Teacher of Righteousness.

Of the later history of the community we know very little. Archaeology tells us of a brief abandonment of the buildings at Khirbet Qumran and of a return there. Successive editing of the texts shows us some of the alterations effected within them, changes to the community structures as well as development of theological beliefs. However, it is not possible to make a historical connection between these 'exiles in the desert' and the tortuous history of Palestine in the 1st century BCE and the 1st century CE. The Qumran group became less and less interested in the transformations of history, in order to focus their energy on study of the Law, and to follow it in accordance with their own interpretation. Only the events of the founding generation seem to have been assumed into a view of their own history, which also belongs to sacred history. In the solitude of the wilderness, the community was to withdraw into itself increasingly. Prayer was to replace temple sacrifice. The requirements of purity were to be emphasized to reach a level enabling communion with the world of angels. The whole life of the community would be stamped with ardent hope for the victory of goodness. This hope was to be nourished principally by reading and studying the sacred texts, as well as compositions emanating from apocalyptic tradition and the Essene movement, and writings composed within the community itself. These compositions as a whole, the voice and essential mainstay of the religious life of the community, were to generate a magnificent library, the remains of which are available here to the interested reader.

VII Further reading

For a first approach to the Dead Sea Scrolls, the Reader from the *Biblical Archaeology Review*, *Understanding the Dead Sea Scrolls* (New York 1992), edited by Hershel Shanks, Joseph A. Fitzmyer, *Responses to 101 Questions on the Dead Sea Scrolls* (Mahwah, N. J. 1992), and James C. VanderKam, *The Dead Sea Scrolls Today* (Grand Rapids 1994) could be very useful.

Standard Introductions in English, although somewhat dated, are the following: M. Burrows, *The Dead Sea Scrolls*, and *More Light on the Dead Sea Scrolls* (New York 1955 and 1958); F. M. Cross, *The Ancient Library of Qumran and Modern Biblical Study* (London 1958); J. T. Milik, *Ten Years of Discovery in the Wilderness of Judaea* (London 1959); A. Dupont-Sommer, *The Essene Writings from Qumran* (Oxford 1961); G. R. Driver, *The Judaean Scrolls* (Oxford 1965); G. Vermes, *The Dead Sea Scrolls: Qumran in Perspective* (London 1977).

More detailed information can be found in the chapter on 'Qumran Sectarian Literature' by D. Dimant, in Michael E. Stone (ed.), *Jewish Writings of the Second Temple Period* (Compendia Rerum Judaicarum II/2)(Philadelphia 1984) 483-550 and in the chapter 'The Writings of the Qumran Community' in E. Schürer, *The History of the Jewish People in the Age of Jesus Christ (175 B. C.-A. D. 135)*. A New English Version revised and edited by G. Vermes, F. Millar and M. Goodman. Volume III.1 (Edinburgh 1986) 380-469.

Notes to the Introduction

1 F. M. Cross, 'The Discovery of the Samaritan Papyri', *BA* 26 (1963) 110-121; – 'Papyri of the Fourth Century BC from Daliyeh: A Preliminary Report on Their Discovery and Significance' in D. N. Freedman and J. C. Greenfield, (eds.) *New Directions in Biblical Archaeology* (Garden City 1971) 48-51; – 'A Report on the Samaria Papyri', in J. A. Emerton, (ed.), *XII Congress of the IOSOT* (Leiden 1988) = Congress Volume Jerusalem 1986.

2 Paul and Nancy Lapp, *Discoveries in the Wadi ed-Daliyeh* (AASOR 41; Missoula 1974).

3 F. M. Cross, 'Samaria Papyrus I: An Aramaic Slave Conveyance of 335 BCE found the in Wadi ed-Daliyeh', *EI* 18 (1985) 7-17.

4 For a complete description of all the manuscripts as well as references concerning publication see the 'List of manuscripts from Qumran' at the end of this book.

5 A frag. of Gn with traces of Gn 47 : 7-11; a frag. of Lv with traces of Lv 4:3-9 and a copy of Pss. On this last MS see G. W. Nebe, 'Die Masada-Psalmen-Handschrift M 1039-160 nach einem jüngst veröffentlichten Photo mit Text von Psalm 81 : 2 – 85 : 6', *RQ* 14/53(1989) 89-97.

6 Y. Yadin, *The Ben Sira Scroll from Masada: With Introduction, Emendations and Commentary* (Jerusalem 1965) [Hebrew].

7 C. Newsom and Y. Yadin, 'The Masada Fragment of the Qumran Songs of the Sabbath Sacrifice', *IEJ* 34 (1984) 77-88.

8 Some of these fragments have been published by S. Talmon, 'Fragments of the Scrolls from Masada', *EI* 20 (1989) 278-286.

9 Only two volumes in the series *Masada reports* have appeared: Yigael Yadin and Joseph Naveh, *Masada I: The Aramaic Coins of Masada* (The Yigael Yadin Excavations 1963-1965: Final Reports) (Jerusalem 1989) and Hannah Cotton and Joseph Geiger, *Masada II: The Latin and Greek Documents* (The Yigael Yadin Excavations 1963-1965: Final Reports) (Jerusalem 1989).

10 Y. Yadin, 'The excavation of Masada – 1963/64: Preliminary Report', *IEJ* 15 (1965) 1-120, esp. 81-82, 103-114.

11 P. Benoit, J. T. Milik and R. de Vaux, *Les Grottes de Murabba'at* (Discoveries in the Judaean Desert II) (Clarendon Press, Oxford 1961).

12 An extensive preliminary report of both campaigns was published in *IEJ* 11 (1961) 3-72 and *IEJ* 12 (1962) 167-262, and of the excavation of the 'Cave of Letters' the definitive report: Y. Yadin, *The Finds from the Bar Kokhba Period in the Cave of Letters* (Judaean Desert Studies) (Hebrew University/Israel Exploration Society, Jerusalem 1963).

13 Y. Yadin, 'Expedition D – The Cave of Letters', *IEJ* 12 (1962) 235-248.

14 H. J. Polotsky, 'The Greek Papyri from the Cave of Letters', *IEJ* 12 (1962) 258-262.

15 H. J. Polotsky, 'Three Greek Documents from the Family Archive of Babatha', *EI* 8 (1967) 46-51 [in Hebrew] and N. Lewis, R. Katzoff, J. C. Greenfield, 'Papy-

rus Yadin 18', *IEJ* 37 (1987) 229-250.

16 *The Documents from the Bar-Kokhba Period in the Cave of Letters.* Greek Papyri edited by N. Lewis. Aramaic and Nabataean Signatures and Subscriptions edited by Y. Yadin and J. C. Greenfield (Judaean Desert Studies II) (Jerusalem 1989).

17 Described and published in part by Y. Yadin, 'The Expedition D', *IEJ* 11 (1961) 40-52. Two of the Greek papyri were published by B. Lifshitz, 'Papyrus grecs du désert de Juda', *Aegyptus* 42 (1962) 240-256. A large part of the Hebrew and Aramaic papyri can be found transcribed and commented on in E. Y. Kutscher, 'The Languages of the Hebrew and Aramaic Letters of Bar Kokhba and His Contemporaries' [in Hebrew] *Lesh* 25 (1960-61) 117-133; 26 (1961-62) 7-23.

18 Described and published provisionally by Y. Yadin, 'Expedition D - The Cave of Letters', *IEJ* 12 (1962) 248-257.

19 See Y. Yadin, *Bar-Kokhba. The Rediscovery of the Legendary Hero of the Second Jewish Revolt against Rome* (Weidenfield & Nicolson London 1971).

20 Y. Aharoni, 'Expedition B - The Cave of Horror', *IEJ* 12 (1962) 186-199; B. Lifshitz, 'The Greek Documents from the Cave of Horror', *IEJ* 12 (1962) 201-207.

21 B. Lifshitz, 'The Greek Documents from the Cave of Horror', *IEJ* 12 (1962) 201-207. The same applies to the Nabataean contract published by J. Starcky, 'Un contrat nabatéen sur papyrus', *RB* 61 (1954) 161-181, identified by Y. Yadin, 'Expedition D - The Cave of the Letters', *IEJ* 12 (1962) 229 as coming from Nahal Hever.

22 E. Tov, *The Greek Minor Prophets Scroll from Nahal Hever (8HevXIIgr)* (The Seiyâl Collection i/Discoveries in the Judaean Desert VIII) (Oxford 1990).

23 Some of the documents in this collection have been published provisionally: the Nabataean contract cited in note 21, edited by J. Starcky; J. T. Milik, 'Un contrat juif de l'an 134 après J.-C.', *RB* 61 (1954) 182-190; J. T. Milik, 'Deux documents inédits du Désert de Juda', *Bib* 38 (1957) 245-268.

24 A certain number of these documents have also been published in provisional form: B. Lifshitz, 'The Greek Documents from Nahal Seelim and Nahal Mishmar', *IEJ* 11 ((1961) 11-24; M. Broshi - E. Qimron, 'A House Sale Deed from Kefar Baru from the Time of Bar Kohkba', *IEJ* 36 (1986) 201-214; Jonas Greenfield has given a general description of the material as yet unpublished: 'The Texts from Nahal Se'elim (Wadi Seiyal)' in: J. Trebolle Barrera and L. Vegas Montaner (eds.), *The Madrid Qumran Congress. Proceedings of the International Congress on the Dead Sea Scrolls* (STJD, 11) (Leiden/Madrid 1992) 661-665.

25 P. Bar Adon, 'Expedition C', *IEJ* 11 (1961) 25-35; B. Lifshitz, 'Three Greek Documents from Nahal Seelim and Nahal Mishmar', *IEJ* 11 (1961) 59-60.

26 Only a few have been published: J. T. Milik, 'Une inscription et une lettre en araméen christo-palestinien', *RB* 60 (1953) 526-539; C. Perrot, 'Un fragment

christo-palestinien découvert à Khirbet Mird', *RB* 70 (1963) 506–555; A. Grohman, *Arabic Papyri from Khirbet el-Mird* (Bibliothèque du Muséon 52) (Louvain 1963).

27 E. L. Sukenik, *The Dead Sea Scrolls of the Hebrew University* (Jerusalem 1955) 13–17; M. Burrows, *The Dead Sea Scrolls* (London 1956) 3–69; J. C. Trever, *The Dead Sea Scrolls. A Personal Account* (Grand Rapids 1977) (an expanded version of his *The Untold Story of Qumran* of 1965); A. Y. Samuel, *Treasure of Qumran. My Story of the Dead Sea Scrolls* (London 1968). Other information is to be found in the articles published by Burrows, Brownlee and Trever in various issues of the *Biblical Archeologist* and of *BASOR* for 1948 and 1949 as well as in *RQ* from 1961 to 1964.

28 See, for example, the chapter 'Discovering the Scrolls' by H. T. Frank in H. Shanks, (ed.), *Understanding the Dead Sea Scrolls* (New York 1992) 4–19, or the more recent and detailed account by H. Stegemann, *Die Essener, Qumran, Johannes der Täufer und Jesus. Ein Sachbuch* (Spektrum 4249) (Freiburg 1993).

29 M. Burrows with the assistance of J. C. Trever and W. H. Brownlee, *The Dead Sea Scrolls of St. Mark's Monastery.* Volume I: The Isaiah Manuscript and the Habakkuk Commentary (New Haven 1950).

30 M. Burrows with the assistance of J. C. Trever and W. H. Brownlee, *The Dead Sea Scrolls of St. Mark's Monastery.* Volume II. Fascicle 2: Plates and Transcription of the Manual of Discipline (New Haven 1951). The first annotated translation of the text by W. H. Brownlee, *The Dead Sea Manual of Discipline* (BASOR Supplementary Studies 10-12) (New Haven 1951) appeared simultaneously.

31 E. L. Sukenik, *'Ozar ham-megilot hagenuzot* (Jerusalem 1954); English version: *The Dead Sea Scrolls of the Hebrew University* (Jerusalem 1955).

32 N. Avigad and Yigael Yadin, *A Genesis Apocryphon. A Scroll from the Wilderness of Judaea* (Jerusalem 1956).

33 The articles by the American team in *BA* and *BASOR*: J. C. Trever, 'The Discovery of the Scrolls', *BA* 11 (1948) 46–57; – 'Preliminary Observations on the Jerusalem Scrolls', *BASOR* 111 (1948) 3–16; – 'A Palaeographic Study of the Jerusalem Scrolls', *BASOR* 113 (1949) 6–23; – 'Variant Readings in the Isaiah Manuscript', *BASOR* 111 (1948) 16–24; 113 (1948) 24–31; W. H. Brownlee, 'The Jerusalem Habakkuk Scroll', *BASOR* 112 (1948) 8–18 as well as the first volume by E. L. Sukenik, *Megilloth Genuzoth* (Jerusalem 1950).

34 D. Barthélemy and J. T. Milik, *Discoveries in the Judaean Desert I: Qumran Cave 1* (Oxford 1955). The photographic reproduction of manuscripts *1Q71-772* did not appear until 1966: J. C. Trever, 'Completion of the Publication of Some Fragments from Qumran Cave 1', *RQ* 5 (1964–66) 323–344, Pl. I–VII.

35 R. de Vaux, 'Fouilles au Khirbet Qumrân: Rapport préliminaire', *RB* 60 (1953) 83–106; –, 'Fouilles au Khirbet Qumrân: Rapport préliminaire sur la deuxième campagne', *RB* 61 (1954) 206–236; – 'Chronique archéologique: Khirbet

Qumrân', *RB*61 (1954) 567-568; – 'Chronique archéologique: Khirbet Qumrân', *RB* 63 (1956) 73-74.

36 Published in 1961: R. de Vaux, *L'archéologie et les manuscrits de la Mer Morte* (London 1961) and in considerably revised form in the English translation of 1973: *Archaeology and the Dead Sea Scrolls* (London 1973).

37 The same conclusion is reached by E. M. Laperrousaz in his detailed analysis of the archaeological evidence: *Qumrân. L'établissement essénien au bord de la Mer Morte* (Paris 1976) and in his contribution on archaeology in the collective article *Qumrân* in the *Supplément au Dictionaire de la Bible* 51, cols. 744-789.

38 See my study: 'Orígenes del movimiento esenio y orígenes qumránicos. Pistas para una solución' in V. Collado-Bertomeu and V. Villar-Hueso (eds.), *Il simposio bíblio español* (valencia-córdoba 1987) 527-556, esp. 535-539.

39 The reader will find a summary of the history of palestine for this whole period in my contribution to the history and institutions of the biblical people from alexander the great to bar kohkba, in the collective work *la biblia en su entorno* (estella 1990) 241-334.

40 R. de Vaux, 'fouilles de feshka: rapport préliminaire', *RB*66 (1959) 223-255 and *archaeology and the dead sea scrolls*, 60-87.

41 J. B. Humbert, 'l'espace sacré à qumrân. Propositions pour l'archéologie', *RB* 101 (1954) 161-214.

42 M. Baillet, j. T. Milik and r. de vaux, *discoveries in the desert of jordan III: Les 'Petites Grottes' de Qumrân* (Oxford 1962).

43 *Discoveries in the Judaean Desert VI: Qumrân Grotte 4 II:* Archéologie, par R. de Vaux. II. Tefillin, Mezuzot et Targums (4Q128-4Q157) par J. T. Milik (Oxford 1977) 3-5.

44 After his death his share of the manuscripts was assigned to E. Puech, who had collaborated with Starcky in the preparation of these texts for many years.

45 John M. Allegro, with the cooperation of A. A. Anderson, *Qumrân Cave 4. I (4Q158-4Q186)* (Discoveries in the Judaean Desert of Jordan v) (Oxford 1969). It comprises an edition which can only be used if the hundred pages of corrections provided by John Strugnell, 'Notes en marge du Volume V des "Discoveries in the Judaean Desert of Jordan"', *RQ* 7 (1970) 163-276 are taken into account.

46 M. Baillet, *Qumrân Grotte 4.III (4Q482-4Q530)* (Discoveries in the Judaean Desert VII) (Oxford 1982).

47 The reader will find the appropriate references in the 'List of manuscripts from Qumran' at the end of this book.

48 In addition to DJD V, VI and VII, quoted already, the first volume of the biblical texts allotted to Skehan has been published: P. W. Skehan, E. Ulrich, J. Sanderson, *Qumran Cave 4. IV (Palaeo-Hebrew and Greek Biblical Manuscripts)* (DJD IX; Oxford 1992). The second volume of Skehan's lot and the first by Cross are forthcoming.

49 Published by J. A. Sanders, *The Psalms Scroll of Qumrân Cave 11 (11QPs^a)* (Discoveries in the Judaean Desert of Jordan IV) (Oxford 1965).

50 Published by D. N. Freedman and K. A. Mathews, with a contribution by R. S. Hanson, *The Paleo-Hebrew Leviticus Scroll (11QpaleLev)* (ASOR 1985).

51 W. H. Brownlee, 'The Scroll of Ezekiel from the Eleventh Qumran Cave', RQ 4 (1963–64) 11–28, Pl. II–III.

52 Published by J. P. M. van der Ploeg and A. S. van der Woude, with the collaboration of B. Jongeling, *Le targum de Job de la grotte XI de Qumrân* (Leiden 1971).

53 Published by J. P. M. van der Ploeg, 'Un petit rouleau de psaumes apocryphes (11QPsAp^a)', *Tradition und Glaube*, 128–139, pls. II–VII, and by F. García Martínez, 'The Last Surviving Columns of 11QNJ', *The Scriptures and the Scrolls*, 178–192, pls. 3–9.

54 See the pertinent references in the 'List of manuscripts from Qumran' at the end of this book.

55 Y. Yadin, *Megillat ham-Miqdash. The Temple Scroll* [in Hebrew] (three volumes with a supplement) (Jerusalem 1977). The ET appeared in 1983.

56 *Materials for the Dictionary. Series I. 200 BCE–300 CE*, The Academy of the Hebrew Language. Historical Dictionary of the Hebrew Language, Jerusalem 1988 [Microfiche].

57 The Aramaic texts are assembled in K. Beyer, *Die aramäischen Texte vom Toten Meer samt den Inschriften aus Palästina, dem Testament Levis aus der Kairoer Genisa, Der Fastenrolle und den alten talmudischen Zitaten* (Göttingen 1984).

58 S. Zeitlin, 'A Commentary on the Book of Habakkuk: Important Discovery or Hoax?', JQR 39 (1949) 235–247; –, *The Dead Sea Scrolls and Modern Scholarship* (JQRMS 3) (Philadelphia 1956).

58 O. R. Seller, 'Radiocarbon dating of Cloth from the ᶜAin Feshka Cave', BASOR 123 (1951) 24–26.

60 F. E. Zeuner, 'Notes on Qumran', PEQ 92 (1960) 27–36. The date given by Zeuner is the year 66 CE since he adds to the date attained about 50 years for the average life of a palm-tree, but, as E. M. Laperrousaz points out, this addition is unnecessary since what Carbon 14 (the Carbon 14 test) determines is the date when the tree was cut down. See E. M. Laperrousaz, 'La datation des objets provenant de Qumrân, en particulier la méthode utilisant les propriétés du Carbone 14' in M. Delcor, (ed.), *Qumrân. Sa piété, sa théologie et son milieu* (BETL 46) (Paris/Leuven 1978) 55–60.

61 D. Burton, J. B. Poole and R. Reed, 'A New Approach to the Dating of the Dead Sea Scrolls', *Nature* 184 (1959) 533–534.

62 C. Roth, *The Historical Background of the Dead Sea Scrolls* (Oxford 1958).

63 In his important book *The Judaean Scrolls. The Problem and a Solution* (Oxford 1965) and in subsequent articles, where he attempts to refute the objections raised against him: 'Myths of Qumran', ALUOS 6 (1966–68) 23–40 and 'Mythology of Qumran', JQR 71 (1970) 241–281.

64 J. L. Teicher, 'The Dead Sea Scrolls–Documents of the Jewish-Christian Sect of Ebionites', *JJS* 2 (1951) 67-99; – , 'The Damascus fragments and the Origin of the Jewish Christian Sect', *JJS* 2 (1951) 115-143; – , 'The Teaching of the pre-Pauline Church in the Dead Sea Scrolls', *JJS* 4 (1953) 1-13, etc.

65 B. E. Thiering, *Redating the Teacher of Righteousness* (Sydney 1979); – , *The Gospels and Qumran. A New Hypothesis* (Sydney 1981); – *The Qumran Origins of the Christian Church* (Sydney 1983).

66 R. Eisenman, *Maccabees, Zadokites, Christians and Qumran* (Leiden 1983) and *James the Just in the Habakkuk Pesher* (Leiden 1986).

67 W. F. Albright, 'A Biblical Fragment from the Maccabaean Ages: The Nash Papyrus', *JBL* 56 (1937) 145-176.

68 S. A. Birnbaum, *The Qumran (Dead Sea) Scrolls and Palaeography* (BASOR Supp. Studies 13-14; New Haven 1952); – , *The Hebrew Script* (Leiden 1971).

69 N. Avigad, 'The Palaeography of the Dead Sea Scrolls and Related Documents' in C. Rabin and Y. Yadin (eds.), *Aspects of the Dead Sea Scrolls* (Scripta Hierosolymitana IV; Jerusalem 1958) 56-87.

70 F. M. Cross, 'The Development of the Jewish Scripts' in G. E. Wright (ed.), *The Bible and the Ancient Near East. Essays in Honor of William Foxwell Albright* (Garden City 1965) 170-264.

71 W. Wölfi, 'Advances in Accelerator Mass Spectrometry', *Nucl. Instrum Meth.* B29 (1987) 1-13.

72 The inclusion of dated manuscripts (a fact unknown to those making the analysis) was for the purpose of checking the accuracy of the technique used.

73 See G. Bonani, M. Broshi, I. Carmi, S. Ivy, J. Strugnell and W. Wölfi, 'Radiocarbon Dating of the Dead Sea Scrolls', *ᶜAtiqot* 20 (1991) 27-32.

74 The only exception is the manuscript of the *Aramaic Testament of Qahat*, for which the Carbon 14 method ascribes a date much earlier than that attributed to it by the palaeographers. Specimens of this manuscript, cleaned by ultrasound, yield dates earlier by about 350 years than specimens of the same manuscripts cleaned chemically, which seems to suggest that the leather became very contaminated by the chemicals used to clean it. This contamination could explain that in this case the date established by the Carbon 14 method (between 388 and 353 BCE) is almost 200 years earlier than the date ascribed to it by palaeographers.

75 Cave 7 is a special case. All the manuscripts recovered from it are in Greek, and to the extent to which they can be identified, they all comprise biblical material.

76 This calendar is to be found as part of several copies of such typical sectarian works as *1QS* or *4QMMT*, is followed consistently in compositions such as *11QTemple*, and is implicit in works such as *1QpHab*, and its organization, its effects and the fact that it was revealed are all made explicit in works such as *CD* and *Jubilees*.

77 N. Golb, 'The Problem of Origin and Identification of the Dead Sea Scrolls',

PAPS 124 (1980) 1-24; –, 'Who Hid the Dead Sea Scrolls?', *BA* 28 (1987) 68-82; –, 'Les manuscrits de la Mer Morte: Une nouvelle approche du problème de leur origine'. *Annales ESC* 40 (1987) 1133-1149; –, 'Who Wrote the Dead Sea Scrolls?', *The Sciences* 27 (1987) 40-49; –, 'The Dead Sea Scrolls', *The American Scholar* 58 (1989) 177-207; 'Khirbet Qumran and the Manuscripts of the Judaean Wilderness: Observations on the Logic of Their Investigation', *JNES* 49 (1990) 103-114.

78 Although expressed independently, this theory of Golb's does little except revive the old and deservedly abandoned hypothesis of K. H. Rengstorf, *Hirbet Qumran und die Bibliothek vom Toten Meer* (Studia Delitzschiana 5; Stuttgart 1960), which conjectured that the manuscripts in question came from the Temple in Jerusalem, and were hidden in the caves for reasons of safekeeping during the revolt against Rome.

79 In F. García Martínez and A. S. van der Woude, 'A "Groningen" Hypothesis of Qumran Origins and Early History', in F. García Martínez (ed.), *The Texts of Qumran and the History of the Community. Vol. III* (Paris 1990) 521-554.

80 This information has been collected in A. Adam and C. Burchard, *Antike Berichte über die Essener* (Berlin 1972²) and in G. Vermes and M. D. Goodman, *The Essenes According to the Classical Sources* (Sheffield 1989).

81 These similarities are to be found both in respect of the structure of the community – prominence of the priestly aspect, admission procedures for members, property in common, preference for celibacy, communal meals, etc. – and in religious belief – predestination (determinism), severe rules for purity, sabbath observance, forswearing of oaths, importance of study of the Law, etc. and even particular points of halakhah ostensibly insignificant, but for that very reason even more telling such as the refusal to use oil or the ban on spitting in the Council. See the summary of parallels drawn up by A. Dupont-Sommer, *Les Ecrits esséniens découverts près de la Mer Morte* (Paris 1983⁴) 51-80 or by G. Vermes, *The Dead Sea Scrolls. Qumran in Perspective* (Philadelphia 1981) 116-136 or the detailed references by T. S. Beall, *Josephus's description of the Essenes illustrated by the Dead Sea Scrolls* (SNTSM 58; Cambridge 1988). H. Stegemann, 'The Qumran Essenes – Local Members of the Main Jewish Union in Late Second Temple Times' in J. Trebolle Barrera, L. Vegas Montaner (eds.), *The Madrid Qumran Congress*, 83-166 have gone so far as to identify the Qumran Essenes with what he calls 'the main Jewish Union', the leading group of Palestinian Judaism.

82 In my contribution to the 'Simposio bíblico de Córdoba', 1985: 'Orígenes del movimiento esenio y orígenes qumránicos. Pistas para una solución', cited above, n. 38.

83 See my study 'Essénisme qumrânien: origines, caractéristiques, héritage' in B. Chiesa (ed.), *Correnti culturali e movimenti religiosi del Giudaismo* (Testi e Studi 5; Rome 1987) 37-57.

84 First advanced at a congress organized by the Polish Academy of Science in Mogilany, in 1987: F. García Martínez, 'Qumran Origins and Early History: A Groningen Hypothesis', *FO* 25 (1988) 113-136.

85 See my book *Qumran and Apocalyptic. Studies on the Aramaic Texts of Qumran* (STDJ 9; Leiden 1992). For a summary view of the connections between the Qumran manuscripts and apocalyptic, see my contribution 'La Apocalíptica y Qumrán' in *II Simposio Bíblico Español*, 603-613.

86 I have discussed some of these topics in detail in 'El Rollo del Templo y la halaká sectaria' in N. Fernández Marcos, J. Trebolle Barrera and J. Fernández Vallina (eds.), *Simposio Bíblico Español* (Madrid 1984) 611-622 and in 'Il problema della purità: la soluzione qumranica' in G. L. Prato, (ed.), *Israele alla ricerca di identità tra il III sec. a. C. e il sec. I d. C.* (Ricerche storico bibliche 1; Bologna 1989) 169-191.

87 See my study 'Profeet en profetie in de geschriften van Qumran' in F. García Martinez, C. H. J. de Geus and A. F. J. Klijn, (eds.), *Profeten en profetische geschriften* (Kampen/Nijkerk 1987) 119-132.

88 Set out in the article by A. S. van der Woude, 'Wicked Priest or Wicked Priests? Reflections on the Identification of the Wicked Priest of the Habakkuk Commentary', *JSJ* 33 (1982) 349-359. My contribution to this part of the 'Groningen Hypothesis' is confined to proving that the title 'Wicked Priest' could equally have been applied to Judas Maccabaeus, '¿Judas Macabeo, sacerdote impío? Notas al margen de 1QpHab VIII, 8-13' in A. Caquot, S. Légasse and M. Tardieu (eds.), *Mélanges bibliques et orientaux en l'honneur de M. Mathias Delcor* (AOAT 215; Kevelaer/Neukirchen-Vluyn 1985) 169-181.

Rules

This chapter contains those texts which can be called 'Rules', texts that serve to establish the group or groups for which they are intended. These writings are not restricted to listing specific regulations concerning the way of life to be followed by the group, to describing the internal hierarchical organization, to setting out disciplinary procedures or how to associate with those who are not members of the sect. They include, in fact, much else besides: theological essays, meditations on biblical history, exegetical commentaries, recommendations on moral issues, and even unmistakably liturgical topics. This unique literary form, previously unknown in ancient Judaism, was to develop extensively within early Christianity and in later monastic communities. These 'Rules' are unquestionably the most typical of all the documents from the Qumran library.

The two principal texts of this chapter, the *Rule of the Community* and the *Damascus Document*, clearly show the marks of the continual revision they have undergone over a long period before reaching the form shown in the best preserved manuscripts. Both documents are composites, and the various copies recovered give us an idea of the different shapes in which these 'Rules' were moulded. Close analysis of these different forms will make it possible to sketch the development and changes which the group (or groups) experienced, of those for which they were intended for different periods, and to establish the connections among these groups.

Reasons of space preclude setting out the fragments of the various copies of each document in synoptic form, using parallel columns. Several of these copies comprise separate versions, but its is impossible to determine whether all the elements preserved in the different copies were at one time present in a single text. Accordingly, it is not feasible to offer a composite version, as a reconstruction of a hypothetical master text, from the material preserved in the different manuscripts.

1 The Rule of the Community

A *The Cave 1 Copy*

1QRule of the Community (1QS)

Col. I   *1* For [the Instructor...] ... [book of the Rul]e of the Community: in order to *2* seek God [with all (one's) heart and with all (one's) soul; in order] to do what is good and just in his presence, as *3* commanded by means of the hand of Moses and his servants the Prophets; in order to love everything *4* which he selects and to hate everything that he rejects; in order to keep oneself at a distance from all evil, *5* and to become attached to all good works; to bring about truth, justice and uprightness *6* on earth and not to walk in the stubbornness of a guilty heart and of lecherous eyes *7* performing every evil; in order to welcome into the covenant of kindness all those who freely volunteer to carry out God's decrees, *8* so as to be united in the counsel of God and walk in perfection in his sight, complying with all *9* revealed things concerning the regulated times of their stipulations; in order to love all the sons of light, each one *10* according to his lot in God's plan, and to detest all the sons of darkness, each one in accordance with his blame *11* in God's vindication. All those who submit freely to his truth will convey all their knowledge, their energies, *12* and their riches to the Community of God in order to refine their knowledge in the truth of God's decrees and marshal their energies *13* in accordance with his perfect paths and all their riches in accordance with his just counsel. They shall not stray from any one *14* of all God's orders concerning their appointed times; they shall not advance their appointed times nor shall they retard *15* any one of their feasts. They shall not veer from his reliable precepts in order to go either to the right or to the left. *16* And all those who enter in the Rule of the Community shall establish a covenant before God in order to carry out *17* all that he commands and in order not to stray from following him for any fear, dread or grief *18* that might occur during the dominion of Belial. When they enter the covenant, the priests *19* and the levites shall bless the God of salvation and all the works of his faithfulness and all *20* those who enter the covenant shall repeat after them: 'Amen, Amen'. *Blank 21 Blank* The priests shall recite the just deeds of God in his mighty works, *22* and they shall proclaim all his merciful favours towards Israel. And the levites shall recite *23* the sins of the children of Israel, all their blameworthy transgressions and their sins during the dominion of *24* Belial. [And all] those who enter the covenant shall confess after them and they shall say:

«We have acted sinfully,
25 [we have transgressed,

we have si]nned, we have acted irreverently,
we and our fathers before us,
inasmuch as we walk
26 [in the opposite direction to the precepts] of truth and justice
    […] his judgment upon us and upon our fathers;

Col. II   *1* but he has showered on us his merciful favour
for ever and ever»
And the priests will bless all *2* the men of God's lot who walk unblemished in
all his paths and they shall say:
«May he bless you with everything good,
3 and may he protect you from everything bad.
May he illuminate your heart with the discernment of life
and grace you with eternal knowledge.
4 May he lift upon you the countenance of his favour
for eternal peace».
And the levites shall curse all the men of *5* of the lot of Belial. They shall begin
to speak and shall say:
«Accursed are you for all your wicked, blameworthy deeds.
May he (God) hand you over to dread
6 into the hands of all those carrying out acts of vengeance.
7 Accursed, without mercy,
for the darkness of your deeds,
and sentenced
8 to the gloom of everlasting fire.
May God not be merciful when you entreat him,
nor pardon you when you do penance for your faults.
9 May he lift the countenance of his anger to avenge himself on you,
and may there be no peace for you
in the mouth of those who intercede».
10 And all those who enter the covenant shall say, after those who pronounce
blessings and those who pronounce curses: «Amen, Amen».
11 *Blank* And the priests and the levites shall continue, saying:
«Cursed by the idols which his heart reveres
12 whoever enters this covenant
leaving his guilty obstacle in front of himself
to fall over it.
13 When he hears the words of this covenant,
he will congratulate himself in his heart, saying:
'I will have peace,
14 in spite of my walking in the stubbornness of my heart'.
However, his spirit will be obliterated,

the dry with the moist, mercilessly.

15 May God's anger and the wrath of his verdicts
consume him for everlasting destruction.

16 May all the curses of this covenant
stick fast to him.
May God segregate him for evil,
and may he be cut off from the midst of all the sons of light
because of his straying from following God

17 on account of his idols and his blameworthy obstacle.
May he assign his lot with the cursed ones for ever».

18 And all those who enter the covenant shall begin speaking and shall say after
them: «Amen, Amen». *Blank 19 Blank* They shall act in this way year after year,
all the days of Belial's dominion. The priests shall enter *20* the Rule foremost,
one behind the other, according to their spirits. And the levites shall enter after
them. *21* In third place all the people shall enter the Rule, one after another, in
thousands, hundreds, *22* fifties and tens, so that all the children of Israel may
know their standing in God's Community *23* in conformity with the eternal
plan. And no-one shall move down from his rank nor move up from the place
of his lot. *24* For all shall be in a single Community of truth, of proper meekness, of compassionate love and upright purpose, *25* towards each other in the
holy council, associates of an everlasting society. And anyone who declines to
enter [the covenant of Go]d in order to walk in the stubbornness of his heart
shall not [enter the Com]munity of his truth, since

Col. III   *1* his soul loathes the restraints of knowledge of just judgment. He has
not remained constant in the transformation of his life and shall not be counted
with the upright. *2* His knowledge, his energy and his wealth shall not enter the
council of the Community because he ploughs] in the slime of irreverence and
there are stains *3* on his conversion. He shall not be justified while he maintains
the stubbornness of his heart, since he regards darkness as paths to light. In the
source of the perfect *4* he shall not be counted. He will not become clean by the
acts of atonement, nor shall he be purified by the cleansing waters, nor shall he
be made holy by the seas *5* or rivers, nor shall he be purified by all the water of
the ablutions. Defiled, defiled shall he be all the days he spurns the decrees
6 of God, without allowing himself to be taught by the Community of his
counsel. For, by the spirit of the true counsel concerning the paths of man all
7 his sins are atoned so that he can look at the light of life. And by the spirit of
holiness which links him with his truth he is cleansed of all *8* his sins. And by
the spirit of uprightness and of humility his sin is atoned. And by the compliance of his soul with all the laws of God his flesh *9* is cleansed by being sprinkled with cleansing waters and being made holy with the waters of repentance.
May he, then, steady his steps in order to walk with perfection *10* on all the

paths of God, conforming to all he has decreed concerning the regular times
of his commands and not turn aside, either left or right, nor *11* infringe even
one of his words. In this way he will be admitted by means of atonement pleasing to God, and for him it will be the covenant *12* of an everlasting Community.
Blank 13 Blank For the wise man, that he may inform and teach all the sons of
light about the history of all the sons of man, *14* concerning all the ranks of
their spirits, in accordance with their signs, concerning their deeds and their
generations, and concerning the visitation of their punishment and *15* the moment of their reward. From the God of knowledge stems all there is and all
there shall be. Before they existed he made all their plans *16* and when they
came into being they will execute all their works in compliance with his instructions, according to his glorious design without altering anything. In his
hand are *17* the laws of all things and he supports them in all their needs. He
created man to rule *18* the world and placed within him two spirits so that he
would walk with them until the moment of his visitation: they are the spirits
of truth and of deceit. *20* In the hand of the Prince of Lights is dominion over
all the sons of justice; they walk on paths of light. And in the hand of the Angel *21* of Darkness is total dominion over the sons of deceit; they walk on paths
of darkness. Due to the Angel of Darkness *22* all the sons of justice stray, and
all their sins, their iniquities, their failings and their mutinous deeds are under
his dominion *23* in compliance with the mysteries of God, until his moment;
and all their punishments and their periods of grief are caused by the dominion
of his enmity; *24* and all the spirits of their lot cause the sons of light to fall.
However, the God of Israel and the angel of his truth assist all *25* the sons of
light. He created the spirits of light and of darkness and on them established
all his deeds *26* [on their p]aths all his labours ⟨and on their paths [all] his
[labours.]⟩. God loved one of them for all

Col. IV   *1* eternal ages and in all his deeds he takes pleasure for ever; of the other
one he detests his advice and hates all his paths forever. *Blank 2 Blank* These are
their paths in the world: to enlighten the heart of man, straighten out in front
of him all the paths of justice and truth, establish in his heart respect for the
precepts *3* of God; it is a spirit of meekness, of patience, generous compassion,
eternal goodness, intelligence, understanding, potent wisdom which trusts in
all *4* the deeds of God and depends on his abundant mercy; a spirit of knowledge in all the plans of action, of enthusiasm for the decrees of justice, *5* of holy
plans with firm purpose, of generous compassion with all the sons of truth, of
magnificent purity which detests all unclean idols, of unpretentious behaviour
6 with moderation in everything, of prudence in respect of the truth concerning
the mysteries of knowledge. These are the counsels of the spirit for the sons
of truth in the world. And the visitation of whose who walk in it will be for
healing, *7* plentiful peace in a long life, fruitful offspring with all everlasting

blessings, eternal enjoyment with endless life, and a crown of glory *8* with majestic raiment in eternal light. *Blank 9 Blank* However, to the spirit of deceit belong greed, frailty of hands in the service of justice, irreverence, deceit, pride and haughtiness of heart, dishonesty, trickery, cruelty, *10* much insincerity, impatience, much insanity, impudent enthusiasm, appalling acts performed in a lustful passion, filthy paths for indecent purposes, *11* blasphemous tongue, blindness of eyes, hardness of hearing, stiffness of neck, hardness of heart in order to walk in all the paths of darkness and evil cunning. And the visitation *12* of those who walk in it will be for a glut of punishments at the hands of all the angels of destruction, for eternal damnation for the scorching wrath of the God of revenge, for permanent error and shame *13* without end with the humiliation of destruction by the fire of the dark regions. And all the ages of their generations they shall spend in bitter weeping and harsh evils in the abysses of darkness until *14* their destruction, without there being a remnant or a survivor among them. *Blank 15 Blank* In these lies the history of all men; in their (two) divisions all their armies have a share by their generations; in their paths they walk; every deed *16* they do falls into their divisions, dependent on what might be the birthright of the man, great or small, for all eternal time. For God has sorted them into equal parts until the *17* last day and has put an everlasting loathing between their divisions. Deeds of injustice are an abhorrence to truth and all the paths of truth are an abhorrence to injustice. There exists a violent *18* conflict in respect of all his decrees since they do not walk together. God, in the mysteries of his knowledge and in the wisdom of his glory, has determined an end to the existence of injustice and on the occasion *19* of his visitation he will obliterate it for ever. Meanwhile, truth shall rise up forever in the world which has been defiled in paths of wickedness during the dominion of injustice until *20* the time appointed for judgment. Meanwhile, God will refine, with his truth, all man's deeds, and will purify for himself the configuration of man, ripping out all spirit of injustice from the innermost part *21* of his flesh, and cleansing him with the spirit of holiness from every irreverent deed. He will sprinkle over him the spirit of truth like lustral water (in order to cleanse him) from all the abhorrences of deceit and from the defilement *22* of the unclean spirit. In this way the upright will understand knowledge of the Most High, and the wisdom of the sons of heaven will teach those of perfect behaviour. For these are those selected by God for an everlasting covenant *23* and to them shall belong all the glory of Adam. There will be no more injustice and all the deeds of trickery will be a dishonour. Until now the spirits of truth and of injustice feud in the heart of man *24* and they walk in wisdom or in folly. In agreement with man's birthright in justice and in truth, so he abhors injustice; and according to his share in the lot of injustice he acts irreverently in it and so *25* abhors the truth. For God has sorted them into equal parts until the appointed end and the new creation. He knows the result of his deeds for all

times *26* [everlas]ting and has given them as a legacy to the sons of men so that
they know good [and evil], so they decide the lot of every living being in compliance with the spirit there is in him [at the time of] the visitation.

Col. V   *1 Blank* This is the rule for the men of the Community who freely volunteer to convert from all evil and to keep themselves steadfast in all he prescribes
in compliance with his will. They should keep apart from *2* men of sin in order
to constitute a Community in law and possessions, and acquiesce to the authority of the sons of Zadok, the priests who safeguard the covenant and to the
authority of the multitude of the men *3* of the Community, those who perse-
vere steadfastly in the covenant. By its authority, decision by lot shall be made
in every affair involving the law, property and judgment, to achieve together
truth and humility, *4* justice and uprightness, compassionate love and seemly
behaviour in all their paths. No-one should walk in the stubbornness of his
heart in order to go astray following his heart *5* and his eyes and the musings
of his inclination. Instead he should circumcise in the Community the foreskin
of his tendency and of his stiff neck in order to lay a foundation of truth for
Israel, for the Community of the eternal *6* covenant. They should make atonement for all who freely volunteer for holiness in Aaron and for the house of
truth in Israel and for those being entered together for the Community for the
lawsuit and for the judgment. *7* They should proclaim as guilty all those who
sabotage the decree. These are the regulations of behaviour concerning all these
decrees when they are enrolled in the Community. Whoever enters the council
of the Community *8* enters the covenant of God in the presence of all who
freely volunteer. He shall swear with a binding oath to revert to the Law of
Moses with all that it decrees, with whole *9* heart and whole soul, in compliance
with all that has been revealed concerning it to the sons of Zadok, the priests
who keep the covenant and interpret his will and to the multitude of the men
of their covenant *10* who freely volunteer together for this truth and to walk
according to his will. He should swear by the covenant to be segregated from
all the men of sin who walk *11* along paths of irreverence. For they are not
included in his covenant since they have neither sought nor examined his decrees in order to learn the hidden matters in which they err *12* by their own
fault and because they treated revealed matters with disrespect; this is why
wrath will rise up for judgment in order to effect revenge by the curses of the
covenant, in order to administer fierce *13* punishments for everlasting annihilation without there being any remnant. *Blank* He should not go into the waters
to share in the pure food of the men of holiness, for they have not been
cleansed *14* unless they turn away from their wickedness, for it is unclean
among all the transgressors of his word. No-one should associate with him in
his work or in his possessions in order not to encumber him *15* with blameworthy sin; rather he should remain at a distance from him in every task, for it is

written as follows: 'You shall remain at a distance from every lie'. None of the men *16* of the Community should acquiesce to his authority in any law or regulation. No-one should eat of any of his possessions, or drink or accept anything from his hands, *17* unless at its price, for it is written: 'Shun the man whose breath is in his nostrils, for how much is he worth?' For *18* all those not numbered in his covenant will be segregated, they and all that belongs to them. No holy man should support himself on any deed of *19* futility, for futile are all those who do not know the covenant. And all those who scorn his word he shall cause to vanish from the world; all his deeds are uncleanness *20* before him and there is uncleanness in all his possessions. And when someone enters the covenant to behave in compliance with all these decrees, enrolling in the assembly of holiness, they shall test *21* their spirits in the Community (discriminating) between a man and his fellow, in respect of his insight and of his deeds in law, under the authority of the sons of Aaron, those who freely volunteer in the Community to set up *22* his covenant and to follow all the decrees which he commanded to fulfil, and under the authority of the majority of Israel, those who freely volunteer to return within the Community to his covenant. *23* And they shall be recorded in the Rule, each one before his fellow, according to his insight and his deeds, in such a way that each one obeys his fellow, junior under senior. *24* And their spirit and their deeds must be tested, year after year, in order to upgrade each one to the extent of his insight and the perfection of his path, or to demote him according to his failings. Each should reproach *25* his fellow in truth, in meekness and in compassionate love for the man. *Blank* No-one should speak to his brother in anger or muttering, *26* or with a hard [neck or with passionate] spiteful intent and he should not detest him [in the stubbornness] of his heart, but instead reproach him that day so as not

Col. VI   *1* to incur a sin for his fault. And in addition, no-one should raise a matter against his fellow in front of the Many unless it is with reproof in the presence of witnesses. In this way *2* shall they behave in all their places of residence. Whenever one fellow meets another, the junior shall obey the senior in work and in money. They shall eat together, *3* together they shall bless and together they shall take counsel. In every place where there are ten men of the Community council, there should not be a priest missing amongst them. *4* And when they prepare the table to dine or the new wine *5* for drinking, the priest shall stretch out his hand as the first to bless the first fruits of the bread {or the new wine for drinking, the priest shall stretch out his hand as the first *6* to bless the first fruits of the bread} and of the new wine. And in the place in which the Ten assemble there should not be missing a man to interpret the law day and night, *7* always, each man relieving his fellow. And the Many shall be on watch together for a third of each night of the year in order to read the book, explain the regulation, *8* and bless together. *Blank* This is the Rule for the session of the

Many. Each one by his rank: the priests will sit down first, the elders next and the remainder of *9* all the people will sit down in order of rank. And following the same system they shall be questioned with regard to the judgment, the counsel and any matter referred to the Many, so that each can impart his wisdom *10* to the council of the Community. No-one should talk during the speech of his fellow before his brother has finished speaking. And neither should he speak before one whose rank is listed *11* before his own. Whoever is questioned should speak in his turn. And in the session of the Many no-one should utter anything without the consent of the Many. And if the *12* Examiner of the Many prevents someone having something to say to the Many but he is not in the position of one who is asking questions to the Community council, *13* that man should stand up and say: 'I have something to say to the Many'. If they tell him to, he should speak. And to any in Israel who freely volunteers *14* to enrol in the council of the Community, the Instructor who is at the head of the Many shall test him with regard to his insight and his deeds. If he suits the discipline he shall introduce him *15* into the covenant so that he can revert to the truth and shun all sin, and he shall teach him all the precepts of the Community. And then, when he comes in to stand in front of the Many, they shall be questioned, *16* all of them, concerning his duties. And depending on the outcome of the lot in the council of the Many he shall be included or excluded. If he is included in the Community council, he must not touch the pure food of *17* the Many while they test him about his spirit and about his deeds until he has completed a full year; neither should he share in the possession of the Many. *18* When he has completed a year within the Community, the Many will be questioned about his duties, concerning his insight and his deeds in connection with the law. And if the lot results in him *19* joining the foundations of the Community according to the priests and the majority of the men of the covenant, his wealth and his belongings will also be included at the hands of the *20* Inspector of the belongings of the Many. And they shall be entered into the ledger in his hand but they shall not use them for the Many. He must not touch the drink of the Many until *21* he completes a second year among the men of the Community. And when this second year is complete he will be examined by command of the Many. And if *22* the lot results in him joining the Community, they shall enter him in the Rule according to his rank among his brothers for the law, for the judgment, for purity and for the placing of his possessions in common. And his advice will be *23* for the Community as will his judgment. *Blank* 24 *Blank* And these are the regulations by which they shall judge him in the scrutiny of the Community depending on the case. If one is found among them who has lied *25* knowingly concerning goods, he shall be excluded from the pure food of the Many for a year and shall be sentenced to a quarter of his bread. And whoever retorts to *26* his fellow with stubbornness and speaks with brusqueness, ruining the footing he has with him, defying the authority of his fellow who is enrolled ahead of him, *27* he has taken the law into his own hands; he will be punished for a year [...] Whoever enunciates the Name (which is) honoured above all [...]

Col. VII   *1* whether blaspheming, or overwhelmed by misfortune or for any other reason, {...} or reading a book, or blessing, will be excluded *2* and shall not go back to the Community council. And if he has spoken angrily against one of the priests enrolled in the book, he will be punished *3* for a year and shall be excluded, under sentence of death, from the pure food of the Many. However, if he had spoken unintentionally, he will be punished for six months. And whoever lies knowingly *4* shall be punished for six months. Whoever knowingly and for no reason insults his fellow will be punished for a year *5* and will be excluded. And whoever speaks to his fellow with deception or knowingly deceives him, will be punished for six months. And if *6 Blank* he is /negligent/ to his fellow he will be punished for three months. However, if he is negligent with the possessions of the Community achieving a loss, he shall replace them {...} *7* in full. *Blank 8 Blank 9 Blank 10* And if he does not manage to replace them, he will be punished for /sixty days/. And whoever feels animosity towards his fellow for no cause will be punished for {six months} /a year/. *11* And likewise for anyone retaliating for any reason. Whoever utters with his mouth futile words, three months; and for talking in the middle of the words of his fellow, *12* ten days. And whoever lies down and goes to sleep in the session of the Many, thirty days. And the same applies to whoever leaves the session of the Many *13* without cause, or falls asleep up to three times during a session shall be punished ten days; however, if ... *Blank 14* and he withdraws, he shall be punished for thirty days. And whoever walks about naked in front of his fellow, without needing to, shall be punished for three months. *15* And the person who spits in the course of a meeting of the Many shall be punished thirty days. And whoever takes out his 'hand' from under his clothes, or if these are rags *16* which allow his nakedness to be seen, he will be punished thirty days. And whoever giggles inanely causing his voice to be heard shall be sentenced to thirty *17* days. And whoever takes out his left hand to gesticulate with it shall be punished ten days. And whoever goes round defaming his fellow *18* shall be excluded for one year from the pure food of the Many and shall be punished; however, whoever goes round defaming the Many shall be expelled from their midst *19* and will never return. And whoever complains against the foundation of the Community they shall expel and he will never return; however, if he complains against his fellow *20* without cause he will be punished six months. The person whose spirit turns aside from the foundation of the Community to betray the truth *21* and walk in the stubbornness of his heart, if he comes back, shall be punished for two years; during the first year he shall not approach the pure food of the Many. *Blank 22 Blank* {...} And during the second he shall not approach {...} /the drink/ of the Many and shall sit at the back of all the men of the Community. *23* When the days of the two years are complete the Many shall be questioned *Blank* concerning his matter; if they admit him, he shall be enrolled according to his rank; and later he will be questioned in connection with judgment *24* {...} However, anyone who has been in the Community council {...} for ten full years. *Blank 25 Blank* {...} *Blank* and whose spirit reverts to betray the Community and go away from the presence *Blank 26* of the Many in order to walk in the stubbornness of his heart, can never return to the Community council. And the person among the men of the Community who fraternises *27* with him in concerns of purity or goods, who [...] the Many, and his sentence will be like his, he shall be exp[elled.]

Col. VIII   *1* In the Community council (there shall be) twelve men and three priests, perfect in everything that has been revealed about all *2* the law to implement truth, justice, judgment, compassionate love and unassuming behaviour of each person to his fellow *3* to preserve faithfulness on the earth with firm purpose and repentant spirit in order to atone for sin, doing justice *4* and undergoing trials in order to walk with everyone in the measure of truth and the regulation of time. When these things exist in Israel *5* the Community council shall be founded on truth, *Blank* like an everlasting plantation, a holy house for Israel and the foundation of the holy of *6* holies for Aaron, true witnesses for the judgment and chosen by the will (of God) to atone for the earth and to render *7* the wicked their retribution. *Blank* It (the Community) will be the tested rampart, the precious cornerstone that does not *Blank 8* /whose foundations do not/ shake or tremble in their place. *Blank* It will be the most holy dwelling *9* for Aaron with total knowledge of the covenant of justice and in order to offer a pleasant /aroma/; and it will be a house of perfection and truth in Israel; *10* {...} in order to establish a covenant in compliance with the everlasting decrees. /And these will be accepted in order to atone for the earth and to decide the judgment of the wicked {...} and there will be no iniquity/. When these have been established in the foundation of the Community for two full years /in/ perfect behaviour *11* /they will be segregated/ (like) holy ones in the midst of the council of the men of the Community. And every matter hidden from Israel but which has been found out by *12* the Interpreter, he should not keep hidden from them for fear of a spirit of desertion. And when these exist /as a community/ in Israel *13* /in compliance with these arrangements/ they are to be segregated from within the dwelling of the men of sin to walk to the desert in order to open there His path. *14* As it is written: «In the desert, prepare the way of ****, straighten in the steppe a roadway for our God». *15* This is the study of the law which he commanded through the hand of Moses, in order to act in compliance with all that has been revealed from age to age, *16* and according to what the prophets have revealed through his holy spirit.

And anyone of the men of the Community, the covenant of *17* the Community, who insolently shuns anything at all commanded, cannot approach the pure food of the men of holiness, *18* and cannot know anything of their counsels until his deeds have been cleansed from every depravity, walking on the perfect path. Then they can include him *19* in the council under the authority of the Many and later they will enrol him according to his rank. And (they shall apply) this regulation to all who enter the Community. *20 Blank* These are the regulations by which the men of perfect holiness shall conduct themselves, each with his fellow. *21* All who enter the council of holiness of those walking along the path of perfection as has been commanded, anyone of them *22* who breaks one word of the law of Moses impertinently or through carelessness will be banished from the Community council *23* and shall not go back again; none of the men of holiness should associate with his goods or his advice on any *24* matter. However if he acted through oversight he should be excluded from pure food and from the council and the regulation applied to him: *25* «He cannot judge anyone and no-one should ask his advice for two whole years». If his conduct is perfect *26* in them, he may return to the interpretation and to the council [according to the authority of the Ma]ny, if he has not sinned again through oversight until two full years have passed. *27 Blank*

Col. IX   *1* For {...} a sin of oversight, then, he will be punished two years; but whoever acts impertinently shall not go back again. Only someone who sins through oversight *2* shall be tested for two full years in respect of his behaviour and of his counsel according to the authority of the Many and shall then be enrolled according to his rank in the Community of holiness. *3 Blank* When these exist in Israel in accordance with these rules in order to establish the spirit of holiness in truth *4* eternal, in order to atone for the fault of the transgression and for the guilt of sin and for approval for the earth, without the flesh of burnt offerings and without the fats of sacrifice – the offering of *5* the lips in compliance with the decree will be like the pleasant aroma of justice and the correctness of behaviour will be acceptable like a freewill offering – at this moment the men of *6* the Community shall set themselves apart (like) a holy house for Aaron, in order to enter the holy of holies, and (like) a house of the Community for Israel, (for) those who walk in perfection. *7* Only the sons of Aaron will have authority in the matter of judgment and of goods, and their word will settle the lot of all provision for the men of the Community *8* and the goods of the men of holiness who walk in perfection. Their goods must not be confused with the goods of the men of deceit who *9* have not cleansed their path, withdrawing from evil and walking on a perfect path. They should not depart from any counsel of the law in order to walk *10* in complete stubbornness of their heart, but instead shall be ruled by the first directives which the men of the Community began to be taught *11* until the prophet comes, and the Messiahs

of Aaron and Israel. *Blank 12 Blank* These are the regulations for the Instructor
by which he shall walk with every living being in compliance with the circumstances of every period and in compliance with the worth of each man: *13* he
should fulfil the will of God in compliance with all revelation for every period;
he should acquire all the wisdom that has been gained according to the periods
and the *14* regulation of the period; he should separate and weigh the sons of
Zadok *Blank* according to their spirits; he should keep hold of the chosen ones
of the period according to his will, as he has commanded; he should carry out
the judgment of each man in accordance with his spirit; he should include each
one according to the purity of his hands and according to his intellect *16* promote him. And thus shall be his love and thus shall be his hatred. *Blank* He
should not reproach or argue with the men of the pit *17* but instead hide the
counsel of the law in the midst of the men of sin. He should reproach (with)
truthful knowledge and (with) just judgment those who choose *18* the path,
each one according to his spirit, according to the circumstances of the time. He
should lead them with knowledge and in this way teach them the mysteries of
wonder and of truth in the midst of *19* the men of the Community, so that they
walk perfectly, each one with his fellow, in all that has been revealed to them.
This is the time for making ready the path *20* to the desert and he will teach
them about all that has been discovered so that they can carry it out in this
moment and so they will be detached from anyone who has not withdrawn his
path *21* from all wickedness. And these are the rules of behaviour for the Inspector in these times, concerning his love and his hatred. Everlasting hatred
22 for the men of the pit in clandestine spirit. To them he should leave goods
and hand-made items like a servant to his master and like one oppressed before
23 someone domineering him. He should be a man enthusiastic for the decree
and for his time, for the day of revenge. He should perform (God's) will in all
that his hand should tackle *24* and in all that he controls, as he commanded.
And all that happens to him he should welcome freely and be gratified by nothing except God's will. *25* He should relish all the words of his mouth, wish for
nothing that he has not commanded and be ever alert to the precept of God.
26 […] he shall bless his Creator and in all that transpires [… and with the of-
fering] of his lips he shall bless him

Col. X   *1* during. *Blank* the periods which (?) he decreed(?).
 At the commencement of the dominion of light,
  during its rotation
  and when retired to its appointed abode.
 At the commencement of the vigils of darkness
2 when he opens his store and stretches them upwards
  and in his rotation
  and when it retires before the light.

When the lights of the holy vault shine out
3 when they retire to the abode of glory.
At the entry of the constellation in the days of the new moon
together with their rotations during their stations
4 renewing each other.
It is a great day for the holy of holies,
and an omen *Blank* of the opening of his everlasting mercies
5 for the beginnings of the constellations in every future age. *Blank*
At the commencement of the months in their constellations,
and of the holy days in their sequence,
as a reminder in their constellations.
6 With the offering of lips I shall bless you,
in accordance with the decree recorded for ever.
At the commencement of the years and in the gyrations of their constellations,
when the decree of their disposition is carried out,
7 on the prescribed day, one after another;
the constellation of the harvest up to summer,
the constellation of seed-time up to the constellation of the grass,
the constellation of the years up to their seven-year periods.
8 At the commencement of the seven-year periods
up to the moment decided for deliverance.
And in all my existence
it shall be a precept engraved on my tongue
like fruit of eulogy
and the portion of my lips.
9 {…} I will sing with knowledge
and for the glory of God shall all my music be,
the playing of my harp for his holy order,
and the whistle of my lips
I shall tune to its correct measure.
10 At the onset of day and night
I shall enter the covenant of God,
and when evening and morning depart
I shall repeat his precepts;
and while they last
I shall set them as my limit
11 with no backtracking.
His judgment reproaches me in conformity with my delights;
they are before my eyes, like graven laws, my sins.
But to God I shall say: «My justice»,
12 and to the Most High: «Foundation of my well-being»,
«source of knowing»,

«spring of holiness»,
«peak of glory»,
«all-powerful one of eternal majesty».
I shall choose what he teaches me,
13 I shall be pleased in how he might judge me.
    When I start to stretch out my hands and my feet
    I shall bless his name;
    when I start to go out and to come in,
14 to sit and to stand up,
    and lying down in my bed
    I shall extol him;
    I shall bless him with the offering that issues from my lips
15 and before stretching out my hand
    to get fat on the tasty fruit of the earth.
    At the onset of fright and dismay
    and in the place of distress and grief,
16 I shall bless him for (his) great marvels
    and shall meditate on his power
    and shall rely on his compassion
    the whole day.
    I realize that in his hand
    lies the judgment of every living thing,
17 and all his deeds are truth.
    When distress is unleashed
    I shall praise him
    just as I shall sing to him
    for his deliverance.
    I shall not repay anyone
    with an evil reward;
18 with goodness I shall pursue the man
    For to God (belongs) the judgment
    of every living being,
    and it is he who pays man his wages.
    I shall have no enthusiasm for the wicked spirit,
19 and my soul shall not crave wealth by violence
    I /shall not be involved/ at all in any dispute
    of the men of the pit
    /until the day/ of vengeance.
20 However, I shall not remove my anger
    from wicked men,
    nor shall I be appeased,
    until he carries out his judgment.

I shall not sustain angry resentment
for someone who converts from transgression,
but I shall have no mercy
21 for all those who deviate from the path.
I shall not comfort the oppressed
until their path is perfect.
I shall not retain Belial within my heart.
From my mouth no vulgarity shall be heard
22 or wicked deceptions;
sophistries or lies
shall not be found on my lips.
The fruit of holiness will be on my tongue,
23 profanity shall not be found on it.
With hymns shall I open my mouth
and my tongue will ever number the just acts of God
and the treachery of men
until their transgression is complete.
24 I shall remove from my lips worthless words,
unclean things and plotting from the knowledge of my heart.
With wise counsel I shall hide /I shall tell of/ knowledge,
25 and with discretion of knowledge I shall enclose him with a solid fence
to maintain faithfulness and staunch judgment
with the justice of God.
26 [I shall share out] the regulation with the cord of the ages
[...] justice and compassionate love with the oppressed,
and to strengthen the hands of the [...]

Col. XI   *1* understanding of those with a stray spirit
in order to instruct in the teaching those who complain
to reply with meekness to the haughty of spirit,
and with a repentant spirit to the men of the stick,
2 those who point the finger
and speak evil,
and are keen on riches.
As for me, in God is my judgment;
in his hand is the perfection of my path
with the uprightness of my heart;
3 and with his just acts he cancels my sin.
For from the source of his knowledge
he has disclosed his light,
and my eyes have observed his wonders,
and the light of my heart the mystery of the future

4 and of the present and of what it is for always.
   There is support for my right hand,
   the path of my steps goes over firm rock,
   it does not waver before anything.
   For the truth of God is the rock of my steps,
5 and his might the support of my right hand.
   From the spring of his justice is my judgment
   and from the wonderful mystery is the light in my heart.
   My eyes have observed what always is,
6 wisdom that has been hidden from mankind,
   knowledge and understanding (hidden) from the sons of man,
   fount of justice and well of strength
7 and spring of glory (hidden) from the assembly of flesh.
   To those whom God has selected he has given them
   as everlasting possession;
   until they inherit them
   in the lot of the holy ones.
8 He unites their assembly to the sons of the heavens
   in order (to form) the counsel of the Community
   and a foundation of the building of holiness
   to be an everlasting plantation
   throughout all future ages.
9 However, I belong to evil humankind
   to the assembly of wicked flesh;
   my failings, my transgressions, my sins, {...}
   with the depravities of my heart,
10 belong to the assembly of worms
   and of those who walk in darkness.
   For to man (does not belong) his path,
   nor to a human being the steadying of his step;
   since judgment belongs to God,
11 and from his hand is the perfection of the path.
   By his knowledge everything shall come into being,
   and all that does exist
   he establishes with his calculations
   and nothing is done outside of him.
   As for me, if I stumble,
12 the mercies of God shall be my salvation always;
   and if I fall in the sin of the flesh,
   in the justice of God, which endures eternally, shall my judgment be;
13 if my grief commences,
   he will free my soul from the pit

and make my steps steady on the path;
   he will draw me near in his mercies,
   and by kindnesses set in motion my judgment;
14 he will judge me in the justice of his truth,
   and in his plentiful goodness
   always atone for all my sins;
   in his justice he will cleanse me
   from the uncleanness of the human being
15 and from the sin of the sons of man,
   so that I can extol God for his justice
   and The Highest for his majesty.
   Blessed be you, my God,
   who opens the heart of your servant to knowledge!
16 Establish all his deeds in justice,
   and raise up the son of your handmaid
   to be everlastingly in your presence,
   as you have cared for the selected ones of humankind.
17 For beyond you there is no perfect path
   and without your will, nothing comes to be.
   You have taught all knowledge
18 and all that exists is so by your will.
   Beyond you there is no-one
   to oppose your counsel,
   to understand one of your holy thoughts,
19 to gaze into the abyss of your mysteries,
   to fathom all your marvels
   or the strength of your might.
20 Who can tolerate your glory?
   What, indeed, is man,
   among all your marvellous deeds?
21 As what shall one born of woman be considered
   in your presence?
   Shaped from dust has he been,
   maggots' food shall be his dwelling;
   he is spat saliva,
22 moulded clay,
   and for dust his longing.
   What will the clay reply
   and the one shaped by hand?
   And what advice will he be able to understand? *Blank*

B   *The Cave 4 Copies*

4QRule of the Community^a (4Q255 [4Qpaps^a])

Frag. 1 (= 1QS I, 1–5)   *1* For [the Instructor…] … Book of the Rule of the Community. *2* [In order to seek God [with all (one's) heart and with a]ll (one's) soul; in order to do *3* [what is good and just in his presence, as com]manded through the hand of Moses *4* [and through the hand of all his servants the Prophets; in order to love all that he selects] *5* [and to hate all that he rejects;] in order to keep oneself dis[tant from all evil,] *6* [and to become attached to all good works;] to bring[about truth…

Frag. 2 (= 1QS III, 7–12)   *1* And by his holy spirit which links him with his truth he is clea[nsed of all] *2* his sins. And by the spirit of uprightness and of humility his s[in is atoned. And by the compliance of] *3* his soul with all the laws of God his fle[sh] is cleansed [by there being sprinkled upon it] *4* cleansing waters and being made holy with the waters of repentance, and [by the steadying of his st]eps *5* in order to walk with perfection on all the paths of God, con[forming to all he has decreed] *6* concerning regular times of his command. He should not [turn aside, either right or] *7* left, nor infringe even on[e of all his words.] *8* In this way he will be admitted by means of pleasing atonement and for him it will be the covenant *9* [of an] everlasting [Community…]

Frag. 3   *1* […] … *2* […] the man *3* […] to him two *4* […] in the judgment *5* […] which

4QRule of the Community^b (4Q256 [4QS^b])

Frag. 1 (= 1 QS I, 16–19)   *1* [… And all those who enter] the Rule of the Community shall institute a coven[ant before God] *2* [in order to carry out all that he commands and in order not to stray from following him] for any [fear, dr]ead or grief [that might occur during] *3* [the dominion of Belial. When they enter the covenant, the priests] and the levi[tes will bless the God of salvation…]

Frag. 2 (= 1QS I, 21–23)   *1* [The priests shall recite the just deeds of God in his] mig[hty works, and they shall proclaim all his merciful] *2* [favours towards Israel. And the levites shall recite the s]ins of the sons of [Israel, all their blameworthy transgressions…]

Frag. 3 (= 1QS II, 4–5)   *1* [May he lift upon you the countenance of his favour for eternal peace».] And the levites [shall curse all the men of the lot of] *2*

[Belial. They shall take up the word and they shall say: «Be accursed for all your wicked, blameworthy] deeds. [May he hand you over ...]

Frag. 4 (= 1QS II, 7–11)   *1* [... Acc]ursed are you, without mercy, for the darkness *2* [of your deeds, and sentenced to the gloom of everlasting fire. May God not be merciful when you entre]at him, nor forgive you when you do penance for your faults. *3* [May he lift the countenance of his anger to avenge himself on you, and may there be no peace for you in the mouth of those who intercede».] And all those who enter the covenant *4* [shall say, after those who bless and those who curse: «Amen, Amen». And the priests and the levites shall continue, saying:] «Accursed

Frag. 5 (= 1QS V, 1–20 ?)   *1* Midrash for the Instructor concerning [...] *2* what he commands. They should keep apart from the congregation of [the men of sin ...] *3* according to the authority of the Many in every affair involving the law, [property and judgment, to achieve together truth and humility, justice and uprightness,] *4* compassionate love and seemly behaviour in all their paths. No-one should walk [...] *5* except in order to lay a foundation of truth for Israel, for the Community for all who [freely volunteer for holiness in Aaron and for the house of] *6* truth in Israel and for those who join them for the Community. Whoever enters the council of the Community ...] *7* to revert to the Law of Moses with all that it decrees, with whole heart and who[le ...] *8* the council of the men of the Community; and to be segregated from all the men of sin who [...] *9* holy, and which he cannot do in the Community. And he is not [...] *10* in every law and precept. And with him [...] is not to enter *11* a man from the holy men [...] *12* [...] is not to [...] *13* [...] ... [...]

4QRule of the Community^{c} (4Q257 [4Qpaps^{c}])

Frag. 1 *col.* II (= 1QS II, 4–11)   *1* And the levites shall curse all the men of the lot of [Beli]al. They shall take up the word and they shall say: «Accursed are you *2* [for all your wicked, blameworthy] deeds. May he (God) hand you over to dread into the hands of those carrying out acts of *3* [vengeance. May he cause to fall upon you destruction at the hand of all those administering punishments. Accu]rsed are you, *4* [without mercy, for the darkness of your deeds, and sentenced to the] gloom *5* [of everlasting fire. May God not be merciful when you entreat him, nor forgive you when you do penance for] your fault. *6* [May he lift the countenance of his anger to avenge himself on you, and may there be no] peace [for you in the mouth] *7* [of those who intercede». And all those who enter covenant shall say after] those who bless [...]

Frag. 1 *col.* III (= 1QS II, 25–III, 5)   *1* shall not [enter the Com]munity of his truth, since his soul loathes the restraints of the knowledge of] *2* just [judgment. He has not remained constant in the transformation of his life and shall not be counted with the upright.] *3* His knowledge, his en[ergy and his wealth shall not enter the council of the Community because he ploughs in the slime] *4* of irreverence and there are sta[ins on his conversion. He will not be justified while he maintains the stubbornness of] *5* his heart, since he regards darkness [as paths to light. In the source of the perfect he shall not be counted.] *6* He will not become clean by the acts of aton[ement, nor will he be purified by the waters of the ablutions, nor will he be] *7* [...] ... [...]

4QRule of the Community^d (4Q258 [4QS^d])

Frag. 1 *col.* I (= 1QS V, 1–20)   *1* Midrash for the Instructor concerning the men of the law who freely volunteer to revert from all evil and to keep themselves steadfast in all he prescribes. *2* They must keep apart from men of sin in order to be together in the law and in possessions and acquiesce to the authority of Many in every affair *3* involving the law and possessions. They must exercise humility, justice and right, compassionate love and se[emly behav]iour in all their paths. *4* [N]o-one should walk in the stubbornness of his heart in order to go astray following his heart in order to establi[sh a foundation of] truth for Israel, for the Community for all *5* who freely volunteer for holiness in Aaron and for the house of truth in Israel and for those who join them for the Community. *Blank* And whoever enters the council *6* of the Community shall make a binding promise to re[vert] to the Law of Moses with all that it decrees, with whole heart and whole soul. All that has been revealed about *7* the regulation [...] the council of m[en...] iniquity, and he is not to approach the pure food of holy *8* [me]n. And he is not to eat (?) [...And] not one of the men of the Community [is to be subject] to his authority in any *9* [law] or regulation, and [...] ... And no-one of the men of holiness is to eat *10* [...] And they are not to support themselves on [any wo]rk of futility, for all those who [do not know] *11* [his covenant] are futility. [And all those who scorn] his word, who vanish from the [world; a]ll their works are uncle[anness before him, there is uncleanness in all their possessions.] *12* [...] the residents. And the Many (?) will verify the oath ...[...] *13* [...] ... [...]

Frag. 1 *col.* II (= 1QS V, 21–VI, 7)   *1* and his deeds in law, under the authority of the sons of Aaron, those who freely volunteer in the Community to set up his covenant and to follow all the decrees which he commanded *2* to carry out, and under the authority of the majority of Israel, those who freely volunteer to be converted within the Community. And they shall record each one in the Rule, before his fellow, each one according to his insight *3* and his deeds in the law, in such a way that each one obeys his fellow, junior under senior. And their spirit and their deeds in the law must be tested, *4* year after year, in order to upgrade each one to the extent of his insight, or to demote him according to his failings. Each should reproach his fellow in compassionate love. *5* And no-one should speak to his fellow in anger or muttering, or with spiteful intent. And in addition, no-one should raise a matter against his fellow in front of the Many *6* unless it is with reproof in the presence of witnesses. In this way shall they behave in all their places of residence, always whenever someone meets his fellow. [The junior shall obey] *7* the senior in work and in [money. They shall eat together,] together they shall bless and together they shall [take counsel. In every place where there are ten] *8* men of the Community council, there should not be a priest missing amongst them; each] one according to his rank, will [sit in front of him, and in this way ask them their counsel on every matter.] *9* And when [they prepare the table to dine or the] new wine [for drinking, the pri]est will stretch out his hand as the first to bless the first fruits of the bread] *10* and the new wine [...]

Frag. 1 *col.* III (= 1QS VI, 9–12)   *1* each can impart his wi[sdom to the council of the Community. No-one should talk during the speech of his fellow before his brother has finished speaking... And in the session of] *2* the Many no-one should ut[ter anything without the consent of the Many. And if the Examiner of the Many prevents someone having something to say] *3* to the Many but [he is not in the position of one who is asking questions to the council...]

Frag. 2 *col.* I (= 1QS VIII, 6–17)   *1* [holies for Aaron, true witnesses for the judgment and chosen by the will (of God) to atone for the earth and to] render the wicked *2* [their retribution. It will be the tested rampart, the precious cornerstone whose foundations do not shake or tremble in] their place. It will be the most holy dwelling *3* [for Aaron with eternal (?) knowledge of the covenant of justice and in order to offer a pleasant aroma; and it will be a house of perfection and truth for Israel;] in order to establish a covenant in compliance with the everlasting decrees. *4* [And these, will be accepted, to atone for the earth and to decide the judgment of the wicked and there will be no iniquity. When these have been established in the fou]ndation of the Community for two full years *5* [in perfect behaviour they will be segregated (like) holy ones in the midst of the council of the men of the Community. And every matter hidden from Is]rael, but which has been found out *6* [by the Interpreter, he should not keep hidden from them for fear of a spirit of desertion.] *Blank* And when these exist [in Israel] they are to be segregated from [within the dwelling] *7* [of the men of sin to walk to the desert in order to open there His path. This is the study of] the law which he commanded through the ha[nd of Moses, in order to d]o all [that has been revealed from age to age,] *8* [and which the prophets have revealed through his holy spirit. And anyone] of the men of the covenant [...]

Frag. 2 col. II (= 1QS VIII, 24–IX, 10)   *1* he should be excluded from pure food and from the council and the judgment for two [who]le years. And he may return to the interpretation and to the council if he does not go *2* sinning through oversight until two full years have passed. Because for a sin of oversight he will be punished two years; but for impertinence he shall not go back again. Only *3* two full years shall he be tested in respect of the perfection of his behaviour and in respect of his counsel according to the authority of the Many and then he will be enrolled according to his rank in the Community of holiness. *Blank 4* [When] these exist in Israel in accordance with these statutes in order to establish the spirit of holiness in truth eternal, in order to atone for the fault of the transgression *5* [and for the disloyalty of sin] and for the approval for the earth [...] of burnt offerings and without the fats of sacrifice, the offerings and the free-will offering of the lips in compliance with the decree will be like the pleasant aroma *6* [of justice and the perfection of behavio]ur will be accept[able] like a freewill offering. *Blank* At this time the house of Aaron set themselves for holiness, for all [...] *7* [Community for Isr]ael, (for) those who walk in per[fection. Only the sons of Aaron will have authority in the matter of jud]gment and of goods. *Blank* And the goo[ds ...] *8* [who wa]lk in perfection. [Their goods] must not be con[fused with the] goods [of the men of deceit] who have not puri[fied their path...] *9* [...] shall be governed by the dir[ectives...]

Frag. 2 col. III (= 1QS IX, 15-X, 3)   *1* and according to his intellect promote him, and thus shall be his love and thus shall be his hatred. He should not reproach anyone or argue with the men of{knowledge}/the pit/ *2* but instead hide his counsel in the midst of the men of sin. He should reproach (with) truthful knowledge and (with) just judgment those who choose the path, each one according to his spirit, according to the circumstances *3* of the time. [He should lead them] with knowledge and in this way teach them the mysteries of wonder and of truth in the midst of the men of the Community, so they walk perfectly, each one *4* [with his fellow, in all that has been revealed to] them. This is the time for making ready the path in the desert to teach them about all that has been discovered so that they can carry it out. *Blank* In this time *5* [they will be detached from any] man who has not withdrawn his path from all wickedness. And these are the rules of behaviour for the Instructor in these times, *6* [concerning his love and] his hatred. Everlasting hatred for the men of the pit in clandestine spirit. To them he should leave goods and hand-made *7* [items like a servant to his master] and like one oppressed before someone domineering him. He should be a man enthusiastic for the precept and for his time, for the day of revenge. He should perform *8* [(God's) will in all that his hand should tackle and in] all that he controls, as he commanded. And all that happens to him he should welcome freely and be gratified by nothing except [God's wi]ll. *9* [He should relish all the words of his mouth, wish for nothing that he has not commanded and be ever alert to the precep]t of God. [...] *10* [...] he shall bless in [...] *11* [...] retired to its appointed abode. At the commencement [...] *12* [...they re]tire before the light. When [the lights of the holy vault] shine out, *13* [when they retire to the abode of glory. At the entry of the constellation in the days of the new moon together with its rotations during its stations,]

Frag. 2 col. IV (= 1QS X, 4–12)   *1* renewing each other. It is a great day for the holy of holies, and an omen of the opening of his everlasting mercies, *2* for the beginnings of the constellations in every future age. At the commencement of the months in their constellations, and of the holy *3* days in their sequence, as a reminder in their constellations. [With the offering of lips] I shall bless you, in accordance with the decree *4* recorded for ever. At the commencement of the years and in the gy[rations of their constellations, when] the decree *5* of their disposition [is carried out,] on the prescribed day, one after another; the cons[tellation of the harvest up to summer, the constellation of seed]time up to the constellation of *6* the grass, the constellations of the years up to their seven-year [periods. At the commencement of the seven-year] periods, up to the times determined for deliverance. *7* And in all my existence it shall be the precept engraved [on my tongue like fruit of eu]logy and the portion [of my lips. I will sing] *8* with knowledge and for the glory of God shall all my music be, the strumming of my harp for his ho[ly order, and the whistle] *9* [of my lips I shall ad]just to its correct scale. [At the onset of] day [and ni]ght I shall enter the covenant *10* [of God, and when evening and morning arrive I shall repeat his precepts;] and while they last I shall go back *11* [...] my sins are before my eyes, like graven laws, my sins *12* [like graven laws. But to God I shall say: «My justice», and to the Most High: «Foundation of my well-being», «source of knowing»,] «place of holiness», «peak *13* [of glory», «all-powerful one of eternal majesty». I shall choose

Frag. 2 col. V (= 1QS X, 12–18)   *1* what he te[aches me, I shall be pleased in how he might judge me. When I start to stretch out my hands] *2* and my feet I shall [bless his name...] on the ta[sty fruits of the earth. At the onset of fright and dismay, in the place of distress] *4* with [grief, I shall bless him for (his) great marvels and shall meditate on his power, on his compassion] *5* I shall rely [the whole day. I realize that in his hand lies the judgment of every living thing, and all his deeds are truth.] *6* When dis[tress is unleashed I shall praise him, just as I shall sing to him for his deliverance. I shall not repay anyone with an evil] *7* reward; [with goodness I shall pursue the man. For to God (corresponds) the judgment of every living being, and it is he who] *8* pays [man his wages...]

4QRule of the Community^e^ (4Q259 [4QS^e^])

Col. I (= 1QS VII, 10–17)   *1* [...] ... [...] *2* [...] *Blank 3* [days] And whoever lies down [and goes to sleep in the session of the Many, thirty days. And the same applies to whoever] *4* [leaves] the session of the Many without [cause, or falls asleep up to three times] *5* [during] a session, he shall be punished [for ten days; however, if ... and he withdraws,] *6* he shall be punished for thirty days. And whoever [walks about naked in front of his fellow, without] *7* [needing] to, [shall be puni]shed for three mon[ths. And the person who spits in the course of a meeting of] *8* the Man[y shall be punished for thirty days. *Blank* (?) And whoever] *9* takes [out his 'hand' from under his] clothes, [or if these are rags which allow his nakedness to be seen,] *10* he will be punished for thirty days. And whoever [giggles inanely causing] *11* his voice [to be heard] shall be punished for thirty [days. And whoever takes out his left hand] *12* to gest[iculate with it shall be punished ten days...]

Col. II (= 1QS VII, 22–VIII, 10)   *1* [... And when the days of] the two years [are complete] *2* [the Many shall be questioned concerning his matter; if they admit him, he shall be enrolled according to his ra]nk; and later he will be questioned *3* [in connection with judgment. However, anyone who has been in the] Community [council] until completion of *4* [ten full years and whose spirit reverts to betray the Community and he goes away from the presence of] the Many in order to walk *5* [in the stubbornness of his heart, may never return to the Community council. And the person from among] the men of the Community who *6* [fraternises with him in concerns of purity or goods, who ... the Many,] and his sentence will be *7* [like his, he shall be expelled. In the Community council (there shall be) twelve men and] three priests, *8* [perfect in everything that has been revealed about all the law to implement truth] justice, judgment, *9* [compassionate love and unassuming behaviour of each person to his fellow to preserve] faithfulness on the earth with firm purpose and with simplicity *10* [and repentant spi]rit, in order to atone for [sin, doing justice and undergoing trials] in order to walk with everyone *11* [in the measure of] truth and the regu[lation of time. When these things exist in] Israel, the Community council shall be founded *12* [on truth like an] everlasting [plan]tation, [a holy house for Israel and the foundation of the] holy of holies for Aaron, *13* true witnesses for the judgment and chosen by the wi[ll (of God) to atone for the earth and to render] the wicked *14* their retribution. It will be the tested rampart, [the precious cornerstone, whose foundations do not shake or] tremble on the spot. *15* It will be the most holy fortress for Aaron [with total knowledge of the covenant of justice and in order to offer] a pleasant [aroma]; and it will be a house *16* of perfection and truth in Is[rael; in order to establish a covenant in compliance with the everlasting dec]rees. When these have been established

Col. III (= 1QS VIII, 11–15+IX, 12–20)   *1* [in the foundation of the Community for two full years in perfect behaviour they will be segregated] (like) holy ones in the midst of the council of the men of [the Community.] *2* [And every matter hidden from Israel but which has been found] out by the Interpreter, he should not [keep hidden from] them *3* [for fear of a spirit of desertion.] And when these exist by means of the sepa[ration of] *4* the men of [sin to walk to the desert in order to open there] the path of truth. As [it is written:] «In the desert, [prepare the way of ****, straighten] in the steppe a roadway for our God». *6* This is [the study of the law which he commanded through the hand of Moses. These are the regu[lations] for the Ins[tructor, so that by them shall walk every living being in compliance with the circumstances of every [period] *8* and in compliance with the wor[th of each man: he should do] the will of God in compliance with all revelation for every period; *9* [he should acquire all the wisdom that has been gai]ned according to the periods and the regulation of the period;] *10* [he should separate and we]igh the sons of justice according to their spirits; [he should encourage] *11* [the chosen ones of the period] according to his will, as he has commanded; [he should carry out the judgment] *12* [of each man in accordance with his spirit;] he should include each one according to the purity of his hands and according [to his intellect] *13* [promote him. And thus shall be his love] and thus shall be his hatred. He should not [reproach] *14* [or argue with the m]en of the pit but instead hide the [counsel of the law] *15* [in the midst of the men of sin.] He should reproach (with) truthful knowledge and (with) just *16* judgment [those who choose the path, each one] according to his spirit and according to the circumstances of the time. He should lead them *17* with kn[owledge and in this way teach them the my]steries of wonder and of truth and give them the secret pa[th of the men of] *18* the Community, [so that they walk perfectly, each one] with his fellow, in all that has been revealed to them. *19* This is the [time for making ready the path] in the desert and he will teach them about all

Col. IV   *1* ... [...] *2* ... [...]

Col. V   *10* [...] ... In the fourth (year of the cycle of) Shebet [...] *11* [...] (the) creation. In the fourth (year), the sign of Gamul. In the Release, the si]gn of *12* [Shekaniah. In the thi]rd, the sign of Gamul. In the sixth, the sign of [Shekaniah. In the second, the sign of Ga]mul. *13* [In the fifth, the sign of Shekaniah. After the Release, the sign of Ga[mul. In the fourth, the sign of Shekan]iah. *14* [In the Release, the sig]n of Gamul, In the third, the sign of Shekaniah. [In the sixth, the sign of Ga]mul. *15* [In the second, the si]gn of She[kaniah. In the fifth, the sign of Ga[mul. After the Rel]ease, the sign of *16* [Shekaniah. In the fou]rth, the sign of Gamul. In the Release, the end of the second jubilee. The signs of the second jubilee *17* [are seventeen signs. From

this in the Release [two] signs (remain) […] the creation *18* […the sig]n of
Shekaniah. In the third year, the sign of Gamul. [In the sixth, the si]gn of
Shekaniah. *19* [In the second, the sign of Ga]mul. In the fifth, the sign of
Shekaniah. After the Re[mission, the sign of Ga]mul.

Col. VI *1* [In the fourth, the sign of Shekaniah. In the Release, the sign of
Gamul. In the third, the sign of Shekaniah.] *2* [In the sixth, the sign of Gamul.
In the se]cond, the sig[n of Shekaniah. In the fifth the sign of Gamul.] *3* [After
the Release, the sign of Shekaniah. In the fou[rth, the sign of Gamul. In the
Release, the sign of] *4* [Shekaniah. In the thi]rd, the sign of Gamul. In the
six[th, the sign of] Shekaniah. [In the second, the end of the] *5* th[ird] jubilee.
The signs of the [third] jubilee are six]teen. From this up to the Release *6* two
signs of (the cycle of) Shekaniah remain. [In the second year, the sign of
Ga]mul. In the fifth the sign of Shekaniah. *7* After the Release, the si[gn of
Gamul. In the fourth, the si]gn of Shekaniah. In the Release, the sign of
Gamul. In the third the sign of [Shekaniah. In the sixth the sign of Ga]mul. In
the second, the sign of Shekaniah. In the fifth, the sign of [Gamul. After the]
Release, the sign of Shekaniah. *10* In the fourth, the sign of Gamul. [In the
Release, the sign of] Shekaniah. In the third, the sign of Gamul. *11* In the sixth,
the sign of Shek[aniah. In the second, the sign of] Gamul. In the fifth, the sign
of Shekaniah. *12* After the Release, the s[ign of the end of the jubilee: Gamul]
The /fourth/ [jub]ilee has seventeen signs: *13* from the last up to the Release
two /signs/ of (the cycle of) [Gamul] (remain). In the fourth year, the sign of
Shekaniah. *14* [In the Release, the sign of Gamul.] *15* In the second, the sign of
Shekaniah. In the fif[th, the sign of Gamul. After the Release, the sign of
Shekaniah.] *16* In the fourth, the sign of Gamul. In [the Release, the sign of
Shekaniah. In the third, the sign of Gamul.] *17* In the six[th, the sig]n of
Shekaniah.] *18* [After the] Release, the sign of Ga[mul. In the fourth, the sign
of Shekaniah, In the Release, the end of the] *19* [fif]th [jubilee] in (the sign of)
Yeshibab. [The signs of the fifth jubilee are seventeen. From this during the
Release,]

Col. VII *1* [three signs (of the Cycle of) Gamul (remain). In the third year, the
sign of Shekaniah. In the sixth, the sign of *2* [Gamul. In the se]cond, the sign
of Shekaniah. In [the fifth, the sign of Gamul. After the Rel]ease *3* the sign of
Shekaniah. In the fourth, the sign of Ga[mul. In the Release, the sign of
Shekaniah.] In the third *4* the sign of Gamul. In the sixth, the sign of
Shekaniah. [In the second, the sign of] Gamul. *5* In the fifth, the sign of
Shekaniah. After [the Release,] the sign of *6* Gamul. In the fourth, the sign of
Shekaniah. In the Rele[ase, the sign of Gamul. In] the third, *7* the sign of
[Shekaniah. In the six]th, the final /sign/ of the [sixth] jubilee […The signs of]
8 the [sixth] jubilee [are six]teen. From this in [the Release] two signs (remain)

[...] *9* ... [...] *10* And on the jub[ilee of Gamul, in the second year, the sign of Shekaniah. In the fifth, the sign of Gamul. After] *11* the Release [the sign of Shekaniah. In the fourth,] the sign of Gamul. [In the Release,] *12* [the sign of Shekaniah. In the third, the sign of] Gamul. In the sixth, the si[gn of Shekaniah.] *13* [In] the second, the sig[n of Gamul.] In the fifth, the sign of Shekaniah. [After] *14* the Release, [the sign of Ga]mul. In the fourth, the sign of Shekaniah. In the Re[lease, the sign of] *15* Gamul. [In the th]ird, the sign of Shekaniah. In the sixth, the sign of [Gamul.] *16* In the se[cond, the sign of Shekaniah.] In the fifth, the final sign of the [se]venth jubilee. *17* [The signs of the] seventh [jubilee] are seventeen. From this in the Release *18* [two signs (remain)...] the sign of the jubilees, the year of the jubilees, according to the days of [...] *19* [...] in Miyyamin, the third Ye[daiah...]

Col. VIII   *1* Gamul [...] *2* Yedaiah [...] *3* Miyyamim [...] *4* Shekaniah [...] *5* Yeshebab [...] *6* Hapzizez [...] *7* Gamul [...]

Col. IX   *1* [... the second] Passover. The [...] of *2* [... the ...] of Jezir [...] *3* [... the ... of] Me^cozaiah, the Passover [...] *4* [... the ... of ...] the day of remembrance [...]

Col. XI   *4* [...] and about the sabbaths *5* [and their days...] and about the feasts *6* [of their days, and about the] months of their [years] and about the signs *7* of their Releases and about their jubilees and the sabbath *8* of the sons of [Gamul], on the fourth day.

4QRule of the Community^f (4Q260 [4QS^f])

Frag. 1 *col.* I (= 1QS IX, 23–24)   *1* [enthusiastic for the decree and for his time, for the day of revenge. He should perform (God's) will in all] that *2* [his hand should tackle and in all that he controls, as he commanded. And] all that happens to him

Frag. 1 *col.* II (= 1QS X, 1–4)   *1* At the commencement of the vigils of [darkness when he opens his store and stretches them upwards and in] his rotation *2* and when it re]tires be[fore the light. When the lights of the holy vault shine out, when they re]tire to the abode *3* of glory. [At the entry of the constellation in the days of the new moon together with their rotations during their stations] renewing *4* [each other. It is a great day for the holy of holies, and an omen of the opening of his everlasting] mercies.

Frag. 1 *col.* III (= 1QS X, 9–11)   *19* the playing of my harp for [his holy order, and the whistle of my lips I shall ad]just to its correct scale. *2* At the [onset of day

and night I shall enter the covenant of God, at the] onset of evening and morning *3* I[shall repeat his precepts; and while they last I shall set them as my
limit,] with no backtracking.

Frag. 1 *col.* IV (= 1QS X, 15–20)   *1* [At the on]set of fright and dismay, [in the
place] of distress and grief, [I shall bless him] *2* for (his) great marvels and shall
meditate on his po[wer and shall rely] on his compassion *3* the whole day. The
judgment of every living thing [is in his hand and all his deeds are truth.] When
4 distress is unleashed I shall praise him, and for his deliverance [I shall sing to
him in the same measure.] I shall not repay *5* anyone with an evil reward; with
goodness [I shall pursue the] man. For to God (corresponds) [the judgment]
6 of every living being, and it is he who pays m[an his wage]s. I shall have [no
enthusiasm for] the wicked *7* [spirit], and my soul shall not c[rave] wealth by
violence. [In the dispute of the men] *8* of the pit I shall not be involved at all
[until the day of vengeance. However, I shall not remove] my anger *9* from
wicked men, [nor shall I be appeased, until] the judgment [is carried out. I shall
not] *10* bear angry resentment for someone who converts from transgression;
[…] of men.

Frag. 1 *col.* V (= 1QS X, 20–24)   *1* [but I shall have no mer]cy for all those who
turn aside from the path. I shall not comfort the oppressed until their path is
2 perfect. I shall not retain Belial within my heart. From my mouth no *3* vulgarity shall be heard or wicked deceptions; sophistries or lies shall not be found on
my lips. *4* The fruit of holiness will be on my tongue, profanity shall not be
found *5* on it. With hy[mns shall I open my] mouth, and the just acts of God
6 my mouth will ev[er number and the treachery of me]n [until their transgression is com[plete.]

4QRule of the Community^g (4Q261 [4QS^g])

Frag. 1 (= 1QS V, 22–24)   *1* [to establish his cove]nant and to [follow all the decrees which he commanded to fulfil,] *2* [and under the authority of the
major]ity of Is[rael, those who freely volunteer to return within the Community
to his covenant. And they shall be recorded] *3* [in the Rule, each one be]fore his
fel[low, according to his insight and his deeds, in such a way that each one
obeys] *4* [his fellow,] junior [under senior. And their spirits must be tested,]
5 [and their de]eds y[ear after year, in order to upgrade each one to the extent
of his insight and the perfection of his path,] *6* [or to demote him acco]rding
to his fail[ings…

Frag. 2 (= 1QS VI, 22–25)   *1* [for the law, for the jud]gment, for pu[rity and for
the placing of his possessions in common. And his advice will be for the Com-

munity as will his judgment.] And these are the regulations] by which they
shall judge him depending on [the case. If one is found among them] *3* [who has
lied knowingly concerning mo]ney, he shall be ex[cluded from the pure food
of the Many] *4* [for a year and shall be sentenced to a quar]ter of his bread. [...]

Frag. 3 (= 1QS VII, 12–16)   *1* [...] ... [...] *2* [And whoever lies down and] goes to
sleep in the sess[ion of the Many, thirty days. And the same applies to whoever
leaves] *3* [the session of the Many] without cause, [or falls asleep up to three
times during a session,] *4* [shall be punished ten d]ays; how[ever, if... and he
withdraws,] *5* [he shall be punished for thirty d]ays. And whoever [walks about
naked in front of his fellow,] *6* without needing to, [shall be punished for three
months. And the person who spits] *7* [in the course of a mee]ting of the Many
[shall be punished thirty days. And whoever takes out] *8* [his 'hand' from
und]er his clothes, [or if these are rags *16* which allow his nakedness to be seen,]

Frag. 4   *1* [...] what he commands. [...] *2* [...] he will stretch out his hand and
[...] *3* [...] and their deeds [...]

4QRule of the Community^h (4Q262 [4QS^h])

Frag. 1 (= 1QS III, 4–5)   *1* [He will not become clean by the acts of aton]ement,
nor shall he be purified by [the cleansing waters,] *2* [nor shall he be made holy
by the seas or rivers, [nor shall he be purified] *3* [by all] the water of the ablutions. Defiled, def[iled shall he be, all the days ...]

4QRule of the Communityⁱ (4Q263 [4QSⁱ])

Frag. 1 (= 1QS VI, 1–3)   *1* [to incur a sin for his fault. And in addition,] no-one
should raise [a matter against his fellow in front of the Many unless] *2* [it is
with reproof] in the presence of witnesses. In this way shall they behave [in all
their places of residence, whenever one fellow meets another.] *3* [The junior
shall obey] the senior in work and in wea[lth. They shall eat together, together
they shall bless and together they shall take counsel.] *4* [In every pl]ace where
there are [ten men of the Community council, there should not be a priest
missing amongst them] *5* [...] ... [...]

4QRule of the Community^j (4Q264 [4QS^j])

Frag. 1 (= 1QS XI, 14–22)   *1* [... he will judge me in the justice] of his truth, and
in his plentiful goodness *2* [always atone for all my sins; in his justice he will
cleanse me from the uncleanness] of the human being, and from the sin of the
sons of man, so that I can extol *3* [God for his justice and The Highest for his

majesty. Blessed be you, my God, who opens] the heart of your servant [to knowledge!] Establish all his deeds in justice, *4* [and raise up the son of your handmaid] to be everlastingly in your presence, [as you have cared for the selected ones of humankind.] For beyond you *5* [there is no perfect path, and without your will, nothing comes to be. You have ta]ught all knowledge, and all that exists *6* [is so by your will. Beyond you there is no-one to oppose your counsel,] to understand one of your holy *7* [thoughts, to gaze into the abyss of your mysteries, to fathom all] your marvels or the strength of your might. *8* [Who can tolerate your glory? What, indeed, is man,] among all your marvellous deeds? The one born of woman *9* [as what will he be considered in your presence? Shaped from dust has he been, maggots' food] shall be his dwelling; he is spat saliva, *10* [moulded clay, and for dust his longing. What will the clay reply and the one shaped by hand?] And what advice will he be able to understand? *Blank*

C *Copies from other caves*

5QRule of the Community (5Q11 [5QS])

Frag. 1 *col.* I (= 1QS II, 4–7)   *1* [... And the levites shall cu]rse *2* [all the men of the lot of Belial. They shall begins speaking and they shall say: «Accursed] are you *3* [for all your wicked, blame]worthy deeds. May he (God) *4* [hand you over to dread at the hands of all those carrying out acts of vengeance. May he cause to fa]ll upon you *5* [destruction at the hands of all those carrying out punishments. Be acc]ursed,

Frag. 1 *col.* II (= 1QS II, 12–14 ?)   *1* When [he hears the words of this covenant, he will bless himself] *2* in his he[art, saying: 'I will have peace, in spite of my walking in the stubbornness of my heart'. However, his spirit will be obliterated, the dry with the moist, mercilessly...]

2 The Damascus document

A *Copies from the Genizah*

Damascus Document (CD-A)

Col. I *1 Blank* And now, listen, all those who know justice, and understand the actions of *2* God; for he has a dispute with all flesh and will carry out judgment on all those who spurn him. *3* For when they were unfaithful in forsaking him, he hid his face from Israel and from his sanctuary *4* and delivered them up to the sword. However, when he remembered the covenant of the very first, he saved a remnant *5* for Israel and did not deliver them up to destruction. And at the moment of wrath, three hundred and *6* ninety years after having delivered them up into the hands of Nebuchadnezzar, king of Babylon, *7* he visited them and caused to sprout from Israel and from Aaron a shoot of the planting, in order to possess *8* his land and to become fat with the good things of his soil. And they realised their sin and knew that *9* they were guilty men; but they were like blind persons and like those who grope for the path *10* over twenty years. And God appraised their deeds, because they sought him with a perfect heart *11* and raised up for them a Teacher of Righteousness, in order to direct them in the path of his heart. *Blank* And he made known *12* to the last generations what he had done for the last generation, the congregation of traitors. *13* These are the ones who stray from the path. This is the time about which it has been written: *Hos 4:16* «Like a stray heifer *14* so has Israel strayed», when 'the scoffer' arose, who scattered *15* the waters of lies over Israel and made them veer off into a wilderness without path, flattening the everlasting heights, diverging *16* from tracks of justice and removing the boundary with which the very first had marked their inheritance, so that *17* the curses of his covenant would adhere to them, to deliver them up to the sword carrying out the vengeance *18* of the covenant. For they sought easy interpretations, chose illusions, scrutinised *19* loopholes, chose the handsome neck, acquitted the guilty and sentenced the just, *20* violated the covenant, broke the precept, colluded together against the life of the just man, their soul abominated all those who walk *21* in perfection, they hunted them down with the sword and provoked the dispute of the people. And kindled was the wrath

Col. II *1* of God against his congregation, laying waste all its great number, for his deeds were unclean in front of him. *2 Blank* And now, listen to me, all entering the covenant, and I will open your ears to the paths of *3* the wicked. *Blank* God loves knowledge; he has established wisdom and counsel before him; *4* discernment and knowledge are at his service; patience is his and abundance of pardon, *5* to atone for persons who repent from wickedness; however,

strength and power and a great anger with flames of fire *6* by the ⟨hand⟩ of all
the angels of destruction against persons turning aside from the path and abom-
inating the precept, without there being for them either a remnant *7* or survivor. For God did not choose them at the beginning of the world, and before
they were established he knew *8* their deeds, and abominated the generations
on account of blood and hid his face from the country, *9* from ⟨Israel⟩, until
their extinction. And he knew the years of their existence, and the number and
detail of their ages, of all *10* those who exist over the centuries, and of those
who will exist, until it occurs in their ages throughout all the everlasting years.
11 And in all of them he raised up men of renown for himself, to leave a remnant for the country and in order to fill *12* the face of the world with their offspring. *Blank* And he taught them by the hand of the anointed ones through his
holy spirit and through seers of the *13* truth, and their names were established
with precision. But those he hates, he causes to stray. *14 Blank* And now, my
sons, listen to me and I shall open your eyes so that you can see and understand
the deeds of *15* God, so that you can choose what he is pleased with and repudiate what he hates, so that you can walk perfectly *16* on all his paths and not
follow after the thoughts of a guilty inclination and lascivious eyes. For many
17 wandered off for these matters; brave heroes yielded on account of them,
from ancient times until now. For having walked in the stubbornness *18* of
their hearts the Watchers of the heavens fell; on account of it they were caught,
for they did not follow the precepts of God. *19* And their sons, whose height
was like that of cedars and whose bodies were like mountains, fell. *20* All flesh
which there was in the dry earth decayed and became as if it had never been,
for having realized *21* their desires and failing to keep their creator's precepts,
until his wrath flared up against them.

Col. III   *1 Blank* Through it, the sons of Noah and their families strayed, through
it, they were cut off. *2* Abraham did not walk in it, and was counted as a friend
for keeping God's precepts and not following *3* the desire of his spirit. And he
passed (them) on to Isaac and to Jacob, and they kept (them) and were written
up as friends *4* of God and as members of the covenant for ever. *Blank* Jacob's
sons strayed because of them and were punished in accordance with *5* their
mistakes. And in Egypt their sons walked in the stubbornness of their hearts,
plotting against *6* God's precepts and each one doing what was right in his own
eyes; and they ate blood, *7* and their males were cut off in the wilderness. He
⟨spoke⟩ to them in Qadesh: *Deut 9:23* «Go and possess ⟨the land⟩». But they preferred the desire⟩ of their hearts, and did not listen to *8* the voice of their creator, the precepts he had taught them and murmured in their tents. And the
wrath of God flared up *9* against their congregation. And their sons died
through it, and through it their kings were cut off and through it their warriors
10 perished and through it their land was laid waste. Through it, the very first

to enter the covenant made themselves guilty and were delivered up *11* to the sword, for having deserted God's covenant and having chosen their whims, and having followed the stubbornness *12* of their heart, each one doing (what was) his desire. *Blank* But with those who remained steadfast in God's precepts, *13* with those who were left from among them, God established his covenant with Israel for ever, revealing to them *14* hidden matters in which all Israel had gone astray: his holy sabbaths and his *15* glorious feasts, his just stipulations and his truthful paths, and the wishes of his will which *16* man must do in order to live by them. He disclosed (these matters) to them and they dug a well of plentiful water; *17* and whoever spurns them shall not live. But they had defiled themselves with human sin and unclean paths, *18* and they had said: «For this is ours». But God, in his wonderful mysteries, atoned for their failings and pardoned their sins. *19* And he built for them a safe home in Israel, such as there has not been since ancient times, not even till *20* now. Those who remained steadfast in it will acquire eternal life, and all the glory of Adam is for them. As *21* God established for them by means of Ezekiel the prophet, saying: *Ez 44:15* «The priests and the levites and the sons of

Col. IV   *1* Zadok who maintained the service of my temple when the children of Israel strayed *2* far away from me, shall offer the fat and the blood». The priests are the converts of Israel *3* who left the land of Judah; and ‹the levites› are those who joined them; and the sons of Zadok are the chosen of *4* Israel, «those called by name» who stood up at the end of days. This is the detailed list *5* of their names, according to their genealogies and the age of their existence and the number of their miseries and the years of *6* their residence, and the detailed list of their deeds… of holiness. ‹These are the very› first, for whom *7* God atoned, and who declared the just man as just, and declared the wicked as wicked, and all those who entered after them *8* in order to act according to the exact interpretation of the law in which the very first were instructed until *9* the period of these years is complete. According to the covenant which God established with the very first, in order to atone *10* for their sins, so will God atone for them. But when the period corresponding to the number of these years is complete, *11* there will no longer be any joining with the house of Judah but rather each one standing up on *12* his watchtower. The wall is built, the boundary far away. And during these years *13* Belial will be sent against Israel, as God has said by means of the prophet Isaiah, son of *14* Amoz, saying: *Isa 24:17* «Panic, pit and net against you, earth-dweller». *Blank* Its explanation: *15* They are Belial's three nets about which Levi, son of Jacob spoke, *16* in which he catches Israel and makes them appear before them like three types of *17* justice. The first is fornication; the second, wealth; the third, defilement of the temple. He who eludes one is caught in another and he who is freed from that, is caught *19* in another. *Blank* The builders of the wall who go after Zaw–

Zaw is a preacher *20* as it is said: *Mic 2:6* «Assuredly he will preach»–are caught twice in fornication: by taking *21* two wives in their lives, even though the principle of creation is *Gen 1:27* «male and female he created them».

Col. v   *1* And the ones who went into the ark *Gen 7:9* «went in two by two into the ark». And about the prince it is written: *2 Deut 17:17* «He should not multiply wives to himself». However, David had not read the sealed book of the law which *3* was in the ark, for it had not been opened in Israel since the day of the death of Eleazar *4* and of Jehoshua, and Joshua and the elders who worshipped Ashtaroth had hidden *5* the public (copy) until Zadok's entry into office. And David's deeds were praised, except for Uriah's blood, *6* and God allowed them to him. And they also defiled the temple, for they did not *7* keep apart in accordance with the law, but instead lay with her who sees the blood of her menstrual flow. And each man takes as a wife *8* the daughter of his brother and the daughter of his sister. *Blank* But Moses said: *Lev 18:13* «Do not *9* approach your mother's sister, she is a blood relation of your mother». The law of incest, *10* written for males, applies equally to females, and therefore to the daughter of a brother who uncovers the nakedness of the brother of *11* her father, for he is a blood relation. *Blank* And also they defile his holy spirit, *12* for with blasphemous tongue they have opened their mouth against the statutes of God's covenant, saying: «they are unfounded». They speak abomination *13* against them. They are all igniters of fire, kindlers of blazes; webs *14* of a spider are their webs, and their eggs are viper's eggs. Whoever is close to them *15* will not be unpunished; the more he does it, the guiltier he shall be, unless he has been compelled. For already in ancient times *16* God visited their deeds, and his wrath flared up against their actions, for it is not an intelligent people; *17* they are folk bereft of advice, in that there is no intelligence in them. For in ancient times there arose *18* Moses and Aaron, by the hand of the prince of lights and Belial, with his cunning, raised up Jannes and *19* his brother during the first deliverance of Israel. *Blank 20 Blank* And in the age of devastation of the land there arose those who shifted the boundary and made Israel stray. *21* And the land became desolate, for they spoke of rebellion against God's precepts through the hand of Moses and also

Col. VI   *1* of the holy anointed ones. They prophesied deceit in order to divert Israel from following *2* God. But God remembered the covenant of the very first, and from Aaron raised men of knowledge and from Israel *3* wise men, and forced them to listen. And they dug the well: *Num 21:18* «A well which the princes dug, which *4* the nobles of the people delved with the staff». The well is the law. And those who dug it are *5* the converts of Israel, who left the land of Judah and lived in the land of Damascus, *6* all of whom God called princes, for they sought him, and their renown has not been repudiated *7* in anyone's mouth. *Blank* And the staff is the interpreter of the law, of whom *8* Isaiah said: *Isa 54:16* «He produces a tool for his labour». *Blank* And the nobles of the people are *9* those who have arrived to dig the well with the staves that the sceptre decreed, *10* to walk in them throughout the whole age of wickedness, and without which they will not obtain it, until there arises *11* he who teaches justice at the end of days. *Blank* But all those who have been brought into the covenant *12* shall not enter the temple to kindle his altar in vain. They will be the ones who close *13* the door, as God said: *Mal 1:10* «Whoever amongst you will close its door so that you do not kindle my altar *14* in vain!». Unless they are careful to act in accordance with the exact interpretation of the law for the age of wickedness: to separate themselves *15* from the sons of the pit; to abstain from wicked wealth which defiles, either by promise or by vow, *16* and from the wealth of the temple and from stealing from the poor of the people, from making their widows their spoils *17* and from murdering orphans; to separate unclean from clean and differentiate between *18* the holy and the common; to keep the sabbath day according to the exact interpretation, and the festivals *19* and the day of fasting, according to what they had discovered, those who entered the new covenant in the land of Damascus; *20* to set apart holy portions according to their exact interpretation; for each to love his brother *21* like himself; to strengthen the hand of the poor, the needy and the foreigner; *Blank* for each to seek the peace

Col. VII   *1* of his brother and not commit sin against his blood relation; to refrain from fornication *2* in accordance with the regulation; for each to reprove his brother in accordance with the precept, and not to bear resentment *3* from one day to the next; to keep apart from every uncleanness according to their regulations, without *4* anyone defiling his holy spirit, according to what God kept apart for them. For all those who walk *5* according to these matters in perfect holiness, in accordance with his teaching, God's covenant is a guarantee for them *6* that they shall live a thousand generations. *Blank* And if they reside in the camps in accordance with the rule of the land, and take *7* women and beget children, they shall walk in accordance with the law and according to the regulation *8* of the teachings, according to the rule of the law which says: *Num 30:17* «Between a man and his wife, and between a father *9* and his son». But all those who despise ‹...› when God visits the earth in order to empty over them the punishment of the wicked, *10* when there comes the word which is written in the words of Isaiah, son of Amoz, the prophet, *11* which says: *Isa 7:17* «There shall come upon you, upon your people and upon your father's house, days such as *12* have ‹not› come since the day Ephraim departed from Judah». When the two houses of Israel separated, *13* Ephraim detached itself from Judah, and all the renegades were delivered up to the sword; but those who remained steadfast *14* escaped to the land of the north. *Blank* As he said: *Am 5:26-27* «I will deport the Sikkut of your King *15* and the Kiyyum of your images away from my tent to Damascus». The books of the law are the Sukkat *16* of the King, as he said *Am 9:11* «I will lift up the fallen Sukkat of David». The King *17* is the assembly; and the plinths of the images ‹and the Kiyyum of the images› are the books of the prophets, *18* whose words Israel despised. *Blank* And the star is the Interpreter of the law, *19* who will come to Damascus, as is written: *Num 24:13* «A star moves out of Jacob, and a sceptre arises *20* out of Israel». The sceptre is the prince of the whole congregation and when he rises he will destroy *21* all the sons of Seth. *Blank* These escaped at the time of the first one's visitation

Col. VIII   *1* while the renegades were delivered up to the sword. Thus will be the judgment of all those entering his covenant but who *2* did not remain steadfast in them; they will have a visitation for destruction at the hand of Belial. This is the day *3* when God will make a visitation. The princes of Judah are those upon whom the rage will be vented, *4* for they hope to be healed but it will cleave to them (?); all are rebels in so far as they have not left the path of *5* the traitors and have defiled themselves in paths of licentiousness, and with wicked wealth, and avenging themselves, and each one bearing resentment *6* against his brother, and each one hating his fellow, and each one despising his blood relative; *7* they have approached for debauchery and have manipulated with pride for wealth and gain. Each one did what was right in his eyes *8* and each one has chosen the stubbornness of his heart. They did not keep apart from the people and have rebelled with insolence, *9* walking on the path of the wicked, about whom God says: *Dt 32:33* «Their wine is serpents' venom *10* and the head of cruel, harsh asps». The serpents are the kings of the peoples and the wine *11* their paths and the asps' head is the head of the kings of Greece, which comes to carry out *12* vengeance against them. But all these things the builders of the wall or those who daub with whitewash, have not understood, for *13* one who raises wind and preaches lies, has preached to them, the one against whose congregation God's wrath has been kindled. *14* And what Moses says: *Dt 9:5* «Not for your justice, or for the uprightness of your heart are you going to possess *15* these nations, but because he loved your fathers and keeps the oath». *16 Blank* And thus is the judgment of the converts of Israel, who turned aside from the path of the people: on account of God's love for *17* the very first who woke up after him, he loves those who come after them, because to them belongs *18* the fathers' covenant. *Blank* And in my hatred for the builders of the wall his anger is kindled. *Blank* And like this judgment *19* will be that of all who reject God's precepts and forsake them and move aside in the stubbornness of their heart. *20 Blank* This is the word which Jeremiah spoke to Baruch, son of Neriah, and Elishah *21* to Giezi his servant. *Blank* All the men who entered the new covenant in the land of Damascus

[The copies from Cave 4 show that the sheets which comprise text A of the Genizah (AD-A) have not been published in the correct sequence. Apparently several sheets have been lost and in any case, columns XV-XVI came before columns IX-XIV. The translation follows this sequence, although for each column it retains the number assigned by the first editor.]

Col. XV   *1* [He will not sw]ear by the Aleph and the Lamed ('EL = God) nor by the Aleph and the Daleth ('ADONAI = The Lord), but by the oath of the youths, *2* by the curses of the covenant. *Blank* Neither should one mention the law of Moses, for [...] *3 Blank* And if he swears and transgresses, he would profane the name. *Blank* And if he sw[ears] by the curses of the covenant [he should do it before] *4* the judges. *Blank* If he transgresses, he will be guilty and will have to confess and make amends but he shall not be liable [for sin and shall not] *5* die. *Blank* Whoever enters the covenant, for all Israel for an eternal law, he must impose upon his sons, *6* who belong to those who are enrolled, the oath of the covenant. *Blank* And such is *7* the regulation, throughout all the age of wickedness, for whoever goes back from his path of corruption. On the day when he talks *8* to the Inspector of the Many, they shall enrol him with the covenant oath which Moses established *9* with Israel, the covenant to rev[ert to] the law of Moses with the whole heart [and with the whole] *10* soul, to what has been discovered that has to be put into practice in all of the a[ge of wickedness]. But no-one should make him know *11* the precepts until he stands in front of the Inspector, lest he appears to be simple when they test him. *12* But when he has imposed upon himself to return to the law of Moses with all his heart and all his soul *13* [they will exact revenge] from him if he should sin. *Blank* And if he fulfils all that has been revealed of the law [for the multitude] *14* [of the camp], the Overseer should teach him and give orders concerning him which he should learn *15* throughout a full year. And in accordance with (his) knowledge ‹he will approach. And no-one› stupid or deranged ‹should enter›; and anyone feeble[–minded and insane,] *16* those with sightless [eyes, the lame or one who stumbles, or a deaf person, or an under-age boy, none of these] *17* should enter [the congregation, since the holy angels are in its midst.] *18* [...]... *19* [...]... *20* [...]...

Col. XVI   *1* with you a covenant and with all Israel. Therefore, the man will make binding upon ‹his› soul to return to *2* the law of Moses, for in it all is defined. *Blank* And the exact interpretation of their ages about the blindness *3* of Israel in all these matters, behold, it is defined in the book «of the divisions of the periods *4* according to their jubilees and their weeks». And on the day on which the man has pledged himself to return *5* to the law of Moses, the angel Mastema will turn aside from following him, should he keep his word. *6* This is why Abraham circumcised himself on the day of his knowledge. *Blank* And as for what he said: *Dt 23:24* «What issues from your mouth, *7* keep it and carry it out». Every binding oath by which anyone has pledged *8* to fulfil the letter of the law, he should not annul, even at the price of death. *Blank* Anything by which *9* he might pledge to turn away fr[om the la]w, he should not fulfil, not even when the price is death. *10* Concerning the oath of a woman. Since he says: *Num 30:7–9* «It is for the husband to annul her oath», *11* no-one should annul an oath if he does not know whether he should carry it out [...]. or annul it. *12* If it is to violate the covenant, he should annul it and should not carry it out. *Blank* And the regulation applies also to her father. *13* Concerning the regulation for freewill-offerings. No-one should dedicate anything, obtained by unjust means, to the altar. Neither *14* should the priests take from Israel (anything obtained by unjust means). No-one should pronounce holy the food *15* [of his mouth for G]od, for this is what he says: *Mic 7:2* «Each one traps his fellow with anathema». *Blank* And no-one should *16* pronounce holy anything of [...] his possession *17* he will pronounce holy [...] will be punished, *18* he who dedicates [...] *19* in order to judge [...] *20* ...[...]

Col. IX   *1 Blank* Every man who gives a human person to anathema shall be executed according to the laws of the gentiles. *2* And what it says: *Lev 19:18* «Do not avenge yourself or bear resentment against the sons of your people»: everyone of those who entered *3* the covenant who brings an accusation against his fellow, unless it is with reproach before witnesses, *4* or who brings it when he is angry, or he tells it to his elders so that they despise him, he is «the one who avenges himself and bears resentment». *5 Blank* Is it not perhaps written that only *Nah 1:2* «he (God) avenges himself and bears resentment against his enemies»? *6* If he kept silent about him from one day to the other, or accused him of a capital offence, *7* he has witnessed against himself, for he did not fulfil the commandment of God which tells him: *Lev 19:17* «You shall *8* reproach your fellow so as not to incur sin because of him». *Blank* Concerning the oath. As for what he *9* said: *1 Sm 25:26* «You shall not do justice with your (own) hand», but whoever forces the making of an oath in the open field, *10* not in the presence of judges or at their command, has done justice for himself with his hand. Every lost object *11* about which it is not known who stole it from the property of the camp in which it was stolen – its owner should make a maledictory *12* oath; whoever hears it, if he knows and does not say it, is guilty. *13 Blank* Every illegal object which should be given back and has no owner – he who gives it back should confess to the priest *14* and it will be for himself, apart from the ram of the sin-offering. *Blank* And in the same way, every lost object which has been found and has *15* no owner, will be for the priests, for he who found it does not know the regulation in its regard; *16* if its owner is not found, they shall keep it. *Blank* Any matter in which a man sins *17* against the law, and his fellow sees him and he is alone; if it is a capital matter, he shall denounce him *18* in his presence, with reproach, to the Inspector, and the Inspector shall write with his hand until he commits it *19* again in the presence of someone alone, and he denounces him to the Inspector; if he returns and is surprised in the presence of *20* someone alone, his judgment is complete; but if they are two, one and one, who testify about *21* a different matter, the man is only to be excluded from the pure food on condition that *22* they are trustworthy, and that on the same day on which he saw him, he denounces him to the Inspector. And concerning riches, they shall accept two *23* trustworthy witnesses. And one, to exclude from the holy food. A witness is not to be accepted

Col. x   *1* by the judges to condemn to death on his word, if he has not completed his days to pass *2* among those who are recruited, and is fearful of God. *Blank* No-one *3* who has consciously transgressed anything of a precept is to be believed as a witness against his fellow, until he has been purified to return. *4 Blank* And this is the rule of the judges of the congregation. Ten men in number, chosen *5* from among the congregation, for a period; four from the tribe of Levi and of Aaron and six from Israel; *6* learned in the book of HAGY and in the principles of the covenant; between *7* twenty-five and sixty years. And no-one over *8* sixty years should hold the office of judging the congregation, for on account of man's sin *9* his days were shortened, and because of God's wrath against the inhabitants of the earth, he decided to remove knowledge *10* from them before they completed their days. Concerning purification with water. *11* No-one should bathe in water which is dirty or which is less than the amount which covers a man. *12 Blank* No-one should purify a vessel in it. And every cavity in the rock in which there is not the amount *13* which covers, if an impure person has touched it, he has defiled the water like the water of a vase. *14* Concerning the sabbath, to observe it in accordance with its regulation. *Blank* No-one should do *15* work on the sixth day, from the moment when the sun's disc is *16* at a distance of its diameter from the gate, for this is what he says: *Dt 5:12* «Observe the *17* sabbath day to keep it holy». And on the day of the sabbath, no-one should say a *18* useless or stupid word. He is not to lend anything to his fellow. He is not to discuss riches or gain. *19* He is not to speak about matters of work or of the task to be carried out on the following day. *20 Blank* No-one is to walk in the field to do the work which he wishes *21* ⟨on⟩ the sabbath. He is not to walk more than one thousand cubits outside the city. *22 Blank* No-one is to eat on the sabbath day except what has been prepared; and from what is lost *23* in the field, he should not eat. And he should not drink except of what there is in the camp.

Col. XI   *1* On the road, if he goes down to bathe, he should drink where he stands. *Blank* But he is not to draw it with *2* any vessel. He is not to send a foreigner to do what he wishes on the sabbath day. *3 Blank* No-one is to wear dirty clothes or (clothes) which are in the chest, unless *4* they have been washed with water or rubbed with incense. *Blank* No-one should fast voluntarily *5* on the sabbath. *Blank* No-one should go after an animal to pasture it outside his city, except for *6* a thousand cubits. *Blank* He is not to raise his hand to strike with the fist. *Blank* If *7* it is stubborn, he should not remove it from his house. *Blank* No-one should remove anything from the house *8* to outside, or from outside to the house. Even if he is in a hut, he should remove nothing from it *9* or bring anything into it. He is not to open a sealed vessel on the sabbath. *Blank* No-one should wear *10* perfumes on the sabbath, to go out or come in. *Blank* In his dwelling no-one should lift *11* a stone or dust. *Blank* The wet-nurse should not lift the baby to go out or come in on the sabbath. *12 Blank* No-one should press his servant or his maidservant or his employee on the sabbath. *Blank* {Not} No-one should help an animal give birth on the sabbath day. *Blank* And if he makes it fall into a well *14* or a pit, he should not take it out on the sabbath. *Blank* No-one should stay in a place close *15* to gentiles on the sabbath. *Blank* No-one should profane the sabbath by riches or gain on the sabbath. *16 Blank* And any living man who falls into a place of water or into a place ‹...›, *17* no-one should take him out with a ladder or a rope or a utensil. *Blank* No-one should offer anything upon the altar on the sabbath, *18* except the sacrifice of the sabbath, for thus is it written: *Lev 23:38* «except your offerings of the sabbath». *Blank* No-one should send *19* to the altar a sacrifice, or an offering, or incense, or wood, by the hand of a man impure from any *20* of the impurities, so allowing him to defile the altar, for it is written: *Prov 15:8* «the sacrifice *21* of the wicked is an abomination, but the prayer of the just is like an agreeable offering». *Blank* And everyone who enters *22* the house of prostration should not enter with impurity requiring washing; and when the trumpets of the assembly sound, *23* he may advance or retreat, but the whole service should not stop...

Col. XII   *1* it is holy. No man should sleep with his wife in the city of the temple, defiling *2* the city of the temple with their impurity. *Blank* Every /man/ over whom the spirit of Belial dominates *3* and he preaches apostasy, will be judged according to the regulation of the necromancer or the diviner. But every one who goes astray, *4* defiling the sabbath and the festivals, shall not be executed, for guarding him *5* belongs to men; and if he is cured of it, they shall guard him for seven years and afterwards *6* he shall enter the assembly. *Blank* He is not to stretch out his hand to shed the blood of one of the gentiles *7* for the sake of riches and gain. *Blank* Neither should he take any of his riches, so that they do not *8* blaspheme, except on the advice of the company of Israel. *Blank* No-one should sell an animal, *9* or a clean bird, to the gentiles lest they sacrifice them. *Blank 10* And he should not sell them anything from his granary or his press, at any price. And his servant and his maidservant: he should not sell them, *11* for they entered the covenant of Abraham with him. *Blank* No-one should defile his soul *12* with any living being or one which creeps, by eating them, from the larvae of bees to every living *13* being which creeps in water. And fish: they should not eat them unless they have been opened up *14* alive, and the[ir blood poured] away. And all the locusts, according to their kind, shall be put into fire or into water *15* while they are still alive, as this is the regulation for their species. And all the wood and the stones *16* and the dust which are defiled by man's impurity, by defilement of oil in them, *17* in accordance with their uncleanness will make whoever touches them impure. *Blank* And every utensil, {nail} nail or peg in the wall *18* which is with a dead person in the house will be unclean with the same uncleanness as tools for work. *19 Blank* Rule for the assembly of the cities of Israel. In accordance with these regulations, to keep *20* the unclean apart from the clean, and distinguish between holy and profane. *Blank* And these are the ordinances *21* for the Instructor, so that he walks in them with every living thing, according to the regulation for every time. And in accordance with this regulation *22* shall the seed of Israel walk and it will not be cursed. *Blank* And this is the rule of the assembly *23* [of the ca]mps. Those who walk in them, in the time of wickedness until there arises the messiah of Aaron

Col. XIII   *1* and Israel, they shall be ten in number as a minimum to (form) thousands, hundreds, fifties *2* and tens. And in the place of ten, a priest learned in the book of HAGY should not be lacking; and by *3* his authority all shall be governed. And if there should not be an expert in them all, and one of the levites is an expert *4* in them, the lot has fallen to all the members of the camp to go out and come in, on his authority. *Blank* But if *5* there is a judgment against anyone about the law of leprosy, the priest shall take his place in the camp *6* and the Inspector shall instruct him in the exact interpretation of the law. *Blank* Even if he is a simpleton, he is the one who shall intern him, for his is *7* the judgment. *Blank* And this is the rule of the Inspector of the camp. He shall instruct the Many in the deeds of *8* God, and shall teach them his mighty marvels, and recount to them the eternal events with their solutions. *9* He shall have pity on them like a father on his sons, and will heal all the strays (?) like a shepherd his flock. *10* He will undo all the chains which bind them, so that there will be neither harassed nor oppressed in his congregation. *11 Blank* And everyone who joins his congregation, he should examine, concerning his actions, his intelligence, his strength, his courage and his wealth; *12* and they shall inscribe him in his place according to his condition in the lot of light. *Blank* No-one *13* of the members of the camp should have authority to introduce anyone into the congregation against the de[cision] of the Inspector of the camp. *14 Blank* And none of those who have entered the covenant of God «should either take anything from or give (anything) to» the sons of the pit, *15* except for «from hand to hand». *Blank* And no-one should make a deed of purchase or of sale without informing *16* the Inspector of the camp and making a contract; and he is not [...] ... *17* [...] And likewise, the one who divorces (?); [...] *18* [...] they shall reply to him and with compassionate love shall not bear resentment against them [...] *19* [...] and the one which is not tied [...] *20* [...] *Blank* And this is the assembly of the camps in all [...] *21* [...] they shall not succeed in dwelling in the land [...] *22* [... These are the regulations] for the Instructor, [to follow them...]

Col. XIV   *1* as have not come since the day on which Ephraim became separated from Judah»; and (to) all those who walk in them, *2* the covenant of God is faithful to save them from all the nets of the pit, for ‹they will come› suddenly and be punished. *3 Blank* Rule of the session of all the camps. All shall be enlisted by their names: the priests first, *4* the levites second, the children of Israel third, and the proselyte fourth; and they shall be inscribed by their [na]mes, *5* each one after his brother; the priests first, the levites second, the children of Israel *6* third and the proselyte fourth. And thus shall they sit and thus shall they be questioned about everything. And the priest who is named *7* [at the he]ad of the Many will be between thirty and sixty years old, learned in the book of *8* [HAGY] and in all the regulations of the law, to say them in accordance with their regulations. *Blank* And the Inspector who is *9* over all the camps will be between thirty years and sixty years of age, master of every *10* secret of men and of every language according to their families. On his authority, the members of the assembly shall enter, *11* each one in his turn; and every affair which any man needs to say to the Inspector, should say it *12* in connection with any dispute or judgment. *Blank* And this is the rule of the Many, to provide for all their needs: the salary *13* of two days each month at least. They shall place it in the hand of the Inspector and of the judges. *14* From it they shall give to the orphans and with it they shall strengthen the hand of the needy and the poor, and to the elder who *15* [is dy]ing, and to the vagabond, and to the prisoner of a foreign people, and to the girl who *16* has no protector, and to the unma[rried woman] who has no suitor; and for all the works of the company, and *17* [the house of the company shall not be deprived of its means]. *Blank* And this is the exact interpretation of the session of [the Many, and these are the foundations] *18* [which the assembly make.] *Blank* And this is the exact interpretation of the regulations by which [they shall be ruled] *19* [until there arises the messiah] of Aaron and Israel. He shall atone for their sins [... pardon, and guilt] *20* [...] in riches, although he knows, and [...] *21* [...] he shall be punished for six days. And he who spe[aks...] *22* [...] without justification, [shall be punished for a] year [...]

Damascus Document*b* (CD–B)

Col. XIX (= CD–A VII, 5–10; VIII, 2–21)   *1* is a guarantee for them that they shall live a thousand generations. *Blank* As it is written: *Dt 7:9* «He keeps the covenant and favour *2* for those who love him and keep his precepts for a thousand generations». And if they reside in the camps in accordance with the rule of *3* the land, as it was since ancient times, and take wives in accordance with the custom of the law, and beget children, *4* they shall walk in accordance with the law. *Blank* And according to the regulation of the teachings, according to the rule of the law *5* which says: *Num 30:17* «/Between/ a man and his wife, and between a father and his son». But (over) all those who despise the precepts *6* and the ordinances, may be emptied over them the punishment of the wicked, when God visits the earth, *7* when there comes the word which is written by the hand of Zechariah, the prophet: *Zech 13:7* «Wake up, sword, *8* against my shepherd, and against the male who is my companion – oracle of God – wound the shepherd and scatter the flock *9* and I shall return my hand upon the little ones». Those who are faithful to him are the poor ones of the flock. *10* These shall escape in the age of the visitation; but those that remain shall be delivered up to the sword when there comes the messiah *11* of Aaron and Israel. As happened in the age of the visitation of the first one, as {Ezekiel} said *12* by the hand of Ezekiel: *Ez 9:4* « {mark} To mark with a tau the foreheads of those who sigh and groan». *13* But those who remained were delivered up to the sword, which carries out the vengeance of the covenant. Thus will be the judgment of all who entered *14* his covenant, but did not remain steadfast in these precepts; they shall be visited for destruction at the hand of Belial. *15* This is the day when God will make a visitation, as he says: *Hos 5:10* «The princes of Judah will be like those who move *16* the boundary, upon them he will pour out his fury like w[ater]». For they entered the covenant of conversion, *17* but did not keep themselves apart from the path of traitors and defiled themselves by paths of licentiousness and with wicked wealth, *18* avenging themselves, each one bearing resentment against his brother and each one hating his fellow, and each one despising *19* his blood relative; they have approached for debauchery and have manipulated with pride for wealth and gain {...} *20* Each one did what was right [in his] eyes and each one has chosen the stubbornness of his heart. They did not keep apart from the people *21* and from their sins. And they have [rebe]lled with insolence, walking on the path of the wicked, about whom *22* God says: *Dt 32:33* «Their wine is serpents' venom and the head of cruel, harsh asps». The serpents *23* are the kings of the peoples and the wine, their paths and the asps' head is the head *24* of the kings of Greece, which comes to carry out vengeance against them. But the builders of *25* the wall have not understood all of these things, nor those who daub with whitewash, because of one who raises up storms, and preaches *26* lies, to the man, the one against whose congregation

God's wrath has been kindled. *Blank* And what Moses says *27* to Israel: *Dt 9:5 and 7:8* «Not for your justice, or for the uprightness of your heart are you going to possess these nations, *28* but because he loved your fathers and keeps the oath». So is *29* the judgm[ent] of the converts of Israel, who turned away from the path of the people on account of God's love. He loves the very first *30* who testified against the people, following God, and those who come after them, because to them belongs *31* the fathers' covenant. And God hates and detests the builders of the wall and his anger is kindled against them and against all *32* those who follow them. And like this judgment will be that of all who reject God's precepts {…} *33* and forsake them and move aside in the stubbornness of their heart. And thus, all the men who entered the new *34* covenant in the land of Damascus and turned and betrayed and departed from the well of living waters, *35* shall not be counted in the assembly of the people and shall not be inscribed in their [lis]ts, from the day of the session {of him who te‹aches› / of the teacher}

Col. xx   *1* of the unique Teacher until there arises the messiah of Aaron and Israel. *Blank* And so is the judgment *2* of everyone who enters the congregation of the men of perfect holiness and is slack in the fulfilment of the instructions of the upright. *3* This is the man who is melted in the crucible. *Blank* When his deeds are evident, he shall be expelled from the congregation, *4* like one whose lot did not fall among the disciples of God. In accordance with his misdeed, all the men *5* of knowledge shall reproach him, until the day when he returns to take his place in the session of the men of perfect holiness {for *6* his lot is not in the midst of}. But when his deeds are evident, according to the exact interpretation of the law in which *7* the men of perfect holiness walked, no-one should associate with him in wealth or work, *8* for all the holy ones of the Most High have cursed him. And (proceed) according to this judgment, with all those who despise, among the first *9* as among the last, for they have placed idols in their heart {and have placed} and have walked in the stubbornness of *10* their heart. For them there shall be no part in the house of the law. *Blank* They shall be judged according to the judgment of their companions, who turned round *11* with insolent men, for they spoke falsehood about the holy regulations and despised *12* the covenant {of God} and the pact which they established in the land of Damascus, which is the first covenant. *13* And neither for them nor their families shall there shall be a part in the house of the law. *Blank* And from the day *14* of the gathering in of the unique teacher, until the destruction of all the men of war who turned back *15* with the man of lies, there shall be about forty years. *Blank* And in this age the wrath *16* of God will be kindled against Israel, as he says: *Hos 3:4* «There shall be no king, no prince, no judge, no-one [who] *17* reproaches in justice». But the converts from the sin of [Ja]cob, those keeping the covenant of God, shall then speak, each *18* to his fellow, each one to make his brother holy, so that their steps become steady in the path of God, and God pays attention to *19* their words. And he will listen; and it will be written in a book of remembrance [before him] for those who fear God and think on *20* his name, until salvation and justice are revealed to those who fear [God. And they shall distinguish] again between the just *21* and the wicked, between whoever serves God and whoever does not serve him. He shows mercy to [thousands,] to whoever loves him *22* and whoever is faithful to him, for a thousand generations. [... those of] the house of Peleg, who left the holy city *23* and leaned on God in the age of Israel's unfaithfulness; but they defiled the temple and turned back *24* to the pa[th] of the people in some things. All these, each one according to his spirit, shall be judged in the holy *25* council. *Blank* And all, among those who entered the covenant, transgressing the limits of the law, when *26* the glory of God is manifested to Israel, shall be cut off from amongst the camp, and with them all the wicked men of *27* Judah in the days of the purges. *Blank* But all those who remain steadfast in these regulations, coming *28* and going in accordance with the law, and listen to the Teacher's voice, and confess before God: «Assuredly *29* have we sinned, both we and our fathers, walking contrary to the ordinances of the covenant; justice *30* and truth are your judgments against us»; and they do not raise their hand against his holy regulations and his just *31* judgments and his truthful stipulations; and they are instructed in the first ordinances, *32* in conformity with which the men of the Unique One were judged; and they lend their ears to the voice of the Teacher of Righteousness; and do not reject *33* the holy regulations when they hear them; these shall exult and rejoice and their heart will be strong, and they shall prevail *34* over all the sons of the world. And God will atone for them, and they shall see his salvation, for they have taken refuge in his holy name.

B *Copies from Cave 4*

4QDamascus Document*a* (4Q266 [4QD*a*])

Frag. 1 (*lines* 2–8 = 4QD*b* 1 I, 1–6; *lines* 9–17 = CD–A I, 1–11)   *1* [....the] final [generations.] Did not, perhaps... [...]? *2* [...] this is his beginning and this, his end [...] *3* [...until] there comes upon them, for ... [...] *4* [... for there is no] before or after in his festivals [...] *5* *Blank* Did he not, perhaps, establish the time of an[ger for those who do not know] *6* [...] will, for those who examine his precepts and [walk on the perfect] *7* path and [... and exami]ne hidden things and open their ears and [hear profound things] *8* and understand everything that happens when it comes upon them. *Blank* [...] *9* Now, then, listen to me, all you who know justice, and understand the deeds [of God; for he has a dispute] *10* [with all flesh,] and will carry out judgment against all those who despise him. For when they were unfaithful in] *11* [abandoning him, he hid his fa]ce from Israel [and] from his sanctuary, and deli[vered] them [up to the sword. But when he remembered] *12* [the covenant of the very] first, he pres[erved a re]mnant for Israel and did [not deliver them up to destruction.] *13* [And at the moment of wrath,] three hundred and nin[ety ye]ars [after having delivered them up into the hands of Nebuchadnezzar,] *14* [king of Babylon,] he visited them and cau[sed to sprout from Isra]el and from Aar[on] a sho[ot of the planting, in order to possess] *15* [his land and to become fat with the good] things of his soil. And they rea[lised their s]in and knew that they were] *16* [guilty men; but they were like blind persons and like those who look] for the pa[th by groping *10* over twenty years. And] *17* [God appraised their deeds, because they sought] him [with a perfect heart and raised up for them a Teacher of Righteousness]

Frag. 2 (= CD – A XIV, 2 – 6)   *1* [and (to) all those who walk in them, the covenant of God is faithful, to save them from a]ll *2* [the nets of the pit, for (they come) suddenly and /.../ Rule of the session of all the camps. All shall be en]listed *3* [by their names: the priests first, the levites second, the children of Israel thi]rd, *4* [and the proselyte fourth; and they shall be inscribed by their [na]mes, each one after his brother; the priests first,] the levites *5* [second, the children of Israel third and the proselyte fourth. And thus shall they sit and th]us shall they be questioned about

Frag. 3   ]...the holy[one(s)

4QDamascus Document^{b} (4Q267 [4QD^{b}])

Frag. 1   *1* [...the so]ns of light to depart from the pa[ths of...] *2* [...] until the completion of time of the visitation [...] *3* [...] all their deeds. The flames [...] *4* ... [...a]ll those who move the boundary, and he shall wreak destruction [...] *5* the evil [...] ... and he shall make them know ... [...] *6* the terrible [...] his marvel (?), he will tell them [...] *7* of man [...] the heavens, who lives ... [...] *8* in the depths of [...] *9* the seal [...] *10-13* [...] *14* in the precep[ts...] *15* in the offering [...] *16* the voice of Moses [...] *17* he slanders the laws and precepts of God [...] *18* the small and the great ... [...] *19* We show, then, [...] *20* he has destroyed you [...] *21* you shall get up and understand [...] *22* [...] they shall reject [...we are dust] *23* and ashes, and whoever [...not] *24* understand [...] *25* ... [...]

Frag. 2 col. I (*lines* 1 – 6 = 4QD^{a} I, 2 – 8; *lines* 6 – 23 = CD – A I, 1 – 20)   *1* [this is his beginning and this is his end...] until *2* [there comes upon them, for ...] for there is no advancing or delaying his festivals. *3* [...] Did he not, perhaps, establish the time of anger for those who do not know *4* [... will, for those who exa]mine his precepts and walk on the perfect path *5* [... and exami]ne hidden things and] open their ears and hear profound things and understand *6* [everything that happens when it comes upon them. *Blank*] Now then, listen, all those of you who know *7* justice, and understand the actions [of God; for he has a dispute with] all flesh and will carry out judgment *8* against all those who spurn [him. For when they were unfaithful in forsaking him,] he hid his fa[ce from Is]rael and from his sanctuary *9* and deliv[ered them up to the sword. However, when he remembered the covenant of the very first, he saved a remnant] for Israel and did not *10* deliver them up to destruction. And at the moment of wrath,] three [hundred and ninety years] after having delivered them up into the hands *11* of Ne[buchadne]zzar, king of Babylon, he visited them [and caused to sprout from Israel] and from Aar[on] a shoot *12* [of the pla]nting, in order to possess [his land and to become fat with the good things of his soil. And they realised their s]in and knew *13* that they were guilty men; [but they were like blind persons and like those who look] for the path by groping over twenty [years. *14* And God appraised their [deeds, because they sought him with a perfect heart and raised up for them a Teacher of Righteousness,] *15* in order to direct them in the path of his heart. [And in order to make known to the last generations what] *16* he had done to the final generation, the congregation of traitors. These are the ones who stray from the path. This is the time *17* about which it has been wri[tten: *Hos 4:16* «Like a stray heifer so has Israel strayed», *18* when 'the sco[ffer' arose, who scattered the waters of lies over Is]rael and] made them stray into a wilderness *19* without path, flattening the everlasting [heights, diverging from tracks of justice and] removing the boundary with which the original ones had marked [their inheritance, so that the cur]ses of his covenant [would adhere to them,] *21* to deliver them up to the sw[ord carrying out the vengeance of the covenant. For they sought] easy interpretations, *22* chose illusions, [scrutinised loopholes, chose the handsome] neck, acquitted *23* [the guilty and sentenced the just, violated the covenant broke the precept,] colluded together against *24* [the life of the just man, their soul abominated all those who walk in perfection, they hunted them down with the sword and provoked the dispute of the people.]

Frag. 2 col II (= CD–A I, 21–II, 21)   *1* And kindled was the wrath of God against his congregation, [laying waste all its great number, for their deeds were unclean] *2* before him. Now, then, lis[ten to me, all who enter the covenant, and I will open your ears to the paths of the wicked] *3* and from all the tracks of s[in I shall divert you. God loves knowledge; wisdom and counsel] *4* has he established before himself; pruden[ce and knowledge are at his service; patience is his and abundance of pardons to atone] *5* for those who turn back from wicke[dness...] *6* without there being service[... For God did not choose them]

7 at the beginning of the world, [and before they were established he knew their deeds, and abominated the generations on account of blood,] *8* and hid his fa[ce from the country... until their extinction. And he knew the years of their existence,] *9* and the number and detail [of their ages, of all those who exist over the centuries, and of those who will exist,] *10* until it oc[curs in their ages throughout all the everlasting years. And in all of them he raised up for himself,] *11* famous pe[ople, to leave a remnant for the country and in order to fill the face of the universe] *12* with their of[fspring. And he taught them by the hand of the anointed ones through his holy spirit and through seers of the truth.] *13* With precision their names [were established. But those he hates, he causes to stray. Now, then, my sons, listen] *14* to me [and I shall open your eyes so that you can see and understand the deeds of God, so that you can choose what] *15* he is [pleased with and repudiate what he hates... so that you can walk] *16* perfectly on all his paths [and not allow yourselves to be attracted by the thoughts of a guilty inclination and lascivious eyes. For many went astray for these things;] *17* brave heroes yield[ed on their account, from ancient times until now. For having walked in the stubbornness of their hearts] *18* the Watchers of the [heavens fell; on its account they were caught, for they did not follow the precepts of God; in the same way their sons fell, whose height was like that of cedars] *19* [and whose bodies were like] mountains. [All flesh which there was in the dry earth decayed and became] *20* as if it had never [been, for having realized their desires and failing to keep their creator's precepts, until] *21* his wrath [flared up against them. *22* [...]

Frag. 3 *col.* I (= CD–A IV, 8–10)   *7* [the law in which the very first were instructed until] the period *8* [of these years is complete. According to the covenant which God established with the very] first, in order to atone *9* [for their sins, so will God atone for them. But when the period is complete] corresponding to [the number]

Frag. 3 *col.* II (= CD–A V, 12–VI, 7)   *9* [God's covenant, saying: «they are unfounded». They speak abomination against] them. [They are all igniters of fire,] *10* [kindlers of blazes; webs of a spider are their webs, and their eggs are vi]per's eg[gs. Whoever is close] *11* [to them will not be unpunished; even more so, if the fault is greater, unless he has been comp]elled. For since ancient [times God visited] *12* [their] deeds, [and his wrath flared up against their actions, «for it is a people] in which there is no intelligence», [they are a nation] *13* [be]reft of counsels [in that there is no intelligence in them. For in ancient] times there a[rose Moses] *14* [and Aa]ron, by the hand of the pri[nce of lig]hts, [and Belial, raised up Jan]nes and [his brother] *15* with his [cunning] {during the wickedness} during the first delive[rance of Israel.] And in the [age of devastation of] *16* [the land there a]rose those who removed the boundary [and made

Israel stray. And they razed the countryside, for they spoke] *17* [of rebellion against] God's precepts through the hand of [Moses and also of the holy anointed ones. They prophesied deceit] *18* [in order to div]ert Israel from following [God. But God remembered the covenant of the very first, and from] *19* [Aaron] raised men of knowledge /and from Israel wi[se men], and forced them to lis[ten.] /as Moses sa[ys: «....] *20* [... with the spa]de». The well is the [law. And those who dug it are the converts of Israel,] *21* [who left the] land of Judah and lived [in the land of Damascus, all of whom God called] *22* [princes, for they sought him, and their renown] has not [been repudiated in anyone's mouth.]

Frag. 3 *col.* III (= CD–A VI, 9–17)   *3* [that the spade decreed, to walk in them throughout the whole age of wickedness, and without whi]ch they will [not] *4* [obtain it, until there arises he who teaches justice at the end of days.] But all those who have been brought *5* [into the cove]nant shall not [enter the temple to kindle his altar in vain.] He is the one who closes the door, *6* as God [said: *Mal 1:10* «Whoever amongst you will close its door so that you do not kind]le my altar in vain!». *7* [Un]less [they are care]ful [to act in accordance with the exact interpretation of the law for the a]ge of wicke[dness: to be keep] apart from the sons of *8* [the p]it; [to abstain from wicked wealth which defiles, either by] promise or by [vow, and from the wealth of the] *9* [temple and from stealing from the poor of the people, from making their wi]dows their spo[ils, and orphans]

Frag. 3 *col.* IV (= CD–A VII, 11–VIII, 9)   *1* as for what he sa[ys: *Isa 7:17* «There shall come upon you, upon your people and upon your father's house, days such as] *2* have not com[e since the day Ephraim separated from Judah». When the two houses of Israel separated,] *3* all [the renegades were delivered up to the sword...] *4* [...] *5* [...] *6* [The King is the as]sembly; [and the plinths of the imag]es are the b[ooks of] the prophets, *7* whose wo[rds Israel despised. And the star] is the Interp[reter of the] law, *8* [who will come] to Damascus, as is written: *Num 24:13* «[A star] moves out [of Jacob *9* and a sceptre ari]ses out of Israel». The sceptre is the prince [of the whole congregation] *10* [and when he rises he will demolish] all the sons of Seth. *Blank* The[se will escape in the age of] *11* t[he first one's visitation.] *Blank* And the renegades will [be delivered up] to the sword. [Thus will be the judg]ment of *12* [all those enter]ing his covenant but do not remain steadfast [in these;] they will have a vis[itation for destruction] at the hand of *13* [Belial.] This is the day when [God] will make a visitation, as [he says:] «Today *14* [...]» the day when *15* [...] all the rebels *16* [in so far as they have not left the path of the traitors and have been defi]led by paths of licentiousness *17* [and by wicked wealth and avenging themselves, and each one bearing resentment against his brother and] each one [hating his] fellow, *18* [and each one despising his blood relative;] they have approached [for debauchery and have manipulated with pride for wealth] *19* [and gain. Each one did what was right in his ey]es and each one has chos[en the stubbornness of his heart.] *20* [They did not keep apart from the people and have rebelled with a raised hand] walki[ng on the path of the wicked]

Frag. 4 (= CD–B XX, 33–34)   *1* [and they shall rejoice] and their heart [will be strong, and they shall dominate all the sons of the world.] *2* [And God will atone for them, and they] shall see his salvat[ion for they have taken refuge in his holy name.] *3* [...]and they shall strengthen

Frag. 5   *1* [... the regu]lations [...] ... *2* [...] for all the upright of heart in Israel *3* [...] the regulations of his justice [...] *4* [...] ... [...]

Frag. 6 *col.* I   *6* [...] and they restore strength in leprosy [...] *7* [the holy men who are str]engthened by his ho[ly] name [...] *8* [and he binds himself to re-turn...]... for in Judah [...] *9* [...] Israel when he arises [...] to instruct *10* [...pe]ace. *Blank* And all those [of Israel] who are [left...] *11* [... for] each one [to appr]oach him according to his spirit [...] for *12* [...] ... they shall depart in accordance with the Inspector [...] *13* [...] in them [shall] walk all the converts of Israel [...] *14* [...] the sons of Zadok, the priests. Behold, [...] *15* [... the exact interpretation] of the last law. And these are the ordinances for the Ins[tructor...] *16* [...] in them for all Israel, for [...] not *17* [...] ... to walk in ... [...]

Frag. 6 *col.* II   *1* [...] And anyone who [speaks weakly or with a faltering sound], *2* [without] separating his words to make [his voice] heard [should not read in the book of] *3* [the Torah], so that he will not lead to error in a capital matter [...] *4* [...] to his brothers, the priests, in service. [...And whoever] *5* of the sons of Aaron has been a captive among the gentiles [...should not enter] *6* to defile it with his impurity. He should not approach the service [...] *7* in the house of the veil, and should not eat of the most holy things [...] *8* Whoever of the sons of Aaron emigrates to se[rve ...] *9* with him in the council of the people, and also to betray ... [... And whoever of the sons of] *10* Aaron has caused the name of truth to fall [... walking] *11* in the stubbornness of his heart to eat of the holy [...] *12* of Israel the council of the sons of Aaron ... [...] *11* he who eats shall incur the fault of the blood [...] *14* in genealogy (?). *Blank* And this is the rule of the session of [...] *15* of holiness in their [camps and in] their cities in a[ll...] *16* [...] the ses[sion of ...]

Frag. 7   *1* [...] of the blood [...] *2* [...] of a man on the he[ad...] *3* [...] a flock in one [...] *4* [...] his eyes [...] *5* [...] ... [...]

Frag. 8   *1* [...]...[...] *2* [...] destroys [...] *3* his betrayal. No-one should keep [...] *4* in the trial of the just man's affliction. No [...] *5* [...] ... [...]

Frag. 9 col. I   *1* [...But if the tumour] or the rash [is deeper] *2* [than the skin ...] and the priest sees in it as it were living flesh or, as it were [...] *3* [...] it is [leprosy] which has taken hold of the living skin. And in accordance with this regulation, *4* [...] The priest shall examine it on the seventh day; if something live has been added *5* [to the dead,] it is malignant leprosy. And the regulation for ringworm of the head or of the beard: *6* [... the priest shall examine it, and] if the spirit enters the head or the beard in one block *7* [...] underneath the hair and changes its appearance to yellowish – for it is like a plant *8* under which there is a worm: cut its root and its fruit turns pale–. And as for what he *9* said: *Lev 13:33* «The priest shall order them to shave their head, but not to shave their ringworm», it is so that *10* the priest can count the dead and living hairs, and see: if *11* living (hairs) have been added to the dead ones during seven days, he is impure; but if liv[ing] (hairs) have not been added *12* to the dead ones and the artery is full of blood, and the spirit of life goes up and down through it, *13* that disease [is healed]. This is the regulation of the law of leprosy for the sons of Aaron, so that they can differentiate [...] *14 Blank* Regulation for the person with gonorrhoea. Everyone who [...] *15* [...]...[...]

Frag. 9 col. II   *1* [...] ... [...] ... *2* [...] she has an impurity; and if, however, is seen, and she does not *3* [...] seven days. She should not eat anything holy or enter *4* the temple until sunset on the eighth day. *Blank 5* And the woman who is pre[gnant] and gives birth to a male [she shall be impure] during seven [days] *6* ... [...] ... [...]

Frag. 10   *1* [...] to separate; and if [...] *2* [...] he shall wash his clothes [...]

Frag. 11   *1* [...] to her [...] *2* [...] she shall not eat [...] *3* [...] penalty of death [...] *4* [...] the wet-nurse in her impu[rity...] *5* [...] If her means do not stretch [to turtle-doves...] *6* [...] ... [...]

Frag. 12   *1* [...] ... [...] *2* [... who drank] lustral water [...It shall be an eternal precept] *3* [for the sons of Is]rael. *Blank* [...] *4* [...] And the bunches of the vi[ne: up to ten ber]ries of the clu[ster] *5* [...] and everything that shoots up [...up to one *seah* per bushel] *6* in which there is no seed [shall be a sacred offering, and] the cluster fallen [from the vine] *7* [...] and on its bunch, up to ten ber[ries, and on the branch] *8* [of the olive... when the branch is complete...] you shall enter it. If [you trample] *9* [in the field, take from it only one from every three, and a]ll that [...]

Frag. 13 ₁ [...] ... [...] ₂ plant of the vi[ne, and eve]ry [fruit tree] and every tree of the fiel[d...] ₃ in accordance with its regulation. [It is a] sacred offer[ing] in the land of residence, and afterwards they shall sell them ₄ to b[uy...] And if a man plants in the third year [...] ₅ he shall consecrate it [...] ₆ what covers it [...] ₇ [...] ... [...] ₈ and he shall add to it [...]

Frag. 15 ₁ [...] each camp [...] ₂ [...] its fourth part. *Blank* [...] ₃ [...] ... [...] ₄ [...] which [...] not ₅ [...] Every one who [...]

Frag. 16 ₁ [...] the camp. *Blank* [...] ₂ [...] interprets ... [...] ₃ [...] whom he rejects [...]

Frag. 17 *col.* I (= CD–A XV, 10–17) ₁ [in all the a]ge of [wickedness. But no-one should show him the precepts until] ₂ he stands in front of the Inspector, so that he appears simple in his instruction. But when ₃ he has imposed upon him to return to the law of Moses with all his heart and all his soul they will exact revenge ₄ [from him] if he should sin. And if he carries out all that has been revealed of the law by for the majority of the camp, ₅ the Teacher should teach him and give orders concerning him and he should learn ₆ throughout a full year. And in accordance with (his) knowledge he will approach. And no-one stupid ₇ or deranged should enter; and anyone feeble-minded and insane, those with sightless eyes, ₈ [and] the lame or one who stumbles, or a deaf person, or an under-age boy, ₉ none [of] these [shall enter] the congregation, for the ho[ly] angels [are in its midst].

Frag. 17 *col.* II (= CD–A XVI, 16–20 + IX, 1–2) ₁ [...his property, pronounce holy...] also ₂ this regulation [... will be punished he who dedicates ...] the sixth part of ₃ money which corresponds [...] {by the regulation} [...] *Blank* [For the judges,] ₄ in order to judge with jus[tice...] behind [...] he is the victim of an accident ₅ until ... and the [violence] is complete if he does not speak ₆ the truth to his fellow, – and until [he is converted ...] ₇ [...] like who does not [...] ₈ *Blank* And as for what he said: *Lev 27:29* [«Every man who gives to anathema a human] ₉ person», [shall be executed] according to the la[ws of the gentiles.] ₁₀ And that matter: *Lev 19:18* [«Do not avenge yourself or bear resentment against the sons of your people»]

Frag. 17 *col.* III (= CD–A X, 1–12) ₁ [he has completed his days to pass among those who are recruited, and is fearful of God. No-one is to be bel]ieved [as a witness against his fellow] ₂ [who has consciously transgressed anything of a precept, u]ntil [he has been purified] to return. [...] *Blank* [...] ₃ And [this is the rule of the judges] of the congregation. [Ten me]n [in number,] chosen from among the congregation, for a period; ₄ fo[ur from the tribe of Levi and of

A]aron and [six from Is]rael; [lea]rned in the book of HAGY *5* and in the princi[ples of the covenant; between] twenty-five and sixty years. And no-one *6* over [sixty years should h]old the office of judging [the congregation, f]or on account of man's sin [his days were short]ened, *7* [and because of God's wrath against the inhabitants of the earth, he decided to re]move [knowledge from them before they completed] *8* [their days. Concerning purification with water. No-one should bathe in water which is dirty or which is le]ss *9* [than the amount which covers a man. No-one should purify a vessel in it. And every cavity in the rock] in which there is no

Frag. 18 *col.* I (= CD–A XII, 14–22)   *1* [their blo]od. And all the locusts, according to their kind, shall be put into fire or into w]ater while they are still [alive,] *2* [as this is the regulation for their species. And all the wood and the sto]nes and the dust which *3* [are defiled by man's impurity, by defilement of oil in them, in accordance with their unc]leanness will make *4* [whoever touches them impure. And every utensil, nail or peg in the wall which i]s with *5* [a dead person in the house will be unclean with the same uncleanness as tools for work. Rule for the asse]mbly of the cities of Israel. *6* [In accordance with these regulations, to keep the unclean apart from the clean, and] distinguish *7* [between holy and profane. *Blank* And these are the ordinances for the Instructor,] so that he walks *8* [in them with every living thing, according to the regulation for every time. And in accordance with this regulation shall the seed of Is]rael walk.

Frag. 18 *col.* II   *1* [And no-one should] do[…] *2* [a me]mber, unless […] *3* which is in the cam[p…] *4* and they will not err. And thus with all those who […] *5* and he stands in the council {and thus} And thus […] *6* he will admonish his sons […] *7* [in] a spirit of poverty and with[…] *8* He shall not bear resentment against them […] *9* with their transgressions […]*10* [in] their judgments […] *11* […]…[…]

Frag. 18 *col.* III (= CD–A XIV, 8–21)   *1* [and in all the regulations of] the [law, to say] them in accordance with their regu[lations. And the] Inspector who is over *2* [all the camps will be between] thirty years and sixty [years of age, master] of every secret *3* [of men and] of every language [according to their families. On his auth]ority, [the members of] the assembly shall enter, *4* [each one in his turn;] and every aff[air which] any [man] needs to say to the assembly, *5* [he shall say it to the Inspector,] in connection with any disp[ute or judgment.] This is the rule of the Many, to provide for all *6* [their needs: the salary] of two [days] at least. They shall place it [in the hand] of the Inspector and of the judges. *7* [From it they shall g]ive to the woun[ded, and with it they shall] strengthen the hand of the needy and the poor, *8* [and to the elder] who is dying, and to the vagabond, and to the prisoner of a foreign people, *9* [and to the girl who] has no protector, and to the unma[rried woman] who has no suitor; and for all *10* [the works of the company,] and the house of the company shall not be deprived of its means. This is the exact interpretation *12* [of the regulations by which] they shall be ruled until there arises the messiah of Aaron and Israel. *13* [He shall atone for their sins ... par]don, and guilt [...]. *Blank 14* [... in riches, although he knows, ... and they shall keep him a]part from the [pure foo]d [...]

Frag. 18 *col.* IV   *1* [he shall be punished for two hundr]ed days, and he shall be punished for ten days. And if, in a capital matter, he bears resentment and does not repent *2* [... And whoever] insults his fellow who is not in the council, they shall keep him apart one year, and he shall be punished *3* for si[x months;] and whoever utters a senseless word with his mouth, shall be punished for ten *4* [days, and they shall keep him apart] for three mon[ths. And whoever speaks in the middle of a fel[low's words, shall be isolated *5* [and shall be punished for ten] days. And whoever lies down and sleeps during the me[eting of the Many...] *6* [shall be kept apart] for thirty days and shall be punished for ten days. [And thus shall they act with whoever] goes away, *7* [who] is not in the council of the Many, without reason, up to three ti[mes] in a session, *8* [shall be pu]nished for ten days; if he goes away [from the session] again [he shall be punished for thirty *9* days. And whoever walks [naked] in front of his fel[low... and whoever walks naked] in front of *10* the creatures, shall be kept apart for six [months... And whoever] *11* takes out {the} 'his hand' from under his cloth[es...] *12* days, and shall be punished for ten; and he who bows [down stupidly, making his] voice [heard, shall be kept apart] *13* for thirty and shall be punished for five [days. And he who takes out] his left hand *14* to gesticulate with it, shall be punished [for ten days.] And whoever goes slandering *15* his fellow [shall be kept apart from the pure food of the Many for one year...]

Frag. 18 *col.* V   *1* about the Many and he will receive his judgment according to his merit, as he says through the hand of *2* Moses about the person who sins through oversight: *Lev 4:27* «they should present *3* their sin-offering or their guilt-offering»; and about Israel it is written: *Lev 26:31* «I shall go *4* to the edges of the heavens, and I shall not smell the aroma of your pleasant fragrances»; and in another place *5a* /and in another place it is written: *Joel 2:13* «Tear your heart and not your clothes»/ *5* it is written: *Joel 2:12* (?) «to return to God in tears and in fasting». And anyone who despises these regulations *6* according to all the precepts which are found in the law of Moses, shall not be counted *7* among all the sons of his truth, for his soul is accursed by those disciplined by justice. In the rebellion he will be expelled from the presence of *8* the Many. And the priest who governs over the Many will speak to him; he will begin to speak, *9* saying:

'Blessed is he who is everything,
and in whose hands is everything,
and he does everything,
who has founded the heavens according to their families,
10 and according to their differences,
and according to their classes.
and he has made them walk through a trackless abyss.
11 You chose the descendants of our fathers
and gave them your truthful regulations
12 and your holy precepts,
so that man could carry them out and live,
and you established frontiers for us,
13 and you curse those who cross them.
And we are the people of your ransom
and the flock of your pasture.
14 You curse those who cross them
but we have raised ourselves up».

And the one who has been expelled will leave, and the man *15* who eats from his riches, and the one who seeks his peace, {the one who has been expelled} and the one who is agreement with him. *16* And his sentence will be written down in the Inspector's hand... and his judgment will be complete. The sons of Levi *17* and the men of the camps will meet in the third month and will curse whoever tends to the right *18* [or to the left of the] law. And this is the exact interpretation of the regulations which they are to observe in every age of *19* [...who] remained firm in all the ages of anger and in their steps, to all those who *20* [dwell in their camps and in their cities. And so, then, all] this is with regard to the exact interpretation of the law.

4QDamascus Document^{c} (4Q268 [4QD^{c}])

Frag. 1 *col.* I   *1* [...] with money [...] *2* [...] ... sent [...] the work [...] *3* [...] and he will not forgive [...] his sins. *Blank* Not to [...] *4* [...] one, for it is an abomination, and as for what he said: *Lev 25:14* «If [you make a sale] *5* [to a fellow, or purchase from the hand of] your fellow, no-one is to harm his fellow». And this is the exact interpre[tation...] *6* [...] in everything that he knows had been found... [...He will not] give *7* [...] and he knows that there is a profit in it, in the man or in the animal. And if *8* [...To the man who joins] anything at all, it will be counted to him. This is why the judgment of [a curse] will come upon him *9* [as he says: *Deut 27:18* «Accursed] whoever leads a blind man astray from the path», and also: «He is not to give, for he is not ready for her», because *10* [he ... two different things... like] a bull and an ass, and woollen and linen

clothing together. *Blank* No-one should enter *11* [...], whoever knows how to do
the work {of the wilderness} in word, and who knows *12* [how to do the work
in her father's] house, or the widow who prostitutes herself after she is widowed. And every *13* [woman who has had] a bad reputation during her maidenhood in her father's house, no-one should take her, unless *14* [on inspection
(the) women are] trustworthy and certain is the knowledge of the decision of
the Inspector who is over *15* [the session of the Many; he is not] to take her and
if they take her, he should proceed in accordance with the regulation of [...]

Frag. 1 *col.* II   *1* [...] of the threshing floor will lower a tenth of the *hom*[*er* and
of the *ephah*] *2* [...] the *ephah* and the *bath* {...} are both the same measure, and
a sixth [of a *homer*] *3* [is a *hin*...] the wood which a man removes in the mountains; of the cattle, one from every hundred *4* [...No-]one should eat [...] and
from the garden. Before this [the pri]ests shall stretch out their hands *5* [...]
first [...] whoever sells ... [...] and if he is free from *6* [...] and [...] the mort-
gaged field *7* [...] one three times. *8* No-one should bring in [flesh... with the
blood of the sacrifices of the gentiles...] in its purity. And of any *9* gold and
silver [and copper and] tin and le[ad with which the gentiles make im]ages, no-
one should bring them *10* into the purity [1] Whoever from [...] enters. [... No-
one should bring in] any skin, or clothing or *11* any utensil [...they work]ed
with them a work which defiles the soul of [man. And if they were sprinkled
according to the regulation *12* [...And this is the rule of] the congregation in the
age of wickedness. Every [... and every insane person] *13* [who mortgages ...
f]or their days were fulfilled to pass to [...]

Frag. 2 *col.* I   *7* [...] the judges *8–10* [...] *11* [...] Israel *12* [...] the age

Frag. 2 *col.* II (*lines* 3 – 16 = CD – A XVI, 1 – 18)   *1* [...] ... [...] *2* and the cov[en-
ant...] the covenant; and about the covenant [...] *3* saying: [in accordance with
these wo]rds I established with you a covenant and with [all Israel. For this the
man will pledge himself] *4* to return [to the law] of Moses, {for} for in it all is
def[ined. And the exact interpretation of their ages about the blindness of] *5*
Israel in all these matters, behold, [it is defined] in the book [«of the divisions
of the periods according to the jubilees and their weeks'»] *6 Blank* And on the
day on which [the man] pledges himself [to return to the law of] Moses, [the
angel] Mastema will leave *7* off following him, should he keep his wo[rds. This
is why Abraham circumcised himself on the] day [of his knowledge. And what]
it says: *Dt 23:24* «What issues *8* from your mouth, keep it and carry it out». Every
mandatory oa[th by which anyone has pledg]ed to fulfil *9* the letter of the law,
he should not [redeem], even at the price of death. [Anything by which he has
ple]dged himself to turn away *10* from the law, he should not ful[fil,] not even
when the price is death. [Concerning the oath of a woman. As for what] he

said: *Num 30:7-9* «It is for the husband *11* to annul her oath», no-one should annul an o[ath if he does not know] whether he should ratify it or *12* annul it. If it is to violate the covenant, he should annul it [and should not ratify it. And the regulation applies also] to the father. Concerning *13* the regulation for freewill-offerings. *Blank* No-one should dedicate [anything, obtained by unjust means, to the al]tar. Neither should the priests take from *14* Israel *Blank* No-one should pronounce holy the fo[od of his mouth for God, for] this is what he says: *Mic 7:2* «Each one *15* traps his fellow with anathema». *Blank* And no-one should pronounce holy anything of [...] and if it is from his fie[ld...] *16* [... his property, which he pronounces holy...] this regulation also [...] he who dedicates the [...will be punished]

Frag. 3 *col.* I (= CD–A XI, 3–XII, 6)   *1* [in the chest, unless they have been wa]shed with water or rubbed with incense. [No-one] should fast voluntarily *2* [on the sabbath. No]-one should go after an animal to pasture it outside his city, exce[pt for a thousand] cubits. *3* [He is not to raise] his hand to strike with the fist. If it is stubborn, [he should not rem]ove [it] *4* [from his house. No-one should remove] anything from the house to outside, or from outside to the house. Eve[n if he is in a h]ut, *5* [he should remove nothing from it] or bring anything into it. He is not to open a sealed vessel on the sabbath. [No-o]ne should wear *6* [perfumes, to go] out or come in on the sabbath. No-one should press his servant *8* [or his maidservant or his employee on the sabbath. No]-one should help an animal give birth on the sabbath day. And if it has fallen into a well *9* [or a pit, he should not take it out on the sa]bbath. No-one should stay in a place close to gentiles on the sabbath. *10* [No-one should profane the sab]bath by riches or gain on the sabbath. And any living man who falls *11* [into a place of water or a we]ll, no-one should take him out with a ladder or a rope or a utensil. No-one should offer anything *12* [upon the altar on the sabbath, except the sacrifice of the sabbath, for th]us is it written: *Lev 23:38* «except your offerings of the sabbath». No-one should send *13* [to the altar a sacrifice, or an offering, or incense,] or wood, by the hand of a man [impure from a]ny of the impurities, so allowing him *14* [to defile the altar, for] it is written: *Prov 15:8* «the sacrifice of the wicked is an abomination, [but the prayer] of the just is like an agreeable *15* [offering». And everyone who enters] the house of prostration should not enter with impurity requiring washing; and when the *16* [trumpets of the assembly sound,] he may advance or retreat, but the whole service should not stop. [All] *17* [the sabbaths are holy.] No man should sleep with his wife in the city of the temple, defiling [the city of the] *18* [temple with their impurity. Ev]ery man over whom the spirit of Belial dominates and he preaches apostasy, will be judged according to [the regulation] *19* [of the necromancer or the diviner.] But every one who goes astray, defiling the sabbath and the fes[tivals,] *20* [shall not be executed, for] guarding him [belongs to m]en;

and if he is cured of it, they shall guard him for [seven] *21* [years and afterwards he shall en]ter the assembly. No-one is to stretch out his hand to shed [the blood...]

4QDamascus Document*d* (4Q269 [4QD*d*])

Frag. 1   *1* [...] ... *2* [...] If *3* [...] you lift up *4* [and you build...] *5* [...they will reject...And w]e are dust and ashes *6* [...] they do not understand *7* [...] and in your mouths *8* [...] all flesh and cre[ature]

Frag. 2 (= CD – A V, 17 – VI, 7)   *1* [For in ancient times there arose Moses and Aaron, by the hand of the] prince of lig[hts,] *2* [and Belial,] with his cunning, [raised up Jan]nes and his brother during the fi[rst] salvation of *3* [Israel]. *Blank* [...] *4* [And in the age of devastation of] the la[nd there arose] those who removed the boundary and made Israel stray. *5* [And they razed the country]side, for they spoke of rebellion against God's precepts through the hand of *6* [Moses] and also of the holy anointed ones. They prophesied deceit in order to divert *7* [Isra]el from following God. But God remembered the covenant of the very first, and raised *8* [from Aaron men of knowledge and from Israel wise men, [and forced them to li]sten. And they dug *9* the well: *Num 21:18* «A well which the princes dug, which *10* the nobles [of the people] struck with the spade». *Blank 11* The well is the law. [And those who dug it] are the converts of Is[rael,] *12* who left the land of Ju[dah and lived in the land of Damascus, all of whom *13* God called princes, for [they sought him, and their renown has not been repudiated *14* in anyone's mouth. *Blank 15* [And the spade is the interpreter] of the law, [...]

Frag. 4 *col.* II (= 4QD*b* 6 I)   *1* [...and they res]tore the stre[ngth in the leprosy]...the holy *2* [me]n who are stre[ngthened by his holy name...] *3* [...] and he is required to return [... for in Judah...] *4* [to Isr]ael when [...] arises [to instruct...] *5* [...pea]ce. *Blank* [...] *6* And all those [of Israel] who rem[ain... for each one to approach him] *7* [ac]cording to his spirit [...]

Frag. 4 *col.* III (= 4QD*b* 6 II, 1–5)   *1* [...] ... [...] *2* [...] or [...] *3* And everyone who [speaks weakly or] with a [faltering] sound, *4* and does not separate his words to [make his voice heard, should not read in the book of] *5* [the Torah, so that he will not lead to error in a capital matter ...] *6* [...] ... [... to his brothers,] *7* [the priests, in serv]ice. And not [...] *8* [And whoever of the sons of A]aron [has been a captive among the gentiles...]

Frag. 9 (= 4D*b* 12:2–9)   *1* [...] ... *2* [It shall be an eternal precept for the sons of Israel. And the bunches of the vine:] up to ten berries of the cluster *3* [... and everything that shoots up …up to one *seah* per bushel] in which there is no seed shall be a sacred offering, *4* [...] *Blank 5* [… If you trample in the field, only take from] it one from every three. *Blank* And all *6* [that… the] field, or you shall burn it with fire and it shall be separated *7* [… up to one *seah* per bushel shall be the tithe, and] if anyone gathers it

Frag. 10 (= CD–A, IX, 5–14)   *1* [he avenges himself against his foes, and he bears resentment against his enemies». If he kept silent about him] from one month to the other, *2* [or accused him of a capital offence, he has testified against himself, for he did not] fulfil the commandment of God *3* [which tells him: *Lev 19:17* «You should reproach your fellow so as not to incur] sin [because of him».] *Blank 4* [Concerning the oath. As for what he said: *1 Sam 25:26* «You shall not do justice with your (own) hand»: wh]oever forces the making of an oath *5* [in the open field, not in the presence of judges or at their command, has done justice for himself with his] hand. Every *6* [lost object about which it is not known who stole it from the property of the camp in which it was stolen –] its owner should make a maledictory *7* [oath; whoever hears it, if he knows and does not say it, is guilty. Every] illegal object *8* [which should be given back and has no owner – he who gives it back should confess to the priest and it will be for himself,] apart from the ram

Frag. 11 *col.* I (= CD–A XIII, 4–14)   *1* [according to his word all the members of the camp. But if there is a judgment against anyone about the law of] leprosy, *2* [the priest shall take his place in the camp, and the Inspector shall instruct him] in the exact interpretation of the law. [Even if] *3* [he is a simpleton, he is the one who shall intern him, for his is the] judgment. *Blank* [...] *4* [And this is the rule of the Inspector of the camp. He shall instruct the Many in the de]eds of God, [and shall teach them] *5* [his mighty marvels, and recount to them the eternal] events with their solutions. He shall have pity *6* [on them like a father on his sons, and shall heal all the str]ays (?) like a shepherd his flock. He shall undo *7* [all the chains which bind them, so that there] is neither harassed nor oppressed *8* [in his congregation. And everyone who joins his congregation, he should examine] concerning his actions, his intelligence, [his strength,] *9* [his courage and his wealth; and they shall inscribe him in his place according to his inh]eritance in the lot of truth. *Blank* No *10* [– one of the members of the camp should have authority to] introduce anyone into the congregation *11* [against the decision] of the Inspector of the camp. And none of those who have entered the covenant] of God «neither

Frag. 11 *col.* II (= CD–A XIII, 22–XIV, 10)   *1* [… These are the regulations for the Instructor, to wal]k in them. *2* [When God visits the] earth [the] word will be ful[filled] which says: *Isa 7:17* «There will come *3* [upon you days such a]s have

not come since the day on which Ephraim became separated from *4* [Judah»;
and (to) all those who wal]k in them, the covenant of God is faithful *5* [to save
them from all the ne]ts of the pit, for they will pass suddenly *6* and they will be
punished. [Rule of the session of] all the camps. Each one shall be enlisted by
his name: *7* the priests [first, the levites] second, the children of Israel *8* third;
and they shall be inscribed [by their names, each one after his brother: the
priests *9* [fi]rst, [the levites second, the sons of] Israel third *10* [and the
pro]selyte fourth. Thus shall they s[it and thus shall they be questioned] about
everything. And the priest who *11* [is na]med at the head of the M[any will be
between] thirty and sixty *12* [years old,] learned [in the book of] HAGY, and in
all the regulations of the law, to say them /for the words/ *13* [in accordance
with] their regulations. And the [Inspector who] is over all the camps will be
between thir[ty y]ears and sixty [years of age, master of every secr]et of me[n
and in every language

Frag. 12   *1* [shall be punished for six days…] And whoever *2* [despises the judgment of the Many, shall leave and] never [ret]urn. *Blank 3* [An whoever takes his
meal outside of the re]gulation, is to give it back to the one *4* [from whom he
took it…]. Whoever approaches *5* [his wife] for lust, [not in accordance with the
regulation, shall leave and] never [retu]rn. *Blank*

4QDamascus Document^e (4Q270 [4QD^e])

Frag. 1 (= CD–A II, 16 – 18)   *1* [by the thoughts of a] guilty [inclination] and lascivious eyes. […] *2* [For many wandered off for these] matters; bra[ve] heroes
[yielded on account of them, from ancient times until now. For having walked
in the stubbornness] *3* [of their hearts the Watchers of the hea]vens fell; on its
account they were [caught, for they did not follow the precepts of God.]

Frag. 2 (= CD–A III, 14)   *1* [hidden matters] in which [all Israel] had gone astray
[: …] *2* [His holy sabb]aths and his glor[ious feasts…]

Frag. 4 (= CD–A IV, 6-8)   *1* [These are the very first, for whom God atoned and
who declared the just man as just, and declared the wi]cked as wicked, *2* [and
all those who entered after them in order to act in agreement with the exact
interpretation of the law in which] the very first [were inst]ructed

Frag. 5 (= 4QD^c 1 I, 8 – 14)   *14* […] To the man who joins [anything at all, it will
be counted to him. This is why] *15* [a jud]gment of a curse [will come upon him
as he says: *Deut 27:18* «Accursed whoever leads a blind man astray from the
path», and also: «He is not to give,] *16* [for he is not re]ady for her», because he
[two different things… like] a bull and an ass, and woollen and linen clothing

together.] *17* [...] *Blank* [No-one] should enter [...] the holy one, *18* [who kn]ows
how to do the work [in word, and who knows how to do] the work [in the house
of] *19* [her fat]her, or the widow who prosti[tutes herself after she is widowed...
And ev]ery *20* [woman who] has had a bad reputation during her maidenhood
in her father's house, no-one should take her, *21* [un]less on inspection (the)
women [are trustworthy and certain is the knowledge of the decision of the
Inspector]

Frag. 6 (= 4QD^b 12:2–9)   *6* [...] this [...] *7* [...] *Blank* [...] *8* [...] *Blank 9* [...] of the
day, and the sun the harvest ... [...] *10* [...] the field [...] who drank the [lustral
water] *11* [...It shall be an eternal precept for the children of Israel. *Blank*] *12* [...
And the bun]ches of the vine: up to te[n berries of the] *13* clu[ster... and everything that shoots up ...] up to one *seah* per bushel in which *14* there is no seed,
shall be a sacred off[ering, and] the cluster fallen from the vine ...] and on its
bunch, up to ten ber[ries,] *15* [and on the bra]nch of the olive [...] when the
gathering is complete [...] *16* [you shall en]ter [it.] If you trample in the field,
[take only from it one from every thr]ee, and all [that which...] *17* [the field, or
you burn with fire, and it will be separated...] up to one *seah* per bushel shall
be the tithe, and if anyone gathers it *18* [...] and gathers one of it on the first
day, the tenth part shall be a sacred offering *19* [...] the cakes of the sacred
offering shall be for all the houses of Israel which eat the bread *20* [...] once a
year a tenth shall be their possession [...] *21* [...] it shall be complete for Israel
once [a year.] Every man

Frag. 7 (= 4QD^e 1 II, 8–10)   *20* [the flesh... with the blood of the sacrifices of the
gentiles... in its pu]rity. And of any gold and [silver] *21* [and copper and tin and
lead with which the] gentiles make images, no-one should bring them into the
purity

Frag. 8   *1* [...And if] a man draws away a woman to curse her *2* [...] he who looks
if he sees the woman from *3* [...] ... *4* [...] ... and if her blood should flow
5 [...] the priests, and will untie *6* [...] ... and he will make drink *7* [...He]
should not take from his hand any *8* [...] the holy ones *9* [... He] should give
anyone *10-11* [...] *12* [...] for the kings *13* [...] with the woman *14* [...] the
/bought/ maid, unless *15* [...] says: « [...] not *16* [...] he shall take her [...]
17 [...] ... [...] *18* [...] his bread [...] *19* [... He should not] lie with

Frag. 9 *col.* I   *9* [...] he will pass or send [...] the sun *10* [...] the days, or he will
consult a necromancer or diviners *11* [...] who curses the name *12-15* [...] *16* [...]
a young girl in house of *17* [... He should not] lie with her after *18* [...He
should not app]roach his wife on the day of *19* [...] or who [...] *20* [...] *21* [...]
all

Frag. 9 *col.* II   *1* concerning [...] *2* to [...] *3* at the place [...] *4* [...] *5* [...] to the mountains [...] *6* [...] the sons of Aaron the plantation [...] *7* [... and he will give] all that there is for them, and a tenth part of the cattle *8* and of the flocks, and the ransom for [the] clean [animal] and the money of the assessments for the ransom of their souls. [...] *10* without returning it, and on top of that a fifth part or [...] *11* in their names, in order to defile his holy spirit [...] *12* or infected by the disease of leprosy or one with an impu[re] discharge. [And whoever] *13* divulges the secret of his people to the pagans, or curses or [preaches] *14* rebellion against those anointed with the spirit of holiness and leads astray [his people, or disobeys] *15* God's word, or slaughters an animal carrying a live foetus, [or] a pregnant woman [...] *17* in the woman's bed [...] *18* enrolled in them in order to make his so[n] pass ... *19* And how, listen to me all you who know justice and ful[fil the] law. *20* I [shall give] you paths of life, but the ways to the pit I shall open for [the wicked and their deeds.] *21* You shall not be made prisoners and [...] in the understanding of my deeds from generation to generation.

Frag. 10 *col.* I (= CD–A XV, 3–5)   *20* [of the covenant, he should do it before the judges. If he should transgress, he will be guilty and will have to confess and make amends,] but not *21* [be burdened with sin nor shall he die. Whoever enters into the covenant, which is for all Israel for eternal law], his sons

Frag. 10 *col.* II (= CD–A XV, 13–18; XVI, 3–8)   [shall exact vengeance for] him if he should sin. And if [he fulfils] all that [has been revealed of the law for the multitude of the camp,] *7* [the Instructor should instruct him and] give orders concerning him which he should learn [for a whole year. And in accordance with (his) knowledge he will approach. And no-one] *8* [stupid or deranged should enter; and any]one feeble-minded or insane, and [those with sightless eyes, the lame or one who stumbles,] *9* [or a deaf person, or an under-age boy, n]one of these [should enter the congregation, since the holy angels are in its midst.] *10* [...] ... the second [...] *11* [...] ... the man [...] *13-16* [...] *17* [in the book] «of the divisions [of the periods] according to their jubilees [and their weeks']». And on the day on which the man has pledged himself *18* [to return] to the law [of Moses,] the angel Mastema [will turn aside from following him], should he keep his word. This is why *19* Abraham circumcised himself on the day of his knowledge. And as for what] he said: *Dt 23:24* «What issues [from your mouth, keep to it and carry it out». Every binding oath by which anyone has pledged to fulfil the letter of the law, he should not annul, even at the price of death. Any*21*thing by which [he might pledge to turn aside from the law, he should not fulfil, even at the price of death.

Frag. 10 *col.* III (CD–A XVI, 18–24; IX, 1–7)   *13* [... to the jud]ges to judge [with justice...he is victim of an accident until] *14* [...] and the violence is complete if he does not tell the tr[uth to his fe]llow, until [he converted ...] *15* [...as] who does not ... [...] And as for [what he says...] *16* [...Every man who gives a ma]n from among men to anathema, shall be executed according to the laws of the gentiles. *17* And as for what he said: *Lev 19:18* «Do not avenge yourself or bear resentment against the sons of your people»–everyone of those who entered the cove[nant, who bri]ngs [an accusation] against his fellow, [this should not be with reproach] before witnesses, or brings it when he is angry, or tells it [to his elders] so that they despise him, he is «the one who avenges himself and bears resentment».] *19* [Is it not perhaps written that on]ly *Nah 1:2* «he (God) [avenges] himself on his foes and bears resentment against his enemies»? If he kept silent about him from one day to the other, or in the heat of his anger *20* [against him...] the matter. Thus [...]

Frag. 10 *col.* IV (= CD–A IX, 10–12; IX, 20–X, 13)   *3* [or at their command, has done justice for himself] with his hand. [Every lost object about which it is not known who stole it from the property of the camp in which it was stolen] *4* [its owner should make a maledi]ctory oa[th; whoever hears it, if he knows and does not say it, is guilty.] *5–10* [...] *11* [someone alone, his judgment is complete; but if they are two, one and one, who testify about a different matter,] the man [is only to be excluded from the pure food,] *12* [on condition that they are trustworthy, and that on the same day on which he saw him, he denounces him to the Inspector. And concerning ric]hes, they shall accept two trustworthy witnesses. *13* [And] on the testimony of one, to exc[lude from the holy food. A witness is not to be accepted] by the judges to condemn to death on his word, *14* [if he has not] completed his days to pass [among those who are recruited, and is fearful of] God. Not to be believed [as a witness] against his fellow, is anyone *15* [who has trans]gressed [knowingly] anything of a precept, [until he has been purified to return. And this] is the rule of the judges of the congregation. *16* Ten men in number, chosen [from among the con]gregation, for a period; [four] from the tribe of Levi and of Aaron and [six from Israel;] *17* learned in the book of HAGY [and in the princi]ples of the covenant; [between] twenty-five and [sixty] years. *18* And no-one over sixty years should hold the office [of judging] the congregation, for on account [of man's] sin *19* his days [were shor]tened, and because of God's wrath against the inhabitants of the earth, [he decided to remove] knowledge [from them] before [they completed their] days. *20* *Blank* Concerning purification with water. No-one [should bathe in water which is dirty or which is less than the amount which covers a man] *21* No-one should purify a vessel in it. [And every cavity in the rock in which there is not the amount which covers, if an impure person has touched it,]

Frag. 10 *col.* V (= CD–A X, 13–19; XI, 7–19)   *1* [he has defiled the water like the water of a vase. Concerning the sabbath, to observe it in accordance with its regulation. No-one should do wo]rk [on the sixth day, from] *2* [the moment when the sun's disc is at a distance of its diameter from the gate, for th]is is what he sa[id: *Dt 5:12* «Observe the sabbath day to keep it holy». And on the day of the sabbath, no-one should say] a useless or stupid word. *4* [He is not to lend anything to his fellow. He is not to discuss riches or gain. He is not to speak about matters of wo]rk or of the task to be car[ried out] *5-12* [...] *13* No-one should re]move [anything from the house to outside, or from outside to the house. Even if] *14* he is in a hut, he should remove nothing from it or bring [anything into it. He is not to open a sealed vessel on the sabbath. No-one should wear] *15* perfumes on the sabbath, to go out or come in. [No-one should lift, in his dwelling, a stone or dust.] *16* [The wet-nurse should] not lift the baby [to go out or come in on the sabbath.] No-one should press] *17* his servant or his maidservant or his employee on the sabbath. [No-one should help an animal give birth on the sabbath day.] *18* And if it falls into a well or a pit, [he should not take it out on the sabbath. No-one should profane the sabbath by] *19* riches or gain on the sabbath. And any living man [who falls into a place of water or into a place,] *20* no-one should take him out with a ladder or a rope or a utensil. No-[one should offer anything upon the altar on the sabbath, except the sacrifice of the sabbath, for thus] *21* is it written: *Lev 23:38* «except your offerings of the sabbath». [No-one should send to the altar a sacrifice, or an offering, or incense, or wood, by the hand of]

Frag. 11 *col.* I (= 4QD^b 18 IV, 9 – 15; V, 1 – 7)   *3* [...] in the house or in the field, walks nak[ed in front of the creatures, shall be kept apart for six months.] *4* [And whoever takes out] 'his hand' from under his clothes and [...] *5* [days, and shall be punished for ten; and he who bows do]wn stupidly, making [his voice] heard, [shall be kept apart for thirty and shall be punished for five] *6* [days. And he who takes out his left ha]nd to gesticulate with it, shall be pun[ished for ten days. And whoever] *7* [goes slandering his fellow shall be kept apart] from the pure food for one year [...] *8* [...and] shall [not] come back again [...] *9* and not [...] and the one whose [spirit] is disturbed [...] *10* about [...] ... [shall be pu]nished for six [days...] *11* [and whoever] despises the judgment of the Many shall leave and [not return again. And whoever takes] *12* his food outside the regulation shall return it to the one from whom he took it [...] Whoever approaches *13* his wife from lust, not in accordance with the regulation, shall leave and not come back again. [...] about the fathers, *14* [shall leave] the congregation and not come back [again. But if it is] about mothers, he shall be punished for ten days because for mothers there is no mingling (?) in the midst of *15* [the congregation ... And these are] the regulations [in which shall walk] all those disciplined and everyone who *16* [... and whoever] enters will inform the priest who is at the fr[ont of the Many and he will receive his judgment according to his merit, as he] *17* says through the hand of Moses about the person who si[ns through oversight: *Lev 4:27* «they should present] their sin-offering or their guilt-offering»; and about *18* Israel it is written: *Lev 26:31* «I shall go to the edges of the hea[vens, and I shall not smell the aroma of your ple]asant fragrances»; and in ano[ther place it is written:] *19 Joel 2:13* «Tear your heart and not your clothes» and it is writt[en: *Joel 2:12* (?) «to return to God in tears and in fasting».] And anyone who des[pises these regulations] *20* according to all the precepts which are found [in the law of Moses, shall not be counted among all the so]ns of his truth, [for his soul is accursed] *21* by those disciplined by justice. *Blank* And al[l …]

Frag. 11 col. II (= 4QD^b 18 V, 16–20)   *11* [The sons of Levi and the men of the camps will meet in] the third month and will cu[rse] *12* [whoever tends to the right or to the left of the law. And th]is is the precise interpretation of the regulations which *13* [they are to observe in every age of …] who remained firm in all the ages of anger *14* and in their steps, to all those who dwell in their camps and all […] in their cities. And so, then, all this is *15* with regard to the last interpretation of [the law.] *Blank 16–21 Blank*

4QDamascus Document^f (4Q271 [4QD^f])

Frag. 1 (= CD–A II, 4–6)   *1* [and the abundance of] pardon, [to atone for those who repent from wickedness; however, strength and power and a great anger with flames of fire] *2* [by the hand of all] the angels [of destruction …]

Frag. 2 (= CD–A III, 6–11)   *1* [and they ate blood, and their males were cut off. He spoke to them in Qadesh: *Deut 9:23* «Go and] possess [the land»….] *2* [… and they did not listen] and did not open their ears [to the voice] *3* [of their creator, to the precepts he had taught them and murmured in their tents. And the wrath] of God flared up against their congregation. And their sons *4* [died through it, and through it their kings were cut off and their warriors perished] through it and through it their land was laid waste. *5* [… Through it] the very first to enter the covenant *6* [made themselves guilty and were delivered up to the sword, for having deserted God's covenant and having chosen] their whims and having followed

Frag. 3 (= CD–A IV, 19–21)   *1* [he is] a preacher, [as it is said: *Mic 2:6* «Assuredly he will preach»–they are caught twice] *2* [in fornic]ation: by ta[king two wives in their lives…]

Frag. 4 col. I (= CD–A V, 20–VI, 2)   *2* [And in the age of devastation of the land there arose those who shifted the boundary and made Israel stray. And they laid waste] the land, *3* for they spoke of rebellion against God's precepts through the hand of Moses and also of the holy anointed ones.] They prophesied *4* [deceit in order to turn Israel away from following God. But God remembered the covenant of the very first, and rai]sed

Frag. 4 col. II (= CD – A VI, 20 – VII, 3)   *1* according to their exact interpretation; to love, [each one, his brother like himself;] *2* to strengthen the ha[nd of the poor, the needy and the foreigner; to seek,] *3* each one, the peace [of his brother and not commit sin against his blood relation;] *4* [to refrain from fornication in accordance with the regulation; to reprove] *5* each one, [his brother in accordance with the precept, without bearing resentment from one day to the next;] *6* to keep ap[art from every uncleanness according to their regulations...]

Frag. 5 (= CD – A VII, 16 – 20)   *1* [the fallen Sukkat of David». The King is the assembly; and the plinths of the ima]ges [are] *2* [the books of the prophets, whose words Israel despised.] And the star [is] *3* [the Interpreter of the law, who will come to Damascus, as is written: *Num 24:13* «A star] moves out of [Jacob] *4* [and a sceptre arises out of Israel». The sceptre is the prince of the wh]ole [congregation...]

Frag. 7 (= 4QD^b 9 I 1 – 4)   *1* [...] ... and if the rash is a wound of wood *2* [or of stone, or any wound through the arrival of the spirit which takes h]old of the artery and the blood returns *3* [upwards or downwards, and the artery ...] behind the blood *Blank 4* [The priest shall examine the skin, living and] d[ead...] *5* [...] seven [days...] *6* [...] says, and the ra[sh ... If the dead (skin) is not deeper that the living (skin)] *7* [he shall confine him until] the flesh grows. The priest shall examine him [on the sev]enth [day;] [if the spirit of life goes up] *8* [and] goes down and the flesh [has grown... is cured... the rash.] *9* [The priest shall not examine] the skin of the fl[esh...] *10* [But if the tumour or the rash is deeper than the skin ...] *11* [and the priest sees in] it as it [were the form of living flesh...] *12* [it is leprosy which has taken hold] of the living skin. [And in accordance with this regulation] *13* [...] The priest [shall examine it on the seventh day...]

Frag. 9 (= 4QD^c 1 I, 8 – 14)   *1* [anything at all, it will be counted to him. This is why the judgment of a curse will come upon him,] as he says: *2* [*Deut 27:18* «Accursed whoever leads a blind man astray from the path», and also: «He is not to give, for he is not ready for her»,] because he, two different things *3* [... like a bull and an ass, and woollen and linen clothing together.] *4* [No-one should enter ...] the holy one, who [knows how to do the work] *5* [in word, and who knows how to do the work in the house of] her father, or the widow who *6* [prostitutes herself after she is widowed... And every woman who] has had] a bad reputation during her maidenhood $_7$ [in her father's house, no-one should take her, unless on in]spection (the) women are trustw[orthy]

Frag. 10 (= 4QD^c 1 II, 7–13) $_1$ [one] three tim[es. No]-one [should bring in flesh...] with the blood of the sacrifices [of the gentiles...] $_2$ [in its purity. And of any gold and] silver [and copper and tin and lead] with which the gentiles make im[ages,] $_3$ [no-one should bring them into the purity ...] from it new [...] No-one should bring in any [skin,] $_4$ [or clothing or any utensil... they work]ed with th[em which defiles the] soul of man. And if they were sprinkled acc[ording to the regulation] $_5$ [...And this is the rule of the congregation in] the age of wic[kedness.... and] every insane person who mortgages

Frag. 12 (= CD–A XV, 4–7) $_1$ [If he transgresses, he will be guilty and will have to confess] and make amends [but he shall not be liable for sin and shall not die.] $_2$ [Whoever enters the covenant, for all Israel for an eternal law, he must impose upon his so]ns who [succeed in passing among whose who are enrolled] $_3$ [the oath of the covenant. And such is] the regulation, [throughout all the age of wickedness, for whoever]

Frag. 13 (= CD–A XIV, 1–22) $_1$ [And this is the exact interpretation of the session of the Many and these are the foundations which make the assem]bly And this is the exact interpretation of $_2$ [the regulations by which they shall be ruled until there arises the messiah of] Aaron and of Israel. $_3$ [He will atone for their sins ... pardon, and guilt...] $_4$ [...in riches, although he knows, and ... and they keep him apart] from the pure food $_5$ [... he shall be punished] for six $_6$ [days....shall be punished] for ten

4QDamascus Document^g (4Q272 [4QD^g])

Frag. 1 col. I (= 4QD^b 9 I, 1–12) $_1$ [... a tumour,] or a rash, or a [white spo]t [...] $_2$ [and the rash is a wound of wood or of] stone, or any wound through the arrival of the spi[rit which takes hold] $_3$ [of the artery and the blood returns] upwards or downwards, and the artery [...] $_4$ [...] ... [...] $_5$ [The priest shall examine the skin,] living and [dead. If the] dead [skin is not deeper] than $_6$ [the living (skin) he shall confine him until] the flesh grows. / [until] the blood returns to the artery, and afterwards he shall compare./ The priest shall examine him $_7$ [on the seventh day: if the] spirit of life goes up [and down and the] flesh has grown $_8$ [he is cured... the] rash. The priest shall not examine the skin of the fl[esh] $_9$ [...] But if the tumour or the rash is deeper $_{10}$ [than the skin and the priest sees in] it as it were the form of living flesh [...] $_{11}$ [it is leprosy which has taken hold] of the living skin. And in accordance with this regulation $_{12}$ [... The priest shall examine it] on the [sev]enth day; if something [live] has

been added *13* [to the dead... it is mal]ignant [leprosy.] *Blank 14* [And the regulation for ringworm of the head or of the beard: ...] the priest shall examine it,
15 [and if the spirit enters the head or the beard in one block ...] underneath
the hair *16* [and changes its appearance to yellowish, for it is like a pla]nt under
which there is a worm: *17* [cut its root and its fruit turns pale.] And as for what
he sa[id: *Lev 13:33* «The priest shall order them to shave] *18* [their head, but] not
to shave [their ringworm»,] it is so that the priest can count *19* [the dead and
living hairs, and see: if] some living (hairs) [have been added] to the dead ones
20 [during seven days, he is impure; but if] living (hairs) [have not been added
[to the dead ones]

Frag. 1 *col.* II (= 4QD^b 9 I, 12–16)   *1* and the artery is full of blood and the spirit
of life goes up and down [through it,] *2* this plague [is healed.] This is [the
reg[ulation for the so]ns of Aaron, [so that they differentiate ...] *3* And the
regula[tion for the man with go]norr[hoea. Everything which ...] *4-6* [...] *7* and
he shall wash his clothes [...] *8* in it. He who touches [...] *9* the discharge of
blood or of se[men...] *10* seven days [...] *11* he who touches [...] *12* and in ...
[...] *13* you shall scrape [...] *14* the water [...] *15* [...] *16* alive [...] *17* his hand
[...] *18* [...]

4QDamascus Document^h (4Q273 [4QD^h])

Frag. 1 *col.* II (= 4QD^g 1 I, 6–15)   *1* ... [...] *2* says [...until the flesh grows. And]
3 the priest [shall examine him on the] seventh [day: if the spirit of life goes up
and down] *4* [and] the flesh has grown, he is cured of [...The priest shall not
examine] *5* [the] skin of the flesh [...] *6* or the rash in it [... and the priest sees
in it as it were the form] *7* of [living] flesh [...] *8* [...] *9* if something live has
been added to the [dead...] it is [malignant leprosy] *10* And the regulation for
ringworm of the he[ad or of the beard...] *11* the priest [shall examine it,] and
if the spi[rit] enters [the head or the beard...]

Frag. 2   *1* [...] ... and she covers [...] *2* [...] ... in her impurity ... for she [...]
3 [...] are [...] eternal. No-one should take [...] *4* [...] ... and he shall count ...
[...] until [...]

c *Copies from other caves*

5QDamascus Document (5Q12 [5QD])

Frag. 1 (= CD–A IX, 7–10)   *1* ... [...] *2* which tells him: *Lev 19:17* «You shall *8*
reproach your fellow so as not to incur sin because of him». *3* Concerning the
oath. As for what [he said: *1 Sm 25:26* «You shall not do justice with your (own)

hand», – whoever forces the making of an oath] *4* in the open field, [not in the presence of judges or at their command, has done justice for himself with his hand.] *Blank* Every lo[st] object

6QDamascus Document (6Q15 [6QD])

Frag. 1 (= CD–A IV, 19–21)   *1* [The builders of the wall who] go [after Zaw–Zaw is a preacher *20* as it is said:] *2* [*Mic 2:6* «Assuredly he will preach» – are] caught [twice in fornication: by taking two wives] *3* [in their lives, even though the principle of crea]tion is *Gen 1:27* «male [and female he created them».]

Frag. 2 (= CD–A V, 13–14)   *1* [They are all ignit]ers of fire, ki[ndlers of blazes; webs of a spider are their webs, and their eggs are] *2* [vip]er's [eggs.] Whoever is close to them [will not be unpunished; the more he does it, the guiltier he shall be, unless he has been compelled.]

Frag. 3 (= CD–A V, 18–VI, 2)   *1* [For in ancient times there arose Moses and] Aaron, by [the hand of the prince of lights and Belial raised up] *2* [Jannes and his brother with his cun]ning during the [first deliv]erance [of Israel. And in the age of devastation of the land] *3* [there arose those who shifted the boundary and] made Israel stray. And they la[id the land waste, for they spoke of rebellion] *4* [against God's precepts through the hand of Mos]es and al[so] of the holy anointed ones. [They prophesied deceit in order to turn] *5* [Israel away from following G]od. But God remembered the covenant of the very fir[st, and from Aaron raised men of knowledge …]

Frag. 4 (= CD–A VI, 20–VII, 1)   *1* [ho]ly [portions] according to their exact interpre[tation; for each to love his brother] *2* like himself; to strengthen [the hand of the poor, the needy] *3* [and the foreigner;] for each to seek [the peace of his brother, and not commit sin] *4* [each one against his bloo]d r[elative;] to [refrain from fornication …]

Frag. 5   *1* […] … […] *2* […Whoever] lies with […] *3* […No-one should lie with a] man as one lies [with a woman …] *4* […] … to cause to pass […] *5* […] the covenant of God in their hearts […]

3 Fragments of other rules

4QSerek Damascus Rule (4Q265 [4QSD])

Frag. 1 *col.* I   *1* [...] ... [...] *2* [...] ... [...] *3* [...] days. *Blank* [...] *4* [...] thirty days [...] *5* to half his bread, for fifte[en...] *6* he shall be punished for three months [...] *7* his fellow what is written in front of him, shall be kept apart [...] *8* in them to half his bread. *Blank* And whoever [...] *9* thirty days. *Blank* And whoever cheats k[nowingly ...] *10* months and shall be punished in them to half his bread [...] *11* knowingly in any matter, shall be punished for thirty days. [...] *12* kn[owingly,] shall be kept apart for six months. *Blank* [...]

Frag. 1 *col.* II   *1* [...] in the session of the Many, shall be punished for th[irty days ...] *2* [...] he shall count him who sleeps up to three times; and if [...] *3* [...And] whoever enters for [...] the council [of the communi]ty [...] *4* [...] the Many, if it falls upon him [...] they shall instruct him and explain for a year [...] *5* [...] the Many shall question him. *Blank* And if [...] is not fou[nd ...] *6* [...] the Inspector of the Many [...] the law and not [...] *7* [...] yet another full year. [And when] the year of [...] [is comp]lete [...] *8* [...] the Inspector of the Many [...] *9* [...] he shall enter [...]

Frag. 2 *col.* I   *1* and [...] *2* on the sabbath day. No-one should [...] dirty [clothes] *3* [...] And whoever (goes) with dir[ty] clothes [or] which have dust on them or [...] *4* [...] sabbath. *Blank* No-one should take out of his tent a vessel or food *5* on the sabbath *Blank* day. No-one should take out an animal which has fallen *6* [into] water on the sabbath day. *Blank* But if it is a man who has fallen into water *7* on the sabbath day, his garment should be thrown to him to lift him out with it. No-one should carry a vessel *8* [...] sabbath. And if ... [...]

Frag. 2 *col.* II   *1* [...] on the [sabbath] day [...] *2* [...] sabbath. And [...] not [...] *3* [...] Whoever is afraid [...] *4* [...it is] a great day and a fast(–day). On the day [...] *5* [...] the animal shall walk two thousand cubits [...] *6* [...from the tem]ple, thirty stadia. Do not rem[ove...] *7* [...] will be in the community council fifteen [...] *8* [And] when the community council is established [... those chosen by its] *9* will, and it shall be the aroma of a pleasant fragrance to atone for the land [...] *10* shall end in the judgment of the times of wickedness [...] *11* *Blank* In the first week [...] *12* for he did not enter the garden of Eden. And their counsel [...] *13* [...] until ... not [...] *14* [...] holy the garden of Eden. And every father who is within it will be holy [...] *15* shall be impure for seven days, as in the days of menstrual impurity, shall be impure. And th[irty ...] *16* of her purification. But if she gives birth to a baby girl, she shall be impure [...] *17* [...] in the blood of her purification. In everything which is holy [...]

5QRule (5Q13)

Frag. 1   *1* [...] ... [...] *2* [...] God of all [...] *3* [...] and he founded upon [...] *4* [...] ... the treasures [...] *5* [...] for them alone, for he made [...] *6* [...] you chose from the sons of the gods [...] *7* [...] and with Noah, your chosen one [...] *8* [...] you have destroyed [...] *9* [...] to understand your works [...] *10* [...] ... the service of [...] *11* [...] ... you commanded him [...] *12* [...] every man of Israel [...]

Frag. 2   *1* [...] ... *2-3* [...] *4* [...] for ever *5* [...] with Abraham *6* [...] you showed yourself to Jacob at Beth El *7* [...] and Levi [you made h]oly and placed to undo *8* [...] you chose the sons of Levi to go out *9* [...] in their spirits in your presence *10* [...] and after two *11* [...] an oath upon *12* [...] to

Frag. 4   *1* [...he] stands before the Inspector [...] *2* [...] and shall not become pure through atonement, [...] *3* [...] Unclean, unclean shall he be all the days [...] *4* [...] these things shall they do, year after year al[l the days ...]

Frag. 5   *1* [...] his reward ... [...] *2* [...] by the hand of Belial, and not [...] *3* [...] Israel when [...] arose

Halakhic Texts

A large part of the contents of the 'Rules' comprises halakhic regulations, actual rules of behaviour obtained from a particular interpretation of Old Testament law–codes. Likewise, many of the texts classed as 'Biblical Interpretation', *The Temple Scroll*, for example, are nothing more than a collection of halakhot. Even within para–biblical stories, such as the book of *Jubilees*, halakhah holds an important position. In spite of this, it has been considered helpful to devote a special chapter to 'halakhic texts'. Included is a unique composition, the *Halakhic Letter*, in which the halakhah differentiating the Qumran group from the rest of Judaism at that time is set out systematically. Included, too, are those fragments which, in the state they have reached us, contain chiefly halakhic regulations. However, due to the loss of the rest of the works to which they belong, it is impossible to know whether these halakhot actually formed part of works of different literary forms, or whether they belonged to compositions intended chiefly to establish and hand on the halakhah of the group.

The *Halakhic Letter*, known by the abbreviation 4QMMT (*4QMiqsat Ma'aseh ha-Torah* = 'Some precepts of the Law'), is important. However, it is difficult to determine with any precision its contents through reading separately the various fragments of the copies preserved. Therefore, here the translation of the fragments of the different manuscripts is prefaced with the translation of the 'composite text' compiled by professors Strugnell and Qimron, who are in the process of editing the different manuscripts in the tenth volume of the Series *Discoveries in the Judaean Desert*. In this way, as in the cases of the *Rule of the Community* and of the *Damascus Document*, it is possible to gain some idea of what each individual manuscript has preserved for us. Although it would be easy to separate it into different sections – a calendar, an introduction, a collection of halakhot and the closing exhortation – each line of the 'composite text' is numbered consecutively, for easier reference to the fragments which have been preserved.

1 Halakhic Letter (4QMMT)

A *Composite text*

1 [...] a sabbath in it; after the sa[bbath, the first and of the second day, a third day] *2* is added. And the year is complete, three hundred and si[xty-four] *3* days. These are some of our regulations [concerning the law of G]od, which are pa[rt of] *5* the precepts we [are examining and] they [a]ll relate to [...] *6* and the purity of [...] ... [Concerning the offering of the] wheat of the Gen[tiles which they ...] *7* and they touch it [...] and they defi[le it: you shall not eat it.] *8* [None] of the wheat of the Gentiles shall be brought into the temple. [...And concerning the sacrifice] *9* which they cook in vessels [of bronze...] *10* the flesh of their sacrifices and [...] in the courtyard the [...] *11* with the broth of their sacrifices. And concerning the sacrifice of the Gentiles: [we say that they sacrifice] *12* [...] which he is pulling towards it. [And concerning the thank-offerings] *13* which they postpone from one day to another, w[e think] *14* that the ce[real]-offering [should be eaten] with the fats and the meat on the day of their sa[crifice, and that the] *15* priests should oversee in this matter in such a way that the [sons of Aaron] do not *16* lead the people into error. And also in what pertains to the purity of the red heifer in the sin-offering: *17* that whoever slaughters it and whoever burns it and whoever collects the ash and whoever sprinkles the [water of] *18* purification, all these ought to be pure at sunset, *19* so that whoever is pure sprinkles the impure. For the sons of *20* [Aaron] ought [to be ...] *21* [And concerning the] hides of cat[tle and the flocks, we think that...] *22* the vessels of [hide...] *23* [in order to bring] them into the tem[ple...] *24* [...] And also concerning the hid[es and the bones of the unclean animals; they shall not make,] *25* [from their bones] and from their hides, handles of ves[sels. And also, concerning the carcases] *26* [of the] clean [animals]: the one who [carries] its carcase [shall not approach the holy purity] *27* [...] And also concerning [...] which they [...] *28* [... for] *29* the priests ought to com[ply with all these] things [so that they do not] *30* lead the people into sin. And concerning what is written: *Lev 17:3* [«When a man slaughters within the camp»– they] *31* [slaughter] outside the camp – «a bull, or a [she]ep or a she-goat»: the pl[ace of slaughter is to the north of the camp.] *32* And we think that the temple [is the place of the tent of meeting, and Je]rusalem *35* is the camp; and outside the camp is [outside Jerusalem;] it is the camp of *34* their cities. Outside the ca[mp...] ... [...] You shall remove the ashes *35* from the altar and bur[n there the sin-offering, for Jerusalem] is the place which *36* [he chose from among all the tribes of Israel...] *37* [...] *38* [... they] do not slaughter in the temple [...] *39* [And concerning pregnant animals, we think that] the mother and son [should not be sacrificed] on the same day *40* [...And concerning who eats, w]e think that one can eat the son *41* [who was in the womb of his mother after she has been slaughtered; and you know that] this is so and that this matter is written down; the pregnant *42* [... And concerning the Ammonite and the Moabite and the bastard and the one with crushed testicles and one with sever]ed penis, if these enter *43* [the assembly... and] take a bone *44* [...] *45* [...] we think *46* [...] concerning these *47* [... that they should not] join them and make them *48* [...] and not be brou[ght] *49* [into the temple... And you know that some] of the people *50* [...some associating with others. *51* [Because the sons of Israel ought to keep themselves from all] uncleanness of the male *52* [and be respectful towards the temple. And also] concerning the blind *53* [who cannot see: they should keep themselves from all uncleanness,] and they do not see the uncleanness of *54* the sin-offering. *55* And also concerning the deaf who do not hear the law or the regulations concerning purity and do not *56* hear the laws of Israel; for whoever neither sees nor hears, does not *57* know how to apply (them); but these are approaching the purity of the temple. And also concerning flowing liquids: we say that in these there is no *59* purity. Even flowing liquids cannot separate unclean *60* from clean because the moisture of flowing liquids and their containers is *61* the same moisture. And into the holy camp dogs should not be brought which *62* could eat some of the bones from the te[mple...] the flesh on them. Because *63* Jerusalem is the holy camp, the place *64* which He has chosen from among all the tribes of Is[rael, since Jer]usalem is the head *65* of the camps of Israel. And also [concerning] the planting of fruit trees: a plant *66* in the land of Israel is like the first-fruits, it is for the priests. And the tithe of the cattle *67* and the flocks is for the priests. And also concerning lepers: we *68* s[ay that] they should [not] enter the holy purity, but instead *69* [reside outside the camp], alone. [And] also it is written that from the moment he shaves and washes he should reside outside *70* [his tent for seven] days. And it happens that when they are unclean, *71* [lepers approach] the holy purity, the house. And you know *72* [...] and apart from him, shall *73* bring [a sin-offering. And concerning him who acts offensively it is wri]tten that he is a slanderer and a blasphemer. *74* [And further: when they have the uncleanness of leprosy] they should not eat any of the holy things *75* until the sun sets on the eighth day. And concerning [the uncleanness of a] *76* corpse: we say that every bone, [whether stripped of flesh] *77* or complete is subject to the law concerning a dead or murdered person. *78* And concerning the fornications carried out in the midst of the people: they are [members of the congregation of perfect] *79* holiness, as it is written: «Holy is Israel». And concerning his [pure animal] *80* it is written that he shall not pair off two species; and concerning clothing, [it is written that no] *81* materials are to be mixed; and he will not sow his field [or his vineyard with two species] *81* because they are holy. And the sons of Aaron are the [holiest of the holy,] *83* but you know that a part of the priests and of the peo[ple mingle] *84* and they squeeze each other and defile the [holy] seed [and also] *85* their (own) [seed] with fornications, be[cause the sons of Aaron]

86 [...] *87* [...] ... [...] who will come *88* and who [...] ... [...] *89* And concerning women: [...] and betrayal [...] *90* for in these matters [... for] violence and for- nication [several] *91* places have been ruined. And [further] it is writ[ten in the book of Moses that] an abomination [is not] to be brought [into a house, for] *92* an abomination is odious. [And you know that] we have segregated ourselves from the rest of the peop[le and (that) we avoid] *93* mingling in these affairs and associating with them in these things. And you k[now that there is not] *94* to be found in our actions deceit or betrayal or evil, for concerning [these things w]e give [... and further] *95* to you we have wr[itten] that you must understand the book of Moses [and the words of the pro]phets and of David [and the annals] *96* [of eac]h generation. And in the book it is written[...] not to *97* [...] And further it is written that [you shall stray] from the path and you will undergo evil. And it is written *98* [...] and we determined [...] *99* [...] And it is written that *100* [all] these [things] shall happen to you at the end of days, the blessing *101* and the curse [... and you shall ass]ent in your heart and turn to me with all your heart *102* [and with a]ll your soul [... at the e]nd [of time] and you shall be [...] *103* [And it is written in the book of] Moses and in [the words of the prop]hets that [blessings and curses] will come upon you] which [...] *104* [the bl]essings which c[ame upon] him in the days of Solomon the son of David and also the curses *105* which came upon him from the [days of Je]roboam son of Nebat right up to the capture of Jerusalem and of Zedekiah, king of Judah *106* [that] he should bring them in [...]. And we are aware that part of the bless- ings and curses have occurred *107* that are written in the b[ook of Mo]ses. And this is the end of days, when they go back to Israel *108* for [ever...] and not return [...] and the wicked will act wickedly and [...] *109* And [...] remember the kings of Israel and reflect on their deeds, how whoever of them *110* who respected [the Torah] was freed from his afflictions; those who sought the To- rah *111* [were forgiven] their sins. Remember David, one of the 'pious' and he, too, *112* was freed from his many afflictions and was forgiven. And also we have written to you *113* some of the precepts of the Torah which we think are good for you and for your people, for in you [we saw] *114* intellect and knowledge of the Torah. Reflect on all these matters and seek from him so that he may sup- port *115* your counsel and keep far from you the evil scheming and the counsel of Belial, *116* so that at the end of time, you may rejoice in finding that some of our words are true. *117* And it shall be reckoned to you as in justice when you do what is upright and good before him, for your good *118* and that of Israel.

B *Translation of the individual copies*

4QHalakhic Letter*ᵃ* (4Q394 [4QMMT*ᵃ*])

Frag. 1 *col.* I (= 4QMMT 1–19)   *1* [...] a sabbath in it; after the sa[bbath, the first

and of the second day, a third day] *2* is added. And the year is complete, three
hundred and si[xty-four] *3* days. *Blank 4* These are some of our regulations [con-
cerning the law of G]od, which are pa[rt of] *5* the precepts we [are examining
and] they [a]ll relate to [...] *6* and purity *Blank* [...] ... [And concerning the offering of the] wheat of the Gen[tiles which they ...] *7* and they touch it [...] and
they defi[le it: you shall not eat it.] *8* [None] of the wheat of the Gentiles shall
be brought into the temple. [...And concerning the sacrifice] *9* which they cook
in vessels [of bronze...] *10* the flesh of their sacrifices and [...] in the courtyard
the [...] *11* with the broth of their sacrifices. And concerning the sacrifice of the
Gentiles: [we say that they sacrifice] *12* [...] which he is pulling towards it. [And
concerning the thank-offerings] *13* which they postpone from one day to another, w[e think] *14* that the ce[real]-offering [should be eaten] with the fats and
the meat on the day of their sa[crifice, and that the] *15* priests should oversee
in this matter in such a way that the [sons of Aaron] do not *16* lead the people
into sin. *Blank* And also in what pertains to the purity of the red heifer in the
sin-offering: *17* that whoever slaughters it and whoever burns it and whoever
collects the ash and whoever sprinkles the [water of] *18* purification, *Blank* All
these ought to be pure at sunset, *19* so that whoever is pure sprinkles the impure. For the sons of

Frag. 1 *col.* II (= 4QMMT 29–35)   *13* the priests ought to be vigilant [in all these]
things [so that they do not] *14* lead the people into sin. And concerning what is
written: *Lev 17:3* [«When a man slaughters within the camp»–they] *15* [slaughter]
outside the camp–«a bull, or a [she]ep or a she-goat»: the pl[ace of slaughter is
to the north of the camp.] *16* And we think that the temple [is the place of the
tent of meeting, and Je]rusalem *17* is the camp; and outside the camp is [outside
of Jerusalem;] it is the camp of *18* their cities. Outside the ca[mp...] ... [...]
You shall remove the ashes from the *19* [al]tar and bur[n there the sin-offering,
for Jerusalem] is the plače which

Frag. 2 (= 4QMMT 40–53)   *6* [...And concerning who eats, we think that one can
eat] the son *7* [who was in the womb of his mother after she has been slaughtered; and you know that this is so and that] this matter is written; *8* [the pregnant ... And concerning the Ammonite and the] Moabite *9* [and the bastard and
the one with crushed testicles and one with severed penis, if these enter] the
assembly *10* [... and] take *11* [a bone ...] we thi[nk] *12* [that...] concerning these
13 [... that they should not join them and] make *14* [... and not be brou[ght]
15 [into the temple... And you know that some] of the people *16* [...some associating with others. *17* [Because the sons of Israel ought to keep themselves
from all] uncleanness of the male *18* [and be respectful towards the temple. And
also] concerning the blind *19* [who cannot see: they should keep themselves
from all uncleanness,] and the uncleanness of

Frag. 3 (= 4QMMT 54–69)   *1* [the sin] offering these do not see it. *Blank 2* [And al]so concerning the deaf who do not hear the law or the precepts concerning purity and do not *3* [h]ear the laws of Israel, for whoever neither sees nor hears, does not *4* [k]now how to apply (them). But these are approaching the purity of the temple. *Blank 5* [And al]so concerning flowing liquids: we say that in these there is no *6* [pu]rity. Neither can flowing liquids separate unclean *7* [from] clean, because the moisture of flowing liquids and their vessels is *8* the same moisture. And into the [ho]ly camp dogs should not be brought which *9* can eat some of the bones from the te[mple with] the flesh on them. Because *10* Jerusalem is the holy camp, the place *11* which he has chosen from among all the tri[bes of Israel, since Jer]usalem is the head *12* of the camps of Israel. And also concerning the planting of] fruit [trees: a plant] *13* [in the land of Israel is like the first-fruits, it is for the pr]iests. And the tit[he of the cattle] *14* [and the flocks is for the priests. And also concerning] lepers: [we] *15* [say that] they should not enter the holy pur]ity, but ins[tead] *16* [reside outside the camp, alone. And also it is written that from the moment he] shav[es and washes he should reside outside]

4QHalakhic Letter*b* (4Q395 [4QMMT*b*])

Frag. 1 (= 4QMMT 10–20)   *1* [the flesh of their sacrifices and … in the courtyard …] *2* to […with the broth of their sacrifices. And concerning the sacrifice of the Gentiles: we say that they] *3* sacri[fice… which he is pulling towards it. And concerning] *4* the than[k-offerings which they postpone from one day to another, we think] *5* that the ce[real-offering should be eaten with the fats and the meat on the day of their sacrifice, and that the priests should] *6* oversee in this matter [in such a way that the sons of Aaron do not lead the people into sin.] *7* And also in what pertains to the purity of the re[d] /heifer/ [in the sin-offering: that whoever slaughters it and whoever burns it and whoever collects] *8* the ash and whoever sprinkles the [water of purification, all these, at sunset,] *9* ought to be pure so that [whoever is pure sprinkles the impure. For the sons of] *10* Aaron ought to be vigilant […] *11* … […]

4QHalakhic Letter*c* (4Q396 [4QMMT*c*])

Frag. 1 *col.* I (= 4QMMT 38–43)   *1* [… they do not] slaughter in the tem[ple.] *2* [And concerning pregnant animals: we think that] the mother and son [should not be sacrificed] on the same day *3* […And concerning who eats: w]e think that one can eat the son *4* [who was in the womb of his mother after she has been slaughtered; and you know that this is] so and that this matter is written down; the pregnant *Blank 5* [… And concerning the Ammonite and the Moabite and the bastard and the one with crushed testicles and one with severed] penis, if these enter *6* [the assembly…] … a bone

Frag. 1 *col.* II (= 4QMMT 52–63)   *1* and to be observant of the temple. [And also concerning the blind] who cannot *2* see: to keep themselves from all uncleann[ess; and the uncleanness of the sin-offering] they cannot *3* see it. *Blank* And also concerning the de[af who do not] hear the law *4* and the precept of purity and do not hear [the laws of] Israel *5* for whoever neither sees nor hears, does not [know] how to apply (them). But these *6* are approaching the purity of the temple. And al[so concerning flowing liquids, we] *7* say that in these there is no [purity. Neither can flowing liquids] *8* separate unclean from cl[ean, because the moisture of flowing liquids] *9* and what contains them is like them. [And into the holy camp] dogs [should not be brought] *10* which e[at some of the bones from the te[mple... with the flesh] *11* [on them.] Because Jerusa[lem is the holy camp, the place]

Frag. 1 *col.* III (= 4QMMT 64–74)   *1* which He has chosen from among all the tribes of Is[rael, since Jer]usalem is the head *2* [of the cam]ps of Israel. *Blank* And also [concerning the planting of] fruit trees: a plant *3* in the land of Israel is like the first-fruits, it is for the priests. And the tithe of the cattle *4* and of the flocks, is for the priests. And also concerning lepers: we *5* s[ay that] they should [not] enter {the pur} the holy purity, but instead *6* [reside outside the camp], alone. And also it is written that from the moment he shaves and washes he should reside outside *7* [his tent for seven] days. And behold, that when they are still unclean *8* [lepers approach] the holy purity, the house. And you know *9* [...] and apart from him, must bring *10* [a sin-offering. And concerning him who acts offensively it is wri]tten that he is a slanderer and a blasp[hemer.] *11* [And further: when they have the uncleanness of leprosy] they should not eat any of the holy things

Frag. 1 *col.* IV (= 4QMMT 75–85)   *1* until the sun sets on the eighth day. And concerning [the uncleanness of the corpse of] *2* a man: we say that every bone, [whether stripped of flesh] *3* or complete, is subject to the law concerning a dead or murdere[d person.] *4* And concerning the fornications carried out in the midst of the people: they are [members of the congregation of perfect] *5* holiness, as it is written: «Holy is Israel». And concerning the [pure animal] *6* it is written that he shall not pair off two species; and concerning clot[hing, it is written that no] *7* materials are to be mixed; and he will not sow his field [or his vineyard with two species] *8* because they are holy. But the sons of Aaron are the [holiest of the holy] *9* [and yo]u know that a part of the priests and of the peo[ple mingle] *10* [and they] squeeze each other and defile the [holy] seed [and also] *11* their (own) [seed] with fornications, [because the sons of Aaron]

4QHalakhic Letter*d* (4Q397 [4QMMT*d*])

Frag. 1 (= 4QMMT 31–36)   *1* [...] ... [...] *2* [...but the place of slaughter is to the nor]th of the camp. [And we think that the temple] *3* [is the place of the tent of meeting, and Jerusalem] is the camp; and outside the [camp is outside Jerusalem.] *4* [It is the camp of their cities. Outside the camp... You shall remove the ash]es [from the altar and burn there the sin-] *5* [offering, for Jerusalem is the place which he chose from among] all [the tribes of Israel...]

Frag. 2 (= 4QMMT 42–49)   *1* [... And concerning the Ammonite and the Moabite and the] bastard [and the one with crushed testicles and one with sever]ed penis, if these enter the assembly *2* [... and] take a bone [...] *3* [...] their impurities. And also, we think [...] *4* [...concerning these ... that they should not] join them and make [...] *5* [... and not be brought into the temple... And you know that some] of the peo[ple ...] *6* [...] ... [...]

Frags. 3 + 4 (= 4QMMT 59–67)   *1* [... Even flowing liquids cannot separate] unclean from clean [because the moisture of flowing liquids and their vessels] *2* [is the same moisture. And into the holy camp] dogs [should not be brought] which could eat some of the bones from the te[mple...] *3* [...] the flesh on [them. Because Jerusalem is the] holy camp, [the place which He has chosen from among all] *4* [the tribes of] Israel, since [Jerusalem is the head of the camps of Israel. And also conc]erning the plan[ting of fruit trees: a plant in the land of] *5* [Isra]el is like the first-[fruits, it is for the pr]iests. [And the tithe of the cattle and the flocks is for the priests.] *6* [...] ... [...]

Frags. 5 + 6 (= 4QMMT 70–82)   *1* [...] ... [...] *2* [... And it happens that when they are uncl]ean le[pers approach the holy purity, the house. And you know ...] *3* [... and apart from him, [shall bring] a sin-offering. [And concerning him who acts offensively it is written that he is a slanderer and a blasphemer.] *4* [And further: when they have the unclea]nness of le[prosy they should not] eat [any of the holy things until] the sun [sets on the eighth day.] *5* [And concerning the uncleanness of a corp]se, we say that every [bone, whether stripped of flesh or complete is subject to the] law concerning a dead or murde[red person.] *6* And concerning the fornications carried out in the midst of the peop[le: they are members of the congregation of perfect holiness,] as it is written: «Holy is [Israel».] *7* [And concerning the pu]re [animal], it is written that he shall not pair off [two species; and concerning clothing, it is written that no] materials [are to be mixed;] and he will not [sow his field] *8* [or his vineyard with two] species because they are [holy. But the sons of Aaron are the holi]est of the holy,

Frags. 7 + 8 (= 4QMMT 86–103)   *1* […] … […] *2* […] … […] who will come *3* and who […] … […] *4* And concerning wom[en…] and betrayal […] *5* for in these matters […] for violence and fornication [several] *6* places have been ruined. And [further] it is writ[ten in the book of Moses that] an abomination [is not] to be brought [into a house for] *7* an abomination is odious. [And you know that] we have segregated ourselves from the rest of the peop[le and (that) we avoid] *8* mingling in these affairs, and associating with [them] in these things. And you k[now that there is not] *9* to be found in our actions deceit or betrayal or evil, for concerning [these things] we give [… and further] *10* to you we have wr[itten] that you must understand the book of Moses [and the words of the] prophets and of David [and the annals] *11* [of eac]h generation. And in the book it is written […] … [… not to] *12* […] … And further it is written that [you shall stray] from the path and you will undergo [evil. And it is written that] *13* a]ll [these] things [shall happen to you at the e]nd of days, [the blessing] *14* [and the curse … and you shall ass]ent in your heart [and will turn to me with all your *15* […] which came […] *16* […] … […]

4QHalakhic Letter^e (4Q398 [4QpapMMT^e])

Frag. 1 (= 4QMMT 104–110)   *1* [the bl]essings which c[ame upon] him in the days of Solomon the son of David and also the curses *2* which came upon him from the [days of Je]roboam son of Nebat and up to the capture of Jerusalem and of Zedekiah, king of Judah *3* [that] he should bring them in […]. And we are aware that part of the blessings and curses have occurred *4* that are written in the b[ook of Mo]ses. And this is the end of days, when they go back to Israel *5* for [ever…] and not return […] and the wicked will act wickedly and […] *6* And […] remember the kings of Israel and reflect on their deeds, how whoever of them *7* respected [the Torah] was freed from his afflictions; those who sought the Torah

Frag. 2 *col.* I   *1–3* […] … *4* […] and we have been established […] *5* And it is written. And this will happen because *6* […] the days of blessing *7* […] all your heart

Frag. 2 *col.* II (= 4QMMT 111–118)   *1* [they were forgiven] their sins. Remember David, one of the 'pious' and he, too, *2* was freed from his many afflictions and was forgiven. And also we have written to you *3* some of the precepts of the Torah which we think are good for you and for your people, for [we saw] *4* in you intellect and knowledge of the Torah. Reflect on all these matters and seek from him so that he may support *5* your counsel and keep far from you the evil scheming and the counsel of Belial, *6* so that at the end of time, you may rejoice in finding that some of our words are true. *7* And it shall be reckoned to you as in justice when you do what is upright and good before him, for your good *8* and that of Israel.

4QHalakhic Letter^f (4Q399 [4QMMT^f])

Frag. 1 *col.* I (= 4QMMT 111–113)   *9* [... Remember David, one of the 'pious' and he, too, was fre]ed *10* [from his many afflictions and was forgiven. And also] to you we *11* [have written some of the precepts of the Torah which we think are good for you] *Blank* for we saw

Frag. 1 *col.* II (= 4QMMT 114–118)   *1* [in you, intellect and knowledge of the Torah. Reflect on all these matters and seek] from him *2* [so that he may support your counsel and keep far from you the] evil scheming *3* [and the counsel of Belial, so that at the end of time, you may rejoice] in finding that some of our words *4* [are true. And it shall be reckoned to you as in justice when you] do what is upright *Blank* before him, *5* [for your good and that of Is]rael. *Blank* *6-11 Blank*

2 Other Halakhic Texts

2QJuridical text (2Q25)

Frag. 1   *1* [...] his mouth [...] is full [...] *2* [...] these obligations [...] *3* [... for] this is what is written in the book of Moses [...]

4QOrdinances*ᵃ* (4Q159 [4QOrd*ᵃ*])

Frag. 1 *col.* II   *1* [...] Not [...] ... [...] *2* [...Isra]el and [their infring]ements and to atone for all their sins. [When someone harvests] *3* [his field and] makes it into a threshing floor or a press, whoever comes to the threshing floor [or to the press, whether levite, foreigner, orphan or widow,] *4* [whoever in Israel owns nothing, that person can eat some and garner for himself; but he is [not to harvest for his household, for «whoever comes into the grain of] *5* a field can eat it himself, but is not to remove it to his house to store it[»...] *6* Concerning [ransom:] the money of the census which one gives as ransom for his own person will be half a *shekel* [corresponding to the *shekel* of the temple, as an offering to God.] *7* Only once will he give it in all his days. The *shekel* comprises twenty *geras* in the [*shekel* of the temple. For all those who enter to be enrolled,] *8* for the six hundred thousand: one hundred *talents*; for the third, half a *talent*, [thirty *minas*; for the five hundreds, five *minas*,] *9* and for the fifty, half a *mina*, [twenty]-five *shekels*. The total [is six thousand and thirty-five and *minas* and half a] *10* mina. [Their peace-offering, according to the enrolled: a thousand m]en, ten *minas*; [one hundred men, one *mina*; fifty men, half a *mina*;] *11* [ten men, five *shekels* – fi]ve (*shekels*) of silver (make) the tenth part of [a *mina*; one man, ten *geras* – ten (*geras*) of silver] *12* [(make) half a *shekel*, since the *shekel* has twenty *geras* at the rate of the *she*]kel of the temple; ha[lf a *shekel* is the offering for God...] *13* [...] *13* [...] the *ephah* and the *bath* are the same measure [...] *14* [...] three tenths [...] *15* [...] *Blank* [...] *16* [...] all the people, and they will raise their ha[nds ...] *17* [...] Israel and he will burn the fa[t...]

Frags. 2–4   *1* [and if he has become poverty-stricken and sells himself to a] foreigner or the descendant of a [foreign] fam[ily, to be a day labourer for a year. He is not to govern him with harshness] *2* in the presence of Isra[el. They] are not to serve gentiles; with [a powerful hand and an outstretched arm he brought them out of the land of] *3* Egypt and commanded them not be sold for the price of a slave. [In an exceptional case, they should go to the ten] men *4* and two priests and be judged by these twelve. [...If there is] *5* a capital offence in Israel, their authority should be consulted, and whoever disobeys them [...] *6* he will be executed, for he acted presumptuously. A woman is not to wear the clothes of a male; every[one who does so commits an abomination;

he is not] *7* to put on a woman's cloak, and he is not to dress in a woman's tunic, for it is an abomination. *Blank* [...] *8* In the case where a man slanders a maiden of Israel, if he says it at the mo[ment] of taking her, they shall examine her; [if] *9* it is proved that he has not lied about her, they shall put her to death; but if he has testified [false]ly against her, they are to fine him two *minas* [and he is not] *10* to divorce her for all the days (of her life). Anyone who [...]

4QHalakhah (4Q251 [4QHalakah*ᵃ*])

Frag. 1   *1* [...] of (the) sin [...] *2* [...] he will compensate for the [enforced unem]ployment and defray the cost of the treatment. *3* [If a bull gores a man or a wom]an and (s)he dies, they shall stone the bull *4* [and its meat is not to be eaten; but the owner will be acquitted. But if the bull had been gor]ing in the past *5* [and, the owner having been warned, had not restrained it and it should kill a ma]n or a woman

Frag. 2   *1* [No-one is to consume grain, wi]ne or oil until [the priest has waved] *2* their first fruits. And no-one is to separate the must, for [wine] *3* is the first of the must, and the grain is the best part of [... And the bread of] *4* the first fruits are the leavened cakes which they have to carry on the day of [the first fruits.] *5* These are the first fruits. No-one is to eat the new wheat [...] *6* until the day of the bread from the first fruits arrives. Not [...]

Frag. 3   *1* [...] ... [...] *2* [...] Not to *3* [...] the *issaron* [...] *4* [...] and the animal [...] *5* [...the first]-born of man and of an unclean animal, *6* [...the bu]ll and ram, and the temple of *7* [...] is like the first-born. And the produce of a tree *8* [... and the oi]l and the olive(‑tree) in the fourth year *9* [...] offering, every holocaust (is) for the priest.

Frag. 4   *1* [...bu]ll or ewe or she-goat which are not perfe[ct] *2* [...] And you shall not eat their flesh, for [...] *3* [...] No-one is to eat the meat of an animal *Blank* *4* [and the de]ad [animal] or the torn animal which is not alive, for *5* [...] to the foreigner, and the fat, to ma[ke...] *6* [...to sa]crifice from it [...] *7* [...] ... [...]

Frag. 5   *1* [...] ... and the woman *2* [...] they shall eat with his bread, only a dove *3* [...] *Blank* Any fraud used to commit fraud *4* [...] to eat, for it is an abomination. *5* [...] an owner (and) has no-one to ransom him

Frag. 6   *1* [...a ma]n with his fellow [...] *2* [...] ... to the unclean [...] *3* [...] the wounded man who falls [...] *4* [...] changes his soul [...] *5* [...] it is a change; everything that is cut [...] *6* [...] in which there is no soul is dead.

Frag. 7   *1* Concerning nakedness: [...] *2* A man is not to take [...] *3* the daughter of his brother or the daughter of [...] *4* a man the nakedness of the sister of his mo[ther...] *5* her father and the brother of her mother [...] *6* A man is not to expose the nakedness of [...] *7* A man is not take the wife [...]

4QPurification rules A (4Q274 [4QTohorot A])

Frag. 1 *col.* I   *1* he shall begin to lay down his [re]quest; he shall lie down in the bed of sorrows, and in the residence of lamentation he shall reside; he shall reside apart from all the impure, and far from the *2* pure food, at twelve cubits; he shall dwell in the quarter reserved for him, to the North-east of every dwelling, at the distance of this measure. *3* Every man of the impure who [touches] him, shall bathe in water and wash his clothes, and afterwards he will eat. For this is what it says: *Lev 13:45-46* «Unclean, unclean, *4* he will shout, all the days that [the con]dition la[sts] him». And she who has a discharge of blood, during the seven days shall not touch the man with gonorrhoea or any of the utensils which the man with gonorrhoea has touched, *5* ‹upon which he has lain› /or/ upon which he has sat. And if she does touch, she shall wash her clothes and bathe, and afterwards, she will eat. And she must not mingle in any way during her seven *6* days, so that she does not contaminate the camps of the holy [ones of] Israel. Nor should she touch any woman [with a discharge] of blood of several days. *7* And the one who counts (their seven days), whether male or female, should not to[uch ...] at the onset of her menstruation, unless she is pure of [her mens]truation, for behold, the blood *8* of menstruation is considered like a discharge [for] him who touches it. And whoever [has an em]ission of semen contaminates through contact. [And whoever tou]ches anyone *9* of these impure persons, during the seven days of [his pu]rification, shall not eat, like whoever is impure through (contact with a) corpse. [He shall bathe in water] and wash, and aft[erwards ...]

Frag. 2 *col.* I   *1* [...] upon whom he sprinkled for the first time, and he shall bathe and wash before *2* [...shall imm]erse upon him the seventh, on the sabbath day. He shall not sprinkle on the sabbath, because *3* [...] on the sabbath; only, he should not touch the pure food until he changes *4* [...] Whoever touches a man's emission of semen shall immerse even all the utensils, and whoever carries it *5* [...] and shall immerse the clothing upon which it was found and the utensils which carry it *6* [...] And if in the camp there is a man whose hand does not reach [...] *7* [...] the clothing which he has not touched; only that he should not touch it, his food. And whoever does touch *8* [...] ... If he does not touch it [...] in water, and if *9* [...] and he shall wash. And concerning all these holy things, he shall wash [...] in water

Frag. 2 col. II   *1* his flesh and thus [...] *2* And if [...] *3* says [...] *4* his bread [...]
5 impure reptile [...] *6* And whoever touches it [...] *7* and all [...] *8* And if [...]
9 who [...]

Frag. 3   *1* [...] Not [...] the apple of his eyes [...] *2* [...] and every regulation
Blank [...] *3* [...] or every [...] *4* [...] ... [...] *5* [...] and is impur[e...] *6* [...] ...
Blank And he shall eat it in purity [...] *7* [...which] they dissolve by rubbing and
its liquid has evaporated, no-one shall eat it [...] *8* [...] the impure among them.
And also from among the greens [...] *9* [...] or a stewed cucumber, the man
who pours [...]

4QPurification rules B (4Q275 [4QTohorot B])

Frag. 1   *1* [... the pre]cept, and shall be put to the test until the week [...] *2* [...]
they will take possession of their inheritance, because ... [...] *3* [...] the truth;
and those who hate the pillaging [...] *4* [... they will] flee so as not to kill a man
[...] *5* [...] the judgment. [...] *6* [...] the place. *Blank* [...] *7* [...] If ... [...]

Frag. 2   *1* [...] they will go by the track [...] *2* [...] those appointed by name [...]
3 [...] in the third month [...] *4* [...] And he shall answer and shall say: *Blank*
[...] *5* [...] and the nations in [...] *6* [...] to them [...] *7* [...] ... [...]

Frag. 3   *1* and the elders with him until [...] *2* and he shall note in the register
[...] *3* The Inspector [will curse... and there shall be no] *4* mercy. Accurs[ed be
...] *5* from his inheritance forever [...] *6* in his destru[ctive] visitation. [...]

4QPurification rules B*b* (4Q276 [4QTohorot B*b*])

Frag. 1   *1* [...] with those which he has not ministered in the holy *2* [of holies...]
and he shall pronounce the clothes guilty, and slaughtered shall be *3* [...] the
heifer before him, and he shall place its blood in a new vessel which [...] *4* on
the altar, and sprinkle some of the blood with his finger. *Blank* Seven *5* [times
...] at the entrance of the tent of meeting. And he shall cast the cedar, *6* [the
hyssop and] scarlet into the midst of its fire. *7* [... and he who coll]ects the
ashes of the heifer *8* [...] ... as a reserve *9* [for the lustral water ...] The priest
shall put on

4QPurification rules B*c* (4Q277 [4QTohorot B*c*])

Frag. 1   *1* [... the cedar,] the hyssop and the [scarlet...] *2* [...] pure from every
impurity of [...] *3* the priest who atones with the heifer's blood and all the [...]
4 [...] and the sewn tunic with which atonement was made for the precept [...]

5 [...] in water [and it will be im]pure till the evening. Whoever carries the vase of the water of purification will be im[pure ...] *6* [...No-one should sprinkle] the water of purification upon the impure, [ex]cept a pu[re] priest [...] *7* [... upon] them, since he atones for the impure. And a wicked man should not sprinkle over the impure. [...] *8* [...] the water of purification. And they shall enter the water and shall be pure from the impurity of the corpse [...] *9* [...] other. The prie[st] shall scatter over them the water of purification to purify *10* [...] rather, they will be purified and their flesh [will be pu]re. And everyone who touches [...] *11* [...] his discharge [...] in the water [...] *12* [...] will be impure [...] his be[d and his] dwelling [...] they touched his discharge, like he who touches the impurity of [a corpse.] *13* [...] Whoever touches [...] [... and will] be impure till the evening, and whoever carries them [shall wash] his clothes and will be impure until the evening.

4QPurification rules C (4Q278 [4QTohorot C])

Frag. 1   *1* [...no-]one is to lie down *2* [...] where he resides *3* [...] If he does not touch it *4* [... the th]ird among them who touch *5* [...] the one who touches the bed *6* [...] ... in the place *7* [...] ...

4QPurification rules D (?) (4Q279 ? [4QLeqet])

Frag. 1   *1* [they shall] glean. And they shall not glean it [...] *2* no-one who touches the drink of the Many, for [...] *3* [they shall] glean, and the figs {...} [...] *4* his drink will come out acc[ording to ...] All shall glean [in purity...] *5* not to [...] And if they mock (?) [...] *6* They are not to ransom a[ll...]... /to run the risk/ until [...] *7* [they shall] glean in purity [...] their work [...]

Frag. 2   *1* [...] ... [...] *2* [...] they shall glean in purity [...] *3* [...] ... and they shall glean, each one [...] *4* [...]...[...] *5* [...] innocent [...] *6* [...] ... [...]

4QDecrees (4Q477)

Frag. 1 *col.* I   *1* [...] and also the men of the community *2* [...] their soul, and to reproach *3* [...] the camps of the Many over *4* [...]

Frag. 1 *col.* II   *1* to [...] *2* which [...because] is one who does evil [...] *3* the Many [...] ... [... *Blank* And they reproached] Johanan, son of Mata[thias because he ...] *4* and was quick for anger, [and ...] with him, and has the evil eye, and also has a boastful spirit. [...] *5* [...] ... to darkness. [...] *Blank* – And they reproached Hananiah Notos because he [...] *6* [...to] reduce the spirit of the commun-i[ty...] and also to mortgage [...] *7* [...] And they reproached [...] son of Joseph, because he has the evil eye , and also because no-one [...] *8* [...] and also he who loves the covering of his flesh [...] *9* [...] – And [they reproached] Hananiah, son of Sime[on...] *10* [...] And also he who loves the [...]

4QOrdinances*b* (4Q513 [4QOrd*b*])

Frags. 1–2 *col.* I   *1* [...] ... *2* [... the *shekel* comprises twe]nty [*geras*] at the rate of the [temple *she*]*kel* [...] The half-*3*[*shekel* has twe]lve *obols*, two] *zuzim* [...] /and also/ from them comes impurity. *4* [The *ephah* and the] *bath* /from these comes impurity/ are of the same size: [ten *issaron*s. Like the *ephah* of] grain, is the *bath* of wine. The *seah* *5* [is of three *issa*]*rons* and a third of an *is/saron*. From them comes imp]urity. And the tenth of the *ephah* *6* [is an *issaron*...]

Frags. 1–2 *col.* II   *1* to approach the holy foodstuffs, for they are unclean [...] *2* ladies of sons of foreigners and all fornication which [...] *3* he chose for himself, to feed them with all the share of [...] *4* and for foo[d (?) of an]gels, and to atone {in them} with them on Is[rael]'s behalf [...] *5* the fornication of their food, he bears the sin because he has defiled [...] *6* they [...] sin in their defilement [...]

Frags. 3–4   *1* [...] ... [...] *2* [...] [holy] convocation [...] the waving of the sheaf [...] *3* [...] on the sabbath day to ... [...] without counting the sabbaths [...] *4* [...] to celebrate the memory of [...] the failure of blindness [...] *5* [...] which ... [...] and not of the law of Moses[...]

Frag. 10   *1* [...] ... [...] *2* and the sons of Israel [...] *3* who should not mingle with [...] *4* them in pu[rity ...] *5* and ... [...] *6* in purity [...] *7* the temple [...] *8* of the sons of Aa[ron ...]

Frag. 13   *1* [...] and the natural cavities in the rock *2* [...] for their pleasing atonement *3* [...] doing and becoming defiled *4* [... becom]ing defiled by oil [...] *5* [...] in their impurity [...] *6* [...] to the dri[nk...] *7* [...] And if [...] *8* [...] of all that [...]

4QOrdinances*c* (4Q514 [4QOrd*c*]?)

Frag. 1 *col.* I   *1* ... [...] a woman [...] *2* he must not eat [...] for all the impure [...] *3* to reckon for [him seven days of ablu]tions; and he shall bathe and wash (his clothes) on the day of [his] purification [... And whoever] *4* has not begun to purify himself of 'his spring' is not to eat [...Nor can he eat] *5* in his original impurity. And all the temporarily impure, on the day of their purification, bathe *6* and wash (their clothes) in water and they will be pure. *Blank* Afterwards, they shall eat their bread in conformity with the law of purity. *7* He is not to eat insolently in his original impurity, whoever has not started to cleanse himself from «his spring», *8* and likewise he is not to eat during his original impurity. All the temporarily impure, on the day of *9* their purification, bathe and wash (their clothes) in water and they will be pure and afterwards they shall eat their bread *10* in con[formity with the law. No-]one is to eat or drink with any woman who prepares *11* [...] in the serv[ice...]

Literature with Eschatological Content

Although eschatology flourishes in one form or another in many of the writings which come from Qumran, it is useful to group together in this chapter a series of texts devoted *completely* to describing or exploring this event, which the texts denote as the 'final days' or 'the end of time', an event which the Qumran community felt as imminent (and, to some extent, as already present) and for which their expectation determined their whole way of life.

The texts collected here are distinguished by content, and not by the literary form they reveal. In fact, the *War Scroll* and the *Rule of the Congregation* could have been included with the other 'Rules'; the *Description of the New Jerusalem* and *4Q246* are genuine 'apocalypses'; *11QMelchisedek*, *4QTestimonia* and *4QFlorilegium* are various forms of thematic pesharim. The decision to present together in this chapter material which in terms of form is so varied, is due to the theme central to all these writings which comprises the various scenarios of the 'final days', the last war and the ensuing peace, the various heavenly agents of salvation, the different messianic characters, the composition of the eschatological community, the new Jerusalem and the new temple, etc.

The various continuous *pesharim* are not included in this chapter, although these works interpret the biblical text in terms of the 'final days', because in those compositions the exegetical aspect is paramount.

As in the case of other Qumran compositions which have been preserved for us in various copies, the different versions of the *War Scroll* exhibit clear signs of a lengthy editorial development. The problem is so severe, that it would be quite in order to ask whether particular manuscripts are in fact different editions of the *War Scroll*. Or it may be that what the manuscripts have conveyed to us are some of the written sources which the author of the *War Scroll* used to produce his work. Or perhaps even these texts are really remnants of other quite different compositions on the same topic. In spite of these problems the designation 4QM (*War Scroll* from Cave 4) has been retained for all the manuscripts which have been published under this label, except for 4Q471. Although published as 4QM*ʰ*, none of the elements preserved in the minuscule fragments of this manuscript compels us to consider the work from which they originate to be a copy of the *War Scroll*.

1 The War Scroll

A *The Cave 1 Copy*

1QWar Scroll (1QM [+1Q33])

Col. I   *1* For the Ins[tructor: The Rule] of the War. The first attack by the sons of light will be launched against the lot of the sons of darkness, against the army of Belial, against the company of Edom and of Moab and of the sons of Ammon *2* and the comp[any of … and of] Philistia, and against the companies of the Kittim of Ashur and [those who assist them from among the wicked] of the covenant. The sons of Levi, the sons of Judah and the sons of Benjamin, the exiled of the desert, will wage war against them. *3* […] against all their companies, when the exiled sons of light return from the desert of the peoples to camp in the desert of Jerusalem. And after the war, they shall go up from there *4* […] of the Kittim in Egypt. And in his time, he will go out with great rage to wage war against the kings of the North, and his anger will exterminate and cut off the horn of *5* [… There] will follow a time of salvation for the people of God and a period of rule for all the men of his lot, and of everlasting destruction for all the lot of Belial. There will be *6* g[reat] panic [among] the sons of Japhet, Ashur shall fall and there will be no help for him; the rule of the Kittim will come to an end, wickedness having been defeated, with no remnant remaining, and there will be no escape *7* [for the so]ns of darkness. *Blank 8* And [the sons of jus]tice shall shine in all the edges of the earth, they shall go on illuminating, up to the end of all the periods of darkness; and in the time of God, his exalted greatness will shine for all the [eternal] times, *9* for peace and blessing, glory and joy, and long days for all the sons of light. And on the day on which the Kittim fall, there will be a battle, and savage destruction before the God of *10* Israel, for this will be the day determined by him since ancient times for the war of extermination against the sons of darkness. On this (day), the assembly of the gods and the congregation of men shall confront each other for great destruction. *11* The sons of light and the lot of darkness shall battle together for God's might, between the roar of a huge multitude and the shout of gods and of men, on the day of the calamity. It will be a time of *12* suffering fo[r al]l the people redeemed by God. Of all their sufferings, none will be like this, from its haste (?) until eternal redemption is fulfilled. And on the day of their war against the Kittim, *13* they [shall go out to destr]uction. In the war, the sons of light will be the strongest during three lots, in order to strike down wickedness; and in three (others), the army of Belial will gird themselves in order to force the lot of *14* […] to retreat. There will be infantry battalions to melt the heart, but God's might will strengthen the hea[rt of the sons of light.] And in the seventh lot, God's great hand will subdue *15* [Belial, and a]ll the angels of his dominion and all the men of [his lot.] *Blank 16* [...] the holy ones, he will shine out to assist the [...] truth, for the destruction of the sons of darkness [...] *17* [...] great [...] they shall stretch out the hand for [...]

Col. II   *1* fathers of the congregation, fifty-two. They shall arrange the chiefs of the priests behind the High Priest and of his second (in rank), twelve chiefs to serve *2* in perpetuity before God. And the twenty-six chiefs of the divisions shall serve in their divisions and after them the chiefs of the levites to serve always, twelve, one *3* per tribe. And the chiefs of their divisions shall each serve in their place. The chiefs of the tribes, and after them the fathers of the congregation, shall have charge of the sanctuary gates in perpetuity. *4* And the chiefs of the divisions with their enlisted shall have charge of their feasts, their new moons and their sabbaths and all the days of the year–those of fifty years and upwards. *5* These shall have charge of the holocausts and the sacrifices, in order to prepare the pleasant incense for God's approval, to atone for all his congregation and in order to grow fat in perpetuity before him *6* at the table of his glory. They shall arrange all /these/ during the appointed time of the year of release. During the remaining thirty-three years of the war, the famous men *7* called to the assembly, and all the chiefs of the fathers of the congregation, shall choose for themselves men of war for all the countries of the nations; from all the tribes of Israel they shall equip for them *8* intrepid men, in order to go out on campaign according to the directives of war, year after year. However, during the years of release they shall not equip themselves in order to go out on campaign, for it is a sabbath of *9* rest for Israel. During the thirty-five years of service, the war will be prepared during six years; and all the congregation together will prepare it. *10* And the war of the divisions (will take place) during the remaining twenty-nine years. During the first year they shall wage war against Aram-Naharaim; during the second, against the sons of Lud; during the third *11* they shall wage war against the remnant of the sons of Aram, against Uz and Hul, Togal and Mesha, who are beyond the Euphrates; during the fourth and fifth, they shall wage war against the sons of Arpachsad; *12* during the sixth and seventh they shall wage war against all the sons of Assyria and Persia, and the eastern peoples up to the great desert; during the eighth year they shall wage war against the sons of *13* Elam; during the ninth they shall wage war against the sons of Ishmael and Ketura; and during the following ten years the war will be divided against all the sons of Ham, *14* ac[cording to their clans, in] their dwellings; and during the following ten years the war will be divided up against all [the sons of Japhet, in their dwe]llings. *Blank 15* [...] *Blank* [...] *16* [...] of alarm for all their services, for [...] for their enlisted men [...] and tens above [...]

Col. III   *1* {the battle formations and the trumpets} / the battle formations and the trumpets/ of rallying, when the gates of battle open for the men of the infantry to go out and the trumpets of alarm of the slain and the trumpets of *2* ambush, and the trumpets of pursuit, when the enemy is struck, and the trumpets of re-assembly, when they retreat from battle. On the rallying trumpets of the assembly they shall write: «Rallied by God». *3* On the rallying trumpets of the commanders they shall write: «Princes of God». And on the trumpets for enlisting, they shall write «Rule of God». And on the trumpets of *4* famous men, {they shall write} chiefs of the fathers of the congregation, when they meet in the meeting house, they shall write: «God's directives for the holy council». And on the trumpets of the camps *5* they shall write: «Peace of God in the camps of his holy ones». And on the trumpets of pulling out they shall write: «God's mighty deeds to scatter the enemy and force all those who hate *6* justice to flee», and «Withdrawal of mercy from those who hate God». And on the trumpets of battle formations they shall write: «God's battle formations for avenging his wrath against all the sons of darkness». *7* And on the trumpets for rallying the infantrymen when the gates of battle open so they can go out up to the enemy line they shall write: «Memorial of revenge at the moment appointed by *8* God». And on the trumpets of the slain they shall write: «God's mighty hand in the battle to fell all the slain of unfaithfulness». And on the trumpets of ambush they shall write: *9* «God's mysteries to destroy wickedness». And on the trumpets of pursuit they shall write: «God has struck all the sons of darkness, he shall not cause his wrath to return, until they are exterminated». *10* And when they retreat from battle to return to the line, they shall write on the trumpets of retreat: «May God re-assemble». And on the trumpets of the path of return *11* from battle with the enemy, to go back to the congregation of Jerusalem, they shall write: «Exultations of God in a peaceful return». *Blank 12 Blank 13* Rule of the banners of all the congregation in order of companies. On the large banner which goes at the head of all the people they shall write: «God's people», and the name of Israel *14* and of Aaron and the names of the twelve tri[bes of Isra]el according to their genealogies. Above the banner of the camp chiefs of the three tribes *15* they shall write: [...] On the banner of the tribe they shall write: «God's flag», and the name of the prince of [the tribe...] *16* [...] the name of the princes of the ten thousand and the names of the pri[nces of ...] *17* [...] ... [...]

Col. IV   *1* And on the banner of Merari they shall write: «God's offering» and the name of the prince of Merari and the names of the commanders of his thousands. And on the banner of the thousand they shall write: «God's Fury unleashed against *2* Belial and against all the men of his lot so that no remnant (is left)» and the name of the commander of the thousand and the names of the commanders of his hundreds. And on the banner of the hundred they shall write: «Of *3* God, hand of battle against all degenerate flesh» and the name of the commander of the hundred and the names of the commanders of his tens. And on the banner of the fifty they shall write: «No longer *4* do the wicked rise, due to God's might», and the name of the commander of the fifty and the names of the commanders of his tens. On the banner of the ten they shall write: «Songs of jubilation of *5* God on the ten-string lyre» and the name of the commander of the ten and the names of the nine men under his command. *Blank 6* And when they go to battle they shall write on their banners: «God's truth», «God's justice», «God's glory», «God's judgment» and after these (names) all the ordered list of their names. *7* And when they approach for battle they shall write on their banners: «God's right hand», «Time appointed by God», «God's confusion», «God's slaughter», and after these the complete list of their names. *8* And when they retreat from battle, they shall write on their banners: «God's glorification», «God's greatness», «God's praise», «God's glory», with a complete list of their names. *Blank 9* Rule of the banners of the congregation. When they go out to battle they shall write on the first banner: «God's congregation»; on the second banner: «God's camps»; on the third, *10* «God's tribes»; on the fourth: «God's families»; on the fifth: «God's battalions»; on the sixth: «God's Assembly»; on the seventh: «Summoned by *11* God»; on the eighth: «God's army»; and they shall write the list of their names in their order. And when they approach for battle they shall write on their banners: *12* «God's battle», «God's revenge», «God's lawsuit», «God's reward», «God's might», «God's prize», «God's power», «God's destruction of all futile nations», and all the list of *13* their names they shall write on them. And when they retreat from battle they shall write on their banners: «God's acts of salvation», «God's victory», «God's help», «God's support», *14* «God's joy», «God's thanksgiving», «God's praise», «God's peace». *Blank 15* [Sizes of the ban]ners: banner of the whole congregation, fourteen cubits long; banner of the th[ree tribes, thir]teen cubits long; *16* [tribal banner], twelve cubits; [banner of the ten th]ousand, eleven [cubits; banner of the thousand, ten cubits; banner of the hundred,] nine cubits; *17* [banner of the fifty, eight] cubits; banner of the ten, seven [cubits. *Blank*]

Col. v   *1* And upon the sh[ield] of the Prince of the whole congregation they shall write his name and the name of Israel and Levi and Aaron and the names of the twelve tribes of Israel, according to their generations, *2* and the names of the twelve commanders of their tribes. *Blank 3* Rule of the formation of fighting battalions. When their army is complete, to fill a front line, the line will be formed of one thousand men, with seven forward *4* formations per line, each formation in its order, each man being behind the other. And all shall be armed with bronze shields, polished like *5* a mirror. And the shield will be surrounded by a plaited border and will have a pattern engraved, a work of art in gold, silver and copper blended together, *6* and precious stones, many-hued decorations, work of a skilful craftsman. Height of the shield: two and a half cubits; and its width, one and a half cubits. And in his hand, a spear *7* and a sword. Length of the spear: seven cubits, including the haft, and the tip of half a cubit. In the haft there will be three rings cut, with an border *8* plaited in gold, silver and bronze intermixed, like a work of art and an engraved pattern. On both parts of the ring, the pattern will be surrounded *9* with precious stones, many-hued decorations, work of a skilful craftsman, and an ear of wheat. And the haft will be engraved between the rings in the style of *10* an artistic column. The point will be of shining white iron, work of a skilful craftsman, and will have an ear of wheat, of pure gold, in the centre of the point pointing towards *11* the tip. The swords shall be of purified iron, refined in a crucible and whitened like a mirror, work of a skilful craftsman; and it will have shapes of an ear of wheat, *12* of pure gold, encrusted in it on both sides. And it will have two straight channels right to the tip, two on each side. Length of the sword: one cubit *13* and a half. And its width: four fingers. The scabbard will be four thumbs; it will have four palms up to the scabbard and diagonally, the scabbard from one part to *14* the other (will be) five palms. The hilt of the sword will be of select horn, craftwork, with a pattern in many colours: gold, silver and precious stones. *15* Blank *16* And when they stand up [...] they shall line up in seven lines, one line behind the other, *17* [...] thirty cubits in which the me[n] shall have *18* [...] the faces [...]

Col. VI   *1* seven times and they shall return to their position. After them, three battalions of infantry shall go out and shall take up position between the lines. The first battalion will hurl against *2* the enemy line seven javelins of war. On the point of the javelin they shall write: «Sheen of the spear by God's might». On the second dart they shall write: *3* «Arrow of blood to fell the dead by God's wrath». And on the third javelin they shall write: «Flame of the sword devouring the wicked dead by God's judgment». *4* All these they shall hurl seven times and go back to their position. And after them, two infantry battalions shall go out and they shall take up position between the two lines. The first *5* battalion will be equipped with a spear and a shield and the second battalion will be equipped with a shield and a sword, to fell the dead by the judgment of God and to humiliate the enemy line *6* by God's might, to pay the reward of their evil towards all the nations of futility. For kingship belongs to the God of Israel and with the holy ones of his people he will work wonders. *7* Blank *8* And seven cavalry formations shall take up position, they also, on the right and on the left of the line. Their formations shall take up position on one side and the other, seven hundred *9* cavalry on one flank and seven hundred on the second flank. Two hundred cavalry shall go out with the thousand soldiers of the infantry of one line. And thus *10* shall they take up position on all the flanks of the camp. In all, four thousand six hundred; and fourteen hundred mounts for the men of the rule of the lines, *11* fifty for each line. The cavalry, including the mounts of the men of the rule, will be six thousand, five hundred per tribe. All the mounts which go out *12* to the battle with the infantry-men shall be stallions, fleet of foot, tame of mouth, long in wind, in the fullness of their days, trained for battle *13* and disciplined to hearing din and the sight of every display. And those who mount them shall be men, hardened in battle, trained in horseman-ship. The range of *14* their days will be from thirty up to forty-five years. The horsemen of the rule shall be between forty and fifty years old. They *15* and their mounts [shall be attired in cu]irasses, helmets and greaves and shall hold in their hands circular shields and a spear of eight cu[bits] *16* [...] and a bow and arrows and war javelins. And all shall be ready *17* [...] to shed the blood of the fallen on account of their wickedness. These are the ones who *18* [...] *Blank* [...].

Col. VII   *1* The men of the rule shall be between forty and fifty years (old). Those governing the camps shall be between fifty and sixty years (old). The supervi-sors *2* shall also be between forty and fifty years (old). And all those who despoil the fallen and those who pillage the loot and those who cleanse the earth and those who protect the weapons *3* and those who prepare the supplies all shall be between twenty-five and thirty years (old). And no young boy or any woman at all shall enter the camps when they leave *4* Jerusalem to go to war, until they return. And no lame, blind, paralysed person nor any man who has an indelible blemish on his flesh, nor any man suffering from uncleanness *5* in his flesh, none of these will go out to war with them. All these shall be volunteers for war, perfect in spirit and in body, and ready for the day of vengeance. And every *6* man who has not cleansed himself of his 'spring' on the day of battle will not go down with them, for the holy angels are together with their armies. And there will be a space *7* between all their camps and «the place of the hand» of about two thousand cubits. And no immodest nakedness will be seen in the surroundings of all their camps. *8* *Blank* *9* When they draw up the battle lines against the enemy, one line opposite another line, out from the central gate towards (the space) between the lines, shall go seven *10* priests of the sons of Aaron, robed with garments of white byssus, a linen tunic and linen trousers, and they shall gird on a belt of intertwined byssus, violet, *11* purple and crim-son, with many–hued patterns, work of a craftsman, and upon their heads (they shall wear) turbans. (These are) the garments of war; they shall not bring them into the sanctuary. *12* The first priest will walk in front of all the men of the line, to strengthen their hands for battle. And the (other) six shall hold in their hand *13* the rallying trumpets, the memorial trumpets, the alarm trumpets, the pursuit trumpets and the trumpets of re-assembly. When the priests go out *14* towards (the space) between the lines, seven levites shall go out with them, with seven ram's horns in their hands. Three supervisors from among the levites (shall go) in front of *15* the priests and the levites. The priests will blow the two rallying trumpets [… of bat]tle upon fifty shields, *16* and fifty infantry-men shall go out of a gate […] the officers of the levites. And with each *17* line they shall go out in accordance with this ru[le… the infan]trymen [shall go out] of the gates *18* [and take up po]sition between the li[nes…] the ba[ttle…]

Col. VIII   *1* The trumpets shall continue sounding, to guide the slingers until they have finished throwing seven *2* times. After, the priests shall blow the trumpets of return for them, and they shall return to the flank of the first *3* line to remain in their position. And the priests shall blow the rallying trumpets and there shall go out *4* three battalions of infantry from the gates and they shall take up position between the lines; at their side, cavalrymen, *5* right and left. The priests shall blow the trumpets with a sustained blast, the signal for battle order. *6* And the columns shall deploy in their formations, each in his own position. When they are in three formations, *7* the priests shall blow for them a second blast, low and sustained, the signal to proceed, until they approach *8* the enemy line and take hold of their weapons of war. The priests shall blow the six trumpets *9* of slaughter with a shrill, staccato blast, to direct the battle. And the levites and all the throng with ram's horns shall blow *10* a single blast, a deafening war alarm, to melt the heart of the enemy. And at the alarm blast *11* the war javelins shall fly, to bring down the slain. The blast of the ram's horns will stop, but with the trumpets *12* the priests shall continue blowing a shrill staccato blast, to direct the fighting hands until they have thrown against the *13* enemy line seven times. Next, the priests shall blow for them the trumpets of retreat, *14* with a low blast, steady and continuous. According to this rule, the priests shall blow for the three battalions. When *15* the first throws, the […], a *16* deafening war alarm to direct the bat]tle […] the priests [shall blow] *17* the trumpe[ts] for them […] in their positions in the line *18* […] and take up positions *19* [… the sl]ain

Col. IX   *1* will begin to strike the fallen with their hands. And all the throng shall stop the alarm signal, but the priests shall continue blowing the trumpets *2* of destruction to direct the battle until the enemy has been routed and turns its back, and the priests shall follow, blowing, to direct the battle. *3* And when they have been routed in front of them, the priests shall blow the rallying trumpets, and all infantry-men shall go out towards them from the midpoint *4* of their front lines. Six battalions shall take up position together with the battalion which is fighting, seven lines in all, twenty-eight thousand *5* warriors and six thousand on horse. All these shall pursue the enemy to exterminate them in God's battle for *6* eternal destruction. The priests shall blow the trumpets of pursuit for them, and they shall divide for the pursuit to destruction of all the enemy. And the cavalry *7* will make them return to the battle zone, until their annihilation. When the dead fall, the priests shall follow, blowing at a distance, and they shall not enter *8* in the midst of the fallen so as not be defiled with their impure blood, for they are holy. They shall not desecrate the oil of their priestly anointing with the blood *9* of futile nations. *Blank 10* Rule for changing the order of the combat battalions. To establish the formation against [...] a semicircle with towers, *11* and an bow of towers and when it advances a little, the heads go out and the wings [go out, on both] sides of the line, to crush *12* the enemy. The shields of the towers shall be three cubits long and the length of their spears will be eight cubits. When the towers *13* go out from the line, (they shall have) one hundred shields on each face of the towers, in all, each tower will be surrounded on its three forward faces *14* by three hundred shields. The tower will have two gates, one on the right and the other on the left. And on all the shields of the towers *15* there will be written: on the first: 'Michael', [on the second: 'Gabriel', on the third:] 'Sariel', on the fourth: 'Raphael'; *16* 'Michael' and 'Gabriel' on [the right, and 'Sariel' and 'Raphael' on the left..] *Blank 17* [...] on the four [...] they shall set an ambush against [...]

Col. x   *1* in our camps and to keep ourselves from any immodest nakedness. And also he told us that you, great and terrible God, will be in our midst to plunder all *2* our enemies before us. And he taught us about our generations from ancient times, saying: *Dt 20:2-5* «When you approach for battle, the priest is to stand up and speak to the people *3* saying: 'Listen Israel, those of you approaching for battle against your enemies. Do not be afraid, and may your hearts not fail; *4* do not fear and do not tremble in front of them, for your God goes with you to do battle for you against your enemies to save you'». *5* Our officers shall speak to all those in readiness for battle: to those with resolute hearts, to strengthen them with God's power, *6* and to all (those) whose heart melts, to send them away and to strengthen together with all the intrepid heroes. For (this is) what you [said] by Moses' hand, saying: *Num 10:9* «When there is a war *7* in your land against the enemy who oppresses you, you shall blow the trumpets and you shall be remembered before your God, *8* and you shall be saved from your enemies.»

Who (is) like you, God of Israel,
in the heavens or on earth,
to do great deeds like your deeds,
9 marvels like your feats?
And who (is) like your people, Israel,
whom you chose
from among all the peoples of the earth,
10 a people of holy ones of the covenant,
learned in the law, wise in knowledge,

[…]
11 alert to the voice of Glory,
  seers of the holy angels,
  with open ears,
  hearing profound things?
  [… You created] the dome of the sky,
  the army of luminaries,
12 the support of the spirits,
  the control of the holy ones,
  the treasures of glory,
  [in the darkness] of the clouds;
  (you are) creator of the earth
  and of the laws of its divisions
13 in desert and steppe,
  of all its products,
  its frui[ts and seeds,]
  of the circle of the sea,
  of the reservoirs of the rivers,
  of the chasm of the abyss,
14 of beasts and birds,
  of man's image,
  of the gener[ations of …],
  of the division of tongues,
  of the separation of peoples,
  of the dwelling of the clans,
15 of the legacy of the nations,
  […]
  of the sacred seasons,
  of the cycle of the years
  and of appointed times
  for ever.
  […]
  We have known this through your knowledge
  that […]
  your heed of our cry,
  for […]
  […] his house […]

Col. XI   *1* For the battle is yours!
  With the might of your hand
  their corpses have been torn to pieces
  with no–one to bury them.

2 Goliath from Gath, gallant giant,
  you delivered into the hands of David, your servant,
  for he trusted in your powerful name
  and not in sword or spear.

  For the battle is yours!
3 The Philistines you humiliated many times
  for your holy name.
  By the hand of our kings, besides,
  you saved us many times
4 thanks to your mercy,
  and not by our own deeds by which we did wrong,
  nor by our sinful actions.

  For the battle is yours!
  And it is from you that power comes,
5 and not from our own being.
  It is not our might
  nor the power of our own hands
  which performs these marvels,
  except by your great strength
  and by your mighty deeds.
6 Thus you taught us from ancient times: *Num 24:17-19*
  «A star will depart from Jacob,
  a sceptre will be raised in Israel.
  It will smash the temples of Moab,
  it will destroy all the sons of Seth.
7 It will come down from Jacob,
  it will exterminate the remnant of the city,
  the enemy will be its possession,
  and Israel will perform feats».
  By the hand of your anointed ones,
8 seers of decrees,
  you taught us the times of the wars of your hands,
  to {fight} /to cover you with glory/ with our enemies,
  to fell the hordes of Belial,
9 the seven nations of futility,
  by the hand of the poor, those you saved,
  with the strength and the peace of your wonderful power.
  The melting heart you open to hope.
  You shall treat them like pharaoh,
10 like the officers and their chariots in the Red Sea.

Like a torch of fire in straw
you shall burn the fallen spirits,
devouring wickedness,
without ceasing,
11 until the sin has been consumed.
From of old you foretold the moment
of the power of your hand against the Kittim: *Isa 31:8*
«Ashur will fall by the sword of no-one,
12 the sword of a nobody will devour it.» *Blank*
13 For you will deliver into the hands of the poor
the enemies of all the countries,
and by the hand of those prone in the dust
you shall fell the powerful ones of the peoples,
you shall give the wicked their reward,
14 on the head of [...]
you shall carry out justice by your truthful judgment
on every son of man,
gaining everlasting renown for yourself among the people.
15 [...] the wars,
in order to show yourself great and holy
in the eyes of the remainder of the peoples,
so that they know [...]
16 [...] you shall carry out sentence on Gog
and on all his gathering [...]
17 [...] for you shall wage war against them from the heavens [...]

Col. XII   1 For there is a multitude of holy ones in heaven
and a host of angels in your holy dwelling
to praise your name.
And the chosen ones of the holy people
2 you have established for yourself in [...]
The [bo]ok of the names of all their armies
is with you in your holy dwelling,
[...] in the dwelling of your glory.
3 And the rewards of your blessings
[...] the covenant of your peace
you engraved for them
with the chisel of life,
in order to rule [...] during all times eternal,
4 to organize the arm[ies] of your chosen ones
in its thousands and in its myriads,
together with your holy ones and your angels,

5 to direct the hand in battle
   [and destroy] the rebels of the earth
   by your great judgments.
   And the people of the chosen ones of the heavens
   will triu[mph]. *Blank*

6 Blank

7 You are a God, awesome in the splendour of your majesty,
   and the congregation of your holy ones is amongst us
   for everlasting assistance.
   [We will] treat kings with contempt,

8 the powerful with jeers and mockery,
   for the Lord is holy
   and the King of glory is with us
   together with his holy ones.
   The heroes of the army of his angels
   are enlisted with us;

9 the war hero is in our congregation;
   the army of his spirits, with our infantry and our cavalry.
   They are like clouds and dew to cover the earth.

10 like torrential rain which pours justice on all that grows.
   Get up, hero,
   take your prisoners, glorious one,

11 collect your spoil, worker of heroic deeds!
   Place your hand on the neck of your foes
   and your foot on the piles of the dead!
   Strike the nations, your foes,

12 and may your sword consume guilty flesh!
   Fill the land with glory
   and your inheritance with blessing:
   herds of flocks in your fields,
   gold, /silver,/ and precious stones in your palaces!

13 Rejoice, Sion, passionately!
   Shine with jubilation, Jerusalem!
   Exult, all the cities of Judah!

14 Open the gates for ever
   so that the wealth of the nations can come in!
   Their kings shall wait on you,
   all your oppressors lie prone before you,

15 [and they shall lick] the dust [of your feet].
   [Daughters] of my people, shout with jubilant voice!
   Deck yourselves with splendid finery!
   Rule over the gover[nment of ...]

16 [...] Israel, in order to reign for ever.
  Blank
17 [...] the heroes of the war, Jerusalem [...]
18 [...] above the heavens, the Lord [...]

Col. XIII   *1* their brothers the priests and the levites and all the elders of the rule
    with him. And from their positions they shall bless the God of Israel and all the
    deeds of his truth and there they shall damn *2* Belial and all the spirits of his
    lot. They shall begin speaking and say:

  «Blessed be the God of Israel
  in all his holy plan
  and in all the deeds of his truth,
  3 and blessed be all who serve him in justice,
  who know him in faith. *Blank*
  4 Accursed be Belial in his malicious plan,
  may he be damned for his wicked rule.
  Accursed be all the spirits of his lot
  in his wicked *Blank* plan
  5 may they be damned for their deeds of filthy uncleanness.
  For they are the lot of darkness
  and the lot of God is for everlasting light.
  6 Blank
  7 You are the God of our fathers,
  we bless your name always.
  We are the people of your [inhe]ritance.
  You established a covenant with our fathers
  and ratified it with their offspring
  8 for times eternal.
  In all the edicts of your glory
  there has been a memorial [of your clemency] in our midst
  in aid of the remnant,
  the survivors of your covenant
  9 and in order to number the deeds of your truth,
  and the justice of your wonderful might.
  You, [have crea]ted [us] for you, eternal people,
  and you have made us fall into the lot of light
  10 in accordance with your truth.
  From of old you appointed the Prince of light
  to assist us,
  and in [...]
  and all the spirits of truth are under his dominion.

11 You created Belial for the pit,
   angel of enmity;
   his [dom]ain is darkness,
   his counsel is for evil and wickedness.
12 All the spirits of his lot
   angels of destruction
   walk in the laws of darkness;
   towards them goes his only desire.
   We, instead, in the lot of your truth,
   rejoice in your mighty hand
13 we exult in your salvation,
   we are happy with your aid and your peace.
   Who is like you in strength, God of Israel?
14 Your mighty hand is with the poor!
   And which angel or prince is like you for aid?
   Since ancient time you determined the day of the great battle
15 [...] to assist truth,
   and destroy wickedness,
   to demolish darkness
   and increase light.
   [...]
16 [...] for an everlasting stay
   to exterminate all the sons of darkness
   and happiness for [...]
17 *Blank*
18 [...] You have destined us [...]»

Col. XIV   *1* like the fire of his wrath against the idols of Egypt. *Blank 2* And when
   they have departed from the slain in order to enter the camp, they shall all sing
   the hymn of return. In the morning they shall wash their clothes and shall wash
   3 off themselves the blood of the guilty corpses. They shall go back to the site
   of their positions, where they arranged their lines before the slain of the enemy
   fell. And there they shall all bless *4* the God of Israel and exalt his name in
   joyful chorus. They shall begin to speak and say:

   «Blessed be the God of Israel,
   the one who keeps mercy for his covenant
   5 and pledges of deliverance
   for the people he has redeemed.
   He has called those who are tottering
   to prodigious [exploits].
   He has gathered an assembly of nations

for destruction with no remnant.
In judgment he has lifted up
6 the melting heart;
he has opened the mouth of the dumb
to sing God's marvels.
The hands of the frail
he has trained in war.
The knees that shake
he gives strength to stand upright.
7 And he girds the kidneys
of those with broken backs.
Among the poor in spirit
[...] to a hard heart.
For the perfect ones of the path
all the wicked nations shall be destroyed.
8 None of their heroes
will remain standing.
Only we, the rem[nant of your people].
Blessed be your name, God of mercies,
guardian of the covenant of our fathers.
9 In all our generations
you have caused your favours to fall on the rem[nant of our people]
during the empire of Belial.
In all the mysteries of his enmity,
he has not separated us from your covenant.
10 You have excluded from us
his spirits of destruction.
You have protected the soul of your redeemed ones
[when the m]en of his empire [were scheming].
You have raised the fallen with your strength,
11 but those who arose, you cut down to humiliate them [...]
For their heroes there is no saviour,
there is no refuge for their swift ones.
To their most esteemed
12 you return scorn.
All their useless *Blank* existence
[you have turned into] nothing.
We, your holy people,
will praise your name
for the deeds of your truth,
13 for your mighty deeds
we will extol *Blank* [your spl]endour,

at [every] moment
and at the times indicated
by your eternal edicts,
at the onset of day and at night
14 at the fall of evening and at dawn.
For great is the p[lan of you]r glory
and your marvellous mysteries on high;
in order to raise from the dust for yourself
15 and subdue gods. *Blank*
16 Rise up, rise up, Oh God of gods,
and be exalted with power, [King of kings!]
17 [...] the sons of darkness,
and your great light [...]
18 [...] like a fire will burn [...]

Col. XV   *1* For there will be a time of suffering for Israel [and a decree] of war
/against/ all the peoples. For God's lot there will be everlasting redemption
2 and destruction for all the wicked peoples. All those who [are ready] for the
war shall go and camp opposite the king of the Kittim and opposite all the
army *3* of Belial, assembled with him for the day [of extermination] by God's
sword. *Blank 4* The High Priest will take up position, and his brothers the
priests and the levites and all the men of the rule shall be with him. And he will
say in their hearing *5* the prayer for the time of war, [as it is written in the
«Bo]ok of the Rule for this time», with all the words of thanksgiving. And he
will array there *6* all the lines, as is wr[itten in the «Book of War»]. And the
priest assigned for the time of vengeance according to the decision *7* of all his
brothers will go forward, and he will strengthen [the heart of the warriors.] He
will begin speaking and say:

«Be strong and valiant,
show yourselves men of valour.
8 Do not be afraid or [tremble,
may your hearts not weaken],
do not be startled, or hesitate in front of them,
9 do not turn back, or [...]
For they are a wicked congregation
and all their deeds are in darkness
10 and to it go their desires,
[...] from their refuge,
their power is like smoke that disappears,
and all the assembly of their hordes
11 [...] will not be found.

All the essence of their being
swiftly vanishes.
12 [...]
Exert yourselves for God's battle
for today is the {day}/time/ of war.
13 [...]
against all flesh.
The God of Israel is raising his hand
with his marvellous power.
14 [...] against all the wicked spirits
[...] heroes of the gods girding themselves for battle,
and the formations of the holy ones
15 [gather] for the day of [...]
16 God of Israel [...]

Col. XVI   *1* until is complete all [...]
The God of Israel has summoned the sword
against all the nations
and with the holy ones of his people
he will perform marvels».

2 Blank 3 They shall act in accordance with all this rule on this [day], when they are positioned opposite the camp of the Kittim. Afterwards, the priest will blow for them the trumpets *4* of memorial, and the gates of battle shall open. The infantrymen shall go out and take up positions in columns between the lines. The priests will blow for them *5* the call of formation, and the columns [shall deploy] at the blow of the trumpets until each man is stationed in his position. The priests shall blow for them *6* a second call [... for the atta]ck. When they are at the side of the Kittim line, at throwing distance, each man will take up in his hand his weapons *7* of war. The six [priests shall blow] the trumpets of slaughter with a shrill, staccato note to direct the battle. And the levites and all the throng *8* with ram's horns shall blow [the battle call] with a deafening noise. And when the sound goes out, they shall set their hand to finish off the severely wounded of the Kittim. And all *9* the throng will interrupt the sound [of the call, and the priests] shall continue blowing the trumpets of slaughter, leading the battle against the Kittim. *10 Blank 11* When [Belial] girds himself to assist the sons of darkness, and there start to fall the dead of the infantry in accordance with God's mysteries, and all those appointed for battle are tested by them, *12* the priests shall blow the rallying trumpets in order to make the other line of reserves go out to fight and they shall take up position between the lines. *13* And for those involved in the fight, they shall blow the withdrawal. The High Priest will approach and take up position in front of the line, and will strengthen *14* their hearts [with the power of Go]d , and their hands in their fight. *Blank 15* And starting to speak he will say:

«[…] the heart of his people
he has tested in the crucible,
[…] your dead,
for from ancient times you heard
16 in the mysteries of God […]
17 […]

Col. XVII   *1* He will place peace for them in the burns
[…]
to those tested in the crucible;
he will whet the weapons of war
and they shall not be blunted until
[all the] wicked [nations are destroyed.]
2 And you, remember the trial
[of Nadab and Abi]hu, sons of Aaron,
a judgment by which God showed his holiness
to the eyes of all the people;
3 while Eleazar] and Itamar
he confirmed in his everlasting covenant.
Blank
4 And you, exert yourselves and do not fear.
They incline towards chaos and emptiness,
and their support is the void[…]
5 [To the God of] Israel what is and will be
[…] in all that always happens.
This is the day appointed to humiliate
and abase the prince of the dominion of evil.
6 He has sent everlasting aid
to the lot redeemed
by the power of the majestic angel
for the dominion *Blank* of Michael
in everlasting light.
7 He will the covenant of Israel shine with joy,
peace and blessing to God's lot.
He will exalt the service of Michael above all the gods
8 and the dominion of Israel over all flesh.
Justice will rejoice in the heights
and all the sons of your truth
will have enjoyment in everlasting knowledge.

And you, sons of the covenant,
9 be strong in God's crucible
until he shakes his hand
and fills up his crucibles,
his mysteries concerning your being».
Blank

10 After these words they shall blow for them /the priests/ in order to arrange the battalions of the line: the columns shall deploy at the sound of the trumpets 11 until each man is in his position. The priests shall blow a second call on the trumpets, the signal for attack. When 12 [the infantry]men reach [the side of the] Kittim line, at throwing distance, each man will take his weapons of war in his hand and the priests shall blow the 13 trumpets of the slain. [The levites and all] the throng with ram's horns shall blow the call for war. The infantry-men will stretch out their hand against the army 14 of the Kittim. [When the sound of the call ends], they shall start to finish off the severely wounded. All the throng will stop at the sound of the call, but the priests 15 shall continue blowing [the trumpets of the slain] and the battle against the Kittim will con-tinue [...] those struck in front of them. 16 In the third lot [...] 17 [...] God [...]

Col. XVIII   1 [...] when the mighty hand of God is raised against Belial and against all the army of his dominion for an everlasting blow. 2 [...] and the call of the holy ones when they pursue Assyria; the sons of Japhet shall fall without rising; the Kittim shall be crushed without a 3 [remnant...] when the hand of the God of Israel is raised against the whole horde of Belial. At this instant, the priests shall blow 4 the memorial trumpets and all the battle lines shall combine against them and shall divide up against all the camps of the Kittim 5 to elimi-nate them. And when the sun travels towards its setting on this day, the High Priest will take up position, likewise the priests and levites who are 6 with him and the ch[iefs of the men] of the rule. And there they shall bless the God of Israel. They shall begin speaking and say:

7 «Blessed be your name, God of gods,
for you have made [your people] great
[in order to work] wonders.
From of old you have kept for us your covenant.
You have opened for us many times
the gates of salvation.
8 By reason of your covenant
[you have removed] our unhappiness
in your goodness towards us.
You, just God, have acted

for the Glory of your Name.
Blank
9 *Blank*
10 [...]
   You have performed with us miracle after miracle.
   From of old there has not been anything similar.
   /For/ you know our appointed time
   and today it shines for us.
11 With us you show a merciful hand
   in everlasting redemption,
   removing for ever the enemy dominion
   with mighty hand.
12 [...] against our enemies
   for complete extermination.
   And now there approaches us the day
   of pursuing their mob,
13 for you [...]
   have overcome the heart of the heroes
   and no-one is able to stand.
   To you the might,
   in your hand the battle,
   and there is no [...]
14 the moment predetermined according to your will [...]

Col. XIX   1 [...] for the heroes.
   For the Lord is holy
   and the King of glory is with us.
   The army [of his spirits
   is with our infantry and cavalry
   like clouds and dew]
2 to cover the land
   like torrential rain which pours down justice
   on every[thing that grows.
   Get up, hero,
3 take your prisoners, oh glorious one,
   co]llect your spoil, wonder-worker!
   Place your hand on the neck of your foes
   and your foot [on the piles of the dead!
4 Strike the nations, your enemies,]
   and may your sword consume flesh!
   Fill your land with glory
   and your inheritance with blessing:

[a herd of flocks in your fields,
5 gold, silver, and precious stones in] your palaces!
Rejoice, Zion, passionately!
Exult, all the cities of Ju[dah!
Open the gates for ever
6 so that] the wealth of the nations [can go in to you!]
Their kings shall wait on you,
[all your oppressors] lie prone in front of you,
and they shall lick the dust of your feet].
7 [Daughters] of my people, shout with jubilant voice!
Deck yourselves with splendid finery!
Rule over the gover[nment of …]
8 […] Israel, in order to reign for ever. *Blank*

9 […] on this night to rest until the morning. And in the morning they shall go
out to the place of the line *10* […] the heroes of the Kittim and the horde of
Assyria and the army of all the peoples […] *11* fallen there by God's sword.
And the High Priest will approach […] *12* […] of war and all the chiefs of the
lines and their enlisted men […] *13* […] the dead of the Kittim. And they shall
praise there the God of [Israel…]

B   *Copies from Cave 4*

4QWar Scroll^a (4Q491 [4QM^a])

Frags. 1–3   *1* Qorah and his congregation […] judgment […] *2* in the sight of all
the assembly [… the judg]ment like a sign […] *3* and the chief of his angels is
with his [armies] to direct the hand in battle […] And this is the regulation (?)
for the mounts and the caval[ry…] *4* And God's hand will strike […] for eternal
destruction […] and they shall atone for you […] all the prin[ces …] shall not
go towards the enemy lines […] *6* This is the rule in their camps and in […]
and in their divisions […] round about, outside […] And the woman, the
under-age boy, everyone who is affec[ted by impurity in his flesh…] *7* […] and
the smiths and the smelters and those enlisted to be […] for their divisions […]
in the line until their return. *Blank* There are to be two thousand cubits between
the ca[mps and the place of «the hand», and no] *8* nakedness shall be seen in its
surroundings. And when they go out to free the battle [to humiliate the enemy,
there shall be] among them (some) allotted {…} by drawing lots, from each
tribe, according to their enlisted men, for each day's task. *9* That day, all the
tribes shall go out of the camps to the house of me[eting…] towards them shall
go the [pri]ests, the levites, and all the chiefs of the camps. *Blank* And they shall
pass there in front of […] *10* in thousands, in hundreds, in fifties and in tens.

And everyone who is not [pure from his «spring»] that night, shall not go with them to battle, because the angels of holiness are together with their rows [...] *11* [In the advan]ce of the line designated for battle on that day, to pass to [...] to the battle. They shall set up three lines, one line behind another, and shall put a gap between the lines [...] *12* [They shall march] to the battle in turns. These are the infantry-men; next to them the men [of the cavalry, who shall stay between the li]nes. If they lay an ambush for one line, three lines wil] be ambushed [at a dis]tance, and they will not ri[se...] *13* [...] the battle. And the trumpets of alarm [...] they will hear them, and the men of [the infantry will set their hand on their sword to bri]ng it down on the guilty badly wounded. Afterwards, the ambush will rise from its position, and it, too, will form up in lines [...] *14* The meeting: on the right and on the left, be[hind and in front, the fo]ur dir[ections...] in the battle of extermination. And all the lines which have approached for battle with the en[emy ...] *15* together. The first line will [go out to battle,] and the second will rem[ain ...] in its position. When the first have carried out their part, they will withdraw and the[y will rise up ...] *16* The sec[ond: ...] organizing itself for the battle. The second line will carry out its part and will withdraw and will re[main in its position.] *17* The th[ird ...] the levites and the m[en of the ru]le. The priests will blow the trumpets every time [...] *18* A belt [of intertwined byssus, violet, purple and crimson, with many-hued patterns, craftwork, and upon their heads (they will wear) tur]bans. [They shall not bring them into the sanctuary, be]cause these are the clo[thes of war.] *19* According to all this rule [...] the chiefs of the camps [...] *20* [...] all [...] they will carry it out to exterminate [...]

Frag. 4   *1* [...] ... [...] ... [...] *2* [...fro]m twenty years old and upwards [...] *3* [...] in accordance with these precepts [...] *4* [...] the enemy, to [...] the horn of wick[edness...]

Frags. 5–6 (= 1QM XII, 1)   *1* [For there is a multitude of holy ones in heaven, and] a host of angels in your hol[y] dwelling [to praise] your name. And the chosen ones of the holy people ...

Frag. 7 (= 1QM XIII, 8–9)   *1* [... for times eter]nal. [In all the edicts of your glory there has been a memorial of your clemency in our midst, in aid of the rem-nant,] *2* [the survivors of your covenant,] and in order to number [the deeds of your truth, and the justice of your wonderful might...]

Frags. 8–10 *col.* I (= 1QM XIV, 4–18)   *1* [his name in joyful] chorus. [...] *Blank* [...] *2* [They] shall begin to speak and say: «Blessed be the Go[d of Israel, the one who] keeps mercy for his covenant and pledges of deliverance for the people. He has called those who are tottering] *3* [to] prodigious exploits. He has gathered an assembly of na[tions] for destruction with no [remnant. In judgment he has lifted up the mel]ting heart, [he has opened the mouth] *4* of the dumb with God's marvels. The hands of the frail he has trained in war. The knees that shake he gives strength to stand upright. And he girds [the kidneys] *5* of those with [broken] backs. [Among the poor in spirit] is the authority over the hard heart. For the perfect[ones of the path all the wicked nations shall be destroyed. [Their] heroes *6* will not remain standing. Only we, the rem[nant of your people.] Blessed be your name, God of mercies, you have caused your favours to fall upon us during the empire of Beli[al.] *7* [In all the mysteries of his enmity, he has not separ]ated us from your covenant. [But his spirits of destruction] you have excluded from us when the men [of his empire] were scheming. *8* [You have protected the soul of] your redeemed ones. And now, you have raised [the fallen with your strength,] but those who arose, you cut down [to humiliate them.] *9* [For their heroes there is no] saviour, there is no refuge for their swift ones. To their most es[teemed you return scorn. All their useless] *10* [existence you have turned into] nothing. We, your people, will praise your name for the deeds of your truth; for your mighty deeds we will extol *11* [your splendour at every mom]ent and at the times indicated by your eternal edicts, [at the onset of day] and at night at the fall [of evening] *12* [and at dawn. For great is] the plan of your glory, and your marvellous mysteries on hi[gh;] in order to raise [from the dust for yourself and subdue] *13* [gods. Rise up, ri]se up, Oh God of gods, and be exalted with power, King of kin[gs!...] you have placed over *14* [...] they scatter before you, the sons of darkness, and your great light [... god]s and men *15* [...like a fire] which lights up the places of darkness and of ruin; in the places of the ruins of Sheol will bu[rn ...] the rebels *16* [...] in all the times appointed for ever. *Blank* [...] *17* [All the hy]mns of battle will they recite there, and afterwards they shall return to the ca[mp ...] there, on the order [...]

Frags. 8–10 *col.* II   *7* ... [...] *8* against the Kittim [...] *9* the infantrymen will set [their hand to finish off the badly wounded of the Kittim ...] *10* the fight against the Kittim [...] *11* the dead of the crucible to fall according to [the myste]ries of God, the priests shall blow the trumpets of recall ... [...] *12* the fight against the Kittim. In the first row [...] *13* The priest designated (?) for battle shall approach and place himself in front [of the first row ...] *14* will strengthen their hands with marvellous feats. He will start speaking and say: [...] *15* vengeance, to devour among gods and men, for [...] not [...] *16* flesh, except dust. And now [...] *17* and will {fire}/consume/ as far as Sheol. And the foundation of wickedness[...]

Frag. 11 *col.* I   *8* [...] has done terrible things marvellously [...] *9* [... in the stre]ngth of his power the just exult and the holy ones rejoice [...] in justice

10 […] he established Israel from eternity; his faithfulness and the mysteries of his prudence in […] courage *11* […] and the counsel of the poor for an eternal congregation. […] the perfect *12* […et]ernal; a throne of strength in the congregation of the gods above none of the kings of the East shall sit, and their nobles not […] silence (?) *13* […] my glory [is incomparable] and besides me no-one is exalted. And he does not come to me, for I reside in […], in the heavens, and there is no *14* […] … I am counted among the gods and my dwelling is in the holy congregation; […my de]sire is not according to the flesh [and] and all that is precious to me is in glory *15* […] holy [pl]ace. Who has been considered despicable on my account? And who is comparable to me in my glory? Who, like the sailors, will come back to tell? *16* […] Who […] sorrows like me? And who […] anguish who resembles me? There is no-one. He has been taught, but there is no comparable teaching. *17* […] And who will attack me when I open [my mouth]? And who can endure the flow of my lips? And who will confront me and retain comparison with my judgment? *18* […] For I am counted among the gods, and my glory is with the sons of the king. To me, pure gold, and to me, the gold of Ophir *19* […] *Blank* […] *Blank* […] *20* the just in the God of […] in the holy dwelling, sound […] *21* […] proclaim in the meditation of joy […] in eternal happiness; and there is no … […] *22* […] to establish the horn of … […] *23* […] to make known his power with strength […] *24* […] … […]

Frag. 11 *col.* II (= 1QM XVI, 3–14; XVII, 10–14)   *1* [with all this rule on this day, when they a]re po[sitioned opposite the camp of the Kittim. Afterwards, the priest will blow] *2* [for them the memorial trumpets, and the gates of ba]ttle shall o[pen. The infantrymen shall go out and take up positions in columns] *3* [between the lines. The priests will blow for them the ca]ll of forma[tion, and the columns shall deploy at the sound of the trumpets] *4* [until each man is stationed in his position. The pr]iests shall blow [for them a second call for the atta]ck. When they are at the side] *5* [of the Kittim line, at] throwing [dist]ance, each man will take up in his hand his weapons of [war. The six priests shall blow the trumpets of] *6* [the slain with a s]hrill and staccato [note] to direct the battle. And the levi[tes and all the throng with ram's horns shall blow the battle call] *7* with a deafening noise. And when the sound goes out, they shall set their ha[nd to finish off the severely wounded of the Kittim. And all the throng will stop the sound of the call …] *8* [and] will continue the battle against the Kittim. *Blank* [… When Belial girds himself to assist] *9* the sons of darkness, and there start to fall the dead of the infantry [in accordance with God's mysteries, and all those appointed for battle are tested by them, the priests] *10* shall blow in order to make the other line of reserves go out to the fig[ht and they shall take up position between the lines. And for those involved in the fight,] *11* they shall blow the withdrawal. The High Priest will approach and ta[ke up position in front of the line, and will strengthen their hearts with the power of God] *12* and their hands in their fight. [And starting to speak he will say: «...] the heart of his people, you have tested them in the crucible, [...your dead,] *13* for from of old you heard in the myste[ries of God ...] be in the thick of things and do not fear when ... [...] *14* [...] he is faithful, and his redeeming help [...] *15* [...the so]ns of truth, to turn aside the heart which melts and strengthen the he[art...] *16* [...the fig]ht this day. The God of Israel will humiliate [...] *17* [...] without it resisting. For God [it is the kingd]om, and for his people, salvat[ion ...] *18* [... of] little time for Belial, and covenant of God of peace for Israel, for all the appointed times [...] *19* After these words the priests shall blow for them to form a second battle against the Kit[tim. And when each man is stationed] *20* in his position, the priests shall blow a second call, the signal to approach. When they reach [the Kittim line, at throwing] *21* distance, each man will take his weapons of war in his hand and the priests shall blow the trum[pets of the slain...] *22* [... The levites and all] the throng with ram's horns shall blow a blast [...] *23* [... to fi]nish off the severely wounded guilty. The sound of [...] *24* [...] ... [...]

Frag. 13   *1* [...with] the gods ... [...] *2* [...] the least amongst you will pursue a thousand [...] *3* [... eter]nal. [After these wor]ds, [the priests] shall blow [the call for formation, and the columns shall deploy] *4* [at the sound of the trum]pets. When they take up position in their battalions, each one in [his position, the priests shall blow a second call] *5* [for the attack. And when they are at the side] of the Kittim line, at throwing distance, [each man] will set his hand [on his weapons of war. The priests shall blow for the continuation] *6* [of the fight, with the trum]pets of the slain, with a shrill and staccato note. And the levites and all [the throng with ram's horns shall blow the battle call. And the rows] *7* [shall fig]ht one behind the other, without a space between them, because [...] All the people will lift up a united voice, saying: [...] *8* [...] ... [...]

Frag. 15   *1* [...] without [...] *2* ... and your praises [...] *3* And we, behold we take up position to approach [...] *4* [...] *Blank* [...] *5* [...] he will begin speaking and say to you: «Be strong and courageous [...] *6* [... for the hand of] God is stretched over all the nations. No [...] *7* [.. to the God Most] High, kingship, and to his people, salvation. [...] *8* [...] their impurity; the gods shall approach upon you [...] *9* [...] to throw all their corpses [...] *10* [...] and all the spirits of their lot [...] *11* [...] eternal together with [...] *12* fight [...]

Frag. 16   *1* [...] ... [...] *2* [...] and among the whole congregation [...] *3* [...] his holy people, a kingdom of prie[sts...] *4* [...] all Israel will gat[her] in Jerusalem [...] *5* [...] they shall exalt the wonders of [...]

4QWar Scroll*b* (4Q492 [4QM*b*])

Frag. 1 (= 1QM XIX, 1–13)   *1* for the heroes. For [the Lord is holy and the King of glory is with us. The host of his spirits is with our infantry and cavalry like clouds] *2* to cover the la[nd, like torrential rain which pours down justice on every[thing that grows. Get up, hero, take your prisoners, oh] *3* glorious one, co[llect your spoil, wonder-worker! Place your hand on the neck of your enemies and your foot on the piles of the fallen! Strike the nations,] *4* your foes, and may your sword [consume fl]esh! [Fill your land with glory and your inheritance with blessing: a herd of flocks in your fields, silver,] *5* and gold in your palaces! *Blank* Rejoice, Zion, passionately! [Exult, all the cities of Judah! Open] *6* the gates for ever so that the wealth of the nations can go in to you! Their kings shall wait on you, [all your oppressors lie prone in front of you, and the dust of] *7* your feet shall they lick. *Blank* Daughters of my people, shout with jubilant voice! Deck yourselves [with splendid finery! Rule over the government of …] *8* your camps. and Israel for an eternal kingdom. *Blank* Afterwards, they shall gather in the camp on this night [to rest until the morning.] *9* [And in the] morning they shall go out to the place of the line where there fell the heroes of the Kit[tim and the ho]rde [of Assyria and the army of all the peoples] *10* [gathered together. If] a large number of the wounded died without burial, (it is) because they fell there by God's sword. [And the High Priest] *11* [and his second, and the priests,] and the levites, [… of war and al]l the chiefs of the lines, [and their enlisted men,…] *12* […] gathered in their positions, over [the dead of the Kittim. And they shall praise] there the God of Israel [saying: …] *13* […] to the God Most High […] … […]

4QWar Scroll*c* (4Q493 [4QM*c*])

1 the war. And the priests, sons of Aaron, shall station themselves in front of the lines *2* and blow the memorial trumpets. And afterwards, they shall open the gat[es] to the soldiers *3* of the infantry. The priests shall blow the battle trumpets [to strike] the lines *4* of the nations. The priests shall go out from among the severely wounded and station themselves [on one side] and on the other of […] *5* on the side of the catapult and the ballista, and they shall not desecrate the oil of their priesthood [with the blood] of the severely wounded, *6* nor shall they approach any of the lines of the soldiers of the infantry. They shall blow a shrill note so that the men *7* of war sally out to approach between the lines of the trumpets of [the slain.] And they shall begin *8* to stretch out the hand for battle. When their part is accomplished, they shall blow for them the trumpets of withdrawal *9* so that they enter the gates; and the second line shall go out. In accordance with this rule the le[vites] shall blow *10* for them during their part: in their sallies, they shall blow the trumpets [of recall] for them,

11 and when they complete (them), the trumpets [of alarm,] and on their withdrawal, they shall blow [for them the trumpets] *12* of assembly. According to [this ord]inance shall they blow for a[ll the li]nes. *Blank* [...] *13* [...] over the trumpets of the Sabbaths [...] *14* [... over the] perpetual [sacrifice] and the holocaust is written [...]

4QWar Scroll^d (4Q494 [4QM^d])

Frag. 1 (= 1QM II, 1–3) *1* [the chiefs of] the tribes [...] *2* And the priests and the levites and the chiefs of [...] *3* the priests; and the same for the levites. And the divisions [...They shall arrange the chiefs of the priests behind the] *4* High Priest and his second, twelve chiefs [to serve in perpetuity before God. And the twenty-six chiefs of the divisions] *5* shall serve in their divisions, [and after them the chiefs of the levites, to serve always, twelve, one per tribe.] *6* [And after]wards, the chiefs [of their divisions shall each serve in their place...]

4QWar Scroll^e (4Q495 [4QM^e])

Frag. 1 (= 1QM X, 9–10) *1* [And who (is) like your people,] Israel, [whom you chose from among all the peoples of the earth, a people of] *2* [holy ones of] the covenant, le[arned in the law...]

Frag. 2 (= 1QM XIII, 9–12) *1* [You,] God, have crea]ted us for you, [eternal people, and you have made us fall into the lot of light in accordance with your truth. From of old, the Prince of light] *2* you appointed to assist us, [and in ...and all the spirits of truth are under his dominion.] *3* You created [Belial for the pit, angel of enmity; his domain is darkness, his counsel is for evil and wickedness. All the spirits of his lot,] *4* angels of des[truction walk in the laws of darkness...]

4QWar Scroll^f (4Q496 [4papQM^f])

Col. 1 *frag.* 3 (= 1QM I, 4–9) *3* [And in his time, he will go out] with great [rage] to wage war against [the kings of the North, and his anger will exterminate] *4* [and cut off the horn of Is]rael. There will follow a time of [salvation for the people of God and a period of rule for all the men of his lot,] *5* [and of everlasting destruction for all the l]ot of Belial. There will be [great] pa[nic among the sons of Japhet, Ashur will fall,] *6* [and there will be no help for him;] the rule [of the Kittim] will come to an end, [wickedness having been defeated, with no remnant remaining,] *7* [and there will be no escape for] /all/ the sons of darkness. And the sons of [justice shall shine in all the edges of the earth, they shall go on illuminating,] *8* [up to the end of a]ll the periods of darkn[ess; and in the time of God, his exalted greatness will shine for all the eternal times,] ₉ [for peace and blessing,] glory and jo[y, and long days for all the sons of light. And on the day on which the Kittim fall, there will be a fight...]

Col. I *frags.* 2 + 1 (= 1QM I, 11–17)   ₂ [The sons of light and the lot of darkness shall battle together for God's might, between the roar of a huge multitude and the shout of] gods ₃ [and of men, on the day of the calamity. It will be a time of suffering for a]ll the people redeemed by God. Of a]ll their sufferings, ₄ [none will be like this, from its haste (?) until eternal redemption is fulfilled. And on the day of] their war ₅ [against the Kittim, they shall go out to destruction. In the war, the sons of light shall be the strongest during three lots, in order to strike down wickedness; and in th]ree (others), [the army of Belial] will gird themselves ₆ [in order to force the lot of ... to retreat. The infantry battalions shall melt the heart, but God's might will stren]gthen the heart of the sons of [light.] ₇ [And in the seventh lot, God's great hand will subdue Belial, and all the angels of] his dominion and al[l the men] ₈ [of his lot. ... the holy ones, he will shine out to assist the ...] truth, for the destruction of ₉ [the sons of darkness ...] ... [...]

Col. II *frag.* 7 (1QM II, 5–6)   ₁ [to prepare the pleasant incense for [God's] approval, [to atone for all his congregation and in order to grow fat] ₂ [in perpetuity before him at the table of] his glory. [They shall arrange all these] ₃ [during the appointed time of the year of] release. During the thirty-[three years] ₄ [remaining of the war,] the famo[us] men [called...]

Col. II *frags.* 6–5 (= 1QM II, 9–12)   ₁ [... During the thirty-five years of service, the war will be prepared during six] years; ₂ [and all the congregation together will prepare it. And the war of the divisions (will take place) during the remaining twe]nty-nine years. ₃ [During the first year, they shall wage war] against Aram-Naharaim; during the second, ₄ [against the sons of Lud; during the third they shall wage war against the remnant of the sons of Aram,] against Uz ₅ [and Hul, Togal and Mesha, who are beyond the Euphrates; during the fourth and the] fifth, ₆ [they shall wage war against the sons of Arpachsad; during the sixth and seventh they shall wage war] against all

Col. III *frag.* 13 (= 1QM II, 13–14)   ₁ [... during the ninth they shall wa]ge war against the sons of Ishmael and Ke[tura;] ₂ [and during the fo]llowing [ten years] the war will be divided [against all the sons of Ham,] ₃ [according to their clans, in their dw]ellings; and during the [following] ten [years] ₄ [the war will be divided up against a]ll the sons of Japhet, in their dwell[ings.]

Col. III *frag.* 18 (= 1QM II, ?–III, 2)   ₂ [...] which [...] ₃ [...] they shall write [...]

4 [...] *Blank* [...] *5* [...the bat]tle formations, and the [rallying] trump[ets of the formations...] *6* [...] and the trumpe[ts of alarm of the slain,... *7* [...] the evil [...] *8* [...] *Blank* [...] they shall write: «Ral[lied by God»....]

Col. IV *frag.* 12 (= 1QM III, 6–7)   *1* [«Withdrawal of mercy from those who ha]te God». [...] *2* [And on the trumpets of] battle [formations they shall write:] *3* [...And] on the trumpets for [rallying] *4* [the infantrymen when the gates of] battle [open so they can go out]

Col. IV *frag.* 11 (= 1QM III, 9–11)   *1* [And on the trumpets of pursuit they shall write:] «God [has struck all the sons of darkness, he shall not cause his wrath to return, until they are exterminated».] *2* [And when they retreat from battle against the en]emy to ret[urn to the line, they shall write on the trumpets] *3* [of retreat: «May God re-assemble». And on the tru]mpets [of the path of return from battle with the enemy, to go back to the congregation of] *4* [Jerusalem, they shall write: «Exultations of God in a peaceful] return» [...]

Col. IV *frag.* 10 (= 1QM III, 13–15)   *1* [Rule of the banners of all] the congregation in order of companies. *3* [On the large] banner /of the chief/ which goes at the head of [all the people they shall write:] *4* [«God's people», and the name of Israel] and of Aaron /and the [name] of the prince./ [Above the banner of the camp chiefs of] *5* three tribes [they shall write: ...]

Col. V *frag.* 16 (= 1QM III, ?–IV, 2)   *2* [...] the trum[pets...] *3* [...] ... [...] *4* [And on the banner of Merari] they shall write: «God's offering» [and the name of the prince of Merari and the names of the commanders of] *5* [his thousands. And on] the banner of the thousand [they shall write: «God's Fury unleashed against Belial and against all the men of] *6* [his lot so that no] remnant [(is left)]» and the [name of the commander of the thousand ...]

C *Texts connected with the War Scroll*

4QWar Scroll^g (4Q285 [4QM^g ?])

Frags. 1–2 (= 11Q14)   *1* [...] before Israel [...] *2* [...] for eternal centuries. [And blessed (be) ...] *3* [And blessed be all his holy angels. May] the Most High God [bless] you, [may he show you his face,] *4* [and for you may he open his] good [treasure] which is in the heavens, [to cause to fall upon your lands rains of] *5* [blessing, dew and] frost, late and early rains in their season, to give [you fruit, the harvests of] *6* [wheat, of wine and of] oil in plenty. And for [you] the land will yield [superb fruits. And you shall eat them] *7* [and be replete. In your land] there will be no miscarriages or [illness; drought and blight] *8* will not be seen in your harvests; there will be no disease [or stumbling blocks in your congregation, and evil will vanish] *9* from the land. There will be no pestilence [in your land.] For God is with [you and the holy angels are in the midst of your Community. And his] *10* holy [name] is invoked over [you …] *11* […] and within you […] interior

Frag. 4   *1* […] *2* […] the Prince of the Congregation and all Is[rael …] *3* […] the Kittim […] *4* […] upon … […] *5* […] the Kittim. *Blank* […] *6* [… the Pri]nce of the Congregation as far as the sea […] *7* […] in front of Israel at that time […] *8* […] (he) will station himself opposite them and take up position against them […] *9* […] they shall return to dry land at the time of […] *10* […] they shall lead him […]

Frag. 5   *1* [… as] the Prophet Isaiah [said] *Isa 10:34*: «[The most massive of the] *2* [forest] shall be cut [with iron and Lebanon, with its magnificence,] will fall. A shoot will emerge from the stump of Jesse […] *3* […] the bud of David will go into battle with […] *4* […] and the Prince of the Congregation will kill him, the bu[d of David …] *5* […] and with wounds. And a priest will command […] *6* […] the destruction of the Kittim […]

11QBlessings (11Q14[11QBer])

1 […] and they shall bless in the name [of the God of] *2* Israel. And they shall start speaking [and say: …] Israel. May they be blessed *3* in the name of the Most High God […] and blessed be your holy Name *4* for everlasting centuries. *Blank 6* May the God Most High bless you, may he show you his face, and for you open *7* his good treasure which is in the heavens, to make it come down upon your lands: *Blank 8* rains of blessing, dew and frost, early and late rains in their season, to give you the fruits, *9* the produce of wheat, of wine and of oil in plenty. And for you the land will produce superb fruits. *10* And you shall eat them and be replete. In your land there will be no miscarriages *11* or sickness: drought and blight will not be seen in your harvests; *12* [there will be neither] stealing of children (?) nor obstacles in your congregation, and evil will vanish from [the land.] *12* [the sword will not pass] through your land. For God is with you and the [holy] angels *13* [are to be found] in your Community. And his holy Name is invoked over you.

4QWar Scroll^h (4Q471)

Frag. 1   *1* […] of all that […] *2* […] each one from his brother; and from the sons of […] *3* […] they shall always be with him and […] *4* a man from each tribe *5* […] and from the levites *6* two […] and they sh[all serve …] always, each

7 [...] so that they will be instructed in the reg[ulations...] *8* [...] in their divisions [...] *9* [...]

Frag. 2   *1* [...] for the time when you commanded them not to *2* [...] and you have been disloyal to his covenant *3* [... and you] said: «Let us fight our battles, for he saves us» *4* [... your ch]ampions shall be subdued and they shall not know that he scorns *5* [...] be men for war and you shall be numbered *6* [...] ... *Blank* You shall ask for a just judgment and the work of *7* [...] you shall extol. *Blank* And he will choose [...] the shout of *8* [...] you shall return [...] sweet

Frag. 4   *1* [...] ... [...] *2* [...] to keep the pledges of your covenant [...] *3* [...] all their armies, slow to anger[...] *4* [...] and to discourage their hearts from every [...] *5* [...sl]aves of darkness, for their judgment [...] *6* [...] in the wickedness of their lots [...] *7* [...] and to choose evil, and to [...] *8* [...] hates God, and he has established [...] *9* [...] all the good which [...] *10* [...] the frenzy of his revenge [...]

Frag. 5   *1* [...] (to) God and to [...] *2* [...] for ever. And he has placed us [...] *3* [... may he] judge his people with justice and [...] *4* [...] in all his precepts [...] *5* [...] for us, in our perversion [...]

4QWords of Michael (4Q529)

1 Words of the book which Michael spoke to the angels of God [...] *2* He said: 'I found there troops of fire [...] *3* [...] nine mountains: two to the Eas[t ...] *4* [and two to the] South. There I saw the angel Gabriel [...] *5* ... and I explained to him his vision'. And he said to me: [...] *6* It is written in my book that the Great One, the Lord Eternal, [...] *7* the sons of Ham to the sons of Shem. And now, the Great One, the Lord Eternal [...] *8* when *keshabin* from *azdara* (?) drip [...] *9* See, a city will be built to the name of the Great [Lord Eternal ...] *10* all that is wicked shall be done before the Great One, Lo[rd Eternal ...] *11* but the Great One, Lord Eternal, will remember his creature [...] *12* [to the Great] One, Lord Eternal; to him the rewards and to him [...] *13* in distant lands there will be a man [...] *14* is he. And he will say to him: 'Look, this [...] *15* to me the silver and the gold [...] ... [...] *16* [...] justice [...]

2 The Rule of the Congregation

1QRule of the Congregation (1Q28a [1QSa])

Col. I   *1* And this is the rule of the congregation of Israel in the final days, when they gather [in community to wa]lk *2* in accordance with the regulation of the sons of Zadok, the priests, and the men of the covenant who have turn[ed away from the pa]th *3* of the people. These are the men of his counsel who have kept the covenant in the midst of wickedness to atone [for the e]arth. *4* When they come, they shall assemble all those who come, including children and women, and they shall read into their ea[rs] *5* all the regulations of the covenant, and shall instruct them in all its precepts, so that they do not stray in their [errors.] *6 Blank* And this is the rule for all the armies of the congregation, for all native Israelites. From his y[outh] *7* [they shall edu]cate him in the book of HAGY, and according to his age, instruct him in the precepts of the covenant, and he wi[ll receive] *8* [ins]truction in its regulations; during ten years he will be counted among the boys. At the age of twenty y[ears, he will transfer] *9* [to] those enrolled to enter the lot amongst his family and join the holy community. He shall not [approach] *10* a woman to know her through carnal intercourse until he is fully twenty years old, when he knows [good and] *11* evil. Then she shall be received to give witness against him (about) the precepts of the law and to take his place in the proclamation of the precepts. *12* And on his completion... *Blank* At the age of twenty-five years, he shall enter to take his place among the «foundations» of the holy *13* congregation to perform the service of the congregation. And at thirty years (of age) he shall approach to arbitrate in disputes *14* and judgments, and to take his place among the chiefs of the thousand of Israel, the commanders of a hundred, commanders of fifty, *15* [commanders] of ten, the judges and the officials and their tribes with all their families, [according to the dec]ision of the sons of *16* [Aa]ron, the priests, and of all the chiefs of the clans of the congregation, as the lot for him comes out, to take his place in the duties, *17* to go out and to come in before the congregation. And in accordance with his intelligence and the perfection of his behaviour, he shall gird his loins to remain steadfast, doing *18* the allotted duty among his brothers. Depending on whether (he has) much or a little, one will be more or less honoured than his fellow. *19* When the years of a man increase, they shall assign him a task in the service of the congregation matching his strength. No man who is a simpleton *20* shall enter the lot to hold office in the congregation of Israel for dispute or judgment, or to perform a task of the congregation, *21* or to go out to war to subdue the nations; merely, his family shall inscribe him in the army register, *22* and he will do his service in the forced labour to the extent of his ability. The sons of Levi shall each stay in his post, *23* under the authority of the sons of Aaron, to make all the congregation come in and go out, each

one in his rank, under the direction of the chiefs *24* of the clans of the congregation, as commanders, judges /and officials/, according to the number of all
their armies, under the authority of the sons of Zadok, the priests, *25* [and of
all] the chiefs of the clans of the congregation. *Blank* And if there is a convocation of all the assembly for a judgment, or for the community council, or for
a convocation of war, they shall sanctify themselves during three days, so that
every one who comes *27* is pre[pared for the cou]ncil. These are the men who
are to be summoned to the community council from ten... *Blank*: all *28* the wi[se
men] of the congregation, the intelligent and those learned in perfect behaviour
and the men of valour, together with *29* [the chiefs of the tri]bes and all the
judges, the officials, the chiefs of thousands, the chiefs of [hundreds,]

Col. II   *1* of fifties and of tens, and the levites, (each one) in the mid[st of his
divi]sion of service. These *2* are the famous men, those summoned to the assembly, those gathered for the community council in Israel *3* under the authority of the sons of Zadok, the priests. No man, defiled by any of the impurities
4 of a man, shall enter the assembly of these; and everyone who is defiled by
them should not be *5* established in his office amongst the congregation. And
everyone who is defiled in his flesh, paralysed in his feet or *6* in his hands,
lame, blind, deaf, dumb or defiled in his flesh with a blemish *7* visible to the
eyes, or the tottering old man who cannot keep upright in the midst of the
assembly, *8* these shall not enter to take their place among the congregation of
famous men, for the angels *9* of holiness are among their congre[gation.] And
if one of these has something to say to the holy council, *10* they shall investigate
it in private, but the man shall not enter in the midst of [the congregation,]
because he is defiled. *11* This is the assembly of famous men, [those summoned
to] the gathering of the community council, when [God] begets *12* the Messiah
with them. [The] chief [priest] of the all the congregation of Israel shall enter,
and all *13* [his brothers, the sons] of Aaron, the priests [summoned] to the assembly, the famous men, and they shall sit *14* befo[re him, each one] according
to his dignity. After, [the Me]ssiah of Israel shall ent[er] and before him shall
sit the chiefs *15* [of the clans of Israel, each] one according to his dignity, according to their [positions] in their camps and in their marches. And all *16* the
chiefs of the cl[ans of the congre]gation with the wise [men and the learned]
shall sit before them, each one according *17* to his dignity. And [when] they
gather at the table of community [or to drink] the new wine, and the table of
18 community is prepared [and] the new wine [is mixed] for drinking, [no–one
should stretch out] his hand to the first-fruit of the bread *19* and of the [new
wine] before the priest, for [he is the one who bl]esses the first-fruit of bread
20 and of the new wine [and stretches out] his hand towards the bread before
them. Afterwards, the Messiah of Israel shall stretch out his hand *21* towards
the bread. [And after, he shall] bless all the congregation of the community,

each [one according to] his dignity. And in accordance with this regulation they shall act *22* at each me[al, when] at least ten m[en are gat]hered. *Blank*

3 Description of the New Jerusalem

2QNew Jerusalem (2Q4 [2QNJ ar])

Frag. 1   [And he led me to the interior of the city and measured each] *1* [block, length and width: fifty-one rods by] fifty-one [in a square,] *2* [three hundred and fifty-seven cubits on each si]de. And a peristyle arou[nd] *3* [the block, the portico of the street: three rods, twenty-one cubits.] Also he showed me all the measurements *4* [of the blocks. Between one block and another there is the street, six rods wide: cubits,] forty-two.

Frag. 3   *1* [...] one [...] *2* [...] and he measured up to the sapphire door [...] *3* [...] which is before [...] *4* [...] the wall [...]

Frag. 4   *1* their flesh [...] *2* as a pleasant offering [...] *3* and they shall bring into the temple [...] *4* eight *sheahs* of finest fl[our ...] *5* and they shall wave the bread [...] [...] *6* to the East upon the alt[ar ...] *7* lined up upon the ta[ble ...] *8* two rows of loa[ves ...] *9* the bread. And they shall take the bread [...] *10* to the West. And they shall be shar[ed ...] *11* And I looked until [...] *12* the list (?) [...] *13* the elders among them and fourteen pri[ests ...] *14* the priests. *Blank* The two loaves which [...] *15* I stood until one of the two loaves was given [...] *16* with him. *Blank* I was watching until it was given to a[ll ...] *18* [...] of the ram to each person [...] *19* [...] until the moment when they sat down [...] *20* [...] in all [...] *21* [...] ... [...]

Frag. 8   *1* [...] ... [...] *2* [...] ten. The fou[rth] row [...] *3* [...] the walls of whi[te] stone [...] *4* [...] the others, the outer side, twenty [...] *5* [...] and they shall make atonement with it upon [it ...] *6* [...] and yet it will not be ended. Each day [...] *7* [...] the courtyard. And he showed me [...] another outside [...] *8* [...] one hundred and ten [...]

4QNew Jerusalem*ᵃ* (4Q554 [4QNJ*ᵃ* ar])

Frag. 1 *col.* I   *9* [...] ... *10* [...] and all those buildings *11* [...from the] East [cor-ner] which is to the North *12* [...] thirty-five stadia; and he secured *13* [... the door of] Simeon; and from this door up to the central door *14* [... and he se-cured this door to what they call door *15* [...] South thirty-five stadia *16* [... and from] this door he measured up to the corner *17* [... and fr]om this corner to the West *18* [...] they call the door of Joseph *19* [... sta]dia, twenty-four. And he secured *20* [... and from] this [do]or he measured up to the door *21* [... the do]or of Reuben and [from] this [do]or *22* [...] and from this corner he mea-sured up to

Frag. 1 *col.* II   7 ... [...] and from the door *8* of the centre [twenty-four] stadia. [...] this [door] they ca[ll] the door of Naphtali. And he measured from this *9* door up to the door which [...:] twenty-four stadia. And he measured this door: they call it *10* door of Asher. And he me[asured from this do]or up to the corner which is to the East: *11* twenty-four stadia. *Blank* *12* And he led me to the interior of the city and me[asured each bl]ock, length and breadth: *13* fifty-one rods by fifty-one, in a square, [all around] three hundred and fifty-seven cubits *14* on each side. And (there was) a peristyle around the block, the portico of the street: *15* three rods, twenty-one cubits. Also he showed me all the measurements of all the blocks; between one block and another *16* there is the street: width, six rods, forty-two cubits; and the main streets which run *17* from East to West: the width of two of these streets is of [ten rods;] cubits: *18* seventy; and he measured the third, which passes to the [left] of the temple: *19* eighteen rods in width, [one hundred and twenty-six cubits.] And the width *20* of the streets that run from South [to North: two of them are] nine rods *21* and four cubits each street, [sixty-seven] cubits. And he measured the width of [the middle one, which is the cen]tre *22* of the city: [thirteen] rods [and a cubit, ninety-two cubits.] And all the streets and the city [were paved with white stone]

Frag. 1 *col.* III   *13* and the wi[dth of ...] its dimensions are: cubits, [... He measured the width of each threshold:] *14* rods, [two; cubits, fourt]een; from the lintel, [one cubit... He measured over each threshold] *15* its jambs, and measured inside the threshold: its length [is thir]teen cubits and its width ten cubits. [...] *16* And he led me to the vestibule. There was another threshold and another door to the side of the inner wall, on the right side, *17* with the dimensions of the outer door: four cubits in width and seven cubits in height, with two rooms. In [front] *18* of this door, the entrance threshold, of one rod in width, seven cubits. The length of the entrance: two rods, cubits, *19* fourteen; and the height: two rods, fourteen cubits. And the door corresponding to this door, the one which opens to the block, has *20* the dimensions of the outer door. To the left of this entry he showed me a stairwell which goes ro[und and up:] its len[gth] *21* and its width are the same size: two rods by two, fourteen cubits. The do[ors which are opposite the other doors are] *22* the same sizes. And the column [within the space,] upon which the staircase goes round and u[p ...]

Frag. 2 *col.* I   *14* [...] two *15* [...] and rods *16* [...] the measurement of *17* [...] the city

Frag. 2 *col.* II   *13* [...] and its foundations, [width:] two rods; [cubits,] *14* fourteen; and its height: seven rods, forty-nine cubits. And all *15* the buildings in it are of sapphire and of rubies, and the windows (?) (are) of gold, and (have) one thousand *16* [four hundred] and thirty-two towers. Their length and their width are the same size: *17* [...] and their height, ten rods, *18* [seventy cubits...] fourteen *19* [...] two *20* [...] ... cubits *21* [...] two, to the door *22* [...] ... three, and the towers project

Frag. 2 col. III   *14* ... [...] *15* after him, and the kingdoms which [...] *16* Kittim (?) after him, all at the end of all [...] *17* many others and the chiefs with them. [...] *18* with them Adom and Moab and the sons of Ammon [...] *19* of Babel, all its land which shall not be fre[ed ...] *20* and they shall do evil to your descendants until the moment that [...] *21* with all the people [...] the kings [...] *22* and the peoples shall d[o] with them [...]

4QNew Jerusalem*b* (4Q555 [4QNJ*b* ar])

Frag. 1   *1* [...] And the staircase which [climbs up at its side] is four cubits wide, and goes round *2* [and upwards to a height of two rods, up to the roof.] *Blank* *3* [And he brought me into the block and showed me the houses there; from one porch to another,] fifteen; eight from the side up to the corner, *4* [and from the corner up to the other porch.] Length of the houses: three rods; cubits, twenty-one; and their width: *5* [two rods, fourteen cubits. And all the rooms the same.] Their height is two rods, fourteen cubits. Their door is in the middle; *6* [it is two rods, fourteen cubits, in width. And he measured the width of the middle of the houses and of their interior,] four cubits; length and height, one rod, seven cubits *7* [... The site is nineteen cubits] in length and twelve cubits in width. The house *8* [has twenty-two beds, and there are eleven lattice windows above the beds.] At their side is the outer gutter. *9* [And he has measured ... from the window: height, two cubits; width, ... cubits, and its thickness is the width of the wall. Height of] its inner part: cubits *10* [... and of the other ... cubits ...] two rods; cubits, fourteen *11* [...] to the South ... *12* [...] and the roof which is over them

5QNew Jerusalem (5Q15 [5QNJ ar])

Frag. 1 *col.* I   *1* [around,] three hundred and fifty-seven cubits on each side. And a peristyle around the block, the portico of the street: three rods, twenty-one cubits. *2* Also he showed me all the measurements of all the blocks. Between one block and another is the street, six rods in width, forty-two cubits. *3* And the main streets which run from East to West; width the streets: of two of them are of ten rods, seventy cubits; and he measured the third, the one which passes to the l[eft] of the temple: eighteen rods in width, [one hundred and twenty-six cubits. And the width of the streets which run from South *5* [to North:] two of them are nine rods and four cubits each one, sixty-seven cubits; the one in the mid[dle, which is in the cen]tre of the city, he measured its width: thirteen rods and a cubit, ninety-two cubits. All the streets of the city are paved with white stone *7* [...] alabaster and onyx. *Blank 8* [And he measured the four hundred] and eighty [posterns:] the wi[dth of] the posterns is two rods, [fourteen cubits...] *9* In each door there were stone jambs; the width of the ja[mbs] is [one] rod, [seven cubits.] *10* [He showed me the dimensions of] the twelve...The width of their doors of three rods, [twenty-one cubits.] *11* [Each door has two jambs;] width of the jambs: one and a half rods, ten and a half cubits ... *12* [On the side of each door were two to]wers, one on the right and the other on the left. Their height and their width [are the same size: five rods by five,] *13* thirty-three cubits. The staircase which skirts the inner door, to the right of the towers, goes up to the height of the to[wers and is five cubits in width. The towers] *14* [and the staircases are five rods by five, and five cubits, forty cubits on each side of the door [...] *15* And he showed me the dimensions of the porches of the blocks; their width is two rods, fourteen cubits; and the wi[dth of ...] their dimensions are ... cubits. *16* [He measured above each] threshold its jambs, and measured inside the threshold: its length is thirteen cubits and its width ten cubits. *18* And he led me inside the vestibule. There was there another threshold and another door to the side of the inner wall; on the right side, with the dimensions of the outer *19* door: four cubits in width and seven cubits in height, with two rooms. In front of this door, the entrance threshold, of one rod in width,

Col. II   *1* seven cubits. The length of the entrance: two rods, fourteen cubits, and the height: two rods, fourteen cubits. And the door *2* corresponding to this door, the one which opens to the block, has the dimensions of the outer door. To the left of this entry he showed me a stairwell *3* which goes round and up: its length and its width are the same size: two rods by two, fourteen cubits. The do[ors which are opposite] *4* the other doors are the same sizes. And the pillar within the space, upon which the staircase goes round and up, its width and its len[gth are six by six cubits] *5* squared. And the staircase which goes up at its side is four cubits in width, and goes round and up to a height of two rods, up to [the roof.] *6* And he brought me [to the interior of] the block and showed me the houses there, fifteen from one porch to another; eight from one side up to the corner, *7* and from the corner up to the other porch. Length of the houses: three rods; twenty-one cubits; and their width: *8* two rods, fourteen cubits. And all the rooms the same. Their height is two rods, fourteen cubits. Their door *9* is in the middle; it is two rods, fourteen cubits, in width. [And he measured the width of the middle] of the houses and of their interior [...] *10* four [cubits;] length and height, one rod, seven cubits [...] The site is nineteen cubits in length *11* and twelve cubits in width. The house has twenty-two beds, and there are eleven lattice windows above [the beds.] *12* At their side is the outer gutter. [And he measured …] from the window: height, two cubits; [width, … cubits,] and its thickness is the width of the wall. [Height of its inner] part: *13* […] cubits [and of the other … cubits.] And he measured the edges of the platforms: nineteen [cubits in length] and twelve cubits in width. *14* […] and their height […] they open above […] two rods, [fourteen] *15* cubits; [their width is] three cubits and their length ten [cubits ..] one and a half cubits, and their height within […]

Frag. 2   *1* […] windows […] *2* […] all the houses which are in the inside […] *3* […] each door, and their thresholds are […] wide *4* […] of the columns, twelve cubits […] *5* […] from one column to another […]

11QNew Jerusalem (11Q18 [11QNJ ar])

Frags. 1 + 2 + 3 I   *1* […] … […] the throne […] *2* […] … […] and he is placed […] *3* […] … […] the temple, and from the blood […] *4* […] … [se]ven rods […] *5* […] by forty […] *6* […] from the tem[ple…]

Frags. 3 II + 4 + 5 + 6   *1* … […] … like all which [… fro]m before the al[tar …] they were taken […] *2* the throne […] … levites … […] … with … […] … seven […] *3* from him … […] it will be for them […] … for him […] until the sun goes down […] *4* the hand […] from [the] festivals […] oil and wine […] offerings […] *5* and over … […] before him [… tw]o bulls […] *6* the temple [… for a plea]sant o[dour…] … […]

Frags. 7 + 8 I   *1* [… al]l Israel […] all the men who […] *2* […] *Blank* And as soon Israel […] they were appointed over them […] *3* […] the Passover sacrifices […] until the sun goes down […] *4* until the sun goes down and all […] together. *Blank* […] *5* […] their peace-offerings […] seven […] *6* […] … […]

Frags. 9   *1* […] the months of Israel […] *2* […] … and in the night […] *3* […] … it will be called […] *4* […] its flesh which […] *5* […] they will be eaten with it and from […] *6* they will be eaten and dr[unk…] *7* […] … […]

Frags. 10 + 11 I   *1* […] the sun […] and from *2* […] the judge from all […] *3* […] which four […] *4* […] over all seed […] *5* all year […] *6* […] … […]

Frags. 11 II + 12   *1* over them and […] over the four horns of the altar, *2* and of the peace-offering […] from it, all the fat *3* of their sacrifices […] the two kidneys *4* and from the knees […] its cakes soaked […] *5* all its multitude [… the al]tar for an odour *6* from all […] […] in the first place *7* [for I]srael

Frag. 13   *1* [… ev]ery seventh day before God, a memori[al …] and their thank-offering *2* […] outside of the temple, to the right of the West, [and it shall be divided …] and they will be accepted. *3* [And I watched until (the bread ?) was di]vided among the eighty-four priests […] *3a* […] from everything the division of the tables filled itself […] *4* [.. the eldest who are among th]em, and fourteen prie[sts …] *5* [priests … Two (loaves) of brea]d [upon which] was the incense […] *6* [I keep watching until one of the two loaves] was given to the [high] priest [… with him.] *7* [And the other was given to the second who was stan]ding apart […]

Frag. 14   *1* the grape when it leaves the palm […] *2* from the radiance in them, and the fi[th] crown […] *3* interior of the cover, and the sixth crown […] *4* seventh [crown], according to the radiance and the […] *5* [And] the High Priest was clothed […] *6* … […]

Frag. 15   *1* […] loosed yet for them, which is […] *2* […] and all who have finished his seven […] *3* […] his brothers entered their place, four hundred […] *4* […] *Blank* And he said to me: to the twenty six […] *5* […] the holy of holies […] *6* [… they] entered […]

Frag. 16   *1* […] the doors which were in front of the temple […] *2* [… on] the seventh day. And on the first day of the m[onth …] *3* […] is holy. The temple and the great glory […] *4* […] for ever. *Blank* *5* […] He started to read to me from a bo[ok …] *6* […] he showed me a book […] *7* […] … […]

Frag. 17   *1* seven cups and bowls to wash […] *2* [to] me, and higher seven caldrons, stoves over the ea[rth…] *3* [and all] of them (are) thirty two thousand and nine hundred […] *4* […] *Blank* […] *5* […] He said to me: See […] *6* […] to his house the joy and to […] *7* […] … […]

Frag. 18   *1* seven by seven. And he sho[wed me …] *2* three rods; and the height of the doors […] *3* to all the twelve door[s…] *4* two [rods,] and its breath is the width of the wa[ll …] *5* the first hundred rods […]

Frag. 19 + 20   *1* […] around the upper room […] and the two doors *2* […] cubits, seven columns [… and the wi]dth of the upper room *3* [… their length] and their [width] are six by six cubits [… and] one; the width of *4* […] and the building built upon it […] And likewise *5* [he showed me …] and all this building […] the stair *6* […] rods […]

Frag. 21   *1* […] in its four feet. And stretch the bull […] *2* [… Wa]sh its feet and its inwards and salt all of them […] *3* […] put them on the fire, and the loaves of sifted fine flour [...] *4* [...a fo]urth of a *seah*, and bring (it) all up to the altar [...] *5* [...a fo]urth of a *seah* and a drink offering to the interior [...] *6* [...] and the flesh is mixed together [...] *7* [...] odour. *Blank* [...] *8* [...] beaten (?) near [...]

Frag. 22   *1* [...] from these and the mixtures (?) which *2* [...] separated and of the tithes *3* [...] separated and prepared *4* [...] *Blank 5* [...] all the West side. *6* [...] the wall *7* [...] ebony *8* [...] in the right

Frag. 23   *1* [... and] its four sides (?) were high: [...] cubits, [...] *2* [... and the chan]nel (?) near the wall which surrounds the [...] *3* [...]its width is two [cubits] and its height two cubits [...] *4* [...] is beautiful and all is of pure gold [...] *5* [...] *Blank* [...] *6* of columns turning from one door to [another door ...] *7* [...] from one door to another in the city-wall [...] *8* [...] in his hand [...]

Frag. 24   *1* [...] living waters *2* [...] this wall is of pure gold *3* [...] water from *4* [...] *Blank 5* [...] all their stones *6* overlay with gold *7* [...] ...

4 Other Texts

4QFlorilegium (4Q174 [4QFlor])

Frags. 1 – 3 *col.* I   *2Sam 7:10 1* [«And] an enemy [will trouble him no mo]re, [nor will] the son of iniquity [afflict him again] as at the beginning. From the day on which *2* [I established judges] over my people, Israel». This (refers to) the house which [they will establish] for [him] in the last days, as is written in the book of *3* [Moses: *Exod 15:17-18* «A temple of the Lord] will you establish with your hands. YHWH shall reign for ever and ever». This (refers to) the house into which shall never enter *4* [...] either the Ammonite, or the Moabite, or the Bastard, or the foreigner, or the proselyte, never, because there [he will reveal] to the holy ones; *5* eternal [glory] will appear over it for ever; foreigners shall not again lay it waste as they laid waste, at the beginning, *6* the tem[ple of Is]rael for its sins. And he commanded to build for himself a temple of man, to offer him in it, *7* before him, the works of the law. And as for what he said to David: *1Sam 7:11* «I shall obtain for you rest from all your enemies»: (it refers to this,) that he will obtain for them rest from all *8* the sons of Belial, those who make them fall, to destr[oy them for their s]ins, when they come with the plans of Belial to make the s[ons of] *9* light fall, and to plot against them wicked plans so that they are trapped by Belial in their guilty error. *Blank 10* And *2Sam 7:12-14* «YHWH de[clares] to you that he will build you a house. I will raise up your seed after you and establish the throne of his kingdom *11* [for ev]er. I will be a father to him and he will be a son to me.» This (refers to the) «branch of David», who will arise with the Interpreter of the law who *12* [will rise up] in Zi[on in] the last days, as it is written: *Amos 9:11* «I will raise up the hut of David which has fallen», This (refers to) «the hut of *13* David which has fallen», who will arise to save Israel. *Blank 14* Midrash of «Blessed the man who does not walk in the counsel of the wicked». The interpretation of this sa[ying: they are those who turn] aside from the path [of the wicked,] *15* as it is written in the book of Isaiah, the prophet, for the last days: *Isa 8:11* «And it happened that with a strong [hand he turned me aside from walking on the path of] *16* this people». And this (refers to) those about whom it is written in the book of Ezekiel, the prophet, that *Ez 44:10* «[they should] not [defile themselves any more with all] *17* their filth». This (refers to) the sons of Zadok and to the men of his council, those who seek jus[tice] eagerly, who will come after them to the council of the community. *18 Ps 2:1* [«Why do] the nations [become agitated] and the peoples plo[t] nonsense? [The kings of the earth [ag]ree [and the ru]lers conspire together against YHWH and against *19* [his anointed one». Inter]pretation of the saying: [the kings of the na]tions [become agitated and conspire against] the elect of Israel in the last days.

Frags. 1–3 *col.* II   *1* It is the time of trial which co[mes ...] Judah to complete [...] *2* Belial, and a remnant will remain [...] for the lot, and they shall put into practice all the law [...] *3* Moses; it is [...] as is written in the book of Daniel, the prophet: *Dan 12:20* «The wicked [act wickedly...] *4a* and the just [...shall be whi]tened and refined and a people knowing God will remain strong [...] *4* ... [...] after [...] which is for them [...] *5* [...] in their descent [...]

Frag. 4   *1* [...] those who devour the offspring of *2* [...fu]rious against them in his zeal *3* [...] This (refers) to the time when Belial will open *4* [...] for the house of Judah difficulties to bear resentment *5* [...] and he will seek with all his might to scatter them *6* [...] he will bring them in to be *7* [... to Ju]dah and to Israel [...]

4QTestimonia (4Q175 [4QTest])

1 And **** spoke to Moses saying: *Dt 5:28-29* «You have heard the sound of the words *2* of this people, what they said to you: all they have said is right. *3* If (only) it were given to me (that) they had this heart to fear me and keep all *4* my precepts all the days, so that it might go well with them and their sons for ever!» *5* *Dt 18:18-19* «I would raise up for them a prophet from among their brothers, like you, and place my words *6* in his mouth, and he would tell them all that I command them. And it will happen that the man *7* who does not listen to my words, that the prophet will speak in my name, I *8* shall require a reckoning from him.» *Blank 9* And he uttered his poem and said: *Num 24:15-17* «Oracle of Balaam, son of Beor, and oracle of the man *10* of penetrating eye, oracle of him who listens to the words of God and knows the knowledge of the Most High, of one who *11* sees the vision of Shaddai, who falls and opens the eye. I see him, but not now, *12* I espy him, but not close up. A star has departed from Jacob, /and/ a sceptre /has arisen/ from Israel. He shall crush *13* the temples of Moab, and cut to pieces all the sons of Sheth.» *Blank 14* And about Levi he says: *Dt 33:8-11* «Give to Levi your *Thummim* and your *Urim*, to your pious man, whom *15* you tested at Massah, and with whom you quarrelled about the waters of Meribah, /he who/ said to his father {...} *16* {...} and to his mother 'I have not known you', and did not acknowledge his brothers, and his son did not *17* know. For he observed your word and kept your covenant. /They have made/ your judgments /shine/ for Jacob, *18* our law for Israel, they have placed incense before your face and a holocaust upon your altar. *19* Bless, ****, his courage and accept with pleasure the work of his hand! Crush /the loins/ of his adversaries, and those who hate him, *20* may they not rise!» *Blank 21 Blank* At the moment when Joshua finished praising and giving thanks with his psalms, *22* he said *Jos 6:26* «Cursed be the man who rebuilds this city! Upon his first-born *33* will he found it, and upon his benjamin will he erect its gates!» And now /an/ accursed /man/, one of Belial, *24* has arisen to be a fowler's trap for his people and ruin for all his neighbours. *25* [...] will arise, to be the two instruments of violence. And they will rebuild *26* [this city and ere]ct for it a rampart and towers, to make it into a fortress of wickedness *27* [a great evil] in Israel, and a horror in Ephraim and Judah. *28* [...And they wi]ll commit a profanation in the land and a great blasphemy among the sons of *29* [... And they will shed blo]od like water upon the ramparts of the daughter of Sion and in the precincts of *30* Jerusalem.

4QAramaic Apocalypse (4Q246)

Col. I   *1* [...] settled upon him and he fell before the throne *2* [...] eternal king. You are angry and your years *3* [...] they will see you, and all shall come for ever. *4* [...] great, oppression will come upon the earth *5* [...] and great slaughter in the city *6* [...] king of Assyria and of Egypt *7* [...] and he will be great over the earth *8* [...] they will do, and all will serve *9* [...] great will he be called and he will be designated by his name.

Col. II   *1* He will be called son of God, and they will call him son of the Most High. Like the sparks *2* of a vision, so will their kingdom be; they will rule several years over *3* the earth and crush everything; a people will crush another people, and a city another city. *4* *Blank* Until the people of God arises and makes everyone rest from the sword. *5* His kingdom will be an eternal kingdom, and all his paths in truth and uprigh[tness]. *6* The earth (will be) in truth and all will make peace. The sword will cease in the earth, *7* and all the cities will pay him homage. He is a great God among the gods (?). *8* He will make war with him; he will place the peoples in his hand and cast away everyone before him. His kingdom will be an eternal kingdom, and all the abysses

4QFour Kingdoms^a (4Q552)

Frag. 1 *col.* I   *1* [...] Which *2* [...] of *3* [...] ... *4* [...] *5* [...] the light of the angels who were *6* [...] he told them what would happen. *Blank* All *7* [...] he has the strength of the seas. *Blank* This *8* [...] *Blank* And he said to me: Oh King, since *Blank* thus *9* [...] how was everything made? They arose *10* [...] He spoke to them and explained to them according to the interpretation *11* [...] and their lords will be destroyed for them.

Frag. 1 *col.* II   *1* Dawn rose and the four trees [...] *2* A tree rose up and they turned away from it. And he said [to me:...Of what] *3* species is it? And I said: How will I see and understand this? [And I saw] *4* a tree of fragrances. [...] *5* And I asked: What is your name? And he answered me: Babel. [And I said to him:] *6* You are the one who rules over Persia. And [I saw another tree] *7 Blank* [He who was be]low us swore by [...] and said *8* that he was different (?). And I asked him: What is your na[me? And he said to me ...] *9* And I said to him: You are the one who [rules over ... and over] *10* the powers of the sea, and over the market [... And I saw] *11* a third tree, and I said to him: [What is your name And he said to me ...] *12* Your vision [...]

Frag. 1 col. III   *1* [...] destroyed. And I said to him: He is the one who [...] from *2* [...] ... [...] And I saw [...] *3-8* [...] *9* [...] they will rejoice *10* [...] the vision *11* [...] ... the word *12* [...] which will escape

Frag. 2   *9* [...] the lord [...] *10* [...] God Most High not [...] *11* [...] which there is above them, and ... [...] *12* [...] the lord of all, he who establishes judges [...]

4QFour Kingdoms^*b* (4Q553)

Frag. 6 col. I   *2* [...] ... my hand *3* [...] for this I will go *4* [...] And he said to me: in the kingdom *5* [...] ... to rebel, and when there is (?) *6* [...] ...

Frag. 6 col. II   *2* [...] to him. And the trees rose up *3* and turned away [from him ...] *Blank* And I said: How will I see and understand *4* this? And I saw [...And I asked: What is] your name? And he answered me: Babel. *Blank* And I said to him: You *5* are [the one who rules over Persia. And I saw] another tree. And I asked him and said to him: What *6* is your name? [And he said to me...]

Frag. 8 col. I   *1* [...] all joy *2* [...] from Moses *3* [...] in the place where *4* [...] ... so that it is called *5* [...] with the name of

Frag. 8 col. II   *1* the markets (?) and over [...] *2* the power of the strength [...] *3* their knowledge [...] *4* to me three [...]

11QMelchizedek (11Q13 [11QMelch])

Col. II   *1* [...] your God ... [...] *2* [...] And as for what he said: *Lev 25:13* «In this year of jubilee, [you shall return, each one, to his respective property», as is written: *Dt 15:2* «This is] *3* the manner (of effecting) the [release: every creditor shall release what he lent [to his neighbour. He shall not coerce his neighbour or his brother when] the release for God [has been proclaimed]». *4* [Its inter]pretation for the last days refers to the captives, about whom he said: *Isa 61:1* «To proclaim liberty to the captives.» And he will make *5* their rebels prisoners [...] and of the inheritance of Melchizedek, for [...] and they are the inheri[tance of Melchi]zedek, who *6* will make them return . He will proclaim liberty for them, to free them from [the debt] of all their iniquities. And this will [happen] *7* in the first week of the jubilee which follows the ni[ne] jubilees. And the day [of atonem]ent is the end of the tenth jubilee *8* in which atonement will be made for all the sons of [God] and for the men of the lot of Melchize-dek. [And on the heights] he will decla[re in their] favour according to their lots; for *9* it is the time of the «year of grace» for Melchizedek, to exa[lt in the tri]al the holy ones of God through the rule of judgment, as is written *10* about him in the songs of David, who said: *Ps 82:1* «Elohim will stand up in the assem[bly of God,] in the midst of the gods he judges». And about him he said: *Ps 7:8-9* «Above it *11* return to the heights, God will judge the peoples». As for what he sa[id: *Ps 82:2* «How long will yo]u judge unjustly and show partiality to the wicked? *Selah.*» *12* Its interpretation concerns Belial and the spirits of his lot, who were rebels [all of them] turning aside from the commandments of God [to commit evil.] *13* But, Melchizedek will carry out the vengeance of God's judges [on this day, and they shall be freed from the hands] of Belial and from the hands of all the sp[irits of his lot.] *14* To his aid (shall come) all «the gods of [justice»; he] is the one [who will prevail on this day over] all the sons of God, and he will pre[side over] this [assembly.] *15* This is the day of [peace about which God] spoke [of old through the words of Isa]iah the prophet, who said: *Isa 52:7* «How beautiful *16* upon the mountains are the feet of the messen-ger who announces peace, of the mess[enger of good who announces salvation,] saying to Zion: 'your God [reigns.»] *17* Its interpretation: The mountains are the pro[phets ...] *18* And the messenger is [the ano]inted of the spirit about whom Dan[iel] spoke [... and the messenger of] *19* good who announces salv[ation is the one about whom it is written that [he will send him *Isa 61:2-3* «to comfo[rt the afflicted, to watch over the afflicted ones of Zion».] *20* «To comfo[rt the afflicted», its interpretation:] to instruct them in all the ages of the worl[d...] *21* in truth. [...] *22* [...] it has been turned away from Belial and it [...] *23* [...] in the judgments of God, as is written about him: *Isa 52:7* «Saying to Zion: 'your God rules'». [«Zi]on» is *24* [the congregation of all the sons of justice, those] who establish the covenant, those who avoid walking [on the pa]th of the people. «Your God» is *25* [... Melchizedek, who will fr]ee [them] from the hand of Belial. And as for what he said: *Lev 25:9* «You shall blow the hor[n in every] land».

Col. III   *1* [Its interpretation ...] *2* and you know [...] *3* God [...] *4* and many [...] *5* [...] ... [...] Melchizedek [...] *6* the law for them [...] the hand [...] and he will announce [...] *7* they shall devour Belial with fire [...] Belial, and they shall rebel [...] *8* the desires of their hearts [...] ... [...] *9* the ramparts of Judah [...] the ramparts of Je[rusalem...] *10-20* (minute traces.)

Exegetical Literature

The exegetical activity of the Community emerges in one way or another in all the writings preserved. Exegesis forms the foundation of the halakhic texts. Interpretation of particular biblical texts peppers the development of the Rules, both in the legislative sections and in the more theological sections. As a matter of course, the biblical text permeates all the ritual texts, and the language of the verse compositions is so steeped in the idiom of the bible that they resemble a patchwork quilt in which biblical sap and personal expression are woven together inextricably.

This chapter comprises a set of compositions of very different types, all of them, though, illustrations of the exegetical efforts of the Community. The *Targum of Job* and the tiny fragments of the *Targum of Leviticus* show us how biblical interpretation permeates the Aramaic translation of biblical texts. *The Temple Scroll* is put forward as a new Deuteronomy, as a sixth book of the Torah. In it, sections from various biblical books are blended with others hitherto unknown and the whole is put forward as the actual word (in the first person) of God.

Perhaps the most typical texts of Qumran exegesis are the *pesharim*, a term used to denote compositions in which the word *pesher* ('interpretation') occurs very often. In essence, this exegesis involves revealing the true meaning of the biblical text, relating it to the actual circumstances of the Community in the last days. In the *pesharim*, the passages from the prophets or from the psalms quoted ealier are commented on, verse by verse. In the other compositions included here, which could be called *thematic pesharim*, texts derived from various biblical books and collected for a specific purpose, are interpreted.

Of course, a number of the compositions in the chapter 'Para-biblical narratives', could just as well have been included in this chapter, since they narrate, explain, expand on or alter the biblical text which sustains the life of the Community. The boundary between interpretation, the result of exegesis and mere paraphrase of the biblical text or incorporation of duplicate traditions, is a movable border where there are no certainties.

1 The Targums

A *Targum of Leviticus*

4QTargum of Leviticus (4Q156 [4QtgLev])

Frag. 1 (= *Lev* 16 : 12–15)   *1* [...And he shall take an incense-burner full of] coals [of fire from the surface of the altar which is before] *2* [YHWH and he shall fill] his two fists with in[cense (?)...] *3* [and shall place them within] the veil... And he shall place [the incense on top of the fire] *4* [before YHWH, and] the cloud shall cover [...] *5* [above the testimony, and] he will not die. [...] And he shall take some of the [blood of the bullock] *6* [and he shall sprinkle with his finger ov]er the mercy-seat. And in front of the mercy-seat, towards the East, *7* [he shall sprinkle] the blood [seven times] with his finger... And he shall slaughter

Frag. 2 (= *Lev* 16 : 18–21)   *1* [... for] him... He shall take [blood from the bull-ock and blood from the he-goat] *2* [and shall put it on] the horns of the altar, ar[ound... And he shall sprinkle upon him the blood] *3* [with his finger sev]en [times] and he shall cleanse it and make it holy [from the im]purities [of the sons of] *4* [Israel...] When [he has finished aton]ing for the holy house, [for] the tent of meeting and [for] *5* [the altar, he shall bring near] the he-goat... Aaron shall lay his two [hands upon] *6* [the head of the] live [he]-goat, ... And he shall confess over it all [...] *7* [...al]l his sin[s...]

B *Targum of Job*

4QTargum of Job (4Q157 [4QtgJob])

Frag. 1 *col.* i (= *Job* 3 : 5–?)   *2* [...] a cloud [should spread] over him *3* [... may it not join the d]ays of the year *4-5* [...] ...

Frag. 1 *col.* ii (= *Job* 4 : 16–5 : 4)   *1* ... [...] *2* Can a man before God [be just?...] *3* and to his angels [he ascribes madness...] *4* which [have their foundations] in dust [...] *5* and without number [...] they die, and not from wisdom. [...] *7* will you consider? *Blank* Perhaps he does not kill the stupid [...] *8* But I have seen a wicked person ...[...] *9* ... [...]

11QTargum of Job (11Q10 [11QtgJob])

Col. I (= *Job* 17 : 14–18 : 4)   *1* [... and my mother and my sister to the mag]got. And what is it, then, that I [...] *2* [...] Perhaps [they shall go down] with me to Sheol? [...] *3* [...in the dust] shall [we] lie down? *Blank* *4* Bildad the Shu[hite answer[ed...] *5* [...] will you finish the word? [...] *6* [...] we resemble animals? [...] *7* [...] Perhaps on your account [...] *8* [...the rock] from its position? [...]

Col. II (= *Job* 19 : 11–19)   *1* Against me his wrath [has flared] up and he regards [me ...] *2* His thieves arrive and flatten [... My brothers from me] *3* have recoiled, and those who know me [... the guests] *4* of my house. My maidservant, like an alien [...] *5* I call my servant and he does not answer [...] *6* I have humbled my spirit in front of my wife [...] *7* The wicked afflict me [...] *8* every man who [...]

Col. III (= *Job* 19 : 29–20 : 6)   *1* [...] evil.*Blank* [...] *2* [...] *Blank* [...] *3* [...and he rep]lied: Behold my heart [...] *4* [...] I will hear my shame, but the spirit [...] *5* [...Do you not] know that from eternity, from [...] *6* [...] Because the exultation of the wicked [...] *7* [...] passes swiftly. [...] *8* [... and] his face [reaches] the clouds [...]

Col. IV (= *Job* 21 : 2–10)   *1* [...] to me [...] my knowing, you mock. [...] *3* surely, therefore, [my spirit] does not get im[patient ...] *4* place your hands over [your mouth! ...] *5* amazement seizes me. How is it that [the wicked...] *6* and increase their riches? Their offspring [...] *7* in front of their eyes. Their houses [...] *8* God upon them. [...] *9* their pregnant (cow) gives birth [and does not abort...]

Col. V (= *Job* 21 : 20–27)   *1* [...] his eyes [...] their downfall and about [...] *2* [...] interest for God in their house [...] [...] *3* [...] the number of his months cut short? Is God [...] *4* [...] him, who judges those most elevated? His flanks [...] *5* [...] the marrow of his bones. Another dies [with bitterness] in his soul [...] *6* [...] without eating; together on [the dust they lie ...] *7* [...] on top of them. Behold, I know [your thoughts ...] *8* [...] you have plotted [against] me. [...]

Col. VI (= *Job* 22 : 3–9)   *1* [...] to God *2* [...] your path *3* [...] will he enter with you? *4* [...] there is no *5* [...] your brothers for nothing *6* [...] to the thirsty not *7* [...] bread. And you said *8* [...] his face *9* [...] of emptiness.

Col. vii (= *Job* 22 : 16–22)   *1* that they died [...] *2* They said to G[od...] *3* to our God [...] *4* But the counsel of the wicked [...] *5* and they laughed and [...] *6* How is it that [...] not [...] *7* Look [...] *8* Receive [...]

Col. VIIa (= *Job* 23 : 1–8)   *1* [...] Job answered and sai[d...] *2* [...] because of my speech which [...] *3* [...] my [groa]ning. Indeed, I would know and I would find him *4* [...] the place of his dwelling. I would speak before [him ...] *5* [...] I would fill my [mouth] with reproof, and I would know [...] *6* [...] and I would understand what he would say to me. [...] *7* [... would he] act unjustly with me? Indeed, until [...] *8* [...] for truth and how [...] *9* [...] If forwa[rd...]

Col. VIII (= *Job* 24 : 12–17)   *1* From their cities [...] *2* he groans: «God [...] *3* in front of him to the fire [...] *4* in its footpaths [...] *5* and to the poor; and in the night [...] *6* the darkness, saying [...] *7* and he will sin. [...] *8* in evil [...] *9* for them [...]

Col. IX (= *Job* 24 : 24–26 : 2)   *1* [...] they have folded, they draw themselves together like the cynodon *2* [...] Who, then, will give me an answer and [...] *3* [...] *Blank* Bildad answered [...] *4* [...] God has dominion and magnificence; he does [...] *5* [...] in his height. Is there confidence for [...] *6* or upon whom does [...] not rise *7* [...] God, and how will he be just [...] *8* [...] pure and the stars [...] not *9* [...] human being, this worm [...] *10* [...] and he said «Can you, perhaps, [...]?

Col. X (= *Job* 26 : 10–27 : 4)   *1* [...] to the edge of darkness; *2* [...] he sieves them and they are alarmed about *3* [...] the sea, and with his understanding he killed *4* [...] he makes it shine; his hand pierced the fleeing serpent. *5* [...] their paths. And it is only an echo that we hear. *6* [...] he will understand». *Blank* *7* [...] *Blank* *8* [...] and said: «May God live [...] *9* [...] to my soul, which while [...] *10* [...] in my nostril, they shall not say [...]

Col. XI (= *Job* 27 : 11–20)   *1* [...] in God's hand and the work of *2* [...] all you have seen it. Why *3* [...] the wicked man *4* [...] they take in front of him. If *5* [...] the sword, they shall open (their) mouth, but it will not be satisfied *6* [...] and their widows [...] no *7* [...] coins, and increases like clay *8* [...] an honest man will share out the wealth *9* [...] like a hut *10* [...] lies down and is not seized *11* [...] like water the evils

Col. XII (= *Job* 28 : 4–13)   *1* foot [...] *3* sapphires [...] *4* not [...] *5* the snake enters [...] *9* man [...]

Col. XIII (= *Job* 28 : 20–28)   *1* the place of wisdom? [...] *2* it hides from the birds of the sky [...] *3* «By hearsay we know your reputation» [...] *4* in it, since he [...] *5* the ends of the earth [...] *6* When he made the wind [...] *7* by one measure. When he made [...] *8* light clouds. Meanwhile [...] *9* And he said to the sons [of man...] *10* and to depart from [...]

Col. XIV (= *Job* 29 : 7–16)   *1* in the mornings, at the gates of the city, in the square [...] *2* Youths, on seeing me, hide, and wise [men...] *3* Great men refrain from speaking and place the palm [...] *4* The leaders concealed their voice; [...] stuck to the palate. *5* He who heard me, praised me; he who saw me [...,] *6* because I freed the poor man from [...] *7* whom no-one helps. The blessing of the lost one [...] *8* in the widow's mouth there was a prayer for me [...] *9* I wore and put on like a tunic [...] *10* [...] and feet for the lame [...] *11* [...] I did not know [...]

Col. XV (= *Job* 29 : 24–30 : 4)   *1* [...] I smiled on them, and they did not believe [...] *2* [...] I chose my path and was a chief [...] *3* [...] at the head of his army, and like a man who [...] the sad ones *4* [...] They made fun of my lads younger than me [...] *5* [...] whose fathers [I would have disdained] to set with the dogs of my flock [...] *6* [...] I did not like them and under their pressure [...] *7* [...] with hunger they go cropping the green of the desert [...] *8* [...] evil, which they ate [...] *9* [...] brooms as their bread [...]

Col. XVI (= *Job* 30 : 13–20)   *1* [...] they come for my ruination, and there is no saviour *2* [...] for them. In the intensity of my boil they come *3* [...] I am bent double [beneath] the evil; it contorts me *4* [...] like the wind my goods and my dignity, and like a cloud *5* [...] my salvation. Now it irritates me *6* [...] days of agony consume me *7* [...] my bones are inflamed and my tendons [...] *8* [...] with violence he seizes me by the garment *9* [...] they surround me and make me go down to the dust *10* [...] to you [...]

Col. XVII (= *Job* 30 : 25–31 : 1)   *1* [...they] boiled [me] and not *4* [...] I walked *5* [...] I shouted *6* [...] for the ostriches *7* [...] of

Col. XVIII (= *Job* 31 : 8–16)   *1* He will eat [...] *2* my heart for a woman [...] *3* She will grind [...] anger *4* and is a sin [...] which up to *5* Abaddon shall consume [...] If I was impatient *6* in the judgment of my servant [...] what will I do *7* when arises [...] Behold *8* he made me [...] oneself. If *9* I denied [...] I ceased to be consumed

Col. XIX (= *Job* 31 : 26–32)   *1* it shone, and at the moon [...] my heart, *2* and my hand kissed my mouth [...] I would have lied *3* to the God of on high [...] I rejoiced *4* in his misfortune [...] *5* my cursed, and he heard [...] in my anger *6* and took [...] *7* my palate sin by asking [...] the men *8* of my house: who [...] *9* (did) not [...]

Col. XX (= *Job* 31 : 40–32 : 3)   *1* in place of wheat [...] *2* of the pine. Completed are [...] *3* Those [...] from answering [...] *4* Job was just [...] *5* *Blank* *6* Meanwhile he grew angry [...] *7* of the clan of Rome [...] *8* and also against [...] *9* words [...]

Col. XXI (= *Job* 32 : 10–17)   *1* my words, I as well. Well then, I waited [...] *2* you finished, while you sought the end of [...] *3* and there was not from you for Job [...] *4* to his words. Perhaps you shall say [...] *5* for this we condemn God and not a man [...] *6* words, and he does not answer him at all [...] *7* and they are silent, while I wait from them [...] *8* they rise and say nothing more [...] *9* I, too, shall set out my words [...]

Col. XXII (= *Job* 33 : 6–16)   *1* [...] Well then, my terror will not startle you [...] *2* [...] heavy. Surely you spoke in my hearing and the voice [...] *3* [...] I am pure and there is no sin in me, I am blameless [...] *4* [...] If he finds sins, he takes me [...] *5* [...] he places my feet in the stocks and fastens me all up [...] *6* [...] because God is greater than man [...] *7* [...] you will utter arrogant words, because in all your actions [...] *8* [...] God knows how to speak in one way or another [...] *9* [...] in dreams, in the depths of the night [...] *10* [...] who is sleeping in his bed [...] *11* [...] ... [...]

Col. XXIII (= *Job* 33 : 24–32)   *1* and he will say: «Free from destruction [...] *2* from the fire which smothers him [...] with *3* youth, and he returns to the days of his youth [...] and he will listen to him *4* and will see his face when healing him [?...] and according to the work *5* of his hands he will reward him. And he will say [...] but *6* he has not rewarded me according to my path. He has preserved [...] *7* will see in the light. Behold [...] *8* [on]ce, twice, three times [to the] man for [...] *9* living (beings). Pay attention to this [...] I will speak. *10* [If] you have words [...]

Col. XXIV (= *Job* 34 : 6–17)   *1* of sin. Who [...] sin? And associates *2* with evildo- ers [...] wicked men. For he says «A man *3* will not change [...] after God». *4* Now, men of [...] Far be from God deceit *5* and doing evil [...] of man, he rewards him *6* [...] Will God, perhaps really *7* lie now, and the Lord [...] him, who made the earth *8* and founded the world? [...] takes his breath away from him, *9* and he will die [...] they shall lie down *10* [...] my words. In deceit, per- haps......?

Col. XXV (= *Job* 34 : 24–34)   *1* [...] to the powerful without end, and put others [...] *2* [...] he knows their deeds and hurls them into the place [...] *3* [...] his path and have not kept to any of his ways [...] *4* [...] of the poor and listens to the lament of the oppressed [...] *5* [...] hides his face, who will answer him about a people [...] *6* [...] the evil man rules. They make [...] stumble *7* [...] I hoped in him, in him alone [...] *8* [...] I did not persist, since [...] *9* [...] you choose and not I [...] *10* [...] words, and man [...]

Col. XXVI (= *Job* 35 : 6–14)   *1* to you.
And when you increase your misdeeds, what do you [do to him?
If you are jus]t, what *2* do you give him,
or what does he gain from your hand?

Your sin (affects) [a man like you],
3 your justice, a son of man.
  Due to the great number [of oppressors]
  they moan and shout *4* in front of many;
  but they do not [sa]y: Where is] God, *5* who made us
  and has given us [...] for our planting *6* during the night;
  who has differentiated us from the ani[mals of the earth]
  and has made us more intelligent than the birds?
7 They shout there, but he does not [answer
  because of the arro]gance *8* of the evil men.
  For God [does not listen to deceit
  and the Lord to] inanity *9* pays [no] attention.
  If you say [...] *10* [...] ...[...]

Col. XXVII (= *Job* 36 : 7–16)   *1* to the kings who sit [on their thrones
  and] their friends are exalted with security.
2 And even those with whom they are fettered [with chains,]
  tied up by the ropes of wretched people;
3 he shows them their deeds
  and their [mis]deeds, for they have elevated themselves.
  He opens *4* their ears for them, so they can learn,
  [and to them he sa]ys:
  «If they are converted from their sins,
5 if they listen and sub[mit,
  they shall end their days] in well-being,
  and their years *6* in honour and delights.
  [But if they do not lis]ten, they shall fall to the sword,
7 and will die without [knowledge]
  [...] their heart in anger *8* upon them
  [...] their city [perishes] because of those who destroy.
9 He will save the poor [...]
  their ears [...] *10* [...] ... [...]

Col. XXVIII (= *Job* 36 : 23–33)   *1* you ac[complished injustice.
  Remem]ber that their deeds are great,
2 men have seen them.
  All men regard them
  and the sons of man *3* look at them from afar.
  God is great and his days are *4* a multitude
  [–we do not] know [them] –,
  and the number of his years infinite.
  For *5* [he counts the] clouds

and commands the squalls of rain;
and their clouds precipitate 6 [drops of water]
[upon] a numerous people.
Indeed, who unfolds 7 the clouds [with great din],
who covers and uncovers [light]
8 [...] covered;
for with them he will judge the na[tions]
9 [...] at his command [...] 10 [...] fold over them [...]

Col. XXIX (= *Job* 37 : 10–19)   1 over the surface of the water.
With them also he causes the clouds to gleam,
and discharges 2 fire from the cloud.
And he says: «They should hear it!»,
and they move to their tasks;
he places them to the fore of everything that he created on the surface of the
world,
whether to smite, 4 or to crush,
or for hunger and hardship,
or when there is an argument 5 over it.
Hear this, Job, and get up;
consider God's wonders.
6 Do you know what God stations above them,
and (how) he makes the light of his cloud shine?
7 Do you know (how) to clothe his cloud with won[ders]?
Since your garment 8 [...]
because he has absolute knowledge.
[Perhaps with him you inflate] the storm clouds
9 [... like a] hard [mir]ror.
He knows [...]

Col. XXX (= *Job* 38 : 3–13)   1 Gird up your lo[ins,] then, like a man
[and I will que]stion [you].
Give me an answer.
2 Where were you when I made the earth?
Tell me, if you know so much.
3 Who marked off its measurements? – if you know it –
or who wielded the measuring tape?
Or 4 upon what are its foundations sunk?
Or who placed its cornerstone
when there shone 5 together the stars of the morning,
and all God's angels cheered in chorus ?
6 Did you secure the sea with doors

when it battled to leave the bosom of the abyss?
7 When did you wear clouds [as vei]ls
and mists as baby clothes?
Was it you who set *8* the sea
its b[orders and law, bolts and gates?]
Did you tell it, this far only,
9 and, you shall not go beyond [...] of your waves?
In your days did you command *10* [...]
the edges of the earth [...]

Col. XXXI (= *Job* 38 : 23–43)   *1* which [I reserve for the] time of danger,
for the day of war and battle?
[...] *2* from where does it come?
Do you blow in front of him over the earth?
Who has imposed *3* a time for rain
and a path for the light clouds,
to make it precipitate on the land *4* of the desert,
where there are no men;
to drench thorns and thickets
5 and cause shoots of grass to grow?
Has the rain a father?
Or who *6* bore the clouds of dew?
From whose belly does frost come?
and the clo[ak of the sky,] *7* who [bore it?]
Like a stone, water is covered with it
and the face of the abyss
8 [...] of the Pleiades,
or you [open] the fence of Orion [...]
9 [...] you undo the Evening Star (?) with his sons?
[...] *10*[...] the clouds [...]

Col. XXXII (= *Job* 39 : 1–11)   *1* the chamois,
or birth-pangs of [...]
their months are *2* concluded;
or do you know the moment of their delivery?
They give birth to their sons and cast them out.
3 Do you cause their young to leave?
They rear their sons and make them leave;
they go away and do not go back *4* to them.
Who set the wild ass at liberty
and untied the bonds of the onager?
5 I have given the desert as a house

and salty soil as a dwelling;
6 and he derides the bustle of the big city
  and to the shouts of the muleteer pays no 7 attention.
  He chooses for himself the mountains for pasture,
  searching out every green patch.
8 Will the buffalo be prepared to serve you,
  or will he spend the night in 9 your stable?
  Will you harness [the buffalo with] its rope
  [and will he till] in the valley 10 behind you [...]?
  Will you trust in him [because his strength] is massive?

Col. XXXIII (= *Job* 39 : 20–29)   *1* [...]
  Do you make him leap with strength
  [...] 2 in his snorting, fright and fear.
  He paws in the valley and canters and revels
3 and hurls himself violently, defying the sword.
  He scoffs at fear and does not 4 waver
  or retreat in front of the sword.
  Over him the quiver is raised,
5 the tip of a spear and a whetted blade.
  At the blast of the trumpet he says 'Aha!'
  and from 6 afar smells battle,
  and exults at the clash of weapons and the shouts of war.
7 Is yours the skill with which the falcon flies
  and stretches 8 his wings to the winds?
  Or does the eagle soar at your commands
9 and the vulture hang his nest high up?
  In the rock he lives and nests
  [...] 10 [...] ... [...]

Col. XXXIV (= *Job* 40 : 5–11)   *1* [...] end. *Blank* [...] 2 God replied to Job
  /from [out of the wind (?)/] and the cloud and told him:
  Gird up your loins, 3 then, like a man,
  and I will question you. Give me an answer.
  Do you presume even 4 to annul judgment
  or condemn me, for you to leave pardoned?
  Or 5 do you perhaps have an arm like God,
  or thunder with a voice like his?
  Abandon, then, greatness and haughtiness of spirit
  and dress in splendour, in glory and in honour.
7 Remove, then, the intensity of your anger.
  Look at every proud person and knock him down;

and every *8* haughtiness of spirit, destroy it.
And wipe out the wicked beneath them.
Bury them *9* in the dust. *Blank*
Tog[ether, cover their faces] with ash.
10 [...] there is

Col. XXXV (= *Job* 40 : 23 – 31)   *1* [... even though] *2* the Jordan [should overflow]
its bank,
he trusted that he will receive it [...]
3 Who will control him when he lifts his gaze
or who will make his muzzle bleed with a claw?
Will you fish *4* the crocodile with a hook
or will you thread his tongue with a rope?
Will you put *5* a ring in his nostril
and pierce his jaw with needle?
Will he speak *6* kindly to you,
or will he speak to you entreating you?
Will he draw up *7* an agreement with you,
or will you take him on as a perpetual slave?
Will you play *8* with him like a bird,
or tie him on a leash for your daughters?
and [...] *9* ov[er him...]
and they shall share him out in the land [of the Canaanites (?)]
10 [...] of fish [...]

Col. XXXVI (= *Job* 41 : 7 – 17)   *1* [...] ... [...]
2 [One] sticks to the other
and the wind does not penetrate between them.
Each one *3* clasped to its neighbour
and they are not separated.
His sneeze ignites *4* the fire between his eyes
like the glow of dawn;
from his cheeks *5* torches emerge,
they leap like tongues of fire;
from his nostrils comes a smoke cloud,
6 flaming torch and an incense burner;
his breath spews coals,
and sparks *7* leap from his cheeks.
In his neck is lodged his brawn
and in front of him *8* runs power.
The folds of his flesh are dense,
cast within him like iron;

and his heart [...] like a stone [...]
10 [...] ... [...]

Col. XXXVII (= *Job* 41 : 25–42 : 6)   *1* [...] ... [...]
2 and he is the king of all reptiles. *Blank*
3 Job answered and said in front of God:
   I know that you *4* can do everything,
   and that nothing powerful or wise
   cannot be achieved by you.
5 I will speak once and I will not insist;
   twice, to that *6* I will add nothing.
   Listen, then, and I will speak to you;
   I will question you *7* and you shall answer me.
   I knew you only from hearsay,
   and now my eyes *8* have seen you;
   for this I will be annihilated and destroyed,
   and I will turn into dust *9* and ash. *Blank*

Col. XXXVIII (= *Job* 42 : 9–12)   *1* [...] and he did [...] *2* God;
   and God heard Job's voice
   and forgave *3* his sins on his account.
   And God turned /to Job/ in his mercy
4 and doubled all his possessions for him.
   And there came to *5* Job all his friends and all his brothers and all his acquaintances and ate *6* bread with him in his house, and comforted him for all the evil
   that *7* God had brought upon him. And each one gave him a ewe *8* and each one
   a gold ring. *9* And God blessed Job in the end, because he had [...]

2 The Temple Scroll

11QTemple Scroll*a* (11Q19 [11QT*a*])

Col. II   *1* [fo]r what [I sha]ll do [to you will be dreadful.] *2* [Behold, I evict before you] the A[morites, Canaanites,] *3* [Hittites, Girgash]ites, Per[izzites, Hivites and] *4* [Jebusites. Bew]are of making a covenant [with the occupants of the country] *5* amongst whom you are going to come, so that they will not be a [trap in your midst. Instead] *6* you shall overturn their al[tars, wreck their stelae] *7* fell their [consecrated trees and burn] the effigies of their go[ds.] *8* You shall not fancy the silver or the gold which [...] *9* you shall [not] take it from him; you shall not [bring an abhorrence into your home] *10* [and become] anathema like it; loathe [it and hate it] *11* [because] it is anathema. Do not bow down in front of [another god, for YHWH has the name Jealous,] *12* he is a resentful God. Avoid making [a covenant with the occupants of the land,] *13* [they whore] after their gods and make sacrifices to [their gods, lest they entice you] *14* [and you eat (part) of their sacrifices and] ac[cept their daughters for your sons;] *15* [their daughters will whore after their gods] and wi[ll make your sons whore after]

Col. III   *1* [...] which in [...] *2* [...] woven violet and purple [...] *3* [...al]l your enemies of [the vicinity...] *4* [... a hou]se in which to set my name a[ll] *5* [...] in it silver and gold from a[ll countries...] *6* [...] and you shall not desecrate it, for if from [...] *7* [... bron]ze and iron and hewn stones in order to bui[ld...] *8* [...] I made all its vessels of pure gold [...] *9* [... the] cover which is on top of it, of pure gold [...] *10* [... the altar] of fragrant incense and the table [...] *11* [...] you shall not remove from the temple. Its salvers [...] *12* [...] and its urns will be of pure gold; and its burners [...] *13* [...] with which fire is inserted inside, and the candelabrum and all [...] *14* [...] *Blank* The whole altar for holocausts [...] *15* [...of] pure [bron]ze and the grille which is on top [...] *16* [...] of bronze [...] in order to see [...] *17* [...] of bron[ze...] ... [...] *18* [...] ... [...]

Col. IV   *1* [...] eig[ht...] *2* [... those] jutting out towards the [...] *3* [...] of the house, fo[ur...] wide *4* [...] and a tiled pavement between the [...] *5* [... be]tween the sixth; a tiled pavement [...] *6* [...] ... *Blank* [...] *7* the width [...] and the height of [...] *8* [...cu]bits, and you shall go into the entrance hall [...] *9* [...] ten cubits, and the wall [...] *10* [...] and sixty cubits high [...] *11* [...] twelve cubits and [...] *12* [...] twenty-one cubits [...] *13* [...] ... twenty cubits square [...] *14* [...]... *Blank* [...] *15* [...] from its half [...] *16-17* [...] ... [...]

Col. V   *1* [...] which are connected [...] *2* [...] cubits [...] *3* [...] the thickness three [...] *4* [...]... according to the size of [...] *5* [...]...for twenty-eight [...] *6* [...]... and also its ceiling [...] *7* [...] cubits the total height [...] *8* [...]... and four gates [...] [...] *9* [...] the gate twelve [...] *10* [...] cubits and all the eaves [...] *11* [... lo]wer, and all encased [...] *12* *Blank* [...] *13* [...]... and made a portico [...] *14* [...] in all [...]

Col. VI   *1* [...] ... [...] *2* [...] upon [...] *3* [...] ... twen[ty-e]ight cubits [...] *4* [...] for[ty] cubits and the cei[ling ...] *5* [...] ten cubits the total height of the eaves, and the wind[ows ...] *6* [...] ... doors of the loft for the four [...] *7* [... twe]lve cubits, and its height ele[ven...] *8* [...] its doors [...] lower and all [...] *9* [...] ... [...] ... [...]

Col. VII   *1* [...] the planks [...] *2* [...] ... [...] *3* [...] the planks of wo[od...] *4* [...] one cubit and ten [...] *5* [...] eighty pla[nks...] *6* [...] on top of all... [...] *7* [...] ... hundred ... [...] *8* [...] ... five cu[bits] in total [...] *9* [...] ... its height, and the cover which is on top [...] *10* [...] ... its width, and two cherubim [...] *11* [...] .. on the other side, stretching out (their) wings [...] *12* [...] ... on top of the ark; and their faces, one [...] *13* [...] *Blank* And you shall make a gold veil [...] *14–15* [...] ... [...] ... [...]

Col. VIII   *1* [...] ... [...] *2* [...] opposite the ark [...] *3* [...] ... seven [...] *4* [...] *Blank* [...] *5* [...] its width, and a cubit [...] *6* [...] ... and you shall make [...] *7* [...] ... [...] *8* [...] ... two [...] *9* [...] ... on top of the two rows [...] *10* [...] this incense over the bread as a reminder [...] *11* [...ab]ove the altar of incense on removing it [...] *12* [...] the bread, you shall place frankincense on it; [...] not *13* [...eter]nal for their generations. This bread will be [...] *14* [...] they shall come [...]

Col. IX   *1* [...] ... *2* [...] their ... and its flowers *3* [...] on its two sides *4* [...] and on one side, three *5* [...] and its hilt *6–7* [...] ... *8* [...] three *9* [...] all the shaft *10* [...] ... three *11* [...] and its snuffers, all of it of two talents *12* [...] they shall light all the lamps and place it *13* [...] and the priests, sons of [...] shall prepare *14* [...] eternal law [for their gene]rations.

Col. X   *1–7* (Traces of letters at the ends of lines) *8* [...] the gate [...] ... *9* [...] ... above the gate *10* [...] ... [...] you shall wear a scarlet cloth *11* [...] and on top of that, columns *12* [...] ... a cloth of red purple, and the capitals *13* [...] *14* and scarl[et...] *15–18* (Traces of letters at the beginnings of lines)

Col. XI   *1–8* (Traces of letters at the ends of lines) *9* [...] ... on the sabbaths and at the beginnings of *10* [...] ... on the feast of the unleavened (bread) and on the day when the sheaf of ears is waved *11* [...] the first-fruits for the offering of wheat *12* [...] ... and on the feast of new oil and on the six days *13* [...] on the feas]t of tents and on the assembly of *14* [...] ... *15–16* (Traces of letters at the beginnings of lines)

Col. XII   *1–7* (Unreadable) *8* [...] ... its dimensions will be *9* [...] ... on one face, and a cubit *10* [...] ... all of it built *11* of sto[nes ...] ... You shall make all *12* [...] ... *13* its hor[ns] and its cor[ners...] You shall make it *14–16* (Traces of letters)

Col. XIII   *1* so that [...] *2* ten cu[bits ...] *3* you shall make [...] *4* and the doors [...] *5* one [...] *6* covered [...] *7* to it a door like [...] *Blank* [...] *9* And the oblation [...] *10* the blood for the people [...] ... [...] *11* without blemish [... a ten]th of *12* finest flour mixed [...] /and its libation of wine of a quar[ter ...]/ *13* for YHWH [...] ... *14* of the burnt [offering] which is for him [...] *15* like the morning off[ering] [...] ... *16* not [...] *17* The sa[bbaths] you shall offer two [...]

Col. XIV   *1* [...] a [...] *2* [and an offer]ing of finest flour mix[ed...] *3* ha]lf a *hin* [...] *4* [...] with a third of a [*hin* ...] *5* [...] a tenth [...] *6* [...] for a lamb [...] *7* [fragrance] which appeases YHWH. At the beginni[ngs ...] *8* the months of the year [...] *9* The first of the month [...] *10* of the year. [You shall do] no menial work [...] *11* Only it will be offered to atone [...] *12* a ram, year[ling] lambs *13* ...[...]... *14* of half a *hin* [...] for libation [...] *15* tenths of finest flour for the mixed offering [...] *16* a thi[rd of] a *hin* for the ram [...] *17* [...] offering [...] *18* [...] a [...] the lambs and for the he-goat [...]

Col. XV   *1* each day [...] *2* seven yearling (lambs) and a he-go[at...] *3* according to this regu[lation [...For the consecration a ram for each day] /and baskets of bread for all the ram[s of the consecration and a basket/ *4* for each [ram]. You shall share out all the sheep and the baskets over the seven [days of the consecration, one for each] *5* day, according to [their divisions. You shall offer to YHWH the right leg,] *6* holocaust of the ram, and [the fat which covers its entrails,] the two *7* kidneys and the fat which is on them, [the fat which is on] *8* the loins and the [whole] tail, cut off at the coccyx, and the lobe of the liver, *9* and its offering and its libation, according to the regu[lation. You shall take up a cake of unleavened bread from the] basket and a cake *10* of oiled bread and a wafer, [and you shall place it all on top of the fat] *11* with the leg of the wave-offering, the right leg. Those who are offering [shall wave] *12* the rams and the baskets of bread, a wave-offering [before YHWH; it is a holocaust,] *13* fire-sacrifice of fragrance which appeases YHWH. [You shall burn everything on the altar, on top of] *14* the holocaust, in order to consecrate their souls (for) the se[ven days of the consecration.] *15* When the High Priest, [who has been consecrated] *16* to don the vestments in succession to his fathers, stands [in order

to serve before YHWH,] he [will offer a bullock] *17* for all the people and another
for the priests. He will first bring near *18* what is for the priests. The elders
from among the priests shall lay [their hands]

Col. XVI   *1* [...] ... [...] *2* [...] they shall put the blood [...] *3* [...] right and they
shall sprinkle [...] *4* [...] they shall be all his days [...] *5* [...] he will [not] defile,
for he is holy [...] *6* [...al]tar, and he will burn the [fat of the first bullock...]
7 [all the fat] which there is upon the entrails and the [lobe of the liver and the
two] *8* [ki]dneys and the fat there is upon them, and the [fat which is upon]
9 the loins and its offering and its liba[tion according to the regulation.] *10* It is
a holocaust, a fire-sacrifice of fragrance which appeases [YHWH.] *11* They shall
burn [the flesh of the bullock] and its hide, with its offal, outside [the city]
12 in a place set aside for the sin-offerings. There they shall bu[rn] it [from head
to feet] *13* with all its entrails; they shall burn everything there, except its fat.
It is a sin-offe[ring.] *14* He will take a second bullock, the one which is for the
people, and with it atone [for all the people] *15* of the assembly with its blood
and with its fat; as he did with the first bullock, [so will he do] *16* with the bullock of the assembly. With his fingers he will smear with blood the horns of the
[altar] *17* and he will sprinkle [all] its blood over the four corners of the rim of
the altar *18* and he will burn in the altar [its fat] its offering and its libation. It
is a sin-offering for the assembly.

Col. XVII   *1* [...] the priests, and they shall place [...] *2* [...] they shall rejoice
because atonement has been made for them [...] *3* [...] and this day will be for
them [...] *4* [...] in all their villages and they will rejoice [...] *5* [...] *Blank* [...]
6 The fourteenth day of the first month, [at twilight,] *7* [they will celebrate the
Passover of YHWH;] they will perform sacrifice prior to the evening offering
and they will sacrifice [...] *8* Those twenty years old and over shall celebrate it,
and they shall consume it at night *9* in the courtyards of the sanctuary. Then
they shall stand up and each one will go to [his tent.] *10* *Blank* The fifteenth day
of this month there will be a ho[ly] assembly. In it you shall do no menial work.
It is the feast of leaven, over seven days, *12* for YHWH. Throughout these seven
days you shall offer, each day, *13* a holocaust to YHWH: two young bulls, a ram,
seven yearling lambs *14* without blemish and a he-goat for the sin-offering,
together with its offerings and libations, *15* according to the regulation for
young bulls, rams, lambs and the goat. The seventh day *16* [there will be a sol-
emn assembly] for YHWH. On it you shall do no menial work.

Col. XVIII   *1* [...] ... [...] *2* [...] for this ram [...] *3* this day and [...] *4* [a he-]goat
for sin-offering [...] *5* [its offering and its libation] according to the regulation:
a tenth of finest flour *6* [and] wine for the libation: a quarter of a *hin*. *7* [It will
atone] for all the sins of the people of the assembly *8* [and they will be forgiven

them. For all their generations] this will be an eternal regulation for them *9* [in all their villages.] Afterwards, they shall offer the single ram, only once, *10* [...] the of day the sheaf-waving. *Blank* You shall count off *11* seven complete sabbaths from the day on which you fetch the sheaf *12* [from the wave-offering,] you shall count off until the day following the seventh sabbath, you shall count off *13* [fifty] days, and you shall fetch a new offering to YHWH from your villages: *14* new leavened [bread] of finest flour, first-fruits for YHWH, wheaten bread, *15* twe[lve cakes;] each cake will be of [two] tenths of finest flour. *16* [The heads of] the clans of the tribes of Israel [will carry them] and offer

Col. XIX   *1* [...] ... [...] *2* [...] the holocaust [...] *3* [...] twelve [...] *4* [...] their offerings and [their liba]tions according to the regulation and they shall lift [...] *5* [...] from the first-fruits, [they shall be for] the priests and they shall eat them in the *6* [inner courtyard, new offeri]ng, bread of the first-fruits. And afterwards [...] *7* [...] a fresh loaf of tendrils of barley and corncobs. [This day] will be *8* [ete]rnal [precept] for their generations. They shall [do] no menial work. *9* It is [the feast] of weeks and the feast of the first-fruits for eternal memorial. *10 Blank 11* From the day on which you carried to YHWH the new offering, *12* the bread of the first-fruits, you shall count off seven weeks, seven full weeks; *13* you shall count off fifty days until the day following the seventh sabbath, *14* and [you shall carry] new wine for the libation: four *hin* for all the tribes of Israel, *15* [...] a th[ird] of a *hin* for each tribe. That day *16* all the heads of a thousand of Israel shall offer [to YHWH with the wine twelve rams]

Col. XX   *1* [...] and the libation and they shall offer [...] *2* [...] fourteen yearling [lambs] [...] *3* [...] the holocaust; they shall make them [...] *4* [and their fat] they shall burn upon the altar [...] *5* [the fat surrounding the entrails] and all the fat there is upon the entr[ails,] *6* [and the lobe of the liver] over the kidneys, will be removed together with the fat [which is on top of them] *7* [and that which there is over the loins and] the tail, cut at the coccyx. And they shall bu[rn] *8* [everything upon the altar,] with their offerings and libations. It is a fire-sacrifice of fragrance which appeases *9* [YHWH.] They shall offer every offering with which a libation is offered according to [the prescription.] *10* [And from all] the offering with which incense is offered or if it is a dry offering, they shall collect *11* [the part of the mem]orial, and they shall burn it on the altar; the remains of it they shall eat in the *12* [inner] courtyard. The priest will eat it with unleavened bread. They shall eat no yeast. They shall eat it on this day *13* [and upon it] the sun [shall not set.] And on all your offerings you shall put salt and the salt shall not cease *14* [upon them.] *Blank* They shall pick out for YHWH as (a) levy *15* [from] the ram and from the lambs the right leg, the breast, the *16* [jawbones, the stomach] and the shoulder blade up to the bone of the upper foreleg. They shall wave them: a wave–offering

Col. XXI   *1* [...] a ram and a lamb; and for each *2* clan [...] one for all the cl[ans of the twe]lve tribes *3* of Israel. And they shall eat [...] before YHWH, *4* the priests shall drink there first and the lev[ites *5* [...] first the chiefs of battalion [...] *6* [...] and after them all the people, from the oldest to the smallest, *7* shall go and drink new wine. [They shall not] eat any grape, sour fruit of the vine, [until] *8* [on] this day they atone for the new wine. The children of Israel shall rejoice in YHWH's presence. *9* Eternal [law] for their generations in all their villages. They shall rejoice on [this day] *10* [at going] to pour out a libation of juice, a new wine, over the altar of YHWH, year by year. *11* *Blank* *12* From this day you shall count off seven times seven weeks. *13* There will be forty-nine days from the seven full weeks up to the day after *14* the seventh sabbath. You shall count off fifty days and you shall offer new oil from the villages *15* [of the clans of the sons of Is]rael: each one of the clans: half a *hin*; refined new oil, *16* [...] virgin oil, over the altar, holocaust of the first-fruits before YHWH.

Col. XXII   *1* [...] they shall burn this oil in the lamps [...] *2* the heads of thousand with the pri[nces...] *3* [...] fourteen [yearling lambs] and their offerings and libations [...] *4* [...] the sons of Levi shall slaughter [...] *5* The priests, sons of Aaron, [shall] sprinkle with its blood [the altar on all its sides] *6* [...] and they shall burn its fat over the altar of holo[causts] *7* [and their offerings] and libations they shall burn over the fat [... fire-sacrifice of fragrance] *8* which appeases YHWH. *Blank* They shall take some [...] *9* the right leg and the breasts of the wave-offering; and as the choicest part [...] *10* and for the priests the jawbones and the stomach, it shall be his share in accordance with the prescription [...] *11* the upper foreleg. Then they shall take it out to the children of Israel. And the children of Israel shall give the priests *12* a ram and a lamb; to the levites a ram and a lamb and to each *13* clan a ram and a lamb. And they shall eat it throughout this day in the outer courtyard *14* in front of YHWH. Eternal precepts for their generations, year after year. Afterwards *15* they shall eat and they shall anoint themselves with the new oil and with the olives, because on this day they shall atone *16* [for all the] virgin [o]il of the land in front of YHWH, once a year. And they shall rejoice

Col. XXIII   *1* [...] ... [...] *2* [...] which [...] *3* [...] holocaust for YH[WH] *4* [...] two he-goats [...] *5* and his offer]ing and libation according to [the prescription ...] *6* [...] a bullock, a ram, a la[mb...] *7* [...] each one of the tribes of the twelve sons of Jacob [...] *8* [...] over the altar after the per[petual] holocaust [...] *9* [...] ... The High Priest will offer the [holocaust of the levites] *10* first, and after it, he will burn the holocaust of the tribe of Judah. [When he is about] *11* to burn it, he shall first slaughter the he-goat in front of it; he shall take *12* its blood to the altar in a sprinkling bowl, and he will anoint with blood, with his fingers, the four horns of the altar *13* of holocaust and the four corners of the rim of the altar; he shall pour out its blood over the base *14* of the rim of the altar on every side and shall burn its fat in the altar; the fat which covers *15* the intestines and what is over the entrails. The lobe of the liver with the kidneys *16* he shall remove and the fat which is over them and which is over the loins; and he will burn *17* everything upon the altar with its offering and its libation. It is a fire-sacrifice, of fragrance which appeases YHWH.

Col. XXIV   *1* [...] the head [...] *2* [...] and it [...] *3* [...] the breast with [...] *4* [...] the paws, and they shall [burn...] *5* [... offer]ing of its oil and libation of [its wine...] *6* [...] the flesh for fragrance [...] *7* [... for each] bullock and for each ram and for [...] *8* and its cuts will be separated and its offering and its libation on top of it. [Eternal] precepts *9* for your generations before YHWH. *Blank 10* In continuation of this holocaust he will offer the holocaust of the only tribe of Judah. In the same way that *11* he offered the holocaust of the levites, so will he do with the holocaust of the sons of Judah after the levites. *12 Blank* On the second day he will offer first the holocaust of Benjamin, and after it *13* he will offer the holocaust of the sons of Joseph together with Ephraim and Manasseh. On the third day he will offer *14* the holocaust of Reuben, only, and the holocaust of Simeon, only. On the fourth day *15* he will offer the holocaust of Issachar only, and the holocaust of Zebulon, only. On the fifth day *16* he will offer the holocaust of Gad, only, and the holocaust of Asher, only. On the sixth day

Col. XXV   *1* [...] he will offer [...] *2* [...] *Blank 3* [For you the first day of the month will be] a great sabbath, a memorial of the blast of trumpets, a [holy] assem[bly]. *4* [You shall make a holocaust of fire of fragrance which appeases] YHWH, and you shall off[er a bullock,] *5* a ram, seven [perfect] yearling [la]mbs and a he *6* [–goat for the sin-offering, and] their offerings and libations according to the prece[pt,] *7* [as well as] the perpetual [hol]ocaust and the monthly [holo]caust. Afterwards [you shall offer] *8* this [holocaust] in the third part of the day. Eternal precepts for your generations [in all your villages.] *9* You shall rejoice on this day. On it you shall do no menial work. This day *10* will be for you a great sabbath. *Blank* The tenth of this month *11* is the day of the atonement. On it you shall afflict your souls, because anyone who does not *12* do penance on this same day will be expelled from his people. On it you shall offer a holocaust *13* for YHWH: a bullock, a ram, seven yearling lambs {...} and a he-*14* goat for the sin-offering. Besides the sin-offering of the day of atonement and its offerings and libations *15* according to the prescription for the bullock, the ram, the lambs, the he-goat and the sin-offering of the day of atonement, you shall offer *16* two rams for the holocaust. One the High Priest will offer for himself and for the house of his father.

Col. XXVI   *1–2* [...] ... [...] *3* [...] The High Priest [will cast lots] *4* [concerning the two he-goats:] one will fall by lot [to YHWH, the other to Azazel;] *5* [and] he will slaughter the he-goat which [has fallen by lot to YHWH and will take] *6* its blood in the golden sprinkling bowl which he has in his hand and will treat [its blood as he treated the blood] *7* of the bullock which was for himself, and with it he will atone for all the people of the assembly. Its fat and the offering of *8* its libation he will burn on the altar of holocausts; but its flesh, its hide and its entrails *9* they shall burn together with his bullock. It is the sin-offering for the assembly *10* and they shall be forgiven. He will wash his hands and his feet from the blood of the sin-offering and will go to the *11* live he-goat and will confess over its head all the sins of the children of Israel with all their guilt together with all their sins; he shall place them upon the head of the he-goat and will send it *13* to Azazel, to the desert, from the hand of man indicated. And the he-goat will take with itself all the sins

Col. XXVII   *1* [...] ... [...] *2* for /all/ the children of Israel, and they shall be forgiven [...] *3* Afterwards he will offer the bullock, the ram and [the lambs according to the] ordinance, *4* upon the altar of holocaust, and the holocaust for the children of Israel will be accepted. Eternal precepts *5* for their generations. Once a year this day will function as a memorial for them, *6* and on it they shall do no menial work, because it is a great Sabbath. Every man *7* who does any menial work on it, or does not do penance will be cut off from the midst *8* of your people. It is a great Sabbath. You shall hold a holy assembly on this day *9* and you will sanctify it as a memorial in all your villages and you shall do no *10* menial work. *Blank* The fifteenth day of this month

Col. XXVIII   *1* [...] ... [...] *2* the altar. It is a fire-sacrifice, [fragrance which appeases YHWH. *Blank* On the] *3* second [day:] twelve bullocks, [two rams, fourteen lambs] *4* and a he-goat [for the sin-offering, and their offerings and libations] *5* according to the ordinance for the bullocks, the rams, the lambs and the he-goat. It is a fire-sacrifice, *6* fragrance which appeases YHWH. *Blank* On the third day, *7* eleven bullocks, two rams, fourteen lambs *8* and a he-goat, for the sin-offering and their offerings and libations according to the ordinance for the bullocks *9* the rams, the lambs and the he-goat. *Blank* On the fourth day, *10* ten bullocks, two rams, fourteen sheep and a he-goat for the sin-offering, and its offerings and libations for the bullocks

Col. XXIX   *1* and its libations [...] *2* These are [...] *3* for your holocausts and your libations [...]. In the house *4* above which I shall make my name reside [they shall offer] the holocausts, [each day what corresponds to] that day according to the ruling of this precept, *5* continually, from the children of Israel, besides their freewill offerings. All that they offer me, *6* all their libations and all the presents which they bring me for acceptance, *7* I shall accept them. They shall be for me a people and I will be for them for ever and I shall establish them *8* for ever and always. I shall sanctify my temple with my glory, for I shall make my glory reside *9* over it until the day of creation, when I shall create my temple, establishing it for myself for ever, in accordance with the covenant which I made with Jacob at Bethel.

Col. XXX   *1* […] and I will sanctify […] *2* […] … […] *3* […] to make, and you shall [make…] *4* […] for the stairways […] in the house which you shall build […] *5* […] … [……you shall] make a spiral staircase to the North of the Sanctuary: a square building *6* of twenty cubits from corner to corner, its four corners matching, located *7* seven cubits away from the wall of the Sanctuary, Northeast of it. Its wall you shall make four cubits in width *8* […] like the Sanctuary; its interior will be twelve cubits from corner to corner. *9* It will have a square pillar within it, in the centre, of four cubits *10* in width on each side […] around which the steps will go up.

Col. XXXI   *1* […] … *2* […] the gate *3* […] … *4* […] the second priest *5* […] … […] … *6* In the loft of this buil[ding you shall make a do]or opening to the roof of the Sanctuary and a passageway made *7* in this door to the opening [of the roof of the] Sanctuary, by which one can enter the loft of the Sanctuary. *8* You shall cover all this building of the spiral staircase with gold: its walls, its gates, its roof both inside *9* and out, its pillar and its steps, and you shall do everything according to what I have told you. *10* You shall make a square building for the laver, to the South-east; all its sides will be twenty-one *11* cubits, at fifty cubits distance from the altar; the width of the wall will be three cubits and the height *12* twenty cubits […] You shall make gates for it to the East, North *13* and West; the width of the gates will be four cubits and their height seven.

Col. XXXII   *1* […] three cubits […] *2-5* […] … […] *6* […] their faults to atone for the people and when they go up *7* […] … and in order to burn *8* the holo[caust] *7* upon the altar *8* […] the wall *9* of this building […] and in the centre of them […] of a cubit in width and its height *10* from the ground will be four cubits, covered over in gold, on which they shall place *11* their clothes with which they will go up on top of the house of […] *12* when they enter to minister in the Holy. You shall make a channel all round the laver within the building. The channel *13* runs [from the building] of the laver to a shaft, goes down and disappears in the middle of the earth so that *14* the water flows and runs through it and is lost in the middle of the earth and no–*15* one should touch it because it is mixed with the blood of the holocaust.

Col. XXXIII   *1* […] they shall enter […] *2* and at the moment when […] *3* […] … and […] *4* […] above them and they shall deposit […] *5* […] … the laver build-

ing and [...] 6 [those who en]ter them and those who go out from them to [...]
7 they shall sanctify my people with the sacred vestments which [...] 8 *Blank* To
the East of the laver building you shall make a building with the same measurements as the la[ver] building. 9 The distance between its walls will be seven
cubits and its constructions and its ceilings will be like those of the laver building. 10 It will have two gates: to the North and to the South, one facing the
other, with the same measurements as the gates of the 11 laver building. In this
whole building, in all its walls on the inside there will be blocked windows;
12 their width will be two cubits by two and their height four cubits, 13 with
doors, niches for the paraphernalia of the altar, for the ewers, the jars, the
tongs, 14 the little silver vessels in which they place the innards and 15 paws
upon the altar. *Blank* When they finish burning

Col. XXXIV   1 [...] in a bron[ze] plate [...] 2 [...] and between column and
col[umn...] 3 [...] which there is between the columns [...] 4 [...] ... between
the whe[els...] 5 [...] ... and they shall close the wheels [...] 6 [...and they shall
tie] the heads of the bullocks to the rings. 7 Afterwards they shall slaughter
them and collect [the blood] in basins 8 and pour it over the base of the altar on
all sides. *Blank* And they shall open 9 the wheels and tear off the hides of the
bullocks from their flesh and they shall chop it 10 into pieces and they shall salt
the pieces with salt. They shall wash 11 the innards and paws, they shall salt
them with salt and they shall burn them in 12 the fire which there is on the
altar: bullock by bullock and its pieces with it and its offering of finest flour on
top of it, 13 and the wine of its libation with it. The priests, sons of Aaron,
shall burn everything 14 upon the altar. It is a fire-sacrifice of fragrance which
appeases YHWH. *Blank* 15 You shall make chains which go down from the ceiling
of the twelve columns

Col. XXXV   1 [...the Ho]ly of Ho[lies...] 2 [...] every man who is not [...] 3 [...]
every man who is not [...] holy 4 [...] ... and every [...] who is 5 not a priest
will be put to death and every one who [...pri]est who enters 6 [...] ... without
putting on the [sacred vestments with which] he was 7 consecrated, these, too,
shall be put to death. They shall not pro[fane the Tem]ple of his God, incurring 8 a sin punishable by death. They shall sanctify what surrounds the altar,
the sanctuary, the laver 9 and the porch. It is sacred for ever and always. *Blank*
10 To the West of the Sanctuary you shall build a circular place, a porch with
columns. The columns 11 for the sin-offering and for the sacrifice for faults,
separated from one another, for the sin-offering of the priests and for the he-
goats, 12 for the sin-offerings of the people and for the sacrifices for faults. No-
one shall proceed from one to the other, 13 for their sites will be separated from
one another, so that 14 the priests do not sin unintentionally with any of the
sin-offering of the people or with the sacrifices for faults, incurring 15 an ac-
countable sin. *Blank* He will offer the birds upon the altar, the turtle-doves

Col. XXXVI   *1* [...] ... [...] *2* [...] the gates and [...] cubits [...] *3* [...] from the corner [...] *4* [up to the ang]le of the gate, [one hundred and twenty cubits;] the width of the gate will be forty *5* [cubits]. Each one of the sides [will have these measurements.] The thick[ness of the wa]ll will be seven cubits, *6* [and its heigh]t forty-five cubits, up to the ceiling of the roof. [The width of the rooms will be] *7* twenty-six cubits from corner to corner. Gates for entry *8* and exit: width of the gate: fourteen cubits; its height, *9* twenty-eight cubits from the threshold to the lintel. Height *10* of the ceiling right from the lintel: fourteen cubits. The beam of the ceiling will be of *11* cedar overlaid with pure gold; and its gates will be covered with quality gold. *12 Blank* From the angle of the gate up to the second corner of the courtyard there will be *13* one hundred and twenty cubits. Thus shall be the measurements of all these gates which give *14* onto the inner courtyard. The gates shall open inwards, towards the inside of the courtyard

Col. XXXVII   *1* [...] ... [...] *2* [...] new from the gardens, for all the [...] *3* [...] between... [...] *4* [...] inside of the edge of the altar which [...] *5* the peace-sacrifices of the children of Israel... and to [...] *6* [...] the corners of the inner porch made...[...] *7* and kit[chens] joined to [...of the] gates, on the two sides of the gate. *8* In the [inner] courtyard you shall make rooms for the priests, and tables *9* in front of the rooms; in the inner courtyard, joined to the wall of the outer courtyard, *10* places made for the priests, for their sacrifices and for the first-fruits and the tithes, *11* and for their peace-sacrifices which they will offer. There shall be no mingling of the peace *12* sacrifices of the children of Israel with the sacrifices of the priests. *13* In the four corners of the courtyard you shall make for them a place for the cauldrons *14* where they shall cook their sacrifices and the sin-offerings

Col. XXXVIII   *1* [...] they shall eat [...] *2* [...] ... [...] *3* [...] they shall eat and drink [...] *4* and they shall eat [...] the grain, the wine and the oil [...] *5* [...] the children of Israel and on the day of the first-fruits [...] *6* they shall eat together in the Western gate [...] *7* [...] the grapes and pomegranates [...] all the wood which enters [...] *8* [...] the offering of the oblations over which there is incense [...] the offering for jealousy. *9* And on the right of this gate [...] *10* ... there they shall eat the products ... [...] *11 Blank 12* You shall make a second court-yard surrounding the inner courtyard, one hundred cubits in width *13* and four hundred and eighty cubits in length on the East side. The same will be the width and length of all *14* its sides, on the South, West and North. The width of the wall will be four cubits and its height *15* twenty-eight cubits. There will be rooms made in the walls on the outside and between one room and another there will be three

Col. XXXIX   *1* [...] ... [...] *2* ... the ceiling of the roof [...] *3* ... [...] and its doors covered with gold *4* ... [...] this courtyard [...] *5* ... [...] the fourth generation. A son of *6* Israel [...] in order to prostrate herself in front of all the assembly of the sons of *7* Israel... [...] No woman shall enter it nor any boy until the day *8* on which [...] by himself to YHWH give half a shekel, eternal law *9* for memorial in their villages. The shekel will be of twenty *geras*. *10* When [...] for me; afterwards shall come those of *11* twenty [years and over...] The na[mes of the] gates of this courtyard will correspond to the nam[es] *12* of the children of Israel: Simeon, Levi and Judah to the East; Reuben, Joseph and Benjamin to the South; *13* Issachar, Zebulon and Gad to the West; Dan, Naphtali and Asher to the North. Between one gate and another *14* the measurement is from the North-east corner up to the gate of Simeon ninety-nine cubits; the gate, *15* twenty-eight cubits; from this gate {of Simeon} up to the gate of Levi, ninety-nine *16* cubits; the gate, twenty-eight cubits; from the gate of Levi up to the gate of Judah,

Col. XL   *1* [...] to wear the gar[ments...] *2* [...] in order to serve [...] *3* [...] the children of Israel and they shall not [die...] *4* [...] this court[yard] ... [...] *5* [...] You shall make a third courtyard [...] *6* [...] to their daughters and to foreigners, who were bo[rn...] *7* [... the wid]th around the central courtyard will be six[hundred cubits (?)] *8* by a length of about one thousand six [hundred] cubits from one corner to the other, on each side, according to these measurements. *9* To the East, to the South, to the West and to the North the thickness of the wall will be seven cubits and its height *10* forty-nine cubits; and it will have recesses, made between the gates, on the outside, at the base of the foundation *11* up to its cornice. In the wall there will be three gates to the East, three to the South, three *12* to the West and three to the North. The width of the gates will be fifty cubits and their height seventy *13* cubits. The [measurement] between gate and gate will be three hundred and sixty cubits. From the corner up to *14* the gate of Simeon there will be three hundred and sixty cubits; from the gate of Simeon up to the gate of Levi, *15* the same measurement; from the gate of Levi up to the gate of Judah, the same measurement; three [hundred] and sixty

Col. XLI   *1* [...] ... [...] *2* [...From the corner] *3* up to the ga[te of Issachar, is three hundred and sixty] cubits; *5* from the gate of Zab[ulon up the gate of Gad,] three hundred and sixty *6* cubits; from the [gate of Gad up to the North corner,] three hundred and *7* sixty cubits. *Blank* From this corner up to *8* the gate of Dan, three hundred and sixty cubits, and the same from the gate of Dan up to *9* the gate of Naphtali, three hundred and sixty cubits. From the gate of Naphtali *10* up to the gate of Asher, three hundred and sixty cubits; from the gate of *11* Asher up to the Eastern corner, three hundred and sixty cubits. *12* The gates shall protrude from the wall of the courtyard outwards seven cubits *13* and will penetrate inwards out of the wall of the courtyard thirty-six cubits. *14* The width of openings of gateways will be fourteen cubits and their height *15* twenty-eight cubits up to the lintel. The rafters will be *16* formed of cedar and covered in gold. Their doors will be overlaid *17* with pure gold. On the inside, between one gate and another, you shall make store-rooms

Col. XLII   *1* [Its length will be] twenty cubits. The wall will be two cubits thick; *2* [its height will be fourteen cubits] up to the beams, and its opening *3* three cubits wide. [So shall you do] with all the store-rooms, their rooms *4* and their por[ches... The wi]dth will be ten cubits. Between one gate *5* and another [you shall make eigh]teen storerooms and their *6* eighteen rooms. *Blank 7* You shall make a stairwell to the side of the walls of the gates in the middle of the *8* porch (with steps) which spiral upwards within the second and third porch *9* and the roof. The store-rooms and their rooms and their porches will be constructed like those below. *10* The second and third floors will be of the same measurements as those below. Above the third roof *11* you shall make columns, furnished with beams from column to column, *12* a place for the huts, eight cubits in height. *13* Year after year, on the festival of the huts, they shall make huts there for the elders *14* of the congregation, for the princes, for the heads of families, for the children of Israel, *15* for the chiefs of a thousand and the chiefs of a hundred, who shall go up *16* and live there until the holocaust of the festival is offered which [corresponds] *17* to the festival of huts, year after year. Between one gate and another there will be

Col. XLIII   *1* [...] ... [...] *2* [...] on the sabbaths and on the days [...] *3* [...] and on the days of the first-fruits of grain, of mu[st and of oil] *4* [and on the feast of the offering of] wood. It will be eaten on these days and will not remain *5* [from one year] for the next. They shall eat it in this way: *6* the grain they shall eat from the feast of the first-fruits of the grain of wheat *7* up to the following year, up to the day of the festival of first-fruits; the wine, from the day *8* of the feast of new wine up to the day of the feast of new wine of the following year; *9* and the oil, from the day of its feast up to the following year, *10* up to the feast of the day of the offering of new oil on the altar. Everything which is surplus from their feasts will be holy, it will be burned on the fire, it shall not be eaten *12* because it is holy. Those who live at a distance of three days from the temple *13* shall carry all that they can carry; if they are unable *14* to convey it they shall sell it for money and shall bring the money and with it they shall buy grain, *15* wine, oil, cattle and sheep, and they shall eat it during the days of the festivals. They *16* shall not eat this on work-days for their own sustenance because it is holy; *17* it will be eaten on the holy days and will not be eaten on the work-days.

Col. XLIV   *1* [...] the inhabitants [...] *2* [...] which there is within the city, up to the Ea[st ...] *3* [...] You shall share out the [... From the gate of] *4* [Simeon] up to the gate of Judah, they shall be for the priest[s] *5* all the right side of the gate of Levi and its left side you shall allot to the sons of Aaron, your brother: *6* one hundred and eight stores and their rooms and their huts *7* which are on top of the roof. To the sons of Judah, from the gate of Judah up to *8* the corner: fifty-four stores and their rooms and the hut *9* which there is above them. To the sons of Simeon, from the gate of Simeon up to the *10* second corner: its store-rooms, its rooms and its huts. To the sons of Reuben, *11* from the corner which is next to the sons of Judah up to the gate of Reuben: *12* fifty-two store-rooms, their rooms and their huts. From the gate of *13* Reuben up to the gate of Joseph, to the sons of Joseph, to Ephraim and Manasseh. *14* From the gate of Joseph up to the gate of Benjamin, to the sons of Kohath, from the Levites. *15* From the gate of Benjamin up to the western corner to the sons of Benjamin. From this corner *16* up to the gate of Issachar, to the sons of Issachar. From the gate

Col. XLV   *1* [...] ... [...] *2* seventy [...] *3* When [...] the second shall enter to the left [...] *4* the first shall go out on the right and one shall not intermingle with the other, nor with their uten[sils...] *5* the priestly course in its place, and they shall camp. He who goes in and he who goes out on the eighth day shall purify the *6* store-rooms, one after another, [at] the moment when the first goes out; and there shall be no *7* mingling there. *Blank* Anyone who has had a nocturnal emission shall not enter *8* the temple at all until three days have passed. He shall wash his clothes and shall bathe *9* on the first day and on the third day he shall wash his clothes /and bathe/ at sunset. Afterwards *10* he shall enter the temple. But they shall not enter my temple which their soiled impurity to defile it. *11* Anyone who lies with his wife and has an ejaculation, for three days shall not enter *12* anywhere in the city of the temple in which I shall install my name. *Blank* No blind person *13* shall enter it throughout his whole life; he shall not defile the city in the centre of which I dwell *14* because I, YHWH, dwell in the midst of the children of Israel for ever and always. *15* Everyone who purifies himself from his gonorrhoea shall count off seven days up to his purification. On day *16* seven he shall wash his clothes and immerse his body completely in running water. Afterwards he shall enter the city *17* of the temple. Anyone who is impure through contact with a corpse shall not enter it until he purifies himself. Every leper *18* and infected person shall not enter it until he purifies himself; when he purifies himself and offers the

Col. XLVI   *1* [...] ... [...] There shall not fly [any] *2* unclean bird over my tem[ple...] ... the roofs and the gates [which lead] *3* to the outer courtyard, and every [...] to be in the middle of my temple for ev[er] *4* and for all the centuries, for [I dwell] among them. *5 Blank* You shall make a platform around the outer courtyard, on the outside, *6* fourteen cubits in width, corresponding to the openings of all the gates; *7* and for it you shall make twelve steps so that the children of Israel can climb up them *8* in order to enter my temple. *Blank 9* You shall make a trench around the temple, one hundred cubits in width, which *10* separates the Holy temple from the city so that they do not suddenly enter *11* my temple and defile it. They shall make my temple holy and respect it, *12* for I dwell among them. *Blank 13* You shall make latrines for them outside the city, where they are obliged to go, *14* outside, to the North-east of the city: houses with beams and wells within them *15* into which excrement shall drop; they shall /not/ be visible from a total distance *16* from the city of three thousand cubits. *Blank* You shall make *17* three zones, to the East of the city, separate from each other, where *18* lepers, those who suffer gonorrhoea and men who have an emission of semen.

Col. XLVII   *1* […] … […] *2* up[wards] and not downwards […] *3* your cities will be pure and […] for ever. The city *4* which I will sanctify, installing my name and my temple [within it] shall be holy and shall be clean *5* from all types of impurity which could defile it. Everything that there is in it shall be *6* pure and everything that goes into it shall be pure: wine, oil, all food *7* and all drink shall be pure. All the hides of pure animal which they sacrifice *8* in their cities they shall not bring into it. In their cities they shall make *9* with these (hides) utensils for all their needs, but they shall not bring them into the city of my temple. *10* Their purity shall be like that of their flesh. You shall not defile the city *11* within which I shall install my name and my temple. With the skins (of the animals) which they sacrifice *12* in the temple, with these very same they shall bring into the city of my temple their wine, their oil and all *13* their food. They shall not defile my temple with the skins of the sacrifices *14* of their abominations which they sacrifice in their land. You shall not purify any city *15* among your cities like my city. In accordance with the purity of their flesh, so shall the skins be pure. *16* What you sacrifice in my temple is pure for my temple; what you sacrifice in your cities is pure *17* for your cities. All the victuals of the temple you shall bring in the skins of the temple and you shall not defile *18* my temple and my city with the skins of your abominations, because I reside within it.

Col. XLVIII   *1* […] … […] *2* […] *Blank* […] *3* [Of your] winged [insects] you can eat: the locust and its species, the bald locust and its species, the cricket *4* and its species, the grasshopper and its species. These you can eat from among winged insects: those which crawl on four paws, which *5* have the hind legs wider than the forelegs in order to leap over the ground with them and to fly with their wings. *6* You cannot eat any carcass of bird or beast; sell it to for-

eigners, but do not eat anything *7* repulsive because you are a holy people for
YHWH your God. *Blank* You are sons *8* for YHWH your God. You shall not gash
yourselves or shave yourselves between your eyes *9* for a dead person, nor shall
you make gashes in your flesh for someone deceased, nor shall you daub yourselves with tattoos because you are a holy people for YHWH your God. *Blank*
You shall not defile *11* your land. *Blank* Do not do as the gentiles do: *12* they
bury their dead all over the place, they even bury them in the middle of their
houses; instead *13* you shall keep places apart within your land where you shall
bury your dead. Among your *14* cities you shall establish a place in which to
bury. In every city you shall make places for those contaminated *15* with leprosy, infection and scabies so that they do not enter your cities and defile them;
and also for those who have gonorrhoea *16* and for women when they are in
their unclean menstruation and after giving birth, so that they do not defile in
their midst *17* with their unclean menstruation. The leper who has chronic
leprosy or scabies and the priest has declared him unclean

Col. XLIX   *1* [...] ... [...] *2* [...] ... to those [...] *3* with cedar wood, with hyssop
and with [...] *4* your cities with the plague of leprosy and infect them. *Blank*
5 When a man dies in your cities, every house in which someone dies shall be
unclean *6* over seven days; everything there is in the house and everything
which goes into the house shall be unclean *7* over seven days; all food over
which water is spilt shall be unclean; every drink *8* shall be unclean; the clay
pots shall be unclean and everything there is in them shall be unclean for every
pure man. *9* The open vessels shall be unclean with all the drink there is them
shall be impure for every Israelite. *10 Blank 11* The day on which they remove
the dead person from the house, they shall cleanse it of every *12* stain of oil,
wine, dampness from water; they shall rub its floor, its walls and its doors;
13 with water they shall wash its hinges, its jambs its thresholds and its lintels.
The day on which *14* the dead person is brought from it, they shall cleanse the
house and all the utensils; the mills, the mortar, *15* all the utensils of wood, iron
and bronze and all the utensils which can be cleaned. *16* They shall wash the
clothes, the sacks and the skins. Every man who has been in the house shall
bathe in water and wash his clothes the first day; *18* the third day they shall
sprinkle over them the waters of purification, they shall bathe and wash their
clothes *19* and the utensils there had been in the house. *Blank* On the seventh
day *20* they shall sprinkle a second time, they shall bathe and wash their clothes
and their utensils and, in the evening, they shall stay purified *21* from the dead
person so that they can approach all the pure things and the men who were not
contaminated by

Col. L   *1* [...] ... [...] *2* because the water of the purifica[tion ...] on mingling
with a dead person [...] *3* shall become impure. In no way ... until they sprinkle

for the second time *4* on the seventh day and are pure in the evening, at sunset. *Blank* Every *5* man who in an open field should touch the bone of a dead person or a stabbed person *6* or a corpse or the blood of a dead person or a burial shall purify himself in compliance with the ruling of this statute, *7* and if he does not purify himself according to the statute of this law he will be impure, *8* his impureness will still persist in him and everyone who touches him shall wash his clothes, bathe and will become pure *9* by the evening. *Blank* *10* When a woman is pregant and her son dies in her womb, all the days which *11* he is dead within her she shall be impure like a grave. Every house which she enters *12* with all its utensils shall stay unclean for seven days; everyone who touches her shall stay impure up to the evening; and if *13* he enters the house with her he will stay impure for seven days; he shall wash his clothes *14* and bathe on the first day; the third day he shall sprinkle, wash his clothes and shall bathe; *15* on the seventh day he shall sprinkle a second time, he shall wash his clothes, bathe *16* and he will become pure by sunset. *Blank* All the utensils, the clothes, the skins and all *17* the objects of goatskin you shall deal with according to the statute of this law. All the vases *18* of clay you shall break because they are unclean; they cannot become clean again, *19* ever. *Blank* *20* Everything which creeps along the ground will be unclean: the mouse, the rat, the lizard and its species, the salamander, *21* the lizard, the chameleon and the wall lizard. Everyone who touches them after they are dead

Col. LI   *1* [what issu]es from them [... will] be unclean *2* [for you nor] will you be contaminated by them. [Everyone who touches them when] they are dead will be impure *3* till the evening; he shall wash his clothes, bathe [and at sun]set he will be pure. *4* Whoever carries their bones or their corpse, the skin or the flesh or the claws, shall wash *5* his clothes and bathe in water at sunset, afterwards he will be pure. Forewarn *6* the children of Israel of every uncleanness. *Blank* They are not to be defiled by those things which *7* I tell you on this mountain. They are not to defile themselves. *Blank* Because I, YHWH, reside *8* among the children of Israel. You shall sanctify them and they shall be holy. They shall not make *9* their souls odious with anything that I have separated from them as unclean and they shall be *10* holy. *Blank* *11* In all your cities you shall install judges and magistrates who judge the people *12* with correct judgment, not show partiality in judgment, and accept no bribe, and not *13* pervert justice, because a bribe perverts justice, corrupts the words of the just person, blinds *14* the eyes of the wise, commits a serious offence and defiles the House with the wickedness *15* of sin. Pursue justice exclusively so that you can live and enter and take possession *16* of the land which I give you so as an inheritance for ever. *17* The one who takes bribes and perverts just judgment shall be killed, and you shall have no qualms *18* in executing him. *Blank* *19* You shall not behave in your land as the nations behave; in any place at all *20* they sacrifice, plant asheroth, set up stelae *21* place hewn stones in order to bow down in front of them and build for themselves

Col. LII   *1* [...] ... you shall not [plant...] *2* [...] You shall not set up for yourself stela [which I loathe] *3* [nor] in all your land make for yourself carved stones in order to bow down in front of them. You shall not *4* sacrifice to me a cow or a sheep which has any serious blemish because it is anathema *5* to me. You shall not sacrifice to me any cow, sheep or she-goat which is pregnant; it is anathema to me. *6* You shall not sacrifice to me a cow or sheep and its young on the same day and you shall not slaughter the mother *7* with its young. *Blank* Every first-born male born to your cattle and sheep *8* you shall consecrate to me. You shall not work with the firstborn of your cow, or shear the firstborn *9* of your sheep. You shall eat it in front of me, year after year, in the place which I shall choose. If there should be *10* any blemish in it: lame or blind or any other serious blem-ish do not sacrifice it to me. *11* You shall eat it in your cities, whether one is pure or impure, like the gazelle or the deer. Only the blood are you not to eat, *12* you shall pour it out on the ground like water and cover it with dust. You shall not put a muzzle on the ox which threshes. *13* You shall not work with an ox and an ass together. You shall not sacrifice any pure cow, sheep or he-goat *14* in any of your cities which are less than three days' walk from my temple, but instead *15* sacrifice them inside the temple, making them into a holocaust and peace offering; you shall eat it *16* and rejoice in front of me in the place where I shall choose to put my name. All *17* pure animals in which there is a blemish you shall eat in your cities, far from my temple *18* at a radius of thirty stadia. You shall not sacrifice near my temple because it is abominable flesh. *19* Within my city, which I make holy by placing my name within it, you shall not eat the flesh of cow, sheep or she-goat *20* which has not come into my tem-ple; they shall sacrifice it there, *21* they shall pour out its blood over the base of the altar of holocausts and they shall burn its fat

Col. LIII   *1* [...] ... [...] *2* [...] the desire of your soul for eating fl[esh] *3* you shall eat fl[esh; you shall slaughter] from your flocks and your cattle according to the blessing which I give you *4* and you shall eat them in your cities, both the clean and the unclean, like the gazelle *5* or the deer. But take care not to eat the blood; you shall pour it out on the ground like water and cover it *6* with dust because the blood is life. You shall not eat the life with the flesh so that *7* it may go well for you and your sons after you, for ever; and you shall do what is up-right and good *8* before me, YHWH, your God. *Blank* *9* Take only your holy things and all your votive offerings and go to the place over which I shall make *10* my name dwell, and sacrifice there in front of me in accordance with what you consecrated or vowed with your mouth. *11* If you make a vow, do not delay in fulfilling it, because I shall certainly demand it from your hand *12* and it shall become a sin to you; but if you refrain and you do not make a vow you shall not have a sin. *13* What your lips have uttered you have to carry out exactly as you promised with your mouth, you have to do *14* as you promised. *Blank* A man who makes a vow to me or promises *15* under oath, binding himself with a formal pledge shall not break his word; he shall act in accordance with all that issued from his mouth. *16 Blank* A woman who makes me a vow or binds herself with a formal pledge *17* in the house of her father, with an oath, in her youth, and her father hears the vow or *18* the formal pledge with which she bound herself and her father says nothing about it, *19* all her vows will remain in force and all the pledges with which she bound herself will stay in force. *Blank* But if *20* her father forbids her on the day when he heard her, all her vows and all her pledges *21* with which she bound herself formally will not remain in force; and I shall pardon her because he forbade her.

Col. LIV   *1* […] … […] *2* his sin […Every vow] or every oath [to do penance] *3* her husband may sanction [it] or her husband may revoke it the day he hears it; and I shall pardon her. *4 Blank* Every vow of a widow or a divorcee, everything by which she binds herself formally *5* will hold good; likewise everything which issues from her mouth. *Blank* All the things which I *6* order you today, take care to carry them out; you shall add nothing to them *7* nor remove anything from them. *Blank 8* If among you there arises a prophet or an interpreter of dreams and gives you a sign or *9* a marvel, and the sign or marvel occurs about which he spoke to you saying: *10* 'Let us go and serve other gods whom you do not know', do not *11* listen to the word of that prophet or of that interpreter of dreams because *12* I am putting you to the test, in order to know whether you love YHWH *13* the God of your fathers, with all your heart and all your soul. *14* You shall follow YHWH your God, serve him and revere him; you shall listen to his voice *15* and attach yourselves to him. And this prophet or interpreter of dreams shall be put to death because he proclaimed rebellion *16* against YHWH, your God, who brought you out from the land of Egypt and saved you *17* from slavery, in order to make you stray from the path on which he ordered you to walk. Thus shall you eradicate *18* the evil in your midst. *Blank* *19* If your brother, the son of your father or the son of your mother, or your son or your daughter *20* or the woman who lies in your embrace or your soulmate provokes you in secret saying: 'Let us go and let us serve other gods whom you do not know'

Col. LV   *1* […] *Blank* […] *2* If in one [of your cities which] I give you so that you res[ide there] you hear *3* it said that there have arisen among you men, sons of Be]lial, and have drawn away all the inhabitants of *4* their city saying: 'Let us go and let us serve other gods whom you do not know', *5* you shall inquire, search and question closely; if the matter is absolutely certain *6* and this atrocity has been committed in Israel, you shall put to the sword all the inhabitants *7* of that city and destroy them; and everything there is in it, and *8* all their animals you shall put to the sword. You shall collect together all their spoils in the middle *9* of the square and set fire to the city and all their spoils entirely for YHWH *10* your God; it shall stay in ruins for ever, it shall not be rebuilt again. There shall not adhere *11* to your hands anything of what has been assigned for destruction. In this way I shall alter the intensity of my anger and shall have *12* mercy on you, take pity on you and increase your numbers as I said to your fathers, *13* if you listen to my voice and keep all the precepts which I enjoin you *14* today in order to do the right and the good before me, YHWH, your God. *15* *Blank* If there happens to be among you in one of the cities which *16* I gave you, a man or a woman who does evil before my eyes *17* breaking my covenant, and goes and serves other gods and bows down in front of them *18* or in front of the sun or in front of the moon or in front of all the legions of heaven, and they tell you it *19* and you hear this thing, you shall investigate and question carefully and *20* if the matter is absolutely certain and this abomination has been committed in Israel, you shall expel *21* that man or that woman and you shall stone them with stones.

Col. LVI   *1* [...] ... [...] *2* the word about you [...] they shall make known to you the sentence. *3* You shall act in accordance with the word *4* which they say to you from the book of the Law. They shall explain it to you accurately *5* from the place I shall select in which to install my name, and you shall take care to act *6* in accordance with everything they tell you. *7* You shall not deviate either to the right or to the left from the law which they explain to you. *8* Whoever does not listen and acts with effrontery in order not *9* to listen to the priest placed there to serve in my presence or the *10* judge, that man shall die. Thus you shall eliminate the evil from Israel and all *11* the people shall listen and fear and no-one will behave insolently in Israel any more. *Blank* *12* When you enter the land which I give you, and own it and live *13* in it and say to yourself: «I shall set a king over myself like all the peoples which surround me», *14* then you shall set over yourself a king /whom I shall choose./ From among your brothers you shall set over yourself a king; *15* you shall not set a foreign man who is not your brother over yourself. But he is not *16* to increase the cavalry or make the people go back to Egypt on account of war in order to *17* increase the cavalry, or the silver and gold. *Blank* I told you «You *18* shall not go back again on this path». He is not to have many wives or *19* let his heart go astray after them. He is not to have much silver and gold; not much. *20* *Blank* When he sits upon the throne of his kingdom they shall write *21* for him this law according to the book which is in front of the priests.

Col. LVII   *1* This is the law [...] the priests. *2* On the day when they proclaim him king, the children of Israel [shall assemble?], from those *3* more than twenty years old up to those of sixty years, according to their banners. And he shall appoint {they shall appoint} *4* at their head chiefs of a thousand, chiefs of a hundred, chiefs of fifty *5* and chiefs of ten in all their cities. From them he shall select a thousand, a thousand *6* from each tribe, to be with him: twelve thousand men of war *7* who will not leave him on his own, so that he will not be seized by the hands of the nations. All those *8* selected, which he selects, shall be men of truth, venerating God, *9* enemies of bribery, skilled men in war; and they shall always be with him *10* day and night and they shall guard him from every act of sin *11* and from the foreign nations so that he does not fall into their hands. He will have twelve *12* princes of his people with him and twelve priests *13* and twelve levites who shall sit next to him for judgment *14* and for the law. He shall not divert his heart from them or do anything *15* in all his councils without relying on them. *Blank* He shall not take a wife from among all *16* the daughters of the nations, but instead take for himself a wife from the his father's house *17* from his father's family. He shall take no other wife apart from her *18* because only she will be with him all the days of her life. If she dies, he shall take *19* for himself another from his father's house, from his family. He shall not pervert justice, *20* or accept a bribe to pervert correct judgment. He shall not crave *21* the field, the vineyard, the wealth, the house or any valuable thing in Israel or purloin

Col. LVIII   *1* [...] ... [...] *2* [...] their men. *Blank* *3* If it happens that /the king/ hears that some nation or people is attempting to despoil Israel of all it owns, *4* he shall send the chiefs of a thousand and the chiefs of a hundred, those stationed in the cities *5* of Israel, and they shall send with him the tenth part of the people so that it can sally out with him to war against *6* their enemies. And they shall sally out with him. If a large number of people comes against the land of Israel they shall send *7* with him a fifth part of the men of war. And if it is a king with chariots and horses and many men, *8* they shall send with him a third part of the men of war. The other two-thirds shall defend *9* their cities and their border so that the troops do not enter their land. *10* If the war against him worsens, they shall send him half of the people, the men of war, *11* but those of the (other) half of the people shall not withdraw from their cities. *Blank* If they overcome *12* their enemies, defeat them and put them to the sword, they shall gathe[r] their spoils and they shall give *13* to the king a tenth part of them; to the priests a thousandth part; to the levites a hundredth part *14* of the whole. And they shall divide the rest into two halves, between those who fought in battle and their brothers, *15* who had to remain in their cities. *Blank* And if he sallies out to war against *16* his enemies, a fifth part of the people shall sally out with him, the men of war, the mighty men of *17* valour. And they shall refrain from every impurity and every immodesty and from every sin and fault.

18 They are not to sally forth until he has entered the presence of the High Priest and he has consulted for him the decision of the Urim *19* and Tummin. On his orders he shall sally out and on his orders he shall (re-)enter, he and all the children of Israel who *20* are with him; he shall not sally out on the advice of his heart until he has consulted the decision of the Urim *21* and Thummim. He will have success in all his paths as long as he goes out in accord with the decision which

Col. LIX   *1* [...] ... [...] *2* they shall disband them over many lands and they shall be a horror, a byword and a gibe; they shall be with a heavy yoke *3* and lacking everything; there they shall worship gods made by the hand of man, of wood and stone, of silver *4* and of gold. In all this period their cities shall be a waste, a gibe and a ruin; *5* their enemies shall leave them razed. They themselves, in the lands of their enemies, shall sigh *6* and scream under the heavy yoke; they shall call and I shall not listen, they shall shout and I shall not reply to them, *7* owing to their evil deeds; I will hide my face from them; they shall be fodder *8* and prey and spoil, and no-one will save them owing to their sins – for they broke my covenant *9* and their soul loathed my law – until they feel guilty of all their faults. Then they shall come back *10* to me with all their heart and with all their soul, in agreement with all the words of this law *11* and they shall be saved from the hand of their enemies and redeemed from the power of those who hate them; they shall be brought *12* into the land of their fathers, redeemed and greater in number; and I will rejoice in them. *13* They shall be my people and I will be their God. *Blank* The king who *14* prostitutes his heart and his eyes, removing them from my commandments, will not find someone who will sit on the throne *15* of his fathers for ever, because over the centuries I shall prevent his line from governing again in Israel. *16* *Blank* But if he walks according to my precepts and keeps my commandments and does *17* what is upright and good before me, there will not be lacking one of his sons who sits on the throne of the kingdom *18* of Israel for ever. I shall be with him and free him from the hand of those who hate him and from the hand *19* of those who seek his life in order to destroy it; I shall place in front of him all his enemies and he will govern them *20* as he pleases and they shall not govern him. I shall make him improve and not diminish, [I shall place him] at the head *21* and not at the tail, and he will extend his kingdom for many days, he and his sons after him.

Col. LX   *1* [...] ... [...] *2* and all their wave-offerings and every firstborn [of their animals,] the males and every [...] *3* for their animals; and all their holy offerings which they consecrate to me along with all their *4* festal offerings; and a levy of tribute upon the birds, animals and fish, one per thousand *5* of all that they catch; and all that they dedicate to the Lord; and a levy on the booty and spoil. *6* *Blank* It shall be for the levites: a tenth of the grain, the new wine and the oil which *7* they consecrate to me first; and the shoulder from those who perform the sacrifice; and the levy on the *8* booty and the spoil; and one percent of the bag of birds, animals and fish; *9* and of the pigeons and of the tithe of the honey, one fiftieth. One percent *10* of the pigeons will be for the priests. For he has chosen them from among all your tribes *11* so that they can be in my presence and serve and bless my name, he and all their sons for ever. *12* *Blank* When the levite who lives in any of the cities of all Israel comes *13* at his own wish to the place where I choose to install *14* my name, he will minister, like all his brother levites who are there in my presence. *15* They shall eat equal portions, not counting the sale of the patrimony. *Blank 16* When you enter the land which I am going to give you, you shall not learn to emulate *17* the depravities of those peoples. Among you there should not be found anyone who makes his son or his daughter pass *18* through fire, anyone who practises divination, astrologers, sorcerers, wizards, anyone who performs incantations, anyone who consults a spirit *19* or oracles or anyone who questions the dead; because all those who do these things are an abomination to me *20* and owing to these abominations I shall dispossess them before you. *21* You are to be perfect before YHWH your God. *Blank* When these nations which

Col. LXI   *1* [who says in my name what I have not ordered him] to say, or who [speaks in the name of o]ther go[ds] *2* that prophet shall be executed. *Blank* If you say in your heart 'How shall we know the word *3* which YHWH has not spoken?' If the prophet speaks in the name of YHWH and the word does not happen *4* and is not fulfilled, it is a word which I did not say; the prophet has spoken it presumptuously. Do not fear him. *5 Blank 6* A single witness may not stand up against a man for any fault or for any sin which he has committed; by the testimony of two *7* witnesses or by the testimony of three witnesses the matter shall be settled. If a false witness should stand up against a man to accuse him *8* of wrongdoing, the two men between whom there is /litigation/ shall appear before me, before the priests and levites and before *9* the judges who will be there on those days. The judges shall investigate and if (it is a question) of a false witness who accused *10* his brother falsely, you shall deal with him as he intended to deal with his brother; thus shall you eradicate the evil from the midst of you. *11* The rest shall hear it and fear and not dare to do a similar thing again in your midst. *12* Your eye shall not take pity on him; life for life, eye for eye, tooth for tooth, hand for hand, foot for foot. *Blank* When *13* you go out to war against your enemies, and you see horses and chariots and a people more numerous than you, do not fear them *14* because I, he who made you come up from the land of Egypt, am with you. When you advance to battle, *15* the priest shall come forward and he will speak to the people and the people shall say: 'Listen, Israel, you are approaching'

Col. LXII   *1-2* ... [...] *3* to speak to the people and they shall say: 'Who is a coward and feeble of heart? He should go and return to *4* his house, lest he weaken the heart of his brother like his own heart' *Blank* When the judges have finished *5* speaking to the people, the military commanders at the head of the people shall be appointed. *Blank* When *6* you approach a city to fight against it, you shall offer it peace; if *7* it answers you with peace and opens up to you, all the people that are in it *8* shall pay you tribute and serve you; however, if it does not make peace with you and makes war, *9* you shall besiege it; I shall put it into your hands and you shall put its males to the sword. However, *10* the women, the children, the flocks and all that there is in the city, all its booty, you shall remove *11* for yourself and you shall consume the booty of your enemies whom I deliver to you. Thus shall you act *12* with all the cities quite far from you, which are not the cities of these peoples. *13* However, of the cities of the peoples which I grant to you as inheritance, you shall leave no-one alive, *14* because you must dedicate them to extermination: the Hittites, the Amorites and the Canaanites, *15* the Hivites and the Jebusites and the Gergasites and the Perizzites, as I have commanded you, so that *16* they do not teach you to do all the abominations which they do for their gods.

Col. LXIII   *1* ... [...] ... *2* the heifer to a torrent of running water which has not been sown or tilled; and there they shall break the heifer's neck. *3 Blank* And the priests, sons of Levi, shall approach because I chose them to serve in my presence and to bless my name, *4* and at their decision every dispute and every quarrel is settled. And all the elders of that city, the nearest to the stabbed person, *5* shall wash their hands over the head of the heifer whose neck was broken in the torrent, they shall begin to speak and shall say: 'Our hands *6* have not spilled this blood and our eyes have not seen anything. Pardon your people Israel whom you redeemed, *7* O YHWH, and do not place innocent blood in the midst of your people Israel', and the blood will be pardoned them. Thus shall you eradicate *8* the innocent blood from Israel, and you shall do the right and good thing before YHWH your God. *9 Blank 10* When you go out to war against your enemies and I place them in your hands and you make prisoners, *11* if among the prisoners you see a woman of beautiful appearance, you desire her and you wish to take her as a wife for yourself, *12* you shall bring her into your house, shave her head and cut her nails; you shall remove *13* the prisoner's clothes from her and she will live in your house. A full month shall she weep for her father and her mother. *14* Then you shall enter her, marry her, and she will be your wife. She is not to touch pure foodstuffs, for *15* seven years, or eat the peace offering until seven years pass; afterwards she may eat

Col. LXIV   *1* ... [...] *2* If a man has a defiant or uncontrollable son who does not listen to his father's voice or his mother's voice, *3* and pays them no attention when they correct him, his father and his mother shall take him and they shall bring him out *4* to the elders of his city, to the gate of his locality; and they shall say to the elders of his city: 'This son of ours is defiant *5* and uncontrollable and does not listen to our voice; he is a glutton and a drunkard'. And all the men of the city shall stone him *6* and he will die. Thus shall you eradicate the evil from your midst, and all the children of Israel shall hear it and fear. *Blank* If *7* there were to be a spy against his people who betrays his people to a foreign nation or causes evil against his people, *8* you shall hang him from a tree and he will die. On the evidence of two witnesses and on the evidence of three witnesses *9* shall he be executed and they shall hang him on the tree. *Blank* If there were a man with a sin punishable by death and he escapes *10* amongst the nations and curses his people /and/ the children of Israel, he also you shall hang on the tree *11* and he will die. Their corpses shall not spend the night on the tree; instead you shall bury them that day because *12* they are cursed by God and man, those hanged on a tree; thus you shall not defile the land which I *13* give you for inheritance. *Blank* If you see your brother's ox or ewe or his ass *14* astray, do not pretend to ignore them; make them go back to your brother. And if your brother is not near *15* you, or you do not know him, you shall take it into your house and it will stay with you until he looks for it.

Col. LXV   *1* ... [...] *2* If you find a bird's [nest] in front of you on the path, in any tree or on the ground, *3* with chicks or eggs and the mother is sitting on the chicks or eggs, *4* you shall not take the mother with the brood; you shall release the mother *5* and take the brood for yourself so that it may go well for you and you lengthen your days. When you build a new house, *6* you shall make a parapet on your roof; in this way you shall not cause blood to fall on your house if anyone falls *7* from it. *Blank* If a man takes a woman and marries her and hates her and covers her with insulting words *8* and causes a bad reputation and says: 'I took this woman and on approaching her *9* I found her not be a virgin', the young girl's father or her mother shall take and bring out *10* the proof of the young girl's virginity to the elders, at the gate. *Blank* The young girl's father will say *11* to the elders 'I have given my daughter to this man /as a wife/ and here he is hating her and *12* covering her with insulting words, saying "I did not find your daughter to be a virgin"'. These are the proofs of the virginity *13* of my daughter'. And they shall spread the garment in front of the elders of that city. And the elders of that city shall take *14* that man and punish him; they shall impose a fine of one hundred silver shekels *15* and they shall be given to the young girl's father, because he caused a bad reputation for a virgin of Israel.

Col. LXVI   *1* [...] ... [...] *2* they shall stone them and they shall be put to death; the young girl because she did not scream *3* in the city, and the man because he raped his neighbour's wife; thus will be eradicated *4* the evil from your midst.

But if it was in a field where the man met /the woman/, in a hidden place far *5* from the city, and he coerced her and lay with her, only the man who lay with her will be put to death. *6* You shall do nothing to the young woman; she has not committed a fault meriting death, because it is the same in this case as when *7* a man rises up against his neighbour and murders him; he met her in the field, *8* the young betrothed girl screamed, but there was no-one to help her. *Blank* If a man violates a young *9* virgin who is not betrothed, and she suits him according to the Law and he lies with her *10* and they are discovered, the man who lay with her will give the girl's father fifty silver shekels *11* and she will be his wife, since he raped her, and he cannot dismiss her all her life. *12* A man is not to take his father's wife or uncover the member of his father. A man is not to take *13* his brother's wife or uncover the member of his brother, of his father's or mother's son, because it is wanton. *14* A man is not to take his sister, the daughter of his father or the daughter of his mother; it is an abomination. *15* A man is not to take his father's sister or his mother's sister because it is depravity. *16* A man is not to take *Blank* *17* his brother's daughter or his sister's daughter because it is an abomination. *Blank* A man is not to take

Col. LXVII   *Blank*

11QTemple Scroll*ᵇ* (11Q20[11QTemple*ᵇ*])

Frag. 1 (= 11QT xv)   *1* [...] seven yearling (lambs) and a he-goat [...] *2* [according to the regulation.] For the dedication of a sheep for each [day...] *3* [... You shall share out] all the sheep and the baskets over the seven [days of the dedication, one for each day,] *4* [according to their divisions.] You shall offer to YHWH the holocaust [of the sheep, and the fat which covers] *5* [the entrails,] the two kidneys and the fat which is on them, [the fat which is on the loins and the whole tail] *6* cut off at the coccyx, and the lobe of the liver, [and its offering and its libation, according to the regulation. You shall take up a cake] *7* [of unleavened bread] from the basket and a cake of oiled bread and a wafer, [and you shall place it all on top of the fat with the leg] *8* [offered in tri]bute, the right leg. Those who are offering shall lift up [the sheep and the baskets of bread,] *9* [lifting up] before YHWH; it is a holocaust, fire-sacrifice of fragrance [which appeases YHWH. You shall burn everything] *10* [on the altar, on top of] the holocaust, in order to consecrate their souls (for) the seven days [of the consecration.] *11* [...] *Blank* When the High Priest, is [about to serve before YHWH, the one who has been] *12* [consecra]ted in order to don the vestments [in succession to his fathers,] he shall offer [a bullock for all the people] *13* [and another for the pr]iests. He shall first bring near what is for the pri[ests. The elders from among the priests shall lay] *14* [their hands upon] his head, and after them the High Pr[iest] and all the [priests. And they shall slaughter] *15* the calf [before

YHWH.] And the elders of the priests shall take some of the blood of the calf and [with their fingers they shall place upon the horns of the altar] *16* the blood [of the calf,] and they shall sprinkle around on the four faces of the base of the [altar…]

Frag. 3   *1* […] …*2* […upon] the thumb *3* […] and of oil

Frag. 4   *1* […] … […] *2* […] and they shall [burn…] *3* […] *Blank* […] *4* […] outside of […]

Frag. 5   *1* [… on the fourth part of the] day they shall sacrifice […] *2* […] perfect, and their offerings and their lib[ations, according to the regulation…] *3* […the first-fruits] will be for the priests, and they shall eat them in the court[yard …] *4* […] new bread of ears [of wheat…] *5* […] and they shall do no menial work […]

Frag. 6 (= 11QT XIX, 12–XX, 9)   *1* [From the day on which you carried to YHWH the new offering,] the bread of the first-fruits, you shall count off seven weeks, *2* [seven full weeks;] you shall count off fifty [days until the day following the] seventh [sabbath,] and [you shall c]arry *3* [new wine for the libation: four *hin* for all the tribes of] Israel, a third of a *hin* for *4* [each tribe. That day all the heads of a thousand of Israel] shall offer to YHWH [with the wine] twelve sheep *5* […she]ep, and the offering, according to the regulation; two *6* [… a third and one] *hin* of oil for the sheep, with that libation. *7* […] seven yearling sheep and a he-goat *8* […] the assembly. *Blank* *9* […] and their libation /according to the regulation/ for the bullocks, and for the sheep. *10* […] to YHWH in the fourth part of that day, and they shall sacrifice *11* […] the sheep and the libation. And they shall sacrifice *12* […] and the fourte[en] yearling lambs *13* […] they shall offer the holocaust *14* […] they shall burn upon the altar *15* [the fat surrounding the entrails and all the fat there is upon] the entrails and the *16* [lobe of the liver over the kidneys will be removed.] *Blank* *17* [And (also) the fat which there is on top of them and what is over the loins and] the tail, cut at *18* [the coccyx. And they shall burn everything upon the altar, with their offerings] and libations. *19* [It is a fire-sacrifice of fragrance which appeases YHWH.] *Blank* *20* [They shall offer all the offering with which a libation is offered according to the regulation] for the offering.

Frag. 7 (= 11QT XX, 13–16)   *1* [… They shall eat it on this day and upon it] the sun [shall not set.] *2* [In all the oblations you shall put salt and it shall not be] missing: covenant of salt /for/ ever. *3* [You shall take for YHWH as tribute, from the ra]ms and from the lambs the right leg, *4* [the breast, the jawbones, the stomach] and the shoulder blade up to the bone of the upper foreleg.

Frags. 8–9 *col.* I (= 11QT XXI, 1–XXII, 5)   *1* [...for the priests] there will be the leg of the offering and the breast *2* [of wave-offering ... the shoulder]-blades, the jawbones and the stomachs of the portions *3* [...] and the lobe and the rest of the shoulder-blade *4* [...] It is eternal law for you and for your descendants. *5* [... and they shall offer for] the heads of thousands [...] of the sheep and of *6* [the lambs; and for ...] a ram and a lamb; and for each one of the clans *7* [a ram and a lamb for each one of the clans of the twe]lve tribes of Israel. And they shall eat *8* [... before YHWH. The pries]ts shall drink there first *9* [and the levites ... the h]eads of the battalions first. *10* [...famous. After them all the people, from the oldest] to the smallest, shall go and drink the new wine. *11* [They shall not eat any grape, sour fruit of the vine, until on] this day they atone for the new wine. And the children of Israel *12* [will rejoice in YHWH's presence. Eternal law for their generations] in all their villages. They shall rejoice on *13* [this day on going to pour out a libation of juice, a new wine, over the altar of YHWH,] year after year. *Blank 14* [*Blank* From this day you shall count off] seven times seven weeks. *15* [There will be forty-nine days from the seven full weeks, up to the day a]fter the seventh sabbath. *16* [You shall count off fifty days and you shall offer new oil from the villages of the clans of the sons of Is]rael: half a *hin 17* [each one of the clans...] ... *18* [...] the sheep [...] *20* [...] with him for all the congregation before *21* [YHWH...] with this oil, half a *hin 22* [... according to the regu]lation it will be a holocaust of fire of *23* [pleasing aroma for YHWH...] they shall burn this oil in the lamps *24* [...] the heads of thousand with the pri[nces] *25* [...fourteen yearling lambs] and their offerings and libations [...] *26* [...] /the priests/ sons of Aa[ron...]

Frags. 8–9 *col.* II (11QT XXII, 8–XXIII, 4)   *1* according to the regula[tion...] *2* to YHWH. [...the right leg and the breasts of] *3* the wave-offering; and as [first-fruits ... and for the priests the jawbones and the stomach; it shall be their share] *4* in accordance with the ordinance. *Blank* [... And the sons of] *5* Israel shall give the priests a [ram and a lamb; to the levites a ram and a lamb and to each] *6* clan a ram and a la[mb. And they shall eat it throughout this day in the outer courtyard in front of YHWH.] *7* Eternal precepts for their generations, [year after year. Afterwards, they shall eat and they shall anoint themselves with the new oil and with the olives] *8* because on this day they shall atone for [all the virgin oil of the land in front of YHWH, once a year. And] *9* all the children of Israel shall rejoice in all [their villages...] *10–11* [...] *12* for the altar [...] *13* the clans of [Levi] and Judah, on [the second day Benjamin and the sons of Joseph, on the thrid day, Reuben and Simeon,] *14* on the fourth day Issachar [and Zebulon, on the fifth day Gad and Asher, on the sixth day, Dan] *15* and Naphtali. *Blank* [... And they shall offer, on the festival of the offering of] *16* the wood, a holocaust for [YHWH...] *17* two he-goats for [...] *18* holo[caust...]

Frag. 10   *1* […] … *2* […] *Blank 3* […] in the fourth part of the day this canal *4* […] perpetual [ho]locaust. *Blank 5* […] a great sabbath of memorial, a holy assembly *6* […] he will do for life *7* […] a sheep, a

Frag. 12 (= 11QT XXXVII, 9–14)   *1* […in front of the rooms. In the inner court-yard,] next to [the wall] of the outer *2* [courtyard, places made for the priests, for their sacrifices and for] the first-fruits and the tithes, *3* [and for their peace-sacrifices which they will offer. There shall be no mingl]ing of the peace sacri-fices of the sons of Is[rael] *4* with the peace [sacrifices of the priests.] *Blank 5* [In the four corners of the courtyard you shall make for them] /a place/ for the cauldrons where they shall [cook] *6* [their sacrifices and the sin-offerings …In the North-]eastern corner […]

Frags. 13–16 *col.* I (= 11QT XLV, 9–XLVI, 18)   *1* [… And on the third day he shall wash his clothes and bathe at sunset.] Afterwards *2* [he shall enter the temple. But they shall not enter my temple with their soiled impurity to defile it. Any-one] who lies [with his wife and has an ejaculation, for three] *3* days [shall not enter anywhere in the city of the temple] in the centre of which I dwell *5* [be-cause I, YHWH, dwell in the midst of the children of Israel for ever and always.] *Blank 6* [Everyone who purifies himself from his gonorrhoea shall count off seven days up to his purification. On day] seven *7* [he shall wash his clothes and immerse his body completely in running water. Afterwards he shall enter the city of the temple. Anyone who is un]clean through contact with a corpse shall not *8* [enter it until he purifies himself. Any leper and infected person shall not enter it until] he purifies himself; when *9* [he purifies himself and offers the …] he shall not enter the temple *10* […] and the temple *11* […] *Blank 12–14* […] *15* [to be in the middle of my temple for ever and for all the centuries, for] I dwell [among them.] *16* […] *Blank 17* [You shall make a platform around the outer courtyard, on the outside, fourteen cubits in width, corresponding to the door]ways; [and for it you shall make] *18* [twelve steps so that the children of Israel can climb] up them in order to enter my tem[ple.] *19* [You shall make a platform around the temple, one hundred cubits in width, which separ]ates the holy [temple from the city,] *20* [so that they do not suddenly enter my temple and defile it.] They shall make my temp[le] holy *21* [and respect it, for I dwell among them.] *Blank 22* [You shall make lat]rines [for them] outside [the city, where they are obliged to go, outside, to the North-east of the city:] *23* [houses with beams] and wells within them, [into which excrement will be dropped; they shall not be visible from a total distance] *24* [from the city of three] thou-sand [cubits. You shall make] three [zones, to the East of the city, separate from each other, where] *25* [lepers, those who suffer gonorrhoea] and men [with a pollution…] *26* […] … […]

Frags. 13 – 16 *col.* II　*1* and those who enter […] *2* ewe […] *3* and all […] *4* affair […] *5* […] *6* and the .. […] *7* Judah […] *8* the cities of […]

Frag. 17　*1* and […] *2* and all […] *3* they purify themselves […] *4* and those with gonor[rhoea …] *5* the clothes […] *6* upon it […] *7* with water […] *7* And if […] *8* until […]

Frags. 18 – 19 *col.* I (= 11QT L, 1 – 11)　*1* […] until the day *2* [… the] seventh day *3* […] in water *4* […] of the dead man *5* […] they shall eat *6* [… they will remain impure.] In any way *7* […] *Blank 8 Blank* [Every man who in an open field should touch the bone of a] *9* dead person or a stabbed [person or a corpse or the blood of a dead person or a burial shall purify himself in compliance with the ruling of this statute, and if he does not purify himself] *10* according to the statute [of this law he will be impure, his uncleanness will still persist in him and everyone who touches him shall wash his clothes, bathe] *11* and will become pure by the [evening. When a woman is pregant and her son dies in her womb, all the days he] *12* is dead within her she shall be impure [like a grave….]

Frags. 18 – 19 *col.* II (= 11QT LI, 5 – 18)　*1* at sunset, [afterwards he will be pure. Forewarn the children of Israel of every uncleanness. They are not to be defiled by those things which I tell] *2* /them/ on this mountain. [They are not to defile themselves. Because I, YHWH, reside among the children of Israel. They shall sanctify themselves and they shall be holy. They shall not make] *3* their souls [odious] with anything [that I have separated from them as impure and they shall be holy. *Blank* In all your cities you shall put] *4* judges and magistrates [who judge the people with correct judgment, and make no distinction of persons in judgment,] *5* and accept no bribe, [because a bribe perverts justice, corrupts the words of the just person, blinds the eyes of the wise] *6* perpetrates a serious offence [and defiles the House with the wickedness of sin. Pursue justice exclusively so that you can live and enter and take possession of the land] *7* which I give you, [so as to own it for ever. *Blank* The one who takes bribes and perverts just judgment] *8* shall [die and you shall have no qualms in executing him….]

Frag. 20 (= 11QT LIV, 19 – 21)　*1* [If your brother, the son of your fa]ther or [the son of your mother, or your son or your daughter, or the woman] *2* [who lies in your embrace or your soul]mate [provokes you in secret saying: 'Let us go and let us serve other gods'] *3* [whom you do not know and neither do your fa]thers, of the gods of [the peoples who surround you, close to you] *4* [or far from] you, from one side of the land to the [other side of the land; you shall not go to him nor] *5* [shall you listen to him, nor shall your sig]ht [take pity] on him, nor shall you have compassion on [him, and you shall not conceal him, but instead you shall kill him;] 6 [your hand will be] the first one [over him] to kill him, and the hand of [all the people after you. You shall stone him with stones,] 7 [because he tried to turn] you aside. *Blank* [...]

3 Pesharim

A *Commentaries on Isaiah*

3QIsaiah Pesher (3Q4 [3QpIs])

1 Is 1:1 Vision of Isaiah, son of [Amoz, concerning Judah and Jerusalem in the period of Uzziah] *2* and of Jotham, of Achaz and of [Hezekiah, kings of Judah. The interpretation of the word which] *3* Isaiah prophesied concerning [...] *4* to [...] king of Ju[dah *Is 1:2* Listen, heavens; pay attention, earth; for the Lord speaks.] *5* [...] *Blank* [Its interpretation: that ...] *6* [the] day of judgment [...] *7* [...] ... [...]

4QIsaiah Pesher*ᵃ* (4Q161 [4QpIs*ᵃ*])

Frag. 1 *col.* I   *20 Is 10:20* [On that day, the remnant of Israel, the survivors of Jacob, will not revert to leaning] *21* [on their assailant but will lean exclusively on the Lord, the Holy One of Israel.] *22* [*Is 10:21* A remnant will return, a remnant of] Jacob to God [the warrior.] *23* [Its interpretation: the remnant of] Israel is [the assembly of his chosen one...] *24* [...] the men of his army [... The remnant of Jacob is...] *25* [...] the priests, since [...]

Frags. 2–6 *col.* II   *1* [*Is 10:22* Even if your people, Israel were like the sand of the sea, only a remnant will return; extermination is decreed,] *2* [but overflowing justice. For it is decided and decreed: the Lord of Hosts is going to do it in the centre of all the earth.] *3* [Its interpretation concerns ...] since [...] the sons of [...] *4* of his people. And as for what he says: *Is 10:22* Even if [your people, Israel were like the sand of the sea,] *5* [only a remnant will return; extermination is decreed,] but justice will overflow. [Its interpretation: ...] *6* [... to des]troy on the day of slaughter]; and many will die [...] *7* [...but they will be] saved, surely, by their plan[ting] in the land [...] *8* [...] *Blank Is 10:24-27* This is why [the Lord God of Hosts] says: [do not be afraid, my people] *9* [li]ving in Zion, [of Assyria: it will hit you with a stick and lift its rod against you in the fashion of Egypt;] *10* [for] very shortly [my anger will end and my wrath will destroy them. The Lord of Hosts] will lash [against them] *11* [the flail as in the destruction of Midian, on the rock of] Horeb, and he will lift his rod [against the sea] *12* [in the fashion of Egypt. And on that day it will happen] that his load will be removed [from your shoulder,] *13* [and his yoke from your neck. The interpretation of the word concerns] ... [...] *14* on his return from the wilderness of the [peoples...] *15* [...] the Prince of the Congregation, and after it will be removed from you [...] *16* [...] *Blank* [...] *17* [*Is 10:28-32* Go up from the side of Rimmon;] come up to Aiath; cross [Migron; at Michmash] *18* [make an inspection of the weapons; traverse] the gorge; spend the night in Geba; fearful [is Ramah; Gibeah of] *19* [Saul deserts. Raise] your voice, Bat-Gallim; pay attention, Laishah; answer, Anathoth.] *20* [Retreat,] Madmenah, the residents of Gebiom flee; this very day [he makes a stopover in Nob,] *21* [already he stretches] his hand towards the mount of the daughter of Zion, towards the hill of Jerusalem. [*Blank*] *22* [The interpretation of] the word concerns the final days, when the [king of the Kittim] comes [...] *23* [...] from his climb from the plain of Akko to do battle against Pa[lestine...] *24* [...] and there is none like her, and in all the cities [...] *25* and up to the boundary of Jerusalem. [...]

Frags. 8– 10 *col.* III   *1* [*Is 10:33-34* See! The Lord God of Hosts will rip off the branches at one wrench; the] tall[est trunks] will be felled, *2* [the loftiest chopped.] The thickest of the wood [will be cut] with iron and Lebanon, with its grandeur, *3* [will fall. Its interpretation concerns the] Kittim, who will be placed in the hands of Israel, and the meek *4* [of the earth...] all the peoples and all the soldiers will weaken and their heart will melt *5* [... and what it says: « The] tallest [trunks] will be destroyed» are the soldiers of the Ki[ttim] *6* [since ...] «and the thickest of the wood will be cut with iron» are *7* [...] for the war of the Kittim. «And Lebanon, with its grandeur, *8* [will fall» are the command- ers of] the Kittim, who will be placed in the hand of their great [...] *9* [...] in their flight before Israel. *10* [...] *Blank* [...] *11* [*Is 11:1-5* A shoot will issue from the stu]mp of Jesse and [a bud] will sprout from its ro[ot.] Over him [will be placed] the spi[rit] *12* [of the Lord; a spirit] of discretion and wisdom, a spirit of ad[vice and courage,] a spirit of knowledge *13* [and of respect for the Lord, and his delight will be in respecting the] Lord. [He will not judge] by appear- ances *14* [or give verdicts on hearsay alone;] he will judge [the poor with justice and decide] *15* [with honesty for the humble of the earth. He will destroy the land with the rod of his mouth and with the breath of his lips] *16* [he will exe- cute the evil. Justice will be the belt of] his loins and lo[yalty the belt of his hips.] *17* [...] *Blank* [...] *18* [The interpretation of the word concerns the shoot] of David which will sprout [in the final days, since] *19* [with the breath of his lips he will execute] his enemies and God will support him with [the spirit of] courage [...] *20* [...] throne of glory, [holy] crown and hemmed vestments *21* [...] in his hand. He will rule over all the peoples and Magog *22* [...] his sword will judge all the peoples. And as for what he says: «He will not *23* [judge by appearances] or give verdicts on hearsay», its interpretation: *24* [...] accord- ing to what they teach him, he will judge, and upon his mouth *25* [...] with him will go out one of the priests of renown, holding clothes in his hand

4QIsaiah Pesher*ᵇ* (4Q162 [4QpIs*ᵇ*])

Frag. 1 *col.* I   *Is 5:5* For now I will tell you what I am going to do with my vine-

yard: *1* [...remove its fence so that it can be used for pasture, destroy] its wall
so that you trample it. *Is 5:6* For *2* [I will leave it flattened; they shall not prune
it or weed it, brambles and thi[stles] will grow. The interpretation of the word:
that he has deserted them *3* [...] and as for what he says: *Is 5:6* «Brambles will
grow, *4* [and thistles»: its interpretation concerns ...] and what *5* [it says: ...]
of the path *6* [...] his eyes

Frag. 1 *col.* II   *1* The interpretation of the word concerns the last days, laying
waste the land through thirst and hunger. This will happen *2* at the time of the
visit to the land. *Is 5:11-14* Woe to those who rise early in search of intoxicants
and carry on until by twilight the wine *3* excites them and with zithers, harps,
tambourines and flutes they feast their drunkenness, but they pay no attention
to God's doings *4* or notice the works of his hands! For this, my people will be
exiled without realising it, their nobles will die of hunger *5* and the ordinary
folk have a raging thirst. For this, the abyss distends its jaws and enlarges its
mouth immeasurably, *6* lowers its nobility and its ordinary people and its revel-
ling throng enters. These are the arrogant men *7* who are in Jerusalem. They
are the ones who: *Is 5:24* «Have rejected the law of God and mocked the word
of the Holy One of *8* Israel. *Is 5:25* For this the wrath of God has been kindled
against his people and he has stretched out his hand against them and wounded
them. *9* The mountains quake, their corpses lie like dung in the middle of the
streets. In spite of this *10* [his anger] is not appeased [and his hand continues
to be stretched out]». This is the Congregation of the arrogant men who are in
Jerusalem. *11* [...] ... [...]

Frag. 1 *col.* III   *1* *Is 5:29-30* and no-one rips [it out. On that day he will roar
against him] *2* like the ro[ar of the sea. He will look at the earth, see deep darkness, even the light is obscured] *3* by the clo[uds...] *4* He is [...] *5* they [...]
6 who co[me...] *7* he has said [...] *8* they have seen [...] *9* ... [...]

4QIsaiah Pesher*ᶜ* (4Q163 [4QIsᶜ])

Frag. 1   *1* [...] ... [...] *2* [...] he is [...] *3* [...] and mistook the path of [...] *4* [...
for it is] written concerning him in Jere[miah...]

Frags. 2 – 3   *1* [*Is 8:7-8* For this, behold, the Lord will bri]ng up against them the
[torrential and violent] water of the river, [the king of Assyria] *2* [and all his
pomp. He will] come up through all the channels and overflow all its banks.
[He will invade Judah, he will flood, he will brim over] *3* [and will reach right
up to the neck.] The opening of his wings will cover the breadth of your land,
[O Emmanuel! The interpretation of the word concerns] *4* [...] ... the law; he
is Rezin and the son of [Romeliah...] *5* [... as it is written in [...] *6* [...] and not
[...]

Frags. 4–6 *col.* I   *14* [*Is 9:17-20* Because evil is burning like a fire] which consumes thistles [and brambles;] it catches fire *15* [in the dense wood and the height] of the smoke coils upwards. [By the wrath of the God] of Hosts devastated is] *16* [the land and the people is fuel for the fire.] No-one [forgives] his brother,] *17* [he destroys to the right and remains hungry, he consumes] to the left and is not replete; *18* [a man eats the flesh of his arm. Manasseh against] Ephraim and Ephraim against *19* [Mana]sseh; [the two] together [against Judah. And with all this] his wrath is not mollified.

Frags. 4–6 *col.* II   *1* [*Is 10:19* A young man] will count them. [...] *2* The interpretation of the word concerns the edict of Babylonia [...] *3* the edicts of the peoples [...] *4* to betray many. He [...] *5* Jerusalem. And what it says: *Is 10:19* «The remainder of the trees of the wood will be a small number and a young man will count them».] *6* Its interpretation concerns the reduction of men [...] *7 Blank* [...] *8 Is 10:20-22* On that day it will happen [that the remainder of the House of Israel and the survivors] *9* of the House of Jacob [will not return to lean on their aggressor but will lean on the Lord, the Holy One] *10* of Israel, in truth. A remnant [will return, a remnant of Jacob, to the warrior God.] *11* Even if your people, [Israel] were to be [like the sand of the sea, only a remnant will return.] *12* The interpretation of the word concerns the fi[nal] days [...] *13* they will go into captivity [...And what] *14* it says: *Is 10:21* [«Even if your people, [Israel] were to be like the sand of the sea, only a remnant will return.»] *15* Its interpretation concerns the reduction [...] *16* Since it is written: [*Is 10:22-23* «Destruction is decreed but justice is overflowing. Because destruction is decreed] *17* the Lord God [of the Hosts will execute it in the midst of the whole earth»] *18 Blank* [...] *19 is 10:24* Therefore, the Lord Go[d of Hosts say as follows: Do not fear, my people who live in Zion]

Frags. 8–10   *1* [The interpetation of the word] concerns the king of Babylon, [since ... as it is written: *Is 14:8* «The very cypresses] *2* [laugh] at you, and the cedars of Lebanon. Since [you lie down, the hewer] *3* [does not come up] against them». The cypresses and the cedars [of Lebanon are ...] *4* [...] the Lebanon. And what it says: *Is 14:26-27* «This [is the strategy decided for] *5* [all] the earth and this is the hand [stretched out against all the peoples.] *6* [For the God] of the Hosts has dec[ided, who will thwart him? His hand is stretched out,] *7* [who] will push it aside?». This is ... [...] *8* [as it is written] in the book of Zechariah ... [*Zac 3:9?* ...] *9* [...] *Blank* [...] *10* [...] *Blank* [...] *11* [*Is 14:28-30*) In the year of the deat]h of king Achaz [this oracle was uttered: Do not] rejoice, *12* al[l Philistia,] that the rod [which injured you] is shattered, [because from the root of the] snake shall [come] *13* [a viper and its fruit will be a] flying [asp. The most destitute] will be fed [and the poor] *14* [will become safe. I will make your root die of hunger and he will kill] your remnant. [...]

Frag. 11 *col.* I   *1* [...] ... *2* [...] servants of *3* [...] they are *4* [...] the insults (?) *5* [...] this

Frag. 11 *col.* II   *1* *Is 19:9-12* those who weave [white cloths. Their masters will be dismayed, all their] *2* labourers knocked [down. How deranged the princes of Zoan; the wise advise] *3* Pharaoh with [inane] advice. [How can you say to Pharaoh: We are sons of wise men,] *4* we are sons of [ancient ki]ngs? [Where are your wise men? Let them announce,] *5* [if they know, what the God of Hosts is planning against Egypt.]

Frags. 15–16   *Is 29:10-11* [For] *1* the Lord pours [upon] you [a breath] of languor and will blinker [your eyes – the prophets – and] *2* he will cover your heads – the seers –. For you [any vision] will be [like the text of a] *3* [sea]led [book:] they give it to someone who can read, tellin[g him: Please read this,] *4* [and he answers: I cannot because] it is sealed. [...]

Frags. 18–19   *1* *Is 29:18-23* [of the book;] without darkness or glo[om the eyes of the blind will see. The oppressed will return to rejoice in the Lord] *2* [and the poor]est of men [will delight in the Holy One of Israel. Because the tyrant is destroyed, the sceptic finished off and] *3* [all] those alert for evil [will be obliterated, those who are going to seize another in speaking and the one who defends in the gate with snares and, for nothing, engulf] *4* [the innocent.] Therefore, so says [the Lord to the House of Jacob, he who ransomed Abraham: No longer] *5* [will] Jacob [be ashamed, no longer will his face smile when he sees that his sons, the work] *6* [of my hands in his midst,] worship my name, because they wor[ship the Holy One of Jacob.]

Frag. 21   *1*[...] *Is 29:17* Perhaps, [in a very little while, *2* [will the Lebanon turn into] an orchard, and will the orchard] seem like [a wood?] The Lebanon are [...] *3* [...] into an orchard and they will turn into [...] *4* [...] by the sword. And what it [says...] *5* [...] ... [...] *6* [...] ... [...] the teacher of [... as it is written:] *7* *Zach 11:11* [It was annulled on that day, and] thus the most helpless of the flock which [was watching me knew] *8* [that it was in fact the word of the Lord.] *Blank* [...] *9* *Is 30:1-5* [Woe to the rebellious sons – oracle of the] Lord – who make plans [without counting] *10* [on me; who sign deals, but] without my spirit, to ad[d sin] *11* [to sin; who proceed to go do]wn to Egypt [without conferring with me, to gain strength] *12* [with the strength of the Pharaoh and shel]ter in the shadow of Egypt! [Their disgrace will be] *13* [the strength of the Pharaoh, and the she]lter of the shadow of Egypt, [their shame. For in Zoan were] *14* [their princes, and their messengers] reached Hanes. [They were all ashamed of a] *15* [powerless people which could neither help] nor [oblige...]

Frag. 23   *1* [...] and they [...] all [...] ... [...] *2* [...] ... [...] *Blank* [...] *3 Is 30:15-18* [For] thus says YHWH, the Holy One of Israel: By turning back and being pla[cid will you be saved;] *4* your courage will comprise composure and trust. But you did not wish and sa[id:] *5* No, let us flee on horseback. Well, then, you need to flee. We will run at a gallop. Well, then *6* those chasing you will run faster. A thousand [shall flee] before the menace of one, before the menace *7* of five shall you flee, until you end up like a flagpole on the peak of a mountain, *8* like a standard upon a hill. This is why the Lord waits to take pity on you, this is why he rises *9* to be lenient with you. For YHWH is a God of justice. Happy are those waiting for! *10* The interpretation of the word, for the last days, concerns the congregation of those [looking] for easy interpretations *11* who are in Jerusalem [...] *12* in the law and not [...] *13* the heart, for in order to crush [...] *14 Hos 6:9* As bandits lie in wait, [the priests scheme]. They have rejected the law [...] *15 Is 30:19-21* [F]or a people living in Zion, [in Jerusalem, will no longer need to weep; the voice will have pity on you at the sound of] *16* on your cry; when he hears [you he will answer you. Even though the Lord were to give you measured bread and rationed water,] *17* no longer will he hide [from your Master, and your eyes will see your Master.] *18* Your ears will [hear a word at your shoulder which says: This is the path, walk on it,] *19* when you need to go to the right [or to the left. The interpretation of the word, for the last days,] *29* concerns the sin of [...]

Frag. 25   *1* [...] the king of Babylon [...] *2* [...] with tambourines and zithers [...] *3* [... downpour and hailstorm, implements of war, they are [...] *4* [...] *Blank* [...] *5* [*Is 31:1* Alas those who go down to] Egypt! In horses [they trust and they rely on chariots] *6* [beca]use they are numerous, and on cavalry, because they are very strong, [without regard for] *7* [the H]oly One of Israel or [consulting YHWH. *Blank*] *8* [Its interpretation: they] are the people which relies [...]

Frag. 26   *1* [*Is 32:5-6* No longer] will they call the fool an aristocrat, or treat the rogue as an aristocrat. For] *2* [the rogue says] roguish things. [His heart plots crime; he commits evil and speaks deceitfully against] *3* [the Lord, leaves the hungry person empty and takes water away from the thirsty...]

4QIsaiah Pesher^d (4Q164 [4QpIs^d])

Frag. 1   *1* [he will trea]t all Israel like «jet» around the eye. *Is 54:11* And your foundations are sapphires. [Its interpretation:] *2* they will found the council of the Community, the priests and the peo[ple...] *3* the assembly of their elect, like a sapphire stone in the midst of stones. *Is 54:12* [I will place] *4* all your battlements [of rubies]. Its interpretation concerns the twelve [chiefs of the priests who] *5* illuminate with the judgment of the Urim and the Thummim [... without] *6* any from among them missing, like the sun in all its light. *Is 54:12* And a[ll your gates of glittering stones.] *7* Its interpretation concerns the chiefs of the tribes of Israel in the las[t d]ays [...] *8* of its lot, their functions [...]

4QIsaiah Pesher*ᵉ* (4Q165 [4QpIs*ᵉ*])

Frags. 1-2 *1* ... [...] ... *2* and Jerusalem [...] And what is written: [*Is 40:11* «He carries them on his chest and leads the mothers».] *3* The interpretation of the word [concerns the Teacher of Righteousness who] reveals just teaching [...*Is 40:12* Who has measured the sea in fistfuls,] *4* or [charted] the sky [in palm-breadths, or the dust] of the earth [by bushels. Who] has weighed [the mountains on the balance or the hills in the scales?]

Frag. 5 *1 Is 21:9-10* [and all the statues of their gods has he smashed] to the ground. [My people, threshed on the threshing floor, what I have heard from the Lord of Hosts, God] *2* [of Israel, I will tell you.] The interpretation of the word concerns [...] *3* [Oracle against Dumah: *Is 21:11-15* Someone sh]outs from Seir: Watchman, what is left of the [night? Watchman, what is left of the night? The Watchman replies: Morning will come and also the night. If you wish to ask, ask,] *4* [come back, return. Oracle against Arabia:] In the scrub of the steppe shall you spend the night, [caravans of Dedan; take out water to meet the thirsty, dwellers in the land of Teman, take bread] *5* [to the refugee, for]/[...] he flees in front of the swords/ in front of the unsheathed sword/ in front of [the taut bow,] / in front of [the fierce fighting. The interpretation of the word concerns ...] *6* [...] the peoples and the bread [...] *7* [...] lays waste [...]

Frag. 6 *1* [...] the chosen ones of Israel [...] *2* [...] eternal. And what is written; [*Is 32:5-7* No longer will they call the fool an aristocrat,] *3* [or] treat [the rogue] as superior. For the r[ogue says roguish things and his heart is dedicated to evil, to commit wicked deeds] *4* [and to speak] absurdities against [the Lord]; to destroy [the soul of the hungry person and take water away from the thirsty. As for the rogue] *5* [his roguish deeds are] illicit and he hatches plots [to destroy the poor with lies] *6* [and the helpless who defends] his rights. Its interpretation concerns [...] *7* [...] ... to the law [...]...[...]

B *Commentaries on Hosea*

4QHosea Pesher*ᵃ* (4Q166 [4QpHos*ᵃ*])

Frag. 1 col. I *1-2* [...] *3* [...] he will show his hostility *4* [...] and they shall commiserate *5* [...] and move far away *6* [...] *Blank 7* [*Hos 2:8* Therefore, he will fence in your path] with brambles and [he will not find] his footpaths *8* [Its interpretation: with madness,] blindness and confusion *9* [of heart will YHWH mutilate them ...] and the era of his betrayal not *10* [...] they are the generation of the visitation *11* [...] the upholders of the covenant. *12* [...] end in the ages of wrath, because *13* [...] *Blank 14* [...] *Blank 15* [*Hos 2:9* And he will say: I shall go and return to my fir]st [husband] because *16* [I was better off then than now. Its interpretation: ...] in the return of the converts *17* [...] pure *18–19* [...]

Col. II   *1* [*Hos 2:10* She did not know that] it was I who gave her wheat, [wine] *2* [and oil.] I increased [the silver] and the gold [out of which they] made [idols] for themselves. [Its interpretation:] *3* they will ea[t and] be replete and forget the God of [justice] *4* they will turn their backs on his precepts which he had sent to them [through the mouth of] *5* his servants, the prophets. They will listen to those who misdirect them and acclaim them [...] *6* and will revere them like gods in their blindness. *Blank* [...] *7 Blank* [...] *8 Hos 2:11–12* Because of this I will collect back my wheat in its time and my wine [in its season,] *9* I will reclaim my wool and my flax which cover [their nakedness.] *10* Now I will uncover her disgrace in the sight of her love[rs and no-one] *11* will free her from my hand. *Blank* [...] *12* Its interpretation: he has punished them with hunger and with nakedness so they will be shame *13* and disgrace in the eyes of the nations on whom they relied. But they *14* will not save them from their sufferings. *Hos 2:13* I will make an end to her joys, *15* her fea[sts, her new] moons and her sabbaths and all her celebrations. Its interpretation: *16* they are to determine [all their celebrations] in agreement with the celebrations of the nations, but [all] *17* [her joy] will be changed into mourning for them. *Hos 2:14* I will devastate [their vines] *18* [and their fig trees about which she said: they are my wages [which] *19* [my lovers gave me;] I will turn them into thickets and the [wild be]asts will eat them.

4QHosea Pesher^a (4Q167 [4QpHos^b])

Frag. 2   *1* [*Hos 5:13* but he cannot heal] your wound. The interpre[tation ...] *2* [...] raging lion. *Hos 5:14* For I will be like a lion [to Ephr]aim [and like a lion cub to the House of] *3* Judah. Its interpretation [concerns] the last priest who will stretch out his hand to strike Ephraim *4* [... his ha]nd. *Blank* [...] *5 Hos 5:15* I will go and return to [my position] until they acknowledge their crime and seek my face; in their distress *6* [they will get up early in search of me. Its interpretation:] God will hide his face from [the land] *7* [...] and they will not listen [...]

Frags. 5–6   *1* [...] the men of [...] *2* [...] their masters [...] upon [...] *3* [*Hos 6:4* What] shall I do with you, [Ephraim;] what [shall I do with you Judah?...]

Frags. 7–8   *1* [*Hos 6:7* They, like Adam,] broke the covenant. Its interpretation: [...] *2* [...] they deserted God and followed the laws of [...] they in all [...]

Frags. 10 + 26   *1* And what [it says]: [*Hos 6:9–10* «They commit evils. [In the House of Israel I have seen something horrifying: there Ephraim prostitutes himself,] *2* Israel [degrades herself»] Its interpretation: [... *3* [the evil]doers of the nations [...] *4* all the [...] *5* upon [...]

Frags. 4 + 8 + 24   *1* [...*Hos 6:11; 7:1* Judah, also] a harvest [is ready] for you, *2* [when the bondage of my people changes. The interpretation concerns ...] on the day of *3* [...] for us *4* [...] *5* [...] and what *6* [it says: *Hos 7:1* «When the bondage of my people changes». Its interpretation concerns ...] since he will make *7* [...] return [...] and humble [...]

Frags. 11 + 12 + 13   *1-2* [...]...[...] *3* [...] (*Hos 8:6*) A sculptor made it [and it is not God.] *4* Its interpretation: they were among the peoples [...] *5* *Hos 8:6* For shattered to pieces was the ca[lf of Samaria. Its interpretation: ...] *6* [Is]rael. *Hos 8:7-8* They sow wind and [reap] storms. [It will not have shoots; the stalk will not have fruit;] *7* [if it did have any,] foreigners would eat it. [They have devoured Israel. Now they are among the nations like a] *8* use[less pot.] *Blank* [...] *9* The interpretation [...] *10* ... [...]

Frags. 15 + 16 *col.* II   *1* [they shall] return. *Hos 8:14* And [Israel] forgot her Maker and built palaces. And Judah] *2* increased her [fortified ci]ies. But I shall send fire against her cities and it will consume her palaces.] *3* *Blank* [...Its inter]pretation: [...] *4* to be [...] each one will collect [...] *5* in front [of...] God does not want [...]

c *Commentaries on Micah*

1QMicah Pesher (1Q14 [1QpMic])

Frags. 1–5   *1* [*Mic 1:2–5* Listen, every people; take notice, earth and what fills it: the Lord G]od [will be] *2* [a witness] against you [the Lord, from his holy temple. For behold,] God [leaves] his place *3* [and descends upon the he]ights of the ear[th. the mountains beneath [him] melt, [and the valleys spli]t a[part,] *4* [like wa]x next to [the fire,] like wat[er poured down a slope.] all [because of Jacob's crime,] *5* because of the sins [of the House of Israel...]

Frag. 6   *1*[...] ... [...] *2* [... in the] last [days [....] *3* [...] the glory [...] *4* [... which] they infringe [...]

Frag. 7   *1* […] Perhaps […] not *2* […] the simple […] *3* […] … in it […]

Frag. 10   *3* [*Mic 1:5-6* What are the 'high places' of Judah? Is it not Je]rusa[lem? I will reduce Samaria] *4* [to a country ruin, to a plot of vines.] The interpretation of this concerns the Spreader of Lies *5* [since he has misdirected] simpletons. *Mic 1:5* 'What are the "high places" of Judah? *6* [Is it not Je]rusalem? The interpretation of this co]ncerns the Teacher of Righteousness who *7* [teaches the law to his council] and to all those volunteering to join the chosen of *8* [God, carrying out the law] in the council of the Community, those who will be saved on the day of *9* [judgment…] … […] *10* […As for what he says: *Mic 1:6-7* I will reduce Samaria] to a country ruin *11* [to a plot of vines; I will tip her stones into the valley and lay bare her foundations. A]ll her idols

Frag. 11   *1* [*Mic 1:8* and I will wail. Its interpretation concerns the priests of] Jerusalem, since they misdirect […] *2* […] their enemies. *Mic 1:8-9* Barefoot and na[ked, I will mourn] *3* [as jackals howl and as ostrich young moan. For it has come as far as Judah, has reached] as far as the gate of my people, as far [as Jerusalem. *4* [… The interpretation concerns the Teacher of Righteousness, since he] will judge his enemies […] *5* […] turning to face towards him […]

Frag. 12   *1* […] *2* […] his glory of Seir […] *3* [… be]cause God will go out from […]

Frags. 17 + 18   *1* […] *2* [*Mic 6:15* … you shall sow and not] reap, [tread olives] *3* [and not anoint yourself, tread grapes and] not drink wine. [The laws of Omri are kept] *4* [and all the procedures of the House of Ahab;] you behave according to his counsels; thus [I shall destroy you] *5* [and hand over your inhabitants to insult. Its interpretation] concerns the last generation [since…] *6* […] … […]

Frags. 22 + 23   *1* […]…[…] *2* […] and he will shine *3* […*Mic 7:15-17* like the] day when you left [the land of Egypt] *4* [I will show you marvels. The peoples shall see it and be ashamed] of all their power, [they shall lift their hands to their mouth,] *5* [cover their ears, bite the dust like sn]akes and creepy-crawlies [of the earth.]

4QMicah Pesher (?) (4Q168 [4QpMic(?)])

Frags. 1 + 3   *1* [of the daughter of] Jerusalem. [*Mic 4:9-12* Now, why do you yell, complaining? Have you no king? Are you lacking a counsellor?] *2* Since [pain] has gripped you [like a woman giving birth, have pain and push (it) out, daughter of Zion, like a woman giving birth, because] *3* now shall you leave the city [and live on waste ground and go right to Babylon. There you shall be redeemed. There,] *4* the Lord will free you [from the hand of your enemies. Now many nations collaborate against you] *5* saying: [be defiled and let us fix our gaze on Zion. They do not know the plans of the Lord or] *6* [understand] his plans.

D *Commentary on Nahum*

4QNahum Pesher (4Q169 [4QpNah])

Frags. 1 + 2   *1* [*Nah 1:3* ... His path is in the hurricane and in the storm, and] a cloud is the du[st of his feet. Its interpretation: ...] *2* [the storms and the hurricanes], vaults of his skies and his earth which he cr[eated...] *3 Nah 1:4* He roars against the sea and dries it up. Its interpretation: the sea are all the Kit[tim], since [...] *4* to carry out judgment against them and to eliminate them from the face of [the earth. *Nah 1:4* And dries up all the rivers.] *5+* /[Its interpretation concerns the Kittim]/ with [all their chi]efs, since his rule will end. *5* [*Nah 1:4* Bashan and] Carmel [become dry] and the bloom of Lebanon shrivels. [The interpretation of the word concerns ... since ...] *6* many will die for him at the height of sin. For [the Kittim] are Bas[han, since ... and his king is called:] *7* [Car]mel and his chiefs: Lebanon; and the bloom of Lebanon is [... since ...] *8* [the sons of his fau]lts, and they will die in front of [...] the chosen of [...] *9* [... a]ll the inhabitants of the world. *Blank Nah 1:5-6* The mou[ntains quake in front of him and the hillocks shake,] *10* the earth [rises] in front of him and before him [the world and a]ll that lives in it. Before his wrath who can endure? And who] *11* [can tolerate] the fire of his anger? Its inter[pretation ...]

Frags. 3 + 4 *col.* I   *1* [... *Nah 2:12*] residence for the wicked of the nations. For a lion went to go into it, a lion cub *2* [without anyone confining him. Its interpretation concerns Deme]trius, king of Yavan, who wanted to enter Jerusalem on the advice of the those looking for easy interpretations, *3* [but he did not go in because God did not deliver Jerusalem] into the hand of the kings of Yavan from Antiochus up to the appearance of the chiefs of the Kittim. But later, it will be trampled *4* [...] *Blank Nah 2:13* The lion catches enough for his cubs and tears prey apart for his lioness; *5* [he fills his cave with prey and his den with spoils. The interpretation of the word] concerns the Angry Lion who struck *6* [the simple folk of Ephraim] with his nobles and the men of his counsel. [And as for what he says: *Nah 2:13* «he fills] his cave [with prey] and his den with spoils», *Blank* Its interpretation concerns the Angry Lion *7* [who filled his den with a mass of corpses, carrying out rev]enge against those looking for easy interpretations, who hanged living men *8* [from the tree, committing an atrocity which had not been committed] in Israel since ancient times, for it is horrible for the one hanged alive from the tree. *Nah 2:14* Here am I against [you]!

9 Orac[le of the Lord of Hosts. I shall burn your throng in the fire] and the sword will consume your cubs. I will eradi[cate] the spoils [from the earth]. *Blank 10* and no [longer will the voice of your messengers be heard. Its inter]pretation: «Your throng» are his gangs of soldiers [...]; «his cubs» are *11* his nobles [and the members of his council, since...] and «his spoils» is the wealth which [the priests of Jerusalem accu]mulated [which] *12* they will deliver [... E]phraim, will be given Israel [...] *Blank*

Frags. 3–4 *col.* II   *1* And his messengers are his emissaries, whose voice will no longer be heard among the nations. *Nah 3:1* Alas the bloody city, all of it [treachery,] stuffed with loot! *2* Its interpretation: it is the city of Ephraim, those looking for easy interpretations, in the final days, since they walk in treachery and lies. *3 Nah 3:1-3* Spoils will not be lacking, nor the noise of the whip nor the din of colliding wheels. Horses at the gallop, chariots bouncing, horsemen lunging, flashing [of swords] *4* and flickering of spears! Masses of wounded and heaps of corpses! Endless corpses, they trip [over] their corpses! Its interpretation concerns the rule of those looking for easy interpretations, *5* since within his assembly there will no lack of the sword of the gentiles, captivity or looting, nor fire in among them, nor exile for fear of the enemy, a mass *6* of corpses will fall in their days; there will be no end to the tally of their wounded and they will even trip over their bodies of flesh because of his mistaken counsel. *7 Nah 3:4* On account of the many fornications of the prostitute, full of elegance and mistress of enchantment, who misleads nations with her sorceries. *Blank 8* [Its] interpretation concerns those who misdirect Ephraim, who with their fraudulent teaching and lying tongue and perfidious lip misdirect many; *9* kings, princes, priests and people together with the proselyte attached to them. Cities and clans will perish through his advice, nobles and le[aders] *10* will fall [due to the fero]city of their tongues. *Blank Nah 3:5* See, here am I against you! – oracle of the Lord of Ar[mies] – You shall hoist *11* [your] skirts up to your face and show the nations [your] nudity and kings your shame. Its interpretation [...] *12* [...] the cities of (the) East, because «the skirts» [...]

Frags. 3–4 *col.* III   *1* The nations with their uncleanness [and the re]fuse of their monstrosities. *Nah 3:6* I will throw refuse on top of you, affront you and make you *2* odious. *Nah 3:7* And what will happen is that all those who see you will run away from you. *Blank 3* Its interpretation concerns those looking for easy interpretations, whose evil deeds will be exposed to all Israel in the final time *4* and many will fathom their sin, they will hate them and loathes them for their reprehensible arrogance. And when the glory of Judah is revealed *5* the simple people of Ephraim will flee from among their assembly and desert the ones who misdirected them and will join the [whole of Is]rael. *Nah 3:7* They shall say: *6* Nineveh is laid waste, who will be sorry for her? Where shall I find comforters for you? Its interpretation concerns those looking for *7* easy interpretations, whose council will die and whose society will be disbanded; they shall not continue misdirecting the assembly and simple [folk] shall no longer support their advice. *Nah 3:8* Do you act better than Am[mon, seated between] the Niles? *Blank 9* Its interpretation: Amon is Manasseh and the Niles are the important people of Manasseh, the nobles of the [people who surround Ma[nasseh] *10 Nah 3:8* Water surrounds the one whose rampart was the sea, and the water her walls. *Blank 11* Its interpretation: they are her men at arms, her mighty warriors. *Nah 3:9* Ethiopia was her strength [and Egypt, without end.] *12* [Its interpretation ...] *Nah 3:9* Put and Libya [were her guards]

Frags. 3–4 col. IV   *1* Its interpretation: they are the wick[ed people of Judah], the house of Peleg, which consorted with Manasseh. *Nah 3:10* She, too, fled to exile, [walked to captivity, also] *2* her children were dashed to pieces at every crossroad and for their nobles they cast lots and all [their] important people [were loaded] *3* with chains. Its interpretation concerns Manasseh, in the last time, since his control over Is[rael] will weaken [...] *4* his women, his children and his babies will go into captivity, his warriors and his nobles [will fall] by the sword. [*Nah 3:11* You, too, will get drunk] *5* and hide away. *Blank* Its interpretation concerns the wicked of E[phraim who ...] *6* since its cup will come after Manasseh [...*Nah 3:11* You, too, will seek] *7* a hideout in the city from the enemy. Its interpretation [concerns ...] *8* their enemies in the city, [... *Nah 3:12* All their fortresses] *9* are fig-trees [laden with figs...]

Frags. 3–4 col. V   *1* [*Nah 3:13* Look, your people are] women a[mong you. The gates of your land are wide open to your enemy, fire has devoured your bars.] *2* [The interpretation ...] the whole border of Israel to the sea [... *Nah 3:14* Stock up with water for the siege;] *3* [reinforce] your defences; tread mud [and stamp on clay, put it in the mould ...]

E *Commentary on Habakkuk*

1QHabakkuk Pesher (1QpHab)

Col. I   *1* [*Hab 1:1-2* Oracle received by the prophet Habakkuk in a vision. For how long, YHWH] will I ask for help without *2* [you hearing me; shout: Violence! to you without you saving me? The interpretation of this concerns the beg]inning of the *3* [final] *2* generation *3* [...] upon them *4* [...they] will shout against *5* [... *Hab 1:3a* Why do you make me see misdeeds and] show [me to]il? *Blank 6* [The interpretation ...] of God with persecution and betrayal. *7* [...*Hab 1:3b* you set violence and destruction in front of me and brawls occur and quarrels arise]. *Blank 8* [The interpretation ...] spoils [...] and brawls *9* [... ar]gument and they [think] destruction *10* [...] *Hab 1:4a* For the Law falls into abeyance. *11* [The interpretation ...] that they have rejected the Law of God. *12* [*Hab 1:4bc* And justice does not emerge as the winner, for the evildoer acc]osts the upright man. *Blank 13* [Its interpretation: the evildoer is the Wicked Priest and the upright man] is the Teacher of Righteousness *14* [who ... *Hab 1:4d* This] is why justice emerges *15* [distorted. The interpretation...] and not [...]

Col. II   *1 Hab 1:5* you reported it. *Blank* [The interpretation of the word concerns] the traitors with the Man of *2* Lies, since they do not [believe in the words of the] Teacher of Righteousness from the mouth of *3* God; (and it concerns) the traito[rs of the] new [covenant] since they did not *4* believe in the covenant of God [and dishonoured] his holy name. *5* Likewise: *Blank* The interpretation of the word [concerns the trai]tors in the *6* last days. They shall be violators of [the coven]ant who will not believe *7* when they hear all that is going [to happen to] the final generation, from the mouth of the *8* Priest whom God has placed wi[thin the Community,] to foretell the fulfilment of all *9* the words of his servants, the prophets, [by] means of whom God has declared *10* all that is going to happen to his people [Israel]. *Hab 1:6* For see, I will mobilize *11* the Chaldaeans, a cru[el and determined] people. *Blank 12* Its interpretation concerns the Kittim, who are swift and powerful *13* in battle, to slay many [with the edge of the sword] in the kingdom of *14* the Kittim; they will vanquish [many countries] and will not believe *15* in the precepts of [God...] *16* and [...]

Col. III   *1* and they will advance over the plain, to destroy and pillage the cities of the country. *2* For this is what he has said: *Hab 1:6* «To vanquish foreign habitations». *Hab 1:7* It is terrible *3* and terrible; from his very self his justice and his preeminence arise. *Blank 4* The interpretation of this concerns the Kittim, due to the fear and dread they provoke in all *5* /the peoples;/ their intrigues are planned ahead, and with cunning and treachery *6* they behave towards all the peoples. *Hab 1:8* Their horsemen are swifter than panthers; they are more savage *7* than wolves at night. *Blank* Their riders leap and hurl themselves from afar. *8* They will fly like the eagle stooping to gorge itself. *Hab 1:9* All of them resort to force; the breath of *9* their faces is like the East wind. *Blank* [Its inter]pretation concerns the Kittim, who *10* trample the land with their horses and their animals *11* and come from far off, from the islands of the sea, to devour all the peoples, like an eagle, *12* insatiable. With fury [they will assemble, and with bu]rning wrath *13* and livid faces they will speak to all [the peoples.] For this is what *14* he has said: [*Hab 1:9* The breath of their faces is like the East wind. And they amass] captives [like sa]nd. *15* [The interpretation of this [...]

Col. IV   *1 Hab 1:10a* they sneer [at kings] and mock leaders. *Blank* Its interpretation:

2 they deride the powerful and despise the honoured men; at kings *3* and princes they mock, and sneer at a great people. *Hab 1:10b* And he *4* laughs at all the strong fortresses, rams down earth and captures it. *5* The interpretation of this concerns the leaders of the Kittim, who despise the *6* fortresses of the peoples and with disdain laugh at them, *7* they surround them with a huge army to capture them. And through dread and fear *8* they surrender to their hands, and they demolish them because of the wickedness of their occupants. *9 Hab 1:11* Then the wind changed and went on. He made his might *10* his God. *Blank* The interpretation of this concerns the leaders of the Kittim, *11* who on the resolution of the House of Bla[me] go by, one *12* in front of the other. [Their] leaders, one after another, will come *13* to raze the earth. *Hab 1:11* He [made] his might his God. *14* Its interpretation […] to the peoples *15* […]

Col. V   *1* [*Hab 1:12b–13a* You have appointed him to judge: Rock, you have installed him to correct. Your eyes are too pure *2* to be looking at evil, you cannot be staring at tyranny. *Blank 3* Interpretation of the word: God is not to destroy his people at the hand of nations, *4* but by means of his chosen ones God will judge all the nations; *5* all the evildoers of his people will be pronounced guilty for the reproof of those who kept his commandments *6* in their hardship. For this is what he has said: *Hab 1:13a* «Your eyes are too pure to look *7* at evil». *Blank* Its interpretation: his eyes have not drawn them to licentiousness in the era of *8* wickedness. *Hab 1:13b* Why are you staring, traitors, and you maintain your silence when *9* a wicked person consumes someone more upright than himself? *Blank* Its interpretation concerns the House of Absalom *10* and the members of his council, who kept silent at the time of the reproach of the Teacher of Righteousness, *11* and did not help him against the Man of Lies, *Blank* who rejected *12* the Law in the midst of their whole Comm[unity.] *Hab 1:14–16* You made man like fish of the sea, *13* like a reptile, to govern him. All of [them] he removes [with a fish]-hook, catches in a net *14* and collects in [a seine. This is why he offers sacri]fices to his net; this is why he rejoices *15* [and is happy and burns incense to his seine; since by them] his portion is fat *16* [and his food rich…]

Col. VI   *1* of the Kittim, and they will garner their wealth with all their loot *2* like the fish of the sea. And what it says: *Hab 1:16a* For this he sacrifices to his net *3* and burns incense to his seine. *Blank* Its interpretation: they *4* offer sacrifices to their standards and their weapons are *5* the object of their worship. *Hab 1:16b* Since by them his portion is fat and his food rich. Its interpretation: they have shared out their yoke and *7* their burden, which is their food, among all the peoples, year after year, ravaging many countries. *Hab 1:17* For this he continually unsheathes his sword *9* to kill peoples without pity. *Blank 10* Its interpretation concerns the Kittim who will cause many to die by the edge of the sword, *11* youths, adults and old people, women and children; not even *12* children at the breast will they pity. *Hab 2:1-2* I will stand firm in my sentry-post, *13* I will position myself in my fortress to see what he says to me, *14* what he answers to my allegation. YHWH answered me *15* and said: Write the vision; inscribe it on tablets so that *16* [he who reads it] takes it on the run. *Hab 2:1-2* [...]

Col. VII   *1* And God told Habakkuk to write what was going to happen *2* to the last generation, but he did not let him know the end of the age. *3 Blank* And as for what he says: *Hab 2:2*] «So that the one who reads it /may run/». *4* Its interpretation concerns the Teacher of Righteousness, to whom God has disclosed *5* all the mysteries of the words of his servants, the prophets. *Hab 2:3* For the vision has an appointed time, it will have an end and not fail. *Blank 7* Its interpretation: the final age will be extended and go beyond all that *8* the prophets say, because the mysteries of God are wonderful. *9 Hab 2:3b* Though it might delay, wait for it; it definitely has to come and will not *10* delay. *Blank* Its interpretation concerns the men of truth, *11* those who observe the Law, whose hands will not desert the service *12* of truth when the final age is extended beyond them, because *13* all the ages of God will come at the right time, as he established *14* for them in the mysteries of his prudence. *Hab 2:4* See, *15* [his soul within him] is conceited and does not give way. *Blank* Its interpretation: they will double *16* [persecution] upon them [and find no mercy] at being judged. *Blank*

Col. VIII   *1* Its interpretation concerns all observing the Law in the House of Judah, whom *2* God will free from punishment on account of their deeds and of their loyalty *3* to the Teacher of Righteousness. *Hab 2:5-6* Surely wealth will corrupt the boaster *4* and one who distends his jaws like the abyss and is as greedy as death will not be restrained. *5* All the nations ally against him, all the peoples collaborate against him. *6* Are they not all, perhaps, going to chant verses against him, explaining riddles at his expense? *7* They shall say: Ah, one who amasses the wealth of others! How long will he load himself *8* with debts? *Blank* Its interpretation concerns the Wicked Priest, who *9* is called by the name of loyalty at the start of his office. However, when he ruled *10* over Israel his heart became conceited, he deserted God and betrayed the laws for the sake of *11* riches. And he stole and hoarded wealth from the brutal men who had rebelled against God. *12* And he seized public money, incurring additional serious sin. *13* And he performed repulsive acts of every type of filthy licentiousness. *Hab 2:7-8* Will *14* your creditors not suddenly get up, and those who shake you wake up? You will be their prey. *15* Since you pillaged many countries the rest of the peoples will pillage you. *16 Blank* The interpretation of the word concerns the Priest who rebelled *17* [...] the precepts of [God...]

Col. IX   *1* being distressed by the punishments of sin; the horrors of *2* terrifying

maladies acted upon him, as well as vengeful acts on his fleshly body. And what
3 it says: *Hab 2:8a* «Since you pillaged many countries the rest of the peoples will
pillage you». *Blank* Its interpretation concerns the last priests of Jerusalem,
5 who will accumulate riches and loot from plundering the peoples. *6* However,
in the last days their riches and their loot will fall into the hands *7* of the army
of the Kittim. *Blank* For they are *Hab 2:8a* «the greatest of the peoples». *8 Hab 2:8b*
For the human blood [spilt] and the violence done to the country, the city and
all its /occupants/. *Blank 9* Its interpretation concerns the Wicked Priest, since
for the wickedness against the Teacher of *10* Righteousness and the members
of his council God delivered him into the hands of his enemies to disgrace him
11 with a punishment, to destroy him with bitterness of soul for having acted
wickedly *12* against his elect. *Hab 2:9-11* Woe to anyone putting ill-gotten gains
in his house, placing *13* his nest high up to escape the power of evil! You have
planned the insult *14* to your house, exterminating many countries and sinning
against your soul. For *15* the stones will shout from the walls, and the wooden
beams will answer. *16* [The interpretation of the quo]te concerns the [priest]
who [...]

Col. X   *1* for its stone to be for repression and the beam of its wood for pillage.
And what *2* it says: *Hab 2:10* «Exterminating many countries and sinning against
your soul». *Blank 3* Its interpretation: it is the house of judgment, for God will
give *4* his judgment among many countries and from there will lead him to
punishment. *5* And in their midst he will proclaim him guilty and will punish
him with sulphurous fire. *Hab 2:12-13* Woe *6* to him who builds a city with blood
and founds a town on a misdeed! Does *7* this not stem from YHWH of Hosts?
The peoples wear themselves out for fire and *8* the nations are exhausted for
nothing. *Blank 9* The interpretation of the word concerns the Spreader of Deceit, who has misdirected many, *10* building a useless city with blood and erecting a community by subterfuge *11* for his own renown, wearing out many by
useless work and by making them conceive *12* acts of deceit, so that their
labours are for nothing; so that *13* those who derided and insulted God's chosen
will go to the punishment of fire. *14 Hab 2:14* For the earth will become full of
the knowledge of YHWH's glory just as water *15* fills the sea. *Blank* Interpretation of the word: *16* in his return [...]

Col. XI   *1* deceit. Afterwards, knowledge will be revealed to them, as plentiful as
the water *2* in the sea. *Hab 2:15* Woe to anyone making his companion drunk,
spilling out *3* his anger! He even makes him drunk to look at their festivals!
4 Blank Its interpretation concerns the Wicked Priest who *5* pursued the Teacher of Righteousness to consume him with the ferocity *6* of his anger in the
place of his banishment, in festival time, during the rest *7* of the day of Atonement. He paraded in front of them, to consume them *8* and make them fall on

the day of fasting, the sabbath of their rest. *Hab 2:16* You are more glutted *9* with insults than with awards. Drink up also and stagger! *10* The cup of YHWH's right hand will turn against you and disgrace come *11* upon your glory. *Blank 12* Its interpretation concerns the Priest whose shame has exceeded his glory *13* because he did not circumcise the foreskin of his heart and has walked on paths of *14* drunkenness to slake his thirst; but the cup of *15* God's anger will engulf him, heaping up [shame upon him.] And the pain

Col. XII   *1 Hab 2:17* will appal you owing to the human blood and the violence (against) the country, the city and all its occupants. *2* The interpretation of the word concerns the Wicked Priest, to pay him the *3* reward for what he did to the poor. Because Lebanon is *4* the Council of the Community and the Animals are the simple folk: of Judah, those who observe *5* the Law. God will sentence him to destruction, *Blank 6* exactly as he intended to destroy the poor. And as for what he says: *Hab 2:17* «Owing to the blood *7* of the city and the violence (against) the country». Its interpretation: the city is Jerusalem *8* since in it the /Wicked/ Priest performed repulsive acts and defiled *9* the Sanctuary of God. The violence against the country are the cities of Judah which *10* he plundered of the possessions of the poor. *Hab 2:18* What use is the sculpture which the craftsman carves, *11* (or) the cast effigy and sham oracle, in whom their crafts-man trusts, *12* to make dumb idols? The interpretation of the word concerns all the *13* idols of the nations which they made, to serve them and bow down *14* in front of them. But they will not save them on the day of Judgment. *Hab 2:19* Woe *15* to anyone [saying to wo]od: Wake up! and to a silent stone: [Get up!]

Col. XIII   *1 Hab 2:20* Silence in his presence, all the world! Its interpretation con-cerns all the nations *2* which serve stone and wood. However, (on) the day *3* of judgment God will obliterate all the worshippers of idols, *4* and all the wicked, from the earth. *Blank 5-15 Blank*

F *Commentaries on Zephaniah*

1QZephaniah Pesher (1Q15 [1QpZeph])

[*1 Zeph 1:18* ... with the fire of] his zeal [all the earth] will be consumed; [because unquestionably he will cause the devastation,] *2* [the obliteration of all the inha]bitants of the earth. *Zeph 2:1-2* Gather together [and huddle up, people, /[before you scatter like] chaff which passes in one day/ *3* [without shame, before] the fire of the Lord's wrath [overtakes you,] *4* [before the day of] the Lord's wrath [overtakes you.] The interpretation *5* [of the word concerns all the occupants] of the land of Judah, since [...] *6* [...] will be [...]

4QZephaniah Pesher (4Q170 [4QpZeph])

1 [Zeph 1:12-13 …] YHWH [does not do] good and does not do evil. [Their wealth] will be plundered [and their houses flattened…] *2* […] he cannot […] Its interpretation [concerns …]

G *Commentary on Malachi*

5QMalachi Pesher (5Q10 [5QpMal(?)])

1 [Mal 1:14 Curse the cheat who has a male in his flock and offers a] maimed [victim] to the L[ord.] *2* [Its interpretation concerns those … who] make fun of animals […] *3* […] *Mal 1:14* Because I am the Great King, s[ays] *4* [YHWH of Hosts, and my name is feared among the peoples. Its interpretation:] he is a living God and […] *5* […]…[…]

H *Commentaries on the Psalms*

4QPsalms Pesher*a* (4Q171 [4QpPs*a*])

Col. I   *20 [Ps 37:6* … He will make your justice come out like the dawn and your rights like] midday. *21* [Its interpretation concerns the congregation of the poor who are ready to do] the will of *22* [God…] the arrogant ones choose *23* [… who l]ove slovenliness and mislead *24* […] wickedness at the hands of E[phra]im. *Blank 25 [Ps 37:7* Be si]lent before [YHWH and] hope in him, do not be annoyed with one who is affluent, with someone who *26* [hatches] plots. Its [interpretation] concerns the Man of Lies who misled many with *27* deceptive words since they thought up absurdities and [did not] listen to the Interpreter of knowledge. This is why

Col. II   *1* they will die by the sword, by hunger and by plague. *Ps 37:8-9* Curb anger and control temper and do not get *2* exasperated; it only leads to evil and those doing evil will be cut off. Its interpretation concerns all who converted *3* to the law, who do not reject their separation from their wickedness, for all the rebels *4* to convert from their sin will be cut off. *Ps 37:9* And those who hope in YHWH will inherit the land. Its interpretation: *5* they are the congregation of his elect who carry out his will. *Ps 37:10* A short while yet and the wicked will no longer exist. *6 Blank 7 Ps 37:10* I will stare at his place and he will no longer be there. Its interpretation concerns all the evil at the end *8* of the forty years, for they shall be devoured and upon the earth no wicked person will be found. *9 Ps 37:11* And the poor shall inherit the land and enjoy peace in plenty. Its interpretation concerns *10* the congregation of the poor who will tolerate the period of distress and will be rescued from all the snares of *11* Belial. Afterwards, all who shall inherit the land will enjoy and grow fat with everything... *12* of the flesh. *Blank 13 Ps 37: 12-13* The wicked plots against the just person, grinding [his teeth] aga[inst him;] YHWH laughs at him because he sees *14* that his day is coming. Its interpretation alludes to the ruthless ones of the covenant who are in the House of Judah, who *15* plot to destroy those who observe the law, who are in the Community Council. But God will not surrender them *16* into their hands. *Ps 37:14-15* The evildoers unsheathe the sword and discharge their bows to bring down the poor and humble, *17* to murder those on the correct path. Their swords shall pierce their own hearts and their bows shall break. *18* Its interpretation concerns the wicked of Ephraim and Manasseh who will attempt to lay hands *19* on the Priest and the members of his council in the period of testing which will come upon to them. However, God will save them *20* from their hands and after they will be delivered into the hands of dreadful nations for judgment. *21 Blank 22 Ps 37:16* Better is the little for the just man than the plenty of the many wicked. [Its interpretation concerns ...]*23* who observes the law, who does not [...] *24* for evil things. *Ps 37:17-18* For the arms [of wicked men will be broken, but YHWH supports just men] *25* YH[WH knows the days of perfect men and their inheritance will last for ever. Its interpretation concerns ...] *26* [their] will [...] *27* [*Ps 37:19* They shall not] be ashamed in [the evil time. Its interpretation concerns...]

Col. III   *1* those who have returned from the wilderness, who will live for a thousand generations, in safety; for them there is all the inheritance of *2* Adam and for his descendants for ever. *Ps 37:19-20* And in the days of famine they shall be replete; for the wicked *3* shall die. Its interpretation: he will keep them alive during the famine of the time of [dis]tress, when many *4* will die because of famine and plague: all who did not leave [there] with *5* the congregation of his chosen ones. /*Blank Ps 37:20* Whoever loves YHWH will be like precious lambs. Its interpretation [concerns...]/ who will be chiefs and princes over [the whole congregation, like shepherds] *6* of ewes in among their flocks. *Blank* [...] *7 Ps 37:20* Like smoke they all vanish. [Its] interpretation concerns the wicked princes who *8* oppress his holy people, who will die like smoke which disapp[ears in the w]ind. *Ps 37:21-22* The wicked asks for a loan but does not pay, *9* while the just man is sympathetic and gives. For those who are blessed by him shall inherit the earth, but those who are cursed by him shall be cut off. *10* Its interpretation concerns the congregation of the poor [for of them is] the inheritance of the whole wor[ld. *11* They will inherit the high mountain of Israel [and] delight [in his] holy [mou]ntain, «but those who are [cursed by him *12* will be cut off». These are the ruthless ones of the co[venant, the wicke]d men of Israel who will be cut off and exterminated *13* for ever. *Blank 14 Ps 37:23-24* For by YHWH [the steps of a man] are secure; he delights in his path: even

though he stumbles he will not *13* fall, for YHWH [supports his hand]. Its interpretation concerns the Priest, the Teacher of [Righteousness, whom] *16* God
chose to stand [in front of him, for] he installed him to found the congregation
[of his chosen ones] for him, *17* [and stra]ightened out his path, in truth. *Ps*
37:25-26 I used to be [young] and am old now; yet I have [not] seen [a just per-
son] *18* deserted or his offspring begging for bread. [Daily] he has compassion
and makes loans, and his off[spring is blessed. The interpretation] *19* of the
word concerns the Teac[her of Righteousness who ...] *20* and [...]

Col. IV   *1* judgm[ent and does not desert his devout ones. They shall be annihilated for ever and the offspring of the wicked will be cut off. Its interpretation:
] they are the ruthless ones *2* [of the covenant who...] the law. *Ps 37:29* The just
[will inherit the earth and live] on it [for] ever. *3* [Its interpretation... they shall
inherit the earth] over a thousand [generations. *Ps 37:30-31* The mouth of the
just man utters] wisdom and his tongue speaks *4* [justice; the law of his God is
in his heart; his steps will not falter. Its interpretation concerns ...] of the
truth, who speaks *5* [...] announces them. *Blank 6 Blank 7 Ps 37:32-33* The wicked
person spies on the just person and tries [to kill him. YH]WH [will not relinquish him into his hand, or] permit them to convict him when he is judged.
8 Its interpretation concerns the [Wic]ked Priest, who spies on the just man
[and wants] to kill him [...] and the law *9* which sent him; but [God will not
desert him] or permit them to convict him when he is judged. But [God] will
pay [him] his reward, delivering him *10* into the hands of dreadful nations so
that they can carry out [vengeance] upon him. [*Ps 37:34* Wait for YHWH] and
observe his path and he will promote you, so that you inherit *11* the earth; and
you shall see the destruction of the wicked. [Its interpretation concerns the
community of the poor] who will see the judgment of evil, and with *12* his chosen one will rejoice in the true inheritance. *Blank 13 Ps 37:35-36* I saw a dreadful
wicked man, who displayed himself [like a leafy tree.] I passed by his place [and
he no longer existed; I looked for him] and did not *14* [find him. Its interpretation alludes] to the Man of Lies [who ...] ... against God's chosen [and tried]
to end with *15* [...] ... [...] to carry out judgment [against him] [...] he acted
impertinently with an arrogant hand *16* [...] ... [*Ps 37:37* Observe the man of
integrity and watch] the upright man, [for there is a future for the man] of
peace. Its interpretation concerns *17* [...] ... [...] peace. *Ps 37:38* But the rebels
18 will be obliterated together, and the future of the [wicked will end up severed. Its interpretation concerns the traitors with the Man of Lies who] will die
and be cut off *19* from among the congregation of the Community. [*Ps 37:39* The
salvation of just men comes from YHWH. He is their refuge in the moment of
danger. YHWH assists them] *20* and rescues them and delivers them from the
wicked [and saves them, because they take refuge in him. Its interpretation ...]
21 God will save them and free them from the hand of the wicked [...] *22 Blank*

23 Ps 45:1 To the choirmaster. According to the Li[lies. A Maskil of the sons of Korah. Love-song. Its interpretation:] They are the seven divisions of *24* the converts of Is[rael who ...] [*Ps 45:2*] My heart [over]flows with a good poem, *25* I re[cite my verses to the king. Its interpretation ...] of the holy spirit, for *26* [...] the books of [...] *Blank Ps 45:2* And my tongue is the pen of *27* [a speedy scribe. Its interpretation concerns] the Teacher of [Righteousness...] before God with eloquent tongue

Col. v   [and] with influe[ntial] mouth [...] to return together to the law w[ith a whole heart...] *2* [...] ... [...] the chosen of Israel [...]

Frag. 13   *1* [[...] ... [...] *2* [...] *Blank* [...] *3* [*Ps 60:8-9 = Ps 108:8-9* G]od spoke [in his sanctuary: I will exult, I will divide up Shechem,] *4* parcel out [the Valley of Suc]coth; mine is [Gilead and mine Manasseh, and Ephraim is the helmet of my head.] *5* [Its interpretation concerns Gi]lead and to the half tribe [of Manasseh which ...] *6* [...] they will be reunited [...]

1QPsalms Pesher (1Q16 [1QpPs])

Frags. 3-4   *1* [...] ... [...] *2* [...] ... they acknowledged ...[...] they observed [...] *3* [...] ... *Ps 68:13* the kings of the armies go fl[eeing, go fleeing; she who lives at home shares out the loot.] Its interpretation: the ho[me is ...] *4* [...] ... the grandeur [...] *5* [...] which they share out [...] *6* [...] ...

Frag. 8   *1* [*Ps 68:26* In the middle go the girls playing tambourines.] Bless G[od] in choirs. [The interpretation ...]*2* [... the ble]ssing of hope for blessing ...[...]

Frag. 9   *1* [*Ps 68:30* To your temple, to Jerusalem, kings bring] gifts. Its interpretation concerns all the ...[...] *2* [...] before him in Jerusalem. *Ps 68:31* Rebuke the savage [beast of the reedbed;] *3* [the herd of bulls are the calves of the peoples, who proceed with ingots of] silver. Its interpretation: the savage beast of the ree[dbed is] *4* [...the Kit]tim for ...[...]

4QPsalms Pesher*^b* (4Q173 [4QpPs*^b*])

Frag. 1   *1* [...] ... [...] *2* [...] who looked for [...] *3* [...] ... of the Teacher of Righteousness [...] *4* [... pri]est in the final era [...] *5* [...] *Blank* [...] *6* [...] and the fever, the inheritance of [...]

Frag. 2   *1* [...] *Blank* The interpretation of the quo[tation...] *2* [...the Te]acher of Right[eousness...]

Frag. 3   *1* [...]... the man [...] *2* [...] who will be ...[...] *3* [...] they shall not be ashamed ...[...]

Frag. 4   *1* [*Ps 129:7-8* which does not] fill the hand of the reaper or [the armful of the one who binds, nor do those who pass by say to him:] *2* [«May YH]WH ble[ss] you. [We bless you in the name of YHWH ...] *3* [...] the wicked [...] ... [...]

4 Other texts

4QTanhumin (4Q176 [4QTanh])

Frags. 1–2 *col.* I   *1* Perform your marvel, do your people justice and … […]
2 your temple. Argue with kingdoms over the blood of […] *3* Jerusalem. See
the corpses of your priests […] *4* there is no-one to bury them. And of the book
of Isaiah: Words of consolation. [*Is 40:1-5* Be consoled, consoled, my people!]
5 says your God; speak to the heart of Jerusalem and sho[ut to her that her
service is done,] that *6* her fault has been forgiven, that from the hand of ****
she has received double for all her sins. A voice shouts: *7* in the wilderness clear
the path of ****, straighten out a roadway for our God in the [the ste]ppe.
Every valley is to be raised, *8* [and every mountain and hi]ll to be flattened; the
rough terrain is to be made into a plain, [and the peaks into] a plateau. *9* [And
the] glory of **** [will be revealed.] *Is 48:1-9* But you, Israel, are my servant,
Ja[cob, whom I cho]se, *10* [seed of Abra]ham, my favourite, whom I took [from
the en]ds of the earth, and [whom I called] from faraway lands; *11* and I [said]
to you: You are my servant, [I chose you and did not reje[ct] you!

Frags. 1–2 *col.* II   *1* [**** who are] loyal, the holy one of Isr[rael, and he has
chosen you. *Is 49:13-17* Celebrate, heavens, rejoice, earth;] *2* erupt with applause,
mountains! For God has consoled [his people, and has compassion on his poor.
But Zion said:] *3* **** has deserted me [and my Lord has forgotten me. Does
a woman, perhaps, forget her suckling child, stop having compassion for the
fruit of her womb?] *4* Even should she forget, [I will not forget you! See, I have
inscribed you on the palms of my hand,] *5* your ramparts [are always before me.
Your rebuilders are in a hurry, your wreckers and your destroyers] *6* depart
from you. […]

Frags. 9–11   *1* … […] … *Blank* *2* [*Is 52:1-3* Wake up, wake up, put on strength,]
Zion; put [on your party clothes, Je]rusalem, holy city, for *3* [no longer will
either uncircumcised or unclean enter you! Shake the dust from yourself, get
u]p, be seated, Jerusalem, undo *4* [the fetters from your neck,] prisoner, [daugh-
ter of Zion! For so] says [****: For nothing have you been sold, and without]
money will you be ransomed. *5* [*Blank* ?] *Is 54:4-10* Do not fear, [for] you will {}
not be asham[ed, do not smile, for] you will not be insulted. Because the indig-
nity of *6* [your spinst]erhood you are to forget and the humiliation of your wid-
owhood you are [not] to remember any more. For your husband will be your
maker, **** *7* [Seba'ot] is his name, your redeemer will be the Holy One of
Is[rael, the one] called [God of all the ea]rth. Because, as a woman, abandoned
8 [and troubled in] spirit has **** called you; and the wife of youth, why
should she be discarded? says **** your God. *9* [A] short [moment] I deserted

you, but with great compassion I will take you back. In a fit of anger [I hid my face] *10* from you [for a moment,] but with everlasting tenderness I took pity on you, says **** your redeemer. As in (the) days of Noah will this be for me; as *11* [I swore] that the waters of Noah would not flood the earth, so have I sworn not to become angry with you again or threaten you. *12* Should [even the moun]tains move or the hills wobble, my compassion will not shift from you [...] *13* [...] *Blank* Lose hope (?) until the words of comfort and of great glory. It is written in [...] *14* [...] among those who love [...] no longer since the time of [...] *Blank 15* [Beli]al to oppress his servants by [...] *16* [...] will rejoice [...] I will raise her who lies [...] *17* [...] ... [...]

Frags. 16 + 17 + 18 + 22 + 23 + 53   *1* and [...] *Blank* And how much more in the temple [...] the possession of his hand, for [man] is not vindicated *2* before [him.] Because he created every [spirit] of the eternal generations, [and with] his commandment [he established] all the paths. The earth *3* he created [with his rig]ht (hand) before it existed, and he con[tinually superv]ises everything [there is in it. And in his] mystery he causes the lot to fall on man in order to give [...] *4* [...] with the angel of [...] holy, and in order to give man's reward bef[ore] *5* [...] eight [...] over those who love him and over those who keep his commandmen[ts.] *6* [...] he showed himself to us since ...[...] forget his covenant. *Blank* And to [...] *7* [...] the Law [...] changes in order to be [...] *8* [...] the Law [...] completing them. [...] *9* [...] ... [...]

4QCatena*ᵃ* (4Q177 [4QCatena*ᵃ*])

Col. 1 (*frags.* 5 + 6 + 8)   *1* [...] the braggarts who [... in the ordeal to co]me upon the men of the Commu[nity,] *2* [as it is written in the book of Isaiah the pro]phet: *Is 37:30* This year what gro[ws of itself] will be eaten, [and the following year the self-seeded yield. And what it s]ays: «what grows of itself», is *3* [...] until the period of the orde[al which comes upon...] After this [...] will arise *4* [...] for all of them are children [...] The braggarts said [...] *5* [... as is written] about them in the book of I[saiah the prophet: ...] for the law of [...] *6* [...] calls them, as [is written about them in the book of Isaiah the prophet: *Is 32:7* He] hatches wicked plots to des[troy the poor] *7* [with cunning words... the] Insolent One to Israel [... *Ps 11:1* For the choirmaster.] Of David. In ʏʜᴡʜ [I trusted.] *8* [For, see, the wicked draw the bow,] notch arrows [to the string, to aim in the darkness at those with an honest heart. Its interpretation:] the me[n of ...] will flee *9* [...and he will flee] like a bird from its spot and will be exi[led from his land. *Blank* And this is what is written about th]em in the book of [...] *10* [*Mic 2:10-11* On account of uncleanness he will ravage you with a dreadful destruc]tion. If a man should run after the win[d and invent untruths: «I foretell strong drink and wine for you» he would be] a preacher for the people. This [is …] *11* […] as is written about them in the book of […] the experts […] *12* […] {…} *Blank* (Ps *12*) For the choirmaster. On the ei[ghth …] for he has no kn[owledge] *13* […] they are the eighth division […] compassion […] *14* [… and] there is [no] peace. For they are […] *15* [as is written in the book of Isaiah, the prophet:] *Is 22:13* Sacrifice of oxen and slaughter of flocks, e[ating meat and drinking wine…] *16* […] the Law, those who make up the Community […]

Col. II (*frags.* 11 + 10 + 26 + 9 + 20 + 7)   *1* [*Ps 12:7* The words of YHWH are pure words, silver purified in a clay crucible, re]fined seven times. As is written *2* [in the book of the prophet Zachariah: *Zac 3:9* Upon this single stone there are seven eyes; see,] its inscription is engraved, oracle of YHWH. What *3* […a]s is written about them: «I shall cure the […] *4* […a]ll the men of Belial and all the rabble *5* […] them, the Interpreter of the law, because there are no *6* […] each one upon his wall when they stand firm *7* […] those who make the sons of light stumble *8* [… *Ps 13:2-3* How long, YHWH?] Are you going to forget me [for ever? How long will you hi]de your face [from me?] How long am I to churn over *9* [worries in my soul, anxieties in my heart each day?] How long [is my enemy to lord it over me?] The interpretation of the word concerns the purification of the heart of the men of *10* [the Community…] in the last days […] to test them and refine them *11* […] them by the spirit, and the spotless and purified […What it] says: «The enemy is not to say *12* [I have proceeded against him» *Blank*] These are the congregation of Those Looking for Easy Interpretations, who […] who seek to destroy *13* [the members of the Community …] by their fervour and their animosity […] as is written in the book of Ezekiel, the prophet *14* [… *Ez 25:8* House of Israel] and of Judah, like all the peoples. [The interpretation of the word concerns the] last [days] when against them will rally *15* […] a just people, but the wicked, the demented and the simpleton […] the men who serve God *16* […who] circumcise the foreskin of their heart in the las[t] generation […] and all that belongs to them, he will pronounce unclean and not

Col. III (*frags.* 2 + 24 + 14 + 3 + 4 + 1 + 31)   *1* [… a]ll their words […] the praises of his glory, as […sa]ys *2* [… *Dt 7:15* YHWH will remove] all illnesses from you. *Ps 16:3* As for the ho[ly ones who are] in the land, they are all the powerful ones [in whom] I delight […] *3* […] will be like him […*Nah 2:11*] and shaking of knees and trembling in every lo[in…] *4* […] *Ps 17:1* Listen, [YHWH, the just,] take notice of my shout, give ear to [my plaint …] *5* […] in the last days, at the time when […] will seek the advice of the Community. He is […] *6* […] The interpretation of the word: A man of the ho[use of …] will arise … […] *7* […] and they will be like fire for the whole world. And these are ones about whom it is written for the last days […] … […] *8* […] rules over the lot of the light which is in mourning during the reign of Bel[ial, and the one who rules over the lot of darkness,] which is in mourning [...] *9* [...] of him [...] return to the chiefs of mourning [...] God of compassion and God of Israel [...] ... *10* [...] who have rebelled against the spirits of Belial and they will be forgiven for ever, and [...] will bless them again {by the hand of} for ever, and [...] will bless them [...] their periods *11* [...] of their fathers, according to the number of their names, according to the precise list of their names, man to man, [...] their years and the period of their service [...] their tongues *12* [...] the descendants of Judah [...] And now, see, everything has been written on the tablets which [...] and showed them the number of [all the genera]tions, and gave him in inheritance *13* [...] to him and to his seed forever. And he lifted him from there to walk from Aram [...] *Hos 5:8* Sound the horn in Gibeah. The horn is the book *14* [of the Law... the trum]pet of alarm is the book of the Second Law which all the men of his council have spurned and they have spoken revolt against him. And he sent *15* [...] great signs {...} over [...] And Jacob will be over the wine-press and will rejoice over the descent of *16* [...] by the sword [...] (to) the men of his council. They are the sword. And as for what he says:

Col. IV *(frags.* 19 + 12 + 13 I + 15)   *1* [...] ... [...] *2* [...] those who do disgusting things come to me [...] *3* [...] spend the night together and [...] *4* [...] wallow [...] *5* [...] I shall gather the anger [...] *6* [...] they shall be converted and [... *Jer 18:18* For] the Law [is not to disappear] from the pr[iest, nor advice from the sage, nor the word] from the prophet *7* [...] for the last days, as David said: *Ps 6:2-3* YHWH, do not scold me in anger. [Take pity on me YHWH,] for I am collapsing. *8* [...] *Ps 6:4-5* My soul is very troubled; but you, YHWH, how long? Take pity on me, save my li[fe...] over *9* [...] Belial, to destroy him in his anger, for there will no longer be [...he will not] give rest to Belial *10* [... Abra]ham, until there are ten just men in the city, for the spirit of truth [...fo]r there are no *11* [...] and his brothers through the scheming of Belial, and he will triumph over them [...] ... *12* [...] the angel of his truth will ransom all the sons of light from the power of Belial [...] *13* their hands [...] to scatter them in a dry and bleak land. This is the period of distress [...] *14* because [...] continually (?) the just man will flee and God's great hand will be with them to rescue them from all the spirits [of Belial...] *15* [...those who f]ear God, they will sanctify his name and enter Zion with joy, and Jerusalem [...] *16* [...] Belial and all the men of his lot will be finished for ever, and all the sons of light will be reunited [...]

Col. V *(frag.* 13 II)   *1-4* [...] *5* Belial [...] *6* for the la[st] days [...] *7* the horn [...] *8* I shall cover them [...] *9* God [...] *10* Belial [...] *11* the men of [...] *12-16* [...]

4QAges of Creation (4Q180 [4QAgesCreat])

Frag. 1   *1* Interpretation concerning the ages which God has made: An age to

achieve [all that there is] *2* and all that will be. Before creating them he determined their operations [according to the precise sequence of the ages,] *3* one
age after another age. And this is engraved on the [heavenly] tablets [for the
sons of men,] *4* [for] /all/ the ages of their dominion. This is the sequence of
the so[ns of Noah, from Shem to Abraham,] *5* [unt]il he sired Isaac; the ten
ge[nerations ...] *6 Blank 7* Interpretation concerning ᶜAzaz'el and the angels who
[penetrated the daughters of man] *8* [and] sired giants by them. And concerning
ᶜAzaz'el [who misled them into fallacy,] *9* [to love] sin and to make them inherit
evil for all the ag[es, for destruction] *10* [for the fervour] of the judgments and
the judgment of the council of [...]

Frags. 2–4 col. II   *1* [... Mount Zi]on on which God resides for e[ver ...] *2* which
[...] attractive for Lot (?), to inherit [...] *3* the earth [...] *Blank* The three men
[who] *4* appeared to [Abra]ham in the oak wood of Mambre are angels. [And
what it] *5* [says: *Gen 18:20-21* The sh]out of Sodom and Gomorrah is loud and
their sin is *6* very serious. I am going down to see: (if it corresponds to) their
shout which comes *7* [right to me, I will wre]ak destruction, and if not, I will
check [it. The interpretation] of the word [concerns all] *8* flesh which [...] and
to every [mouth] *9* which speaks [...] and I will check it, for everything [is inscribed in conformity with the ages of] *10* [their plans, since] before creating
them he knew their thou[ghts.]

Frags. 5–6   *1* [... for e]ver. *Blank* [...] *2* [... And what is wr]itten concerning the
earth [...] *3* [...] two days' journey [...] *4* [...] is Mount Zion, Jerusalem [...]
5 [... and wh]at is written concerning Pharaoh [...]

4QAges of Creation (4Q181 [4QAgesCreat])

Frag. 2   *1* [to Abraham until he sire]d Isaac; [the ten generations. ᶜAzaz'el and the
angels who penetrated] *2* [the daughters of] man and sired gian[ts by them [...]
3 to Israel in the seventieth week to [...] *4* to love sin and to make them inherit
evil [...] *5* in the eyes of all those knowing [...] *6* and his goodness is unfathomable [...] *7* these are the wonders of knowledge [...] *8* he measured them by his
truth and [...] *9* in all their ages [...] *10* their creatures [...]

Frag. 1   *1* for guilt in the Community with a counsel of sin, to wallow in the sin
of the sons of man, and for great judgments and vile maladies *2* in the flesh.
According to the powerful deeds of God and in line with their evil, according
to the foundation of their impurity, he delivered the sons of the heavens and
the earth to a wicked community until *3* the end. In accordance with God's
compassion and in accordance with his goodness and the wonder of his glory
he approaches some from among the sons of the world [...] so that they can be

considered with him in [the community of] *4* the gods like a holy congregation
in the position of eternal life and in the lot of his holy ones [...] *5* [the mysteries
of] his wonder, each man according to the lot assigned to him [...] *6* [...] for
eternal life [...]

4QCatena*ᵇ* (4Q182 [4QCatena*ᵇ*])

Frag. 1   *1* [Its interpretation for] the last days concerns [...] *2* [...] who stiffened
their necks [...] *3* [...] and remove restraint with arrogant hand to defile [...]
4 [as is wr]itten about them in the book of Jere[miah: *Jer 5:7* Why should I have
to forgive you?] *5* [Your so]ns have deserted me and have sw[orn by what is not
a god...]

Frag. 2   *1* [...] ... for the last days [...] *2* [...] to destroy them[...]

4QHistorical Work (4Q183)

1 their enemies. And they defiled their temple [...] *2* of them, and they arose
for wars, one man [against his brother. But those who remained loyal] *3* to his
covenant, God saved and set free [...And he selected the chosen of] *4* his be-
nevolence, and gave them the heart to walk [on the path of his heart and so that
they would detest] *5* any wicked wealth. And they went away from the path [of
the people and taught all] *6* those with misguided spirit, and with the language
of truth [they spoke to ...] *7* and atoned for their sins through their sufferings
[...] *8* their sins. *Blank* [...] *9* As for what he says: [...]

4QGenesis Pesher*ᵃ* (4Q252 [4QpGen*ᵃ*])

Col. I   *1* [In the y]ear four hundred and eighty of Noah's life, Noah reached the
end of them. And God *2* [sa]id: 'My spirit will not reside in man for ever'.
Their days shall be fixed at one hundred and twenty *3* [y]ears until the end of
the waters of the flood. And the waters of the flood burst over the *Blank* earth
in the year six hundred *4* of Noah's life, in the second month, on the first (day)
of the week, on its seventeenth (day). On that day *5* all the springs of the great
abyss were split and the sluices of the sky opened and rain fell upon *6* the earth
forty days and forty nights, until the twenty-sixth day of the third *7* month, the
fifth day of the week. One hundred and fifty days did the wate[rs] hold sway
over the [ea]rth, *8* until the fourteenth day in the seventh month, the third (day)
of the week. At the end of *9* one hundred and fifty days, the waters came down
(during) two days, the fourth day and the fifth day, and the sixth *10* day, the ark
rested in the mountains of Hurarat, the seventeenth of the seventh month.
11 And the waters continued [di]minishing until the [ten]th month, on its first

(day), the fourth day *12* of the week. And the peaks of the mountains began to be visible at the [e]nd of forty days. *13* And Noah [op]ened the window of the ark the first day of the week, which is the tenth *14* of the el[eventh] month. And he sent out the dove to see whether the waters had diminished, but it did not *15* find a place of rest and returned to him, [to the] ark. And he waited yet a[nother] seven days *16* and again sent it out, and it returned to him, and in its beak there was a cut olive branch. [It was day twenty-] *17* four of the eleventh month, the first (day) of the wee[k. And Noah knew that the waters had diminished] *18* over the earth. And at the end of another seven days, [Noah sent the dove out, but it did not] *19* come back. It was the [fir]st day [of the twelfth] month, [the first day] *20* of the week. And at the end of the th[irty-one days from Noah having sent out the do]ve which did not re[turn to him] *21* again, the wat[ers] dried up [from upon the earth and] Noah removed the cover of the ark *22* and looked, and behold [they had dried up on the fourth day,] on the first (day) of the first month.

Col. II   *1* in the year six-hundred and one of Noah's life. On the seventeenth day of the second month *3* the land dried up, on the first (day) of the week. On that day, Noah went out of the ark, at the end of a complete *3* year of three-hundred and sixty-four days, on the first (day) of the week. On the seventh *4 Blank* one and six *Blank* Noah (went out?) from the ark, at the appointed time of a complete *5* year. *Blank* And Noah awoke from his wine and knew what *6* his youngest son had done. And he said: 'Cursed be Canaan; he will be, for his br[others], the last of the slaves!' [But he did not] *7* curse Ham, but only his son, for God had blessed the sons of Noah. And they dwelt in the tents of Shem. *8* He gave the land to Abraham, his beloved. *Blank* Terah was one hundred and [for]ty years old when he left Ur of the Chaldees and came to Haran, and Ab[ram was se]venty years old. Abram lived five years *10* in Haran, and afterwards [Abram] went [to] the land of Canaan. Six[ty five years (?).] *11* The heifer, the ram and the he-g[oat ...] Abram to God [...] *12* the fire when he crossed [...] *13* for Ab[ram] to go [to the land of] Canaan [...]

Col. III   *1* As it is written: [...] twe-*2*lve me[n ...] and also *3* this city. [...The] just *4* [I will] not [destroy them...] only those will I exterminate. *5* If there are not found there [...] that is found in it and its booty *6* and its children. And the remnant [...] forever. And Abraham *7* stretched out his hand [...] *8* And he told him: [...] *9* your only [...] *10–11* [...] *12* El-Shaddai will [bless] you [...] *13* the blessing of your father [...] *14* [...] ... [...]

Col. IV   *1* Timnah was the concubine of Eliphaz, Esau's son, and she bore him Amaleq. It was he whom Saul sl[ew], *2 Blank* as he said *Blank* through Moses in respect of the last days: *Dt 25:19* «I will erase the memory of Amaleq *3* from under the heavens». *Blank* Blessings of Jacob: *Gen 49:3-4* «Reuben, you are my first-born *4* and the first-fruits of my manhood, pre-eminent in stature and pre-eminent in strength; you seethe like water; you shall not enjoy supremacy. You mounted *5* your father's bed; then you defiled it, for he had lain in it». *Blank* Its interpretation: That he reproved him, because *6* he lay with Bilhah, his concubine. And as for what he said: «You are my first-born» [...] Reuben *7* was the first of his order [...]

Col. V   *1 Gen 49:10* A sovereign shall [not] be removed from the tribe of Judah. While Israel has the dominion, *2* there will [not] lack someone who sits on the throne of David. For «the staff» is the covenant of royalty, *3* [the thou]sands of Israel are «the feet». Until the messiah of justice comes, the branch *4* of David. For to him and to his descendants has been given the covenant of royalty over his people for all everlasting generations, which *5* he has observed [...] the Law with the men of the Community, for *6* [...] it is the assembly of the men of [...] *7* [...] He gives

4QGenesis Pesher*ᵇ* (4Q253 [4QpGen*ᵇ*])

Frag. 1   *1* [...] Israel [...] *2* [...] of the ark [...] *3* [...] to show to all [...]

Frag. 2   *1* the impurity [...] *2* ... [...] *3* the clean (animals) of creation [...] *4* his holocaust according to his will, for we shall take [...] *5* for him the highest gates, since [...]

Frag. 3 *col.* I   *1* [...] and he will pay attention *2* [... *Mal 3:16-18*] And they shall be for me *3* [my possession on the day that I prepare. I will have pity o]n them, as *4* [a man has pity on the son who serves him. You shall return, then, to differentiate] between the just and the wicked, *5* [between who serves him and who does not serve him ...] justice and upon

Frag. 3 *col.* II   *1* and {he who} /a man of/ Israel who ea[ts ...] *2* and approaches its blood, who does not [...]

Frag. 4   *1* [...] ... [...] *2* [...] Belial, and as [...] *3* [...] and he will abandon [...]

4QGenesis Pesher*ᶜ* (4Q254)

Frag. 1   *1* And what he says: [...] *2* upon the openings, and [... And Noah awoke from his wine] *3* and knew what [his youngest son had] done. And he said: 'Cursed be Canaan;] *4* the last of the slaves [will he be for his brothers!' ...]

Frag. 2   *1* and for his bread and for [...] *2* your countenance does not [...] *3 Blank*
[...] *4* what he gathers [...] *5* [and] to separate from [...]

Frag. 4   *1* [...] to them, and to the people [...] *2* [...] the two sons of the oil of
anointing which [...] *3* [...] those who observe God's precepts [...] *5* [...] for the
men of [...]

Frag. 5   *1 Gen 49:15* And he bent [his shoulder to the burden and was reduced to
(the) tribute] of a slave. *Blank* [...] *2* which [...] the great ones [...] *3* servant ...
[... *Gen 49:17* Dan will judge] his people like one of the ju[dges of Israel ...
4 Dan will be a ser[pent on the path, an asp on the w[ay...] *5* the horse's heels
[...]

Frag. 6   *1* [... *Gen 49:24-26* And] his bow [remain]ed steady [and his arms and his
hands stayed agile, by virtue of the hands of the Strong One of Jacob,] *2* [by the
name (?) of the Shep]herd, the Stone of Israel. [...] *3* [...blessings of the
heaven] above, [...] *4* [...] ... [...]

Frag. 15   *1* [...] the sevente[enth] of the [second] *2* month [...] Noah went out of
the ark at the appointed time of the complete (?) days *3* [...] *Blank* *4* [...And he
sent out the ra]ven and it went out, going to and fro and returned, to show to
the la[st] generations *5* [...] before him, for the raven went out, going to and fro
and ret[urned] *6* [...] the dove [...] *7* And this is the plan of the construction of
the ar[k: three hundred cubits will be the len]gth of the ark, and fift[y cubits]
8 the width, and thirty [the height...] *9* And the measurement of the ark [...]
10 [...] ... [...]

Para-biblical Literature

This chapter also gathers together material differing greatly in literary form and in origin: reports, apocalypses, testaments, etc. Even so, all the compositions from which this material comes could be classed as 'para-biblical literature', literature that begins with the Bible, which retells the biblical text in its own way, intermingling it and expanding it with other, quite different traditions. Every one of these compositions has its starting point in specific texts of the Torah or of the Prophets but, unlike the exegetical literature, rather than interpreting the biblical text, they elaborate on it, augmenting it with other material.

Fidelity to the original biblical text varies greatly from composition to composition. While the *Paraphrases of the Pentateuch* do not seem to be much more than a collection of literal quotations of various passages from the Pentateuch, interwoven with other traditions previously undocumented (to the extent that it would be reasonable to wonder whether, in fact, we have found atypical variants of biblical manuscripts) the connection with the original text of other compositions included here is weaker or more remote. In some compositions, such as the *Genesis Apocryphon* or the *Book of Jubilees*, the biblical plot is still distinguishable with ease. In many others, such as the pseudepigrapha, the modifications effected are such that the biblical origin is only visible as a fine thread running throughout the work. Other compositions seem, rather, to be self-contained developments around certain biblical characters. The starting point continues to be the biblical text, but the development results in independent compositions. In the last texts to be included, such as those with the title 'proto-Esther', the connection is even more tenuous and remote. It is really literature which is parallel to, earlier than, or simultaneous with, the biblical text, but with no direct connection to it.

Some of these texts, such as the *Books of Enoch* or the *Book of Jubilees*, have reached us at the periphery of the official Bible. Of other compositions, such as *Pseudo-Ezekiel*, it appears possible to trace some echoes in the literature of primitive Christianity. Others, such as the *Aramaic Testament of Levi*, seem to have served as the model for later compositions. Most of them, though, have been lost for ever. Their retrieval, even in this fragmented condition, allows us to envisage the breadth of para-biblical literature in circulation.

It is hard to determine exactly the origin of each particular work. Some compositions preserve clear evidence of a Qumranic origin. Of others it can be stated without a doubt that they were produced outside the Qumran community. For most of the works represented, it is impossible, even so, to specify the milieu in which they arose, or the kind of reader for which they were intended.

1 Paraphrase of the Pentateuch

A 4QReworked Pentateuch*ᵃ* (4Q158 [4QRP*ᵃ*])

Frags. 1–2   *1* [...] because of this [...] *2* [...] you shall fight and [...] *3* [...] *Gn 32:25-30* And [Jac]ob remain[ed] alone there, and [a man] was fi[ghting] with him until first light. Since he saw that he could not prevail against him, he seized him in the thigh joint] *4* [and Jacob's thigh joint was dislocated] while he struggled with him and he caught hold of him. And said to him: [Let me walk, for dawn is breaking. But Jacob replied: I shall not let you walk] *5* [unless you have blessed] me. He asked him: What is your name? And [he told him: Jacob. He said to him: Now you will no longer be called Jacob, but Israel, for you have fought] *6* [with God and with] men and you have won. And Ja[cob] asked him and said: Tell me your na[me] /please/! *7* [And he said to him: Why do you ask me [my name?] And he blessed him right there. And he said to him: May YHWH make you fertile and bl[ess] you [... May he fill you with] *8* [knowle]dge and intelligence; may he free you from all violence [...] *9* until this day and for everlasting generations [...] *10* And he walked on his way after having blessed him there. [*Gn 32:31-33* Jacob named the place Penu'el: Because I saw God face to face and in spite of that my life has remained safe. And there rose] *11* the sun as he passed Penu'el [and he went on with a game thigh...] *12* on that day. And he said to him: You shall not ea[t...] *13* above the two joints of the thigh until the present [day...] *14 Ex 4:27-28* to Aaron saying: Go and find [Moses in the desert! He went, then, and coming across him on God's mountain he kissed him. Moses repeated to Aaron all] *15* the words of YHWH which he had transmitted to him, and all [the signs which he had commanded...] *16* YHWH to me, saying: When you make leave [...] *17* in order to go like slaves. And see, these are the thi[rty...] *18* YHWH God [...] *19* ... [...]

Frag. 3   *1* And Jacob called [...] *2* in this earth [...] *3* my fathers in order to enter [...]

Frag. 4   *1* [...] he commands you [...] *2* the people of Egypt: you shall s[erve...] *3* according to the number of the twelve tribes of [Israel...] *4* and he offered the holocaust on the altar [...*Ex 24:6* And Moses took half the blood and put it] *5* in earthenware bowls and the (other) half of the blood he poured over the al[tar...] *6* as I showed Abraham and [Jacob] [...] *7* to them, so that God would be for them and for their descendants [...] *8* for ever [...]

Frag. 6   *1* [*Ex 20:19-21 Samaritan* in the midst of one like us.] You, [approach and listen to all that YHWH our God tells you and you shall transmit to us all that YHWH our God tells you] *2* [and we will hear it and carry it out. But God] is not to talk to u[s, in case we die. Moses answered the people: Do not fear, for in order to test you] *3* Go[d] has come [and] so that fear of him [be with you and you shall not sin. And the people kept their distance, while Moses approached the thick fog in which] *4* God [was]. And YHWH [spoke] to Moses sa[ying: I have heard the noise of the words of this people, what they have said to you: all they have said to you is good. Who gave them] *5* and placed in them this heart, to fear me [and keep my statutes all their days, so that it will go well with them and their children for ever! And you, hear] *6* the sound of the words which I tell them: [I will raise up] a prophet [like you for them from amongst their brothers, and I will place my words in his mouth and I will tell them everything I command him. And it will happen that the man] *7* who does not listen to the words [which he will utter in my name, I will call him to account. But the prophet who dares to speak in my name what I have not commanded him] *8* to say, or who sp[eaks in the name of other gods, that prophet shall die. And if you say in your heart: How will I know the word which YHWH has not spoken?] *9* If what [the prophet] says [in the name of YHWH does not occur, or does not happen, it is a word which YHWH has not pronounced; the prophet has pronounced it daringly; have no fear of him.]

Frags. 7–8   *1* [*Ex 20:12-17* your fat]her and your mother [so that your days on the soil which YHWH your God gives you are lengthened. You shall not kill. You shall not commit adultery. You shall not rob. You shall not give] *2* false evidence against your fellow man. You shall not covet the wife of [your neighbour, or his house, or his servant, or his maid, or his ass, or anything of what belongs to your neighbour.] *3* And YHWH said to Moses: *Dt 5:30-31* Go and tell them: Go back to [your tents! You, however, stay here with me, for I am going to explain to you all the commandments, the laws] *4* and the statutes, so that they can be taught and put into practice in the land [which I give them so that they can possess it...] *5* And the people did return, each man to his tent. But Moses remained in the presence [of YHWH...] *6 Ex 20:22-26* You have seen that from the heavens have I spoken. You shall not make [alongside me gods of silver or gods of gold, do not make them! You shall construct for me an earthen altar, and sacrifice] *7* on it their holocausts and their peace-offerings, their flocks [and their cattle. In any place where I make you commemorate my name, I shall come to you and bless you. If] *8* you construct [an altar of stone] for me, you are not to chisel it in the manner of blocks of stone, for by passing [your chisel over each one of them you will desecrate it. Nor are you to climb to my altar by steps, in case you reveal your nakedness] *9* on it. *Blank Ex 21:1-10* These are the statutes which you are to propound to them. [When you purchase a Hebrew slave he will serve for six years, but on the seventh he shall go away free] *10* [for nothing.] If he came in alone he will go away alone; if [he was married, his wife will go with him. If his master gave him a wife and she bore him sons or daughters] *11* [the wife and her children will be] for the master and he [will go away alone. But if the slave should say clearly: I love my master, my wife and my children; I do not wish to go away free,] *12* [his master] will lead [him before God, place him near the door or the jambs…His master will pierce] *13* his ear with an awl, [and he will serve him for ever. When a man sells his daughter as a slave-girl, she is not to leave as the slaves leave. If she turns out to be unpleasant in the eyes of her master, who had intended her for himself, he shall allow her to be] *14* redeemed; [he cannot sell her to] a foreign peo[ple, having been disloyal to her. If he intends her for his son, he shall treat her according to the norm for daughters. If he takes another (girl) for himself,] *15* he is not [to take from (the first) her food, her clothing] [and her conjugal rights…]

Frags. 10–12   *1* […*Ex 21:32-37* If the bull gores a slave or a slave-girl, their owner is to be paid] thirty sil[ver] shekels [and the bull shall be stoned.] *2* [When a man opens a well or digs a well and not having covered it, a bull or an ass falls into it, the owner] of the well will pay [him; he will compensate] *3* [their owner with money, and the dead animal will be for him. When someone's bull wounds his neighbour's bull, so that it dies, the live bull will be sold and] its price [shared out,] and [the dead animal will] also [be shared out.] *4* However, if it was kno[wn, that [in the past] that bull used to] gore, [and its owner did not keep it in, the latter must repay, bull for bull, and the carcass will be for him.] *3* If anyone steals a bull or a ewe, and slaughters it or se[lls] it, [he is to pay five beasts for the bull and four sheep for the ewe. *Ex 22:1-13* If] *6* [the thief was surprised during the break-in,] and was wounded and died, he will not be the subject of blood vengeance. If the sun was shining, he will be the subject of blood vengeance. [He is to repay, of course; if he owns nothing, he will be sold for what he stole. If] *7* [the stolen property is found in his possession, should it be a] live [bull,] ass or ewe, he will pay double. When a man uses [a field or vineyard for pasture, and leaves his flock loose to graze in the field of someone else] *8* [he is to make repayment from his own field, depending] on its produce; if he used the whole field, [he is to repay] with the best of his (own) field or the best of his vineyard. [When a fire breaks out and, encountering thorns,] *9* [a hayrick or the cornfields or the field are consumed,] whoever lit the fire has to pay damages. When a man entrusted [his neighbour] with [money, or objects for safekeeping, and they were stolen from that person's house, if the thief is found he is to pay double.] *10* [If the thief is not found,] the owner of the house [shall approach] the house of God (to swear) that he did not put his hand on the property [of his neighbour. Whatever the object of the felony might be, whether a bull, an ass, a sheep,] *11* [clothing or anything else lost,] about which one could say: /This is it,/ the affair of both parties shall come to YHWH: [the one which God convicts is to pay his neighbour double.] *12* [When someone has given his neighbour an ass,] or bull or ram, or any animal for safekeeping, [and it should die or suffer injury or be stolen without an eyewitness, the oath of YHWH shall intervene] *13* [between both parties: if he did not reach out his hand] to his neighbour's property, the owner of the beast must concede and he shall not [pay. However, if] it was stolen from beside him, [he shall pay damages to its owner. If it was torn to pieces] *14* [he is to show the torn animal as evidence, and shall not pay.] When someone takes a loan of an animal from a friend [and it is torn to pieces or dies] its owner not being with it [he has to repay.]

Frag. 14   *1* [...] ... *2* [...al fle]sh and all the spirits *3* [...] for blessing for the land *4* [...] the peoples [...] and the land of Egypt *5* shall have desolation [...] the yoke of /the hand/ of Egypt, and I shall free them *6* from their hands and I shall make them a people for myself for [eternal gener]ations [...] of Egypt. And the seed *7* of your sons shall [possess the la]nd in security [...And Egypt I shall hurl into] the middle of the sea, into the depths *8* of the abyss [...] who dwell *9* in it [...] the frontiers (?)

B 4QReworked Pentateuch*b,c* (4Q364–365 [4QRP*b,c*])

Frag. 3   *1* you (Rebecca) shall see him [...] *2* you shall see in peace [...] *3* your death, and your eyes [...Why should I have to remain deprived of] *4* you two? And [Isaac] called [Rebecca, his wife,... and showed] *5* her all the wo[rds...] *6* after Jacob, his son [...] *7* *Gn 28:6* And Esau saw that [Isaac had blessed Jacob, and had sent him to *8* Pa[dan-]Aram in order to acquire [a wife] there [...]

Frag. 6 *col.* II   *1* you despise (?) [...] *2* for the majesty of [...] *3* you are great, the saviour [...] *4* the enemy's hope has died and he is for[gotten...] *5* they have died in the copious waters, the enemy [...] *6* and he raised her to the heights [...] and gave [...] *7* [...] majesty. *Blank* [...] *8* *Ex 15:22-26* And he made Moses leave for Is[rael] from the sea, and they walked through the desert for three [days and did not find water.] *9* And they reached Marah, [but] they were [un]able to drink the waters of Marah because they were bitt[er. This is why that place is called Marah (bitterness)] *10* And the people complained aga[inst Moses] saying: What will we drink? And Moses called to [YHWH and YHWH showed him] *11* a log. He threw it in the [water] and the waters became sweet. There he imposed on him the law and [the statute, and there he put him to the test. And he said:] *12* If you lis[ten care]fully to the voice of YHWH your God, and do what is right in his eyes, and [lend an ear] *13* [to his commandments and keep] all his laws, all the plagues which he imposed on Egyp[t] *14* he will not impose on you, for I am YHWH, the one who] heals [you]. *Blank*

Frag. 7   *1* *Ex 15:16-20* until [your people] pa[sses *Blank* YHWH, *Blank* until *Blank* the people you gained passes. *Blank* You will bring them in and plant them] *2* in the mountain of your inheritance, *Blank* in the place [you prepared] for your resi[dence *Blank* YHWH, *Blank* the temple, Lord, *Blank* which your hands founded.] *3* YHWH will rule for ever and ever. *Blank* When [the Pharaoh's cavalry *Blank*, with its chariots and horses] went into the sea, *Blank* *4* YHWH [overturned] *Blank* the waters of the sea upon them. *Blank* And the so[ns of Israel *Blank* walked with dry feet *Blank* in the middle of the sea,] *5* [and the wa]ters form[ed a wall] on their left and on their right. *Blank* And [Miriam, the prophetess, Aaron's sister,] took [the timbrel in her hand] and all the women came out behind her with [timbrels and in choirs.]

Frag. 25   *1* Lv 23:42-24:2 you shall live [in hu]ts for seven days; all those natives of Israel shall stay in huts, so that your gen[erations may] know *2* that your fathers lived [in hu]ts when I took them out of the land of Egypt. I am YHWH, your God! *3* *Blank* And Moses promulgated the feasts of YHWH to the children of Israel. *Blank* *4* And YHWH spoke to Moses saying: Command the children of Israel, saying: When you enter the land which *5* I will give you as inheritance, and you live safely in it, you will offer wood for the holocaust and for all the work of *6* [the ho]use you are to build in the land, in order to arrange it upon the altar of sacrifice. And the holocausts *7* [...] for the passover sacrifices and for the peace offerings, for the sacrifices for sins and for the freewill offerings and for the holocausts, each thing according to [its order] *8* [...] and for the gates and for all the work of the house they shall off[er...] *9* [...] and for the feast of oil, the twelve [...] shall offer the wood the twe[lve...] *10* [...] ... those who offer on the first day, Levi [...] *11* [...Reu]ben and Simeon [and on the four]th [day...]

Frag. 28 *col.* I   *2* [...] for the wheat and for the oil *3* [...] the children of Israel and on the day of first produce *4* [...] the grapes and the pomegranates *5* [...] the offering of the sacrifices upon which one places *6* [...offering] for jealousy, and to the right of this gate *7* [...] ... they will eat the offerings for sins *8* [...] *Blank* *9* [...] and the distance up to the side *10* [...] and the distance in every direction *11* [...] between recess and recess, three and a half cubits

Frag. 28 *col.* II   *1* one hundred cubits; from the gate of Zabulon up to the gate of Gad, three [hundred and sixty cubits]; from the gat[e of G]ad up [to the North corner, three hundred] *2* and sixty cubits. From this corner up to the gate of Dan, three [hundred] and sixty cubits; and the same [from the gate of Dan up to] *3* the gate of Nephtali, three hundred and sixty cubits; and from the gate of Nephtali up to the gate of Asher, three hundred and [sixty cubits...] *4* and from the gate of Asher up to the Eastern corner [...] three hundred and sixty cubits. And [the gates of the courtyard wall] will project [outwards] *5* seven cubits [and] in the inside /it will penetrate/ from the courtyard wall thirty-six cubits. The width of the gatew[ays will be fourteen] 6 cubits and their height twenty-five cubits up to [the crossbeams] and likewise the lintel. And [the beams] will be encased [with cedarwood] 7 and encased in gold. Their doors will be encased in pure gold. Between one door and another you sh[all make storage places and rooms and porches on the inside.] 8 The width of a storage place will be ten cubits; its length twenty cubits and its height four[teen cubits. They will be encased with timber from] 9 cedarwood. The width of the wall will be two cubits and on the outside, the rooms. The width of a room will be ten cubits; its length] 10 twenty cubits. The width of the wall will be two cubits [...] 11 of cedarwood and its entrance three cubits wide [...]

c Other texts

2QApocryphon of David(?) (2Q22 [2QapDavid?])

Col. I   1 [... and I did not need to begin anew because] YHWH our God [had destroyed him] with the edge of the [sword.] 2 [...and I made] deadly catapults with bows and (did) not 3 [... the ba]ttle to seize fortified cities and to terrify 4 [...] ...

Col. II   1 [...] ... because I knew [...] 2 for his kindness towards Israel [...] 3 he in all his paths /words/ and not [...] 4 he will deliver them to judgment. And al[l...]

4QExhortation based on the Flood (4Q370)

Col. I   1 And he crowned the mountains with produce and rained food upon them and satisfied every living thing with good fruit. « May all those who do what I want, /eat and be satisfied»/ says YHWH 2 «and bless my [holy] name». «But now they have done what is evil in my eyes», says YHWH. And they rebelled against God with their deeds. 3 And YHWH judged them according to all their ways and according to the thoughts of the [evil] inclination of their heart and thundered against them with his might. And all 4 the foundations of the earth shook, and the waters overflowed from the abysses; all the sluice-gates of the heavens were opened and the abysses overflowed with mighty waters; 5 and the sluice-gates of the heavens poured out rain. And he destroyed them with the flood. [...] all of them...[...] 6 This is why everything there was on dry land [vanished,] and men, the [animals and all the] birds, all winged things [died.] And the gi[a]nts did not escape. 7 [...] ... And God made [a sign of (the) covenant and] placed the rainbow [in the clouds] to remember the covenant 8 [...and never again will] the water of the flood [come] for [destruction, or] will the turmoil of the waters be opened. *9* [...] they made, and clouds [...] for (the) waters [...] *10* [...] ... [...]

Col. II   *1* of sin, they will seek [...] *2* YHWH will justify [...] *3* and he will cleanse them from their sins [...] *4* their evil and their knowledge [...] *5* They jump, but their days are like a shadow [...] *6* and he is compasionate for ever [...] *7* YHWH's marvels; remember the won[ders...] *8* due to his fear and [your] soul will rejoice [...] *9* those who support you. Do not disobey [YHWH's] words...

4QApocryphon of Joseph (4Q372 [4QapocrJoseph*ᵃ*])

Frag 1.   *1* [...]...[...] *2* he who does [...]...; foreigners [...] *3* and the priests of foreign gods and they honour those who serve [idols...] *4* the Most High, and he delivered them into the hands of the nations in order to [... and he dispersed them] *5* in all the countries and among all [the peoples he scattered them... They did not enter...] *6* Israel. And he uprooted them from the land [...] ... [from the place ... to him; they did not allow them to rest...] *7* The nations were given a place in the valley of the vision and ... [... Zion, and they made... and turned] *8* Jerusalem into ruins and the mountain of my God into a wooded height [...] ... [... the laws...] *9* God and Judah as well, together with him, and he stood at a crossroads, to d[o...] *10* to be together with his two brothers. And in all this, Joseph was thrown into lands which he did not kn[ow...] *11* among a foreign people, and they were scattered in the whole world. All the mountains were appalled at them [...fools...] *12* building a high place for themselves on a very high mountain to arouse the jealousy of Israel. And they spoke words [...] *13* the sons of Jacob, and they terrified them with the words from their mouths, blaspheming against the tent of Zion; they spoke [false] wor[ds and all] *14* the deceitful words, they spoke them to anger Levi, Judah and Benjamin with their words. And in all this, Joseph [was delivered] *15* into the hand of foreigners, consuming his strength and breaking all his bones up the time of his end. And he shouted [and his call] *16* summoned the powerful God to save him from their hands. And he said: «My father and my God, do not abandon me in the hands of gentiles, *17* do me justice, so that the poor and afflicted do not die. You have no need of any people or of *18* any help. Your finger is bigger and stronger than any there are in the world. For you choose truth and in your hand there is no *19* violence at all. And your tenderness is great and great is your compassion for all who seek you; they are stronger than me and all my brothers who *20* are associated with me. An enemy people lives in it and [...] and they open their mouth against *21* all the sons of your beloved Jacob with insults for [...] *22* the moment of their destruction of the whole world and they shall be delivered [...] *23* I will arise to do right and just[ice... to do] *24* the will of my creator, to offer sacrifices [of thanksgiving...]

25 to my God. And I will declare his compassion [...] *26* I shall praise you, YHWH, my God and I shall bless all [...] *27* the first things, and in order to teach sinners your statutes and your law to those who forsake you [...] *28* and the evil, so that your witnesses do not reproach me and to declare your ju[st] words [...] *29* For God is great, holy, powerful, glorious, terrifying and wond[erful] are [his... the heavens] *30* and the earth and even in the depths of the abyss. Splendour and [majesty...] *31* I know and understand and ... [...] *32* ... [...]

Frag. 2   *1* [...] ... [...] *2* [...] YHWH in the heavens [...] *3* [...]in the depths and in all the abyss [...] *4* [...who may tr]ain his hand for war, who may come [...] *5* [... who] gives him intelligence to understand knowledge [...] *6* [... to d]o his delights for ever, according to the greatness of [...] *7* [...] time. For he gave you strength to over[come...] *8* [...] and he placed them in the hand of his people in the judgment [...] *9* [...mou]ntain of Bashan...[...] and all their cities [...] *10* ... you shall be placed in [...] *11* [...] whoever does to his people trust in [...] ... [...] *12* [...Is]rael, for it has been scattered in his presence [...] *13* [...] his head with a dead[ly] stone [...] *14* [...] not [...]

4QApocryphon of Joseph (4Q373 [4QapocrJoseph*ᵇ*])

1 [...] his... and he [...] *2* all his servants with Og [...XXX] *3* and a half cubits was his height and two [cubits his girth ..., a sword like a cedar...] *4* and a shield like a tower. The light-footed [...] *5* whoever moves seven stadia away. I did not stand [...] *6* and I did not do it a second time, but YHWH, our God, crushed him; with the edge of the sword [...] *7* I made deadly catapults wi[th bows and not ...] *8* for [...war to take fortified cities and to terrify...] *9* [... and now...]

4QNarrative (4Q462)

1 [...] *2* [...Shem,] Ham and Japhet [...] *3* [...] for Jacob, and he [...] and re-membered [...] *4* [...] ... for Israel [...] *Blank* Then it will be said: [...] *5* [...] ... we were empty-handed; for, to seize [...] *6* [...] like slaves for Jacob. With love [...] *7* [... he] will give to many in inheritance. ****, who governs ... [...] *8* [...] his glory which from one will fill the waters and the earth [...] *9* [...] ... [...] the control; they captured his people; the light was with them and over us there was [...] *10* [...the peri]od of darkness [has gone] and the period of light has arrived. And they will rule for ever. That is why it will be said: [...] *11* [...] to Israel, for in the midst of us was the people of the beloved Jacob [...] *12* [...] ... and they served and gave support and shouted to **** [...] *13* [...] and behold, they were delivered up to Egypt a second time in the period of the kingdom

and sup[ported...] *14* [... the inhab]itants of Philistia and of Egypt for spoil and
devastation and they shall raise her [...] *15* [...] ... to set wickedness on high so
that it contracts uncl[eanness...] *16* [...] and the hardness of her face will
change into brilliance and her «uncleanness» and her clothes [...] *17* [...] and
what he did to her, so will be the uncleanness of [...] *18* [...] she was loathed as
she was prior to her construction [...] *19 Blank* And he will remember /Israel/
Jerusalem [...]

6QGenesis (?) (6Q19)

1 of the sons of Ham [...] *2* [...] the peoples [...] *3* [...] ... [...]

4QWork with Place Names (4Q522)

Frag. 6   *1* [...] And Sime[on ...] ... [...] *2* [...] to them. And Dan, neither was he
destroyed [...] *3* [...] And Issachar to ... And Asher [...] *4* [... to] Dazan (?) ...
[...]

Frag. 7   *1* [...] ... [...] *2* [...] and the Canaanites who [...] *3* [...] from the Vale of
Achor [...]

Frag. 8 col. I   *2* [...] and to Ain Qeber, Bet ... *3* [...] Beqaᶜa and to Bet Zippor,
to *4* [...] ... and to all the valley of Mizvah, to *5* [...] to Heikal Yzad, to Yaᶜapor
and to *6* [...] ... and to Mani, to En Kober *7* [...Moun]t Garizim, to Chadita
and to ᶜOshel *8* [...] ... [... to Ma]don, which *9* [...] ... and to [...to] Ashkelon
10 [... to] Galilee and the two S[... and] to the Sharon *11* [... to Ju]dah, to Beer-
Shebaᶜ and [to] Beᶜalot *12* [...] to Qeᶜilah, to Adullam and to *13* [...] Gezer, to
Temni and to Gimzon and to *14* [...] Chiqqar and Qitron and Ephronim and
to Soccoth *15* [...] Bechoron, Lower and Upper, and to *16* [...] to Gilat, Upper
and Lower

Frag. 8 col. II   *1* [...] ... [...] *2* ... [...] to establish there the tent of me[eting ...]
3 of the times. For, behold, a son is born to Jesse, son of Perez, son of Ju[dah
...] *4* the Rock of Zion, and he will drive out from there /all/ the Amorites,
from [...] *5* to build the house for YHWH, God of Israel. Gold and silver [...]
6 he will bring cedar and cypress [from] Lebanon for its construction; but his
son, the younger, [...] *7* the first will officiate there [...] and to him [...] *8* [...]
of watc[hers ...] The beloved of YHW[H will] dwell in safety [...] *9* [the] days,
[and] his people will dwell forever. But now, the Amorites (are) there, and the
Canaan[ites ...] *10* dwellers who have made them sin, because I have not explained [the pre]cept [...] *11* of you. And the Shilonite and the [...] I have made
the servant of [my pe]ople [...] *12* And now, let us establish the t[ent of

mee]ting far from [...] *13* Eleazar [to transpor]t the [tent of me]eting from the house of [...] *14* salvati[on ... to the ch]ief of the army [...]

6QDeuteronomy (?) (6Q20)

1 Blank [...] *2* For the ea[rth ...] *3* a land of to[rrents ...] *4* the house of [...] *5* the abysses [...] *6* new and [...] *7* and you shall inherit [...]

4QNarrative (4Q458)

Frag. 1   *1* [...] to the beloved [...] *2* [...] the beloved [...] *3* [...] in the tent [...] *4* [...] they did not know [...] *5* [...] burns of fire [...] *6* [...] and they arose with him from [...] *7* [...] he spoke to the first, saying: [...] *8* [...] the first angel will send to those living [...] *9* [...] burnt, and he will destroy the tree of wickedness [...] *10* [... from] Egypt to the house of [...]

Frag. 2. col. I   *2* [... the mo]on and the stars *3* [...] the years *4* [...] the flight ... *5* [...] impurity *6* [...] fornication.

Frag. 2 col. II   *3* and he destroyed him, and his strength [...] *4* and she devoured all the uncircumcised ones and ... [...] *5* and he justified him and went on high [...] *6* anointed with the oil of kingship [...]

4QBiblical Chronology (4Q559)

Frag. 1   *1* [...I]saac, Ja[cob ...] *2* [... XXX] 5 in the la[nd of ...] *3* [...] ... years [...]

Frag. 2   *1* [Abraham was 99] years old [when he begot Isaac.] *2* [And I]saac was [60 years old when he begot Jacob. And Jacob] *3* [was] 65 ye[ars old when he begot Levi ...] *4* [...] ... [...]

Frag. 3   *7* [...And Levi was 3]4 [years old] when he [begot Qahat.] *8* [And Qahat was 2]9 years old when he begot ᶜAmram. And ᶜAmram [was] *9* [110 years old when he begot] Aaron. And Aaron left Egy[pt...] *10* [...] these: 11 thousand and 536 *Blank*

Frag. 4   *1* [...] ... [...] *2* [...] from the lan[d of ...] *3* [...] years [...] *4* [... Joshua the Jo]rdan [as far as ...] ... [...] *5* [...] 35 years in Gilgal [...] *6* [... in Timnath Ser]ah (for) 20 years. And from the death [of Joshua ...] *7* [...] Cushan-rishathaim, king of Aram-naharaim ...] *8* [...] *8* [ye]ars. Othniel, son [of Kenaz ...] *9* Eglon, king of Moab, [...] *10* [...E]hud, son of Gera, 80 years; Sham[gar, son of ᶜAnath ...]

Frag. 5   *1* [...] *2* [Gideon, son of Joash,] 40 y[ears;] To[la, son of Pua ...] *3* [...] ... [...]

2 Genesis Apocryphon

1QGenesis Apocryphon (1Q20 [1QapGen ar])

Frag. 1 *col.* I   *1* [...] you shall pour out you anger and tear out (?) [...] and who is he who *2* [...] the fury of your anger. *Blank 3* [...]and those who have been wiped out and those who have fallen, bereft and [...] *4* [...] and now, look, I have oppressed the prisoners *5* [...] ... *6* [...] *Blank 7* [... the Great] Holy One *8* [...] all that he *9–10* [...] ...

Frag. 1 *col.* II   *3* day of [...] *4* all [...] *5* ... [...] *6* land of [...] *7* ... [...] *8* and the evil for [...]

Frag. 2   *1* [...] ... *2* [...] and they were struck from behind *3* [...] *Blank 4* [...] ... *5* [...] in front of the Lord of the Universe.

1QGenesisApocryphon (1QapGen ar)

Col. I   *1* [...] ... and with the sowing *2* [...] ... not even the mystery of evil which *3* [...] ... the mystery which

Col. II   *1* Behold, then, I thought in my heart that the conception was the work of the Watchers and the pregnancy, of the Holy Ones, and it belonged to the Gian[ts, ...] *2* and my heart within me was upset on account of this boy. *Blank* [...] *3* Then I, Lamech, was frightened and turned to Bitenosh, my wife, [and said: ...] *4* [Swear to me] by the Most High, by the Great Lord, by the King of the Uni[verse, ...] *5* [...] the sons of heaven, that you will in truth let me know everything, if [...] *6* You will [in truth] and without lies let me know whether this [... Swear to me] *7* by the King of all the Universe that you are speaking to me frankly and without lies [...] *8* Then Bitenosh, my bride, spoke to me very harshly, she wep[t ...] *9* and said: Oh my brother and lord! Remember my pleasure [...] *10* [...] the time of love, the gasping of my breath in my breast. I [shall tell you] everything accurately [...] *11* [...] and then within me my heart was very upset. *Blank* [...] *12* When Bitenosh, my wife, realized that my counte-nance had altered [...] *13* then she suppressed her anger, speaking to me and saying to me: O my lord and [brother! Remember] *14* my pleasure. I swear to you by the Great Holy One, by the King of the hea[vens...] *15* that this seed comes from you, that this pregnancy comes from you, that the planting of this fruit comes from you, *16* and not from any foreigner or watcher or son of heaven. [Why is the expression] *17* of your face so changed and distorted, and your spirit so depressed? [...] *18* I speak truthfully to you. *Blank* [...] *19* Then I, Lamech, /ran/ to my father, Methuselah, and [told] him everything, [so that he would go and ask Enoch,] *20* his father and would know everything for certain from him, since he (Enoch) is liked and well-liked [... and with the holy ones] *21* his inheritance is found and they show him everything. When Methuselah heard [these things] *22* [he ran] to Enoch, his father, in order to know everything reliably [...] *23* his will. And he left for the higher level, to Parvaim, and there he met [Enoch, his father...] *24* He said to Enoch, his father: O my father and my lord, to whom I [...] *25* [...] I tell you: Do not be annoyed with me because I came here to [you...] *26* fear (?) before you [...]

Col. III   *3* For in the days of Jared, my father [...]

Col. V   *3* I, Enoch [...] *4* [not from the sons of] heaven but from Lamech [your son...] *9* Now I tell you ... I let you know [...] *10* Go, tell Lamech, your son [...] *24* When Methuselah heard [...] *25* and with Lamech, his son ... he spoke [...] *26* When I, Lamech [...] *27* which he brought out of me [...]

Col. VI   *2* and all my life I have behaved correctly [...] *6* [...] I, Noah, a man [...]

Col. VII   *1* [you will rule] the earth and all there is in it, over the seas [...] *7* [...] and I was happy at the words of the Lord of the heavens [...]

Col. X   *12* [...] the ark settled [on] one of the mountains of Hurarat [...] *13* [...] I atoned for all the whole earth [...] *15* [...] I burned incense on the altar [...]

Col. XI   *17* [...] You shall eat no blood of any kind [...]

Col. XII   *1* [...] and it was for me a sign in the cloud [...] *2* [...] the earth *3* [...] was revealed to me *4-7* [...]... *8* [...] in the mountains of Hurarat; afterwards I descended to the base of these mountains, I, my sons and my sons' sons *9* [...] for desolation was great in the earth [...] after the flood *10* [...] was born first Arpachsad two years after the Flood [...] all the sons of Shem, all of them *11* [...] Put and Canaan [...] *12* [...] seven. *Blank* And the sons of Japhet, Gomer, Magog, Madai, Yavan, Tubal, Mosok, Tiras and four daughters. *13* I, and all my sons began to till the earth and I planted a huge vineyard on Mount Lubar and four years later it produced wine for me. *14* [...] *Blank* And when the first feast occurred, on the first day of the first feast of the month, *15* [...] my vineyard; I opened the pitcher and began to drink it on the first day of the fifth year. *16* [...] On that day I called my sons, and my sons' sons, and all our wives and their daughters and we got together and we went *17* [...] And I blessed the Lord of the Heavens, the God Most High, the Great Holy One, who saved us from destruction.

Col. XVI   *11* [...] all the land of the North until he reached [...] *12* [...] this frontier, the waters of the Great Sea [...] *16* [...] the river Tina [...]

Col. XVII   *8* [...] towards the West, towards Ashshur, until it reached the Tigris [...] *9* to Aram, the land which [...] until it reached the upper part of [...] *10* [...] this mountain of the Bull, and he crossed this portion towards the East, until he reached [...] *11* [...] and over the upper part of the three portions [...] To Arpachsad [...] *16* [...] to Gomer he gave the Eastern part in the North, until it reached the river Tina and its crown; to Magog [...]

Col. XIX   *7* [...There I built an altar and called on the name of God] there and said: You are *8* for [me the eternal God] ... Until now I have not reached the holy mountain. I left, then, *9* as far as [...] and kept on walking towards the South [...] until I reached Hebron. [At that time] Hebron had been built, and I lived *10* [there two ye]ars. *Blank* However, a famine occurred in this whole country. I heard that there was grain in Egypt, and left *11* to [enter] the land of Egypt [...] I reached the river Carmon, one of the *12* branches of the river [...] now we [...] our land. And I crossed the seven branches of this river which [...] *13* [...] Then we cross our land and we enter the land of the sons of Ham in the land of Egypt. *14 Blank* I, Abram, dreamt a dream, on the night of my entry into Egypt. And in my dream I saw a cedar and a palm-tree. *15* [...] Some men arrived intending to cut and uproot the cedar, leaving the palm-tree alone. *16* But the palm-tree shouted and said: Do not hew down the cedar, because both of us are of the same family. And the cedar was saved thanks to the palm-tree, *17* and was not hewn down. *Blank* I woke up from my slumber during the night and said to Sarai, my wife: I have had *18* a nightmare [... and] I am alarmed by this dream. She said to me: Tell me your dream so that I may know it. And I began to tell her the dream. *19* [And I let her know the interpretation] of the dream. I said: [...] they want to kill me and leave you alone. This favour only *20* [must you do for me]: every time we [reach a place, say] about me: He is my brother. And I shall live under your protection and my life will be spared because of you. *21* [...] they will try to separate you from me and kill me. Sarai wept because of my words that night. *22* [...] the Pharaoh [Zoan ... so that] Sarai [did not wish] to go to Zoan *23* [with me, because she greatly feared] within herself that anybody could see her. After these five years *24* three men of the princes of Egypt [came...] from Pharaoh Zoan on account of my [words] and of my wife. They gave me *25* [many presents expecting from me] goodness, wisdom and truth. I read in front of them the [book] of the words of Enoch *26* [...] concerning the famine which [...] and not [...] and they arrived, urging until [...] to her [...] the words of [...] *27* [...] with much eating and drinking [...] wine [...]

Col. xx   *1* […]…[…] *2* […] How dazzling and pretty is the shape of her face, and how […] *3* […,] how smooth the hair of her head! How lovely are her eyes; how pleasant her nose and all the animation *4* of her face […] How graceful is her breast and how lovely all her whiteness! How beautiful are her arms! And her hands, how *5* perfect! How alluring is the whole appearance of her hands! How pretty are the palms of her hands and how long and supple all the fingers of her hands! Her feet, *6* how lovely! How perfect her legs! No virgin or wife who enters the bridal chamber is more beautiful than her. Above all *7* women her beauty stands out; her loveliness is far above them all. And with all this beauty there is in her great wisdom. And everything she does with her hands *8* is perfect. When the king heard the words of HRKNWS and the words of his two companions, since the three of them spoke in unison, he desired her greatly and sent *9* with all speed for them to fetch her. He saw her and was amazed at all her beauty, and took her for himself as a wife. He tried to kill me, but Sarai said *10* to the king: He is my brother, so that I could profit at her expense. I, Abram, was forgiven on her account and I was not killed. But I wept *11* bitterly that night, I, Abram and my nephew Lot with me, because Sarai had been taken away from me by force. *Blank* *12* That night I prayed, pleaded and entreated and said in my distress, while my tears flowed: Blessed are you, O God Most High, my Lord, through all the *13* universe. For you are Lord and Master of everything and rule all the kings of the earth, to judge them all. Now *14* I lodge a complaint before you, my Lord, against Pharaoh Zoan, king of Egypt, because my wife has been taken away from me by force. Do justice for me against him and show your mighty arm *15* against him, and against all his house. During this night, may he not be able to sully my wife, separated from me; and so they shall know you, my Lord. For you are the Lord of all the kings *16* of the earth. And I wept and stayed silent. That night, the God Most High sent him a chastising spirit, to afflict him and all the members of his household, an evil spirit *17* that kept afflicting him and all the members of his household. And he was unable to approach her, much less have sexual intercourse with her, in spite of being with her *18* for two years. At the end of two years, the punishments and plagues, against him and against all the members of his household, increased and intensified. And he sent *19* for all [the wise men] of Egypt to be called, and all the wizards as well as all the healers of Egypt, (to see) whether they could heal him of that disease, [him] and the members *20* of his household. However, all the healers and wizards and all the wise men were unable to rise up and heal him. For the spirit attacked all of them and *21* they fled. *Blank* Then HRKNWS came to me and asked me to come and pray for *22* the king, and lay my hands upon him so that he would live. For [he had seen me] in a dream. But Lot said to him: Abram, my uncle, cannot pray for *23* the king while Sarai, his wife, is with him. Go, now, and tell the king to send back his wife to her own husband and he will pray for him and he will live. *24* *Blank*

When HRKNWS heard Lot's words, he went and said to the king: All these plagues and punishments 25 with which the king my Lord is afflicted and punished are on account of Sarai, Abram's wife. They should return Sarai, then, I beg you to Abram, her husband, 26 and this plague and the spirit of purulent evils will cease to afflict you. (The Pharaoh) called me to him and said to me: What have you done to me with regard to Sarai? You told me: 27 She is my sister, when she is your wife; so that I took her for myself for a consort. Here is your wife; take her away! Go! Depart from 28 all the cities of Egypt! But now pray for me and for my household so that this evil spirit will be banished from us. I prayed for [...] 29 and laid my hands upon his head. The plague was removed from him; [the evil spirit] was banished [from him] and he lived. 30 The king got up and informed me [...] The king swore an oath to me that not [...] Then, they [brought to] me 31 Sarai. The king gave her much gold [and silver] and many clothes of fine linen and purple [...] 32 in front of her and also Hagar. He handed her to me, and appointed men to escort me out [of Egypt.] 33 I, Abram, walked with much cattle and also with silver and gold. I left [Egypt ... Lot] 34, my brother's son, [was] with me. Lot, too, had acquired many flocks and had taken for himself a wife from among the daughters [of Egypt. I camped with him]

Col. XXI   *1* in all my (old) camp-sites until I reached Bethel, the place where I had built an altar, and I built it once again. *2* Upon it I offered holocausts and an offering to the God Most High, and invoked the name of the Lord of the Universe there; I praised God's name and blessed *3* God. I gave thanks there in God's presence for all the flocks and wealth which he had given me, because he had acted well towards me, and because he had returned me *4* in peace to this land. *Blank 5* After that day, Lot parted from me on account of the behaviour of our shepherds. He went and settled in the Jordan Valley (taking) all his flocks *6* with him. And I even added many to his. He pastured his flocks and reached Sodom and bought himself a house in Sodom *7* and lived there, while I lived in the mountain of Bethel. It distressed me that Lot, my brother's son, should have parted from me. *8 Blank* God appeared to me in a night vision and said to me: Go up to Ramat Hazor, which is to the North of *9* Bethel, the place where you are living; raise your eyes and look to the East, to the West, to the South and to the North. Look at all *10* this land, which I am giving you and your descendants for ever. The following morning I went up to Ramat Hazor and looked at the land from *11* that height, from the River of Egypt up to Lebanon and Senir, and from the Great Sea up to Hauran, and all the land of Gebal up to Qadesh, and all the *12* Great Desert which there is to the East of Hauran and Senir as far as the Euphrates. And he said to me: I shall give all this land to your descendants and they will inherit it forever. *13* I will multiply your descendants like the dust of the earth which no-one can count. In the same way, your descendants will be innumerable. Get up, walk its length and breadth, *14* and see how great is its length and how great is its width. For, I shall give it to you, to you and to your descendants after you, for all the centuries. *Blank 15* I, Abram, went out to traverse and see the land. I began the traverse at the River Gihon. I went along the edge of the sea until *16* I reached the mountain of the Bull. I walked from [the coast] of this Great Sea of Salt, skirting the mountain of the Bull towards the East, through the breadth of the land *17* until I reached the River Euphrates. I proceeded towards the East along the bank of the Euphrates, until reaching the Red Sea. I continued walking along the shore *18* of the Red Sea until arriving at the branch of the Sea of Reeds which issues from the Red Sea, and continued towards the South until I reached the *19* River Gihon. Then I turned back and arrived at my house in peace and found everyone well. I went and settled next to the oaks of Mamre, in Hebron, *20* to the North-east of Hebron. There I built an altar, and upon it I offered a holocaust and an offering to the God Most High. And I ate and drank there, *21* I and all the people of my household. I invited, Mamre, Arnem and Eshkol, three Amorite brothers, my friends, and they ate together *22* with me and drank with me. *Blank 23* Before those days there came Chedorlaomer king of Elam, Amraphel, king of Babylonia, Arioch, king of Cappadocia, Tidal, king of Goiim, which is Mesopotamia, and they declared war on Bera, king of Sodom, Birsha, king of Gomorrah, Shinab, king of Admah, *25* Shemiabad, king of Zeboiim and the king of Bela. All these formed an alliance to do battle in the Valley of Siddim. However, the king of *26* Elam and the kings allied with him were victorious over the king of Sodom and all his allies, and they imposed tribute on them. Over twelve years they continued *27* paying their tribute to the King of Elam but in the thirteenth they revolted against him. In the fourteenth year, the king of Elam positioned himself at the head of all *28* his allies, they climbed up the desert road and were ravaging and laying waste from the river Euphrates. They routed the Rephaites of Ashteroth-*29*karnaim the Zumzumites of Ammon, the Emim of Shaveh-kiriathaim and the Horites of Mount Gebal until they reached El-*30*paran, in the desert. They returned [...] in Hazazon-tamar. *Blank 31* The king of Sodom went out to meet him, together with the king [of Gomorrah,] the king of Admah, the king of Zeboiim and the king of Bela. [They engaged] battle *32* in the Valley [of Siddim] against Chedorlaomer, [and the allies] who were with him. But the king of Sodom was defeated and fled; the king of Gomorrah *33* fell in the pits [...] The king of Elam pillaged all the property of Sodom and of *34* [Gomorrah...] and they captured Lot, the son of the brother

Col. XXII   1 of Abram, who was living in Sodom, together with them and all his cattle. One of the shepherds of the flock *2* which Abram had given Lot, who had escaped captivity, came to Abram – at that time Abram *3* was living in Hebron – and told him that Lot, the son of his brother and all his flocks had been captured, but that he was not dead, and that *4* the kings had taken the road of the Great Valley up to his city, taking prisoners, ravaging, killing and proceeding *5* as far as the city of Damascus. Abram wept for Lot, the son of his brother. Abram gained courage, stood up *6* and chose from among his servants those most fit for war: three hundred and eighteen. Arnem, *7* Eshkol and Mamre were with him. He went in pursuit of them until he reached Dan and found them *8* camped in the Valley of Dan. He fell upon them by night from (all) four sides. He killed *9* some during the night. He destroyed them and chased them and they were all fleeing before him *10* until they reached Helbon which lies north of Damascus. He retrieved from them all that they had captured, *11* all that they had looted and all their own goods. He also saved Lot, his brother's son, and all his flocks and brought back all *12* the captives they had taken. The king of Sodom heard that Abram had brought back all the captives *13* and all the loot and went up to meet him. He went to Salem, which is Jerusalem. Abram was encamped in the Valley of *14* Shaveh, which is the Valley of the King, the Valley of Bet ha-Kerem. Melchizedek, king of Salem, brought out *15* food and drink for Abram and for all the men there were with him. He was a priest of the Most High God. He blessed *16* Abram and said: Blessed be Abram by the Most High God, Lord of heaven and earth and blessed be the Most High God, *17* who has delivered your enemies into your hands. And (Abram) gave him a tithe of all the flocks of the king of Elam and his allies. *18* *Blank* Then, the king of Sodom approached and said to Abram: My Lord Abram, *19* give me the people who are mine, who are captive with you, whom you have rescued from the king of Elam. All the wealth, *20* keep for yourself. *Blank* Then Abram answered the king of Sodom: *21* I swear this day by the Most High God, Lord of heaven and earth, that I will not accept a thread or a sandal thong *22* or anything of what belongs to you so that you will not say: From my wealth do *21* Abram's riches (come), *23* apart from what my boys who escort me have eaten, and apart from the share of the three men who *24* came with me; they are owners of their share to give to you. Abram gave back all the wealth and *25* all the captives and gave (them) to the king of Sodom. And all the prisoners who were with him from that area he released *26* and freed them all. *Blank* *27* After these events, God appeared to Abram in a vision and said to him: See, *28* ten years have passed since the day you left Haran; you have spent two years here, seven in Egypt and one *29* since you came back from Egypt. Now inspect and count up all you possess and see how many times *30* everything which left with you on the day of your move from Haran has increased. Now, do not fear, I am with you and for you I shall be *31* support and strength. I shall be your shield and your buckler against one stronger than you. Your riches and your flocks *32* shall increase enormously. *Blank* Abram replied: My Lord God, great are my riches and my flocks; but what use is all this to me? *33* When I die

I shall go naked and without sons. One of my servants will inherit from me, *34* Eliezer [...] ... But he answered him: He will not inherit from you but (some)one who has left

3 The Book of Jubilees

4QJubilees*a* (4Q216 [4QJub*a*])

Frag. 1 *col.* I (= *Jub* 1 : 1–2.4–7)   *3* [Sinai, when he went up to] re[ceive the stone tablets, the Torah and the statute] by the word of YHWH [according to which he told him:] *4* [Go up] to the top of the moun[tain. In the first year] of the so[ns of Israel] leaving *5* [Egypt, in the] thir[d month, the sixteenth of this month] YHWH spoke to *6* [Moses saying: Come up to me] on the mountain [and I will give you the two tablets] of stone, the Torah *7* [and the statute which I have written in order to te]ach [you. And Moses climbed the mountain of YHWH and] the glory of YH[WH settled] *8* [on top of Mount Sinai and for six days the cloud covered it...] *9–10* [...] *11* [...And he showed him the divisions [of per]iods for the Law *12* [and for the testimony. And he said to him: Pay attention to all the wo]rds which I tell you *13* [on this mountain and write them in a book so that] their generations may [know] that he has not forsaken them *14* [for all the evil which they did by breaking the covenant which] I set up to-day between me and you *15* [for their generations on Mount Sinai. And when] all these things happen to them *16* [they will know that I have been just with them in all] their jud[gments and in all] their curses and they will know *17* [that in truth I was with them. And you, write] all these wo[rds...]

Frag. 1 *col.* II (= *Jub* 1 : 7–15)   *2* in the land [which I promised to their fathers, to Abraham and to Isaac and to Ja]cob, *3* saying: To your offspring [I will give a land which flows with milk and ho]ney. They will eat and be replete [but they will turn back] *4* after other gods [who did not save them from any trou]ble. And the [testimony] will reply to this testimony; bec[ause they will forget all my statutes, all that I] commanded you and they will go [after] *6* [the nat]ions and [after their foulnesses and after their disreputableness]. And they will serve other go[ds who to them will be a hindrance,] *7* trouble, [affliction] and [trap. Many will be destroyed.] They will be captured and fall [into the hand of the enemy for] *8* [they will forsake] my laws and [my statutes, the festiva]ls of my covenant [and my sabbaths and the holy things] *9* which they will dedicate to me in the mid[st of them and my tent and my] temple [which I made holy for myself in the midst] *10* of the earth in order to place [my name] in it [and reside there]. They made for themselves burial mounds, sacred woods and idols] *11* and grovelled in front of a[ll the work]s of their wickedness. [And they will sacrifice their sons to the devils and to all the works of the wickedness of their heart.] *12* I shall send them witnesses [to testify against them, but they will not listen and will kill the witnesses] *13* They will harass those who study the Torah [and they will alter everything and will start to do what is evil] *14* in my eyes. And I shall hide my face from them and will con[sign] them [into the hand of the nations for imprisonment,] *15* [for ru]in [and so they can be consumed. I will remove them from the midst of the land and] scatter them among all the nations. *16* [They will forget all my laws and all my statutes] and all my teachings and they will forget [the month, the sabbath] *17* [the feast, the jubilee and the covenant. After this they will come back] to me from among the nati[ons with all their heart ...]

Frag. 1 *col.* IV (= *Jub* 1 : 26–28)   *3* [...the first and the] last *4* [and what will come in all the divisions of the periods for the] Law and for the test[imony] *5* [and for the weeks and the jubilees for ever until I come down] and stay with [them] *6* [for all the centuries of centuries. And he told the angel of the] presence to dictate *7* [to Moses from the beginning of creation until] my temple is built *8* [in their midst for all the centuries of the centuries. YHWH will reveal himself to the eyes of] everyone and they will [all] know *9* [that I am the God of Israel and the father of all the sons of] Jacob and the king *10* [on Mount Zion for all the centuries of centuries And Zion and Jerusa]lem [will be holy...]

Frag. 1 *col.* V (= *Jub* 2 : 1–4)   *1* [And the angel of the presence told Moses at God's command: Write all the wo]rds of the creation: h[ow] *2* [on the sixth day YHWH Elohim finished all his works and all that he had created] and observed the sabbath on the [seventh] day *3* [and made it holy for all the centuries and placed it as a sign for all] his works. *Blank 4* [*Blank* For on the first day he created the] upper hea[vens,] the earth, *5* [the waters and all the spirits who serve before him: the angels] of the presence, the angels of ho[liness,] *6* the an[gels of the spirits of fire, the angels of the spirits of the win]ds and the angels of the spirits of the [clouds] *7*, darkn[ess, ice, frost, dew, snow, hail and hoar]frost; and the angels of thu[nder] *8* and the angels of the [storm-]winds [and the angels of the winds of cold and of] heat, of winter and of summer, [all] *9* the spirits of his creatures [which he made in the heavens and which he made in the ea]rth and in everything, the aby[sses] *10* the darkness, the dawn [the light, the dusk which he prepared with his know]ledge. Then we saw his deeds and [blessed him] *11* on account of all his deeds and [we praised him in his presence because he had ma]de seven great works [on the first day.] *12* And on the [second d]ay [he made the vault in the middle] of the waters [and the waters were separated on that day. Half] *13* went up on to[p of the vault and half went down below the vault which was in its midst, on top of the face of all] *14* the earth [...]

Frag. 1 *col.* VI (= *Jub* 2 : 7–12)   *2* [... and the po]ols and all the d[ew of the earth] *3* [the seed for sowing with its seed, every shoot and tree that gives fruit, the] woods and the garden of Eden [in Eden] *4* [for pleasure and for eating. These four great works] he did on the thir[d] day. *5* [*Blank* On the fourth day YHWH made the] sun, the moon and the stars. [He placed them] *6* [in the vault of the

sky so that could give light to the whole earth] to regulate day and night and to
separ[ate] *7* [light and darkness. And he placed the sun as a] great [sign above
the earth] of the days, the weeks, the mon[ths] *8* [the feasts, the years, the weeks
of years and the ju]bilees and of all the ag[es of the years.] *9* [It separates light
from darkness and is the vitality by which everything] that sprouts and grows
in the ea[rth prospers.] *10* [These three great works he did on the fourth day.]
Blank *11* [On the fifth day he created the] grea[t cetaceans in the core of the
abys]ses of the wa[ters, for these] *12* [were the first works of flesh by his hands;
and everything that moves in] the waters, fish and all [the birds] *13* [which fly
and all their species. The sun shone over them for] vigour and over everything
there was on the earth, [everything] *14* [that sprouted from the earth and every
tree that yields fruit and all flesh. These] three great [things] *15* [he did on the
fifth day. *Blank*]

Frag. 1 *col.* VII (= *Jub* 2 : 13–24)   *1* [On the] sixth [day he made] all the anim[als
of the earth and all the cattle and everything that slithers over the earth. After
all these] *2* he made man, male and fe[male he made them, and gave them control over everything there is on the earth and in the seas and over everything
that flies] *3* over the animals and over everything that slithers [creeping over the
earth, and the cattle and over all the earth. Over all these he gave them control.]
4 He made these [four] types [on the sixth day. And in all there were twenty-
two types. And he finished all his works on the sixth day: everything] *5* there
is in the heavens and on the earth [and in the waters and in the abysses, in the
light and in the darkness and in everything. And he gave us a huge sign, on the
day of the] *6* sabbath on which he left off doing [all the works which he had
created over the six days...] *7* they were made in six days [...] *8* and we observe
the sabbath on the seventh [day (refraining) from all work. For we, the angels
of the presence and all the angels of – these] *9* two classes – he commanded us
[to observe the sabbath with him in the heavens and on the earth. And he said
to us: I am going to isolate for myself] *10* a people among my peoples. And
[they will keep the sabbath and I will consecrate them as my people and I will
bless them. They will be my people and I will be their God.] *11* And I chose the
descendants of Jacob among [all those I saw. And I registered him for me as the
first-born son and consecrated him to me] *12* for ever and ever. The [seventh]
day [I will teach them so that they keep the sabbath on it above all. For I
blessed them and consecrated them as an exceptional people] *13* among all the
nations so that together [with us] they keep [the sabbath. And he lifted up his
statutes like a pleasant perfume which is acceptable in his presence] *14* every
day. *Blank* [There are twenty-two patriarchs] *15* from Adam to him and twenty
two typ[es of works were done up to the seventh day. One is blessed and holy
and the other is blessed] *16* and holy. One and the other were made together for
holiness [and for blessing. To this one was granted to be blessed and holy forever.] *17* And this is the testimony and the first Law. [...]

11QJubilees (11Q12 [11QJub])

Frag. 1 (= *Jub* 4 : 7–11)   *1* [And in the] fourth [year] of the fif[th week they re-joiced and Adam knew his wife once again] *2* and she bore a son for him and he named him [Seth for he said: YHWH has raised a seed for us] *3* [in the] earth, another in place of Abel, since [Cain] killed him. [In the sixth week she bore] *4* [Azu]ra, her daughter. And Cain took his sister [Awan as his wife and she bore Enoch for him] *5* [at the end of the] fourth [ju]bilee. *Blank* [In the first year of the first week] *6* [of the fifth jubilee] they built houses in the la[nd and Cain built a city and gave it] *7* [the name of his s]on Enoch. And Ad[am knew his wife Eve and she gave birth to *8* [nine more children. And in the fi]fth we[ek …]

Frag. 2 (= *Jub* 4 : 13–14)   *1* [And she gave birth to a s]on [for him] in the [third ye]ar [of the fifth week and gave him the name] *2* [Cainan. And] at the end of the [eighth ju]bilee [Cainan took for himself a woman, Muhalelet] *3* [his sister] as a wife. [And she gave birth to a son for him in the ninth jubilee, in the first week] *4* [in the thi]rd [year] of [that week.]

Frag. 3 (= *Jub* 4 : 16–17)   *1* [in the fifth wee]k [of the fourth year of the jubilee and called him Enoch.] *2* [*Bla*]*nk*. He was the first (person) [to learn writing…]

Frag. 4 (= *Jub* 4 : 29–30)   *1* [the first to be bur]ied in [the earth, seventy years short of one thousand] *2* [years, for] a thousand years [are like one day in the testimony of heaven. This is why] *3* [it was written concerning the tr]ee of knowledge: For on [the day on which you eat from it, you shall die. This is why] *4* [he did not complete the] years of that day […]

Frag. 5 (*Jub* 5 : 1–2)   *1* [… those fal]len. And [brutality on earth] increased [and all flesh perverted] *2* [its way from men to] animals, the bea[sts, the birds and everything that moves] *3* [over land; all these pe]rverted their ways and their standa[rds and began to consume each] *4* [other and brutality increased upo]n earth. […]

Frag. 6 (= *Jub* 12 : 15–17)   *1* and [his sons in order to go to the country of Leba-non and the country of Canaan and he settled in Haran. And Abram stayed] *2* [in Haran] with [Terah his father during two 'weeks' of years. *Blank* And in the sixth week] *3* in his fifth [year] Abram kept vigil during the night of the first day of the seventh month to observe *4* the sta[rs from the evening to the morn-ing, in order to see what the yearly cycle would be in relation to the rains. And it happened that] *5* while he [was sitting alone, watching, a voice came to his heart and said to him: All the signs] *6* of the sta[rs…]

Frag. 7 (= *Jub* 12 : 28–29)   *1 Blank* And it happened that in the sev[enth year] of the sixth week he spoke to his father and told him] *2* [that] he was leaving [Haran to go to the land of Canaan to see it and to return to him.] *3* [And his father] Terah [said] to him [:Go in peace. May the eternal God direct your path] *4* [and may YHWH be with] you and kee[p you from every evil; may no son of man overpower you] *5* [to mis]treat you. [...]

4QJubilees^c (4Q220 [4QJub^c])

(= *Jub* 21 : 5–10)   *1* [... You, my son, keep his pre]cepts [his decrees and his judgments; do not go after] idols or after [carved or cast effigies.] *2* [And] do not [eat any blo]od of an animal, cattle or any bird which [flies in the sky. If you sacrifice] *3* [a victim for] a holocaust or a free-will offering, [you will sacrifice it and pour the blood over the altar. And all] *4* [the fat] which is for the holocaust you shall offer upon the al[tar] with the finest flour of its offering mixed with [oil] *5* [and its libation. And] you will burn everything upon the altar, a fire-offering with a pleasant fragrance before Elohim. [...] *6* You will offer on the fire which is upon the altar, and the fat [...] *7* [...] and all the fat which there is upon the entrails and the kidneys and the [...] *8* and the appendix of the liver and from the kidneys you shall remove [...] *9* with the offering and the libation for the plea[sant fragrance...] *10* [You are to eat the flesh the] same [day] and the following morning and not [...]

4QJubilees^d (4Q219 [4QJub^d])

Col. I (= *Jub* 21 : 14–16)   *11* [And in the sixth year, in] the seventh [week of this jubilee, Abraham called Isaac, his son,] and commanded him saying: I am old [and I do not know the day of my death, for I have completed] *13* my days. Behold, I am [one hundred and seventy-]two [years, and throughout all the days of my life I have been remembering] *14* our Elohim always and I have been [seeking him with all my heart...] *15-31* [...] *32* [upon] the altar [with the finest flour of its offering mixed with oil and its libation. And you will burn everything upon] *33* the al[tar, a fire-offering with a pleasant fragrance before Elohim. And the fat of the thanksgiving sacrifice you will of]fer *34* [on the fire which is upon the altar, and the fat which is upon the belly, and] all the fat *35* [which is upon the entrails and the kidneys and] all the fat which is upon them and that which *36* [is on the loins and the appendix of the] liver with the kidneys you shall remove. You shall offer *37* [the whole for a pleasant fragrance before Elo]him, with its offering and its libation [for a pleasant (fragrance), the bread] *38* [of the fire-offering to YHWH. You are to eat its flesh] the same [day] and the following mor[ning, and (the sun) will not set upon it.]

Col. II (= *Jub.* 21 : 14 – 16.18 – 22 : 1)   *11* [...and the aroma of its fragrance does not ri]se to heaven. Keep *12* [this commandment and carry it out, my son, so that you will be upr]ight in all your actions. *13* [And at every time be pure in your flesh and wash yourself with water before] going to offer *14-16* [...] *17* [You are not to eat blood any more] because the blood is [the life, and you are not to eat any blood. You are not to accept] *18* [a bribe for any blood] of men which is poured out [for no reason, without judgment, because the blood which is poured out] *19* [defiles the earth, and the] earth cannot be [purified from the human blood except with the blood] *20* [of the one who shed it. Do not take a bri]be or atonement for [human blood: blood for blood, and it will be acceptable] *21* [before YHW]H, God Most High. He will be custodian for [the goodness, and so you will keep yourself from every] *22* [evil and He will] protect you from every pestilence. *Blank* [...] *23* [My son: I see that all the labours [of the human race are evil and sinful and all] *24* [their actions are uncleanness, abomination] and filth, and there is no truth in them. *Blank* Be[ware, lest you walk] *25* [in their ways and] tread in their paths and commit a deadly misdeed [in front of God Most High] *26* [and He hide his face] from you, give you into the hands of your fault and obliterate you [from the earth] *27* [and your progeny from] beneath the sky. And your name and your memory will vanish from the whole [earth.] *28* [Refrain from all] their deeds and from all their abominations, and keep the regula[tions of God] *29* [Most High and do] His will, and you will be succesful in everything. He will bless you in all your deeds, [and will cause to sprout] *30* [from you a plant of] truth in the earth for all the generations of the earth. And [my name] *31* [and your name] will not cease [from beneath] the sky for all the days. *Blank* Be upright, my son, in pea[ce. May he strengthen] *32* [you, the God] Most High, my God and your God, to perform his will and to [bless your progeny] *33* and the [remnant of your pro]geny for all the eternal generations with every blessing [of truth so that you might be] *34* a blessing [in all the earth.] *Blank* And he went out from him rejoicing. *Blank* *35* [...] In the first week of the [forty-]third [jubilee, in its] *36* [second year, which is] the year in which Abraham died, [Isaac and Ishmael] came *37* [from Beer Sheba to celebrate] the feast of [weeks] which is the fes[tival of the first fruits.]

4QJubilees*f* (4Q221 [4QJub*f*])

Frag. 1 (= *Jub* 21 : 22 – 24)   *1* Be[ware of walking in their way]s and committing [a deadly misdeed in front of God Most High] *2* [lest] He hide his face from you, give you [into the hands of your fault and obliterate you] *3* [from the earth] and your progeny from beneath the sky. [*Blank* ...] *4* And your name and your seed will vanish from the whole earth. [Refrain from all their deeds and from all] *5* their abominations; keep the regulations of God Most High, [and do His will and you will be successful] *6* [in everything.] ⟨and from all their abomina-

tions; keep [the regulations of God Most High, [and do his will] *7* [and you
will] be successful in everything.⟩ He will bless you in all [your deeds, and will
cause to sprout from you a plant of truth] *8* [in the earth for all the generations
of the ear]th. And [my name and your names will not cease from beneath the
sky] *9* [for al]l the days.

3QJubilees (3Q5 [3QJub])

Frags. 3 + 1 (= *Jub* 23 : 6 – 7.12 – 13)   *1* [...and this] was heard in [Abraham's
house. *Blank*] *2* [And Ishmael his son got up and] fled to A[braham his father.
And he wept for Abraham] *3* [his father, he and all the me]n of the house(hold)
of A[braham; they wept a great deal. And] *4* [Isaac and Ishmael his sons] buried
him in the cave of Mac[phelah next to Sara, his wife.]

2QJubilees*ᵃ* (2Q19 2QJub*ᵃ*])

[= *Jub* 23 : 7 – 8]   *1* [...And Isaac and Ishmael his sons buried him in the cave of
Mac]phelah ne[xt to Sara, his wife.] *2* [And for him wept] for forty days all the
me[n of his household, and Isaac and Ishmael and all their sons and all the sons
of Qetura] *3* [in their places.] *Blank* [And the mourning ended,] *4* [the lament for
Abra]ham. He had lived for three jubilees and fo[ur weeks of years, one hundred and seventy-five years and he ended] *5* [the days of his life] old and replete
with days. [...]

4QJubilees*ᶠ* (4Q176 fragments 19 – 21 [4QJub*ᶠ*])

Frags. 19 – 20 (= *Jub* 23 : 21 – 23)   *1* [... They invoke the great name, however
neither in tru]th nor in justice, *2* [and they defile the Holy of Holies with his
impur]ity and with the de[solation of abomination.] Great punishment there
will be against the works of this generation *3* [on the part of the Lord who will
deliver them] to the sword, to the judgment, to [the bondage] to pillage and to
be devoured. He will rouse against them *4* [the sinners of the nations who will
have neither mercy nor compas]sion towards them, and [who will not] respect
any[body nor]

Frag. 21 (= *Jub* 23 : 30 – 31)   *1* And their ene[mies] will see [all their judgments]
2 in all their cur[se. Their bones will rest in the earth] *3* and their spirits [will
rejoice exceedingly and they will know that] *4* a God exists who administers
[justice and has mercy] *5* to the thous[ands] and the my[riads who love him.]

1QJubilees*a* (1Q17 [1QJub*a*])

[= *Jub* 27 : 19–21]   *1* [...] *Blank* [...] *2* [And Jacob left Beersheba to] go to Haran
in the first [year of the second week of the forty-fourth jubilee] *3* [and reached
Luz] which is on the mountain – it is Bethel – [the first (day) of the first month
of that week.] *4* [And he reached] the pl[ace in the eve]ning and he moved off
the path, to the ri[ght, that night and spent the night there, because the sun had
set.] *5* [And he to]ok one of the stones of that place [and placed it as a pillow
under the tree and lay there] *6* [for he] travelled alone. [...]

1QJubilees*b* (1Q18 [1QJub*b*])

[= *Jub* 35 : 8–10]   *1* [...with] me about your death. *Blank* [...] *2* [And she fled to
Isaac and said to him: One request] I ask of you. Make Esau swear that *3* [he
will not bully Jacob, his brother and that he will not harass] him with enmity,
for you know Esau's nature which is *4* [evil from his youth and you know all
that he has do]ne from the day on which [his brother Jac]ob fl[ed] to Haran
[right till today.]

2QJubilees*b* (2Q20) [2QJub*a*])

[= *Jub* 46 : 1–3]   *1* [... And they were very fruitful] *2* [and multiplied greatly
during ten] weeks of years, a[ll the days of Joseph's life.] *3* [And he had neither
rival nor any evil] all the days of Joseph's life whic[h he lived after] *4* [his father
Jacob, for all Egypt] paid hono[ur to Jacob's sons] *5* [all the days of Joseph's
life. And Joseph died at the age of] one hundred and te[n years]

4QPseudo Jubilees*c* (4Q227 [4QPsJub*c*])

1 [...] Enoch, after we had taught him *2* [...] six jubilees of years *3* [...] of the
earth, among the sons of men and he gave witness against them all *4* [...] and
also against the Watchers and he wrote everything *5* [...] of the heavens and the
paths of their armies and [...] *6* [...] so that they would not stray [...]

4 The Books of Enoch

4QEnoch*a* (4Q201 [4QEn*a* ar])

Col. I (= 1 *Enoch* 1 : 1 – 6)   *1* [Words of blessing with which] Enoch [blessed] the chosen [just ones, who will be present on the day of distress to eliminate all the enemies and wicked people,] *2* [while the just will be saved. Enoch, a just man to whom a vision of the Holy One and of heaven was revealed, announced] his oracles saying: [The vision of the Holy One of heaven] *3* [was revealed to me, and I heard] all the words of the Wat[chers] and of the Holy Ones [and because I heard it from them, I knew and understood everything] *4* [I will not speak for this] generation but a future generation. [Now I speak about the chosen, concerning them I declare my oracle, saying:] *5* The Great Holy One will leave [his dwelling and the eternal God will descend upon the earth and will walk to Mount Sinai and will appear] *6* [with his great army] and will rise in the strength of his might [from the height of the heavens. All the Watchers will shake and will be punished in secret places] *7* [in all the lim]its of the earth; all the limits of the earth will split [and they will be seized with shuddering and fear as far as the edges of the earth. They will split and fall] *8* [and] the peaks [will melt] and [the high mountains will be flattened...]

Col. II (= *Enoch* 2 : 1 – 5 : 6)   *1* [they appear in their constellations] and they do not overstep his command. Notice the earth and scrutinise his works *2* [from the first to the] last, how none alter and everything is obvious to you. Notice the indications *3* [of the summer: ...] above it. And the indications of winter: how all the earth *4* [is filled with water] and the clouds drip rain. Notice how all the trees turn white *5* [and lose all their leaves, ap]art from fourteen trees whose leaves survive *6* [and do not renew their leaves until] two or three years [go by]. Notice the indications *7* [of summer: how then (in it) the sun burns] and warms and you look for shade and relief from it *8* [upon the scorching face of the earth] without finding a way of walking through the dust or the stones owing to *9* [the heat. Notice and understand all the] trees; in all of them green leaves sprout and cover *10* [the trees, and all their fruits are for] decoration and show. Exalt and contemplate all these works *11* [and realise that God, who lives [for eternity. has made all these works. Year *12* [after year his works do not alter, instead] they all carry out his word. However, you alter your works *13* [and do not carry out his word, instead you offend] against him with great and harsh [words] with your unclean mouth *14* [against his greatness. Hard-hearted ones] there will be no peace for you! This is why you will curse your days and *15* [the years of the your life will perish...] The years of your destruction will increase with an everlasting curse. There will be no mercy *16* [or peace for you. This is why your name will be] (an) everlasting curse [for all the just ones and through you will be cursed] *17* [all the accursed; and all the sinners and evil ones will swear by you,] and to all [the sinners...]

Col. III (= 1 *Enoch* 6:4–8:1)   *1* They will all say to him: We take [an oath and swear, all under oath, one to another not to] *2* go back on this enterprise [until we have completed this work. Then they] *3* all [took an oath] together and they promised [each other. They were two hundred, all who went down] *4* in the time of Yared upon the [peak of Mount] Hermon. [They called the mountain 'Hermon'] *5* because they took an oath and swore under oath [with each other upon] it. These are [the names of their chiefs] *6* Shemihazah, who [was his chief; 'Ar'teqo]f, second to him; Ramt'el, [third] *7* to him; Kokab'el, [fourth to him; ...-'el, fif]th to him; Ra'ma'el, [sixth to him;] *8* Dani'el, seventh [to him; Zeq'el, eighth] to him; Baraq'el, ninth [to him;] *9* ᶜAsa'el, tenth [to him; Hermoni, eleventh] to him; Matar'el, twelfth [to him;] *10* Anan'el, thirteenth [to him; Sato'el, four]teenth to him; Shamshi['el, fift]*11*eenth to him; Sahari'el, sixteenth to him; Tumi'el, sevent[eenth to him;] *12* Turi'el, eighteenth to him; Yomi'el, nineteenth to him; [Yehadi'el, twentieth to him.] *13* These are the chiefs of the chief-of-tens. They and their chiefs [all took for themselves] *14* women, choosing (from) among (them) all, and [they began to penetrate them, and be defiled by them] *15* and taught them sorcery, [incantations and the cutting of roots and to explain herbs.] *16* They became pregnant by them. and [gave birth to giants, some three thousand cubits tall, who] *17* were born upon the earth [in keeping with their infancy and grew at the rate of their growth and consumed] *18* the work of all the sons of men, without [the men being able to supply them. The giants] *19* plotted to kill the men [and to consume them. They began to sin and to ...] *20* against all the birds and animals of the earth [and against the reptiles who move upon the earth and in the waters] *21* and in the sky and the fish of the sea and for some to consume the flesh [of the others and drink the blood. Then] *22* [the earth denounced the] wicked [for all that had been done to it.] *23* ['Asa'el taught men] to [apply...]

Col. IV (= *Enoch* 8:3–9:3.6–8)   *1* Shemihazah taught incantations [and (how) to cut roots; Hermoni taught (how) to undo magic,] *2* sorcery, magic and skills; [Baraq'el taught the signs of the shafts; Kokab'el taught] *3* the signs of the stars; Zeq'el [taught the signs of the lightning; 'Ar'teqof taught the signs of the earth;] *4* Shamsi'el taught the signs of the sun; [Sahari'el taught the signs of] the moon. [All began] *5* [to reveal] secrets to their wives. Since [a section of men] was expiring on the earth, their outcry *6* went right up to [the sky. Then] Michael, [Sariel,] Raphael, Gabriel gazed *7* from the sanctuary [of the heavens to the earth and saw] much blood spilt [upon the earth] and all [the earth] *8* was filled with the [evil] and violence perpetrated upon it. [Hearing this the four of them went] *9* and said to themselves [that the] outcry and the wail for the [destruction of the sons of the earth went right up to] *10* [the gates of heaven. [And the holy ones of heaven said: It is now to you, holy ones of heaven] *11* to whom [the souls of the sons of men appeal saying:] *12–18* [...] *19* [... in the ear]th and [every trick in] *20* [the dry land. For they have taught the eternal mysteries which exist in heaven so that the cognoscenti] *21* [from among men] perform them. And (see) Shemihazah, to whom you gave jurisdiction] to rule over all [his fellows.] *22* [They have gone to the daughters of men of the earth and have slept with those women] becoming defiled [by them.]

Col. V (= 1 *Enoch* 10:3–4)   *3* [...Teach] the just man [what he had to do and the son of Lamech] to save [his soul for life] *4* [and to escape] for [ever. And] for him a plant will be planted and all the generations] of the world [will be founded.] *5* [He said to Raphael;] Go, [then, Raphael and bind Azael hand and foot and hur]l him into [darkness.]

Col. VI (= 1 *Enoch* 10:21–22)   *3* [And all the sons of men will succeed in being] just [and all of them will worship me; every nation] *4* [will bless me] and grovel. [The whole earth will be cleansed of all defilement and all] *5* [impurity. And] I shall [not again] send [upon them either anger or punishment for all the generations] *6* [of the world...]

4QEnoch*ᵇ* (4Q202 [4QEn*ᵇ* ar])

Col. II (= 1 *Enoch* 5:9–6:4 + 6:7–8:1)   *1* [a]ll the days [of your life...] *2* It happened that when [in those days the sons of men increased,] *3* pretty and attractive [daughters were born to them. The Watchers, sons of the sky, saw them and lusted for them] *4* and said [to each other: Let's go and pick out women from among the daughters of men and sire for ourselves] *5* [sons. However, Shemihazah, who was their chief, said to them: I am afraid you do not want to carry out] *6* [this deed and I alone will be guilty of a great sin. They replied and all] said [to him:] *7* We [all take an oath and all swear under oath to each other not to go back on this] venture [until] *8* we have performed [this deed...] *9–14* [...] *15* ['Anan'el, thirteenth to him; Sato'el, fourteenth] to him; [Shamshi'el, fifteenth] *16* [to him; Shahari'el, sixteenth to him; Tu]mi'el, seventeenth to him; {Yomi'el} Turi'el, *17* [eighteenth to him; Yomi'el, nineteenth] to him; Yehadi['el, tw]entieth [to him. /They] are the chiefs of the chief-of-tens.]/ *18* [They and their chiefs all took for themselves] women, choosing (from?) among all and they began *19* [to penetrate them and be defiled by them and teach them] sorcery, incantations [and the cutting of roots] *20* [and to explain herbs. They became pregnant by them and gave birth to giants, some three] *21* [thousand cubits tall, who were born upon the earth in keeping with their infancy and grew at the rate of their growth and] consumed *22* [the work of all the sons of men, without the men being able to supply them. The giants] *23* [plotted to kill the men and to consume them and they began to sin and to ... against] *24* [all the birds and animals of the earth and] the reptiles [which move upon the earth and in the sea] *25* [and in the skies and the fish of the sea/ and for some to consume the flesh of the others and] drink the blood./ *25*b [Then the earth denounced the wicked for all] that had been done on it. *26* 'Asa'el taught [men] to manufacture swords of iron and breast-[plates of copper and showed them] *27* what is dug up [and how] /they could work the go[ld to leave it rea]dy;/ /and as for/ silver, /to emboss it/ for brace-lets [and other jewellery for women.] *28* [To the women he divulged] about antimony and eye-shadow [and all the precious stones] *29* [and about dyes...]

Col. III (= *Enoch* 8:2–9:4)   *1* [wickedness became great and they] stray[ed in all their paths. Shemihazah] taught [incantations] *2* [and (how) to cut roots; Hermoni] taught (how) to remove magic, [sorcery, magic and skills; Baraq'el] taught [the signs of] *3* [the rays; Kokab'el] taught the signs of the stars; [Zeq'el taught the signs of the lightning; ...'el taught] *4* [the signs of ...; 'Ar']taqof taught the signs of the earth; [Shamshi'el taught the signs of the sun; Sahari'el] *5* [taught the signs of the moon.] And all began to reveal [secrets to their wives. Since] *6* [a section of men was expiring on the earth,] their outcry [went right up to the sky.] *7* [Then] Michael, Sariel, [Raphael and] Gabriel gazed from the sanctuary [of the heavens] to the earth *8* [and saw much blood spilt] upon the earth; [and all the earth was filled with the evil and violence perpetrated] *9* [upon it. Hearing this the four of them went and said to themselves that the outcry and the wail] *10* [for the des]truction of the sons of the earth [went] right [up] to the gates [of heaven. And they said to the holy ones of heaven: It is now to you,] *11* [holy ones of heaven] to whom [the souls of the sons of men appeal saying: Take our case in front of the Most High] *12* [and our destruction in front of the Majestic Glory and in front of the Lord of all the lords in re-spect of majesty.] *13* [Ra]phael and Michael, [Sariel and Gabriel] went [and said in front of the Lord of the world:] *14* [You are] our great Lord, [you are] the Lord of the world; [you are the God of gods and the Lord of lords and the King of kings.] *15* [The heavens are the throne] of your glory for all the genera-tions which exist since eternity [and all the earth is the footstool in front of you for all of eternity] *16* [and your name is great and] holy and blessed for eve[r...]

Col. IV (= 1 *Enoch* 10:8–12)   *1–4* [...] *5* [all] sin. [And to Gabriel] the Lord [said]: Go [to the bastards and the sons of whoring and exterminate] *6* [the son]s of the Watchers [from among the sons of men; involve them in] a war of attrition [for there will not be] lo[ng days for them.] *7* [Absolutely no] re[quest in their favour will be granted to their fathers; for they hope to li]ve an [everlasting] life [or that] *8* [each one of them will live five hundred years. And to Michael the Lord said: Go, Michael and] tell *9* [Shemihazah and all his friends] who coupled with [women to be defiled by them in their uncleanness that] *10* their sons will expire and they will [see the extermination of their loved ones; chain them up for] seventy ge[nerations in the valleys] *11* of the earth until the great day [of his judgment...]

Col. VI (= *Enoch* 14:4–6)   *1–4* [...may your request] *5* [not be granted to you for all the days of eternity, and] the verdict against y[ou be decided and pronounced;] *6* [right from now may you not] return [to heaven or ascend for all] *7* [eternity;] ver[dict is pron]ounced to shackle you in the prisons of the earth for all the days of eternity;] *8* [before this may you see] all your loved ones and all their sons [go to destruction] *9* and [not enjoy] the belongings [of your loved ones and their sons,] *10* may they fall bef[ore you by the destructive sword...]

4QEnoch^c (4Q204 [4QEn^c ar])

Col. I (= 1 *Enoch* 1:9–5:1)   *1–15* [...] *16* [when he comes with] the myriads of his holy ones [to carry out the sentence against everyone; and he will destroy all the wicked] *17* [and he will accuse all] flesh for all their [wicked deeds which they have committed by word and by deed] *18* [and for all their] arrogant and wicked [words which wicked sinners have directed against him. Weigh up] *19* all the deeds [and notice] the work of [the heavens and the luminaries which do not alter their courses] *20* in the locations of their lights; how they all [rise and set, each one of them in its turn.] *21* Notice the earth and weight up its works, [from the first to the last; how none] *22* alters and everything is evident to you. [Notice the signs...] *23* [...] which all [...] *24* [...] apart from fourte[en trees whose] *23* [leaves survive until] two or three years [go by. Notice] *26* [the indications of summer: how (in it) the] sun burns and warms [and you look for shade and relief] *27* [before it upon the] scorching [face] of the earth without finding a way of walking through the dust or the stones owing to the heat. *28* [Notice and understand] all the trees; on all of them green [leaves sp]rout and on them *29* [they become green, and all their fruits] are for decoration and show. Exalt and [contemplate all these works] *30* [and realise that the living God,] who [lives] for all the everlasting [centuries has made everything.]

Col. II (= 1 *Enoch* 6:7)   *1–23* [...] *24* These are the names of their chiefs: [Shemihazah, who was his chief; 'Ar^cteqof, second to him; Rama'el,] *25* third [to him;] Kokab'el, fourth to him; [...-'el, fifth to him; Ra^cma'el, sixth to him;] *26* Dani'el, se[venth to him;] Zeq'el, eighth [to him; Baraq'el, nin]th to him; ^cAsa'[el, tenth to him;] *27* and Hermoni, [el]eventh to him; Matra['el, twelfth to him;] ^cAnan'el, thirteenth to him; Sato'el, *28* [four]teenth [to him;] Shamshi'el, [fifteenth to him;] Sahari'el, sixteenth to him; *29* Tu[mi'el, seventeenth to him; Turi'el, eighteenth to him; Yomi'e]l, nineteenth to him; *30* [Yehadi'el, twentieth to him. These are the chiefs of ten…]

Col. V (= *Enoch* 10 : 13 – 19 + 12 : 3)   *1* [and to] torture and to [confinement in the] everlasting [prison]. Everyone to be sent[enced will be lost right from now; he will be shackled with them until the destruction] *2* [of his generation.] And at the moment [of the judgment by which] I shall judge they will die for all the [generations. Exterminate all the spirits of the bastards and of the sons of] *3* [the Watchers, because they have caused evil to be done to men.] Exterminate the sin from [the face of the earth, make every evil deed disappear] *4* [and make the] plant of justice [appear; it will be a blessing and the deeds of just men will be planted in enjoyment for ever.] *5* [At that time all the just] will escape and live [until they sire thousands]. All the days of *6* [your youth and of] your old age will be achi[eved in peace…] *7* [Then all the earth will be tilled] in justice and it will all be planted [with trees and filled with blessing. All the trees] *8* [of the earth which they wish for will be planted in it and in it they will plant vines and each vine] planted it in *9* [will yield a thousand amphoras of wine and each seed sown in it will yield] a thousand [*seah*s for every] *10* [*seah* …] *11-18* […] *19* [I, Enoch, was starting to bless the Lord of Majesty, the King of the Centuries, when] here there was the Watcher *20* [of the Great Holy One…] *21-30* […]

Col. VI (= 1 *Enoch* 13 : 6 – 14 : 16)   *1* with [all] their request for their souls for each and all of [their deeds and for all those who asked: for them there might be] *2* [forgiveness and long life.] I fled [and sat next to the waters of Dan, in the country of Dan, which is to the south of] Hermonim at its Western side, *3* [and I was reading the book of records] of their requests [until I fell asleep. Behold, dreams came to me and visions fell upon me] so that [I lifted] *4* my eyelids to the portals of the [palace of heaven…] *5* And I saw a vision of the severity of the punishment. [And a voice came and said to me: Speak to the sons of heaven to admonish them. When I woke up I went] *6* to them. They were all assembled together and seated and [weeping in Abel-Maya (The Spring of Weeping) which is between the Lebanon and Senir, with covered faces.] *7* *Blank* In front of them I related all [the visions which I had seen in dreams and I began to speak] *8* with words of justice and of vision and to admonish the [heavenly] Watchers. *9* *Blank* Book of the words of truth [and of the admonishing of the Watchers who had always existed, according to the command of] *10* [the Great Holy One] in the dream which [I dreamt. In that vision I saw in my dream what I now speak with a tongue of flesh, with the breath of my mouth,] *11* which the Great One gave the sons [of men so they can speak [with it and so they can understand in (their) heart. So just as God has intended and created the sons of men so they can understand] *12* the words of knowledge, he has intended and made and created me to adm[onish the Watchers, the sons of heaven. I wrote down your request, Watchers,] *13* and in a vision was revealed to me that [your request will not be granted to you for all the days of eternity and that there will be a verdict against you by decision] *14* and pronouncement; that right from now [you will not return to heaven or ascend for all the ages; and that the verdict has been pronounced] *15* [to shackle you in the prisons of the earth] for all the days of eternity; [but that before you will see that all your loved ones will go to destruction with all] *16* their sons; and you will not enjoy use of the possessions of your loved ones [and of their sons; they will fall in your presence by the sword] *17* of destruction, for your request for [them will not be granted you just as it is not granted to yourselves. You will carry on] *18* asking and entreating [...You are not to utter even one word] *19* of the writing which I have written. [This was revealed to me in the vision: Behold, in the vision, the clouds were calling me, the mists] *20* shouted to me and the thunders and lightnings [urged me and ... In the vision, the winds caused me to fly, they lifted me up] *21* on high, they took me and placed me in [the heavens. I entered them until I reached the wall of a building made of hailstones] *22* and encircled, so as to be completely surrounded by tongues of fire [which began to alarm me and to ... I entered through these tongues of fire] *23* [until] I reached a huge house [made of hailstones; the walls of this house were like stone planks; they were all] *24* [of snow and the floor w]as made of snow. [The roof was like thunders and lightnings and between them, cherubim of fire; and its sky was of water.] *25* [A burning fire surrounded] all the walls [encircling them completely. And the doors were of burning fire. I entered this house which was as hot] *26* [as fire and as cold as] snow; [in it were none of the pleasures of life. Fear shrouded me and trembling clutched me.] *27* [I was shivering and shaking] and fell [on my face and a vision was revealed to me: Behold I saw another door which opened] *28* [in front of me and another house which] was larger than this, all of it [made of tongues of fire. All of it was so much better than the other in grandeur, glory] *29* [and majesty that I] cannot describe to you [its grandeur and majesty. Its floor was of fire,] *30* [its upper part was of thunders and lightnings and its roof of burning fire. It was revealed to me and in it I saw a raised throne and its appearance...]

Col. VIII (= 1 *Enoch* 18:8–12)   *1–12* [... the top] *27* of the throne was [of sapphire. I saw a burning fire; beyond those mountains there is a place on the other side of the great earth,] *28* and there [the heavens e]nd. [Then I was shown a great abyss between pillars of heavenly fire and I saw] *29* in it pillars [of fire which go down to the bottom: its height and its depth were immeasurable. And beyond] *30* this a[byss ...]

Col. XII (= 1 *Enoch* 30:1–32:1)   *1–22* [...] *23* [...and beyond] them I went away, *24* [very much to the east, and I saw another huge place with valleys with abundant water in] which there were sweet-smelling reeds *25* [comparable to the mastic; and on the sides of these valleys I saw] the aromatic cinnamon. And beyond [these] valleys *26* [I went on to the East. I was shown] other mountains and in those, too, I saw trees from which issued *27* [the resin called *tsaru* and galbanum.] Further from this mountain I was shown [another] mountain *28* [to the East of the limits of the earth, and] all the trees were full of ..., which is comparable to almond peel. *29* [When... in these trees] there comes from them a fragrant aroma; when these peels are ground up, *30* [they are superior to any fragrance. Beyond these mountains,] towards the North-east of them, I was shown mountains

Col. XIII (= 1 *Enoch* 35 (?) + 36 : 1–4)   *1–22* [...] *23* the open doors [...] *24* their number. *Blank* Then [...] *25* From there I was conveyed to the South of the e[nds of the earth, and there I was shown their three open doors] *26* for the South wind, for the dew and the rain [and for... From there I was conveyed to the East of the ends of the earth and there] *27* I was shown their three doors, [open to the East...] *28* of the sky. *29* *Blank* *30* Then ... [...]

Frag. 4 (= 1 *Enoch* 89 : 31–37)   *1* [...] And they were all startled and shaking [in front of him.] *2* [And they shouted to the lamb, which was its second,] which was in their midst: «We are unable to be in front [of the Lord».] *3* [Then the lamb who led them turned,] and climbed for a second time to the top of that rock. But the flock began to go blind *4* [and move off the path which he had indicated to them] without the lamb realising these matters. The Lord of the flock grew extremely angry against [the flock] *5* [and the lamb knew it and came down from the top of that rock] and came to the flock and found most of them blind *6* [and astray. When they saw him they began to get alarmed in fr]ont of him, trying to return to their pens. *7* [The lamb took other lambs with him and came to the] flock. They butchered all the strays and they began to tremble *8* [in front of him ... Then] this lamb made all the stray flock return to their pens. *9* [When the stray flock had returned to their pens, this lamb] busied himself with scolding, killing and punishing whoever had sworn by *10* [...I continued seeing this dream until] that lamb turned into a man, built a Taber[nacle] *11* [for the Lord of the flock and took all the flock to that Taberna-cle. I continued looking until] that lamb who had joined [him fell asleep.]

Frag. 5 *col.* I (= 1 *Enoch* 104 : 13–106 : 2)   *1–19* [...] *20* [... They shall believe in them and exult in them;] all [the just] will exult *21* [in learning from them all the paths of justice. In those days the Lord counted them] among the sons of the earth *22* [to read to them and to give them witness concerning their wisdom, saying: Show it to him si]nce you will be *23* [their guides and you will be re-warded among all the sons of the earth. You shall have] all *24* [reward. Exult, then, sons of justice …] *25* […] *26* [After a time, I, Enoch, took a woman for Methuselah, my son and she bore him a son to whom I gave] the name Lamech *27* [saying: «Surely justice has been demeaned until this day». When he reached adulthood, Methuselah took] a woman [for him] and she *28* [became pregnant by him and gave birth to a son for him. When the child was born his flesh was whiter than the snow and] redder *29* [than the rose and all his hair was white like pure wool, lush and shiny. When he opened his eyes he lit up the] whole *30* [house like the sun …]

Frag. 5 col. II (= 1 *Enoch* 106 : 13 – 107 : 2)   *1-15* […] *16* […Then I, Enoch, replied saying:] *17* Surely [the Lord] will [restore his law upon the earth, according to what I saw and related to you, my son.] In the days of Yared, my father, *18* they infringed [the word of the Lord … they si]nned and infri[nged … they changed in order to go *19* [with women and sin with them; they married some of them who gave birth to creatures not like the spirits but made of flesh.] *20* There will be [great anger and flood over the ear]th [and there will be great devastation for a year. But this boy] *21* born to you [and his three sons] will be sa[ved when those there are above] the earth [die. Then will rest] *22* the earth, and it will be cleansed from the great corruption. [Now say to Lamech: He is your son] truly [and … this] *23* boy [who was born.] He is to be called [Noah, for he will be your repose when you repose in him;] *24* [and he will be your deliverance, for] he [and his sons] will be delivered [from the depravity of the earth – caused by the actions of all sinners] *25* [and by the wicked of the earth – which] will occur in his days. Subsequently there will be even worse wickedness [than this which will have taken place] *26* in his days. For I know the mysteries [of the Lord which] the Holy Ones have told me and have shown me [and which] *27* I read in [the tablets] of heaven. In them I saw written that generation after generation will perpetrate evil in this way and there will be wickedness [until there arise] *28* generations of justice and the wickedness and corruption end and violence [vanishes] from the earth, and until [goodness comes to the earth] *29* above them. *Blank* Now, go to Lamech, your son, and [say to him] *30* that this boy is in truth and without lies his son. [*Blank*].

4QEnoch*d* (4Q205 [4QEn*d* ar])

Frag. 1 col. I (= 1 *Enoch* 22 : 13 – 24 : 1)   *1* […] on the day of judgment they will be tormented outside [of there and they will not be removed] outside of there. *2* [Then I blessed the Lord of Majesty] and said: Blessed be the judgment of justice [and blessed be the Lord] of Majesty *3* [and Justice, who is the Lord of the World.] From there I was conveyed to another place, [to the West of the ends of the earth and I] was shown *4* [a fire which flows without resting] or interrupting its flow [either by day or by night,] remaining steady at the same time. *5* [I asked, saying: What is that which has] no rest at all? [Ra'u'el answered me: This is its] purpose: this fire *6* [which flows towards the West directs the luminaries of the] sky. [And he showed me mountains:] the ground between them [was of burning fire] *7* [which flamed up at night ...]

Frag. 1 *col.* II (= 1 *Enoch* 25 : 7 – 27 : 1)   *1* [he gets up] in front of him, who prepares [such things for men, for the just ones.] These things [he has created and has promised to give them. From there] *2* [I was conveyed to the] centre of the earth and saw a blessed place] in which there were trees [whose branches blossomed continuously.] *3* [There I was shown a holy mountain; and there was water coming out] from underneath [the mountain, from the East, and going down towards the South.] *4* [...] *Blank* [...] *5* [And I saw in the East another mountain, much higher] than this and between them a deep ravine [which had no breadth, through which flowed] *6* [the water which came from underneath the mountain. And to] its [West] another mountain [much lower than this, with no height,] *7* [and a deep, dry ravine beneath it and] between them [there was another ravine between the three mountains. All the ravines were deep] *8* [and of hard rock and there were no trees planted in them.] I was amazed at the mountains [and I was amazed at the ravines, I was absolutely amazed.] *9* [Then I said: Why is this land] blessed [and completely covered with trees...?]

Frag. 2 *col.* I (= *Enoch* 89 : 11 – 14)   *1-23* [...] *24* [... and they began to bite and] chase one *25* [another. The white bull which had been born in their midst sired a wild ass and also a white bullock.] And the wild asses *26* [increased in number. The white bullock, which had been sired by the white bull, sired] a black wild boar and a [white] ram. *27* [The wild boar sired several wild boars and the ram sired twel]ve [ewes.] *28* [When these twelve ewes had grown, they gave one ewe] from among them to the wild asses and the wild asses *29* [gave this lamb to the wolves. And the ewe grew up among wolves. The ram guided] all the ewes

Frag. 2 *col.* II (= 1 *Enoch* 89 : 29 – 31)   *1-26* [...] *27* [and then we climbed to the top] of a high [rock and the Lord of the flock sent her in the middle of the flock;] *28* [and they all kept their distance.] *Blank* [...] *29* [Then I looked and behold the Lord of the flock got up in front] of the flock: his aspect was mighty, magnificent and dreadful, [and all] *30* [the flock saw him and became afraid in front of him. They were all] quaking and frightened [in front of him]

Frag. 2 *col.* III (= 1 *Enoch* 89 : 43 – 44)   *1-25* [...] *26* [...and this ram began] *27* to butt [and to chase with his horns, to hit the foxes and then the wild boars; and he destroyed *28* many wild boars [and then set the dogs free. The ewe, whose eyes had opened, gazed] *29* at this ram [until he abandoned his path, and began to strike the flock and throw them to the ground and he began to walk off] *30* the path. *Blank* [...]

4QEnoch*e* (4Q206 [4QEn*e* ar])

Frag. 1 (= 1 *Enoch* 22 : 3 – 7)   *1* [the souls] of all the sons of men. Thus, then, these are the wells which function as a prison for them. *2* They are made in this way up to the day on which they will be judged, up to the instant of the last day on which *3* the Great Judge will deal with them. *Blank* There I saw the spirit *4* of a dead man, blaming; and his lament rose up to heaven, shouting and blaming. *5* [Then I asked Raphael,] the Watcher and Holy One who [was with me] *6* [and said to him:] Whose is [this spirit which is blaming, whose groan in this fashion] *7* [rises up to heaven, shouting and blaming? He answered] me [saying: This is]

Frag. 2 (= 1 *Enoch* 28 : 3 – 29 : 2 + 31 : 2 – 32 : 3)   *1–2* […] *3* […] one [… which flowed towards the North-east, taking the water and the dew to every section.] *4* [From there] I went to another place [in the desert and I moved away] *5* [a great deal] to the East [from this] location. [There I saw uncultivated trees which] *6* gave off [an aroma of incense and myrrh…] *7–13* […] *14* [… in] it, it is full of resin and is like the bark] *15* [of the almond tree. When] their bark is crushed it is superior to any fragrance. Beyond] *17* these [mountains] towards the North-east of them, I was shown (still) other mountains *18* [full of] choice nard, mastic, cardamum and pepper. *Blank* From there I went on *19* [to the] East of all those mountains, far from them, to the East of the land; I was taken *20* [above] the Red Sea and I moved very far from it; I crossed at the height of *21* darkness, far from it, and was taken to the side of the Paradise of Justice.

Frag. 3 (= 1 *Enoch* 32 : 3 – 6 + 33 : 3 – 34 : 1)   *1* And I was shown fr[om afar, trees in it, over-abundantly numerous and huge trees] *2* differing [from each other. There I saw a tree which was different from all the others, very large] *3* and [beautiful and splendid…] *4–9* […] *10* [and] your first mother, and they learnt [wisdom and their eyes opened and they understood] *11* that they were naked. […] *12–18* […] *19* […Uriel, one of] the Watchers. And [he showed] me *20* [and wrote down everything for me; he even wrote down their names for me,] in accordance with their times. *21* [From there I was conveyed to the North of the edges of the earth] and I was shown great works.

Frag. 4 *col.* I (= *Enoch* 88 : 3 – 89 : 6)   *1–9* […] *10* [… I continued watching in my dream, when, behold one] of *11* [the four who had left received a command from heaven and he took all the] numerous stars *12* [whose sexual organs were like those of horses, and he] bound [them] all hand and foot and hurled them *13* [into an abyss in the earth. One of the four] went to one of the [white] bulls *14* [and instructed him. He bu]ilt for himself a boat, and the boat was covered and roofed *16* [above them. I was] watching and behold, seven streams pouring out *17* [abundant water over the earth.] And behold, the reservoirs in the interior of the earth opened and they began *18* [to spout and lift up the water over it.] I continued to watch until the earth was covered by the water *19* [and by darkness and mists (?) which] hung over it. The bulls were submerged and swallowed *20* [and destroyed by that water.] The boat floated on top of the water and all the bulls, *21* [the wild asses, the camels] and the elephants sank in the water.

Frag. 4 *col.* II (= 1 *Enoch* 89 : 7 – 16)   *1*[Once again I watched in] my dream, until [those streams shut off from that elevated roof] *2* [and the sluices] of the reservoirs closed [and other reservoirs opened. The water began] *3* to sink to its interior, until [the water] vanished [from the surface of the land, and it emerged, and the boat] *4* rested upon the land; [darkness withdrew and there was light. *5-8* [...] *9* [... and there was born] *10* in the midst [of them a white bull. And they began to bite and chase one] *11* another. [The white bull sired a wild ass and also a white bullock. And the wild asses increased in number.] *12* The [white] bullock, [which had been sired by the white bull, sired a black wild boar and a white ram;] *13* [the wild boar sired several wild boars and the ram sired] *14* twelve ewes. [When they had grown, they gave one from among those ewes to the wild asses,] *15* and the wild asses gave [that lamb to the wolves. And that ewe grew up among the wolves.] *16* The ram took [all eleven ewes to live and graze with him] *17* among the wolves; and they increased [in number and changed into a flock with many ewes. And the wolves] *18* began to harass the flock [even causing their kids to die and to hurl their kids] *19* [into a] stream of water. Then [the ewes began to shriek for their young and to wail] *20* [in front of their Lord. One] ewe, which had evaded [the wolves, fled and went to the wild asses. And I watched while *21* [the flock groaned and shrieked horribly] until the Lo[rd of the flock] came down.

Frag. 4 *col.* III (= 1 *Enoch* 89 : 27 – 30)   *1-12* [...] *13* [...] water [...] *14* [I continued watching until all the] wolves who went on chasing that flock [died] *15* [sinking and drowning, and] the water covered them. The fl[ock moved away from] *16* [that water and we]nt to a barren place [in which there was no] *17* [water or grass] and their eyes opened [and they saw. I watched] *18* [until the Lord of the flock fed them] and gave them water and grass [and the ewe] *19* [went and led them. The ewe] climbed to the top of a high rock and the Lord *20* [of the flock sent her to the middle of the flock and] they all kept their [distance. Then] *21* [I watched and behold the Lord of the flock rose up in front of the flock] and [his aspect was mighty]

4QEnoch*f* (4Q207 [4QEn*f* ar])

Frag. 1 (= 1 *Enoch* 86:1–3)   [... Again I was] *1* [staring in the dream and I saw the heaven] above [and behold] a star [fell from the sky in the middle] *2* [of the great bulls and ate and grazed] in the midst of them. And then I saw [those bulls, large] *3* [and black; all of them exchanged their feeds,] their stables and their bullocks [and began to live with each other.] *4* [I looked again in my dream and watched the sky] and behold many stars [came down and fell from the sky] *5* [in the middle of the first star and were turned into] bulls in the middle [of those bullocks and grazed with them and among them]

4QEnoch*g* (4Q212 [4QEn*g* ar])

Col. II (= 1 *Enoch* 91:18–92:2)   *1–13* [...] *14* [...] and he will go [...] *15* [...] they will give it glo[ry...] *16* and the earth shall rest [...] *17* all future generations. [And now I am going to speak to you, my sons and show you all] *18* the paths of justice [and all the paths of violence and again I shall show you them so] *19* you know what is going to happen. [Now, then, my sons, listen to me and choose the tracks] *20* of justice in order to walk on them and [...] *21* because they are going to utter destruction [all those who walk on the path of injustice.] *22* What he wrote and gave to Methu[selah, his son, and to all his brothers, Enoch, the celebrated scribe] *23* [and the wis]est of men, the chosen one among the sons of [the earth to judge their deeds. He wrote to the sons] *24* of their sons and to future generations, to all who [dwell on dry land so that they will achieve good] *25* [and peace: «Do not] upset yourselves [in your spirit on account of the times] *26* [because the Great Holy One] has given [a time for everything ...]

Col. III (= 1 *Enoch* 92:5–93:4)   *1–15* [...] *16* [...] darkness [...] *17* [...] from this day [...] *18* [... When he was delivering his letter] Enoch resumed his speech and said: «I, [Enoch, was born] on the seventh day [in the] first [week] *24* and until my time justice [was] still] [strong. After me will come the] *25* second [week] when deceit and violence will increase. [...]

Col. IV (= 1 *Enoch* 93:9–10 + 91:11–17)   *1–10* [...] *11* [... but all] their deeds will be at fault. *12* [At its close] the chosen ones will be selected as witnesses of the justice of the plant *13* of everlasting justice; they shall be given wisdom and knowledge sevenfold. *14* They shall uproot the foundations of violence and the work of deceit in it in order to carry out [justice.] *15* After this, the eighth week will come, the one of justice, in which [a sword] will be given to all the just, for them to carry out just judgment against the wicked *17* who will be delivered into their hands. At its close, they will gain riches in justice *18* and there will be built the temple of the kingship of The Great One, in his magnificence, for all eternal generations. *19* And after that, the ninth week. [In it] will be revealed jus[tice and just judgment] *20* to all the sons of the whole earth. All those who ac[t wickedly will vanish] from all *21* the whole earth and they shall be hurled into the [eternal] well. All [men will see] *22* the just eternal path. And after [that, the tenth week. In its seventh part] *23* there will be eternal judgment and the moment of the great judgment [and he will carry out revenge in the midst of the holy ones.] *24* In it, the first heaven will pass away [and there will appear a new heaven and all the forces] of heaven *25* will rise throughout all eternity, shining [seven times more. After that there will be] many weeks *26* [the number of which will not] have an end [ever, in which goodness and justice] will be achieved

Col. v (= 1 *Enoch* 93 : 11 – 94 : 2)   *1–13* [...] *14* [... Who, among all men] *15* [... ca]n understand the commandment of [...] *16* can hear the words of the Holy One [without being upset or can visualise his thoughts?] *17* Or who, among all men, [can consider all the works of the heavens or the] *18* angular [columns] upon which they rest; [or who sees a soul or a spirit and can] *19* go back to tell about [it? Or go up and see all their extremities and think or act like them?] *20* Or who [among the sons of men can know and measure what is] *21* the length and breadth of all the earth? Or [to whom has all its ... been shown] *22* and its shape? Who, among all men, can [know what the extent of the heavens is, and what] *23* their height is, or how they are supported, [or how large is the number of the stars?] *24* Now I tell you, my sons: [love justice and walk in it, because] *25* the paths of justice [are worthy of being approved, but the paths of wickedness will be destroyed and will vanish. To the sons] *26* of men [...]

5 The Book of Giants

1QBook of Giants*a* (1Q23 [1QEnGiants*a* ar])

Frags. 1 + 6 + 22   *1* [...two hundred] *2* donkeys, two hundred wild asses, two hun[dred...] *3* rams, two hundred he-goats, two hundred [...] *4* of each animal, of each [...] *5* of dilute wine [six] thousand, of [...] *6* [...] Then [...]

Frags. (9 + 14 + 15   *1* [...] *2* [...] and they knew the mysteries ... [...] *3* [...] great in the earth [...] *4* [...] in the earth [...] *5* [...] the giants [...] of [...]

4QBook of Giants*a* (4Q203 [4QEnGiants*a* ar])

Frag. 1   *1* When I arise [...] *2* Baraq'el [...] *3* my face still [...] *4* I arise [...]

Frag. 2   *1* over them [...] *2* *Blank* [...] *3* Mahaw[ai] replied [...]

Frag. 3   *1* [...] *2* their friends [...] *3* Hobabes and ADK [...] *4* What will he give me to ki[ll ...?]

Frag. 4   *1* [...] in them. [...] *2* [...] *Blank* [...] *3* [Then] 'Ohyah said to Ha[hyah, his brother ...] *4* [...] on top of the earth [...] *5* [...] the earth. When [...] *6* [...] they bowed down and wept in front of [Enoch ...]

Frag. 5   *1* [...]... [...] *2* [...] violence done to men [...] *3* [...] they were killed [...]

Frag. 6   *1* [...] ... [...] *2* [...] went for us [...] *3* [...] ... [...]

Frag. 7 *col.* I   *1-2* [...] *3* and your power [...] *4* *Blank* [...] *5* Then 'Ohyah [said] to Hahyah, [his brother ...] Then he punished not *6* us but Azazel and made him [... the sons] of the Watchers, *7* the Giants; and none of their [beloved beings] will be forgiven [...] he has seized us and has captured you.

Frag. 7 *col.* II   *1-4* [...] *5* [...] to you, Maha[wai ...] *6* the two tablets [...] *7* and the second has not been read up till now [...]

Frag. 8   *1* The book [...] *2* *Blank* [...] *3* Copy of the second tablet of the l[etter ...] *4* written by the hand of Enoch, the celebrated scribe [...] *5* and holy, to Shemihazah and to all his [companions ...] *6* Know that [...] not *7* your deeds and those of your wives [...] *8* they and their sons and the wives of [their sons ...] *9* for your prostitution in the land. It will happen to you [...] *10* and accuse you regarding the deeds of your sons [...] *11* the corruption with which you have corrupted [...] *12* until the coming of Raphael. Behold, there will be destruction [...] *13* those who are in the deserts and those who are in the seas. The explanation of your task [...] *14* upon you for evil. Now, then, unfasten your chains [...] *15* and pray. *Blank* [...]

Frag. 9   *1* [...] and all [...] *2* [...] ... before the splendour of your glory [...] *3* [... your glo]ry, for you know all the mysteries [...] *4* [...] and nothing is stronger than you [...] *5* [...] before you. *Blank* Now, then, the Ho[ly One of the heavens ...] *6* [...] your glorious rule for the [everlasting centuries ...] *7* [...] *Blank* [...]

Frag. 10   *1* [...] And now, my Lord [...] *2* [...] you have multiplied and [...] *3* [...] your wishes and [...]

Frag. 11   *1* [...] *2* the dew and the frost [...]

Frag. 13   *1* [They pros]trated themselves in front of [Enoch ...] *2* [Th]en he said to them: [...] *3* [may there not] be peace for you [...] *4* [...] to be [...]

4QBook of Giants*b* (4Q530 [4QEnGiants*b* ar])

Col. II   *3* [...] Then two of them had nightmares, *4* and the dream fled from their eyes. They [arose ...] *5* and went [to Shemihazah their father and told him] their dreams *6* [...] In my dream which I saw tonight [...] *7* [...] gardeners; they were watering [...] *8* [...] numerous roots issued from its trunk [...] *9* [...] I watched until the springs closed up [...] *10* [...] all the water and the fire burned in everything [...] *11* [...] *12* [...] Here the dream ended. *13* [...] the Giants were searching for someone who would explain *14* [the dream] to them [... to Enoch,] the celebrated scribe and interpret *15* the dream for us. *Blank* Then 'Ohyah, his brother, acknowledged and said in front of the Giants: *16* I also saw something amazing in my dream last night: The Power of the heavens came down to earth *17-19* [...] *20* [...] ... here the dream ended. [Then] all the Giants [and the Nephilim] became alarmed, *21* and they called to Mahawai and he came to them. They implored him and sent him to Enoch, *22* [the celebrated scribe] and they said to him: Go [...] ... and death for you, who *23* [...] hears his voice and tell him to [explain to you] and interpret the dream [...]

Col. III   *3* on one (tablet) the evidence of the Giants [and on the other (tablet) ...] *4* like the hurricane, and flew with his hands like an eagle [provided with wings ...] *5* the earth and crossed Desolation, the great desert [...] *6* and saw Enoch, he called him and said to him: «An oracle [...] *7* here. For a second time I beg you for an oracle [...] *8* your words, together with all the Nephilim of the earth. If he removes [...] *9* from the days of their [...] and may they be punished [...]

10 [so] we know its explanation from you. [... Then Enoch said:] *11* [The two] hundred trees which have come from heaven [...]

4QBook of Giants^c (4Q531 [4QEnGiants^c])

Frag. 1   *1* [...] they were defiled [...] *2* [...] the Giants and the Nephilim and [...] *3* they shall sire [...]. And if all [...] *4* [...] in his blood. And according to the power [...] *5* [... the Giants] which was not enough for them and for [their sons ...] *6* [...] and they demanded much to eat [...] *7* [...] *Blank* [...] *8* [...] the Giants destroyed it [...]

Frag. 2   *3* [...] powerful. And with the strength of my powerful arm and with the might of my power *4* [...] all flesh, and waged war on them. But not *5* [...] I found support to strengthen me, for my accusers *6* [...] (they) reside in the heavens and live with the holy ones and not *7* [...for they] are more powerful than me. *Blank* *8* [...] the roar of the wild beasts has come and they bellowed a feral roar *9* [...] 'Ohyah spoke as follows to him: «My dream has depressed me *10* [...] the dream [has fled] from my eyes at seeing the vision. Surely I know that

6QBook of Giants (6Q8 [6QEnGiants])

Frag. 1   *1* [...] *2* [...] 'Ohyah, and said to Mahawai [...] *3* [...] and do not quake. Who has shown you everything? [...] *4* [...] Baraq'el, my father, was with me. [...] *5* [...] hardly had Mahawai finished telling what he [...] *6* [... said to him:] «I have heard wonders. If a barren person can give birth [...]

Frag. 2   *1* its three roots [... and he was watching] *2* until [...] ca[me..] *3* this whole garden and not [...]

6 The Book of Noah

1QNoah (1Q19 [1QNoah])

Frag. 1   *1* [...] he was [...] *2* [...] they increased in number upon the earth and [...] *3* [... because all men had lost] their path on the earth [...] *4* [... when they perished, they started to cry out] and their cries came before God and [...]

Frag. 2   *1* [Holy Ones] of heaven [...] *2* [saying: Present] our case to [the Most High ...] *3* [...] *4* [and Michael, Sariel, Rapha]el and Gabriel [said to the Lord: ...] *5* [Lord] of Lords and Mighty One [of Mighty Ones *6* [...] of the centuries [...]

4QElect of God (4Q534 [4QMess ar])

Col. I   *1* from the hand two [...] a mark; red is *2* his hair and he has moles upon [...] *Blank 3* and tiny marks upon his thighs [...] different from each other. He will know ... *4* During his youth he will be ... [... like] one who knows nothing, until the time when he *5* knows the three books. *Blank 6* Then he will obtain prudence and will know [...] ... of the visions in order to reach the upper sphere. *7* And with his father and with his ancestors [...] life and old age. With him there will be advice and discretion *8* and he will know men's secrets. His wisdom will extend to all the peoples. He will know the secrets of all living things. *9* All their plans against him will fail, although the antagonism of all living things will be great. *10* [...] his plans, for he is the one chosen by God. His birth and the exhalation of his breath *11* [...] his plans will last for ever. *Blank 12* [...] lest [...] *13* the plan [...] *14–17* [...]

Col. II   *1* [...] which [...] fell in ancient times. The sons of the pit [...] *2* [...] evil. The spot [...] *3* [...] *4* [...] in order to go [...] *5* [...] fle[sh ...] *6* [...] *7* and the exhalation of his breath [...] *8* for ever [...] *9–10* [...] *12* and the cities [...] *13* and they will destroy [...] *14* The waters will end [...] they will destroy ... from the heights. They will all come [...] *15* [...] *Blank 16* [...] and they shall all be destroyed. His work will be like that of the Watchers. *17* Instead of his voice [...] he will establish his foundation upon him. His sin and his error *18* [...] the Holy One and the Watchers [...] to say *19* [he will sp]eak against him [...]

4QAramaic N (4Q535)

Frag. 1   *1* when ... [...] *2* Baraq'el [...] *3* my face once more [...] *4* I arose [...]

Frag. 2   *1* [...] the time of birth [...] *2* [...] the walls of the house of [...] *3–4* [...] ... [...]

Frag. 3   *1* [...] he is born. They are joined in the evening [...] *2* [...] he is born in the night and comes out complete [...] *3* [...with] a weight of three hundred and fifty shekels [...] *4* [...] he sleeps until the middle of the day and ... [...] *5* [...] during the day until he completes the years of [...] *6* [...] he separates from it for him [...]

4QAramaic C (4Q536)

Frag. 1 *col.* I   *1* [...] they will be [...] *2* [...the ho]ly ones will remem[ber] *3* [...] to him will be revealed the lig[hts] *4* [...] all their teaching which *5* [...] the wisdom of man, and every wise man *6* [...] in the region, and he will be great *7* [...] the man will tremble and until *8* [...] he will reveal mysteries. Like Elyonin *9* [...] with the understanding of the mysteries *10* [...] and also *11* [...] in the dust *12* [...] firstly [...] the mystery goes up *13* [...] may he count me among the number of [...] the portion

Frag. 1 *col.* II   *7* of [...] *8* he made. [...] *9* of which you are afraid for all ... [...] *10* he will strengthen its concealment at the end of your powers. Their possessions [...] *11* and he will not die in the days of evil. And wisdom shall issue from your mouth. I will praise you [...] *12* is condemned to die. Who will write the words of God in a book which does not wear out? And my sayings [...?] *13* You will go towards me, and in the time of the wicked he will know you for ever. A man who [...] your servants, [your] sons

Frag. 2   *1* [...] he sleeps until the middle of the day *2* [...] during the day until he completes the years of [...] *3* [...] he separates from it for him [...]

7 Books of the Patriarchs

A *Visions of Jacob*

4QApocryphon of Jacob (4Q537 [4QAJa ar])

Frag. 1   [And I had a vision at night. Behold, an angel of God came down from heaven carrying seven tablets in his hand, and he said to me: God has blessed you, you and] *1* your descendants. And all just men will survive and the upright [...and absolutely no] *2* debauchery [is to be practised] and absolutely no deceit is to be found among [...] *3* And now, take the tablets and read everything [which is written on them. And I took the tablets and read. There were written all my privations] *4* and all my troubles and all that was to happen to me [over the one hundred and forty seven] years of my life. [Again he said to me: Take the tablets from my hands.] *5* [And I] took those tablets from his hand [and read everything.] And I saw written in them that [this place was not to be built as a temple,] *6* [for] you would leave there and on the [eighth] day [your offerings would not be] invalid before [the Most High God...] *7* [...] ... [...]

Frag. 2   *1* [...] And how the building will be [... And how its] priests will dress, and *2* [their hands] purified. [And how] they will offer sacrifices on the altar. And how, as food, they will eat a part of their sacrifices in the whole land. *3* [...] who leave the city and from beneath the walls, and where they [...] *4* [...] *Blank* [...] *5* [...] before me a land of two quarter parts [...]

B *The Aramaic Testament of Judah*

3QTestament of Judah (?) (3Q7 [3QTJuda?])

Frags. 5 + 3 (TestJud 25 : 2?)   *1* [...] ... [...] *2* [Simeon, the] fifth; Issa[char, the sixth; and to all the remainder, each according to his rank. The Lord] praised [Levi;] *3* [to me, (Judah, he allocated)] the angel of the presence, [to Simeon, the power of the glory, to Reuben the heavens, to Issachar] the globe, to Zebu[lon the sea] *4* [...] ... [...]

4QApocryphon of Judah (4Q538 [4QAJu ar])

Frag. a   *1* [... T]hen he devised a plan a[gainst ...] *2* [... ag]ainst me/him; and why in their heart there is [...] against [me/him] *3* [...] ... together they entered ... [...] *4* [...] they will revere. Then he knew that there was no [...] *5* [...] ... and he could not ... again [...] *6* [...] ... on my neck and hugged me ... [...] *7* [...] Joseph again; and all [...] *8* [...] ... [...]

Frag. b   *1* [...] ...[...] *2* [...] *Blank* After I had been brought and introduced *3* [...] their heads, and before Joseph *4* [... an] evil [sp]irit and he could not again *5* [...] ... [... ag]ainst his brothers *6* [...] fearing *7* [...] and not

C *The Aramaic Testament of Joseph*

4QApocryphon of Joseph (4Q539 [4QAJo ar])

Frag. 2   *1* [...] Jacob [...] *2* [And now, l]isten, my son [...hear] me, my loved ones, [...] *3* [... the s]ons of my uncle Ishmael [...] my father Jacob observed mourning [...] *4* [...] count coins, and the slave [...] eighty of the kind [...] *5* [...] to them; if he ask[s ...] to scorn the messenger [...] *6* [...] this. Why do you [wait...] my brother, to scorn [...] *7* [...] mercy ... [...] the men [...]

D *Aramaic Testament of Levi*

1QAramaic Levi (1Q21 [1QTLevi ar])

Frag. 1   *1* [...] for they will be threefold [...] *2* [...] the sovereignty of the priesthood will be greater than the sovereignty of [...] *3* [...] ... [...]

Frag. 3   *1* [and for the sovereignty of the] sword, [the war ...] *2* [sometimes] you shall work and other times you sh[all rest. Sometimes ...] *3* [the greatness of] an eternal peace [...]

Frag. 7   *1* [...] until you *2* [...] you shall rule with whomever *3* [...] he seeks

Frag. 8   *1* [...] and he rewarded. *Blank* And I [...] *2* [...] he rewarded, and every man [...] *3* [...] I [...]

Frag. 30   *1* [...] ... [...] *2* [...] not for fornication [...] *3* [...] to seek [...]

4QAramaic Levi*ᵃ* (4Q213 [4QTLevi*ᵃ* ar])

Frag. 1 *col.* I   *1-5* [...] *6* [...] I *7* [...I wa]shed and all *8* [...] I lifted to heaven *9* [...] and the fingers of my hands and my arms *10* [...] and I said: Lord, you *11* [...] only you know *12* [...] paths of truth; remove *13* [...] evil, fornication; turn aside *14* [...] wisdom in intelligence and strength *15* [.. to] find favour before you *16* [...] what is beautiful and good before you *17* [... may] no foe rule over me *18* [...] to me, Lord, and approach me so that it may be for you

Frag. 1 *col.* II   *1-5* [...] *6* Lord, you have bless[ed ...] *7* tr[ue] offspring [...] *8* the prayer of your ser[vant ...] *9* true judgment for a[ll the centuries ...] *10* to the son of your servant be[fore me ...] *11* Then I went to [...] *12* to my father Jacob and [...] *13* of Abel-Mayin. Then, [...] *14* I lay down and settled upon [...] *15* *Blank* Then I saw visions [...] *16* seeing this vision, I saw heaven [...] *17* underneath me. It rises to reach up to heaven [...] *18* to the gates of heaven, and an angel [...]

Frag. 2   *2* [...] the men *3* [...] the woman and she will defile her name and her father's name *4* [...] ... and all *5* [... the young] woman of the destruction of her name and of the name of her fathers for all her brothers *6* [...] her father, and the name of her disgrace will not be disclosed for all her people for ever *7* [... it will be cu]rsed for all eternal generations. [...] the holy one of the people *8* [...] holy tithe, an offering for the God of

Frag. 3   *1* [...] your priesthood of all flesh *2* [...] I awoke from my dream. Then *3* [... and I saw] this, too, in my heart and did not [reveal it] to any person. *4* [...] When my father Jacob was separating the tithe *5* [...] and he gave to me among his sons *6* [...] ...

Frag. 4   *10* [...Again you shall wash your hands and] your feet [from the blood,] *11* [and you shall begin to offer the sal]ted [portions. The head [will be offered] *12* [first; cover it with fat,] and [the blood of slaughter] *13* [of the cow should not be seen. Afterwards, the neck. And after the neck, the shoulder blades,] and after the shoulder blades, [the breast] *14* [with the ribs. And after the shoulder blades,] the hips and the b[ack.] *15* [And after the hips, the wa]shed [hooves,] with the entrails. And a[l]l *16* [salted with salt, in the way which] is fitting [for them.] *Blank* And af[ter this,] *17* [flour mixed with oil. And] after everything, [pour] wine, *18* [and incense should be wafted over them,] so that your service may be in or[der and all the offerings...]

Frag. 5 col. I   *1* [And in the year one hundred and eighteen of my life, the year] in which [my brother Joseph] died, *2* [I summoned my sons and their sons, and I began to explain] to them *3* [all that there was in my heart. I began speaking and said to my sons: «Listen to] the word *4* [of Levi, your father, and pay attention to the precepts of the beloved of God.] I, to you *5* [my sons, give orders, and to you I show the truth, my beloved ones. The beginning of] all your deeds *6* [should be the truth, and] justice and truth rem[ain for ever,] *7* [... go]od. Whoever sows goodness, harvests good, *8* [and whoever sows evil, against him his see]d [turns.] *Blank* But now, the book and the instruction and wisdom *9* [teach them to your sons, and wisdom will be for you] for eternal honour. He who teaches wisdom will be honoured *10* [by it, but he who despises wisdom] will be given to insult and scorn. See them, my sons, *11* [...] wisdom for honour and for greatness and for the kings *12* [...] Do not renounce wisdom for the teaching *13* [...] Every man who teaches wisdom, all *14* [his days will be lengthened and multiplied will be his re]nown. In each region and province to which he goes, *15* [he will have a brother, and will not be a foreigner] in it, and will not be likened in it to every alien, nor *16* [be likened to a foreigner. Instead, all] shall give him glory for it, for all desire *17* [to learn from his wisdom. His fri]ends are many, and numerous those who desire his good *18* [And they shall seat him upon a throne of glory, to] listen to the words of his wisdom. *19* [A great richness of glory is wisdom for] whoever knows it, and a treasure *20* [for all who acquire it. If] powerful [kings come and a [great] people and an army *21* [of horsemen and many chariots with them, and they take the possessions of the region and of the province] *22* [and steal everything there is in them, they cannot steal the treasure of wisdom, nor will they find]

Frag. 5 col. II *1* its secrets, nor enter its gates, nor [...nor] *2* will they be able to destroy its ramparts, nor [...] *3* will they see the well of its treasure [...] *4* and there is no price compared to her [...] *5* seek wisdom [...] *6* which has hidden itself from it [...] *7* and there is no lac[k ...] all those who seek *8* truth [...] the book and the instruction *9* and wi[sd]om, teac[h them to them...] you will instruct them *10* [...] great. You shall give *11* [...glo]ry. *Blank* *12* [...] also in the books *13* [...you sh]all be chiefs and judges *14* [...] and servants *15* [...] and also priests and kings *16* [...] your kingdom *17* [...] will have no end *18* [...] will pass from you until all *19* [...] with great glory

Frag. 5 col. III *1* [...] all the peoples *2* [...] the moon and the stars *3* [...] of *4* [...] the moon *5* [...] you will become dark [...] *6* Did not Enoch accuse [...?] *7* [...] And upon whom will the blame fall, *8* [...] except upon me and upon you, my sons? Then you will know *9* [...] you will forsake the paths of justice and all the ways of *10* [...] you will renounce and you will walk in dark[ness] *11* [...] a great tribulation will come upon you, and you will be delive[red up] *12* [...] strong and [...] and they shall be for those knowing

4QAramaic Levi*b* (4Q214 [4QTLevi*b* ar])

Frag. 1 *1* [When you go to offer upon the altar, wash hands and feet again. Offer the] split [wo]ood; *2* [but scrutinise it fi]rst for all [the worms and af]terwards, [offer] it. [For] thus I saw Abraham, *3* [my father, looking out for] any obstacle. *Blank* [Twe]lve (kinds of) wood did [he show] me [of those] which can be offered upon the altar, *4* [whose aroma] rises, pleasing. And these are their nam[es: ce]dar, juni[per,] almond, *5* [tamarind, pine, ash, cypress, fig, olive, lau]rel, myrtle *6* [and balsam.] These are what he sho[wed] me, [from which one could make offerings] under the offering *7* upon the altar. *Blank* [When you offer] any of these (kinds of) woo[d] upon the al[tar and the fi]re st[arts] *8* to bur[n them, then you shall begin to sprinkle the blood] upon the sides of the altar. Again, [you shall wash] *9* [your hands and your feet from the blood and you shall begin to offer] the sal[ted por]tions, the hea[d, first.]

Frag. 3 *col.* II   *1* and from the provinces [and they steal everything there is in them, they cannot steal the treasure of wisdom,] *2* nor will they find [its secrets ...] *3* and there is no pr[ice compared to her ...] *4* from it, and [it has] not been] hidden from it [...] *5* ... the book and the [instruc]tion and wi[sdom, teach them to them ...] *6* ... [...]

4QAaronic Text A = Testament of Levi^c (?)
(4Q540 [4QAhA = 4QTLevi^c])

1 [...] Again distress will come upon him and the little one will lack goods and will [ask ...] *2* [...] fifty-two weeks. Again, a famine will come upon him, and he will lack goods [...] *3* [...] and he will not resemble a merchant of goods, but instead like the great sea [...] *4* [...] he will leave the house in which he was bred, and another dwelling [...] *5* [...and he will rebuild, like] a servant of God, [with] his goods, another sanctuary which will be consacrated [...]

4QAaronic Text A = Testament of Levi^d (?)
(4Q541 [4QAhA = 4QTLevi^d ?])

Frags. 1 + 2 *col.* I   *3* the totality has meditated upon [...] ... *4* he will cause the idols to fall [...] *5* and all their sighs [...] he will utter words, and in conformity with the will *6* of God, he will keep [...he has ad]ded a further book for me *7* and a second [...] and he will speak about him in enigmas *8* [...] and he approached me, but remaining at the time far from me *9* [... such that] his vision [was not se]cret. And I said: the fruits of

Frag. 2 *col.* II + 3 + 4 *col.* I + 5   *1* uncertain. Behold [...] *2* from before God [...] *3* you will take the smitten [...] *4* I will bless you. A holocaust [...] the foundation of his peace [...] ... *5* your spirit, and you will rejoice [...] To you I address my poems [...] ... *6* Behold a wise man who [rises] to st[udy the instruction of wisdom] and understands the depths and utters enigmas. *7* ... [...] he will come before you whom you have taken from the nest, and the bird *8* he has hunted and he has asked it for [...] to eat it. See, you will be very happy, and greatly the place of

Frag. 4 *col.* II + 6   *1* [and] the earth [...] *2* to the son of Jos[eph ...] those smitten for [...] *3* here [...] your judgment and you will not be gui[lty ...] *4* your blood

[…] the blows of your pains (?) which […] *5* for the captives […] your rest has not lessened and all […] *6* of […] your heart of […]

Frag. 7   *1* and he will reveal [the secr]et of the abysses […] *2* who does not understand the written text […] *3* and he will make the great sea be silent for […] *4* Then, he will open the books of wisdom […] *5* his word. And, like the wicked, the wise [man …] *6* [his] teac[hing …]

Frag. 9 col. I   *1* […] the sons of the generation […] *2* […] his wisdom. And he will atone for all the children of his generation, and he will be sent to all the children of *3* his people. His word is like the word of the heavens, and his teaching, according to the will of God. His eternal sun will shine *4* and his fire will burn in all the ends of the earth; above the darkness his sun will shine. Then, darkness will vanish *5* from the earth, and gloom from the globe. They will utter many words against him, and an abundance of *6* lies; they will fabricate fables against him, and utter every kind of disparagement against him. His generation will change the evil, *7* and […] established in deceit and in violence. The people will go astray in his days and they will be bewildered

Frag. 9 col. II   *4* who has seen a […] *5* seven rams (?) watc[hing…] *6* one part of their sons will go […] *7* and they will be added to […]

Frag. 24 col. II   *1* […] … […] *2* Do not mourn for him […] and do not […] *3* And God will notice the failings […] the uncovered failings […] *4* Examine, ask and know what the dove has asked; do not punish one weakened because of exhaustion and from being uncertain a[ll …] *5* do not bring the nail near him. And you will establish for your father a name of joy, and for your brothers you will make a tested foundation rise. *6* You will see it and rejoice in eternal light. And you will not be of the enemy. *Blank 7 Blank*

4QTestament of Naphtali (4Q215 [4QTNaph])

Frag. 1   *1* with the sisters of Bilhah's father, my mo[ther … and] Deborah, who suckled Rebe[cca …] *2* And he went to captivity, but Laban went and freed him; and he gave Hana to him, one of his maidservants [who begot for him the first] *3* daughter, Zilpah. He gave her the name of Zilpah, the name of the city in which he had been prisoner. […] *4* And she conceived and gave birth to Bilhah, my mother. Hana gave her the name of Bilhah, for when she was born [straight away] *5* hurried to suck. And she said: 'How my daughter hurries!' And from then she called her Bilhah (hurried). *6 Blank* When Jacob, my father, came to Laban fleeing away from his brother Esau, … […] *8* of the father of Bilhah, my mother. And Laban led Hana, my mother's mother, and the two daughters, [and he gave one] *9* [to Leah] and the other to Rachel. And as Rachel did not bear sons [...] *10* [... to Ja]cob, my father. And he was given Bilhah, my mother, and she bore Dan, my brother [...] *11* [...] to the two sisters [...]

Frag. 2 col. II   *1* [...] ... from the well, *2* and the dread of the precipice, and the anguish of the pit. And they shall be refined in them to (be) chosen of justice ... *3* on account of his pious ones; for the age of wickedness had expired and all injustice will pass [away.] *4* The time of justice has arrived, and the earth will be filled with the knowledge and the praise of God. In the da[ys ...] *5* the age of peace arrives, and the laws of truth, and the testimony of justice, to instruct [them] *6* in God's paths and in the marvels of his deeds [...] for eternal centuries. Every [creature ?] *7* will bless him, and every man will bow down before him, [and they will have] a single heart. For he [knows ?] *8* their actions before they were created, and [makes] of the service of justice the division of their frontiers *9* for their generations. For the dominion ‹of justice› of goodness has arrived, and he will raise the throne of [...] *10* and knowledge is exalted; intelligence, prudence and success are proved by the deeds of [his] holiness *11* [...] ... [...]

Frag. 3   *1* of his holiness will establish them for [...] *2* he creates them to ren[ew ...] *3* of their days. And the darkness [...] *4* for their feasts ... darkness [...] *5* for the feasts before [...] *6* [...] his will [...]

Frag. 4   *1* [...] ... [...] to destroy the earth with his anger and to renew [...] *2* [...] the wall of his knowledge, because [...] *3* [...] the weak [...]

E *The Aramaic Testament of Qahat*

4QTestament of Qahat (4Q542 [4QTQahat ar])

Col. I   *1* and God of gods for all the centuries. And he will make his light shine upon you and make you know his great name *2* and you will know that he is the God of the centuries, the lord of all works, and has control *3* over all, to deal with them as he pleases. And he will give you glory and happiness to your sons in the generations of *4* justice for ever. And now, my sons, make note of the inheritance which has been transmitted to you *5* and which your fathers have given you, and do not give your inheritance to foreigners or your riches *6* to pretenders, to be induced into humiliation in their eyes, for they will scorn you because *7* they would be residents for you and they would be chiefs over you. Comply with the words of Jacob, *8* your father, and ... the directives of Abraham and the justice of Levi and mine, and be holy and pure *9* from all [un-cleanness] ..., complying with the truth and walking in uprightness and not with a double heart, *10* but with a pure heart and with a truthful and good spirit. And you, my sons, will give me a good name, and there will be glory *11* for Levi and joy for Jacob and rejoicing for Isaac and honour for Abraham, because you have kept *12* and taken the inheritance which your fathers gave you, truth, justice, uprightness, *13* perfection, purity, holiness and the priesthood according to all that he commanded you and according to all that

Col. II   *1* I taught you in truth from now and for all [the centuries ...] *2* all the word of truth will come upon you [...] *3* eternal blessings will rest upon you and will be [for you ...] *4* will be for all the eternal generations and there will be no more [...] *5* of your punishment and you will rise to make the judgment [...] *6* and to see the sin of all the sinners of the world [...] *7* in the fire and in the abysses and in all the caves so as not to [...] *8* in the generations of justice; and all the sons of wickedness will vanish [...] *9* And now, to you, ⁽Amram, my son, I order you [...] *10* and your sons and their sons; I order you [...] *11* that they give to Levi, my father and which Levi, my father has gi[ven] me [...] *12* all my writings as evidence, so that you will wait for them [...] *13* for you in them great worth, using them to guide you. *Bla[nk ...]*

Col. III   *5* [... in order to] read and [...] *6* [...] their sons [...] *7* [...] men and li[fe ...] *8–9* [...] ... [...] *10* [upon] them and upon [...] *11* darkness and ... [...] *12* and the light, but [...] *13* and I ... [...]

F   *Visions of Amram*

4QVisions of Amram^*a*^ (4Q543 [4Q^*c*^Amram^*a*^ ar])

Frag. 1   *1* Copy of the writing of the words of the visions of ⁽Amram, son of [Qahat, son of Levi. All that] *2* he revealed to his sons and what he advised them on [the day of his death, in the year one hundred] *3* and thirty-six, the year of [his death: in the year one hundred] *4* and fifty-two of the ex[ile of Isra]el to Eg[ypt...] *5* upon him and he sent [and called to Uzzi'el] his youngest brother [...] *6* to him Miriam [his daughter and said: You (f.) are] thirty [years old.] *7* [And he gave a feast for seven days and ate and drank during] the fea[st.] *8* [Then, when the days of the feast were completed, he s]ent [and called]

Frag. 2   *1* [...] from your lord will give you [...] *2* for ever will give you wisdom [...] *3* [...] ... [...]

Frag. 3   *1* [...] you will be God, and angel of God will you be cal[led] *2* [...] and you will do in this land, and a judge [...] *3* [...] ... your name for all [...] *4* [...] for eternal generations [...] *5* [...] ... you will do [...] *6* [...] ... [...]

Frag. 4   *1* [... your fathers,] and [my father Qahat] left me [there ...] *2* [...] from the land [of Canaan ...]

Frag. 5   *1* Therefore (?) [...] *2* and with all this [...] *3* my protection [...] *4* I have taken [...]

Frag. 6   *1* [...] ... [...] *2* [... I ra]ised my eyes and saw that one of [...] *3* [... and his clo]thing was coloured and obscured [by darkness...] *4* [...] *Blank* And I looked at the other, and be[hold...] *5* [...] and his face was smiling and he was covered with [...] *6* [...] ... [...] and all their eyes [...]

4QVisions of Amram*b* (4Q544 [4Q*c*Amram*b* ar])

Frag. 1   *1* Qahat there to stay and to dwell and to bui[ld the tombs of our fathers...] *2* a man, and about our work it was very much until [we have buried the dead ... and they retreat (?) *3* quickly, and they do not build the tomb which their fathers [...] *4* until we build. *Blank* And it was war between [...] *5* And they closed the [bor]der of Egypt and it was not possible to [...] forty-one years, and we could not [...] *7* between Egypt and Canaan and Philistia. *Blank* [...] ... [...] *8* and she was not. *Blank* I, myself, ano[ther] woman [...] *9* all: that I will return to Egypt in peace and I will see the face of my wife [...] *10* in my vision, the vision of my dream. And behold, two were quarrelling over me and they said: [...] *11* and they entered into a great debate over me. And I asked them: You, why are you [...over me? And they replied and said: We] *12* [have received] control and control all the sons of Adam. They said to me: Which of us do you [choose ...? I lifted my eyes and saw] *13* [that one] of them had a dreadful appearance [...] and his clothing was coloured and obscured by darkness [...] *14* [And I looked at the other, and behold [...] in his appearance and his face was smiling and he was covered with [...] *15* a great deal, and all their eyes ...]

Frag. 2   *1* [...] ruling over you [...] *2* [...] this, who are you? And he said to me: This [...] *3* [...] and Melki-resha*c*. *Blank* I said: My Lord: What [...] *4* [...] dark and all his work is dark, and in darkness he [...] *5* [...] you see. And he rules over all darkness, and I [...] *6* [... from the] upper [regions] up to the lower regions, I rule over all that is bright and all [...]

Frag. 3   *1* [of his favour and of his peace. And I] have acquired power [over all the sons of] light. I asked him and said to him: What [are your names?] *2* [...He replied and] said to me: My three names [are ...]

4QVisions of Amram^c (4Q545 [4Q^{c}Amram^c ar])

1 Copy of the [writing of the words of the visi]ons of ^{c}Amram, son of Qahat, son of Levi. All *2* that [he revealed to his sons and what he advised] them on the day of [his death, in the] year *3* one hundred and thirty-six, the year of his death: [in the ye]ar one hundred *4* and fifty-two of the exile of Israel to Egypt. [... upon him and he sent] *5* and called Uzzi'el, his youngest brother [...] to him [Miriam,] his daughter [and said:] *6* You are thirty years old. And he gave a feast for seven [day]s *7* and ate and drank during the feast. Then, when *8* the days of the feast were completed, he send and called Aharon, his son. He was [...] years old *9* [...] to him: Call Malachiyah [...] from the house of *10* [...] above [...] him. *11* [...] I *12* [...] my father *13* [...] from *14* [...] growing *15* [...] ... *16* [...] he steals *17* [... you will be old, and an]gel of God *18* [you will be called ... from] this [earth and] *19* [a judge...] your name to all

Frag. 1 *col.* II　　*11* in this land, and I went up to [...] *12* to bury our fathers. And I went up [... Qahat there] *13* to stay and to dwell and to build [...] *14* many from the sons of my uncle, together [... a man, and about] *15* our work it was very much un[til we have bu]ried the dead [...] *16* rumour of war, frightening those of us [retur]ning to the land of Eg[ypt ... and they retreat (?)] *17* quickly, and they do not bu[ild the to]mb which their fathers [...] *18* and to build and to obtain for them [...fr]om the land of Canaan [...] *19* we ourselves build. And war [broke out between Canaan and] Philistia and Egypt and was winning [...]

Frag. 2　　*1* [...] and I will show you [...] *2* [...] See, God ... and also [...] *3* and I will show you the mystery of his service, holy judgment [...] *4* holy for him will be all his descendants for all [eternal] generations [...] *5* the seventh of the men of His will [and he will] call and he will [...] *6* he will choose as eternal priest. *Blank* [...]

4QVisions of Amram^e (4Q547 [4Q^{c}Amram^e ar])

Frag. 1　　*1* [...] ... [...] *2* [...] I rescued [...] *3* [...] he built [...] *4* [...] in Mount Sinai [...] *5* [...] great upon the bronze altar [...] *6* [...] the priest will be exalted among all my sons for ever. Then [...] *7* [...] and their sons after him for all eternal generations in tru[th ...] *8* [...] And I awoke from the sleep of my eyes and I wrote the vision [...] *9* [...] and from the land of Canaan. And it happened to me as he said [...] *10* [...] ... and afterwards he took twen[ty ...] *11* [...] ... [...]

Frag. 2　　*1* [...] ... you will take off and when you rise [...] *2* [...] the first to the second [...] *3* [... over] his soul they were twisting between the two of them [...] *4* [...] ... [...] *5* [...] ... the friend and a great [...] *6* [...] the friend to [...]

4QVisions of Amram^f (4Q548 [4Q^{c}Amram^f ar])

1 [...] staffs [...] to them and all [their] ways [...] *3* [...] them from their healers [...] *4* [...] them from death and from an[nihilation ...] *5* [...] for you, sons of the blessing [...] *6* [...] all generations of Israel for all [centuries ...] *7* [...] [...] rejoice in me, because the sons of ri[ghteousness ...] *8* you will be ca[lled ...] your [name?,] sons of lie and not sons of [truth ...] *9* I will [let you know the] desirable [way,] I would let you know [... For the sons of light] *10* will be brilliant, and all the sons of darkness will be dark. [For the sons of light ...] *11* and for all their knowledge they will be [...] but the sons of darkness will be destroyed [...] *12* For all senselessness and ev[il are dark,] and all [pea]ce and truth are brilliant. [This is why the sons of light] *13* will go to the light, to [everlasting] happiness, [to rejoicing;] and all the sons of dark[ness will go to the shades, to death] *14* and to annihilation. [...] There will be light for the people and they shall live [...] *15* And they will make kn[own ...] from darkness. For all [the sons of ... and all] *16* the sons of [...] and all the sons of light [...]

Frag. 2 col. I   *1-8* [...] ... *9* [...] to the East *10* [...] elect for the truth *11* [...] there, and the deeds of the truth *12* [...] all the end of dark annihilation *13* [...] the evil. And from every senseless *14* [...] he is [...] *15* [...] darkness [...] *16* [...] ... [...]

Frag. 2 col. II   *1-6* [...] *7* they will be [...] *8* progeny [...] *9* to the month [...] *10* ... [...] *11* weighed [...] *12* they will come from [...] *13* his portentous work from one to the [other ...] *14* of the tenth day. And in [...] *15* [...] of the dawn; and the sons of [...] *16* [...] ... [...] *17* [...] ... [...]

Frag. 3   *1* [...] great [...] *2* and you will be strangled [...] *3* When the man from the likeness [...] *4* and he will see no more the shame [...] *5* [gr]eat [...] ... [...]

G *Hur and Miriam*

4QHur and Miriam (4Q549)

Frag. 1   *1* [...] ... [...] *2* [...] to Egypt [...] *3* [...] ... [...]

Frag. 2   *1* what he ate, he and his sons [...] *2* her husband eternal sleep [...] *3* upon him and they found him [...] *4* his sons and the sons of his broth[er...] *5* and they went back outside a moment, [...] *6* to leave for the eternal dwelling. [...] *7* *Blank* And from [...] *8* ten. And from Miriam he sired a people [...] *9* and to Sitri. *Blank* And Hur married [...] *10* And from her he sired Ur and Aa[ron ...] *11* from her four sons [...]

8 Pseudo-Moses

A *Words of Moses*

1QWords of Moses (1Q22 [1QDM])

Col. I   *1* [And God spoke] to Moses in the year [forty] of the departure of the children of Israel from [the land of] Egypt, in the eleventh month, *2* the first day of the month, saying: [Muster] all the congregation, climb [Mount Nebo] and stay there, you *3* and Eleazar, Aaron's son. *Blank* Interpret [for the heads of] families of the levites and for all the [priests] and decree to the sons of *4* Israel the words of the Law which I commanded [you] on Mount Sinai to decree to them. [Proclaim] in their ears everything *5* accurately, for [I will require] it from them. [Take] the heavens and the [earth as witnesses] for they will not love *6* what I have commanded them, they and their so[ns, all the] days [they live upon the ea]rth. [However] I announce *7* that they will desert me and ch[oose the sins of the na]tions, their abominations and their disreputable acts [and will serve] *8* their gods, who for them will be a trap and a snare. They will [violate all the] holy [assemblies], the sabbath of the covenant, [the festivals] which today I command [to be kept. This is why] I will strike them with a great [blow] in the midst of the land for *10* the conquest of which they are going to cross the Jordan there. And when all the curses happen to them and strike them until they die and until *11* they are destroyed, then they will know that the truth has been carried out on them. *Blank* And Moses turned towards Eleazar, son of *12* [Aaron] and to Joshua [son of Nun, saying] to them: Speak [all the words of the Law, without leaving any out. Be silent,]

Col. II   *1* Israel, and listen! On this day [you are going to become the peo]ple of God, your G[od. Ke]ep [my rules], my stipulations, [my commandments] which *2* today [I] am commanding you [to carry out. And when you cross the Jordan] for me to give you large [and good] cities, *3* houses full of every [wealth, vineyards and olive groves] which you [did not plant, wel]ls bored which you did not *4* dig, and you eat and become replete, [bew]are of raising your heart and fo[rgetting what] I command you today; *5* [for] it is your life and your old age. *Blank* [And] Moses [spoke] and [said to the sons of Is]rael: Forty *6* [years] have passed [from the] day of our departure from the land [of Egypt, and] to-day God, our G[od has caused these wo]rds [to issue] from his mouth *7* [all his pre]cepts {and all his precepts} How [shall I alone carry] your burden, [your weight, your qua]rrels? *8* [When] the covenant [has been estab]lished and the path [on which you must] walk has been decreed, [choose for yourselves wise men who] will explain *9* [to you and your so]ns all the words of this Law. [Be] very [careful,] for your lives, [to keep them, lest] the wrath *10* [of your God] against you be enkindled and reach you, and it closes the skies above, which make rain fall upon you, and [the water] from under[neath the earth which gives you *11* [the harv]est. *Blank* And Moses [continued speaking] to the so[ns of Is]rael: Th[ese are the command]ments [which God] commands you to carry out *12* […]… […]

Col. III   *1* [Every seven years you shall leave the land] at rest, [and the yield of the land's rest will provide you] with food, you [and your animals and the beasts of the] field. *2* […And what] remains will be for the po[or from among your brothers] who are in the la[nd. No]-one will so[w his field] or prune [his vine.] *3* [No-one will harvest his harvest or] gather [anything. Keep al[l the words of] this covenant *4* [carrying them out,] for […] in order to do […] And in this year you shall grant a release. *5* [Every creditor] who [has lent something to] someone, or [who possesses something from his brother,] will grant a re[lease to his fell]ow for *6* [God], your [God, has proclaimed the release. You are to demand restitution] from the fore[igner, but from your brother] you shall not demand restitution, for in that year *7* [God will bless you, forgiving you your si]ns …] *8* […] in the year […] of the month of *9* […] on this day […Because your fathers] wandered *10* [in the wilderness until the tenth day of the month {the[… on the te]nth [day] of the month} *11* You shall refrain [from all work.] And on the tenth day of the month, you shall atone […] of the month *12* […] they shall take […]

Col. IV   *1* in the congregation of the gods [and in the council of the holy] ones, and in [… in favour of the sons of Is]rael and on behalf of the la[nd] *2* [And you shall] take [the blood and] pour [it] on the earth […] *3* […] and it will be forgiven them [… And] Moses [spoke saying:] Do […] *4* […] eternal precepts for your generations […] And on the […] day *5* […] he will take […] the children of Israel […] *6* […] all that which […] for all *7* […] of the […] year the person who […] *8* […] upon the book […] the priest […] *9* […] he will lay his ha[nds …] all this *10* […] in the […] year these *11* […] of the two … […]

B *Pseudo-Moses*

1QLiturgy of the Three Tongues of Fire (1Q29)

Frag. 1   *1* […] … […] *2* […] the stone. When […] *3* […] by tongues of fire. […] *4* [… until] the priest […] stops speaking *5* […who] speaks to you. Behold […] *6* […] who speaks. Dwell […] *7* […] YHWH, God of […]

Frag. 2   *1* […] … […] *2* [… the] right st[one] when the priest leaves […] *3* […] three tongues of fire […] *4* […] And after he shall go up and remove his shoes […]

Frags. 3–4   *1* [...] ... [...] *2* [...] YHWH, your God, [...] *3* [...] all Israel [...] *4* [...] with all. Your name [...] *6* [...] the greatness of the power of the glorious ones [...]

Frags. 5–7   *1* [...] these words, according to all [...] *2* [...] the priest will explain all his will to all [...] *3* [...] the assembly. *Blank* [...] *4* [... Children of] Israel, keep these words [...] *5* [...] to do all [...] *6* [...] the number of ... [...] *7* [...] ... [...]

4QApocryphon of Moses A (4Q374 [4QapocrMoses A])

Frag. 2 *col.* II   *1* together and [...] *2* And the nations will rise in anger [...] *3* through their deeds and through the impurity of their actions [...] *4* and for [you] there will be neither remnants nor survivor; and for their descendants [...] *5* and he planted for us, his chosen ones, in a land preferable to all other lands [...] *6* And he made him like God for the powerful ones, and a fright for the Pharaoh [...] *7* And their hearts melted and trembled and their entrails dissolved. [But] he took pity on [them...] *8* And when he made his face shine upon them for healing, to strengthen their hearts anew and *9* and no-one knew you, but they melted and trembled. They were startled at the voice [...] *10* [...] to them [...] for salvation

4QApocryphon of Moses B (4Q375 [4QapocrMoses B])

Col. I   [you shall do] *1* [all that] your God commands you by the prophet's mouth, and you shall keep *2* [all these pre]cepts, and shall return to YHWH, your God with all *3* [your heart and with all] your soul, and your God will repent of the fury of his great wrath *4* [in order to save] you from all your troubles. However, the prophet who rises up to preach *5* [apostasy] to you, [to make you] move far from God, shall die. And if the tribe *6* from which he comes should rise up and say: «He is not to die, for he is a just man, he is a *7* trustworthy prophet», you shall come with that tribe and your elders and your judges *8* to the place which your God will choose in one of your tribes before *9* the anointed priest upon whose head the oil of anointing has been poured

Col. II   *1–2* [...] *3* and he shall take [a young bullock from the herd and a ram ... and he shall sprinkle] *4* with his fingers [over the surface of the place of atonement ...] *5* the flesh of the ram [...] and the he-goat *6* for the sin-offering, he shall ta[ke] it [and slaughter it, and at]one for all the congregation. And Aa[ron shall sprinkle with the blood] *7* in front of the veil of the curtain and shall approach] the ark of the testimony and shall study [all the precepts of] *8* YHWH concerning all [... which] have been hidden from you. And he shall go out before a[ll the chiefs] *9* of the assembly [...]

4QLiturgy of the Three Tongues of Fire (4Q376)

Col. I   [...in front of the anointed priest, upon whose head the oil of anointing has been poured] *1* [... and in front of the seco]nd of the anointed priest *2* [... a bu]llock, young of the herd and a ram [...] *3* [...] to the Urim

Col. II   *1* they will provide you with light and he will go out with him, with tongues of fire; the stone of the left side which is at its *2* left side will shine in the eyes of all the assembly until the priest finishes speaking. And after [the cloud(?)] has been removed *3* [...] and you will keep and d[o al]l [that] he tells you

Col. III   *1* in accordance with all this judgment. And if there were in the camp the Prince of the whole congregation [...] *2* his enemies, and Israel is with him, or if he marches to a city to besiege it or in any affair which [...] *3* to the Prince [...]... [...] the field is far away [...]

4QPseudo-Moses*b* (?) (4Q387a)

Frag. 1   *1* [...] ... so they serve me with all their heart *2* and with a[ll ...] you will instruct them *3* in the service of the deeds [...] until ten *4* jubilees of years are complete. And I will bring them to madness [...] ... and confusion *5* of heart and the destruction of the generation. I will liberate the kingdom from the hand of the powerful ones. *6* [...] ... [...] others of the people. Afterwards, he will govern *7* ... [...] all the country and the kingdom of Israel will perish in those *8* days [...] a blasphemer and will perform abominations. And I will split *9* [the] kingdom apart [...] the kings, and my face the hidden ones of Isra‹el› *10* [...] many peoples [...] Israel the cries *11* [...] to them

Frag. 2   *1* [..Isra]el from the people. [In their days] I will destroy the kingdom of [Egypt] *2* [...] and I will destroy Israel [and Egypt and deliver them up to the sword...] *3* [... coun]try, and I have removed the ma[n ...] *4* [...] the country in the hands of the angels of destruction. And I will hide [...] *5* [...Is]rael. And this will be the sign for them in the day of abandonment of the la[nd ...] *6* [...] the priests of Jerusalem to serve other gods. [...] *7* [...] house of [...]

4QPseudo-Moses*c* (4Q388 [4QpsMoses*c*])

Frag. 1   *1* ... [...] *2* the covenant which [I established] with Abraham, with Isaac [and with Jacob. In] those [days] *3* a blasphemous king will arise [for the na]tions and will do evil things. [...] *4* to Israel from the people. In his days I will destroy the kingdom of Egypt [...] *5* I will destroy Egypt and Israel and deliver them up to the sword [...] *6* I have removed the man and I have abandoned the country into the ha[nds of the angels of destruction ...] *7* to serve other gods. [...] ... [...] *8* three who will re[ign ...] *9* [the] sanctuary [...] *10* [what is upr]ight and what is just [...]

4QPseudo-Moses*d* (4Q389 [4QpsMoses*d*])

Frag. 1   *1* [...] ... [...] *2* [...] and the reign will return to the peop[les ...] ... and the children of Israel *3* [...] a heavy yoke in the lands of their exile, and there will not be *Blank* a saviour for them *4* because and only because they have rejected my precepts and their soul despised my law. For this I hid *5* my face [until] they make good their faults. *Blank* And this will be the sign for them that they have made good *6* their faults [...] I have abandoned the earth because they hardened their hearts against me and did not know *7* [...] and they did evil. *Blank* From [the] first [days] *8* [.. the covenant which I established] with Abra[ham, with Isa]ac and with *9* [Jacob ...] A blasphemous king will rise up for the nations and will do evil things *10* [...] I will destroy [...]

c *Pseudo-Moses Apocalypse*

4QPseudo-Moses Apocalypse*e* (4Q390 [4QpsMoses*e*])

Frag. 1   *1* [...]...[...] *2* vio[lating ... And I will] go back [to deliver them] into the hand of the sons of Aa[ron...] seventy years [...] *3* And the sons of Aaron will rule over them, but they will not walk [in the pa]ths which I command you so that *4* you can caution them. And also they will do what is evil in my eyes, everything that Israel did *5* in the earliest days of its kingdom, apart from those who were the first to go up from the land of captivity in order to build *6* the temple. But I will speak to them and send them precepts and they will understand all that *7* they have lost, they and their fathers. And when this generation passes, in the seventh jubilee *8* of the devastation of the land, they will forget the law, the festival, the sabbath and the covenant; and they will disobey everything and will *9* do what is evil in my eyes. And I will hide my face from them and deliver them to the hands of their enemies and abandon them *10* to the sword. But from among them I will make survivors remain so that they will not be exterminated by my anger and by the concealment of my face *11* from them. And over them will rule the angels of destruction and [...] and they will come back *12* and do [...] evil before my eyes and walk according to the des[ires of their heart...] *13* [...] .... [...]

Frag. 2 *col.* I   *1* [...]... [...] *2* [and my] house, [my altar and] my ho[ly] temple [...] *3* and so it was done [...], for all these things will happen to them [...] and there will come *4* the dominion of Belial upon them to deliver them up to the sword for a week of yea[rs... During] this jubilee *5* they will break all my laws and all my precepts which I will command them [and I will send them by the hand of] my servants the prophets; *6* and they will begin to argue with one another for seventy years, from the day on which they break this vow and the covenant. And I shall deliver them *7* [to the hands of the an]gels of destruction and they will rule over them. And they will not know and will not understand that I am annoyed with them for their transgressions *8* [for they will des]ert [me] and do what is evil in my eyes and what I do not want them to choose: domineering for money, for advantage *9* [and for wickedness,] one stealing what belongs to his neighbour and one persecuting his neighbour; they will defile my temple *10* [they will loathe my sabbaths and] my festivals and with the sons of [foreigners] they will debase their offspring; the priests will rape *11–12* [...] ... [...]

Frag. 2. col. II   *1–3* [...] *4* the asc[ents (?) ...] *5* and with the word [...] *6* we [...] *7* they shall know and I will send [...] *8* and with arrows in order to se[ek...] *9* in the interior of the land and over ...[...] *10* their belongings, and they will sacrifice in [...] *11* they will desecrate it, and the al[tar...

D *Other Texts*

2QApocryphon of Moses (?) (2Q21 [2QapMoses ?])

1 [... Na]dab and Abihu, Eleazar and Ita[mar...] *2* [... in order to do you] justice in truth, and in order to reprove with faithfulness [...] *3* [...] *Blank* [...] *4* [And Moses went out]side the camp and pleaded with YHWH and bowed down [before ...] *5* [And he said: YHWH God,] how can I look at you, and how can I lift my face [towards you...] *6* [...] in order to make a single people for your deeds [...] *7* [...] ... [...]

9 Pseudo-Joshua

4QPsalms of Joshua^a (4Q378 [4QPsJoshua^a])

Frag. 3 col. II   *3* and he took out [...] *4* and this very day [...] *5* and we listen to Moses [...] *6* great and just man [... chiefs of] *7* hundreds, chiefs of fif[ties...] *8* and (to) the inspectors [...] *9* and he heard and (did) not [...Do not fear] *10* and do not be afraid, be strong and reso[lute because you] will cause [this people] to take possession [... YHWH is not] *11* to leave you or desert you [...] the strength of his hand [...] *12* to leave [at the head of the people...]

Frag. 6 col. I   *4* [...] a prayer for our sins *5* [...]... Do not resemble the brothers who descend *6* [...] your evil deeds for ever, for during eternity (?) *7* [...] your fault. Woe, brothers, upon you

Frag. 11   *1* [...] because YHWH [your God] ... [...] *2* [... in order to] establish the word which he gave *3* [...] he swore to Abraham to give *4* good and spacious [...], a land of streams of water, *5* [of springs and well-heads which gush in] the plain and on the mountain, a land of wheat and grain, [of vineyards] *6* [of fig-trees and herds, a land of olive oil and] honey, for it is a land which flows with milk and honey *7* [... of st]ones of iron and of mountains of copper [...] *8* [...] to inspect and take possession of [...] *9* [...]...[...]

Frag. 14   *1* [...] And the sons [of Israel] wept [over Moses] in the steppes of Moab] *2* [above the Jordan, close to] Jericho, in Bet-hishimot [as far as Abel ha-Shittim, for thirty days and they completed] *3* [the days of lament] and mourning for Moses. And the children of [Israel...] *4* [... the covenant] which YHWH established with [...] *5* [...fe]ar and trembling before you [...]

Frag. 22 *col.* I   *1* [...] Moses, my God. And he did not destroy them for their faults *2* [...] with you by means of Joshua, minister of your servant Moses *3* [...] ... by means of the oracle of God, Joshua, on behalf of your people *4* [...] ... which he agreed with Abraham *5* [...] compassion with a thousand

Frag. 26   *1* [...] he has the knowledge of Elyon and sees [the vision of Shaddai...] *2* [...] compassion for us, man of God, according [...] *3* [...] and the assembly of Elyon; they heard the voice of Mo[ses...] *4* [...]...[...] God Elyon [...] *5* [...] vast and large; and in the heat he kept back [...] *6* [...] man of the pious ones and for ever may he remember [...] *7* [...] ... [...] *8* *Blank* *9* [...] ... [...]

4QPsalms of Joshua*b* (4Q379)

Frag. 1   *1* […] and you made him exult with twe[lve…] *2* […] eternal to Levi, the beloved, […] *3* […] to Reuben and Ju[dah… *4* […] to Gad and Dan and […] *5* […] the twelve tribes of [Israel…]

Frag. 12   *1* […the waters] which come down …[…] *2* [… the waters] which come down will linger in a barrier *3* […] they will cross dryshod in the *4* [fi]rst month of the forty-first year of their departure from the land of *5* Egypt; this was the year of the Jubilees from the start of their entry into the land of *6* Canaan; and the Jordan floods all its banks with water and overflows *7* its water from the month … […] until the month of the wheat harvest *8* […] … […]

Frag. 17   *2* […]… and blessing […] *3* […] with his words and he was faithful to the Law […] *4* […] Abraham, Isaac and Jacob; to Moses *5* […] Eleazar and Itamar. I will rejoice…

Frag. 22 *col.* II   *5* Blessed be YHWH, God of [Israel…] *6* … … […] *7* At the time when Joshua finished pra[ising and giving] thanks with his prai[ses, he said:] *8* «Cur[sed be the ma]n who rebuilds this city! With his first-born (son) [he will lay its foundations] *9* and with his [youngest so]n [he wil]l set up its gates» *Blank* So, then, cur[sed be the man of Belial,] *10* [who rises] to be a bird-trap for his people and a reason for destruction by all his neighbours. And there will arise *11* […] for both to be instruments of violence. They will return and rebuild *12* [that city,] and will establish a wall and towers in it, to make it [a refuge of evil] *13* [in the land,] a great evil/ in Israel, a horror in Ephraim [and in Judah;] *14* [they have made an abomination] in the land and a great sin / among the sons of Jacob; they have caused [blood to flo]w/ like wa[ter on top of the ram-parts of the daughter of Zion and in the precincts of Jerusalem.]

10 Pseudo-Samuel

4QVision of Samuel (4Q160 [4QVisSam])

Frag. 1   *1* […] For I swore to the House of [Eli that the sin of the House of Eli would not be atoned for, either by sacrifices] *2* or by of[ferings, for ever.] Samuel heard the words of […] *3* […] Samuel was lying down before Eli, and he arose and opened the do[ors…] *4* […] to explain the oracle to Eli. But Eli answered him: […] *5* […] Let me know the vision of God! Do not[hide it from me, please! May] *6* [God do this to you, and this to you in addition] if you hide one wor[d of all the words which he told you…] *7* […] Samuel […]

Frags. 3–5 *col.* II   *1* […] your servant. I did not control my strength before this, because *2* […may they be re]united, my God, with your people; be assistance for him and raise him up *3* […] free his feet from the [clinging] bar and establish for them a rock from of old, for your praise *4* [above all the pe]oples. Your people will take shelter [in your house] and […] In the anger of those who hate your people you shall exalt your splendour *5* [and] over the lands and the seas […] and your fear will be over every […] and kingdom. And all the peoples of your lands will know [that] *6* you did create them. […] your holy ones whom you made holy […]

Frag. 7   *1* […] and there will be […] *2* I lived with him my feasts and joined /him/ […] *3* […] I did not solicit his favour with estates, riches or merchandise […] *4* […] my lord, and I chose to lie down in the presence of… […]

6QApocryphon on Samuel-Kings (6Q9)

Frag. 21   *1* [… to li]sten to his voice and ke[ep …] *2* […] his precept. […] *3* [… in the bo]ok of the Law […]

Frag. 32   *1* […] the Philistines […] *2* his heart, and they fought in front of […] *3* […] … […]

Frag. 33   *1* […] … […] *2* […] and they delivered them into the hands of […] *3* […] and fled from there to the king of Moab […] *4* […]… […]

11 Pseudo-Jeremiah

4QApocryphon of Jeremiah C (4Q385b [4QapocrJer C)

Frag. 1 *col.* I   *1* [...] *Blank* *2* [...] Jeremiah the prophet before YHWH, *3* [...w]ho were made prisoners of Jerusalem and were led *4* [...] to destroy Nabuzardan, chief of the escort, *5* [...] ... and he took all the vessels from the temple of God, and the priests *6* [...] the children of Israel and led them to Babylon. And Jeremiah the prophet went *7* [...] he laughed and told them what they had to do in the country of exile *8* [...] by the voice of Jeremiah, concerning the words which God had decreed for him. *Blank* *9* [...] they will keep the covenant of the God of their fathers in the country of *10* [exile ...] what they and their kings and their priests did *11* [...] God [...]

Frag. 1 *col.* II   *1* in Taphnes [...] *2* And they said to him: «Interpret [...] *3* to them Jere[miah ... but] do not interpret these things for them [...] *4* entreaty and prayer.» And Jeremiah settled [in Taphnes (?) ...] *5* [and dwel]t in peace. *Blank* [...] *6* Jeremiah in the country of Taphnes which is in the land of E[gypt ...to] *7* the children of Israel and the children of Judah and Benjamin [...] *8* ... and they will keep my laws and my precepts [...] *9* after ... of the nations, which [...] *10* He will not free [...] not [...]

4QApocryphon of Jeremiah D (4Q387b [4QapocrJer D)

Frag. 1   *1* [...] the land of [...] *2* [...] concerning [...] *3* [... a]ll who fall in the land of E[gypt ....] *4* [... Je]remiah, son of Hilkiah, from the country of Egypt *5* [the XXX]-six years of exile from Israel. ... the words of [...] *6* [...] Israel concerning the torrent Sor. *Blank* In the position of [...]

12   Pseudo-Ezekiel

4QPseudo-Ezekiel^a (4Q385 [4QpsEz^a])

Frag. 2   *1* [And they shall know that I am YHWH,] who rescued my people, giving them the covenant. *Blank 2* [And I said: «YHWH,] I have seen many in Israel who have loved your name and have walked *3* on the paths of [justice.] When will these things happen? And how will they be rewarded for their loyalty?». And YHWH said to me: *4* «I will make the children of Israel see and they will know that I am YHWH». *Blank 5* [And he said:] «Son of man, prophesy over the bones and say: May a bone [connect] with its bone and a joint *6* [with its joint».] And so it happened. And he said a second time: «Prophesy, and sinews will grow on them and they will be covered with skin *7* [all over».] And so it happened. And again he said: «Prophesy over the four winds of the sky and the winds *8* [of the sky] will blow [upon them and they will live] and a large crowd of men will rise and bless YHWH Sebaoth who [caused them to live.»] *9* [*Blank*] And I said: «O, YHWH, when will these things happen?» And YHWH said to me [...] *10* [...] a tree will bend over and straighten up [...]

Frag. 3   *1* [...] under my grief [... and my heart] *2* disturbs my soul. And the days will pass rapidly until [all the sons of] *3* man *2* say: *3* «Are not the days hastening on so that the children of Israel can inherit [their land?»] *4* And YHWH said to me: «I will not shun your face, Ezekiel; see, I measure [time and shorten] *5* the days and the years [...] *6* a little, as you said to [...] *7* [For] the mouth of YHWH has said these things»[...]

Frag. 4   *1* and my people will be [...] *2* with a whole heart and a [satisfied so]ul [...] *3* and hide a minute [...] *4* and cleaving [...] *5* The vision which Ezekiel saw [...] *6* the gleam of the chariot and four living creatures; a living creature [... and when they walk they do not turn] *7* backwards; each living creature walked on two, and their two fe[et...] *8* ... [...] was a spirit and their faces were each joined to the ot[her. And the shape of] *9* their fac[es was: one a lion, o]ne an eagle, one a calf and one a man. And each one [had a] *10* man's [hand] attached at the back of the living creatures and fastened to [the wings] and the wh[eels...] *11* one wheel attached to another wheel while walking, and from the two sides of the whe[els streams of fire came out] *12* and there were living beings in the middle of the embers, like embers of fire, [like torches in the middle of] *13* the wheels and the living beings and the wheels. And [over their heads] there was [a vault like] *14* awful ice. And there was a sound [on top of the vault...]

4QPseudo-Ezekiel^b (4Q386 4QpsEz^b])

Col. I (= 4Q385 2)   *1* [And I said: «YHWH,] I have seen many in Israel who have l]oved your name *2* [and have walked on the paths of justice. When will these things happen? And] how will they be rewarded for their loyalty?». *3* [And YHWH said to me: «I will make] the children of Israel see and they shall know *4* [that I am YHWH». *Blank* And he said: «Son of man, prophe]sy over the bones *5* [and say: «May a bone connect with its bone and] a joint with its joint». And it happened] *6* [thus. And he said a second time: «Prophesy, and flesh will grow on th]em and they will be covered with skin *7* [all over...] and the sinews will grow on them *8* [... And so it happened. And again he said: «Prophesy ov]er the four winds *9* [of the sky and the winds of the sky will blow upon them and they will live, and] a large crowd of men *10* [will rise and bless YHWH Sebaoth who caused them to live.»] *Blank*

Col. II   *1* And they will know that I an YHWH. *Blank* And he said to me: «Consider, *2* son of man, the land of Israel.» And I said: «I have seen, YHWH; behold it is desolate. *3* And when will you assemble them?» And YHWH said to me: «A son of Belial will plot to oppress my people, *4* but I will not allow him to and his dominion will not exist; but he will defile a multitude. Offspring will not remain. *5* And from the grapevine there will be no new wine, nor will the bee make honey. [...] And the *6* wicked man I will kill in Memphis and I will make my sons go out of Memphis. And I will turn myself toward their remnant. *7* Thus, as they will say: «There is peace and order», they will say «[...] the land, *8* as there was in the days of ancient [...]». Then ... [...] *9* [to the fo]ur winds of the hea[vens ... to [...] *10* [...] consuming [fi]re [...]

Col. III   *1* and he will not have pity on the poor, and will lead (him) to Babylon. Babylon is like a pot in YHWH's hand, like dung *2* he will throw her [...] *3* in Babylon and there will be [...] *4* the dwelling of your fields. [...] *5* desolate [...] *6* ...[...]

13 Pseudo-Daniel

A *Pseudo-Daniel*

4QPseudo-Daniel*ᵃ* (4Q243 [4QpsDan*ᵃ* ar])

Frag. 1   *1* [...] ... [...] *2* [...] over the tower and [...] *3* [...in order to] examine the sons of [...] *4* [...]... [...]

Frag. 2   *1* [...fo]ur hundred [years...] *2* he [...] them ... and ... [...] all of them and they shall depart from within *3* Egypt at the hand of [...] he will cause them to cross the River Jordan *4* [...] and their sons [...]

Frag. 3   *1* [...] the children of Israel preferred his presence to [God]'s *2* [and they sacrif]iced their sons to the devils of delusion. God grew angry against them and ordered them to be consigned *3* to the hands of Ne[buchadnezzar, king of Ba]bylon [to devastate their land] among them, from the hands of [...]

Frag. 4   *1* [...] oppressed (for) seventy years [...] *2* [... this] great [kingdom] and he will rescue them [...] *3* [...] strong (ones) and a kingdom of peoples [...] *4* [...] This is the fi[rst] kingdom [...]

Frag. 5   *1* [... has] ruled [...] years *2* [...] BLKRWS [...]

Frag. 6   *1* [...] years [...] *2* [...] RHWS, son of [...] *3* [...] WS, [...] years *4* [...] to speak [...]

Frag. 7   *1* [...] of sin, they made [...] stray *2* [...in] that [period] the ones called will reunite [...] *3* [... the kings] of the peoples, and from the day [...] there will be *4* [... the holy] ones and the kings of the peoples [...] *5* [...] slaves until the day [...]

Frag. 8   *1* They asked Daniel, saying: [...] *2* YHWH will give [...] *3* ... [...]

4QPseudo-Daniel*ᵇ* (4Q244 [4QpsDan*ᵇ* ar])

Frag. 1   *1* [...] before the ministers of the King, and he said [...]

Frag. 3   *1* [...] ... [...] *2* [...] after the flood *3* [...] Noah [...] from [Mount] Lubar [...] *4* [...] a city

Frag. 4   *1* [...] the children of Israel preferred his presence to [God's] *2* [and they sacrificed their sons to the de]vils of delusion. God grew angry against them and or[dered them] *3* [to be consigned to the hands of Nebuchadnezzar, king of Ba]bylon, and to devastate their land among them by the hands of [...] *4* [...] the sons of the exile [...]

4QPseudo-Daniel*ᶜ* (4Q245 [4QpsDanᶜ ar])

Frag. 1 *col.* I   *1* [...] ... *2* [...] and what *3* [...] Daniel *4* [...] a book that he gave *5* [...] Qahat *6* [...] ... Uzz[iah] *6* [...] A[bia]thar *7* [...] ... *8* ... *9* [...] Simeon *10* [...] David, Solomon *11* [...] ...

Frag. 2   *1* [...] ... [...] *2* [...] in order to eradicate sin *3* [...] those shall stray in their blindness *4* [... th]ey shall arise *5* [...] the holy ones and return *6* [...] iniquity. *Blank*

B *Prayer of Nabonidus*

4QPrayer of Nabonidus (4Q242 [4QPrNab ar])

Frags. 1–3   *1* Words of the prayer which Nabonidus, king of the la[nd of Baby-lon, [a great] king, prayed [when he was afflicted] *2* by a malignant inflamma-tion, by decree of the G[od Most] High, in Teiman. [I, Nabonidus,] was af-flicted [by a malignant inflammation] *3* for seven years, and was banished far [from men, until I prayed to the God Most High] *4* and an exorcist forgave my sin. He was a Je[w] from [the exiles, who said to me:] *5* Make a proclamation in writing, so that glory, exal[tation and honour] be given to the name of the G[od Most High. And I wrote as follows: When] *6* [I was afflicted by a malig[nant] inflammation, [and remained] in Teiman, [by decree of the God Most High, I] *7* prayed for seven years [to all] the gods of silver and gold, [of bronze and iron,] *8* of wood, of stone and of clay, because [I thought] that they were gods [...]

Frag. 4   *1* [...]...I had a dream *2* [...] has gone far off, the peace of [...] *3* [...] my friends. I could not [...] *4* [...] as you were like [...]

c *Daniel-Susannah (?)*

4QDaniel-Suzanna (?) (4Q551)

Frags. 1 + 3   *1* [...] knowledge [...] ... *2* [... t]hen an old man[...] it is from *3* [...] son of Jonathan, son of Jeshua, son of Ishmael, son of [...] After this *4* [...] and all the men of the city gathered in front of the house and said to him: «Make

[...] come out [...] God». And they said: 5 [...] ... He [said] to them: «My brothers, do not do evil [...] here 6 [...]...[...] for them 7 [...] which 8 [...] my spirit

14 Aramaic Proto-Esther

4Q550

4QProto Esther*a* (4QprEsth*a* ar)

1 [and they ob]eyed your father Patireza [...] *2* and among the attendants of the
royal wardrobe [...] performing *3* the service of the King according to all that
[...] ... At that time *4* the lengthening of the King's spirit... [...] the books of
his father were to be read in front of him; and among *5* the books was found a
scroll [sealed with] seven seals of the ring of Darius, his father. The matter
6 [...] ... [... of Da]rius the King to the attendants of the Empire of the whole
earth, peace». I read the beginning and found written in it: «Darius the King
7 [...] will rule after me and to the attendants of the Empire, peace. Know that
every tyrant and deceitful

4QProto Esther*b* (4QprEsth*b* ar)

1 a man; but the King knows whether there is [...] *2* and his good name will not
pass away, and his loyalty [...] *3* of the King will be for Patireza, son of
Ya'[ir...] *4* there fell upon him the dread of the house of Safra [...] *5* herald of
the King. May it be said and it will be given [...] *6* from my house and from my
belongings and all that which [...] *7* be measured; and you shall receive your
father's service [...]

4QProto Esther*c* (4QprEsth*c* ar)

1 [...] herald of the King. He must say to the princess [...] bani[shed ...] *2* [...]
Patireza [your] father, of Hama who rose above the attendants of the [kingdom]
before the King [...] *3* [...] he served with justice and with [...] before her [...]
4 [...] and the herald said [...] *5* [...] the purp[le ...] *6* [...] ... [...]

4QProto Esther*d* (4QprEsth*d* ar)

Col. I   *1* Look, you know [...] and for the failings of my fathers *2* who had sinned
before you, and [...] peaceful [...] and left [... of his at]tendants, a *3* Jew, from
the chiefs of Benjam[in...] one of the diaspora, stands up for an accusation and
wishes [... a] good divi[ner], *4* a good man, [...] attendant. What can I do for
you? You know [...] possible *5* to a Kutean man the return [...] of your kingdom, rising after you rise [...] *6* However, what you wish command it of me
and when you die I will bury you in [...] *7* ravaging (?) everything. Is it possible
that the rise of my service means [...] all that [...]

Col. II   *1* [...] the decision of [...And] the second ones will pass [...] *2* [... the plagues and the third ones will pa[ss...] in the [royal] wardrobe [...] *3* [...] the crown of g[old upon his h]ead, And five years will pass [...] *4* [...] alone and [... and the sixth] ones will pass, bl[ack] *5* [...] all silver and all gold and all the wea]lth which belongs to Bagoshe, doubled, [...] *6* and the seve[nth ones will pass...Th]en Bagasro entered in peace into the court of the King [...] *7* Bagosh[e retur]ned to [...] his judgment was judged [and the verdict] announced and he was executed. Then Bagasro entered the sev[enth] court of the King [...] *8* And he took his hand [...] on his head [...] and hugged him, answering him and saying: «In [...] Bagasro of [...]

Col. III   *1* [...] the Most High who you revere and venerate, is the one who governs [the whole] earth. All that one who approaches should wish [...] *2* [...] every man who utters a bad word against Bagasro [...] will be killed, because he has nothing [...] *3* [...] a barrier for ever. [...all] that he had seen in the two [...]. And the King said to him: «Wri[te...] *4* [...] Emp[ire...] they in the inner courtyard of the royal palace [...] *5* [...] they shall rise after Bagasro, the readers of this written text [...] *6* [...ev]il, evil has returned against his [head...] *7* [... his desce]ndants. *Blank*

4QProto Esther*ᵉ* (4QprEsth*ᵉ* ar)

1 [...] before the King [...] *2* walk in the area [...] *3* [...] upon [your] faces [...] *4* [...Ba]gasro [...]

4QProto Esther*ᶠ* (?) (4QprEsth*ᶠ* ar (?))

1 [...] Look, from the North comes the evil [...] *2* [...] founded the building of Zion, and there all the unassuming of his people will take refuge. *3* [...] *Blank* *4* [they] rose above him, they grew great between Media and Persia, Assyria and the Sea. *5* [...] *Blank*

15 Tobit in Aramaic and Hebrew

4QTobit*a* (4Q196 [4QTob*a* ar])

Frag. 1 (= *Tob* 1:17)   *1* [...] the wall of Nineveh [...]

Frag. 2 (= *Tob* 1:19–2:2   *1* [And one of] the Ninevites [went] and informed the
king that I [was bu]rying [them,] but I found out. And when I knew that *2* [the
king] knew [about me] I took fright and hid. [And] all that I had [was seized],
and I was left with no relations *3* [... except An]na, my wife, and Tobias, my
son. However, [fort]y days had not [passed] *4* [when his two so]ns [killed him.]
And they fled to the mountains of Ararat and af[ter him] *5* [Esarhaddon, his
son] ruled. And to Ahikar, son of my brother Anael, he gave power over all the
6 [treasures of the kingdom, so that he held control] over them and over all the
king's finances. And Ahikar interceded *7* [for my life and I could return to
Nineveh. Ahikar was the chief of the cupbearers and the keeper of the seals and
the treasurer *8* [and] the administrator before Asharyarib, king of Assyria, while
Esarhaddon made him his second-in-command. See, *9* he was my brother's son
and from my father's house and from my family. And in the days of king Esarhaddon, when I had returned *10* [to my ho]me and Anna, my wife, had been returned to me, and Tobias, my son, on the day of the Feast of Wee[ks, they prepared for me] *11* a good banquet, and I reclined to [eat.] They brought the table
near, in front of me, and I saw that the dishes that they placed *12* upon it were
many. And I sa[id to Tobias, my son: My son, go and fetch all those you find
from among our brot[hers] *13* [...] My son, go and fetch them, so they may
come and eat [together with us ...]

Frag. 5 (= *Tob* 3:11–15)   *1* [...and may my father not hear re]proaches again in
my lifetime. *2* [And then she spread her hands] towards the window [and
prayed] *3* [saying: Blessed be you, merciful God, and blessed (be)] your holy
and glorious name [for ever, and] may *4* [all your works] bless you [for ever.
And now,] to you I lift my face and my eyes: say that I may be freed from *5* [the
earth and not return to hear reproaches. You kn]ow that I am clean in my bones
from every [impurity] *6* [of a male, that I have not def]iled my na[me or my
father's name in all the land of deportation; *7* [I am my father's only daughter,
he has no] other son to be his heir, nor (has he) a brother or a relative *8* [that I
should keep] my soul for a son, [to be] his wife. Already there have been

Frag. 11 *col.* I (= *Tob* 6:14–17)   *2* [... And I have heard that the people said that
a demon] killed them. *3* [And now I am afraid to die and that sorrow for me
bring to the grave the li]fe of my father and of my mother. *4* [And they have no
other son] who could bury them. *5* [And he said to him: Do you not remember

the precepts of] your father who commanded you *6* [to take a wife from your father's house? Now,] listen to me, my brother, *7* [do not fear this demon and take her. I know that in] this night *8* [she will be given to you as a wife. And when you enter the bridal chamber, ta]ke some of the heart *9* [of the fish and (some) of its liver, place it upon the embers of the incense and the smell will come out,] the demon will [smell it,] fl[ee]

Frag. 11 *col.* II (= *Tob* 6 : 19 – 7 : 3)   *1* much [and his heart grew fond of her. And when they arrived within Ecbatana, Tobias said to him:] *2* Azarias, my brother, [take me straight to the house of Raguel, our brother. And he took him and they entered the house of Raguel.] *3* And they found Raguel seated in [front of the door of the courtyard, and first they wished him peace. And he said to them:] *4* In peace you came and in peace shall you go, [my brothers. And he made them enter his house. And he said to Edna, his wife,] *5* How [like Tobit, my uncle's son, is this young man! And Edna] aske[d them and said: Where are you from, brothers?] *6* And they said to her: [From the sons of Naphtali, from the exiles in Nineveh ...]

Frag. 15 *col.* II (= *Tob* 13 : 6 – 14)   *1* your heart and [with all] your soul to [act truthfully before him. Then, he will turn to you] *2* and no [longer hide his face] from you. [And now, consider what he has done for you and give him thanks] with your whole mouth, *3* and ble[ss the Lord of] justice and exa[lt the eternal king. I, in the land] of exile, give you thanks *4* and dec[lare] his power and his great[ness to a nation of sinners. Turn, you sin]ners, and with all your heart ac[t] *5* just[ly] before him. [...] ... [...] *6* [...] my soul to the k[ing of heaven ...] all the days [...] *7* [...] his greatness. They will chant psalms *8* [...] the holy city ... *9* [...] of justice. Give thanks [...] *10* [...] ... [...] *11-12* [...] *13* [...] genera-tions will pass on to generations [their joy] for you *14* [and] the name of your great[ness to] eternal [ge]nerations. Cursed be all those who say] harsh things and all those who against you *15* [...] Cursed be those who [...] and all [...] ...

Frag. 15 *col.* III   *1* [...] and all those who make [your towers] fall [...] *2* [...] be happy and rejoice in the sons of [...] *3* [...Blessed] those who love you and bles[sed ...] *4* [... a]ll those who suffer for you [...] *5* [...] the great king who [...] *6* [...] from my descendants [...] *7* [...] you will be built of sapphire [...] *8* you will be built [of go]ld and your wo[od ...] *9* [...] and stone from [Ophir ...] *10* [...] for all eternity [...] *11* [...] for ever. Those who are in you will bless [...] *12* [...To]bit and died in peace [...] *13* [...eigh]ty-five years [...] *14* [...] his eyes he lived well and with all [...] *15* [...] *** and praise the gr[eat ...] *16* [...] his sons and he commanded [...]

4QTobit^b (4Q197 [4QTob^b ar])

Frag. 3 *col.* I (= *Tob* 5 : 19 – 6 : 12)   *1* [... May] our son's money not be added [to our money]! And now [it is not enough] *2* [to live as has been granted us by the Lord to live.] He said to him: Do not fear, my sons will leave in peace *3* [and he will return to us in peace. Your eyes will see him on the day when he returns to you] in peace. Do not fear and do not be worried for him, my sister, *4* [for a good angel will go with him, his path will be successful and he will return in peace.] And she wept no more. *Blank 5* [The young man left and the an]gel went with him; [the dog left with them, and the two walked] together. And *6* [the angel] commanded them [to spend the night close to the river] Diqlat (the Tigris). And the young [man] went down [to the river Tigris to bathe his feet, and] a great fish [leapt] from the *7* [water which tried to con]sume the young man's foot. [The young man shouted, but the angel said to him: Catch and] grasp the fi[sh. And] the young man cau[ght] *8* [the fish and grasped it and brought it] out on dry land. [And the angel said to the young man: Spli]t it and remove [its skin, its heart] *9* [and its liver, and keep them in your] hand, but [throw away] its guts, [for its skin, its heart] and its liver [are a good medicine.] And [the young man [split the fish] *10* [and removed the skin, the he]art and [the liver. The young man cooked part of the] fish and ate it, and also [for the journey he prepared another part] *11* [with salt. And] the two walked together [until they appro]ached Media. *Blank* [Then] *12* [the young man questioned the angel and] said to him: Azarias, my brother, what good medicine is there in the heart of the fish and in its liv[er and in its skin? And he said to him:] *13* [As for the heart of the fish and its liver] make it depart in smoke before a man or a woman attacked by a demon or by an [evil] spirit [and from them will flee] *14* [every kind of attack and] they will [not] approach them and their vicinity ever. As for the skin, it is to anoint the ey[es of the man on whom burns had been caused,] *15* the burns [shall fall away from him] and they shall be cured. And when they came within Media and were now [going to Ecbatana] *16* [Raphael said to the young] man: Tobias, my brother. And he answered him: Here I am. And he said to him: [We are going to spend the night] in Raguel's house] *17* [tonight, for] he is a man from your father's house and has a beautiful daughter [whose name is Sarah. *Blank* *18* [And] he has [no] other son or daughter except Sarah, and you are the closest relative to h[er from all men] *19* [... and to take her] for yourself as a br[ide] and you have the right [to inherit all the property]

Frag. 3 *col.* II (= *Tob* 6 : 12 – 19)   *1* [of her father, the young woman is sensible, and vivaci]ous and very beautiful, and her father loves her [and ...] *2* [...] of her father. And as for you, a lawful right has decided [that you take her. And now] *3* [listen to me, my brother.] Tonight we will speak about this young woman,

we will install her so that you take her for a wi[fe, and when we return] *4* [from
Rages we will celebrate] the nuptial feast. I know that Raguel will not be able
to deny her to you because he knows *5* [that it pertains to you to secure] and
take his daughter more than to any other ma[n, and he also] knows that if he
gives her to another man *6* [he deserves death according to the sentence of the
book of Mo]ses. And now, [listen to me and we will speak about this young]
woman tonight, we will install her *7* [so that you accept her as a wife and take
her to your home. And Tobias answered and said to Ra]phael: Azarias, my
brother, I have heard *8* [that she has already been given to seven men who died
in her bridal chamber. In the night in which] they approached her, they *9* [died.
And I have heard that the people said it was a demon who killed them. And
now,] I am afraid [of the] demon who *10* [did no harm to her, but kills everyone
who tries to approach her. I am an only son for my] father and for my mother
11 [and I am afraid of dying and that sorrow for me might bring to the grave the
life of my father and of my mother. And they have no] other son *12* [who could
bury them. And he said to him: Do you not remember the pre]cepts of your
father who commanded you *13* [to take a wife from your father's house? Now,]
listen to me, my brother, do not fear] this demon and take her. *14* [I know that
in this night she will be given to you as a wife. And when you enter her bridal
chamber, take some of the heart of the fish and of its liver,] *15* [place it upon the
embers of the incense and the smell will come out, the demon will smell it, flee
and will not return to appear near her ever again.] *16* [And when you go to be]
with her, [first stand up, both of you, to pray; ask the Lord of heaven that upon
you may come mercy] *17* [and salvation. And] do not fear, [for] she has been set
apart and to you [she belongs from eternity. *Blank*] *18* [And you will sa]ve [her
and she will walk with you; and] think that for you there will be [sons from her,
and] that they will be *19* [like brothers for you. So, then, do not be afraid. And
when] Tobias heard the words of Rapha[el that Sarah was] his sister and from

Frag. 3 *col.* III (= *Tob* 6:19–7:10)　　*1* [the descendants of his father's house] he
loved her much and his heart grew fond of her. And when they arrived within
Ecbata[na,] *2* Tobias [said to him:] Azarias, my brother, [take me straight to the
house of Raguel, our brother. And he took him and they entered [the house]
3 of Raguel. And they found Raguel seated in front of the door of the courtyard, and first they wished him peace. And he said to them: In peace *4* you
came and in peace shall you go, my brothers. And he made them enter [his
house.] *5* And he said to Edna, his wife, How like Tobit, my uncle's son, is this
young man! And Edna asked them and said: Where are you from, brothers? *6*
And they said to her: From the sons of Naphtali, from the exiles in Nineveh.
And she said to them: Do you know Tobit, our brother? *7* They said to her: We
know him. Is he well? They said to her: [He is well and healthy. And] Tobias
[said:] *8* He is my father. Raguel jumped up, kissed him and wept. [And he

answered him and said to him: Be blessed, my son, son of the] *9* good man! A pity [that] a just man [has gone blind! [... And he sprang] *10* into the arms of Tobias [his brother and wept. And Edna his wife and Sarah his daughter also wept for him. And he killed] *11* a splendid bull calf [...] *12* to eat and to drink [...] *13* [...] And he heard [...]

Frag. 4 (= *Tob* 8:21–9:4)　　*1* [...] you shall take her with you to your father's house [...] *2* my son, I am your father and Edna [is your mother ...] *3* [... do not] fear, my son. *Blank* [...] *4* [Then Tobias called Raphael and said to him:] Azarias, my brother, take with you from here fo[ur servants and two camels] *5* [and go to Raguel.] Approach Gabael, give him the document, [receive the money, and take it with you for the wedding,] *6* [for you know that my father] is counting the days, and if I delay [one day ...]

4QTobit*e* (4Q198 [4QTob*e* ar])

Frag. 1 (= *Tob* 14:2–6)　　*1* justice and continued fearing God and prais[ing ...] *2* his sons and he commanded him and sa[id] to him: [... because he trusted in the word of] *3* God who sa[id ...] *4* ... [...] *5* Everything will happen in its time [...] *6* in all that God has said, [everyth]ing will occur and will hap[pen ... And our brothers] *7* who dwell in the land of Israel, all of them [will be deported ... And all the land of] *8* Israel will be deserted and Sama[ria ... until] *9* the time when he will cause them to return [...] *10* [and] not like the first time. *Blank* [...] *11* [they will build] Jerusalem with glo[ry ...] *12* [as the prophets said] of her [...] *13* [...] and they shall cast away all their idols [...]

Frag. 2 (= *Tob* 14:10 ?)　　*1* not [...] *2* he left [...] *3* ... [...] *4* fell into the trap of [death ...] *5* ... [...]

4QTobit*d* (4Q199 [4QTob*d* ar])

Frag. 1 (= *Tob* 7:12 ?)　　*1* [...And To]bias [said:] I shall not eat anything here [...]

4QTobit*e* (4Q200 [4QTob*e* hebr])

Frag. 1 *col.* I (= *Tob* 3:6)　　*1* [... and may I return to the] dust; *2* [for it is better for me to die] than to live, for *3* [I have heard false] reproaches [and there is much sorrow] with me. Command that I be freed *4* [from this conflict ...] ...

Frag. 1 *col.* II (= *Tob* 3:10–11)　　*1* they may reproach [my father ...] *2* whether for you [...] *3* concerning me. It is not convenient [...] *4* I will hear and he will not hear [...] *5* [the wi]ndow and begged [...]

Frags. 2–3 (= *Tob* 4:4–7)   *1* [...] ... [...] *2* [...] and she carried you in her wo[mb ...] *3* [...] *Blank* And all your days /my son/ God [...] *4* of his word. *Blank* [Act] truthfully all the days [of your life] *5* [and do not walk on pat]hs of deceit, for in the practice [of the truth success will be] with you. *6* [...] According to the size of your hands, my son, be [generous in doing] just deeds (alms), and do not wit[hdraw] *7* [your face from any poor] person, so that from you [the face of God does] not [withdraw.] If, my son, you have [much,] *8* [do] ju[st] deeds with it. [*Blank*] If you have little, according to the lit[tle] *9* [do just deeds, and do not fear to do a small] just deed: a [good] store

Frag. 5 (= *Tob* 10:8–9)   *1* [When] the fourteen days of [the wedding feast] ended *2* which Raguel had sworn to have for Sarah, his daughter, Tobias came [to him] *3* and said to him: Allow me to leave, for I know that [my father] *4* [and that] my mother also do not believe that they are going to see me again. /And now/ I beg you, *5* [yes you], my father, that you allow me to leave and I will go to my father. Already *6* I have told you how I left him. And Raguel said to Tobias: My son, *7* stay with me and I will send messengers to Tobit, your fat[her and they shall] tell [him]

Frag. 6 (= *Tob* 11:10–12)   *1* [...] to approach his son until [...] *2* [... the sk]in of the fish in his hand, and he destroyed [...] *3* [... he said] to him: Do not fear, my father. [...] *4* [...] his eyes, and rubbed [...] *5* [...] his eyes, and he saw [...]

Frag. 7 (= *Tob* 13:)   *1* [...] this event and what has happened to you. *Blank* [...] *2* [...] to him. And they {were astonished} blessed [...] *3* [...] his great deed, and they were astonished that there had appeared [to them [...] *4* [...] *Blank* Thus spoke Tobit and wrote a hymn with praises to G[od, and he said:]
5 [Blessed be the] living [God],
    whose kingdom is for all the centuries;
6 he is the one who [punishes
    and he is the one who] has pity,
    he brings down to the deepest Sheol
    and brings up from the abyss
7 [immense and great.]
    Who escapes from his hand? *Blank*
    Give him thanks, children of Is[rael,]
8 [before all the nations,]
    for he scattered you among them;
    and there tell [his greatness,]
9 [and exalt him before every] living creature,
    for he is your Lord,
    and he is your God.

Frag. 8 *col.* I (= *Tob* 13 : 15 ?)   *1* [...] Then shall you be happy and rejoice *2* [...] and blessed be *3* [...] all

Frag. 8 *col.* II (= *Tob* 13 : 18 ?)   *1* Jerusalem a hymn [...] *2* the God who [...] *3* who [...] *4* And ... [...]

Frag. 9 (= *Tob* 14 : 2 ?)   *1* [... Je]rusalem [...] *2* [... and he die]d in peace [...] *3* [...] eighty-five [years] old [...] *4* [...] and after fo[ur ...]

Poetic Texts

Due to our ignorance concerning the actual development of liturgical practice in the Qumran Community, it is not possible to make a precise distinction between verse compositions intended for liturgical use, and others which seem rather to have been written in order to inspire collective or individual meditation, or to express personal feelings. The fact that compositions such as the *Community Rule* also include sections in verse obviously intended for the communal celebration of the feast of covenant renewal and the use of various literary forms within a single composition, as happens in the *Hymns* of Cave 1 (*1 QHodayoth*), makes any attempt at classifying the texts even more speculative.

The arrangement of the texts in this chapter and the next is, then only a suggestion and is based on the predominance within one composition of one element or other.

The texts in this chapter are poetic in character without a shadow of doubt, though their liturgical nature is not actually stated.

Due to the bad state of preservation of part of this material, there is no point in setting it out in strophic form. Nevertheless, the layout highlights the poetic nature of the best preserved texts, leaving the more fragmentary parts as continuous text.

The origin of these texts varies enormously. While there is no doubt at all that the *Hodayoth* originate from within the Qumran Community, the origin of the other compositions, in particular the different *Apocryphal Psalms*, is rather more uncertain. The use of the compositions, here called *Psalms against demons*, as psalms of exorcism, seems to be certain.

For the *Hymns* from Cave 1, the reconstruction of the original manuscript suggested by E. Puech has been used, and this applies also to the insertion of a large number of isolated fragments within the original scroll. See E. Puech, 'Quelques aspects de la restauration du Rouleau des Hymnes (1QH)', *JJS* 39 (1988) 38-55. Due to the different arrangement and the insertion of fragments, the line numbering does not always match that of Sukenik's *editio princeps*. To assist the reader the correlation with the columns of the *editio princeps* has been indicated in parentheses.

1 Apocryphal Psalms

A *Apocryphal psalms included in copies of the biblical psalter*

4QPsalms*ᶠ* (4Q88 [4QPsᶠ])

Col. VII (*Hymn to Zion* = 11Q5 XXII, 1–3)   *14* [*Blank* I rem]ember you, [Zion] for
   blessing;
15 I have loved you [with all my powers.]
   [May your memory be blessed for ever!]
16 Great is your ho[pe, O Zion;]
17 [peace will come and the prosp]ect [of your salvation.]

Col. VIII (*Hymn to Zion* = 11Q5 XXII, 8–15)   *1* [Your hope does not die, O Zion]
2 [nor is your wait forgotten.]
3 [Who] is it [that died being just]
4 [or who] is the one who has been saved [in his iniquity?]
   [Man is examined] according to his path
5 each one is rewar[ded according to his de]eds.
6 All round you, O Zion, your enemies are quelled
7 and all those who hate you are scattered.
8 It is pleasant to hear your praise, O Zion,
   throughout the whole world.
9 Many times I remember you
10 [and I bless you] Zion;
   with all my powers I love you.
11 You shall receive everlasting justice
12 and accept the blessings of the glorious ones!
13 Accept a vision spoken in your regard
14 a prophets' dream requested for you!
   May you be glorified and magnified, O Zion!
15 [Praise the Mos]t H[igh, your Saviour!]
16 [May my soul be happy in your glory!]

Col. IX (*Eschatological hymn*)   *1–3* …[…]
4 […] many […]
5 and may they praise the name of YHWH.
   Because he comes to judge all things,
6 to obliterate evil-doers from the earth;
7 [the sons] of wickedness will find no [rest].
8 The heavens [will give] their dew,
9 and there will be no corrupt dealing in their frontiers.

10 The earth [will give] fruit in its season,

11 its crops will not fail.

12 The fruit-trees […] of their vineyards,

13 and their springs will not deceive.

14 The poor will eat

  and those who fear YHWH will be replete.

Col. x (*Hymn to Judah*)   *4* […] …

  5 […] meanwhile the heavens and earth will exult together.

  6 May all the stars of dusk, then, rejoice.

  7 Be happy, Judah, be happy!

  8 Be happy and burst with joy!

  9 Observe your feasts, fulfil your vows

  10 because within you there is no Belial.

  11 Lift up your hand, strengthen your right hand!

    See, your enemies perish

  12 and all who work evil will be scattered.

  13 And you, YHWH, for ever!

  14 Your glory shall be for ever and ever!

11QPsalms*ᵃ* (11Q5 [11QPs*ᵃ*])

Col. XVIII (*Psalm* 154)   [With powerful voice give glory to God,

  in the assembly of the Many proclaim his Glory;

  among the throng of the just give glory to his Name

  and with the faithful sing his greatness.]

  1 [Unite] your souls with the good ones and with the perfect ones

    to glorify the Most High.

  2 Join together to make his salvation known

    and do not hesitate to proclaim his power

  3 and his glory to all ordinary people.

    For, wisdom has been granted

    so that YHWH's glory can be proclaimed

  4 and so that his many deeds can be recounted

    has she been taught to man:

    so that his power can be proclaimed to ordinary people

  5 so that his might can be explained to those lacking judgment:

    those found to be far from his gates,

  6 removed *Blank* from his entrances.

    For the Most High is the Lord

  7 *Blank*

  8 *Blank*

9 of Jacob
  and his glory beyond all his deeds.
  The man who gives glory to the Most High
10 is accepted like one who brings an offering
  like one who offers goats and bullocks.
11 like one who makes the altar greasy with many holocausts,
  like the sweet fragrance of the just man's hand.
12 Her voice is heard in the gates of just men
  and in the assembly of devout men, her song;
13 they speak about it when they eat to bursting,
  when they drink, all meeting together;
14 their meditation is on the Law of the Most High,
  their words, to proclaim his power.
15 How distant from the wicked is his word
  from all the arrogant his knowledge!
16 See, YHWH's eyes
  have pity on good people;
  he increases his compassion on those who give him glory;
17 he frees their soul at the instant of danger.
  Bless YHWH
  who ransoms the humble from the foreigner's hand
18 [and frees the perfect from the wicked man's hand;
  who raises a horn from Jacob]
  and judges [the peoples from Israel,
  who pitches his tent in Zion
  and remains for ever in Jerusalem.]

Col. XIX (*Entreaty for deliverance* = 11QPs^b *frags. a + b*)
1 For not even a maggot could give you thanks,
  or a worm tell of your goodness.
2 The living, the living *Blank* can praise you,
  even the ones who stumble extol you.
  You teach them, revealing to them
3 your goodness and justice,
  for in your hand is the soul of every living being;
4 you give all flesh its breath.
  Deal with us, O YHWH, according to your kindness,
5 according to your abundant compassion
  and the great number of your just acts.
6 YHWH has heard the outcry of those loving his Name
  and has not denied them his goodness.
7 Blessed be YHWH who performs just deeds

8 and crowns his devout with goodness and compassion.
   Cry out, my soul, to extol /your/ Name
   to announce your good deeds with shouts,
9 to proclaim your loyalty;
   your praise is mysterious.
10 For my sins I was on the point of dying
   and my iniquities sold me to Sheol.
11 But you, YHWH, saved me
   according to your abundant compassion
   and the great number of your just acts.
12 I too have loved your Name
   and I have looked for sanctuary in your shade.
   The memory of your power strengthens my heart
13 I relax in your goodness.
   Pardon my sins, YHWH,
14 and cleanse me from my iniquity.
   Bestow on me a faithful and knowing spirit;
   may I not be disgraced in the calamity.
15 May Satan not rule over me
   or an unclean spirit;
   may neither pain nor evil purpose
16 take possession of my bones.
   Because you, YHWH, are my praise
   and in you I hope all day.
17 May my brothers be happy with me
   and my father's house,
   whom you baffled by your favour
18 ... [...]
   in you shall I be happy for ever.

Col. XXI (*Hymn to wisdom = Ben Sira* 51 : 13 – 19)   *11 Aleph* <u>A</u>lthough still young,
   before going astray
   I searched for her.
   Beth <u>B</u>eautiful she came to me
12 when at last I found her.
   Ghimel As falls the flower when <u>g</u>rapes are ripening
   making the heart happy,
13 *Daleth* <u>d</u>irectly walked my foot
   for since my youth I have known her.
   He <u>H</u>ardly my ear I bent
14 and found great allure.
   Waw <u>W</u>et-nurse was she for me

on my mistress I conferred my honour.

15 Zain Zealous for good,
I decided to enjoy myself
ceaselessly.

Heth Charred was my soul for her
16 I did not give in.

Teth Torrid my desire for her
and on her heights I was not serene.

17 Yodh Yes, 'my hand' opened [her doors]
and I inspected her nakedness.

Kaph Cleansed then 'my hand' [...]

Col. XXII (*Hymn to Zion* = 4QPs11ᶠ VII–VIII)   *1* (*Aleph Blank* Ah, I remember you,
Zion, for blessing;

2 Beth beloved to me with all my powers.
May your memory be blessed for ever!

Ghimel Great is your hope, O Zion;
3 peace will come and the longing for your salvation.

Daleth Dwell shall generation after generation in you,
generations of the devout shall be your splendour;

4 He hungering for the day of your salvation
Waw with the greatness of your glory shall they rejoice,

5 Zain suckle shall they at your splendid breasts,
they shall scamper about your marvellous squares.

Heth Cherish will you the goodness of your prophets
6 you will revel in the deeds of your devout ones.

Teth (Then purge ferocity from within you,
7 may lying and sin be eradicated from you.

Yodh Your sons will rejoice within you
and your loved ones will be united with you.

8 Kaph Keenly they have waited for your salvation;
how your perfect ones have observed mourning for you!

Lamed Lo, your hope does not die, Zion,
9 nor is your longing forgotten.

Mem Might anyone have died through being just?
Might anyone have been saved in his sin?

10 Nun Anent his path is a man examined
each one rewarded according to his deeds.

Samek Suppressed, O Zion, are your enemies around you
and all those who hate you are scattered.

Ain A lovely scent, O Zion, is your praise
12 which rises in all the world.

Peh Past counting the times I remember you for a blessing,
with all my heart I bless you.

13 Sade Secure eternal justice
and receive the blessings of the glorious ones!

14 Qoph Acquire the vision spoken in your regard
the prophets' dreams requested for you!

   Resh Rank glorified and magnified, O Zion!

15 Praise the Most High, your Saviour!

   Tau Thrill may my soul in your glory! *Blank*

Col. XXIV (*Psalm* 155)   *3* YHWH, I call to you, listen to me;

4 I extend my hands to your holy dwelling;
bend your ear and grant my plea,

5 and my entreaty, do not reject it;

   Beth? build up my heart and do not erode it
or forsake it in the presence of wicked men.

6 Ghimel Grant that the judge of truth
turn away from me
the recompenses of evil.

7 O YHWH, do not judge me by my sin
because no-one living is just in your presence.

8 He Have me instructed, YHWH, in your law,
and teach me your precepts

9 Waw whereby many hear your deeds
and the peoples honour your glory.

10 Zain Recognize me and do not forget me
or lead me into difficulties.

11 Heth From me childhood sin remove
and may my offences not be remembered against me.

12 Teth Turn me pure, YHWH, from the evil taint
may it stop coming back to me;

13 Yodh dry up its roots in me
may its leaves not become green again over me.

   Kaph Glory are you, YHWH,

14 therefore my plea is achieved in your presence.

   Lamed To whom may I shout and he would grant it to me?

15 The sons of men: what can their strength do?

   Mem My trust is in you, YHWH.

16 I called «YHWH» and he heard me
[and healed] my broken heart.

17 Nun Now I slumbered and slept;
I dreamt and, well: [woke up!]

Samek? [Sustained me, YHWH, you have
and I called to you], YHWH, [my deliverer.]
18 Ain? [And now I rejoice in his shame;
I trusted in you and have not been disillusioned.
Peh Pay for Israel, your devoted ones, O YHWH,
and the house of Jacob, your chosen ones.]

Col. XXVI (*Hymn to the Creator*)   *9* Great and Holy are you, YHWH,
the Holiest of Holy Ones, from generation to generation.
In front of him walks glory
10 and behind him boom copious waters.
Goodness and truth surround his face,
11 truth, uprightness and justice are the base of his throne.
He separated light from darkness
established the dawn with the knowledge of his heart.
12 Then all his angels saw him and sang
for he showed them what they had not known.
13 He covered the mountains with produce
perfect nourishment for all the living.
14 Blessed be he who made the earth with his strength
establishing the world with his wisdom.
With his knowledge he spread out the heavens
15 and brought out [the wind] from his storehouses:
[with (the) lightning flashes] he unleashed [the rain]
and made the clouds from the end [of the earth] go up.

Col. XXVII (*Compositions of David* › 2 *Sam* 23:7)   *1* and the haft of his spear
and he cast them in the fire
leaving no trace of them.
2 Blank And David, son of Jesse, was wise, a luminary like the light of the sun,
learned, *3 Blank* knowledgeable, and perfect in all his paths before God and
men. And to him *4 Blank* YHWH gave a wise and enlightened spirit. And he
wrote psalms: *5* three thousand six hundred; and songs to be sung before the
altar over the perpetual *6* offering of every day, for all the days of the year:
three hundred *7* and sixty-four; and for the sabbath offerings: fifty-two songs;
and for the offering for the beginning *8* of the month, and for all the days of the
festivals, and for the day of atonement: thirty songs. *9* And all the songs which
he composed were four hundred and forty-six. And songs *10* to be sung over
the possessed: four. The total was four thousand and fifty. *11* He composed
them all through the spirit of prophecy which had been given to him from
before the Most High. *Blank*

Col. XXVIII (*Psalm* 151)   *3* Halleluia of David, son of Jesse.
  I was smaller than my brothers
  and younger than my father's sons;
 4 he put me as shepherd of his flock
  and master of his kid goats.
  My hands made a flute.
  my fingers a lyre,
 5 and I gave glory to YHWH.
  I said to myself:
  the mountains do not witness in his favour,
 6 nor do the hills proclaim on his behalf,
  nor the trees his words
  or the sheep his deeds.
 7 Who, then, is going to announce
  and who will speak
  and who will narrate the deeds of the Lord?
  God saw everything
 8 he heard everything
  and listened.
  He sent his prophet to anoint me
 9 Samuel, to make me great.
  My brothers went out to meet him
  well built,
  very presentable.
  They were quite tall,
 10 they had attractive hair,
  but YHWH God did not choose them,
  instead he sent to fetch me from following the flock
 11 and anointed me with holy oil
  and set me as leader of his people
  /and chief of/ the sons of his covenant.
 12 Blank
 13 Beginning of David's exploit,
  after God's prophet had anointed him.
  Meanwhile I saw a Philistine
 14 threatening from [...]
  I [...]

11QPsalms*b* (11Q6 [11QPs*b*])

Frag. a (= 11Q5 XIX, 1–9)   *1* [poor] and weak am I,
  for [...]

2 [For] not even a grub can give you thanks
[or a maggot narrate your goodness.]
3 [The live person,] the live person can praise you.
[They shall extol you those who stumble.]
4 [You teach them, revealing to them]
your goodness and your justice,
[for in your hand is the spirit of every] living thing;
5 you give all flesh its food.
[Deal with us, O YHWH, in accordance with your kindness
in accordance with your abundant comp]assion
6 and your numerous just deeds.
[YHWH has heard the cry of those loving his Name]
7 [he has not removed] from them his goodness.
Bles[sed be YHWH who performs just deeds]
8 [and crowns his devoted ones] with goodness and compassion.
[May my soul shout to extol your Name,]
9 [to proclaim] with cheers your acts of goodness
to ann[ounce your constancy;]

Frag. b (= 11Q5 XIX, 12–15)   *1*[and in your shade] I have looked for shelter.
The memory of [your power strengthens my heart,]
[I rest in your acts of goodness.]
2 Forgive my sins, YHWH,
[and cleanse me from my iniquity.]
3 Adorn me [with a spirit of loyalty and knowledge;]
may I not be disgraced in the calami[ty.]

B *Independent collections of apocryphal psalms*

4QNon-Canonical Psalms A (4Q380)

Frag. 1 *col.* I   *1* [...] *2* [...Jerusalem is *3* [the city chosen by YH]WH for ever and
ever *4* [...] holy ones *5* [Because the Na]me of YHWH is invoked over her, *6* [and
his glory] is seen over Jerusalem *7* [and] Zion. Who will utter the Name of
8 YHWH? And who shall proclaim all [his] praise? *9* YHWH [remem]bered him
in his favour and visited him *10* in order to make him see the good *11* [of his
chosen] ones in order to che[er him in the joy of his people.]

Frag. 1 *col.* II   *1* He made a man for you [...] *2* Because he is the one [whose
wo]rds they keep [...] *3* which is for all the children of Israel [...] *4* May your
hand rescue you, for God's power [...] *5* doing good and hating the wicked.
Until [when...] *6* will you take pleasure in doing evil? Unless the wicked person

expires [...] *7 Blank 8* Hymn of Obadiah. God [...] *9* the truth in it and his kindness [...]

Frag. 2   1 [...] ... [...] *2* [...] mountains and hills [...] *3* [...] those who rely on
them shall shudder [...] *4* [... and they shall shout to] YHWH in their distress.
From their difficulties ...] *5* [... and he will free them. For] with the devout
YHWH is compassionate. [...] *6* [...] to the man [...] *7* [...] ... [...]

Frag. 4   1 Hymn of [...] *2* You shall repel the [...] *3* He will make [...] wise *4* and
... [...]

4QNon-Canonical Psalms B (4Q381)

Frag. 1   1 [...] I proclaimed.
And I reflected on his wonders
which for me shall be (the) teaching of justice.
2 [...] my mouth;
and to the simple, and they shall understand,
and to those without heart, and they shall know YHWH.
How power[ful...]
3 wonders!
He, in his day, made the heavens and the earth.
With a word from his mouth [...]
4 and torrents;
they shall channel their streams (?),
pools and every whirlwind,
and ... [...]
5 the night, the stars and the constellations;
and he caused [...] to shine (?) [...]
6 tree and every fru[it of the vi]ne
and all the produce of the field.
And according to his words ... [...]
7 to [his wi]fe.
And by his spirit he established them
to control all of them in the earth,
and with all [...]
8 month by month, feast by feast, day by day,
to eat its fruit ...[...]
9 [...]
and the birds and all that is theirs
to eat the best of everything.
And also [...]

10 [...] in them
and all his armies and his an[gels...]
11 [...] in order to serve man
and help him and [...]

Frag. 15   *1* [...] you shall change my heart and [...]
2 [...Turn your face to me
and have pity on me,
give your strength to your servant]
and save the son of your maidservant.
3 Show me [a sign for good,
so that those who hate me see it and are bewildered,
because you,] my God, did help me
and I made my case to you, my God.
4 [...You control the de]pths of the sea
and you calm its waves;
5 you [crushed Rahab like a corpse,
with your powerful arm you scattered your enemies.
The world and] what fills it, you established
6 You have a [powerful] arm;
[strong is your hand;
upraised is your right.
Who in the heavens is like you] my God?
And who among the sons of gods?
7 And in the whole [company of the holy ones?...
For you] are the glory of its grandeur,
and I, your anointed, have understood.

Frag. 24   *4* Hymn of the man of God.
YHWH God [...]
5 He has redeemed Judah from all hardships,
and of Ephraim [...]
6 generation.
The mighty shall praise you and say:
'Arise, my God [...]...[...]
7 Your Name is my salvation;
my rock, my fortress and my deliverer [is YHWH...]
8 On the day of [my hardship] I will call to YHWH
and my God will answer me;
my help [...] those who hate me.
And [...] will say: *9* because [...] to the people, and I [... (may) my sh]out before him reach his ears.

Frag. 31   *1* [...] in the net which they hide [...] ... [...] I will sing to you, YHWH, [...] *2* [...] I will praise your wonders [...] before you. [...] You will rescue me and extricate me from the teeth of death. And you [...] (to) the heights of all [...] *3* [...] of all his path [...] in a holy place. [...] *Blank*

4 [Prayer of ...] King of Judah:

Listen, [my] God [...] ... my strength

[...] I will narrate before those who fear you

[...] ... with me [...]

5 [... Your th]oughts,

who can understand them?

For my enemies are before you.

You have humiliated them and the ones who detest my life

you have overturned them before your eyes,

I shall live, for, [...]

6 [... You will not] hide (the) sin from those who have knowledge.

You will destroy them.

God of my salvation, the days of my service are counted.

What can I do?

Here I am, weak,

7 [... You will deliver] to the sword those waiting for me;

on the day of wrath, those who say ...

They have plaited a crown for my head.

I shall know the fruits of their glory,

8 and their ornaments [...]

a question on my lips [...]

from the book of life [...]

those who bully me will stop

my enemies will die,

and not [...]

9 [...]...song of thanksgiving

[...] with you [...] *Blank*

Frag. 33   *1* [...] and for her there will be no offspring [...] ... [...] *2* And you will establish for my times and ... [...Above the heavens, rise, YHWH, and ... [...] *3* and we will revel in your might, because [your wisdom] is unfathomable [...] ... your reproach will be *4* eternal [...] for me and for your glory. For my faults are too many for me and [...] ... But you, my God, will send your spirit and [have pity] *5* on the son of your maidservant, and compassion on the servant who approaches you. And [...] I will sing and rejoice in you in the presence of those who fear you, for [you will judge] *6* your servants in your justice according to your compassion [...] to set free ... [...] (to) you. *Selah. Blank 7 Blank* *8* Prayer of Manasseh, king of Judah, when the King of Assyria put him in

prison. [...]
My God [...] near,
my salvation is in front of your eyes;
[...]
9 I await the salvation of your presence.
I yield to you for my sins,
for you have incr[eased your compassion],
whereas I have added to my fault,
and so [have separated myself] from everlasting joy.
10 You have not looked at the goodness of my soul,
for [...]

Frag. 45   1 And I shall understand and teach whoever does not understand. Him
[...] and I shall fear you and purify myself 2 from all the abominations that I
am aware of. And I shall humble my soul in your presence [...] They increased
sin, plotted against me 3 to confine me. But I trusted in you [...] 4 Do not pronounce sentence against me, my God [...] 5 Those conniving against me open
a deceitful tongue [...] 6 for me. The deeds of [...] 7 ... [...]

Frag. 46   1 [...] against me [...] 2 Your abundant favours [...] ... [...] a horn is
given to me [...] 3 with you. And I ... [...] idols. Your laws, your splendour and
your beauty [...] 4 will spread out like clouds over the face [of the earth ...] and
our sandy places, and they will be scattered in great numbers, until [...] 5 Man
will not be prevail, nor will [...] arise [...] you test everyone. The chosen (ones),
like the offerings, you will purify in your presence. Those who are hated 6 you
will reject like uncleanness. A storm wind [...] their deeds. But those who fear
you will be before you forever. Their horns are horns of 7 steel with which they
gore many. They will gore [...] You will make their hooves of bronze, and
sinners 8 will be trampled like dirt on the face of the earth. [...] They will be
hurled from before [...] And your spirit [...] 9 [...] and a searing fire [...] ...
[...]

Frag. 69   1 [...] (to) them because [...] When he saw that the peoples of the earth
behaved abominably 2 [...] all the earth went from impure defilement to impure
defilement. And wonderfully, from the beginning, 3 [...] conferred with his
heart to destroy them from upon it and to create on it a people for himself
4 [...] And through his spirit he gave you prophets to teach you and show you
5 [...] /he came down from heaven and spoke to you to teach you and keep you
away from the deeds of the inhabitants of/ he gave you laws, instructions and
commandments of the covenant which he established through the hand of
[Moses ...] 6 [...] to reside on the earth. Then it will be purified and [...] 7 [...]
to consider among yourselves if you will be for him, or if [...] 8 [...] and break

the covenant which he established with you, and act like foreigners and [...]
9 [...] against wickedness and alter his words from his mouth. [...] 10 [...] ...
[...]

Frags. 76–77   1 [...] for me. Animals and birds, be gathered [...] 2 [...] with the
sons of man, following the inclination of the thou[ghts of their heart ...] 3 [...]
will be destruction [...] 4 [...] fire and annihilation. And [...] not 5 [...] the
people of its belongings. [...] 6 [...] ... [...] *Blank* 7 [...] congregation of the
Holy of Holies, lot of the King of Kings [...] 8 [...] my word. You will pay
attention to the wisdom which issues from my mouth, and will understand [...]
9 [...] and the honest judge and the reliable witness. Do you perhaps have the
strength to answer him? [...] 10 [...] to proclaim. Who among you will reply
and dispute with him? [...] 11 [...] because those who judge you are many and
those who bear witness against you are countless. But is [...] 12 [...] YHWH will
sit in judgement with you to judge in truth and without injustice [...] 13 [...]
his spirits, to render you judgments of truth. Is there knowledge, for you to
learn it? [...] 14 [...] Lord of Lords, hero, wonderful. There is no-one like him.
He has chosen you [...] 15 [... from among] many [peoples] and from among
great nations so that you will be a people for him, to rule over everyone [...]
16 [...] heaven and earth, and to be at the summit of all the nations of the earth,
and to [...]

2 The Hymns

1QHymns^a (1QHodayoth^a [1QH^a])

Cols. I–III [*Nothing has been preserved.*]

Col. III (= *frags.* 16 + 11)

Frag. 16   *1* [...] turning himself round [...] *2* [...] the oppressed [...] *3* [...] his gentleness with the poor [...] *4* [...] And who can measure [...] *5* [...] ? And who can measure the strength of [...] *6* [...] eternal. Who plots [...] *7* [...] previous [...] *8* [...] ... [...]

Frag. 11   *1* [...] ... [...] *2* [...] it has stood for all the years of eternity [...] *3* [...] from your hand every seal ... [...] *4* [...] ... the sons of man according to their intelligence [...] *5* [...] his kingship. Who has made all these things? [...] *6* [...] for you the pleasure. In justice shall you place [...] *7* [...] in your presence [...] and the creature of clay [...] *8* [...] he will answer. You are glorified above all the go[ds ...] *9* [...] holiness, and according to what there is in your soul [...] *10* [...] for your name. You [...] in the congregation of the holy [ones...]

Col. IV (= XVII + *frag.* 14)   *1* [...] a low measure [...] *2* [...] revealed, without judg[ment, for] by the spirit *3* [...] a fire which consumes the fl[esh of] their dead without *4* [...] in the dry earth [...] without judgment *5* [...] striking suddenly, unexpectedly [...] as wax *6* [melts in front of the fire ...] judgment by the spirit which seeks you. And there will arise *7* [...] you shall throw into [...] the commandment. *Blank* By the spirit [...] ... *8* [...] by the blows of [...] *Blank* [...] *Blank*
9 [I give you thanks, Lord,]
for the secrets which [...]
which do not [...] reach
10 [...] and by the judgment of [...]
thoughts of wickedness [...]
11 [...] and by the judgment [...]
[You have purified] your servant from all his sins
[by the abundance of your co]mpassion,
12 [as y]ou said through the hand of Moses,
[forgiving rebellion,] iniquity, sin,
atoning for [failings] and disloyalty.
13 [Even though you burn] the foundations of mountains
and fire [sears] the base of Sheol,
those who [keep] your regulations [are saved.]

14 [You protect] the ones who serve you loyally,
    so that their posterity is before you all the days.
    You raise an [eternal] name for them,
15 [forgiving them all] sin,
    eliminating from them all their depravities,
    giving them as a legacy all the glory of Adam
    and plentiful days. *Blank*
16 Blank
17 [I give you thanks, Lord,]
    for the spirits you have placed in me.
    I shall find the reply on (my) tongue
    to recount your (acts of) justice,
18 the patience [of your judgments,]
    the deeds of your mighty right (hand),
    to confess my former sins,
    to bow low and beg favour
19 for […] of my deeds
    and the depravity of my heart.
    Because I wallowed in impurity,
    [I separated myself] from the foundation [of truth]
    and I was not allied with […]
20 […]
    To you does justice belong,
    blessing belongs to your Name for ever!
    [Act according to] your justice,
21 free [the soul of your servant,]
    the wicked should die!
    However, I have understood
    that [you establish] the path of the one whom you choose
22 and in the insight [of your wisdom]
    you prevent him from sinning against you,
    you restore his humility through your punishments,
    and by your ord[eals streng]then his heart. *Blank*
23 [You, Lord, prevent] your servant
    from sinning against you,
    from tripping over all the words of your will.
    Engrave your com[mandments in him,]
    so that he can hold himself up against [fiendish] spirits,
24 so that he can walk in all that you love
    and loathe all that you hate,
    [so he can do] what is good in your eyes
25 […] in my vitals,

for your servant is a spirit of flesh. *Blank*

26 [I give you thanks, Lord, because] you have spread your holy spirit upon your servant [...] ... [...] his heart *27* [...] and I will consider every human treaty [...] they shall find it *28* [...] and those who love it [...] for ever and ever.

Col. V (= XIII + *frags.* 15 + 31 + 17 + 20 + 33)   [Chant for the Ins]tructor for [...] God's deeds *2* [...] and to make the simple understand [...] eternal *3* [...] of knowledge, to make the man [...] of flesh understand, and the council of the spirits [...] they walked *4* [...Blessed] are you, Lord, because the spirit of flesh is forgiven through your mer[cies ...] with the strength of your power, *5* [the greatness of] your favour, with the abundance of your goodness, [the slowness] of your wrath and the zeal of your judgment [... without] limit. Every*6*[one who has been chosen by] the knowledge of all intelligence will understand [...] and the mysteries of your plan and the beginning of [...] you have established. *7* [For] to you belongs holiness before the centuries and for ever and ever. You are [...] holy ones *8* [...] And in your wonderful mysteries you have instructed me for your glory, and the depth of [...] of your knowledge (does) not *9* [...] But you have revealed the paths of truth and the deeds of evil, wisdom and folly, [...] *10* [...] their deeds: truth and insight, sin and folly. They have all walked [...] *11* [comp]assion and everlasting favour for all the periods of peace, and ruin for all [...] *12* his judgments. Everlasting glory, delight and unending enjoyment for a [good] deed [... but ...and puni]shment for *13* a bad de[ed.] *Blank*

These are those you fou[nded before] the centuries,

14 to judge through them all your works before creating them,
together with the host of your spirits and the assembly of [the gods,]
with the holy vault and all its hosts,

15 with the earth and all its produce,
in the seas and in the deeps,
according to all their designs for all the eternal ages

16 and the final visitation
For you have established them
before the centuries,
and [in them you have enha]nced the action of [man]

17 so that they can recount your glory throughout all your kingdom;
for you have shown them what they had never seen,
[overcoming] what was there from of old
and creating new things,

18 demolishing ancient things
and erecting what would exist for ever.
For you have established them
and you will exist for ever and ever.

19 In the mysteries of your insight
you have apportioned all these things,
to make your glory known.
However, what is the spirit of flesh
to fathom all these matters
20 and to appreciate your great and wondrous secret?
What is someone born of a woman among all your awesome works?
21 He is a structure of dust shaped with water,
his base is the guilt of sin,
vile unseemliness, source of impurity,
over which a spirit of degeneracy rules.
22 *Blank*
If he brings about evil it will be an eternal [sign,]
a portent for generations,
shame for all flesh.
23 Only by your goodness is man acquitted,
[purified] by your abundant compa[ssion.]
You embellish him with your grandeur,
you install him in your abundant pleasures,
24 with everlasting peace and lengthy days.
For [you are the truth,]
and you do not go back on your word. *Blank*
And I, your servant, have known
25 thanks to the spirit you have placed in me
[…]
and all your deeds are just,
and you do not go back on your word,
26 and all your periods are fixed
[…] chosen for their pleasures.
And I know […]
27 the wicked […] so that he may realise […] *28* […] your spirits […] *29* […] …
[…]

Col. VI (= XIV + *frags.* 15 + 18 + 22 + 44 + 9)   *1* […] his instructions […] in your
people […] … *2* […] our ears […]
[Fortunate,] the men of truth,
those chosen by jus[tice, those probing the] mind,
3 those searching for wisdom, those bui[lding …]
[those who l]ove compassion, the poor in spirit,
4 those refined by poverty and those purified by ordeal,
the com[passionate … those who keep the]ir nerve until the time of judgment,
5 those alert for your salvation.

And you [...] have strengthened your precepts through their hands
6 to make judgment on the world,
   so that all inherit your jus[tice...]
   holy for everlasting generations.
7 And all [...] of their deeds,
   with [...] the men of your vision. *Blank*
8 *Blank*
   [I give you thanks,] Lord,
   for putting wisdom in the heart of your servant
9 to know these matters,
   to unders[tand...]
   to be encouraged in the face of the assaults of evil,
10 to bless, in justice, all the chosen ones of your will
   [... to love all th]at you love,
   and hate all that you [loathe.]
11 You teach your servant
   [...] of the spirits of man,
   for corresponding to the spirits
   you allot them between good and evil,
12 and set over them [...
   to sho]w them their actions.
   But I,
   I have known, thanks to your insight
13 that in your kindness towards man
   you have enlarged his share with the spirit of your holiness.
   Thus, you make me approach your intelligence,
14 and to the degree that I approach
   my fervour against all those who act wickedly
   and (against) men of guile increases;
   for everyone who approaches you,
   does not defy your orders,
15 and everyone who knows you
   does not change your words.
   For you are just,
   and all your chosen ones are truth.
   All sin and wickedness
16 you obliterate for ever,
   and your justice is revealed to the eyes of all your creatures.
   Blank
17 But I,
   I have known, thanks to the wealth of your goodness,
   and with an oath I have enjoined my soul

not to sin against you
18 and not to do anything which is evil in your eyes.
In this way I force all the men of my counsel
to make progress in the community.
19 According to his intelligence I promote him,
I love him in proportion to his abundant inheritance.
I do not lift my face to evil,
or consider a wicked gift.
20 I do not exchange your truth for wealth,
or for a gift all your judgments.
Quite the reverse, to the degree [...] I love him,
21 and to the extent that you remove it from him, I hate him. *Blank*
I will not admit into the council [of your truth]
22 someone distant from your covenant.
Blank
23 I give you thanks, Lord,
according to your great strength
and your abundant wonders
from eternity and for eternity.
You are lofty, great, lavish in favours,
24 you are someone who forgives those who turn away from sin
and someone who punishes the depravity of the wicked.
[You love the truth] with a generous heart
25 and you hate depravity, for ever.
And myself, your servant, you have favoured me
with the spirit of knowledge
[so that I can love] truth [and justice,]
26 so that I loathe all the paths of wickedness.
I love you liberally, with (my) whole heart,
27 [with (my) whole soul I look for] your wisdom,
because these things happen at your hand
and without [your approval nothing exists.]
28 [...] flesh will rule it [...] ... [...] *29* [...] him, and he will construct with help,
the [...] *30* [...] of the vault upon the wings of the wind [...]

Col. VII (= XV + *frags.* 10 + 32 + 34 + 42)   *1* [...] ... [...] *2* [...] ... I have received
intelligence [...] *3* [... to your won]ders what reply shall we make? For you have
dealt [kindly] with us and have done wonders [with us...] *4* [...] they will not
gather the strength to know {in} your glory [or to tell] of your wond[ers...]
5 [...] ... according to their intelligence. And in accordance with this knowledge
[and by] your glory [...] *6* below [...] unceasingly. And from age to age he will
make ... hear [...] *7* [...] And we have collected together as a Community, and

with those who know [...] ... /for you/ ... *8* your compassion [...] the people
of your heroes, and before your wonders we shall sing together [...] ... *9* at the
time of [...] our harvests [...] sons of man. And among [the sons of] Adam
10 because [...] wonderful to the utmost. *Blank* [...] *Blank* *11* in [...] ... *12* [...]
13 [...] they will love you for all days [...] *14* [...] I love you lavishly, with (my)
whole heart and with all (my) soul I purify [...] *15* [... not] to turn aside from
all that you have commanded. I have joined the Many [... so as not] *16* to desert
all your precepts. *Blank*
But I,
I have known, thanks to your intellect,
that it is not by a hand of flesh that the path of man [is straightened out,]
17 nor can a human being establish his steps.
I know that every spirit is fashioned by your hand,
18 [and all its travail] you have established
even before creating him.
How can anyone change your words?
You, you alone, have created the just man.
19 For him, from the womb, you determined the period of approval,
so that he will keep your covenant and walk on all (your paths),
20 to [empty] upon him your plentiful compassion,
to open all the narrowness of his soul to eternal salvation
and endless peace, without want.
21 Upon flesh you have raised his glory. *Blank*
But the wicked you have created for the time of wrath,
from the womb you have predestined them for the day of annihilation.
22 For they walk on paths that are not good,
they reject your covenant,
their soul loathes your decrees,
they take no pleasure in what you command,
23 instead they choose what you hate.
You have established all those [who hate your law]
to carry out great judgments against them
24 in the eyes of all your creatures,
so they will be a sign and an omen
[for] eternal [generations,]
so that all will know your glory
25 and your great might.
What, then, is flesh, to understand [your wonders?]
And how can dust direct its steps?
26 You have fashioned the spirit
and have organised its task.
From you comes the path of every living being.

But I, I have known
27 that utter wealth cannot compare to your truth,
 and I have [...] your holiness.
 I know that you have chosen them above all
28 and they will serve you forever.
 You do not take [gifts for evil deeds,]
 or accept a bribe for wicked acts.
29 For you are God of truth
 and you [destroy] all sin.
 [...]
 will no longer exist in your presence.
 I know that [...] belongs to you
30 [...] ... [...] 31 your holiness [...] 32 because in [...]

Col. VIII (= XVI + frag. 13)   1 [...] all [...] 2 [...] admits into the number of 3 [...]
 in heaven and on earth 4 [...] and in your hand is the judgment of all 5 [...] and
 what he think of them? ... 6 [...] and nothing is done 7 [...] according to your
 advice you visited them 8 [...] with ... 9 [...] ... 10 for your spirit of ho[liness
 ...] ... [...] and 11 your spirit of holiness 10 is unable to 11 [...] the fullness of
 heaven and earth [...] your glory. The fullness [...]
12 I know that in your kindness towards man
 you have multiplied [...]
 your truth in all [...]
13 and the stance of justice [...]
 which you have positioned over him [...]
 to stumble in all [...]
14 Through my awareness of all this
 my tongue will find a reply
 to [...] my sin
 to look for the spirit [...]
15 to be strengthened by the spirit of holiness,
 to adhere to the truth of your covenant,
 to serve you in truth, with a perfect heart,
 to love your [will.]
16 Be blessed, Lord,
 creator [of all things,]
 [mighty] in acts,
 everything is your work.
 You have resolved, in fact, to take pity [on your servant,]
17 to show me favour by the spirit of your compassion
 and by the splendour of your glory.
 To you belongs justice

because you done all [this.]

18 And since I know that you have recorded the spirit of the just man,

I have chosen to purify my hands in accordance with your will

and your servant's soul detests every work of sin.

19 I know that no-one besides you is just.

I have appeased your face by the spirit which you have given me,

20 to lavish your favour on your servant for [ever,]

to purify me with your holy spirit,

to approach your will according to the extent of your kindnesses.

21 ...[...]

the stance of your will which you have chosen

for those who love you,

and for those who keep your precep[ts ...]

22 in your presence for ever.

[May ...not]

associate with the spirit of your servant

or with all their works for [ever!]

23 [...]

May no affliction [come] upon him

so he does not stumble on the precepts of your covenant!

For [...] glory.

24 And you, you are [a lenient] and compassionate [God,]

slow to anger, full of favour and of truth,

who forgives sin [...]

25 and has pity on the [evil of those who love you]

and keep your precepts,

those who turn to you with trust

and a perfect heart [...]

26 to serve you [and to do what] is good in your eyes.

Do not turn your face away from your servant,

[do not reject] the son of your maidservant!

[...]

27 [...]

And I, through your word I have approached

[...]

28 [...]

Col. IX (= I)   *1–2* ... [...] *3* eternal [...] *4* in it, and the judgment [...] for [...] ...

5 source of po[wer ...] great counsel [...] without number, and your zeal *6* be–

fore [...] long for (the) anger in the judgment [...] just in all your works.

7 In your wisdom you es[tablished] eternal [...];

before creating them you know all their deeds

8 for ever and ever. [...]

[Without you] nothing is done,

and nothing is known without your will.

9 You have fashioned every spirit

and [...]

and the judgment of all their deeds.

Blank

10 You have stretched out the heavens for your glory.

Everything [which it contains you have established] according to your approval:

powerful spirits, according to their laws,

11 before they changed into [holy] angels [in their residences,]

into eternal spirits in their realms,

the luminaries in their mysteries,

12 the stars in their circuits,

the stormy winds in their roles,

lightning and thunder in their duties

13 [you have established] the deposits of the computations in th[eir] purposes

[...] in their secrets.

Blank

You have created the earth with your strength,

14 seas and deeps [...]

you have founded them with your wisdom,

everything which is in them

15 you have founded with your will.

[...]

so that the spirit of man rules over the world

16 for all days everlasting and unceasing generations,

so that [...] in their seasons.

You have shared out their tasks in all their generations

17 and the regulation at predetermined times

to ru[le...]

generation after generation

just like the visitation of this punishment

18 with all its agonies.

[...] you share it out

among all their descendants

according to the number of their eternal generations

19 for all the endless years.

[...]

And in the wisdom of your knowledge

you have determined their course

before they came to exist.

20 And with [your approval] everything happens,
  and without you nothing occurs.
  Blank
21 These things I know through your knowledge,
  for you opened my ears to wondrous mysteries
  although I am a creature of clay, fashioned with water,
22 foundation of shame, source of impurity,
  oven of iniquity, building of sin,
  spirit of mistake, astray, without knowledge,
23 terrified by your just judgments.
  What will I be able to say which is not known?
  What will I be able to declare which has not been told.
24 Everything has been engraved in your presence
  with the stylus of remembrance
  for all the incessant periods
  in the eras of the number of everlasting years
  in all their predetermined times,
  and nothing will be hidden,
  nothing will remain away from your presence.
25 How will a man count his sin?
  How will he defend his infringements?
26 How will he answer every just judgment?
  To you, God of knowledge,
  belong all the works of justice
27 and the foundation of truth;
  to the sons of man,
  the service of sin and the deeds of deception.
  Blank
28 You created breath on the tongue,
  you know its words,
  you instituted the fruits of lips,
  before they came to be;
  you placed a rhythm for words,
29 and a cadence to the puff of breath from the lips;
  you make the rhythms emerge by their mysteries
  and the puffs of breaths by their measures,
30 to declare your glory and tell your wonders,
  in all the deeds of your truth and of your just judgments,
  to praise your name through the mouth of all.
31 And they will know you by your intellect
  and they will bless you for [everlasting] centuries.
  Blank

And you, in your compassion,
32 and in the vastness of your mercy,
   have strengthened the spirit of man
   before his miseries,
   you have [...] him
   you have purified him from abundant evil
33 so that he can tell your wonders before all your works.
   Blank
   [...]
   the judgments which torment me,
34 and to the sons of man, all the wonders
   which you have achieved [...]
   Blank
35 Listen, wise men,
   and you, meditating with knowledge,
   and (you) cowards,
   be of staunch purpose!
   [...] increase caution!
36 Just men, finish with injustice!
   And all of you, of perfect way,
   strengthen [...] the poor!
37 Be slow to anger,
   and do not spurn [...]
   his heart does not understand these matters
38 *Blank*
   [...]
39 [and the bru]tal will grind their tee[th ...]

Col. X (= II)   *1–2* [...] ... [...] *3* [...] all the deeds of wickedness [...] *4* [...] ... [...]
[of truth] /of justice/ in all [...] *5* [...] overwhelmed [...] those who announce
joy to the mourner, the [...] *6* [...,] to all destruction [...] the strong, to mollify
my heart, the dynamic, *7* before the [calam]ity.
   But you give the tongue's reply
   to my uncircumcised lips,
   you support my soul
   strengthening my kidneys
8 and increasing strength;
   you guide my steps on the frontier of evil.
   I am a trap for offenders,
9 medicine for everyone who turns away from sin,
   discretion for simple folk,
   staunch purpose for the timorous at heart.

10 You have set me as a reproach and a mockery of traitors,
foundation of truth and of knowledge
for those on the straight path. *Blank*
On account of the offence of the wicked
11 I have been the target of slander in the mouth of violent men,
and the scoffers grind their teeth.
You have made me into a laughing-stock for sinners,
12 the assembly of the wicked is roused against me,
they roar like the turbulence of the seas
when their waves beat
13 and spew out ash and mud.
But you have set me like a flag
for the elect of justice,
like a wise sower of secret wonders. *Blank*
14 To put to the test [all the men of] truth,
to refine those who love learning.
To those who spread fallacies I am a man of dissent,
15 [but a man of peace] to all true observers.
I have turned into an ardent spirit
against all the interpreters of flat[tering] things.
16 [All] arrogant men mutter against me
like the mighty din of turbulent water;
[all] their thoughts are devilish schemes.
17 They throw the life of a man into the ditch
the one whom you established through my mouth
and to whom you have imparted knowledge.
18 In his heart you have put the opening of the source of wisdom
for all those who understand.
But they have changed them
19 by uncircumcised lip and weird tongue
into a people without understanding,
and so they go astray in their delusions. *Blank*
20 Blank
I give you thanks, Lord,
because you put me in the bag of life
21 and have protected me from all the traps of the pit,
for vicious men have ambushed my soul
22 when I relied on your covenant.
They are a council of futility,
a devilish assembly.
They do not know that through you I subsist
23 and in your compassion you have saved my life,

because from you come my steps.
They – they attack my life on your account,
24 so that you will be honoured by the judgment of the wicked,
and you will make yourself great through me
before the sons of man
25 because through your compassion I do subsist.
I have said:
heroes have set up camp against me
surrounded by all their weapons of war;
26 they loose off arrows without any cure;
the tip of the spear, like fire which consumes trees.
27 Like the crash of turbulent water
is the roar of their voices,
like a hurricane storm
which destroys many.
Right up to the stars
28 burst emptiness and nothing
when their waves heave upwards.
But you, when my heart turned to water
confirmed my soul in your covenant.
29 And the net which they spread for me
has entangled their feet,
in the trap they set for my life
they have fallen.
«My foot remains on the right path,
30 in his assembly I shall bless your Name».
Blank
31 I give you thanks, Lord,
for your eye [keeps watch] over me.
You have freed me from the zeal of the sowers of deceit,
32 from the congregation of the interpreters of flattering things.
You have freed the life of the poor person
which they thought to finish off,
pouring out his blood while he was at your service.
33 But they did not know
that my steps come from you.
They have put me as a mockery and a reproof
34 in the mouth of all the interpreters of trickery. *Blank*
But you, my God,
have freed the soul of the poor and needy
35 from the hand of someone stronger than him;
from the hand of the powerful you have saved my soul,

and at their taunts you have not let me lose heart

36 so as to desert serving you

from fear of destruction by the wicked

and exchange a firm purpose for follies

37 which […]

the edicts, and by witness given to their ears

38 […]

to all their descendants

39 […]

among your followers.

Col. XI (= III + frag. 25)   *1–2* […] … […] *3* […] you have made my face shine […]

4 […] to you, with everlasting glory, together with all […] *5* […] your mouth,

and you have freed me from […] and from […]

6 Blank Now, my soul […]

they have counted me, and have put the soul

like a boat in the depths [of the sea],

7 like a besieged city positioned opposite [its enemies].

I was in distress

like a woman giving birth the first time

when her birth-pangs come on her

8 and a pain racks her womb

to begin the birth in the «crucible» of the pregnant woman.

Since sons reach the frontiers of death

9 and the woman expectant with a man is racked by her pains,

for from the shores of death

she gives birth to a male,

and there emerges from the pains of Sheol,

10 from the «crucible» of the pregnant woman

a splendid counsellor with his strength,

and the man is freed from the womb.

Into the woman expectant with him rush all the spasms

11 and the wrenching pains of his birth;

terror (seizes) those giving birth,

and at his birth all the pains come suddenly,

12 on the «crucible» of the pregnant woman.

And she who is pregnant by the serpent

is with a wrenching pain;

and the edge of the pit

is with all the deeds of terror.

13 The foundations of the wall shake

like a ship on the surface of the sea,

and the clouds echo with the uproar.
And both he who lives in the dust
14 and he who sails upon the sea
are terrified by the din of the water.
For them their wise men are like sailors on the deeps,
15 for all their wisdom is perplexed
by the roar of the sea,
by the welling up of the deeps
upon the springs of water;
[they churn] to form huge waves,
16 the gates of the water, with clamorous sound.
And when they are wild, [Sheol and Abaddon] open;
all the arrows of the pit
17 make their voice heard while going down to the abyss;
the gates of [...] open
[...] the deeds of the serpent.
18 And the gates of the pit close
upon the woman expectant with wickedness,
and the everlasting bolts
upon all the spirits of the serpent. *Blank*
19 *Blank* I thank you, Lord,
because you saved my life from the pit,
and from Sheol and Abaddon you have lifted me up
20 to an everlasting height,
so that I can walk on a boundless plain.
And I know that there is hope
21 for someone you fashioned out of clay
to be an everlasting community.
The corrupt spirit you have purified
from the great sin
so that he can take his place
22 with the host of the holy ones,
and can enter in communion
with the congregation of the sons of heaven.
You cast eternal destiny for man
with the spirits of knowledge,
23 so that he praises your name together in celebration,
and tells of your wonders before all your works.
And I, a creature of clay,
24 what am I?
Mixed with water, with whom shall I be counted?
What is my strength?

For I find myself at the boundary of wickedness
25 and with those doomed by lot.
   The soul of the poor person lived amongst great turmoil,
   and the calamities of hardship are with my footsteps.
26 When the traps of the pit open
   all the snares of wickedness are spread
   and the nets of the doomed are upon the surface of the sea.
27 When all the arrows of the pit fly without return
   they hit without hope.
   When the measuring line for judgment fails,
   and the lot of anger against the forsaken
28 and the outburst of wrath against the hypocrites,
   and the period of anger against Belial,
   and the ropes of death approach with no escape,
29 then the torrents of Belial will overflow their high banks
   like a fire which devours all those drawing water (?)
   destroying every tree, green or dry, from its canals.
30 He revolves like flames of fire
   until none of those who drink are left.
   He consumes the foundations of clay
31 and the tract of dry land;
   the bases of the mountains does he burn
   and converts the roots of flint rock
   into streams of lava.
   It consumes right to the great deep.
32 The torrents of Belial burst into Abaddon.
   The schemers of the deep howl with the din
   of those extracting mud.
33 The earth cries out at the calamity with overtakes the world,
   and all its schemers scream,
   and all who are upon it go crazy,
34 and melt away in the great calamity.
   For God thunders with the thunder of his great strength,
   and his holy residence echoes with the truth of his glory,
35 and the host of the heavens adds its noise,
   and the eternal foundations melt and shake,
   and the battle of heavenly heroes spans the globe,
36 and does not return until it has terminated
   the destruction decided forever.
   There is nothing like it. *Blank*
37 *Blank*
   I give you thanks, Lord,

for you are a massive rampart for me

38 […] against destroyers and against all […] *39* […] you hide me from the calamities of the commotion […] *40* […] steel bars they shall not enter […] *41* […] around it, unless … […]

Col. XII (= IV + frag. 43)   *1-2* […]… […] *3* […] my foot upon the rock […] *4* […] eternal path, and /on/ the tracks which you have chosen […] *5* *Blank*
I give you thanks, Lord,
because you have brightened my face with your covenant
6 and […] I have looked for you.
Like perfect dawn you have revealed yourself to me with your light.
But (to) them, your people,
7 [interpreters of deceit, with their wo]rds they lure them,
sowers of fraud [misdirect them]
and make them fall without them being aware.
8 For in folly they carry out their deeds.
Because I have been an object of ridicule for them,
and they do not esteem me
when you make yourself great through me.
For they evict me from my land
9 like a bird from the nest;
all my friends and my acquaintances have been taken away from me,
and rank me like a broken jug.
But they are sowers of deceit
10 and seers of fraud,
they have plotted evil against me {…}
to alter your Law, which you engraved in my heart,
by flattering teachings for your people;
11 they have denied the drink of knowledge to the thirsty,
in their thirst they have given them vinegar to drink
to consider their mistake,
12 so they may act like fools in their feasts
so they will be caught in their nets.
But you, O God, abhor all the scheming of Belial
13 and your counsel remains,
and the plan of your heart persists endlessly.
But they, hypocrites, plot intrigues of Belial,
14 they look for you with a double heart,
and are not firmly based in your truth.
There is in their thoughts a root which produces poison and wormwood,
15 with stubbornness of heart they inquire,
they look for you among the idols,

place in front of themselves the stumbling-block of their offences,
16 they go to look for you in the mouth of prophets of deceit
attracted by delusion.
They speak to your people with stuttering lip and weird tongue
17 to convert to folly all their deeds with tricks.
For they have not chosen the path of your heart
nor have they listened to your word.
18 They said of the vision of knowledge: It is not certain!
and of the path of your heart: It is not that!
But you, O God, will answer them, judging them with your power
19 according to their idols and their numerous sins,
so that in their schemes are caught
those who deviate from your covenant.
20 At the judgment you will annihilate all the men of deception,
there will no longer exist seers of delusion.
For there is no folly in all your acts,
21 and there is no deception in the intentions of your heart.
Those in harmony with you,
will persist in your presence always;
those who walk on the path of your heart,
22 will be established permanently.
And I, when I lean on you,
I remain resolute and rise above those who scorn me,
and my hands succeed against all those who mock me;
23 for they do not value me,
even though you exhibit your power in me
and reveal yourself in me with your strength to enlighten them.
You have not covered in disgrace
24 the face of all those looking for me,
those who unite /together/ for your covenant.
Those who walk on the path of your heart have listened to me,
25 they have aligned themselves with you in the council of the holy ones.
You will make his right triumph,
and truth through justice.
You will not mislead them at the hand of the doomed
26 as they have schemed against them;
instead you will put their fear into your people
and the scattering of all the peoples of the lands,
to destroy, at the judgment, all who violate your word.
27 Through me you have enlightened the face of the Many,
you have increased them, even making them uncountable,
for you have shown me your wondrous mysteries.

28 By your wondrous advice you have strengthened my position
   and worked wonders in the presence of the Many
   on account of your glory,
29 and to show your power to all living things.
   What is flesh compared to this?
   What creature of clay can do wonders?
   He is in sin from his maternal womb,
30 and in guilty iniquity right to old age.
   But I know that justice does not belong to man
   nor the perfect path to the son of man.
31 To God Most High belong all the acts of justice,
   and the path of man is not secure
   except by the spirit which God creates for him
32 to perfect the path of the sons of man
   so that all his creatures come to know the strength of his power
   and the extent of his compassion
   with all the sons of his approval.
33 And dread and dismay have gripped me,
   all my /bones/ have fractured,
   my heart has melted like wax in front of the fire,
   my knees give way like water which flows down a slope,
34 for I have remembered my faults
   with the disloyalty of my ancestors,
   when the wicked rose up against your covenant
35 and the doomed against your word –
   I said «For my sin I have been barred from your covenant».
   But when I remembered the strength of your hand
36 and the abundance of your compassion
   I remained resolute and stood up;
   my spirit kept firmly in place
   in the face of my distress.
37 For you have supported me by your kindnesses
   and by your abundant compassion.
   Because you atone for sin
   and cle[anse man] of his fault through your justice.
38 It is not possible for man [...]
   you made [...].
   For you created the just and the wicked
   [...]
39 [...] I will tie myself to your covenant until [...]
40 [...] for you are the truth
   and all [your deeds] are justice.

Col. XIII (= V + frag. 29)   *1* on the day of a people [...] *2* your pardons and the great number of [your (acts of) compassion ...] *3* And when I knew this I gained comfort [...] *4* by your approval, and in your hand is the judgment of all. *Blank*

5 I give you thanks, Lord,
  because you did not desert me when I stayed among a [foreign] people [...]
6 [and did not] judge me on my fault,
  nor did you abandon me to the plottings of my desire
  but you saved my life from the pit.
  You put [the soul of the poor and wretched]
7 right among lions,
  intended for the sons of guilt,
  lions which grind the bones of strong men,
  and drink the blood of champions.
8 You made my lodging with many fishermen,
  those who spread the net upon the surface of the sea,
  those who go hunting the sons of iniquity.
  And there you established me for the judgment,
9 and strengthened in my heart the foundation of truth.
  The covenant, therefore, for those looking for it.
  You closed the mouth of the lion cubs,
10 whose teeth are like a sword,
  whose molars are like a sharpened spear,
  they are vipers' venom,
  all their scheming is to lay waste.
11 They lay in wait for me, but did not open their mouths against me.
  For you, my God, hid me from the sons of man,
  concealed your law in me,
12 until the moment of revealing your salvation through me.
  For in the distress of my soul you heard my call,
13 you identified the outcry of my pain in my complaint
  and saved the soul of the poor man in the lair of lions,
  who sharpen their tongue like swords.
14 And you, my God, you closed {their tongue} their teeth
  so they would not rip up {my} the soul of the poor and wretched;
15 their tongue has been drawn in like a sword into the scabbard,
  so that it would not [destroy] the soul of your servant.
  And to show your greatness /through me/ before the sons of man,
16 you did wonders with the poor,
  you placed him like gold in the crucible,
  under the effect of fire
  like purified silver in the furnace of the jeweller

to be refined seven times.

17 The powerful wicked hustle me with their harassment,
and the whole day they crush my soul. *Blank*

18 But you, my God, have changed {my soul} the storm to a calm
and have freed the soul of the poor
like [...]

19 from the power of the lions. *Blank*
Blank

20 {I give you thanks} /Be blessed/ Lord,
because you did not desert the orphan
nor have you slighted the wretch.
For your might [is unfathomable]

21 and your glory measureless.
Wonderful heroes are your attendants,
and a people of simple folk is in the mud before your feet;
[You have performed wonderfully] with those apprehensive of justice,

22 to raise from the uproar
the community of all {the faithful} the poor of compassion.
But I have been the target of sl[ander for my rivals,]

23 cause for quarrel and argument to my neighbours,
for jealousy and anger to those who have joined my covenant,
for challenge and grumbling to all my followers.
[Even all those who e]at my bread

24 have raised their heel against me;
they have mocked me with a wicked tongue
all those who had joined my council;
the men of [my congregation] are stubborn,

25 and mutter round about.
And with the mystery which you have concealed in me
they go slandering towards the sons of destruction.
But to sh[ow my p]ath

26 and because of their guilt
you have concealed the source of knowledge
and the foundation of truth.
They plot evil in their heart,
[men of] Belial have opened a lying tongue,

27 like vipers' venom which stretches for periods
like those who throw themselves in the dust they cast a spell,
serpent's venom, against which there is no incantation.

28 They have become incurable pain,
a wasting disease in the innards of your servant,
which makes [the spirit] stagger

29 and makes an end of strength,
> so that he is unable to remain in his place.
> They have overtaken me in narrow places where there is no escape,
> though not di[viding the gro]ups.

30 They announce the charge against me with the harp,
> their grumblings with verses in harmony,
> with demolition and destruction.
> Resentment has taken hold of me
> and torments like the pangs of giving birth.

31 My heart is in turmoil within me.
> I have dressed in black
> and my tongue sticks to my palate,
> because they surround me with shame of their heart;

32 their intention is obvious to me in bitterness.
> The light of my face has become gloomy with deep darkness,
> my radiance has changed into gloom. *Blank*
> And you, my God,

33 have opened a broad space in my heart
> but they have increased the narrowness
> and have wrapped me in darkness.
> I have eaten the bread of weeping,

34 my drink is tears without end.
> For my eyes are blinded by the grief
> and my soul by the bitterness of the day.
> [Agony] and pain surround me,

35 shame covers my face,
> my bread has turned into quarrel
> and my drink into argument,
> they have entered my bones

36 to make my spirit stagger
> and make an end of strength
> in accordance with the mysteries of sin
> which, by their evil, have altered the deeds of God.
> For I have been tied with ropes

37 which could not be untied,
> with chains which could not be broken;
> a [strong] rampart [surrounds me,]
> iron bars and [bronze] doors [imprison me]

38 [my gaol] is tied to the deep
> without there being [a chance of escape ...]

39 [...]
> [...] of Belial surround my soul [...]

Col. XIV (= VI + frag. 26)   *1* ... [...] *2* my heart in scorn [...] *3* and misfortune
without limit and destruction without [end ...]

4 [But you, my God,]
have opened my ears [to the instruction]
of those who judge with justice
[...]

5 of the assembly of futility and of the council of violence.
You have brought me into the council of [...]
[...] blame.

6 And I know that there is hope for whoever is converted from wickedness
and relinquishes sin [...]

7 to walk on the path of your heart,
without injustice.
I will take comfort above the noise of the people
and the uproar of kingdoms,
when they join together [against me.]

8 [I know] that shortly you will raise
a survivor among your people,
a remnant in your inheritance.
You will purify them to cleanse them of guilt. *Blank*

9 For all your deeds are in truth
and with mercy you judge them
with great compassion and plentiful forgiveness.
According to your mouth you teach them,

10 and according to the correctness of your truth,
to establish them in your council for your glory.
For your own sake have you done (it),
to enhance the law,
[...]

11 the men of your council amongst the sons of man,
to tell everlasting generations your wonders,
and your exploits they will contemplate unceasingly.

12 All the nations will know your truth
and all the peoples your glory.
For you have brought [your truth and your] glory

13 to all the men of your council
and in the lot, together with the angels of the face,
without there being an mediator
between the intelligent and your holy ones.

14 [...]
They will return under your glorious commands,
your princes will be in the lot of [your holy ones.]

15 [Their root] will sprout like a flower [of the field] for ever,
  to make a shoot grow
  in branches of the everlasting plantation
  so that it covers all the world with its shade,
16 [and its tip reaches] up to the skies,
  and its roots down to the abyss.
  All the streams of Eden [will make] its branches [grow]
  and it will be [a huge tree without] limits;
17 the glory of the wood will be over the whole world, endless,
  and [deep] as down to Sheol [its roots.]
  The source of light will be an eternal spring, inexhaustible,
18 in its shining flames
  all the sons [of iniquity] will burn
  [and it will be turned] into a searing fire
  of all the men of guilt
19 until destruction.
  But those, followers of my testimony,
  have allowed themselves to be enticed by those spread[ing lies]
  [and they have discontinued] in the service of justice,
20 even though you, God, commanded them to seek fortune far from their paths,
  [walking] on your holy path,
  on which the uncircumcised, the unclean, the vicious,
21 do not travel.
  They have staggered off the path of your heart
  and in [boundless] misfortune they languish.
  Belial is the counsellor of their heart,
22 and following the schemes of iniquity
  they wallow in guilt.
  [I am] like a sailor in a ship
23 in the raging sea,
  its waves and torrents roar over me,
  a whirlwind [without a] lull for taking breath,
24 without tracks which direct the path over the surface of the sea.
  The deep thunders at my sigh,
  [my soul nears] the gates of death.
25 I am like someone entering a fortified city,
  and looking for shelter in the rampart until salvation.
  My God, I lean on your truth,
26 for you place the foundation upon rock,
  and the beams to the correct size,
  and the plumb line [...]
  tested stone for a strong building

27 which will not shake.
  All those who enter there will not stagger,
  for a foreigner will not penetrate it;
  its gates are armoured gates
28 which do not permit entry;
  the locks are massive,
  and cannot be broken.
  No band at all with its weapons of war will enter,
  even though it is loaded [with weapons]
29 of the wicked battle.
  Then the sword of God will pounce
  in the era of judgment,
  and all the sons of his truth will awaken,
30 to destroy wickedness,
  and all the sons of blame will no longer exist.
  The hero will bend his bow
  and break the encirclement
31 to an endless broad place.
  (He will open) the everlasting gates
  to take out weapons of war,
  and they will rule from one end to the other.
32 There will be no salvation for guilty inclination,
  it will be trampled to destruction
  without there being a remnant.
  There is no hope in the profusion [of their weapons,]
33 nor for all the heroes of war will there be shelter. *Blank*
  For to God Most High [the battle belongs]
  [...]
34 Those who lie in the dust will hoist the flag,
  and the worms of the dead will raise the banner
  for [...]
35 in the battles of the insolent.
  He will make an overwhelming whiplash pass,
  but it will not invade the fortress.
  [...]
36 [...] for plaster, and the beams for [...] *37* of ... [... *38* the truth ... [...]

Col. XV (= VII)   *1* [...] I remain silent [...]
 2 [...] my arm is broken at the elbow,
  my feet sink in the mud,
  my eyes are blind from having seen evil,
 3 my ears, through hearing the shedding of blood,

my heart is horrified at wicked schemes,

for Belial is present when the inclination of their being becomes apparent.

4 The foundations of my building have crumbled,

my bones have been disjointed,

my entrails heave like a boat in the rage of the storm,

5 my heart pulsates to destruction,

a whirlwind overwhelms me,

due to the wickedness of their sin. *Blank*

6 *Blank*

I give you thanks, Lord,

because you have sustained me with your strength,

7 you have spread your holy spirit over me so that I will not stumble,

you have fortified me against the wars of wickedness,

8 and in all their calamities you have not discouraged (me) from your covenant.

You placed me like a sturdy tower,

like a high wall,

you founded my building upon rock,

9 and everlasting foundations as my base,

all my walls are like a tested wall

which will not shake.

10 And you, my God, you have placed me for the downtrodden

as your holy council;

you have established me in your covenant

and my tongue is like your disciples.

11 But there is no word for the spirit of destruction,

nor is there a reply in the tongue of all the sons of guilt,

for deceitful lips will be silent.

12 For, at the judgment you pronounce as guilty all those who harass me,

separating the just from the wicked through me.

13 For you know the inclination of every creature,

and scrutinise every reply of the tongue.

14 You establish my heart with your disciples and in your truth,

to straighten my steps on the paths of justice,

to walk in your presence on the frontier of life

15 along tracks of glory {and life} and peace without [end]

[which will ne]ver stop.

16 And you, you know the inclination of your servant,

that I […] not […]

17 uplifting the heart and seeking shelter in strength;

I do not have the defences of flesh,

[…] there is no justice,

18 to be saved [from sin, except] through forgiveness.

And I lean on [...]
[...] and hope in your kindness,
to make salvation thrive,
19 and make the shoot grow;
    to seek refuge in strength
    and [...] in your justice.
    You have established me in your covenant
20 and I have clung to your truth,
    and [...]
    You have made me like a father for the sons of favour,
21 like a wet-nurse to the men of portent;
    they open their mouth like a child [on the breast of its mother,]
    like a suckling child in the lap of its wet-nurse.
22 You have exalted my horn above all those who denounce me,
    [you have scattered] those who fight me,
23 and those who bring a complaint, like straw in the wind,
    and those who dominate me [...]
    You have saved my life,
    and lifted my horn to the heights.
24 I am radiant with sevenfold light,
    in the light prepared for your glory,
25 for you are my everlasting luminary,
    and have established my foot on the right path. *Blank*
26 *Blank*
    I give you [thanks, Lord,]
    because you have taught me your truth,
27 you have made me know your wonderful mysteries,
    your kindness with [sinful] men,
    your bountiful compassion with the depraved of heart.
28 Who is like you, Lord, among the gods?
    Who is like your truth?
    Who, before you, is just when judged?
29 No spirit /host/ can reply to your reproach,
    no-one can stand up against your anger.
30 All the sons of your truth
    /you take/ to forgiveness in your presence,
    you purify them from their sins
    by the greatness of your goodness,
    and in your bountiful mercy,
31 to make them stand in your presence,
    for ever and ever. *Blank*
    For you are an eternal God

and all your paths remain from eternity to eternity.
32 And there is no-one apart from you.
What is empty man, owner of futility,
to understand your [great] wondrous deeds?
33 *Blank*
34 [I give you thanks,] Lord,
because you did not /make/ my lot /fall/ in the congregation of falsehood,
nor have you placed my regulation in the counsel of hypocrites,
35 [but you have led me] to your favour and your forgiveness,
[…]
and in your bountiful mercy,
to all the judgments of […]
36 […] depravity, and in the regulation

Col. XVI (= VIII)   *1* […] … […] *2* […] your justice is constant for ever, because
[…] not […] *3* […] … *Blank*
4 [I give you thanks, Lord,]
because you have set me in the source of streams in a dry land,
in the spring of water in a parched land,
5 in the canals which water a garden [of delights in the middle of the desert,]
[so that] a plantation of cypresses and elms [may grow,]
together with cedars, for your glory.
6 Trees of life in the secret source,
hidden among the trees of water.
They must make a shoot grow
in the everlasting plantation,
7 to take root before it grows.
Its roots reach as far as the gully,
and its trunk opens to the living waters
8 to be an everlasting spring.
On its buds all [the animals] of the wood will feed,
its trunk will be pasture for all who cross the path,
9 and its leaves for all winged birds.
Above it will rise all the trees of water
for they will grow in its plantation
10 although its roots do not reach the stream.
However, he who causes the holy shoot to grow in the true plantation
hides and seals its secret
11 so it will not be noticed or known. *Blank*
But you, O God,
you protect your fruit with the mystery of powerful heroes,
12 of spirits of holiness,

so that the flame of the searing fire
[will] not [reach] the spring of life,
nor with the everlasting trees
13 will it drink the waters of holiness,
nor produce its fruit with [the help] of the clouds.
For it sees, but does not know,
14 notices, but does not believe,
in the spring of life,
and gives eternal [...]
But I had become the mockery of the raging torrents
15 which throw their mire over me. *Blank*
16 But you, my God,
you have placed in my mouth as it were early rain for all [...]
spring of living water;
17 the skies will not cease to open,
they will not stop,
but will become a torrent overflowing [into every river]
and into the seas, without end.
18 They will swell suddenly from secret hiding-places,
[...]
they will serve to water [every tree,] green and dry,
19 a marsh for every animal.
The [wicked] trees [will sink] like lead in powerful waters,
20 [they will all be victims] of fire and dry up.
But the plantation of fruit [...]
eternal [...] for the glorious garden
and will [bear fruit always.]
21 By my hand you have opened their spring with channels [of water]
[putting them in] straight] lines, correctly
22 the planting of their trees with the plumb-line of the sun,
so that [...] with foliage of glory.
When I stretch my hand to dig out its ditches,
23 its roots pierce the rock of silex,
[its stems sink] into the earth,
and in the time of heat it retains its vitality.
24 But if I remove my hand
it will be like the aca[cia in the desert,]
its stump like nettles in salt flats,
25 its furrows will make thorns and reeds grow,
brambles and thistles [...]
[the trees] of its banks will turn into sour vines;
26 in the heat its leaves rot,

they do not open in the rain.
[My] residence is with the sick,
my heart knows diseases,
27 and I am like a forsaken man in [pain,]
there is no refuge for me.
For my disease increases in bitterness,
28 in incurable pain which does not stop,
[…] over me like those who go down to Sheol,
29 and with the dead my spirit hides,
because my life has gone down to the pit.
[Within me] my soul languishes day and night,
30 without rest.
And grows like a searing fire enclosed in my [bones]
whose flame consumes as far as the seas,
31 devouring strength by periods,
destroying the flesh by seasons,
the waves rush against me.
32 My soul within me has weakened right to destruction,
for vitality leaves my body,
my heart pours out like water,
33 my flesh melts like wax,
the vitality of my loins has turned into listlessness,
my arm is broken at the elbow
without my being able to wave my hand,
34 my foot has been caught in the snare,
my knees slide like water,
and it is impossible to move one step forward
nor are there footfalls to the tread of my feet,
35 […]
in chains which cause stumbling.
You have made the tongue in my mouth strong,
it cannot hold back;
36 it is impossible [for me] to raise my voice
[with the tongue of] instruction
to give life to the spirit of those who stagger.
The voice of my lips is silent.
37 […] with chains of judgment […] my heart […] in bitterness […] 38 […] to the
sea […] the circuit of the globe 39 […] have been silenced like nothing 40 […]
man not

Col. XVII (= IX)   1 […] … […]
2 […] my eye does not sleep at night […]

3 [...] without compassion. In anger his zeal is aroused, and for destruction [...]
4 The waves of death [surround me,]
Sheol is upon my bed,
my couch drones a lament,
my bed, a sighing sound;
5 my eyes are like the smoke in an oven,
my tears, like streams of water,
my eyes are worn out by rest,
[my strength] is kept far away from me,
6 and my life at a distance.
As for me,
from ruin to annihilation,
from sickness to disease,
from pains to tortures,
7 my soul reflects on your wonders;
you, in your favour, have not rejected me,
8 from one moment to the next my soul delights
in your bountiful mercy,
and I can give a reply to whoever wishes to devour me
9 and a rebuke to someone who envies me.
I have pronounced his trial as wicked,
but your judgment I have pronounced just.
10 For I have admitted your truth.
I have chosen my judgment,
I have been pleased with my ordeal,
because I hoped for your favour.
11 You have placed a plea in the mouth of your servant,
you have not threatened my life,
nor have you removed my peace,
nor have you deserted my expectation;
12 rather, in the face of the ordeal you have upheld my spirit,
you know my intentions,
13 in my troubles you comfort me.
I delight in forgiveness,
I console myself for former sin.
14 I know that there is hope, thanks to your kindness,
and trust, through the fullness of your strength,
for no-one is pronounced just in your judgment,
15 or inno[cent] at your trial;
one man is more just than another man,
a fellow is wiser [than a fellow,]
16 the flesh is respected more than one made from [clay,]

one spirit is more powerful than another spirit;
but before your might, nothing is strong,
17 and nothing is [comparable] to your glory,
and to your wisdom there is no measure,
and your fait[hfulness has no end;]
18 to everything which is excluded from it
[...] *Blank*
But in you I [...]
19 my position and not [...] *20* when against me they devise [...] for shame of face
21 to me, but you [...] my enemy grows great against me to make me fall [...]
22 men of war [...] confusion of face and shame for those who plot against me.
Blank
23 For you, my God, [...]
you argue my case.
For in the mystery of your wisdom
you have rebuked me,
24 you have hidden the truth a while,
[your favour, until] the ordained time.
Your rebuke has been changed into happiness and joy for me,
24 my disease into everlasting healing and unending [bliss,]
the scoffing of my rival into a crown of glory for me,
and my weakness into everlasting strength.
26 For, by your name [you created light for me,]
and through your glory, my light becomes visible,
for from darkness you make my light shine,
27 to [change] my bruises [to everlasting happiness,]
my weakness to wonderful force,
28 the constriction of my soul to everlasting expanse.
[For you, my God, you are] my refuge,
my protection, the rock of my strength, my fortress.
29 In you I will be guarded from every [foe,]
[you will be] salvation for me unto eternity. *Blank*
For you have known me since my father,
30 from the vitals [you have established me,]
[from the womb of] my mother you have filled me,
from the breasts of her who conceived me
your compassion has always been upon me,
31 from the lap of my wet-nurse [you have looked after me,]
from my youth you have shown yourself to me in the intelligence of your judgment,
32 and with certain truth you have supported me.
You have delighted me with your holy spirit,

and until this very day you have guided me.

33 Your just reproach escorts my path,
  your peace watches over the salvation of my soul,
  with my steps there is bountiful forgiveness

34 and great compassion when you judge me,
  until old age you support me.

35 For my mother did not know me,
  and my father abandoned me to you.
  Because you are father to all the sons of your truth.

36 In them you rejoice,
  like one full of gentleness for her child,
  and like a wet-nurse,
  you clutch to your chest all your creatures. *Blank*

37 *Blank*

38 [...] you have enlarged without number 39 [...] your name for doing wonders
  40 [...] thinking [...] 41 [...] ... [...]

Col. XVIII (= X + 30)   1 [...] the plan of your heart [...]

 2 And without your will they shall not be.
  And no-one understands all your wisdom,

 3 and your wonders, no-one contemplates them.
  What, then, is man?
  He is nothing but earth.

 4 From clay is he fashioned
  and to dust he must return.
  But you teach him about wonders like these
  and make him know the foundations of your truth.

 5 I am dust and ashes,
  what can I plan if you do not wish it?
  what can I devise without your agreement?

 6 How can I be strong if you do not make me stand?
  How can I be learned if you do not mould me?

 7 What can I say if you do not open my mouth?
  And how can I answer if you do not give me insight?

 8 See, you are prince of gods and king of the glorious ones,
  lord of every spirit, owner of every creature.

 9 Without your will nothing happens,
  and nothing is known without your wish.
  There is no-one besides you,

10 no-one matches your strength,
  nothing, in contrast with your glory,
  there is no price on your might.

11 And who among all your wonderful great works
   will have the strength to stand before your glory?
12 And what, then, is someone who returns to dust
   to retain strength?
   Only for your glory have you done all this.
13 *Blank*
14 Be blessed, Lord,
   God of compassion and of abundant favour,
   because you have made me know these things
   so that I recount your marvels,
15 and I do not keep silent day and night.
   [...]
   To you all power [...]
16 by your pity in your great goodness
   and in the abundance of [your compassion ...]
   I will delight in your forg[iveness ...]
17 for I have leaned on your truth,
   [...]
18 your position, and there is no [...]
   without your threat there is no fall,
19 nor is there disease that you do not know.
   [...] *Blank*
20 And I, in accordance with what I know of your truth,
   [extol your great name,]
   in contemplating your glory
21 I recount your wonders,
   on understanding [your secrets
   I trust in the] abundance of your compassion
   and hope in your forgiveness.
22 Because you have fashioned my sp[irit,]
   you have established me in accordance with your approval.
   You have not placed my support in robbery,
23 nor in wealth [have you anchored my hea]rt,
   nor have you put, as my refuge, one fashioned from flesh.
24 The strength of heroes lies in abundant gratification,
   [their might, in abund]ant grain, wine, oil;
25 they take pride in their belongings and possessions,
   [they grow like] verdant [trees] in the streams of water
   to produce branches and increase leaves,
   for they select [the best of the sons of] man
   for all to grow fat from the earth.
27 But to the sons of your truth

you have given intelligence,
[so that they know you for ever] and ever;
and to the extent of their knowledge they are honoured,
28 the one more than the other.
And so for the son of man
[...]
you have increased his legacy
29 in the knowledge of your truth,
and according to his insight and corresponding to his understanding
[he will be glorified.]
The soul of your servant loathes wealth and robbery,
30 and is not pleased with the glorification of pleasures.
My heart rejoices in your covenant
31 and your truth delights my soul.
I flourish like an iris,
my heart opens to an everlasting spring,
32 my support is in an elevated refuge.
[...] grief,
and wilts like a flower in the heat.
33 My heart flutters in anxiety,
my kidneys in alarm,
my sigh reaches down to the abyss,
34 even pierces the caverns of Sheol.
I am appalled to hear your verdict against the powerful heroes,
35 your trial against the host of your holy ones.
[...]
36 your judgment against all your works,
justice and [...]
37 -39 [...]

Col. XIX (= XI)   *1* [...] in terror [... the grief has not been] hidden from my eyes,
and the sor[row ...] *2* in the meditation of my heart. *Blank*
3 I give you thanks, my God,
because you have done wonders with dust;
with the creature of mud you have acted
in an immeasureably /very/ powerful way.
And I, what am I?
4 For you have taught me the basis of your truth,
you have instructed me in your wonderful works.
You have put thanksgiving into my mouth,
praises on my tongue,
5 my uncircumcised lips in a place of jubilation.

I will chant your kindness,
I will ponder your might the whole day,
6 I will bless your name continually,
I will declare your glory among the sons of man,
7 and in your abundant goodness my soul will delight.
I know that truth is in your mouth,
and justice in your hand,
8 and in your thoughts, all learning,
and all glory is with you,
and in your wrath all punishing judgment,
9 and in your goodness, abundance of forgiveness,
and your compassion for all the sons of your approval.
For you have taught them the basis of your truth,
10 and have instructed them in your wonderful mysteries. *Blank*
For your glory, you have purified man from sin,
11 so that he can make himself holy for you
from every impure abomination and blameworthy iniquity,
to become united with the sons of your truth
and in the lot of your holy ones,
12 to raise the worms of the dead
from the dust, to an [everlasting] community
and from a depraved spirit, to your knowledge,
13 so that he can take his place in your presence
with the perpetual host
and the [everlasting] spirits,
to renew him with everything that will exist,
14 and with those who know
in a community of jubilation. *Blank*
Blank
15 I give you thanks, my God,
I exalt you, my rock,
and in your working wonders [...]
16 because you have made me know the foundation of truth.
[...]
17 you have revealed [your wonders] to me
and I have contemplated [...]
[...] of your favour.
18 And I have known that in you there is justice,
and in your favour there is [...]
and destruction without your compassion.
19 A source of sorrow has opened for me,
bitterness [without end distresses me,]

grief has not been hidden from my eyes,
20 when I knew man's instincts,
   the return of mankind [to dust,]
   [his inclination] towards sin
   and the anguish of guilt.
21 These things have entered my heart,
   they have penetrated my bones,
   […]
   to plunge me into the meditation of anguish.
22 /I have sighed on the harp of lament
   for every sorrow of anguish,/
   with bitter plaint,
   until iniquity is destroyed,
   and [fraud comes to] an end,
   and there are no more ravaging diseases.
23 Then will I sing with the harp of salvation,
   the zither of happi[ness,]
   [the tambourine of j]oy
   and the flute of praise,
   without cease.
24 And who among your creatures
   can recount [all your glo]ry?
   In the mouth of everyone is your name praised,
25 for ever and ever they bless you, to the extent of their knowledge,
   [day after] day they proclaim together, with a joyous voice.
26 There will be neither distress nor sighing,
   iniquity [and fraud will exist no longer.]
   But your truth will be displayed
27 for endless glory and eternal peace.
   Be blessed, Lord,
28 because you have given your servant
   the insight of knowledge
   to understand your wonders
   [and your deeds without] number
   through the abundance of your favour.
29 Be blessed, God of compassion and kindness,
   though your great goodness,
   through the abundance of your truth.
   and through your great kindness
30 towards all your works.
   Gladden the soul of your servant with your truth
   and purify me with your justice,

31 since I have trusted in your goodness
and I have hoped in your favour.
32 By your forgiveness you will open my hope,
in my distress you will comfort me,
for I have leaned on your compassion.
33 Be blessed, Lord,
because you have done these things.
You have put into the mouth of your servant
thanksgiving, [praises,]
34 entreaties and the reply of the tongue.
For me you have established actions [and deeds,]
[…]
35 I have had [the strength …] *36* And you […] *37–48* … […]

Col. XX (= XII + *frags.* 54 + 60)   *1* […] you swell my soul […]
2 In happiness and [joy will I live] safely
in the holy residence,
in rest and peace.
3 [Praise] and blessing
in your tents of glory and salvation.
Among those who fear you, I will praise your name.
4 [For the Instruc]tor,
praises and prayers,
to bow down and entreat always,
from period to period:
when the light comes from his residence;
5 in the positions of the day, according to the regulation,
in accordance with the laws of the great luminary;
at the return of the evening, at the departure of light,
6 when the realm of the shades begins;
at the appointed moment of the night, in their stations;
at the return of dawn,
7 at the moment when it withdraws to its quarters before the light;
at the departure of night when day enters;
continually,
8 in all the births of time
in the foundation of the period,
in the positions of the stations in the commands of their signs
9 through the whole realm,
in accordance with the decree established through God's mouth,
and through the witness of what is.
And this will be, and nothing more;

10 besides him there is no other, nor will there ever be another.
For the God of knowledge
11 has established it
and no-one else with him. *Blank*
And I, the Instructor, have known you, my God,
12 through the spirit which you gave to me,
and I have listened loyally to your wonderful secret
through your holy spirit.
13 You have opened within me
knowledge of the mystery of your wisdom,
the source of your power,
[…]
14 […] abundance of grace, zeal for annihilation […] *15* […] the majesty of your
glory like light […] *16* […] wicked and there will be no fraud […] *17* […] ruin,
for […] not *18* […] there will be no more annihilation, because before […]
19 […] and there is no-one just with you […] *20* to understand all your mysteries and to be able to answer […] *21* your reproach, and they will be attentive to
your goodness because in your favour […] *22* and they know you and in the era
of your glory they rejoice, and in accordance with their k[nowledge …] and to
the extent of their intellect *23* you let them improve and in accordance with
their domain they serve you, and corresponding to their divisions […] … *24* so
as not to transgress your word.

And I: from the dust you have gathered me,
[and from clay] you have made [me,]
25 to be a source of uncleanness,
and of vile filth,
a pile of dust,
kneaded with water,
[…]
a lodging of shades.
26 The creature of clay must return to the dust
at the end of his days.
[…]
[and must revert] to the dust
27 from which he has been taken.
What will the dust reply?
[…]
28 How will he stand up to someone who reproaches him?
[…]
29 […] eternal,
storehouse of glory,

spring of wisdom,
power [of wonder.]

30 They cannot recount all your glory,
or stand up in front of your anger.

31 There is no reply at all to your reproach,
for you are just
and there is no-one before you.
Who is he, who returns to his dust?

32 I have kept silence.
What can I say about these matters?
I spoke in accordance with my knowledge,
with the rights of one fashioned from clay.

33 What will I say if you do not open my mouth?
How can I understand if you do not teach me?

34 What can I propose if you do not open my heart?
How will I walk on the right path
if you not steady [my feet?]

35 [How] will my steps stay secure
[if you do not] strengthen [me] with strength?
And how will I rise [if you do not ... me]

36 and everything [...] in waters ... [...] *37* ...[...] *38* in [...] *39* ... [...]

Col. XXI (= XVIII [*lower section, col.* I] + *frag.* 3   *1* [...the wic]kedness of one born
from wo[man] *2* [...] your justice *3* [...] I saw this *4* [...] How will I see if you
do not open my eyes, and hear *5* [if you do not open my ears?...] My heart is
perturbed, because the word has been disclosed to an uncircumcised ear and
a [...] heart. *6* And I know that you, my God, have done these things for yourself. And what is flesh *7* [... to perform] wonderfully, and in your plans to
strengthen and establish everything for your glory. *8* [...] the host of knowledge
to proclaim exploits to flesh and solid precepts to the one born of *9* [woman ...]
You have brought him into the covenant with you and you have opened the
heart of dust so that he will avoid *10* [...] the traps of judgment, by reason of
your mercies. And I, I am a creature *11* [of clay ... of du]st and heart of stone.
With whom will I be reckoned until these things? For *12* [...] to the ear of dust,
and you have inscribed for ever what is to happen in the heart of *13* [...] you
have made stop, to bring into the covenant with you and so that he will continue *14* [in your presence ...] in the everlasting residence, in the light of dawn
for ever, without darkness *15* [...] with no end, and eras of peace without li[mits
...] *16* [...] And I, I am a creature of dust [...] *17* [...] I will open [...] *18* [...] ...
[...]

Frag. 3   *1* [...] ... [...] *2* [...] ... [...] the path is open for [...] *3* [...] the tracks of peace, and with flesh to perform wonders […] *4* […] my steps over hiding-places of traps. And he who stretches […] *5* […] I and I preserve the one fashioned from dust from being scattered, and in the the midst of wax […] *6* […] heap of ash, how can I stand firm before the hurricane? […] *7* […] and he protects him by the mystery of his will. For he knows […] *8* […] until destruction. They have hidden trap upon trap, the nets of wickedness […] *9* […] in sinfulness. And every creature of deception will end. For […] not *10* […] And there will be no more wicked intention and deeds of deception. […] *11* […] *Blank* And I, creature of c[lay…] *12* […] How will it appear strong before you? You are the God of knowledge […] *13* […] You have made them, and without you nothing is made […] *14* […] of dust. I have known by the spirit which you have given me […] *15* […] all sinfulness and fraud will be driven out, and presumption will end […] *16* […] deeds of impurity [will be punished] by illnesses and judgments of diseases and destruction […] *17* […] … Yours is indignation and zeal […] *18* […] … […]

Col. XXII (= XVIII [*lower section, col.* II] + *frags.* 1 I + 52 + 4 + 47)   *1* [… hol]iness which is in heaven *2* great […,] and is a wonder. They cannot *3* […] but he will not prevent them knowing everything *4* [… which go]es back to its dust. I, I am a man of sin, wrapped *5* [in impurity … in] wicked guilt. In the periods of anger I *6* […] to endure before my diseases and to be preserved from *7* […] you have taught me these things. For there is hope for man *8* […] you loathe. And I, I am a creature of clay. I have leaned *9* … […] my God. I know that truth *10* comes from your mouth […] behind. And I, in my era, will keep *11* your covenant […] You have kept me in my position, for *12* […] man, and you have made him turn back. Why … *13* […] creature of clay […] you increase and … *14* […] he will instruct (?) … not […] *15* […] I, I am a creature [of clay …]

Frag. 47   *1* […] he will rejoice […] *2* and the volunteers do not […] *3* for me since the time when I was established for […] *4* he will not enter, for […] *5* like my building, and my entrails […]

Frag. 4   *1* […] … […] *2* […] which […] *3* […] evening and morning with […] *4* […] of the man and of […] *5* […] they keep watch and over their turns […] *6* […] your threats to every dishonest and dsetr[uctive] opponent […] *7* […] And you, you have opened my ear, for […] *8* […] and the men of the covenant have been seduced by them and have entered […] *9* […] before you. And I, I have been disturbed at your judgment […] *10* […] Who will be innocent in your judgment? How will I open [my mouth] *11* […] I in your judgment? Who goes back to his dust like […] ? *12* […] you have opened my heart to your knowledge, and you open my ear *13* […] to lean on your goodness. But my heart is disturbed […] *14* […] and my heart melts like wax on account of fault and sin.

15 [...] ... Be blessed, God of knowledge, who has established *16* [...] this happens to your servant on your account. Because I have known *17* [...] I hope with
all that I am. Always I will bless your name *18* [...] .... [...] Do not desert
me in the time of *19* [...] your glory and your goodness. *20* [...] upon [...]

Col. XXIII (= XVIII [*upper portion, col.* I] + *frag.* 57 I + 1 II + 2 I)   *1* your light, and
you have established the lum[inaries...] *2* your light, without cease. [...] *3* Because light is with you for [...] *4* You open the ear of dust [...] .... *5* the
plan you have made [...] to kn[ow] .... and have entrusted to the ear of
6 your servant for ever. [...] your wonderful pronouncements to show yourself
7 to the eyes of all those who listen to you [...] by your powerful right (hand),
to take care of the weak *8* by the strength of your might [...] by your name and
to show yourself mighty in your power.
  9 Do not withdraw your hand,
    [keep your arm stretched] out
    for the one who holds fast to your covenant
  10 and stands up before you!
    [...]
    You have opened a spring in the mouth of your servant,
  11 on his tongue you have inscribed the cord [...]
    [to] announce your knowledge to your creature,
  12 to explain these matters to dust such as me.
    You have opened a spring to correct
    the path of the creature of clay,
    the guilt of the one born of woman
  13 according to his deeds,
    to open [the source of] your truth to the creature
    whom you have supported with your power,
  14 to [be,] according to your truth,
    [...] herald of your goodness,
    to proclaim to the poor
    the abundance of your mercies,
  15 [to........] of the spring [...]
    to the repentant at heart
    and to the downtrodden, everlasting delight.
  16 [...]...[...]

Frag. 2   *1-2* [...] ...[...] *3* [...] and in your land and among the sons of gods and
among the sons of [...] ... *4* [...] to praise you and to tell of all your glory.
    And I, what am I?
    From the dust you took me
  5 and to the [dust I will return.]

For your glory have you done all this.
According to the abundance of your graces
of the observance of your justice.
6 [...]
continually, until salvation.
The interpreters of knowledge
are with all my steps,
the reproachers of truth
7 [...]
For, what is dust in your pal[ms?]
The works of dust between your hands?
They are [nothing.] But you
8 [...] clay [...] your approval. Upon stones (?) do you put me as a test 9 [...]
and upon the dust you stretch out the spirit 10 [...] in the mud [...the sons of]
gods, to be in communion with the sons of heaven. 11 [...] without return to
darkness. For 12 [...] you have revealed light, but not in order to make [...]
return 13 you have stretched out [your] holy [spirit] to cover the fault 14 [...]
with your army and those who walk 15 [...] before your presence, because they
have been established in your truth 16 [...] you have done these wonders for
your glory and for your justice 17 [...] ... the depravity of the hateful creature.
18 [...] hateful creature.

Col. XXIV (= XVIII [*upper portion, col.* II] + *frags.* 57 II + 9 + 50 + 45 + 6 + 2 II)
1 [...]...[...] 2 and you will place [...upon] (a) creature of flesh 3 your hand [...]
and bend it double 4 in your judgment [...] (to) the angels 5 ... [...] the secrets
of sinfulness /to convert/ 6 flesh into [...] planned upon it all 7 the angels of
[...] through the cords of the spirit, and humbled 8 the gods from the place of
[...] in the dwelling of your glory. And you, you 9 to the man upon [...] I will
withdraw until the times of your approval, 10 and to send [...] the power and
the abundance of the flesh, to sentence as guilty 11 in the age of [anger...] to
establish in council with you 12 [...] the bastards, all the 13 [...] ...

Frag. 45   1 [...] justice [...] 2 [...] to the pit in the time of sinfulness [...] of every
opponent and the destruction [...] 4 [...] on their heads and to send peoples to
them [...] 5 [...] the presumptious man in very many disloyalties [...] 6 [...]
with contempt. Because all the spirits [...] 7 [...] (they) will be condemned as
guilty during their lives [...]

Frag. 6   1 [...] wicked 2 [...] and in the judgments 3 ... [...] the bastards to condemn the flesh as guilty 4 ... [...] their spirit to save 5 [...] you have revealed
the wonder of your mysteries 6 to the so[ns of ...] to the flesh, and I have
known 7 for [...] wickedness in the time of 8 all [...] and everyone who consid-

ers *9* [...] and he will not hide *10* [...] you have worked more than the sons of *11* God [...] the iniiquities of the peoples *12* in their inheritance [...] increasing the guilt *13* of every [...] you have abandoned them into the hand *14* ... [...] ...

Col. XXV (= *frags.* 8 + 5)

Frag. 5   *1* [...] your judgment of justice against [...] *2* [...] he will scatter them from the position of [...] *3* [...] with the congregation of the holy ones. In the wonder of [...] *4* for ever. You will make the spirits of wickedness dwell (?) outside [...] *5* and he will no longer exist. You will destroy the place of [...] *6* the spirits of wickedness who have been oppressed by sorrow [...] *7* and delight for everlasting generations. And when wickedness arises to [...] *8* its oppression has grown right to destruction. And opposed to all your works [...] *9* your graces, and to know everything in your glory, and to [...] *10* the judgment of your truth. You have revealed to the ear of flesh [...] *11* your heart. And you have made known the time of the witness [...] *12* and to the dwellers of the land, upon the land. And also [...] *13* darkness. You will make a lawsuit to pronounce the ju[st man ju]st and sen[tence the guilty...] *14* and not to scatter [...] your word [...] *15* ...[...]

Frag. 8   *1-2* ...[...] *3* you exalt [...] *4* counsel [...] *5* those who serve [...] *6* and those who acknowledge [...] *7* to praise [...] *8* I have told and *9* the knowledge [...] *10* For the Instructor, so[ng...] *11* because [...]

Col. XXVI (= *frag.* 7 II)   *1* more. [...] ...[...] *2* height, without there being a remnant. [...] *3* and high in its elevation, with [...] *4* everlasting. And those who stumble on earth [...] *5* and everlasting enjoyment in his place [...] *6* {to make known the power} ...[*7* in his knowledge of the covenant of grace [...] *8* God of justice and of knowledge [...] *9* with the strength of might [...] *10* What is flesh before these things? [...] *11* to settle in their positions [...] *12* to make a reply [...] *13* ...[...]

1QHymns*b* (1Q35 [1QH*b*])

Frag. 1 (= 1QH*a* XV, 27–38)   [I give you] thanks, Lord, because you have taught me your truth, you have made me know your wonderful mysteries, *1* [your kindnesses with sinful men, the abundance of your compassion with] the perverted [of heart.] *2* Who is like you, Lord, among the gods? Who (is) like your truth? Who is just before you] when he is judged? *3* [No host could reply to your reproach, no-one could endure] before *4* [your anger. All the sons of your truth you bring to forgiveness in your presence, you cleanse from their sins *5* [by the greatness of your goodness and in the abundance of your compassion, to make them be in your presence for ever and ever.] For you are an eternal God, 6 and all your paths remain from eternity to eternity. And there is no-one apart from you. What 7 is empty man, owner of futility, to understand] your wonderful great deeds? *Blank 8* [...] *Blank 9* [I give you thanks, Lord, because you have not let my lot fall in the congregation of deceit,] and in the council of hypocrites 10 [you have] not [put my regulation, but you have led me to your grace and your forgiveness,...] and, in [the abundan]ce of 11 [your compassion, to all the judgments of...] I have been taught about the offen[ces] 12 [...] since my youth in blood, and up to 13 [... corruption, and in the regulation ...] your heart and to hear 14 [...] ...

Frag. 2 (= 1QH*ᵃ* XVI, 12 – 13)   1 [so that the flame of the searing fire will not reach] the spring of life, 2 [*Blank* (?) with] the everlasting trees it will not drink 3 [the waters of holiness, or produce its fruit with the help of the clouds.]

4Q427 (4QHodayot*ᵃ* [4QH*ᵃ*])

Frag. 1 (= 1QH*ᵃ* XIX 17–25)   1 [... to me have you re]vealed [your wonders]
and I have contemplated [...]
[...] of your favour.
2 [And I have known that in you there is justice,
and in your favour there is ...]
and destruction without your compassion.
[A source of sorrow] has [opened for me,
bitterness without end distresses me,...
3 grief has not been hidden from my eyes,
when I knew the instincts of] man,
and considered the reply of mankind,
and have deepened [sin
4 and the anguish of guilt.
These things have entered my heart,
they have penetrated my bones...
to plunge] me into the meditation of angu[ish.
I have sighed] on the harp of lament
for every sorr[ow of anguish,
5 with bitter plaint,
until iniquity is destroyed,
and fraud comes to an end,
and there are no more ravaging diseases.
Then will I sing with the harp of] salvation,
the zither of [happiness,]
the tambourine of j]oy

6 [and the flute of praise,
without cease.
And who among your creatures
can recount all your glory?
In the mouth of everyone is your name pra]ised,
7 [for ever and ever they bless you, to the extent of their knowledge,
day after day they will proclaim together, with a joyous voice...]

Frag. 3 col. I (= 1QH^a VII 5 – 9) *1* [...] ... [...] *2* [... according to their intelligence.] And in accordance with their knowledge by your glory [...] *3* [... unceasingly. And from age to age] they will cause to hear and from festivity to
festivity [...] *4* [... And we have gathered together in a community, and] with
those who know we allow ourselves to be reproached by you and we acclaim
5 [... the people of your heroes.] Before your marvels we will sing together in
the assembly of God and with *6* [... and our descendants] will inform the sons
of man in the midst of the sons of Adam. *7* [...] *Blank 8* [...] a great cry through
the ruins of *9* [...] ... *10* [...] the man *11* [...] light, dominion *12* [...] For he
purifies *13* [...] for ever. And the lamp of blessing *14* [...] anguish. I have
moaned *15* [...] his mercy.

Frag. 3 col. II (= 1QH^a XX 3 – 15) *3* ... [...]
4 with the spirits eter[nal ...
in his tents of glory and salvation.
Among those who fear you, I will praise your name.]
5 For the Instructor,
praises [and prayers,
to bow down and entreat always,
from period to period:
6 when] the light comes to his king[dom
in the positions of the day, according to the regulation,
in accordance with the laws of the great luminary;
7 at the return of evening,] at the departure of light,
when the realm of the sha[des begins;
at the appointed moment of the night, in their stations;
at the return of dawn,
8 at the moment when it withdraws] to its quarters before the light;
at the de[parture of night when day enters;
continually,
in all the births of time,
in the foundations of the period,]
9 in the positions of the stations [in the commands of their signs
through his whole realm,

in accordance with the decree established through God's mouth,
and through the witness] of what is.

10 And this [will be, and nothing more;
besides him there is no other, nor will there ever be another.

11 For the God] of knowledge
has esta[blished it
and no-one else with him. *Blank*

12 And I, the Instruc[tor, have known you, my God,
through the spirit which you gave to me,
and I have listened loyally to your wonderful secret]

13 through [your holy] spirit.
[You have opened within me
knowledge of the mystery of your wisdom,
the source of your power,...]

14 abun[dance of grace, zeal for destruction...
the majesty of your glory like light]

15 eter[nal...]

Frag. 7 *col.* I   *6–7* [...] ... *8* [...] among the divinities *9* [...] he will summon me
with the tongue *10* [...] evil to the holy ones, and he will not come [...] *11* [...]
and he will not be able to compare with my glory. As for me, my place is with
the divinities, *12* [and glory or splend]our for myself I do not [buy them] with
gold or with refined gold or precious metals *13* [...] will not be counted to me.
Sing, favoured ones,
sing to the king of [glory,

14 be happy in the assem]bly of God,
exult in the tents of salvation,
praise in the [holy] residence,

15 exalt together with the eternal hosts,
ascribe greatness to our God
and glory to our King;

16 [san]ctify his name with stalwart lips
and powerful tongue,
raise your voices in unison in all the periods,

17 cause the sound of the shout to be heard,
rejoice with everlasting happiness,

18 and bow down unceasingly in the united assembly.
Bless the one who does amazing wonders,
and shows the might of his hand

19 sealing up the mysteries
and revealing hidden things,
raising up those who stumble

and the ones who give in,

20 [con]verting the behaviour of those who await knowledge
and lowering the exalted meetings of the eternally proud,

21 [con]firming the mysteries of majes[ty]
and establishing the [porten]ts of glory.
He who judges with destructive wrath

22 [...] with tenderness, justice,
and with great mercy, entreaty

23 [...]
mercy for those who enjoy the goodness of his greatness
and source of [...]

Frag. 7 col. II   *3* [...] oppression [...]

4 deceit [ends]
and there is no wickedness that is not known;
light is evident
and enjoyment [flourishes;]

5 sorrow [disappears]
and anguish flies away;
peace is evident,
terror ceases,
there opens the fount of [perpetual bles]sing,

6 and of wellbeing for all the eternal periods;
wickedness ends,
the plague ceases
and there is no illness;
[evil is eliminated]

7 and there is no more [guilt.]
Proclaim and say:
[Great is the God who works wonders,]

8 for he brings down the arrogant spirit
without even a remnant;
and he raises the poor from the dust [to an eternal height,]

9 and extols his stature up to the clouds
and cures him together with the divinities
in the congregation of the community;
[...]

10 wrath for eternal destruction. *Blank*
Those who fall to earth he lifts up
with no price,

11 [perpetual po]wer [is in] their steps
and eternal enjoyment in their dwellings,

perennial glory,
unceasing [for ever and ever.]
12 They will say: Blessed be God
who works mighty wonders,
who does great things to display power,
13 [who declares just] in the knowledge of all his creatures,
who [performs] goodness upon their faces,
so that they know the abundance of his kindn[esses
14 and] his [many] mercies
with all the sons of his truth.
We have known you, God of justice,
15 and we have seen your zeal in the strength of your power
and we have recognized [your justice in the abundance of] your mercies
16 and in the wonder of your forgiveness.
What is flesh before these things?
How will [dust and clay asp]ire
17 to tell these things from period to period,
or set in their positions [...]
18 the sons of the heavens?
There is no intermediary to make reply [to your commands]
[...]
19 for you,
for you have established us by your wi[ll
in the frontier of ...]
20 strength, to ⟨reply⟩/hear your wonders/
[...]
21 to you we speak and not to a cham[pion ...
[...]
22 [And you paid] attention to the outcry of our lips.
De[clare and say:
[...]
23 the heavens with his strength,
and all their plans he established with his force,
the earth with his power [...]

4Q428 (4QHodayot*b* [4QH*b*])

Frag. 7 (= 1QH*a* XV 34–36; 1QH*a* XVI 1–5)   [I give you thanks,] Lord,
because you did not make my lot fall in the congregation of falsehood,
1 nor have you placed] my regulation [in the counsel of hypocrites,]
but you have called me [to your favour and your forgiveness,
...]

2 and in your bountiful mercy,
   to al[l the judgments of ...]
3 I plunged into the fault of [...]
   [depravity, and into the regulation ...]
4 with abundant impurity,
   and since my youth in [...]
5 My God, you steady my feet in your paths
   [...]
6 my ear and my heart to understand your truth
   [...]
7 the ear in your teaching until [...]
8 you establish knowledge in my vitals
   and you glori[fy me ...]
9 to him more for the stumbling-block of sin
   for [...]
   [your justice is constant]
10 for ever, because not [...] your paths [...]
11 *Blank* I give you tha[nks,] Lord,
   because [you have set me in the source of streams]
   in a dry land,
   in the spring of water in a [parched] land, [...]

4Q429 (4QHodayot^c [4QH^c])

Frag. 1 *col.* I (= 1QH^a XIII 7–9)   *1* [lions which grind the bones of strong men,
   and drink the blood of champ]ions.
   You made my lodging [with many fishermen,
2 those who spread the net upon surface] of the sea,
   those who go hunting [the sons of iniquity.
3 And there you established me for the judgment,
   and the foundation of tr]uth you strengthened

Frag. 1 *col.* II (= 1QH^a XIII 15–18)   *1* in me, [to show before the sons of man,
   you did wonders with the poor,
2 you placed him like g]old in the crucible,
   [under the effect of fire
   like purified silver in the furnace] of the jeweller
3 to be refined [seven times.
   They hustled me, the wicked of]
4 the nations with their harassment,
   [and the whole day they crushed my soul.
5 But you, my Go]d, have changed the storm to [calm
   and have freed the soul of the poor.]

Frag. 1 *col.* III (= 1QH*ᵃ* XIII 26 – 28)   *7* [you have concealed the source of know]ledge

[and the foundation of truth.

8 They] plot [evil in their heart,]

and the words of Be[lial have opened a lying tongue]

9 like vipers' venom which stretches for periods

10 like those who throw themselves in the dust they cast to trap

glints of serpents,

11 against which there is no [inca]ntation.

They have become incurable pain,

12 a wasting disease [in the innards of] your servant,

which makes the spirit stagger and makes an end of

Frag. 1 *col.* IV (= 1QH*ᵃ* XIII 29 – 38)   *1* [strength, so] that he is unable to remain in his pl[ace.

They have overtaken me in narrow places where there is no escape,

though not dividing the groups.]

2 They announce the charge against me with the harp,

[their grumblings with verses in harmony,

with demolition and destruction.]

3 Resentment has taken hold of me

and torments [like the pan]gs of [giving birth.

My heart is in turmoil within me.

I have dressed in black]

4 and my tongue sticks to my palate,

because they surround me with the sha[me of their heart;

their intention is obvious to me in bitterness.]

5 The light of my face [has become gloomy] with deep darkness,

my radiance [has changed into gloom.

And you, my God,]

6 have opened [a broad space] in my heart,

but they have increased the narrowness

[and have wrapped me in darkness.

7 I have eaten] the bread of weeping,

my drink is tears [without end.

For my eyes are blinded by the grief

8 and my soul by the bitterne]ss of the day.

Weeping and pain sur[round] me,

[shame covers my face,

9 my bread has turned into quarrel]

and my drink into argument,

[they have entered my bones

10 to make my spirit stagger
   and make an end of strength
   in accordance with the mysteries of sin
   which, by their evil, have altered] the deeds of [God.
   For I have been tied with ropes
11 which cannot be un]tied,
   with chains which cannot [be broken;
   a strong rampart surrounds me,
12 iron bars and bronze gates] which cannot be opened
   [my gaol is tied to the deep
   without there being a chance of escape]

4Q430 (4QHodayot^d^ [4QH^d^])

Frag. 1 (= 1QH^a^ XII 13 – 19)   *1* [But they, hypocrites, plot intrigues of Belial,]
   they loo[k for you with a double heart,
   and are not firmly based in your truth.
2 There is in their thoug[hts a root which produces poi]son and wormwood,
   with stubbornness of heart they inquire,
3 [they look for you among the idols,]
   place in front of themselves the stumbling-block of their offences,
4 [they go to look for you in the mouth of prophets of] deceit
   attracted by delusion.
   [They speak to your people with stuttering lip and weird tongue
5 to convert to folly al]l their deeds [with tricks.
   For they have not chosen the path of your heart
6 nor have they listened to your word.]
   They said of the vision of knowledge: [It is not certain!
   and of the path of your heart: It is not that!
7 But you, O God,] will answer them, [judging them with your power
   according to their idols and their numerous sins.]

4Q431 (4QHodayot^e^ [4QH^e^])

Frag. 1 (= 4Q427 *Frag.* 7 II 2 – 10)   *1* and wickedness perishes [...] *2* in it oppression ceases, with indignation [...]
3 [and there is no] wickedness that is not known;
   light is evident
   and enjoyment [flourishes;]
   sorrow disappears
4 and anguish flies away;]
   peace is evident,

terror ceases,
there opens the fount of [perpetual bles]sing,
5 [and of wellbeing for all the] eternal [periods;]
wickedness ends,
the plague ceases
and there is no illness;
6 [evil is eliminated]
and there is no more [guilt.]
Proclaim /and/ say:
Great is the God who works [wonders,
7 for he brings down the] arrogant [spirit]
without even a remnant;
and he raises the poor *Blank* from the dust
8 [to an eternal height,
and up to the clo]uds extols his stature
and [treats him together] with the divinities
9 in the community of the congregation;
[... wrath] for eternal destruction,
and those who fall to earth

3 Hymns against Demons

A *Songs of the Sage*

4QSongs of the Sage^a (4Q510 [4QShir^a])

Frag. 1   *1* [...] praises.
   Bless[ings to the Ki]ng of glory.
   Words of thanksgiving in psalms of [...]
2 to the God of knowledge,
   to the resplendence of the powerful,
   God of gods,
   Lord of all the holy ones.
3 His rea[lm] is above the powerful mighty
   before the might of his power all are terrified,
   they scatter and flee before the radiance of his dwelli[ng]
4 of his glory and majesty. *Blank*
   And I, the Sage,
   declare the grandeur of his radiance
   in order to frighten and terr[ify]
5 all the spirits of the ravaging angels
   and the bastard spirits,
   demons, Liliths, owls and [jackals...]
6 and those who strike unexpectedly
   to lead astray the spirit of knowledge,
   to make their hearts forlorn and ...
   in the era of the rule of wickedness
7 and in the periods of humiliation of the sons of light,
   in the guilty periods of those defiled by sins
   not for an everlasting destruction
8 but rather for the era of the humiliation of sin [...]
   Rejoice, righteous ones, in the God of wonders.
9 My psalms are for the upright. *Blank*
   May all those of perfect path praise you. *Blank*

Frag. 2   *1* [...] and in the lot of wickedness. And all [...] *2* [...] God of salvation.
   And the holy ones [...] *3* [...] eternal. And all the spirits [...] *4* [...] eternal fire,
   burning in [...] *5* [...] ... [...]

4QSongs of the Sage^b (4Q511 [4QShir^b])

Frag. 1   *1* [...] in their domains *2* [...on the ear]th

3 and in all the spirits of his domain for ever.
   In their eras may the seas bless
4 and all their living things.
   May they declare [...] beauty, all of them;
5 may they exult before the God of Justice
   in [...] saving acts.
6 Because there is no exterminator in their borders,
   and their evil spirits do not walk in them,
7 for the glory of the God of knowledge shines out in their words,
8 and not one of the sons of wickedness is able to resist.

Frag. 2 col. I   *1* Of the Sage. Song [...]
   [Praise the name of] his holiness
2 and extol him all of you who know [justice...]
3 He has concluded with the chief of demons
   and has not [...]
4 eternal and lasting life
   to make the light shine [...]
5 His lot is Jacob's best,
   and the inheritance of God [...]
   Israel [...]
6 [they] follow the path of God
   and the way of his holiness.
   For the holy ones of his people
7 intelligence lies in knowledge of God.
   He located Israel in twelve camps [...]
8 [...] the lot of God with the angels of the luminaries of his glory.
   In his name the praises of
9 [...which] he instituted for the feasts of the year;
   and in the unique dominion,
   so that they would walk in the lot of [God]
10 according to his glory,
   and serve him in the lot of the people of his throne.
   For, the God of [...]

Frag. 2 col. II   *1* ... [...] *2* and they will seek for [...] *3* and the congregation of the
   bastards. All [...] *4* and the shame of ones face. According to the number of
   [...] *5* God ... with might [...] *5* God's mysteries, who knows them? [...] *6* The
   God of the powers has united them [...] *7* like them. And the impure, according to their impurity [...] *8* knows the uprightness of the upright [...] *9* and in
   Israel ... [...]

Frag. 3   *1* [...] through the centuries. For, [...] *2* [...] your abominations. *Blank*
After, [...] *3* [...] the periods of wickedness [...] *4* [...] the powers. And, like a
wise man [...] *5* [...] I will not have peace for you [...] *6* [...] their dwelling.
And they will all be startled [...] *7* [...] the heavens and the earth will be split
[...] *8* [...] and all[...]

Frag. 8   *1* [...] ... [...] *2* [...] they will exult in God. [...] *3* [...] *Blank* [...] *4* [For
the Instructor.] Second song to startle those who terrify [...] *5* [...] their straying in humiliations, but not for [eternal] destruction [...] *6* [...] of God in the
secret of Shaddai [...] *7* [...] he will hide me [...] *8* [...] among his holy ones
[...] *9* [...] together with his holy ones [...] *10* [...] giving thanks to God. *Blank*
Because [...] *11* [...in] the houses of his glory will they be gathered [...] *12* [...]
You are the God of gods [...]

Frag. 10 (= 4Q510 1)   [And I, the Sage,
   declare the majesty of his radiance
   in order to frighten and terrify
1 all the spirits of the ravaging angels
   and the bastard spirits,
   demons,] Liliths, [owls and jackals...
2 and those who strike unexpectedly]
   to lead astray the spirit [of knowledge,
3 to make their hearts forlorn and ...]
   in the era of the rule of wickedness
4 [and in the periods of humiliation of the sons of light,]
   in the guilty periods of those defiled [by sins;]
5 [not for an everlasting destruction]
   but rather for the era of [the humiliation of sin]
6 [...] *Blank*
7 [Rejoice, just people,] in the God of wonders.
   For the upright the psalms of his glory.
8 [*Blank*]
   May all those of perfect path praise you.
   Blank
   With the lyre of salvation they shall open their mouth
9 for God's kindnesses.
   They will search for his manna. *Blank* Save me, O God!
10 [He who keeps fav]our in truth for all his works,
   he who rules with justice
11 those who exist for ever
   and will exist for centuries.
   He judges in the council of gods and men.

12 In the heights of the heavens (is) his reproach
and in all the foundations of the earth
the judgments of his hand.

Frag. 18 *col.* II   *1–3* [...] . *4* [...] *Blank* *5* [Are there, perhaps, needs] in my words?
There are none. In what issues from my lips? There is no foe. *6* [...] and the
spirit of my intelligence ... deed of wickedness, for *7* God examines me. I
loathe all my deeds of impurity. For, *8* God makes the knowledge of intelligence shine in my heart. My arbiter *9* is just with my depravities, and my judge
is faithful in all the sins *10* of my guilt. For, God is my judge, and in the profane hand, no

Frag. 18 *col.* III   *6* in ... [...] *7* and God ... [...] *8* judgment [...] *9* and when I
stumble (?) [...] *10* my wings towards you [...]

Frag. 30   *1* you have sealed [...] ... [...] *2* and deep are [...] the heavens and the
abysses [...]
3 You, my God have sealed them all for ever,
and nobody opens them.
And for what reason [...]
4 Perhaps with the hollow of a man's hand
the copious waters can be measured?
And [the span of the heavens] be calculated in palms?
[Who, with a third of a measure]
5 will accommodate the dust of the earth,
weigh the mountains with scales,
or the hills with a balance?
6 Man does not do these things.
How, then, can man measure
the spirit [of God?]

Frag. 35   *1* God in all flesh,
and a judgment of vengeance to exterminate wickedness,
2 and through the rage of God's wrath
against those (who have been) purified seven times.
3 Among the holy ones, God makes (some) holy for himself
like an everlasting sanctuary,
and there will be purity amongst those purified.
4 And they shall be priests, his holy people,
his army and his servants,
the angels of his glory.
5 They shall praise him with fantastic marvels. *Blank*

6 And as for me, I spread the fear of God in the ages of my generations
to exalt the name [...]
7 [to terrify] with his power
all the bastard spirits,
to subjugate them by fear [...]

Frag. 42   *1* [...] ... [...] *2* [...] he will do everything [...] *3* [...] *Blank* And on the
eighth I will open [my mouth...] *4* [...] the generations of my guilt, and I will
keep [...] *5* [...] And upon the foundations of the earth [...] *6* [...] its dust. I
know your thought [...] *7* [...] Because it is in your hand to open [...] *8* [...] but
the eye. [...] not *9* [...] and if [...]

Frags. 48–59 *col.* II   *1* in God's council. Because [...] He has placed his intelligence in my heart [...] *2* the praises of his justice. [...] And through my mouth
he startles [all the spirits of] *3* the bastards, to humiliate [...] from impurity.
For in the members of *4* my flesh is the foundation of [... and in] my body the
wars. The laws of *5* God are in my heart, and I surpa[ss] all the wonders of
man. The deeds of *6* guilt I pronounce wicked [...] God of ... *Blank* He
7 knows, and in his mysteries [...] ... the disputes of all *8* the spirits [...] ...
[...]

Col. III   *1* [...] ... And you, my God, [you are a merciful and compassionate
God,] slow to anger, bountiful in favour, foundation of tru[th..] *2* [...] to Adam
and to his sons [...] source of purity, deposit of glory, great in just[ice ...] *3* [...]
... [...] judgments for the deeds of all, and he who returns blessings [...]
4 [...Blessed are you,] my God, king of glory, because from you comes judgment [...] *5* [...] and from you, the foundation of all those who fear you [...]
6 [...] ... [...] You [...] *7* [...] from your threat [...] in the abundance of [...]
8 [...] ... [...]

Frags. 63–64 *col.* II   *1* [...] God's deeds of my redemption,
[...] in the foundations of [...]
2 ... and in all this ... I will bless your name,
and in the festivals of my stipulations
3 I shall recount your marvels and engrave them,
the laws of praise of your glory.
At the start of every venture of the heart
4 lies knowledge,
and the offering of the utterance of just lips,
and being ready for every service of truth.
5 And with all the men of the covenant [...]
My peace is in thanksgiving,
I [...] the deed, and in all

Col. III   *1* As for me, my tongue will extol your justice
    because you have unfastened it.
    You have placed on my lips a fount of praise
  2 and in my heart the secret of the start of all human actions
    and the culmination of the deeds of the perfect ones of the path,
  3 the judgments of all the works that they do,
    to vindicate the just one in your faithfulness
  4 and pronounce the wicked guilty for his fault;
    in order to announce: Peace to all men of the covenant
    and to shout with a terrifying voice:
    Woe on all those who break it.

Col. IV   *1* May all your works bless
  2 always. May your name be blessed
  3 for eternal centuries. Amen. Amen.

B *Psalms of exorcism*

11QApocryphal Psalms*ᵃ* (11Q11[11QPsApᵃ])

Frag. A   *1* [...] and who weeps for him *2* [...] the oath *3* [...] by YHWH *4* [...] the
    dragon *5* [...] the ea[rth...] *6* [...] exor[cising ...] *7* [...] to [...] *8* [...] this [...]
    9 [...] to the dev[ils...] *10* [...] and he will dwe[ll...]

Col. I   *2* [Of David. Concerning the words of the spell] in the name of [YHWH...]
    3 [...] of Solomon, and he will invoke [the name of YHWH] *4* [to set him free
    from every affliction of the sp]irits, of the devils, [Liliths,] *5* [owls and jackals.]
    These are the devils, and the pri[nce of enm]ity *6* [is Belial,] who [rules] over
    the abyss [of dark]ness. *7* [...] to [...] and to mag[nify the] God of *8* [wonders...
    the sons of] his people have completed the cure, *9* [... those who] have relied
    on your name. Invoke *10* [... guardian of] Israel. Lean *11* [on YHWH, the God
    of gods, he who made] the heavens *12* [and the earth and all that is in them,]
    who separated [light] *13* [from darkness...] ... [...]

Col. II   *1* [...And you shall say to him: Who] *2* are you? [Did you make the heav-
    ens and] the depths [and everything they hold,] *3* the earth and every[thing
    there is upon the] earth? Who has ma[de these portents] *4* and these won[ders
    upon the] earth? It is he, YHWH, [the one who] *5* has done a[ll this by his
    power,] summoning all the [angels to come to his assistance,] *6* every [holy se]ed
    which is in his presence, [and the one who judges] *7* [the sons of] heaven and
    [all the] earth [on their account,] because they sent *8* sin upon [all the earth,]
    and [evil] upon every ma[n. But] they know *9* [his wonder]ful [acts,] which none

of them [is able to do in front of YHW]H. If they do not *10* [tremble] before YHWH, so that [... and] obliterate the soul, *11* YHWH [will judge them] and they will fear that great [punishment (?)]. *12* One among you [will chase after a thousand ...] of those who serve YHWH *13* [...] great. And [...] ... [...]

Col. III   *1* [and] great [...] summoning [...] *2* and the great [...And he will send a] powerful [angel] and will ev[ict] you [from] *3* the whole earth. [...] heavens [...] *4* YHWH will strike a [mighty bl]ow which is to destroy you [for ever,] *5* and in the fury of his anger [he will send] a powerful angel against you, [to carry out] *6* [all his comm]ands, (one) who [will not show] you mercy, who [...] *7* [...] above all these, who will [hurl] you to the great abyss, *8* [to the] deepest [Sheol. Fa[r from the home of light] shall you live, for *9* the great [abyss] is utterly *8* dark. *9* [You shall no] longer [rule] over the earth *10* [but instead you shall be shut in] for ever. [You shall be cursed] with the curses of Abaddon, *11* [and punished by] the fury of Y[HWH]'s anger. [You shall rule over] darkness for all *12* [the periods of] humiliation [...] your gift *13* [...]

Col. IV   *1* [...] ... [...] *2* which [...] those possessed [...] *3* the volunteers of your tr[uth, when Ra]phael heals them. [...] *Blank* *4* Of David. Conc[erning the words of the spe]ll in the name of YHWH. [Call on] *5* the heavens [at a]ny time. [When] Beli[al] comes upon you, [you] shall say to him: *6* Who are you, [accursed amongst] men and amongst the seed of the holy ones? Your face is a face *7* of futility, and your horns are horns of a wre[tch]. You are darkness and not light, *8* [s]in and not justice. [Against you,] the chief of the army. YHWH will [shut] you *9* [in the] deepest She[ol, he will shut] the two bronze gates through which] no *10* light [penetrates.] [On you there shall] not [shine the light of the] sun, which [rises *11* [upon the] just man [to illuminate his face.] You shall say to him: [Is there not] perhaps [an angel] *12* [with the just] man, to go [to judgment when] Sa[tan] mistreats him? [And he will be freed] from dark[ness by] *13* [the spirit of tru]th, [because jus]tice is with him [to uphold him at the judgment.] *14* [...] not [...]

Col. V (*lines* 3–14 = *Ps* 91)   *1* [...] ... [...] ... [...] ... *2* [...] ... [...] ... [...] for ever *3* [all the] sons of Be[lial. Amen. Amen.] *Selah.* [Of David. He who stays] in the shelter [of the Most High, [lives] in the sha]dow of the Powerful, *4* he who says: YHWH is my refuge and my fortress, [my God] is the safety in which I trust.] *5* [For] he will free you from the hun[tsman's net,] from the dead[ly] pestilence. [With] his feathers he will cover you, and under *6* his [wings] shall you lodge. His pity for you will be your shield, and his truth your breastplate. *Selah.* You shall not fear *7* the dread of the night, or the arrow which flies by day, or the plague which fells at noon, or the pestilence which proceeds *8* in darkness. A thousand will fall at your side, [ten thousand at your ri]ght, but it will not make reach you. Only [lo]ok *9* with your eyes [and you shall see] the reward of the vil]lain. You have called on your shelter, you have made him your happiness. *10* You will *9* [not] see [evil upon you, the plague] will not reach your tents. Because he has commanded his angels] *11* to safeguard you on your [paths. They shall lift you] upon their palms, so that your foot does not [trip on a st]one. [Upon] *12* vipers [and asps shall you] walk, trample [lions] and dragons. You have joined YHWH and he will rescue you.] Thus [he will exalt you and sh]ow [you] his salva[tion. *Selah.*] *Blank* [...] *14* And they shall ans[wer: Amen. Amen.] *Selah. Blank* [...] *15 Blank*

B *Incantations*

4QAgainst Demons (4Q560)

Col. I   *1* [...] and to the heart, and as [...] *2* and you gave birth to rebellion, begotten (through) the visitation of evil. [...] *3* [...] he who enters the flesh, the male penetrator and the female penetrator *4* [...] iniquity and guilt, fire and frost, and the heat of the heart *5* [...] in sleep, he who crushes the male and she who passes through the female, those who dig *6* [...] the wicked [...] *7* [...] ... [...]

Col. II   *4* before him and ... [...] *5* And I, to the spirit of the oath [...] *6* I enchant you, spirit, [...] *7* in the earth and in the clouds [...] *8* [...] ... [...]

4 Wisdom poems

4QWiles of the Wicked Woman (4Q184)

1 She […] utters futility
  and in […]
  She is always looking for depravities,
  and whets the words of her mouth,
2 and implies insult,
  and is busy leading the community astray with nonsense.
  Her heart weaves traps,
  her kidneys [nets.]
3 [Her eyes] have been defiled with evil
  her hands go down to the pit
  her feet sink to act wickedly
  and to walk towards crimes.
6 [Her…] are foundations of darkness,
  and there are sins a-plenty in her wings.
  [Her…] are night gloom
  and her clothes […]
5 Her veils are shadows of the twilight
  and her adornments diseases of corruption.
  Her beds are couches of corruption
6 […] of deep ditches.
  Her lodgings are couches of darkness
  and in the heart of the night are her tents.
  In the foundations of gloom she sets up her dwelling
7 and camps in the tents of silence.
  In the midst of eternal fire is her inheritance,
  and those who shine do not enter.
8 She is the start of all the ways of wickedness.
  Alas! She is the ruination of all who inherit her,
  and the calamity of all those who grasp her.
9 For her paths are paths of death,
  and her roads, tracks to sin.
  Her trails lead astray towards wickedness
10 and her pathways, to the guilt of transgression.
  Her gates are the gates of death,
  and in the entrance to her house, Sheol proceeds.
11 All those who go to her will not come back,
  and all those who inherit her will sink to the pit.
  She hides in ambush, in secret places

12 [...] all [...]
    In the city squares she veils herself,
    and stations herself in the gates of the village,
13 and there is no-one who interrupts her in [her] incessant [fornicating.]
    Her eyes scan hither and yon,
    and she raises her eyebrows impudently,
    to spot the just man and overtake him,
14 and the important man, to trip him up.
    To contort the path of the upright,
    to divert the righteous chosen from its precepts,
15 to make those who rely on her, fall into ridicule,
    to alter the standard of those who walk honestly.
    To make the simple rebel against God,
16 to turn their steps off the paths of justice,
    to lead the [...] into a trap,
    so that they do not persist in correct paths.
17 To sidetrack man into the paths of the pit,
    and seduce the sons of men with smooth words.

4QSapiential Work (4Q185)

Col. I   *3* [...] ... [...] *4* [...] pure and holy [...] *5* and according to his anger [...]
6 [...] up to ten times [...] *7* [...] And there is no strength to stand before her
or anybody who endures *8* the bitterness of her anger. [...] And who can endure to be in front of his angels? For, like *9* burning fire will he judge [...] of
his spirits. But you, O sons of man, woe to you!
10 For see, (man) sprouts like grass
    and his loveliness blooms like a flower.
    His grace makes the wind blow over him
11 and his root shrivels,
    and his leaves: the wind scatters them,
    until hardly anything remains in his place,
12 and nothing but wind is found. *Blank*
    They will look for him and not find him,
    and no hope remains;
13 their days are like a shadow on the earth.
    And now, please, hear me, my people!
    Simpletons, pay attention to me!
14 Draw wisdom from the great power of God,
    remember the miracles he performed in Egypt,
15 his portents [in the lands of Ham]:
    And may your heart quake in front of his terror

Col. II   *1* and do his wil[l...]
> [...] your souls according to his good favours
> and look for a path towards life,

2 a road [...]
> a remnant for your sons after you.

3 Why do you give your soul to futility
> [and your ...] of judgment?
> Listen to me, my sons,
> and do not defy the words of YHWH

4 or walk in [...]
> [but in the road which he established for] Jacob
> on the path which he commanded to Isaac.
> Is a day [in his house] not better

5 [...?]
> [...] to revere him,
> and not be afflicted by the trap and the net of the hunter.

6 [...] to be separated from his angels, for there is no darkness *7* [...] and his
> knowledge. And you, *8* what [...?] before him shall the evil go to all people?
> Blessed is the man to whom she has been given, *9* the son of man [...]
> The wicked person should not brag, saying:
> She has not been given to me

10 and I [shall not look for her.]
> [God has given her] to Israel,
> and like a good gift, gives her.
> He has saved all his people,

11 but has destroyed ... [...]
> Whoever glories in her will say:
> he shall take possession of her

12 and she will find him
> [...]
> With her there are long days,
> and greasy bones,
> and a happy heart.

13 Her youth [increases] favours and salvation.
> [...]
> Blessed the man who does it,
> and does not [...]

14 and does not look for her with a fraudulent spirit,
> or grow fond of her with flattery.
> As it was given to their fathers
> so will he inherit her.

15 [He will grow fond of her] with all force of his strength and with all his vigour without restraint.

And he will give her in inheritance to his descendants.

I know the struggle it takes to do good.

Col. III   *1–10* [...]

11 Did not God make the heart,

and does he know [its thoughts?]

12 [God sees] all the chambers of the stomach,

and puts their kidneys to the test.

God made the tongue,

13 and knows its word.

God made hands,

[and knows their deeds.]

14 [...] good or evil [...]

[...] ... [...]

15 [...] ... [...]

4QCryptic A: Words of the Sage to the Sons of Dawn (4Q298)

Col. I   *1* [Wo]rds of the Sage to the Sons of Dawn: Listen to [me a]ll men of heart *2* [and those who pur]sue justice. Understand my words and you shall be seekers of truth. Hear my words with all *3* [streng]th. Pay [attention ... you shall] know the paths of [...] life [...] *4–5* [...] ... [...]

Col. II   *1* their roots ri[se ... into] the upper heaven *2* and into the lo[wer] abyss [...] in it. *3* Consider [...] the dust *4* [...] God has given *5* [...] in all the globe *6* [...] has measured their positions *7* [... un]der the name *8* [...] their positions to walk *9* [...] the store of knowledge *10* [...] and that which

Col. III   *1* [...] and the number of their frontiers *2* [...] so as not to be on high *3* [...] the upper heaven. And now *4* listen [...] and hear, those of you who know. And the men *5* of intelligence [...] and those who seek justice, discretion *6* to contend [...] increase the pressure. And the men of *7* truth pursue [justice] and love piety. Increase *8* patience. [...] of the secrets of the testimony which *9* interprets [...] with the purpose that you understand the time of *10* eternity and you examine the ancient things, to know

4QSapiential Work (4Q413)

Frag. 1   *1* Song [...] and he will teach you wisdom. They will understand the paths of man and the deeds *2* of the sons of ma[n ...] God will make man great, he will give him in inheritance the knowledge of his truth, and in accordance with his rejection *3* of all evil [...] he will neither hear nor see *Blank* And now *4* grace [...] the first ones and afterwards their sons, generation after generation, as God showed.

4QSapiential Work A^b^ (4Q416 [4QSap.Work A^b^])

Frag. 1 *1* ... [...] *2* for the measurement of his pleasure [...] *3* feast after feast [...] *4* according to his hosts [...] *5* and the kingdom for [...] *6* and according to the lack of his hosts [...] *7* and the host of the heavens establishes [...] *8* and through his marvels and wonders [...] *9* one to another, and all his commands [...] *10* He passes judgment in the heavens upon every evil deed and takes pleasure in all the sons of truth [...] *11* their end, and all those who wallow in it will tremble and shout, for the heavens [...] *12* the waters and the abysses will tremble and all the spirits of flesh will strip naked, and the sons of the heavens [...] *13* his judgment, and all injustice will end at one go and the time of truth will be complete, [...] *14* in all the periods of eternity, for he is the God of truth, and before the centuries [...] *15* so that the just man may distinguish between good and evil [...] all [...] *16* the inclination of the flesh, and those who understand [...] *17-18* ...

Frag. 2 *col.* I (= 4Q417 *Frag.* 1) *1* [... he will act, for, how unique is he in every deed,] without *2* [... Do not consider the wicked as a help, nor whoever hates ...] without *3* [... the evil of his deeds he will make them known in his visitation. Walk with him ...] Take *4* [...do not turn your heart aside or move far off alone ...] in your head *5* [... for, what is more trivial than poverty? Do not rejoice in your sorrow lest you become tired] in your life. Consider the mystery of existence *6* [and take the offspring of salvation and know who will inherit glory and injustice. Is not ...] and for his sorrows *7* [he will have eternal happiness. The contender will be at your disposal and will not have ...] for all your perversities. Pronounce *8* [your judgments like a just chief. Do not ... and do not pass] over [your failings] *9-15* [...] *16* [... Do not lie to him; why will you commit a sin? And also of the reproach ...] and no longer trust *17* [... his neighbour and in your lack he will close his hand ...] and as he takes a loan. He knows ... *18* [... And if a misfortune happens to you ...] Do not hide from [...] *19* [Behold he will reveal ...] ruling over him. Then they will not strike *20* [with the stick ...] and he will stop once more. And also *21* [you ...] it will pass. If you hasten, he will flatten you *22* [...] Beg your nourishment, for he

Frag. 2 *col.* II *1* he opens his rewar[ds ...] all his scarc[ity graciously (?) and gives nourishment] *2* to every living creature. There is no [...If] he closes his hand, the spirit [withdraws] from all *3* flesh. Do not ta[ke ...] and before his reproach you will cover your face, and for the folly *4* of the prison like [...also the money

... And whoever has a debt with him, quickly] should pay it. And you, reach an agreement with him, for the purse *5* of your treasures [... for your creditor in favour of your fellow ...] all your life with him. Pay quickly so that *6* he does not take your purse. And in your affairs do not demean] your spirit with any wealth. Do not embitter your holy spirit, *7* for it has no price [...Ma]n is not inclined freely, seek his face and in his tongue *8* he speaks. Then you will find your pleasure [...] do not forsake your laws and be careful in your mysteries. *9* [...] If he entrusts you with his service, [do not rest ... and] sleep [should not enter] your eyes until you have fulfilled *10* [...] do not add. And if there is for the hu[mble ...] do not add for him; even wealth without *11* [... lest it changes into disgrace and he falls ...] and see, for excessive zeal *12* [of a man confuses the heart...] Also, for his will, increase his service, and the wisdom of his kindness *13* [...] ... and there will be for him a firstborn son. He will take pity on you like a man on his only begotten *14* [... For you ...] And do not be trusting: why resemble him? And do not stay awake for your riches (?) *15* [...] Neither depress your soul with good wealth, it is working with the wind and serving your oppressor for nothing. *18* Do not sell your glory for money, and do not pass it on as your inheritance, lest your body becomes impoverished. Do not fill yourself with bread; *19* and if there are no glasses, do not drink wine; and if there is no food do not seek delicacies. (If) *20* you lack bread, do not glory in your lack; you are poor, do not *21* despise your life. Neither should you lighten a vessel [...]

Frag. 2 *col.* III   *1* [...] ... *2* and remember that you are poor. [...] and what you need *3* you will not find. In your unfaithfulness [...] he has appointed for you. *4* Do not stretch out your hand lest you burn yourself and your body is consumed by his fire. According to [what he t]ook, so has it been given back to him. *5* You will rejoice if you are free of him. Nor should you take money from a man you do not know, *6* lest you increase your poverty. If he determined your death, you will not corrupt your spirit *7* for that. Then will you repose with truth, and in your death he will pro[duce ...] your memorial and your succession will inherit *8* the enjoyment. [If] you are poor, desire nothing except your portion, and do not be consumed for it, lest you shift *9* your boundary. And if he restores you in glory, walk in it, and investigate among its offspring about the mystery of existence. Then you shall know *10* its inheritance and walk in justice, for God exalts his ... in all your paths. Give honour to those who glorify you *11* and praise his name always. For from poverty he lifted your head and seated you among the nobles. Over an inheritance *12* of glory he has given dominion to you, always seek his will. (If) you are poor, do not say 'I am poor and *13* cannot seek knowledge'. Bend your shoulder to all discipline and in all [...] refine your heart and in much knowledge *14* your thoughts. Investigate the mystery of existence, consider all the paths of truth and examine all the roots of evil. *15* Then you shall know what is bitter for man and what is sweet for a man. Honour your father in your poverty *16* and your mother in your steps, for like grass for a man, so is his father, and like a pedestal for a man, so is his mother. For *17* they are the oven of your origin, and just as they have dominion over you and form the spirit, so you must serve them; and just as *18* he has opened your ears to the mystery of existence, (so) you must honour them, for your own glory. [...] honour his presence *19* for your own life and the duration of your days. *Blank* And if you are poor [...] *20* without law. *Blank* If you take a wife in your poverty, take her from the offspring of [...] *21* of the mystery of existence. In your association walk together with the help of your flesh [...]

Frag. 2 col. IV   *1* his father and his mother, [... one of] *2* your signs will rule over her and you [...] *3* will not rule over her. From the separated mother and you [...] *4* for you for the flesh. He will separate your daughters one by one, and your sons [...] *5* and you, together with the wife who reposes in your bosom, for she is the remnant of your na[kedness ...] *6* and if another than yourself rules over her, he will remove the boundary from his life. [...in her spirit] *7* which rules you to walk according to your will, without adding a vow or a freewill sacrifice [...] *8* to change your spirit according to your will, and every obligatory oath to offer a vow [...] *9* to violate what issues from your mouth, and according to your will ... [...] *10* from your lips lifted up on your account. Do not multiply [...] *11* your glory in your inheritance [...] *12* in your inheritance, lest *Blank* [...] *13* the wife who reposes in your bosom and the reproach [...] *14* [...] ... [...]

4QSapiential Work A*c* (4Q417 [4QSap.Work A*c*])

Frag. 1 *col.* I   *1* in every time, lest you are satisfied, and his spirit speaks in him, lest [...] *2* without suitable reproach he pardons him. And what is tightly tied [...] *3* And further, his spirit will not be consumed for he spoke in a whisper [...] *4* and he reckons his rebuke quickly. Do not cause work through your transgressions [...] *5* and he is just like you, for you are a prince among the prin[ces ...] *6* he will act, for, how unique he is in every deed, without [...!] *7* *Blank* Do not consider the wicked as a help, nor whoever hates [...] *8* the evil of his deeds he will make them known in his visitation. Walk with him [...] *9* do not turn your heart aside or move far off alone [... in your head ...] *10* for, what is more trivial than poverty? Do not rejoice in your sorrow lest you become tired in your life. [Consider the mystery of] *11* existence and take the offspring of salvation and know who will inherit glory and injustice. Is not [...] *12* and for his sorrows he will have eternal happiness. The contender will be at your disposal and will not [...] *13* for all your perversities. Declare your judgments like a just chief. Do not [...] *14* and do not pass over your failings ...

judgment [...] *15* take. Then God will see and change his wrath and pass over your sins, for before [...] *16* he will not maintain everything. And who will be just in his judgment, and without release [...] *17* the poor. And you, if you need nourishment, your lack and your abundance [...] *18* Leave what grows for his subsistence according to his desire, and you take from your inheritance, but do not add [...] *19* And if you need, do not ... from your lack, for his treasure is not lacking [...] *20* his mouth everything succeeds. Eat what he offers you but do not add [...] *21* [...] your life [...] If you take borrowed money from men for your necessities, do not [...] *22* day and night, and do not give your soul rest [...] and he will make you go back to [...] Do not lie to him; *23* why will you commit a sin? And also of the reproach [... and no longer trust ...] his neighbour *24* and in your lack he will close his hand. [... and as he takes a loan. He knows ...] *25* And if a misfortune happens to you [... Do not hide ...] *26* behold he will reveal [... ruling over him. Then] *27* they will not strike with the stick [... and he will stop] *28* once more, and also you [...]

Frag. 1 *col.* II   *1* If you hasten, he will flatten you without [... Beg] *2* your nourishment, for he opens his rewards [...] *3* all his scarc[ity graciously (?) and gives nourishment to [every living creature. There is no ...] *4* [If] he closes his hand, the spi[rit] withdraws from all flesh. Do not ta[ke ...] *5* [... and before his repro]ach you shall cover your fa[ce, and for the folly of the prison like ...also the money ...] *6* And whoever has a debt with him, quickly should pay it. And you, [reach an agreement with him, for the purse of your treasures [...] *7* for your creditor in favour of your fellow ...[all your life with him. Pay quickly so that he does not take] *8* your purse. And in your affairs do not demean [your spirit with any wealth. Do not embitter your holy] *9* [spi]rit, for it has no price [...] *10* [Man] is not inclined freely, seek his face and in his tongue he speaks. Then you will find your pleasure [...] *11* [...] ... do not [forsake your laws and be careful in your mysteries... If] *12* [he entrusts] you [with his service, do not rest ... and sleep should not enter your eyes] *13* [until] you have fulfilled [... do not add. And if there is for the humble ... do not *14* [add] for him; ev[en wealth without ... lest it changes into disgrace and he falls ...] *15* [... and see, for excessive zeal of a man confuses the heart...] *16* Also, [for his wi]ll, increase [his service, and the wisdom of his kindness ...] *17* [...] will counsel him and will be for him [a firstborn son. He will take pity on you like a man on his only begotten ...] *18* For you [... And do not be trusting: why resemble him? And do not stay awake for your riches (?)] *19* ... [Neither depress your soul to whoever does not resemble you,] but be for him [... Do not strike whoever does not have your strength lest you stumble] *21* and are humiliated excessiv[ely. Do not magnify your soul with good wealth, it is] *22* working with the wind and serving your oppressor for nothing. Do not sell your glory for money,] *23* and do not pass it on as your inherit[ance, lest your body becomes impoverished. Do not fill yourself with bread; and if there are no] *24* glasses, do not drink wine; and if there is no fo[od do not seek delicacies. (If) you lack bread,] *25* do not glory in your lack; [you are poor, do not despise your life. Neither should you lighten] *26* a vessel [...]

Frag. 2 col. I   *1* [...] you understand [...] *2* in the wond[erful] mysteries [...Teach poverty to those who fear ...] *3* [...] ... [... before, why will it exist and what will exist in them?...] *4* [...] ... [...] *5* [...Why were they and why will they be in them? ...] in all [...] you shall do [...] *6* [... day and night meditate on the mystery of exis]tence and always investigate. Then you shall know truth and injustice, wisdom *7* [...] ... [...] in all his paths with his visitations through all the eternal periods, and the eternal *8* visitation. To the woman who does [...] to all [...] her inclination and the rule of her deeds *10* to all ... she spreads her understanding to every creature so that it walks *11* in the inclination of its knowledge. And he will explain [...] And in the prosperity of understanding ... the secrets of *12* his thought while they walk [perfect in all] their deeds. These are always black and will show insight in all *13* their departures. Then you shall know e[ternal] glory [with] his wonderful mysteries and the might of his deeds. And you, *14* understand the poverty of your deeds in the memory of tim[e, for] the engraved decree will come and every visitation will be written, *15* for the decree has been engraved by God through all [times for] the sons of Seth. And the book of memorial is written in his presence *16* for those who keep his word. And this is the vision of the meditation of the book of memorial: he will give his spirit as inheritance to the weak of the people, for *17* the holy ones are formed as a model, and he will no longer give meditation to the spirit of flesh, for it does not differentiate between *18* good and evil according to the law of his spirit. *Blank* And you, son, understand; pay attention to the mystery of existence and know *19* [the inhe]ritance of every living creature. And they will walk and administer [...] *20* [...] between the much and the little in their foundations [...] *21* [...] in the mystery of existence [...] *22* [...] every vision of knowledge and in every [...] *23* and always encourage yourself. Do not exert yourself in wickedness [...] *24* in it, it will not empty the handfuls of its inheritance [...] *25* for with intelligence they will understand your secrets [...] *26* its foundation with you [...] with the recompense [...] *27* They will not choose after their hearts /and after/ their eyes [...]

Frag. 2 col. II   *1–2* [...] *3* in the mystery of existence [...] *4* compassion(s) [...] *5* to walk [...] *6* Bless his name [...] *7* in your happiness [...] *8* the great mercies of God [...] *9* Praise God and for every plague ble[ss ...] *10* it happens through his will /and/ he understands [...] *11* he will observe all your paths *12* Do not be deluded with the thought of an evil inclination [...] *13* investigate the truth. Do not be deluded [...] *14* the intelligence of the flesh does not /command/. Do not stray [...] *15* you will think [...] Do not say [...] *16* for [...]

4QSapiential Work A*ᵃ* (4Q418 [4QSap.Work Aᵃ])

Frag. 2 (= 4Q416 1)   *1* [...] one to [another, and all their commandments ...] *2* [...
He judges in] the heavens upon [every evil deed and takes pleasure in] all the
sons of truth ...] *3* [... their end,] and all those who wa[llow in it] will tremble
and shout, [for the heavens ...] *4* [...the waters] and the abysses will tremble
[and all the spirits of flesh] will str[ip naked, and the sons of the heavens ...]
5 [... his judgm]ent, and all injustice will end at one go and [the time of truth]
will be complete [...] *6* [...] in all the periods of eternity, for he is the God of
truth [and before the centuries ...] *7*, [...] so that the just man may distinguish
between good and evil [...]

Frag. 7 (= 4Q417 1 I–II)   *1* [...take. Then] God [will see and change his wrath and
pa[ss over your sins, for before ...] *2* [... he will not support everything. And
who will be jus]t in his judgment, and [without release ...?] *3-4* [...] *5* And if
you need, do not ... from your lack, for his treasure is not lacking ...] his
mouth *6* [everything succeeds. Eat what he offers you but do not add ...] your
life *7* [If you take borrowed money from men for your necessities, do not ...
day and ni]ght, and do not give rest *8* [to your soul... and he will make you go
back to ... Do not lie to him; why will you com]mit a sin? And also *9* [of the
reproach ... and no longer trust ... his neighbour and in] your lack he will close
10 [his hand ... and as he takes a loan. He knows ... And] if a misfortune happens to you *11* [... Do not hide ... behold he will reveal ...] *Blank* *12* [... ruling
over him.] Then they will not [strike] with the stick *13* [...] and he will stop
again, *14* [and also you ...] If *15* [you hasten, he will flatten you without ...] Beg
your nourishment, *16* [for he opens his rewards ...] all their lack

Frag. 8 (= 4Q416 2 II)   *1* [...If] he closes [his hand, the spirit withdraws from all
flesh. Do not take] *2* [...] and before his re[proach you shall cover your face,
and for the folly of the prison] *3* [like ...] also the money [... And whoever has
a debt with him, quickly should pay it.] *4* [And] you, rea[ch an agreement with
him, for the purse of] your treasures [... for your creditor in favour of your
fellow ...] *5* all your life [with him. Pay quickly so that] he does not take your
purse. And [in your affairs do not demean] *6* [your spirit with any wealth. Do
not] embitter your holy spirit, for [it has] no [price ...] *7* [... Man is not in-
clined] freely, seek his face [and in his tongue he speaks. Then] *8* [you will find
your pleasure ... do not forsake] your laws [and be careful in your mysteries.]
9 [... If he entrusts you with his service,] do not rest [... and sleep should not
enter your eyes *10* [until you have fulfilled ... do not add.] And if there is for
the humble [...] *11* [do not add for him; even weal]th without [...] lest it
changes into disgrace and he falls [...] *12* [... and see, for] excessive zeal of a
man confuses the heart [...] *13* [Also, for his will, increase] his service, and the

wisdom of his kindness [...] *14* [... and (there) will be for him a firstborn son. He will take pity] on you like a man [on his only begotten ...]

Frag. 9 (= 4Q416 2 III)   *1* ... [...] *2* he has appointed for you. [Do not stretch out] your hand [lest you burn yourself and your body is consumed by his fire. According to what] *3* he took, so [has it been given back to him. You will rejoice if you are free of him. Nor should you take money from a man] *4* you do not [know, lest you increase your poverty. If he determined] *5* your death, [you will not corrupt] your spirit [for that. Then will you repose with truth,] *6* and in your death he will produce [...] your memorial [and your succession will inherit the enjoyment. If] you are poor, *7* desire nothing except [your portion, and do not be consumed for it, lest you shift your boun]dary. And if *8* he restores you in glory, walk in it. *Blank* [And investigate among its offspring about the mystery of existence.] Then *9* you shall know its inheritance and walk in justice, for God exalts [his ... in all] your paths. To those who honour you *10* ... [...] ... *12* give honour and praise his name always. For from poverty he lif[ted your he]ad and among the nobles *13* he seated you. Over an inheritance of glory he has given dominion to you, always seek his will. *Blank* *14* [If you are po]or, do not say 'I am poor and cannot seek knowledge'. To all discipline *15* [bend your shoulder] and in all [...] refine your heart and in much knowledge your thoughts. *16* [Investigate the mystery of existence, consider] all the paths of truth and examine all the roots of evil. *17* [Then you shall know what is bitter for man] and what is sweet for a man. *Blank* Honour your fa[ther in your poverty and your mother] in your steps, for like grass for a man, so is his father, *19* and like a pedestal [for a man, so is his mother. For] they are the oven of your origin, and just as they have dominion over you

Frag. 10 (= 4Q416 2 IV)   *1* [and just as he has opened] your ears to the mystery of e[xistence, (so) you must honour them, for your own glory ... honour his presence] *2* [for your own life and the duration of] your days. [And if you are poor ... without law.] *3-4* [...] *5* [...] one, and he will not [rule over] you [in her and you ...] *6* [... for you for] the flesh. [He will separate] your daughters one [by one, and your sons ... and you] *7* [together with the wife] who reposes in your bosom, for she is the rem[nant of your nakedness ... and if another than yourself rules over her,] *8* [he will remove the boundary from his life. ...] in her spirit which rules you [to walk according to your will, without adding a vow] *9* [or a freewill sacrifice ... to change your spirit] according to your will, and [every obligatory oath to offer a vow ...] *10* [to violate what issues from your mouth, and according to your] will ... [...]

Frag. 43 (= 4Q417 2 I)   *1* [... in the wonderful mysteries ...] Teach poverty to those who fear [...] *2* [...] before, why will it exist and what will exist in them?

[…] *3* […] Why were they and why will they be in them? […in all …] *4* [… day] and night meditate on the mystery of existence [and always investigate. Then you shall know truth and injustice, wisdom] *5* [… in a]ll his paths with his visitations [through all the eternal periods, and the eternal visitation. Then you shall differentiate between] *6* [good and evil according to his deeds, for] God will spread knowledge of the foundation of truth [and of the mystery of existence. To the woman who does …] *7* [all…] her inclination and the dominion of her deeds to [all …] *8* [she spreads her understanding to every creature so that] it walks in the inclination of her kno[wledge. And he will explain … And in the prosperity of understanding …] *9* [the secrets of his thought while they wa]lk [perfect in all their deeds. These are always black and will show insight in all their departures. Then you shall know] *10* [eternal glory with his wond]erful [mysteries] and the might [of his deeds. And you, understand the poverty of your deeds] *11* [in the memory of time, for] the engraved dec[ree will come] and [every visitation will be] written, [for the decree has been engraved by God for all the times for the sons of Seth.] *12* [And the book of the memorial is written in his prese]nce for those who keep his wor[d. And this is the vision of the meditation of the book of the memorial: he will give his inheritance to the man with spirit] *13* [for the holy ones are formed as a model, and he will no] longer [give meditation to the spirit of flesh, for it does not differentiate between good and evil according to the law of his spirit.] *14* [*Blank* And you, son, understand; pay] attention to the mystery of existence [and know the inhe]ritance of every living creature. And they will walk and administer …] *15* […] between the much and the little in their founda[tions …] *16* […] in the mystery of existence […]

Frag. 55   *1* […] and his soul […] *2* […] *Blank* […] *3* his paths are dug in pain. We will rest *4* […] and there will be watchfulness in our hearts […] knowledge will trust in all our paths. *Blank 5* […] and they have not sought intel[ligence, and wisdom] they have [not] chosen. *Blank* Is not the God of knowledge *6* […] above truth to understand all […] intelligence? He divides between the heirs of truth *7* […] watchfulness in […] Are not peace and quiet *8* […] if you do not listen to him, for the angels of holiness […] in the heavens *9* […] the truth. And they will go after all the roots of understanding and will watch over *10* […] his knowledge, and they will honour a man more than his fellow, and according to his intelligence his glory will increase. *11* […] They are like the man who is slothful and like the son of man who is ruined. Is not *12* [… ?] But they will inherit an eternal possession. Will you not see ?

Frag. 69   *1* […] … *2* […] and you will understand […] … with *3* […] … Do they not walk in the truth? *4* […] and in the knowledge of all their rejoicings. *Blank* And now, crazy ones at heart, what is good which does not *5* […? And what is]

quietness which is not destruction? And what is the judgment which is unfounded? And what will the dead sigh about [...] *6* ... [...] you were formed,
and you will return to eternal destruction, for [...] ... [...] *7* The dark places
will cry out for your abundance and all will be for ever. Those who seek the
truth will rise for the judgment [...] *8* All the crazy at heart will be annihilated
and the sons of iniquity will be found no more, and all those who strengthen
evil will be dried up [...] *9* During your judgment, the foundations of the firm-
ament will cry out and deafen all [...] ... [...] *10 Blank* And you, the chosen ones
of truth and the pursuers of [...] the guardians *11* of all knowledge, will you
say: We exert ourselves for understanding and are watchful to pursue knowledge [...] in all [...] *12* but he does not fly for all the years of eternity? Does he
not delight in truth for ever? And knowledge [...] you will serve it and [...]
13 the heavens, whose inheritance is life eternal. Will they say: We exert ourselves in the deeds of truth and we are weary *14* in all the periods? Do they not
walk in eternal light? [...] glory and much honour. You [...] *15* in the firmaments [...] the foundation of the pillars, all [...] *Blank* And you, sons [...]

Frag. 81   *1* Open the spring of your lips to bless the holy ones, and you, praise
in the eternal spring [...] He has separated you from all *2* spirit of the flesh; and
you, keep separate from all that he hates and keep yourselves apart from all
abomination of the soul; for he has made everything *3* and causes each man to
inherit his portion. He has destined a portion to you (and has placed) your inheritance among the sons of man [and over their in]heritance he makes you
rule. And you, *4* in this you give him glory, when you make yourself holy for
him. When he placed you like the holy of holies [...] ... *5* He makes your lot
fall and glorifies you outstandingly, and he will establish you like a firstborn in
[...] *6* and he will give you my goodness. Is not his goodness for you? Always
walk in his faithfulness. [...] *7* your deeds. And you, investigate his judgments
with a whole hand (?) and multiply [...] *8* love him, and with ‹eternal› piety and
with mercy for all who keep his word. [...] *9* And you, he has opened knowledge for you and makes you rule over his treasure, and has determined a measure of truth [...] *10* they for you, and by your hand to change the wrath of the
men of his favour and to administer [...] *11* with you, before you take your
inheritance from his hand, the glory of his holy ones, and be[fore ...] *12* he
opened [...] all his holy ones and all those called by his name, [...] *13* with all
the periods, his honour and his beauty for the eter[nal] planting [...] *14* ... all
who will inherit the earth will walk, for in the he[avens ...] *15* And you, understand; if through the wisdom of hands he has given you dominion, [...] *16* ex-
tension (?) for every man who walks. And from there he will administer your
nourishment [...] *17* Understand the praised one, and by the whole hand of
your sages add [...] *18* Show your lack to all those who seek delicacies. Then
you will understand [...] *19* Fill and be replete with the abundance of goodness

and the wisdom of your hands [...] *20* for God has divided the inheritance [of every living creature] and all those wise at heart understand [...]

Frag. 88   *1* Keep yourself steady [...] *2* In your life he will fill you with abundance of yea[rs ...] *3* he who guards you. Why will you change [...] *4* he will judge iniquity and with the strength of your hands [...] *5* he will close his hand in your lack [...] *6* to the sole of your feet. For God seeks kno[wledge ...] *7* by your hand the animals and gathers them when they suffer [...] *8* and in truth will he fill up your inheritance. [...]

Frag. 103 *col.* II   *1* [...] ... [...] *2* the workers until all [...] *3* bring into your baskets and into your stores all [...] *4* it will produce, epoch after epoch, seek them; and do not cease to [...] and do not [...] *5* for they all seek them in their epochs. And man, according to his taste [...] will find companions of [...] *6* like a spring of living waters which contains [...] Do not change your lack which [...] *7* lest it be a hybrid like the mule, or like a garm[ent of two materials, or] (with) wool and with linen, or (lest) your work (be) like he who tills *8* with an ox and an ass together, neither let your produce be like those who sow hybrids; for the seed and harvest and the produce *9* [of the vine] are ho[ly ...] Your wealth with your flesh together will end your life and in your life you will not find

Frag. 123 *col.* II   *1* ... [...] *2* at the entrance of the years and the departure of the periods [...] *3* all that will happen in it, because it is and what it [...] *4* its period, for God opens the ears. Those who understand the mystery of existence [...] *5* And you, understand; in your consideration of all these things [...] *6* ... he weighs your deeds with [...] *7* [...] he governs you. He observes much [...] *8* [...] ...

Frag. 126 *col.* II   *1* [...] None of his armies will rest [...] *2* [...] in truth. In the hand of every lovable man [...] *3* [...] ... the truth. And with the scales of justice God measures all [...] *4* he separates them in truth. He positions them and examines their delights [...] *5* and hides all. Neither will they exist without his approval ... [...] *6* judgment to carry out vengeance on all the evildoers and the visitation [...] *7* to confine the wicked for ever and to lift up the head of the weak [...] *8* with eternal glory and perpetual peace, and the spirit of life to separate [...] *9* all the sons of life, and with the power of God and the abundance of his glory, with his goodness [...] *10* and in his faithfulness. They will bow down the whole day, they will always praise his name [...] *11* *Blank* And you, walk in the truth with all those who seek [...] *12* and in your hand is his lovableness (?) and from your hamper you will seek his delight. And you, [...] *13* and if he does not stretch out his hand to your lack, and your lack ... [...] *14* [...] and he will not place some of his delight, for God [...] *15* your hand to increase, and the explosion of your zeal [...] *16* always ... [...]

Frag. 127   *1* […] from your spring, and you will not find what you need, and your soul will languish for every goodness until death […] *2* […] all day. And your soul will wish to approach his gates, and will cover the tomb […] *3* […] … and it will be a tooth for food and a flame for heat against […] *4* […] pleasure and the oppressors in his behaviour. And you also […] *5* for yourself, for God does all his pleasure simply, and regulates them in truth […] *6* […] with the balance of justice he weighs all their knowledge, and in truth […] *7* […] … […]

4Q Sapiential Work B (4Q419 [4QSap.Work B])

Frag. 1   *1* which you will do in accordance with all the precep[ts …] *2* to you by the hand of Moses, and what he will do […] *3* by the hand of his priests, for they are those who keep the coven[ant …] *4* he he will make known what […] and what […] *5* […] and he will choose among the descendants of Aaron […] *6* his paths and to approach [the fire] which appeases […] *7* and he will give them … […] with him […] *8* and they will go out […] *9* the throne which rises in splendour […] *10* he lives for ever and his glory for centu[ries …] *11* you will seek, and the abomination of impurity […] *12* the love of them and they will wallow in all […]

4QSapiential Work C (4Q424 [4QSap.Work C])

Frag. 1   *1* […] … […] *2* […] *Blank* If […] *3* […] outside and decides to build it and covers the wall with plaster, he also […] *4* [and] from it rain will fall. *Blank* If it is hidden, do not take a law, and if it is […,] do not *5* enter the oven, for like lead so will it melt you and it will not resist before the fire. *Blank 6* In the hands of the slothful do not place an affair, for he will not follow your orders; and do not send him *7* to collect something, for he will not level off your paths. *Blank* Do not trust in the collector of taxes *8* to collect money for your necessities. *Blank* Do not entrust the man with twisted lips *9* with your trial; certainly he will distort with his lips, he will not be favourable to the truth […] *10* with the fruit of his lips. *Blank* Do not entrust wealth to the avaricious man […] *11* and he adjusts what remains to you to your pleasure […] … […] *12* and in the time of harvest he is found (to be) a hypocrite. *Blank* The impatient person […] *13* the simple, for certainly he will consume them. *Blank* The man […]

Frag. 2   *1* […] from the spring of judgment … […] *2* […] Do not mortgage it in the midst of the poor […] *3* […] likewise the pigeon. *Blank* The man […] *4* […] … Do not […] *5* […] he will do […]

Frag. 3   *1* and he will not do his work in proportion to his weight. The man who judges before investigating is like he who believes before [examining.] *2* Do not

place him to govern those who pursue knowledge, because he does not understand their judgments to justify the just man and condemn [the wicked;] *3* he
too will be despised. *Blank* Do not send the man with tearful eyes to observe the
upright [...] *4* Do not send the hard of hearing to investigate the judgment, for
he will not weigh up the men's dispute. Like he who winnows in the wind
[grain] *5* which does not separate out, so is he who speaks to an ear which does
not listen or he who recites to the sleepyhead, to one who is asleep in spirit [...]
6 Do not send the man with a coarse heart to differentiate thoughts, for the
wisdom of his heart is hidden and will not rule [...] *7* and he will not find the
knowledge from their hands. *Blank* The prudent man will receive kn[owledge.]
Blank The wise man will obtain wisdom. *Blank* *8* The upright man will take pleasure in judgment. *Blank* The man [...] *Blank* The brave man will be zealous for
[...] *9* [he] will be the master of the lawsuit with those who shift boundaries.
Blank [...] ... *10* [...] fear all who lack riches, the sons of justice [...] *11* [...] with
all wealth [...]

4QMessianic Apocalypse (4Q521)

Frag. 2 col. II   *1* [for the heav]ens and the earth will listen to his Messiah, *2* [and
all] that is in them will not turn away from the holy precepts. *3* Be encouraged,
you who are seeking the Lord in his service! *Blank* *4* Will you not, perhaps, en-
counter the Lord in it, all those who hope in their heart? *5* For the Lord will
observe the devout, and call the just by name, *6* and upon the poor he will place
his spirit, and the faithful he will renew with his strength. *7* For he will honour
the devout upon the throne of eternal royalty, *8* freeing prisoners, giving sight
to the blind, straightening out the twisted. *9* Ever shall I cling to those who
hope. In his mercy he will jud[ge,] *10* and from no-one shall the fruit [of] good
[deeds] be delayed, *11* and the Lord will perform marvellous acts such as have
not existed, just as he sa[id] *12* for he will heal the badly wounded and will make
the dead live, he will proclaim good news to the meek *13* give lavishly [to the
need]y, lead the exiled and enrich the hungry. *14* [...] and all [...]

Frag. 2 col. III   *1* and the law of your favour. And I will free them with [...] *2* ...
the fathers towards the sons [...] *3* who blesses the Lord in his approval [...]
4 May the earth rejoice in all the places [...] *5* for all Israel in the rejoicing of
[...] *6* and his sceptre ... [...] *7* ... [...]

Frag. 5 col. II   *1* [...] see all [that the Lord] *2* [has made: the earth] and all that is
in it, the seas [and all] *3* [they contain,] and all the reservoirs of waters and torrents. *Blank* *4* [...] those who do good before the Lord *5* [...] like these, the accursed. And they shall be for death, [when] *6* [he makes] the dead of his people
[ri]se. *Blank* *7* And we shall give thanks and announce to you the just acts of the

Lord, who[...] *8* the de[a]d and opens [...] *9–10* ... [...] *11* and reveals [...] *12* and the bridge of the abys[s ...] *13* the accursed have coagulated [...] *14* and have found the heavens [...] *15* and all the angels [...]

Frag. 8   *1* [...] and a wall between *2–4* [...] *5* [...] they will appear *6* [...] to Adam *7* [...] Jacob *8* [...] and all the holy utensils *9* [...] and all his anointed ones *10* [...] and /they will speak/ the word of the Lord and [...] *11* [...] to the Lord *12* [...] the eyes of

4QWisdom Text with Beatitudes (4Q525 [4QBéat])

Frag. 1   *1* [... which he has said] with the wisdom God gave him [...]
2 [... in order to kn]ow wisdom and discipline, in order
3 [...] in order to increase kn[owledge...]

Frag. 2 col. II   *1* [Blessed is the one who speaks the truth] with a pure heart,
and does not slander with his tongue.
Blessed are those who adhere to his laws,
2 and do not adhere to perverted paths.
Blessed are those who rejoice in her.
and do not explore insane paths.
3 Blessed are those who search for her with pure hands,
and do not importune her with a treacherous heart.
Blessed is the man who attains Wisdom,
4 and walks in the law of the Most High,
and dedicates his heart to her ways,
and is constrained by her discipline
and always takes pleasure in her punishments;
5 and does not forsake her in the hardship of [his] wrongs,
and in the time of anguish does not discard her,
and does not forget her [in the days of] terror,
6 and in the distress of his soul does not loathe her.
For he always thinks of her,
and in his distress he meditates on [the law,]
7 [and throughout] his [whole] life [he thinks] of her,
[and places her] in front of his eyes
in order not to walk on paths [of evil...]
8 [...] together,
and on her account eats away his heart [...]
9 [...] and with kings it shall make him s[it...]
10 with his sceptre over [...] brothers [...]
11 *Blank* [...]

12 [Now, sons, listen to me]
   do not reject [the words of my mouth]
13 [...] ... [...]

Frag. 2 col. III   *1* it is like her the whole day [...] *2* She cannot be obtained with
   gold [...] *3* with any precious stone [...] *4* they stay silent before the beauty of
   her face [...] *5* flowers, purple with [...] *6* scarlet, with all the clothes [...] *7* and
   with gold and pearls [...]

Frag. 4   *2* [...] in the time of n[eed...] *3* [...] of his trial [...] *4* [...] *Blank* [...]
   5 [...of pu]rity ... [...] *6* [...Do n]ot seek her with [wic]ked heart [...] *7* [...Do
   n]ot se[ek her] with arrogant heart [...Do not]
8 abandon [your inh]eritance to the na[tions,]
   or your lot to the sons of foreigners.
   For, the wise [man...]
9 they instruct with tenderness.
   Those who fear God keep her paths
   and walk in
10 her laws,
   and do not reject her reproaches.
   Those who understand will acquire [...]
11 Those who walk in perfection keep away from evil
   and do not reject her admonishments [...]
12 they bear him.
   The skilful dig her paths, [...]
   and in her depths, they ris[e up...]
13 they watch.
   Those who love God humble themselves for her
   and in her paths [...]

Frag. 7 col. II   *1* ...and for the zeal of...[...] *2* so that he may not understand. Of
   the spirit ... *3* of knowledge; of the spirit which circumcises [...] *4* he blesses;
   and whoever stumbles and does not [...] *5* certain; and whoever seeks and does
   not [...] *6* pride, and arrogance of hea[rt...]

Frags. 8–9   *1* ... the lament and the sorrow [...] *2* *Blank* [...] *3* Pay attention to me,
   all the sons of [...] *4* [...] humility and uprightness ... [...] *5* and he loves the
   enemy and does not justify all flesh [...] *6* If you are good, it will go well with
   you [...] you will return [...] *7* all [...] knowledge [...]

Frag. 10   *1* [...] the creature, lest [...] *2* [...] of the fate of the spirit [...] *3* [...]
   (the) judgment. On the pit [...] *4* [...] ... [...]

Frag. 12   *1* […] abundance of peace [with] all the blessings […] *2* […] … glory for all those who cling to me […] *3* […] perfect in all the paths, and to … […] *4* […] and with the whole spirit […]

Frag. 13   *1* […] and the sons of … […] *2* […] in the evils of the eye […] *3* […] … to shed blood … […] *4* […] you will inherit pride and in entrails […] *5* […] all her inheritance […] *6* [… Li]sten to me, all […]

Frag. 14 *col.* II   *1* […] … […] *2* upon the throne of evil and upon the heights […] *3* […] they will praise your head […] *4* […] before your word and […] *5* in full glory and she desires […] *6* drawn near in your paths. You will not hesitate […] *7* you will be blessed. At the time of your staggering you will meet […] *8* and the insult of whoever hates you will not approach you […] *9* together, and those who hate you and those who intend to destroy you […] *10* your heart, and you will rejoice over […] … […] *11* to the space of your foot, and you will walk upon the heights of […] *12* your soul; he will free you from every evil and fear will not enter you […] *13* and your inheritance; he will fill your days with goodness, and with abundant peace […] *14* you shall inherit honour, and when you are snatched away to eternal rest they will inherit […] *15* and in your teaching, all those who know you will walk together. […] *16* together they will stray, and in your paths they will remember you, for you were […] *17* Blank […] *18* And now, understand and listen to me and apply your heart to *19* grant knowledge deep within you … […] meditate […] *20* with just humility pronounce your words; may you not give […nor] *21* may you answer the words of your fellow, so that he does not […] you *22* and answer according to what you have heard. Like a merchant, there rises in him the [… Do not] *23* utter sighs before having heard his words […] *24* excessively. *Blank* First hear his words and afterwards, answer with [… and with] *25* patience bring them out; and in the midst of princes, answer correctly […] *26* with your lips, and be very careful against a slip of the tongue […] *27* lest you be condemned by your (own) lips and trapped together with […] *28* … […] indiscretion […] from me, and … […]

Frag. 15   *1* […] darkness […] poverty and in the number […] *2* […] serpents […] (he) will go to him, and you will enter *3* […] fire. And the serpent devours its lords […] *4* […] in it they stand firm. Eternal curses and vipers' venom […] *5* […] snake; and in him fly the demons of death; at his entrance […] *6* […] darkness. Flames of sulphur are his foundation, and from *7* […] his […] are shameful reproaches; his bolts are the fasts of the pit […] *8* […] they will not reach the tracks of life […] *9* […] the couches […]

Frag. 16   *1* […] … […] *2* the chiefs of […] *3* those who understand stray in her […] *4* and the cheats […] *5* blood…. […] *6* with treachery and oppression […]

Frag. 21   *1* [...] darkened, and we will be abandon[ed...] *2* [...] those who annoy God alwa[ys...] *3* [...] the wicked [...] *4* [...] and you choose disgrace [...] *5* [...] in him. They get conceited and parade themselves [...] *6* [...] those saturated with terror *7* [...] ... her source, the source of [...] *8* [...] amass wrath and with long [...] *9* [...] certainly, and he becomes annoyed [...]

Frag. 22   *1* they will seize their entrails before G[od...] *2* has been expelled. And on the day decreed [...] *3* and to descend to the bottom of the pit, and to [...] [...] ... *4* in the oven of wrath. *Blank* For I [...] *5* God has commanded for the wise men [...] *6* in their favour. From knowledge of wisdom [...] *7* to change, lest they whisper with [...] *8* he abhors him and with insolent men [...] *9* of justice, and like a rock for stu[mbling ...] [...] *10* For G[od] is annoyed with me [...]

Frag. 23 *col.* II   *1* [...] he utters words [...] of your people, *2* the heart. Pay attention to me and [...] *3* has established. And drink from [...] *4* my house is a house of [...] *5* [...] my house. He dwells in [...] *6* for ever. And they will go up [...] *7* they will co[llect] their harvests [...] *8* he will burn it, and every thicket [...] *9* a well of waters [...]

5 Other Compositions

1QMysteries (1Q27 [1QMyst])

Frag. 1 *col.* I   *1* [...] all [...] *2* [...] the mystery of sin
3 [...]
   And they do not know the future mystery,
   or understand ancient matters.
4 And they do not know what is going to happen to them;
   and they will not save their souls from the future mystery.
   Blank
5 And for you this will be the sign /that this is going to happen./
   When those born of sin are locked up,
   evil will disappear in front of justice
   as darkness disappears in front of light.
6 As smoke disappears, and no longer exists,
   so will evil disappear for ever.
   And justice will be revealed
   like a sun which regulates the world.
7 And all those who curb the wonderful mysteries will no longer exist.
   And knowledge will pervade the world,
   and there will never be folly there.
8 This word will undoubtedly happen,
   the prediction is truthful.
   And by this he will show you that it is irrevocable:
9 Do not all peoples loathe sin?
   And yet, they all walk about under its influence.
   Does not praise of truth come from the mouth of all nations?
10 And yet, is there perhaps one lip or one tongue which persists with it?
   What people would wish to be oppressed by another more powerful than itself?
11 Who would wish to be sinfully looted of its wealth?
   And yet, which is the people not to oppress its neighbour?
   Where is the people which has not looted another of its wealth?
12 [...] the exits [...]

Frag. 1 *col.* II   *1* [...] ... [...] *2* ... [...] for him the schemes advantageous [...]
   3 ... [...] are for [...] *4* except he who does good and he who does evil. If [...]
   5 He will have no success in anything. So all the good, his riches [...] *6* without
   wealth, and will be sold without them paying him, because [...] *7* What are [...]
   except all [...] *8* rest, and n[o pri]ce will be enough for [...] *9* *Blank* [...] *10* To
   all the peoples [...] *11* God knows all [...] *12* [...] ... [...]

Frag. 6   *1* [...]... [...] *2* [...] ... he will atone for the mistakes of [...] *3* [...] for ever before his face to atone [...]

Frags. 9–10   *1* Today [...] ... [...] *2* for, if [...] What is [...] *3* the kings of the peoples have heard [...] in him, and like him *4* in all the judgments [...] he and [...] *5-6* ... [...]

4QMysteries*ᵃ* (4Q299 [4QMyst*ᵃ*])

Frag. 2 col. II   *1* [...] ... [... the poor man.] *2* How will we call [...] and the deed [...] *3* and every deed of the just man has been made [unclean. And how will we call the man [...] *4* wise and just, for it does not suit man [...] and not [...] hidden wisdom, except *5* the wisdom of prudence. Evil [...] *6* the deed which he will no longer do. For [...] *7* they fulfilled the word. And what will the ma[n] do [...] *8* he who rebels against the word which they fulfilled. He will erase his name before [...] *9* *Blank.* Listen, those who support [...] *10* eternal and the decisions about every deed. And what [...] *11* every mystery and place of all thought. He does all [...] *12* He is first always. It is his name and [...] *13* [...] thought. He opens the house of the begotten [...] *14* [...] the sons of the proof and will give us as inheritance [...] *15* [...] every mystery and the pains of every deed [...] *17* [...] ... [...]

4QMysteries*ᵇ* (4Q300 [4QMyst*ᵇ*])

Frag. 1 col. II   *1* [... the wiz]ards, learned in iniquity, speak the parable and declare the divination before it is spoken. Then you shall know if you have seen; *2* and the signs of the he[avens ...] your madness, for upon you has been marked the seal of the vision and you have not seen the eternal mysteries, and knowledge you have not understood. *3* Then you shall say to [...] ... [...] for you have not seen the root of the vision. And if you open the vision *4* [to you will be] closed [...] all your wisdom, for to you [...] his name, for it is a hidden *5* wisdom. [...] there will be no [...] *6* vision [...]

Frag. 3   *1* [... all] *2* the difference between go[od and evil ... the mystery of iniquity ...] *3* all its wisdom. And they do not kn[ow the mystery of existence, nor understand ancient things. And they do not know what is going to happen to them;] *4* and they will not save their souls from the mystery of ex[istence. And this will be for you the sign that this is happening. When the begotten of iniquity are confined,] *5* wickedness will vanish before justice as [darkness] van[ishes before the light. As smoke vanishes, and no longer exists, so will] *6* [wicke]dness [vanish] for ever. And justice will be revealed like a sun [which regulates the world. And all those who restrain the wonderful mysteries will no longer exist.]

4QMysteries*c* (4Q301 [4QMyst*c*])

Frag. 2   *1* the judgment of the mad (person) and the inheritance of the sage [...] And what is the enigma for you? ... in the roots of knowledge. *2* What does the heart honour? It is the proverb [...] proverb. What is glory for you? It is [...] without strength and it will rule him in a rebuke without price. Who will say *4* [...?] Who among you seeks the face of the light, and the luminary [...] *5* [...] the model of the memorial which does not [...] *6* [...] with the angels of [...] *7* [...] those who praise [...]

Frag. 3   *1-3* [...] *Blank* [...] *4* [...] and he is glorified for the slowness of his anger and he is great for the abundance of his fury, [and he is honoured] *5* [...] he in his great mercy, and he is terrible for the shrewdness of his face. He is glorified [...] *6* [...] and in the earth of his dominion. And God is glorified in the people of his holy ones *7* [...] his chosen ones, and he is honoured [...] his holiness. He is great in blessings [...] *8* [...] ... [...] in the destruction of the period of wickedness [...]

3QHymn (3Q6)

Frag. 1   *1* [...] all those who will rejoice [...][...] *2* [...] their songs will please you *3* [...] they will praise you for ever. [...]

4QApocryphal Lamentations A (4Q179 [4QapocrLam A])

Frag. 1 *col.* I   *2* [...] all our sins. *5* and loves the enemy and does not justify all flesh [...And we can do nothing, because we have not liste[ned] *3* [... at the time of] the visitation, so that all these things will happen to us in the evil of [...] *4* his covenant. *Blank* Woe to us! *5* [...] It has been burned by fire and ravaged *6* [...] our honour, and in it there is nothing pleasant [...] *7* [...] and our holy courtyards were *8* [...] ... Jerusalem, city *9* [... In the well [...] has ended up in ruins, as a la]ir of animals and there is no [...] And her squares *10* [...] Alas! All her palaces are desolate *11* [...] and those who used to come to the festival are not in her. All the cities *12* [...] Our inheritance has been turned into a desert, land which does not *13* [...] the sound of joy is not heard in her. And he who is looking for *14* [...] for his incurable wound. All our debts *15* [...] our transgressions [...] our sins.

Frag. 1 *col.* II   *1* Woe to us, because the wrath of God has gone up [...] *2* and has been defiled by the dead [...] *3* like a detested woman [...] *4* the children of her breast. The daughter of my people is cruel [...] *5* of her youth. The sons of my people are desolate [...] *6* before the winter, when their hands are weak [...]

7 dunghills are the lodging where they spend the night [...] *8* they ask for water and there is no-one to give it [...] *9* evicted ... [...] *10* and there is no delight at all in him. «Those who used to wear purple [...] *11* and jewellery of pure gold; those who wear clothes of *12* and silk, purple and brocade [...] *13* The {pretty} dainty daughters of Sion ... [...]

Frag. 2   *1-2* [...] ... [...] *3* [...] in (the) tents [...] *4* [How] lonely has the city been left [...] ... [...] *5* [...] the princess of all the nations is desolate like an abandoned woman; all her daughters have been abandoned, *6* like a woman without sons, like a wounded and abandoned woman. All her palaces and her sq[uares] *7* are like a barren woman, and all her paths like an imprisoned woman [...] like a bitter woman, *8* and all her daughters like those mourning for {for} their hus[bands...] like those bereft *9* of their only sons. How Jeru[salem] must weep [... the tears will flow] down her cheek for her sons *10* [...] and her sigh

4QLiturgy (4Q409)

Col. I   *1* [...Praise and bless in the] days of the first-[fruits (?)] *2* [of the new wheat, of the new wine and of the new oil, with the] new [of]fering, *3* [and bless his holy Name. Pr]aise and bless on the days of *4* [the festival of (fire)wood, with the offering] of (fire)wood for the sacrifice, *5* [and bless his Name. Praise and bless] on the day of remembrance with cheering *6* [... and bless the Lo]rd of all. Praise *7* [and bless... and bless] his holy Name *8* [...and ble]ss the Lord of all. *9* [...Praise and bless] on these days *10* [...] Praise and bless and give thanks *11* [...Praise and bless and] give thanks with branches of a tree

Col. II   *1* [...] ... [...] *2* Praise and ble[ss ...] *3* and rams [...] *4* in *5* when you bu[rn ...] *6* your creator [...] *7* and bless [...] *8* upon the altar [...] *9* with cheering [...] *10* to your God [...]

4QBenediction (4Q500)

1 [...] may your mulberry trees blossom ... [...] *2* [...] your winepress, built of stone [...] *3* [...] at the gate of the holy height [...] *4* [...] your plantation and the channels of your glory [...] *5* the branches of your delights [...] *6* [...] ...
Blank [...]

4QApocryphal Lamentations B (4Q501)

1 [...]
Do not give our inheritance to foreigners,
or our produce to the son of a foreigner.

Remember that we are [...]
2 of your people
the forsaken ones of your inheritance.
Remember the sons of your covenant,
the desolate,
3 [...] the volunteers,
the wanderers, for whom there is no return,
the sorely wounded, for whom there is no cure,
4 [those bent double, with no straig]htening up.
The wretched ones of your people have surrounded us
with their lying tongue, and they have been turned [...]
5 your foliage to one born of a woman.
Look and see the affront of the sons of [your people]
6 for our skin [is burning,]
indignation rules us,
on account of the tongue of the insolent.
7 [...] not [...] in your commandments.
Their posterity will not be with {among the sons of} the covenant.
8 [...] against them the might of your strength,
and avenge yourself on them.
9 [...] They have not placed you before them,
but they act the bully against the poor and needy.

5QCurses (5Q14)

1 [...] and over the seas. Also over [...] 2 [...] May your eyes fall out [...] 3 [...]
May you fall down in all the falls [...] 4 [...] May they obliterate you from
among all the [...] 5 [...] may there be little for you and may you not have
enough. Because [...]

6QAllegory of the Vine (6Q11)

1 [...] ... [...] 2 [...] with [...] 3 [...] I came at the time of the grape harvest [...]
4 [... from mor]ning to evening [...] 5 [...] the girl destroyed and destroyed the
boy [...] 6 [...] And you shall say: I have planted a vineyard, I shall guard it [...]

6QHymn (6Q18)

Frag. 2   1 [...] ... [...] 2 [...] eternal life and glory [...] 3 [...] darkness and gloom
[...] 4 [...] darkness are your inclinations [...] 5 [...] to whom lives for ever.
And may [...] be 6 [...] for glory [...] 7 [...] the son of Isaac [...] 8 [...] with
ever[lasting] praise [...]

8QHymn (8Q5)

Frag. 1   *1* [...] In your Name, O Powerful One, I sow dread [...] *2* [...] this man, who is from the sons of [...] *3* this [...]. And how will you reflect his light on ... [...] *4* [...] to the constellations of the heavens [...]

Frag. 2   *1* [...] ... [...] *2* [...] and the rep[ly ...] *3* [...] YHWH. [...] *4* [...] is great above all [...] *5* [...] the persecutions and the judgments [...] *6* [...] and all the spirits before you [...]

11QHymns^a^ (11Q15)

1 [...] ... [...] *2* [...] which they will establish, and ... [...] *3* [...] and you will show...[...] *4* [...] in your rooms; in their names [...] *5* [...] his glory; and their deeds and their grief [...] *6* [...] you created all the spirits [...]

Liturgical Texts

This chapter contains a set of poetic texts which differ in some way from the texts of the foregoing chapter in that they provide signs of having been intended for liturgical use.

Both the *Daily Prayers* and the *Festival Prayers* include exact information on the days or the feasts for which these prayers were intended. Unfortunately, most of the copies of these works which have reached us were copied onto papyrus and survive in an extremely fragmentary condition. Although the preserved fragments from each one of these compositions can be numbered in hundreds, there are very few which provide enough text for a translation. This is why the details in respect of the liturgical celebrations for which they were intended, although significant, are scarce indeed.

In spite of the title (preserved on one of the fragments, suggesting a connection with the heavenly or angelic world), the *Words of the Luminaries* is a composition that is very similar to the previous two. Like them, it has actual information on the days for which these prayers were intended. The details which survive do not allow us to determine either the origin of these works, which turn out to be imbued with biblical themes, or the date of composition.

Very different is the *Songs of the Sabbath Sacrifice*, a composition which transports us straight to the world of angels and has an undeniably mystical character. Even so, its sectarian origin and its liturgical use within the Qumran Community seem to be certain. The collections of blessings and curses included here have this same clear sectarian setting. These blessings and curses have reached us as separate works, in spite of being very like the blessings and curses which have been included within other principal works such as *1 QS* or *1 QM*.

The last texts included in this chapter appear to contain the remains of separate rituals. *4 Q512* comes from a purification ritual, and *4 Q502* was published as a wedding ritual. Although this is not certain, it is in any case a text intended for a joyful celebration.

1 Daily Prayers

4QDaily Prayers*a* (4Q503 [4QPrQuot])

Frags. 1–6 *col.* III   *1* And at the rising of the [sun...] to the vault of the heavens, they shall bless. Starting to speak [they shall say:] *2* Blessed be the God [of Israel...] Today he ren[ews ...] *3* in the fourth [gate of light...] for us the rule [...] *4* [...]teen [...] the heat of the [sun...] *5* when it crosses [... with the streng]th of his powerful hand [... peace be with you] *6* /Israel/. In the fifth [of the month, in the] evening, they shall bless. Starting to speak, they shall say: Blessed be the God [of Israel *7* who hides [...] before him in each unit of his glory. And that night [...] *8* [...] eternal and to give him thanks. And our deliverance at the beginning of [...] *9* [...] the rotations of the shining objects [...] Today, fourte[en ...] *10* [...] the light of the day. Peace be [with] you, Israel. *Blank 12* And at the ri[sing of the sun ...] to shine on the earth, they shall bless. And should there still (remain) *13* the number of [... ele]ven days until the festivals of joy and the ceremonies of glo[ry.] *14* Then [that d]ay is in the fiftieth of the gates [of light ...] *15* the festivities of glo[ry...] in the divisions of the night [...] *16* its resplendence will be complete [...] *17* Israel. [...] *Blank* [...] *18* And on the sixth of the month [in the evening, they shall bless. Starting to speak, they shall say: Blessed be the God of] Israel [...]

Frags. 7–9 *col.* IV   *1* [...] the light of day so that we may know *2* [...] in the sixth gate of the light *3* [... And we,] the sons of your covenant, bless [your name,] *4* with all the companies of [the light ... with] all the tongues of knowledge. Blessed be [...] *5* the light. Peace [be with you, Israel ...] ... [...] *6* The seventh of the [month, in the evening, they shall bless. Starting to speak, they shall] say: Blessed be the God of Is[rael ...] *7* justice [...] we know all these things through [...] *8* ... [...] Blessed be the God [of Israel...]

Frags. 10–11 *col.* V   *1* [And when] the sun [ascends] to illuminate the earth, [they shall bless ...] *2* [...] with the companies of light. Today [...] *3* [...] the ninth day [...] *4* [...] *Blank* [...] *5* [The twel]fth of the month, in the evening, [they shall bless ...] *6* [...] And we, his holy people, exult this night [...] *7* [...] and with us the witnesses in the service {in the service} of the day [...]

Frags. 13–16 *col.* VI   *1* [...] God of lights [...] *2* [...] the light, and the witnesses [...] *3* [...] the light of day [...] *4* [...Blessed be] your name, God of Israel, in all [...] *5* [...] *Blank* [...] *6–7* [...] ... [...] *8* [... holy of] holies in the heights [...] *9* [...] his holy name [...] *10* [...] and glory in the holy [of holies ...] *11* [...] and witnesses for us in the holy of holies [...] *12* [...] in the dominion of the light of the day. Blessed [...] *13* [...] peace be with you, [Israel ...] *14* [... Bles]sed be the God of Israel, he who performs won[ders ...] *15* [...] the earth. And the night [...] *16* [...] who for us adds [...] *17* all their divisions [...] *18* God of Is[rael ...] *19* [...]your holiness [...] *20* [...] in thir[teen ...] *21* [...] twelve *22* [...] Israel [...] *23* [...] Israel [...] *24* [...] your holiness [...]

Frags. 21–28 *col.* VII   *1* [...] in the light of his glory, and gladdens us [...] *2* [...] telling us [...] *3* [... holy of] holies [...] *4* [...] *Blank* [...] *5-7* [...] ... [...] *8* [And when the sun climbs to give light] to the earth, they shall bless. [Starting to speak, they shall say: Blessed be] *9* [the God of Israel] who has chosen us from among all the nations [...] *10* [...] for a fe[ast] of rest and of delights (?) [...] *11* [... jo]yful [...] *12* [...] the lights [...] *13* [...] ... [...] ... [...] first *14* [...] his works [...] in the sky [...] He has created the evening [and the morning ...] *15* [...] his holiness [...] he thinks [...] for centuries. *Blank* [...] *16* [...] ... [...] they shall bless [...] Israel, and a[ll ...] *17* [...] holy of holies [...] we [...]

Frags. 29–32 *col.* VIII   *1* and the peace [of God be with you, Israel...] *2* The seven[teenth of the month, in the evening, they shall bless. Starting to speak, they shall say: Blessed be the God of Israel, who] *3* has made you holy [...] *4* And the night [...] with [...] *5* ... [...] valuable to us. Peace [...] *6* [...] God will bless Yeshurun [...] *7* [And when the sun climbs up to shine on] the earth, they shall bless. [Starting to speak, they shall say: Blessed be the God of Israel] *8* [...] of light will rejoice in [...] *9* [pr]aising your name, God of lights, who renewed [...] *10* [...] gate of light. And we, in the acclamation of your glory [...] *11* [the compa]nies of the night. The peace of God be with you, Israel at the ascen[t of the sun...] *12* [The] seventeenth of the month, in the evening, they shall bless. They shall start speaking [and say: Blessed be the God of Israel] *13* [...] to praise [...] *14-16* [...] *17* [And when the sun rises to shine on the earth, they shall bless. Starting to speak, they shall say: Blessed be the God of Israel] *18* [... our] joy [...] *19* [...] the companies of night [...] *20* [...] Today we [...] *21* [...The peace of God be with you] Israel, for all [time eternal ...] *22* The eig[hteenth of the month in the evening they shall bless. Starting to speak, they shall say: Blessed be the God of Israel ...] *23* [... holy of ho]lies. That night [...] *24* [...] ... [...]

Frags. 33–34 *col.* X   *1* [... the] light of day *2* [...ex]alting *3* [...] holy *4* [...] the feasts of *5* [...] ... *6* [...] which *7* [...] glory. And the night *8* [...] for the kingdom of *9* [...] in the rotation of *10* [...] peace *11-15* [...] *16* [... and we will] remain in the lot of [...] *17* [Peace be with you, Israel.] *Blank* [...] *18* [The twenty-first day] of the month, in the evening, they shall bless. Starting to speak, they shall say: [Blessed be the God of Israel] *19* [...] and for us the night is the beginning of the rule of da[rkness ...] *20* [... Bless]ed be you, God of Israel, who has established [...] *21* [Peace be with you, Israel,] at all moments of the night. *Blank* [...]

Frags. 33–36 *col.* XI *1* When the sun rises over the ea[rth, they shall bless. Starting to speak, they shall say: Blessed be you, God, who] *2* renews our joy with the light [of day ...] *3* ... as the day [...] *4* in your gladness, keeping itself [...] *5* Peace be with you, Israel [...] *6* [On the twenty-]first [day of the month, in the evening, they shall bless. Starting to speak, they shall say: Blessed] *7* be you God, who [...] *8* ... [...] *9* ... [...] Israel [...] *10* [And when] the sun [rises] over the [earth, they shall bless ...] *11* [...] Blessed be the God who [...] *12* [... peace] be with you, Is[rael ...] *13-20* [...] *21* [...] sixth day *22* [... jus]tice. *23* [...] Blessed be the God *24* [...] in the festival of glory.

Frags. 37–38 *col.* XII *1-11* [...] *12* for ever. *Blank* [...] *13* On the twenty-fifth day [of the month, in the evening, they shall bless and say: Blessed be *14* the God of all the holy ones [...] *15* holiness and rest for us [...] *16* in the lot of his dominion [...] *17-18* [...] *19* holy ones [...] *20* twenty[...] gate of [light ...] *21* praising with us [...] *22* our glory. Peace [...] *23* On the twenty-sixth day [...] *24* ... [...]

Frag. 39 *col.* XIII *1* [...] ... [...] *2* [...] Because /it is the night of [...] until it hides .../ thirteen lots of darkness [...] *3* [... the com]panies of the evening and the morning ... our peace. Peace be with you, [Israel ...]

Frags. 40–41 *1* And you [...] *2* and in the rule [...] *3* the name of the God of [Israel. Peace be with you,] Israel, at all mom[ents of the night.] *4* And when [the sun] rises [to shine on the earth...] the third for [...] *5* our glory [...] rest of holiness [...] *6* and they shall praise you [...] and your name will be praised [...] *7* all the holy [ones ...] the holy ones [...] *8* the glory [...] ... [...]

Frags. 48–50 *1* [...] ... [...] *2* [... Peace be with you, Is]rael. *Blank* [...] *3* [On the ... of the month, in the evening, they shall praise. Starting to speak, they shall say: Blessed] be the God of Israel, who *4* [...] our joy and [...] *5* [... and this night] is the third among the fe[asts of] our joy. And you [...] *6* [...] your salvation. Peace be with you, Israel. *Blank* [...] *7* [And when the sun goes out to sh]ine on the earth, they shall bless. Starting to speak, they shall s[ay:] Blessed be the God of Is[rael,] *8* [the God of all the armies of the] gods, who with the sons of justice, justi[fies...] God over all [...]

Frags. 51–55 *1* [...] ... [...] *2* [...] lots of [...] ... [...] *3* [...] explanation, thanksgiving [...] for ever [...] *4* [...] ... [...] *5* [...] the [...]teenth of the gates of glo[ry ...] *6* [...] /the light of day. Peace be with [you, Israel.]/ [In the ... of the month, in the evening, they shall bless. Starting to speak] they shall and say: Blessed be the God of Is[rael...] *7* [...] ... [...] *8* [...] the companies of the light [...] *9* [...] you have taught us the praises of your glory [...] *10* [... at all] times of the night. Peace be with you, [Israel.] *11* [...] *Blank* [...] *12* [...] and they shall say: Blessed be the God of Israel [...] *13* [...] He has let us know the great plans of his intellect [...] *14* [...] the lots of light so that we may know the signs [...] *15* [...]... [...] *16* [...] *Blank* [...] *17* [...] and they shall reply [...] *18* [...] his glory [...] *19* [...] the fifth [...]

Frag. **64**   *1* [...] in the evening [...] *2* [...] our ... [...] *3* [...] the priesthood of [...] *4* [...] a sign for us, for the night of the festival of [...] *5* [...] the night, to be /praising/ with us [...] *6* [...] *Blank* [...] *7* [And when the sun rises,] to shine on the earth, they shall bless. [...] *8* [...] time eternal. Today [...] *9* [...] the company of [...]

2   Festival Prayers

1QFestival Prayers (1Q34 [1QPrFêtes])

Frags. 1–2 (= 4Q509 3)   *1* […] the time of our peace. [… For you console us from our distress, and you gather together our exiles] *2* for the time […] and our scattered ones (you assemble) for the age of [… your mercies upon our assembly, like dr[ops of water] *3* upon the earth in se[ed-time …] like rain upon the [field in the time of grass … We will sing of your wonders] *4* from generation to generation. Blessed be the Lord who makes us rejoice […] *5* *Blank* […] *6* Prayer for the day of atonement. Remember, Lord, […] *7* […] … […]

Frag. 3 *col.* I (= 4Q508 1)   *1* […] … […] *2* […] in the lot of the just and to the wicked in the lot of *3* […] in their bones a disgrace for all flesh. But the just *4* [… in order to flou]rish, thanks to the clouds of the sky and to the produce of the earth, in order to discriminate *5* [between the jus]t and the wicked. Of the wicked you shall make our ransom, while for the upright *6* [you will bring about] the destruction of all our enemies. And we, we will celebrate your name for ever *7* [and ever,] for this is why you have created us. And this is why [we will answer] you: Blessed *8* *Blank* […] *9* […] … […]

Frag. 3 *col.* II   *1* […] the great light for [day]-time, [and the small one for night-time …] *2* […] without their laws being broken. And all of them […] *3* […] and his dominion over the whole world. But the offspring of man has not understood all that you have given them as inheritance, and they have not known you, *4* to do your word and they act more wickedly than anybody. They do not understand your powerful strength. This is why you reject them, because you do not like *5* sin, and the wicked person will not endure before you. However, you have chosen a people in the period of your favour, because you have remembered the covenant. *6* You established them, isolating them for yourself in order to make them holy among all the peoples. And you have renewed your covenant with them in the vision of your glory, and in the words of *7* your holy spirit, by the works of your hand. Your right hand has written to let them know the regulations of glory and the everlasting deeds. *8* [… You raised up] a loyal shepherd for them […] poor and […]

4QFestival Prayers*ᵃ* (4Q507 [4QPrFêtes*ᵃ* ?])

Frag. 1   *1* … […] … […] *2* But we are in sin from the womb, and from the breast, in gu[ilt …] *3* And while we exist, our steps are impurity […]

Frag. 2   *1* […] all the […] *2* Blessed be the Lord […] *3* *Blank* *4* […] … […]

Frag. 3   *1* [...] Blessed be the Lord [...] *2* [...] everlasting generations. Amen. Amen. [...] [...] Rem[ember, Lord, that ...]

4QFestival Prayers*ᵇ* (4Q508 [4QPrFêtesᵇ])

Frag. 1 (= 1Q34 1)   [... But the just ...in order to flourish, thanks to the clouds of the sky and to the produce of] *1* [the earth, in order to discriminate] between the just and the wicked. [The wicked] you shall make [our ransom, while for the upright] *2* [you will complete the destruction] of all our enemies. And we, we will celebrate your na[me for ever and ever, for this is why] *3* [you have created us. And this is why we will answer] you: [Blessed ...]

Frag. 2 (= 1Q34 1 ?)   *1* [...] and you will remain in our midst [...] *2* [...Prayer for the day of atonem]ent. Remember, Lord, the feast of your compassion and the time of the return [...] *3* [...] for us you established a festival of fasting, [et]ernal law [...] *4* [...] and you know secret matters and revealed matters [...] *5* [...] you know our inclination [...] *6* [...] our getting] up and our lying down [...]

Frag. 3   *1* [...] we have acted wickedly [...] *2* [...] and for their multitude. With Noah you established [a covenant ...] *3* [... with Isa]ac and with Jacob your loyalty [...] *4* [...] you have remembered the times of [...]

Frag. 13   *1* [...] Lord, because in your love *2* [...] in the feasts of glory and to make holy *3* [...] the wheat, the wine and oil

4QFestival Prayers*ᶜ* (4Q509 [4QPrFêtesᶜ])

Frags. 1–4 *col.* I (= 1Q34 1–2)   *1-2* [...] ... [...] *3* [... the b]ar of the wheels [...] *4* [... in your pre]sence we issue our compla[int ...] to all [...] *5* [...] ... [...] in the period of [...] for ever. And he has made us glad [...] *6* [...] ... [...] Lord, who makes us understand [...] *7* [...for ever] and ever. Amen. Amen. [...] *8* [...] Moses, and you told him [...] *9* [...] ... upon him who [...] *10* [...] (you) who commanded [...] *11* [...] your people [...] *12-14* [...] *15* [...] and his sorrow [...] *16* [...] the time of our peace [...] *17* [For you comfort us] from our grief, and you assemble [our exiles for the time of ...] *18* [...] and our scattered women you gather for [the age of ...] *19* [...] your favours upon our congregation like dr[ops of water upon the earth in the season at seed-time] *20* [...] *Blank* [...] *21* [like rain upon] the meadow in the time of grass [...] *22* [And we, we will sing] your wonders from generation to generation. [...] *23* [... Bless]ed (is) the Lord, who makes us rejoice [...] *24* [...] ... [...]

Frags. 5–7 *col.* II   *1* [...] ... [...] *2* [...] our blood in the period [...] *3* [...] to tell us everything [...] *4* ...[...] You know everything [...] *5* You divide and utter [...] all the curses [...] *6* in us, as you have said [...] *7* Behold, you lie down with [...] *8* [...] ... [...] *9–14* [...] *15* [and] in the abysses and in every [...] *16* For, from eternity you hate [...] *17* together in your presence [...] *18* at the end of time [...] *19* [the op]ponent ... [...] *20* [...] to observe [...] *21* [...] ... [...]

Frags. 8–13 *col.* III   *1* [...] the work of [...] *2–3* [...] ... [...] *4* [... of] our earth in order to wave [...] *5* [...] at the beginning of [...] *6* [...] much ... [...] *7* [...] and we simple people [...] *8* [...] the dominion of [...] *9–15* [...] *16* the exiles who wander without [anyone making them return ...] *17* without strength, the fallen, without anyone [to lift them up...] *18* without anyone to undertsand them, the wounded, without anyone [to heal them...] *19* in sin. And there is no doctor [...] *20* consoling those who have stumbled in their sins [...Remem]ber *21* the sadness and weeping. You are the companion of prisoners [...]

Frags. 10–16 *col.* IV   *2* ... [...] *3* You have made [...] appear *4* in your [...] *5* and your angels [...] *6* and your inheritance [...] *7* Lord [...] *8* Prayer for the festival of [...] *9* [...] which [...] *10* [...] ... [...] *11* [...] all [...] *12* [...] ... [...] *13–16* [...] *17* [...] in all their sorrows [...] *18* [...] take pity on his grief *19* [...] the sadness of our older folk and of our nobles *20* [...] of the youths who have mocked them *21* [...] they did not realise that you *22* [...] our wisdom [...] *23* [...] and we [...]

Frags. 97–98 *col.* I (= 1Q34 II)   *1* [...] However, man's offspring [has not under-stood] *2* [everything you have given them in inheritance, and they have not known you] to do {to do} *3* [your word, and they act more wickedly than any. They do not under]stand your *4* [mighty] *3* power. *4* [For this you reject them, because you do not like] sin [and the wicked person] *5* [will not endure in front of you. But you have chosen a people in the age of your approval] *6* [because you remembered your covenant. You established them, isolating them for] yourself to make them holy *7* [among all the peoples. And you have renewed] your covenant with them in the sight of *8* [glory and in the words of your holy spirit, for] the works of your hand. Your right (hand) has written *9* [to make them know the regultions of glory and the eternal works.]

Frags. 131–132 *col.* II   *1* [...] ... [...] *2* [...] your glory [...] *3* [...] Amen. A[men...] *4* [...] *Blank* [...] *5* [Prayer for the day] of the first fruits. Remember, Lord, the feast *6* [...] and he pleasant, free-will offerings which you have pre-scribed *7* [...] to present before you the first fruits of your works *8* ... [...] upon the earth to be [...] *9* [...] ... For on the day of [...] *10* ... [...] you have made holy [...] *11* [...] the young of [...] *12–14* ... [...] *15* with [...] *16* holy [...] *17* in all [...] *18–20* ... [...]

3 Words of the Luminaries

4QWords of the Luminaries*a* (4Q504 [4QDibHam*a*])

Title of the work on the reverse of Frag. 8: *Words of the Luminaries.*

Frags. 1–2   *Col.* I   *1-6* […] *7* […] Amen. Amen. *8* […] your marvels *9* […] of Egypt *10* […] the desert

Col. II   *1-5* […] *6* […]… […] *7* O Lord, act, then, in accordance with yourself, in accordance with your great power. You, who did forgive *8* our fathers when they made your mouth bitter. You became angry with them in order to destroy them; but you took pity *9* on them in your love for them, and on account of your covenant–for Moses atoned *10* for their sin–and so that they would know your great power and your abundant kindness *11* for everlasting generations. May your anger and your rage for all their sin turn away from your people Israel. Remember *12* your marvels which you performed in view of the peoples, for we have been called by your name. *13* […] … with all (our) heart and with all (our) soul and to implant your law in our heart, *14* [so that we do not stray] either to the right or to the left. For, you will heal us of madness, blindness and confusion *15* [of heart…] For our faults were we sold, but in spite of our failings you did call us *16* […] and you will free us from sinning against you. *17* […] and to make us understand the stipulations *18* […] and their behaviour

Col. III   *1-2* … […] *3* Behold, all the peoples are like nothing in front of you; they are reckoned as chaos and nothing in your presence. *4* We have invoked only your name; for your glory you have created us; *5* you have established us as your sons in the sight of all the peoples. For you called *6* Israel «my son, my first-born» and have corrected us as one corrects *7* a son. You have made us {fat} great *Blank* over the years of our generations *8* […] evil illnesses, famine, thirst, plague, the sword *9* [… loy]alty of your covenant, for you chose us *10* [to be your people amongst all] the earth. For this you have poured on us your rage *11* [and your jea]lousy with all the intensity of your anger. And he has clung to us *12* […] which Moses wrote and your servants *13* the prophets whom you sent, so that evil would overtake us in the last *14* days. Because […] *15* and our kings, for […] *16* to take our daughters […] *17* and they acted pervertedly with […] *18* your covenant […] *19* the seed of Israel […] *20* You are just for […] *21* …[…]

Col. IV   *1* […] *2* in your residence […] rest *3* in Jerusalem [the city which you c]hose from the whole earth *4* for your Name to be there for ever. For you loved *5* Israel more than all the peoples. And you chose the land of *6* Judah, and established your covenant with David so that he would be *7* like a shepherd, a prince over your people, and would sit in front of you on the throne of Israel *8* for ever. And all the countries would see your glory, *9* for you have made yourself holy in the midst of your people, Israel. And to your *10* great Name they will carry their offerings: silver, gold, precious stones, *11* with all the treasures of their country, to honour your people and *12* Zion, your holy city and your wonderful house. And there was no opponent *13* or bad luck, but peace and blessing [...] *14* And they ate and drank and were replete [...] *15* [...] ... [...]

Col. v   *1* [...] ... [...] *2* the source of living water [...] *3* and they served a foreign god in their land. And their land, too, *4* was sacked by their enemies; because your rage *5* and the intensity of your anger, in a fire of your jealousy, over-flowed to form a desert *6* with no comings or goings. But in spite of all this you did not reject *7* the descendants of Jacob and did not hurl Israel *8* to destruction, breaking the covenant with them. For you are *9* a living God, you alone, and there is no other apart from you. You remembered your covenant, *10* for you redeemed us in the eyes of the nations and did not desert us *11* amongst the nations. You did favours to your people Israel among all *12* the countries amongst whom you had exiled them, to introduce *13* into their heart turning to you and listening to your voice, *14* in agreement with all that you commanded through the hand of Moses, your servant. *15* For you have poured your holy spirit upon us, *16* to fill us with your blessings, so that we would look for you in our anguish, *17* [and whis]per in the grief of your reproach. We are coming into anguish, *18* [we were str]uck and tested by the anger of the oppressor; for *19* we too have wearied God by our sins, we have wearied the Rock with our failings. *20* [But] for our profit you did [not] enslave us away from our paths, on the path *21* [on which we were obliged to walk. But] we did not pay attention [to your precepts.]

Col. VI   *1* [...] *2* [...] You have removed from us all our failings and have purified us *3* from our sin, for yourself. To you, to you, Lord, justice; for *4* you are the one who has done all this. And now, on this very day *5* on which our heart has been humbled, we atone for our sin and the sin of *6* our fathers, together with our disloyalty and rebellion. We have not rejected *7* your trials and punishments; our soul has not despised them to the point of breaking *8* your covenant, in spite of all the anguish of our soul. For you, who sent our enemies against us, *9* have strengthened our heart so that we can recount your mighty works to *10* everlasting generations. *10* O Lord, since you do wonders from eternity to *11* eternity, may your wrath and rage withdraw from us. Look at our [distress,] *12* our grief and our anguish, and free your people Isr[ael from all] *13* the countries, both near and far, [to where you have exiled us]. *14* All that is written in the book of life [...] *15* to serve you and give thanks to [...] *16* from all their pursuers [...] *17* those who make them stumble [...] *18-19* ... [...]

Col. VII *1* [...] ... [...] *2* who has freed us from all our anguish. Amen. [Amen ...] *3* *Blank* [...] *4* Hymns for the sabbath day. Give thanks [...] *5* his holy Name for ever [...] *6* all the angels of the holy vault [...] *7* to the heavens, the earth and all those who think [... the] *8* great abyss, Abaddon, the water and all that there [is in it ...] *9* all its creatures, always, for centuries [eternal. Amen. Amen.] *10* *Blank* [...] *11* of his holiness. Sing to God [...] *12* glory and ... [...]

Frag. 3 col. II (= 4Q505 124)   *1* [...] ... [...] *2* [...] Blessed is the God who makes us rest [...] *3* [... Amen.] Amen. *Blank* [...] *4* [...] *Blank 5* [Prayer for the] fourth day. Remember, Lord, [...] *6* [...] you are made holy in glory [...] *7* [...eye] to eye have you been seen in our midst [...] *8* [...] and we have heard your holy words [...] *9* [...] upon our faces so as not [...] *10* [... the] great [Name] of your holiness [...] *11* [...] the earth [...] *12* [...] and so that we believe [...] *13* for ever. And you established a covenant with us on Ho[reb ...] *14* upon all these decrees and precepts [...] *15* and the go[od ones...] and the holy ones [...] *16* who [...by the hand of] Moses ... [...] *17* in all [...] face to face /you spoke/ to him [...] *18* the glory [...] you were kind to him. And they fo[und favour in your eyes ...] *19* [...] in his hand to our eyes [...]

Frag. 4 (= 4Q506 131–132)   *1* [...] ... [...] *2* [...] which you demanded [for] the generations [...] *3* [...] the earth, and the work of all [... you have given to him] *4* [in the joy of his heart]. For you are the God of knowledge and all the thoughts of [...] *5* [before you.] These things we know because you have favoured us with a [holy] spirit. [Take pity on us] *6* [and do not] remember [against us the sins of] the very first in all their wicked [behaviour, nor that] *7* [they were stiff]-necked. You, acquire us and forgive, [please,] our iniquity and [our sin] *8* [...] ... the law which you commanded through the hand of Moses [...] *9* [...] which [...] in all [...] *10* [... a kingdom of] priests and a holy people [...] *11* [...] which you chose. Circumcise the foreskin of [our heart ...] *12* [...] ... again. Strengthen our heart to do [...] *13* [...] to walk in your paths [...] *14* [... Blessed is] the Lord who makes us know [...] *15* [...] Amen. Amen. *Blank* [...] *16* [...Blessed,] Lord, your holy name [...] *17* [...] on your account, and by the word [...] *18* [...] ... [...] *19* [...] the fault [...] *20* [...] the spirit [...] *21-22* [...] ... [...]

Frag. 5 col. I   *1* [...] your gifts *2* [...] you have made *3* [...] eternal name, and to see *4* [...] your marvels for [everlasting] generations. *5* [...] *Blank* [...] *6* [...] for you in the heavens and on the earth *7* [...] ... *8* [...] astray

Frag. 5 *col.* II (= 4Q506 124)   *1* their descendants among them for [...] *2* holy, being in your presence [...] *3* Remember, Lord, that [...] *4* [...] let us celebrate our redemp[tion...] *5* for our faults and to seek in [...] *6* what is evil in your eyes. You commanded [...] *7* [...] and how to your soul [...] *8* [...] to your intelligence [...]

Frag. 6   *1* [...] ... [...] *2* [...] and the fruit of thought [...] *3* [...] to understand all your decrees [...] *4* [...] his possession, in order to understand [...] *5* [...] ... in his exploits always. [...] *6* [...] Remember, please, that we are all your people. You have lifted us wonderfully *7* [upon the wings of] eagles and you have made us enter to you. And like the eagle which urges its brood *8* circling over its chicks, stretches its wings, takes it and lifts it upon [its feathers] *9* [...] we remain aloof and one does not count us among the nations. [...] *10* [...] You are in our midst, in the column of fire and in the cloud [...] *11* [...] your holiness, which walks in front of us, and your glory in our midst [...] *12* [...] in front of Moses, your servant [...] *13* [...] For you [...] *14* [...] and you do not acknowledge innocent [...] *15* [...] as one punishes a son [...] *16* [...] the holy ones and the pure ones [...] *17* [...] the man and lives in them [...] *18* [...] the oath which you [swore ...] *19* [...] in your face [...] *20* [...] Blessed, Lord, [...] *21* [...] we will examine your splendours [...] *22* [...] the spirit of every living thing [...]

Frag. 7   *1* [...] straightening *2* [...] the marvels which you have done *3* [...] /Israel/ so that the everlasting generations can tell *4* [...] the works of your hands *5* [...] for your glory *6* [...] it has not been shortened *7* [...] is [not] impossible for you *8* [...] he is *9* [...] you placed a treasure *10* [...] and (you) do not desert us *11* [...] and in your compassion *12* [...] we have found *13* [...] which you have forgiven *14* [...] who rebelled *15* [...] and they poured it out as a libation, and they found you *16* [...] they did not believe *17* [...] they saw *18* [...] the eyes *19* [...] blessed

Frag. 8   *1* [...] Remember, Lord, that [...] *2* [...] And you, he who lives for ever, [...] *3* [...] the marvels of old and the portents [...] *4* [... to Adam,] our father, you fashioned in the image of your glory [...] *5* [... a breath of life] you blew into his nostril, and intelligence and knowledge [...] *6* [... in the gard]en of Eden, which you had planted. You made him govern [...] *7* [...] and so that he would walk in a land of glory [...] *8* [...] he looked. And you imposed on him not to turn [away...] *9* [...] he is flesh, and to dust [...] *10* [...] *Blank* And you, you know [...] *11* [...] for everlasting generations [...] *12* [...] a living God, and your hand [...] *13* [...] man on the paths of [...] *15* [... fill] /the earth/ with violence and shed [innocent blood ...] *16* [...] ... [...]

4QWords of the Luminaries*b* (4Q505 [4QDibHam*b*])

Frag. 124 (= 4Q504 3 II, 11–13 *and* 5 II 1–2)   *1* […] … […] *2* […] the earth […]
3 […] and so that we believe […] *4* [… forever.] And you with us you established [a covenant on Horeb …] *5* […] … […] *6* [for Abraham,] for Isaac and
for Ja[cob. And you chose his descendants after them to …] *7* holy […,] being
in your pr[esence …] *8* […] … […]

4QWords of the Luminaries*c* (4Q506 [4QDibHam*c*])

Frag. 124 (= 4Q504 5 II)   *1* […] all […] *2* [You chose his descendants] after them
to [holy …, being in your presence …] *3* […] Remember, [Lord, that …] *4* […
let us celeb]rate our redemption [… for our faults and to seek in […] *5* […] to
do what is evil [in your eyes. You commanded …] *6* […] … […]

Frags. 131 – 132 (4Q504 4)   *1* […] … […] *2* […] we […] *3* […] woman. […]
4 [wo]rks of your hands. […] *5* You gave us […] *6* man born in […] *7* [which
you wis]hed [for the generations …] *8* [the ea]rth, and the wo[rk of all …to him
have you] given in the joy *9* [of his he]art. For you are the God of knowl]edge,
and all *10* [the tho]ughts of […]before you. These things we know, *11* [bec]ause
you have favoured us [with a] holy [spirit. Have pity on us *12* [and do not] remember [against us the sins of] our first fathers *13* [in a]ll their ev[il behaviour,
nor that they were] stiff-necked. *14* [You, acquire us and please forgive our
iniquity and] our sin.

4 Songs of the Sabbath Sacrifice

4QSongs of the Sabbath Sacrifice*a* (4Q400 [4QShirShabb*a*])

Frag. 1 *col.* I   *1* [Of the Instructor. Song for the holocaust] of the first [sabbath,] the fourth of the first month. Praise *2* [the God of ...,] you, the gods, among the holy of holies; and in the divinity *3* [of his kingdom, rejoice. Because he has established] the holy of holies among the eternal holy ones, so that for him they can be priests *4* [who approach the temple of his kingship,] the servants of the Presence in the sanctuary of his glory. In the assembly of all the deities *5* [of knowledge, and in the council of all the spirits] of God, he has engraved his ordinances for all spiritual works, and his *6* [glorious] precepts [for those who establish] knowledge of the people of the intelligence of his glory, the gods who approach knowledge. *7* Eternal [...]. And from the holy source of the sanctuaries of the holy of *8* [holies...] priests who approach, to serve in the presence of the holy king of *9* [the holy ones ...] of his glory. And they confirm each regulation for the seven *10* [eternal counsels. Because he] set them up for himself as the ho[ly of the holy ones, who serve in the holy of] holies. *11* [...] approached them in the council [...] of the knowledge of *12* [...] holy of holies, pr[iests ...] They are princes *13* [...] in the temples of the king. [...] in their territory and in their inheritance *14* [...] They do not tolerate anyone whose path is [warped.] There is no impurity in their holy offerings. *15* For them he has engraved ho[ly precepts] by which all the holy ones become perpetually holy; and he purifies the pure *16* [shining ones, so that they deal] with all those of depraved path. And they shall appease his will, in favour of all those converted from sin. *17* [...] knowledge in the priests who approach, and from their mouths (come) the teachings of all the holy ones, with the precepts of *18* [his glory...] his favours for compassionate, eternal forgiveness, and [to destroy] in the vengeance of his jealousy *19* [...] He has established priests for himself, who approach the holy of holies. *20* [... God] of the divine ones, priests of the exalted heights, who approach *21* [...] ... [...]

Frag. 1 *col.* II   *1* your exalted kingdom [...] *2* the heights [...] the beauty of your kingdom [...] *4* in the gates of the exalted heights [...] *5* ... spirit of all [...] *6* the holy ones of the holy of hol[ies ...] *7* king of the gods and the seven [...] *8* the glory of the king. *Blank* [...] *9* glory in the council of the go[ds ...] *10* on the seven pathways [...] for judgments of silence [...] *12* eternal. *Blank* [...] *13* And they extol his glory [...] *14* king of the princes [...] *15* holy [...] *16* holy [...] *17* divine beings [...] *18* justice. *Blank* [...] *19* priests [...] *20* the affections of God [...] *21* to be made holy by [...]

Frag. 2   *1* to praise your glory wondrously with the gods of knowledge, and the praises of your kingship with the holy ones of the holy o[nes.] *2* They are honoured in all the camps of the gods and paid reverence by the councils of men, a wonder *3* among gods and men. And they will recount the splendour of his kingdom, according to their knowledge, and they will extol [his glory in all] *4* the heavens of his kingdom. And in all the exalted heights [they will sing] wonderful psalms according to all [their knowledge,] *5* and they will tell [of the splendour] of the glory of the king of the gods in the residences of their positions. *Blank* And [...] *6* how will he be regarded amongst them? And how will our priesthood (be regarded) in their residences? [...] *7* ... What is the offering of our tongue of dust (compared) with the knowledge of the divinities? *8* [...] for our song. Let us extol the God of knowledge [...] *9* [...] holiness. And his understanding is beyond all those who know [...] *10* [...] holiness. The holiness of the first [...] *11* [...] ton[gues of] knowledge, precepts [...] *12* [...] glory [...] *13-14* [...]

4QSongs of the Sabbath Sacrifice*b* (4Q401 [4QShirShabb*b*])

Frags. 1–2   *1* Of the Instructor. So[ng of the sacrifice of the fourth sabbath, the] twenty-[fifth of the first month.] *2* Praise God [...] ... [...] *3* and ... [...] who are before [...] *4* the kingdom [...] with all the ch[iefs ...] *5* king of the go[ds ...] *6* ... [...]

Frag. 14 *col.* I (= 4Q400 2, 1–2)   *1-3* [...] *4* [...] its height is exalted above [...] divine beings [...] *5* the chiefs of his dominion [...] the heaven of the kingdom of his glory [...] *6* to praise your glory wondrously [with all the divinities of knowledge, and the praises of] your kingship with the holy ones of the holy ones. *7* They are honoured in all the camps of the gods and rever[ed by the coun]cils of men, a wonder

Frag. 14 *col.* II   *1* [...] ... [...] *2* his wondrous mysteries [...] *3* shout of jubilation [...] *4* they cannot [...] *5* [G]od fortress [...] *6* princes of [...] *7* they make their hidden things heard [...] *8* what issues from the lips of the king [...]

4QSongs of the Sabbath Sacrifice*c* (4Q402 [4QShirShabb*c*])

Frag. 1   *1* [...] in the co[ming ...] *2* [...] when they come with the gods of *3* [...] together with all the wonderful stipulations *4* [...] their powers to the strong heroes *5* [...] all the councils of rebellion *6-7* [...]

Frag. 4 (*completed from the copy of ShirShabb found in the excavations of Masada*) *1* [...] ... [...] *2* [...] and share out knowledge [...] *3* [... according to] his understanding he commanded pre[cepts ...] *4* [...] being impure [...] not [...] *5* [...]

and it will not be [...] to the Community [...] 6 [...] who keeps his plan. And
the knowledge of the holy [of holies ...] 7 [...] the war of the gods in the
per[iod ...] 8 [...] for to the God of the divinities belong the weapons of war
[...] 9 [...] the gods run to their positions, and a powerful noise [...] 10 [...] the
gods in the war of the heavens. And it will happen [...] 1 [...] new wondrous
deeds. He has done all this wondrously [with things hidden forever, and not]
12 [... all the words of knowledge;] because from the God of knowledge comes
all [that existed for ever. And through his knowledge] 13 [and through his decisions all the predestined exist for ever.] He does the first things [in their ages
and the final (things)] 14 [in their appointed periods. And nobody, among those
who have knowledge,] can understand [his wonderful revelations] before he
[does them. And when he acts, those who apply justice cannot understand]
15 [his proposals. For they are part of his glorious deeds,] before they [existed,
are part of his design.]

4QSongs of the Sabbath Sacrifice*d* (4Q403 [4QShirShabb*d*])

Col. I (= 4Q404 1–5; 4Q405 3–6; Masada ShirShabb)   1 [Psalm of celebration on
the tongue of the] third of the sovereign princes. He will celebrate the God of
the exalted angels seven times, with seven words of wonderful exaltations.
2 Psalm of praise, on the tongue of the fourth, to the Powerful One who is
above all [the gods] with his seven wonderful powers. He will praise the God
3 of the powers seven times, with seven words of [wonderful] praise. [Ps]alm
of thanksgiving on the tongue of the fifth, to the King of glory, 4 with seven
acts of wonderful thanks. [Psalm] of exultation 5 on the tongue of the sixth, to
the God of goodness, with seven [wonderful] exultations. He will exult in the
King of goodness seven times, [with seven words] of wonderful exultation.
6 *Blank* Psalm of singing on the tongue of the seventh of the [sovereign] princes,
a powerful song [to the God] of holiness with se[ven wonderful songs. 7 He will
have to sing to the King of holiness seven times with seven words of [wonder-
ful son]gs. Seven psalms [of his blessings.] Seven 8 psalms of glorification o[f
his justice. Seven psalms of exaltation of his kingdom. [Seven] psalms [of praise
of his glory. Seven psalms of thanksgiving for his wonders.] 9 [Seven psalms
of exult]ation in his power. Seven [psalms of song] of his holiness. [...] 10 [won-
derful words, words of ... The first] among the sovereign princes will bless in
the glorious name of God al[l the... with seven wonderful words;] 11 [he will
bless all the councils] in his [holy] temple [with] seven wonderful words; [he
will bless those who know] eternal [things]. [The second] 12 [among the sovereign princes will bless in the name] of his loyalty all the st[ations with seven]
wonderful words; [he will bless] with seven wonderful words; 13 [and he will
bless all who celebrate] the King with seven wo[rds of the glory of his wonders,
all] the everlastingly pure. The th[ird] 14 [among the sovereign princes will

bless in the name] of his exalted kingship [all the exalted] ones of knowledge with se[ven wo]rds of exaltation, and all [...] *15 Blank 16* [...] He will bless with seven wonderful words; he will bless all [destined] for justice [with seven] wonderful words. [The fourth] *17* among the sovereign princes will bless, in the name of the King's majesty, all who walk straight, with majestic words; he will bless all who establish majesty with seven *18* [wonderful] words; he will bless all the di[vinities who appro]ach the knowledge of his loyalty with seven words of justice for his glorious mercy. The fifth *19* among the [sovereign] princes will bless in the name of his [wonderful] majesty all [who know the mysteries of ...] purity with seven words of his exalted *20* loyalty; [he will bless] all who hasten (to do) his will with seven [wonderful words; he will bless] all who acknowledge him with seven majestic words *21* for [wonderful] thanksgiving; The sixth among the sovereign princes will bless in the name [of the powers] of the divinities all the powerful of intellect with seven *22* words of his wonderful powers; he will bless all whose path is perfect with seven wonderful words so that they are constantly with all those who exist *23* for ever; he will bless all who hope in him with seven wonderful words for the return of his merciful compassion. The seventh among the sovereign princes *24* will bless in the name of his holiness all the holy ones who make the foundation of knowledge with seven words of his wonderful holiness; he will bless all who exalt *25* his precepts with seven wonderful words for sturdy shields; he will bless all those destined for justice who praise his glorious kingship [...] for ever *26* with seven [wonderful wo]rds [for] everlasting peace. And all the [sovereign] princes [toge]ther [will bless] the God of the divinities in the name [of his holiness] with all *27* [their] sevenfold [stipulations] and they will bless those destined for justice and all the blessed [... the bl]essed for eve[r ...] *28* for him. Blessed be the Lord, the king of all, above all blessing and pr[aise. And may he bless all the ho]ly ones who bless him, [and proclaim him just] *29* in the name of his glory. And he will bless those permanently blessed. *Blank 30* Of the Instructor. Song of the sacrifice of the seventh sabbath of the seventeenth of the month. Praise the God of the august heights, you august ones among the *31* divinities of knowledge. May the holy ones of God make holy the king of glory, who makes holy with his holiness all the holy ones. The chiefs of the praises of *32* all the gods, praise the God of magnificent praises, for in the magnificence of the praises is the glory of his kingdom. From it come the praises of all the *33* divinities, together with the splendour of all his majesty. And exalt his exaltation to the heights, gods of the august divinities, and the divinity of his glory above *34* all the august heights. For he is the God of the gods of all the chiefs of the heights, and king of kings of all the eternal councils. {By the consent} *35* {of knowledge} By their words a[ll the august divinities] exist; by what issues from their lips, all the eternal spirits; by the will of his knowledge, all his creatures *36* in their enterprises. Sing with joy, those of you enjoying his knowledge, with rejoicing among the wonderful gods. Make festival of his glory with the tongue of all those who make a festival with knowledge, and their wonderful songs, *37* with the mouth of all who make a feast [in him. For he is] God of all who sing {with knowledge} for ever, and judge, in whose power are all the sprits of under-standing. *38* Give thanks, all the divinities of majesty, to the king of majesty; for through his glory all the divinities of knowledge proclaim, and all the spirits of justice proclaim his truth. *39* And they make his knowledge acceptable according to the judgment of his mouth and his proclamations, when his powerful hand returns for the judgment of reward. Chant to the powerful God *40* with the chosen spiritual portion, so that it is [a melody] with the joy of God, and celebration with all the holy ones, for a wonderful song in eternal happiness. *41* You, praise with them all the found[ations of the holy of] the holy ones, the supporting columns of the highest vault, and all the corners of his building. Sing *42* to the God who is awesome in power [all the spirits of knowledge and of light], to exalt together the splendidly shining vault of the santuary of his holiness. *43* [Praise him,] divine spirits, praising [for ever] and ever the main vault of the heights, all [its beams] and walls, all its *44* shape, the work of its construction. The spirits of the holy of the holies, the living gods, the spirits of everlasting holiness above *45* all the holy ones [... marvellous wonder of splendour ... and the glory] in the most perfect light, and the knowledge *46* [... in all the wonderful sanctuaries. The spirits of the gods around the residence of the king of truth and justice. All its walls ...]

Col. II   *1* perfect light, the mingled colours of the spirit of the holy of holies [...] *2* high places of knowledge. And at its feet [...] *3* the manifestation of the glorious form of the chiefs of the kingdom of the spirits. [...] *4* [...] his glory. And the gates, in all their movements (?) [...] *5* the shaft of lightning (?) [...] to crush. The gods [...] *6* among them run gods in the form of embers [of fire ...] *7* going around. The spirits of the holy of holies [...] *8* of the holy of holies, spirits of the gods, eternal vision [...] *9* and the spirits of the gods, forms of flames of fire around [...] *10* wonderful spirits. And the tabernacle of greater height, the glory of his kingdom, the *debir* [...] *11* And make holy the seven august holy ones. And the voice of the blessing of the chiefs of his *debir* [...] *12* And the voice of the blessing {is heard} is glorified when the gods hear it, and the foundations of [...] *13* of the blessing. And all the decorations of the *debir* hurry with wonderful hymns ... [...] *14* wonder, *debir* to *debir*, with the sound of crowds of holy multitudes. And all their decorations [...] *15* And the chariots of his *debir* praise together, and his cherubim and *ofanim* bless wonderfully [...] *16* the chiefs of the structure of the gods. And they praise him in his holy *debir*. *Blank* [...] *17* *Blank* [...] *18* Of the Instructor. Song of the sabbath sacrifice of the twent[y-third of the second month. Praise the God of all the august heights, all you his] eternal [holy ones,] *19* those second among the priests who approach him, the second council in the wonderful dwelling among the seven [... among all those having knowledge of] *20* eternal things. And exalt him, you chiefs of the princes with his wonderful portion. Praise [the God of the divinities, the seven priests who approach...] *21* height, seven wonderful territories, in the regulations of his sanctuaries, {the chiefs of the princes of the wonderful pri[esthoods]} [...] *22* seven priesthoods in the wonderful sanctuary for the seven holy counsellors [...] *23* the prince, the angels of the king in their wonderful residences. And the comprehensive knowledge of the seven [... of the] [...] *24* chief, [...] of the priest who approaches. And the chiefs of the congregation of the king in the assembly [...] *25* and exalted praises to the king of glory, and exaltation of Go[d ...] *26* to the God of the divinities, to the king of purity. And the offering of their tongues [...] *27* seven mysteries of knowledge in the wonderful mystery of the seven regions of the hol[y of holies ... The tongue of the first will be strengthened seven times with the tongue of the second. The tongue of the second will be strengthened] *28* seven times with (that) of the third compared to [him. The to]ngue of the third will be strengthened seven times [with (that) of the fourth compared to him. The tongue of the fourth will be strengthened seven times with the tongue of the fifth compared to him. The tongue of the fifth will be strengthened seven times with the tongue of] *29* the sixth compared to him. The tongue [of the sixth will be strengthened seven times with the tongue of the seventh compared to him. The tongue of the seventh will be strengthened ...] *30* And according to the seven w[ords ...] *31* with wonderful hymns with wo[rds ... *32* wonder. *Blank* [Psalm o]f blessing on [the tongue of the first ...] *33* wonder, and praise the Lord of all the div[inities...] *34* his wonderful choice [...] for great praise [...] *35* to those who make knowledge shine among all the gods of light [...] *36* of praise on the tongue [...] *37* wonder. [Psalm of thanksgiving on the] ton[gue of the fifth ...] *37* thanksgiving [...] *38-48* ... [...]

4QSongs of the Sabbath Sacrifice*ᵉ* (4Q404 [4QShirShabb*ᵉ*])

Frag. 1 (= 4Q403 1, 6–8)   *1* [...Psalm of] song on the ton[gue of the seventh of the sovereign princes, a powerful song [to the God] of holiness with seven *2* wond[erful songs]. He will have to sing [to the King of holiness seven times, with seven words of wonderful songs. Seven psalms of his blessings.] *3* [Seven ps]alms of exaltation of his justice. Seven psalms of exaltation of his kingdom...]

Frag. 2 (= 4Q403 1, 20–28)   *1* [he will bless all those who hurry (to do) his will with seven] wonderful words; he will bless all [those who confess with seven majestic words] *2* [for wonderful thanksgiving. The sixth among] the sovereign princes will bless, in the name of the powers of the divinities, all [those powerful in intellect, with seven] *3* [words of their] wonderful [powers;] he will bless all whose path is perfect with seven wond[erful words so that they are continually with those who exist] *4* [for ever;] he will bless all who hope in him with seven wonderful words [for the return of merciful compassion. The seventh] *5* [among the sovereign] princes will bless, in the nam[e of his holiness, all the holy ones who form the foundation of knowledge, with seven words of his wonderful] *6* [holiness;] he will bless all who exa[lt his precepts with seven wonderful words for sturdy shields; he will bless all those destined *7* [for jus]tice who praise [his glorious kingship ... for ever with seven wonderful] *8* wo[rds] for eternal peace. [And all the sovereign princes will, together, bless the God of the divinities in the name of his holiness] *9* [with] all their sevenfold testimonies [and they will bless those destined for justice and all those blessed ...] *10* [the bl]essed for ever [...by him. Blessed be the Lord, the king of all, above all blessing and praise. And may he bless all] *11* [the holy ones] who bless him [and declare him just...]

Frag. 3 (= 4Q403 I, 30–31)   *1* [...] ... [...] *2* [Of the Instructor. Song of sacrifice of the seventh sabbath, of the six]teenth of the month. [Praise the God of the august heights, you august ones among the] *3* [divinities of knowledge. May the holy ones, the holy ones of God, [make holy] the king [of glory who, with his holiness, makes holy all his holy ones ...]

Frag. 4 (= 4Q403 I, 35–40)   *1* [By his words] a[ll the august divinities exis]t; by what issues from his lips, all the eternal spirits;] *2* [by the wi]ll of his knowledge, [all his creatures in their enterprises. Sing with joy, those of you enjoying his knowledge,] *3* [with rej]oicing among the [wonderful] gods. [Make festival of his glory with the tongue of all those who make a feast] *4* [with knowledge; their [wonderful] songs, [with the mouth of all who make a feast in him. For he is] *5* God of all [who sing for ever, and judge in whose power are all the spirits of understanding.] *6* Give thanks, all the divinities [of majesty, to the king of majesty; for through his glory all] *7* [the divin]ities of knowledge proclaim, and all the spirits of justice proclaim his truth.

Frag. 5 (= 4Q403 I, 44–47)   *1* [its form, the work of its construction.] The spirit of the holy of the holy ones, *2* [the living gods, the spirits of] everlasting holiness above *3* [all the holy ones ...] marvellous wonder of splendour ...*4* [...] and glory in the most perfect light, knowledge *5* [...] in all the wonderful sanctuaries. The spirits of the gods *6* [around the residence] of the king of truth and justice. All its walls *7* [...] of the holy [...] *8* [...] the structure [...]

4QSongs of the Sabbath Sacrifice*f* (4Q405 [4QShirShabb*f*])

Frag. 3 col. II (= 4Q403 I, 11-17)   *1* [he will bless] those who know eternal things. [The second among the sovereign princes will bless, in the name of his loyalty, all the stations with seven] *2* wonderful words; he will bless with seven [wonderful] words; [and he will bless all who celebrate the King with seven] *3* words of the glory of his wonders, all the everlastingly pure. [The third among the sovereign princes will bless in the name] *4* of his exalted kingdom all the exalted ones of knowledge with seven words of exaltation, and all [...] *5* He will bless with seven wonderful words; he will bless all destined for justice with se[ven wonderful words. The fourth] *6* among the sovereign princes will bless in the name of the King's ma[jesty all who walk straight with majestic words;] *7* he will bless all who establish majesty with seven [wonderful words; he will bless all the di[vinities who approach the knowledge of his loyalty] *8* with seven words of justice for his [glorious] mercy. [The fifth among the sovereign princes will bless in the name of his wonderful *9* [majesty] all who know the mysteries of [... purity with seven words of his exalted loyalty; he will bless all] *10* who hasten (to do) his will with seven [wonderful words; he will bless all who acknowledge him with seven] majestic [words] *11* for [wonderful] thanksgiving. The sixth [among the sovereign princes will bless in the name of the powers of the divinities all the powerful] *12* *Blank* [...] *13* of intellect with seven words [of his wonderful powers; he will bless all whose path is perfect with seven wonderful words] *14* so that they are constantly with all [those who exist for ever; he will bless all who hope in him with seven wonderful words for the return of] *15* his merciful compassion. The se[venth among the sovereign princes will bless in the name of his holiness all the holy ones who found] *16* knowledge with seven words [of his wonderful holiness; he will bless all who exalt his regulations with seven wonderful words] *17* for sturdy shields; he will bless [all those destined for justice who praise his glorious kingship ... for ever with seven] *18* [wonderful wo]rds for [everlasting] peace. [And all the sovereign princes together will bless the God of the divinities in the name of his holiness] *19* with all [his] sevenfold stipulations [and they will bless those destined for justice and all the blessed ...]

Frags. 4-5 (= 4Q403 I, 33-36)   *1* [...And exalt his exaltation] to the heights, gods [of the august divinities, and the divinity of his glory above] *2* all the august [heights. For he is the God of the gods of all the chi]efs of the heights, and king [of kings of all the eternal councils. By the words] *3* of his mouth a[ll the august divinities] exi[st; by what issues from his lips, all the] eternal [spirits]; by the wi[ll of his knowledge, all his creatures in their enterprises.] *4* Sing with j[oy, those of you enjoying his knowledge, with rejoicing among the wonderful gods. Make festival of his glory with the tongue of all] *5* those who make [a feast...]

Frag. 6 (= 4Q403 I, 40–45)   *1* [...for a wonderful song] in [eternal] happiness. *2* You, praise with them all the found[ations of the holy of the ho]ly ones, [the] supporting [columns] of the highest vault, and all the corners *3* [of his building. Sing to the God, who is awesome in power, all spirits] of knowledge and of light, to exalt together the splendidly [shining] vault [of the sanctuary] *4* [of his holiness. Praise him, divine spirits, praising] for ever and ever the main vault of the heights, [all its beams] *5* [and walls, all its form, the work of its structure.] The spirits of the holy of the holy ones, the living gods, the spirits of [everlasting] *6* holiness [above all the holy ones ...] impressive wonder of splendour [...] and the glory in the *7* [most perfect] light, [and the knowledge ...] wonderful sanctuary. The spirits of God around the residence *8* [...] in the holy of the holy ones [...] ... *9* [...] ... *10* [...] the sound of *11* [...] they shall cause to hear

Frags. 8–9 (= 4Q403 II, 18–22)   *1* [...Of the Instructor. Song of the sacrifice of the] fifth sabbath [of the twenty-third of the second month.] *2* Praise the God of all [the august heights], all [you] his [eternal] holy ones [the second among the priests who approach him,] *3* the second council in the wonderful dwelling among the sev[en ...] among all those having knowledge of *4* eternal things. And exalt him you [chiefs of the princes with his wonderful portion. Praise the God of the divinities,] the seven *5* priests who approach [... height, seven wonderful territories, in the regulations of their sanctuaries, the chi]efs of the princes *6* of the [wonderful priest]hoods [...] the sanctuaries *7* [...] the priesth[oods ...]

Frag. 11 (= 4Q403 II, 27–29)   *1* [...] ... [...] *2* [...] holy ones [...The tongue of the first will be strengthened seven times with the tongue of the second.The tongue] *3* of the second will be strengthened [seven times] with that of the third compared to him. The tongue of the third will be strengthened [seven times with (that) of the fourth compared to him. The tongue] of the fourth will be strengthened *4* seven times with the tongue of the fifth compared to him The tongue of the fifth will be strengthened se[ven times with the tongue of the sixth] compared to him. The tongue of the sixth *5* will be strengthened seven times with the tongue of the seventh compared to him. The tongue of the seventh will be st[rengthened ...] the sanctuary *6* [...] ... [...]

Frags. 14–15   *1* [...] spirit of glory [...] *2* [...] wonderful likeness of the spirit of the holy of holies, embroidered [...] tongue of blessing. And the likeness *3* [of God,] the voice of blessing for the king of those who exalt. His wonderful exaltation is for the God of the divinities [...] his adornment. And they sing *4* [...] the lobbies of their entrances, spirits who approach the holy of holies [...] always. *5* [The likeness] of the living gods is engraved in the lobbies when the king enters, forms of shining spirits [...] king, forms of glorious light, [wonderful] spirits. *6* In the middle of the spirits of splendour, wonderful embroidered work, forms of the living gods [...] in the *debirim* of glory, the structure *7* [of the sanctuary of the ho]ly of holies, in the *debirim* of the king, forms of the divinities. And of the likeness [...] holy of holies *8* [...] ... [...] the *debir* of the king [...]

Frags. 15–16 *1* the fringes of the hem [...] *2* and streams of light [...] ... [...] *3* the aspect of flames of fire [...] ... above the veil of the *debir* of the king [...] *4* in the *debir* of his face, the embroidered [...] all that is engraved [...] forms of the div[inities ...] *5* of the glory of both sides [...] the veils of the wonderful *debirim*. And they will bless [...] *6* their sides, And they will cause wonderful [...] to be heard the *debir* [...] *7* [...] to the king of glory with joyful voice [...]

Frag. 17 *1* [...] ... [...] *2* [...] wonders [...] *3* [...] spirits of knowledge and understanding, truth *4* [...of] purity, angels of glory for the power of *5* [...] angels of beauty and spirits of *6* [...] ... of holiness, seats of *7* [...] works of *8* [...] glory *9* [...] ...

Frag. 18 *1* [...] spirits [...] *2* [...] to sustain the holy ones. The *debir* [...] *3* [...] with the serene spirit of God [...] *4* [...] ... they hurry to the voice of glory [...] *5* [...] wonderful psalms in a serene voice [...] *6* [...] ... [...]

Frag. 19 *1* [...] ... [...] *2* And forms of the divinities praise him, spirits of [...], forms of glory, the dais (?) *3* of the wonderful *debirim*, spirits of the eternal divinities. All [...] of the king. The works of the spirits of the wonderful vault are *4* intermingled purely, spirits of knowledge of the truth and of the justice of the holy of holies, effigies of living gods, effigies of shining *5* spirits. All their works are of holy things wonderfully interwoven [...] embroidered [...] shapes of the figures of the divinities, engraved *6* around his glorious tiled pavement, glorious effigies of the works [...] of splendour and majesty [...] Living gods with all their works *7* and the images of their forms are holy angels. Beneath the wonderful *debirim*, the serene sound of silence, the gods blessing *8* [...] the king [...always praise] ...

Frags. 20–21–22 *1* [they do not withdraw when they arise ...] all the priests who approach [...] *2* in [the law. They re]main secure to ser[ve ...] the seat of the throne of his kingship [in the *debirim* of his glory. They do not sit down ...] *3* the chariots of his glory [...] holy cherubim, shining *ofanim*, in the de[bir ... spirits of gods ... purity ...] *4* holy. The works of its ang[les ...] of his kingdom [...] the glorious seats of the chariots [... wings of knowledge ... wonderful power ...] *5* truth and eternal justice [...] the chariots of his glory when they

move [... they do not turn aside at all... they go straight...] *6 Blank* Of the
Ins[tructor. Song for the sacrifice of the] twelfth sabbath, [the twenty-first of
the third month. Praise the God of ...] *7* wonderful [...] and exalt him ... the
glory in the te[nt of the God of knowledge. The cherubim lie prostrate before
him, and bless when they rise. The voice of a divine silence is heard, *8* and
their is the uproar of excitement when they raise their wings, the voice of a
divine silence. They bless the image of the throne-chariot (which is) above the
vault of the cherubim, *9* and they sing [the splen]dour of the shining vault
(which is) beneath the seat of his glory. And when the *ofanim* move forward,
the holy angels go back; they emerge among *10* the glorious wheels with the
likeness of fire, the spirits of the holy of holies. Around them, the likeness of
a stream of fire like electrum, and a luminous substance *11* with glorious
colours, wonderfully intermingled, brightly combined. The spirits of the living
gods move constantly with the glory of the wonderful chariots. *12* And (there
is) a silent voice of blessing in the uproar of their motion, and they praise the
holy one on returning to their paths. When they rise, they rise wonderfully;
13 when they settle, they are ready. The voice of glad rejoicing beomes silent
and there is a silent blessing of the gods in all the camps of the gods. And the
voice of praises *14* [...] from among all their divisions [...] and all their enrolled
ones exult, each one in his place.

Frag. 23 col. I   *1* [...] their tasks [...] *2* [...] when they rise [...] *3* [...] the throne
of the glory of his kingdom and all the assembly of whose who serve *4* [...]
wonderfully. The gods will not shudder for ever *5* [...] for they are steady in
the tasks of all, because the gods of the offering *6* [...] his offering. The gods
praise when they begin to rise, and all the spirits of the pure vault *7* rejoice in
his glory. And there is a voice of blessing from all their divisions which counts
the vaults of his glory. And the gates praise *8* with jubilant voice. When the
divinities of knowledge enter through the gates of glory, and in all the departures of the holy angels to their domains, *9* the gates of the entrance and the
gates of the exit declare the glory of the king, blessing and praising all the spirits *10* of God in the exits and in the entrances through the gates of holiness.
And among them there is no-one who omits a regulation or who *11* opposes the
precepts of the king. They do not deviate from the path nor do they go far
from his territory. They do not esteem themselves above their duties *12* nor do
they demean themselves. For he will have compassion during the rule of the
severity of his obliterating wrath. He will not judge while his glorious wrath
resides. *13* The fear of the king of the gods is dreadful for all the gods. [He sent
them] on all his missions in order *Blank* ... And they go *14* [...] ... [...]

Frag. 23 col. II   *1* [...] the beauty of the engravings [...] *2* [...] the king, when
they serve before [...] *3* king, and write his glory [...] *4* holiness, the sanctuary

of all [...] *5* their *ephods*; they scatter [...] *6* the holy ones, the approval [...] ...
the spirits of the holy [ones...] *7* his holy ones. *Blank* In their wonderful positions there are spirits (with) many-coloured (clothes), like woven material engraved with splendid pictures. *8* In the midst of the glorious appearance of
scarlet, the colours of the light of the spirit of the holy of holies remain fixed
in their holy position before *9* the king, spirits of [pure] colours in the midst of
the appearance of the whiteness. And the substance of the spirit of glory is like
work from Ophir, which diffuses *10* light. And all their decorations are mixed
purely, like a work plaited with artistry. They are the chiefs of those wonderfully ordained for service, *11* the chiefs of the kingdom ‹of the kingdom› of the
holy ones of the holy king in all the heights of his sanctuary of the kingdom
12 of his glory. *Blank* In the chiefs of the offerings are the tongues of knowledge.
They bless the God of knowledge in all the works of his glory. *13* [And the
regulations] of their divisions in all their holy *debirim* [he engraved in] the
knowledge of his understanding and in the inelligence of his glory.

11QSongs of the Sabbath Sacrifice (11Q17 [11QShirShabb])

Col. I (= 4Q505 19)   *1* [...] . [...] *2* [... And forms of the gods praise him, [the
spirits of ... the fo]rms of glo[ry, the dais (?) *3* of the [wonderful] *de*[*birim*, spirits of the] eternal [divinities. All ... of the king.] The works [of the spirits of
the] wonderful vault are *4* intermingled purely, [spirits of knowledge of the
truth and] of justice [in the holy of holies, effigies of] living [gods, effigies of
shin]ing spirits. All *5* their wo[rks are of holy things wonderfully interwoven
...] embroidered [... shapes of the figures of the gods,] engraved around [his
glorious tiled pavement, glorious] effigies *6* of the wo[rks of spelndour and
majesty. Living] gods [with all their works and the images of] their forms are
ho[ly angels.] Beneath the [wonderful *deb*]*irim*, *7* the [serene] sound [of silence,
the gods blessing ... the king ...] always pra[ise ...] *8 Blank* [...] in the second
[...] *9* [...] wonderful splendour [...]

Col. II (= 4Q505 20–22)   *1* [...] his face [...] above the august throne [...] *2* [...]
they do not withdraw when they arise [... all the priests who approach ...]
Blank [...] *3* [...] in the law. They remain firm to serve [... the seat of the throne
of his kingship] in the *debirim* of his glory. They do not sit down [...] *4* [the
chariots of] his glory [...] holy [cheru]bim, [shining *ofanim*, in the *de*[*bir* ...]
spirits of go[ds ...] purity [...] *5* [holy.] The works of its angels [... of his kingdom. The [glorious] seats [of the chariots ...] wings of knowledge [...] wonderful power [...] *6* [truth and] eternal justice [... the chariots] of his glory [when
they move ... they do not] turn aside at all [...] they go straight [...] *7 Blank*
[...] *Blank* [...] *Blank* [...] *8* [Of the Ins]tructor. Song [for the sacrifice of the]
twelfth sabbath, the twenty-first of the third month. [Praise the God of ...]

9 [and exa]lt him [… the glory in the tent of the God of knowledge. The cherubim bow down before him, and] bless when they rise.

Col. III   *1* […] and wonder, knowledge and understanding …] the wonderful
vault […] *2* […] with light of lights, the splendour of […] all the figures of the
wonderful spirits […] *3* […] gods, of awesome strength, all […] his wonders
with the strength of eternal God. *8* And exalting the powerful works of the God
of […] of the four foundations of the wonderful vault *5* they proclaim with the
raised sound of the gods […] blessing and praising the God of *6* gods. The
noise […] the heights […] king of glory […] for the wonderful foundations *7* …
[…] God of […] and all their bases […] the holy of *8* holies […] their wings
[…] their heads. *9* And they declare […] the positions of […]

Col. IV   *1* […] the approval […] all his works […] *2* […] for the sacrifices of the
holy ones […] the aroma of their offerings […] *3* […] and the aroma of the
libations according to the nu[mber of …] of purity with a spirit of holiness,
4 […] always, spl[endour and] majesty […] wonder, and the form of the breastplate *5* […] many-coloured, like [plaited] work […] intermingled purely, of the
colour *6* […] with forms […] *ephod* *7* […] … […] …

Col. V   *1* […] the heights of his [glory …] … […] *2* his prize in the judgments of
[…] his compassion with the honour […] his stipulations *3* and all the blessings
of his peace [… the glo]ry of his works and with the light […] and with the
splendour *4* of his praise in all the vault […] light and darkness in the figures
of […] the holiness of the king of *5* glory towards all the works of his truth […]
the angels of knowledge in all […] holy proclamation *6* for the thrones of his
glory, and the footstool of [his feet, and all the ch]ariots of his majesty, and the
holy *debirim* […] and for the entry portals *7* [of the king] with all his exits from
[…] the corners of the structure and for all […] for the temples of his glory and
for the vaults of

5 Blessings and Curses

1QRule of the Blessings (1Q28b [1QSb])

Col. I   *1* Words of blessing. Of the Instructor. To bless those who fear [God, do] his will, keep his commandments, *2* remain constant in his holy covenant and walk with perfection [on all the paths of] his truth, those he has chosen for an eternal covenant *3* which endures for ever. May [my Lord] bless you [from his holy residence.] For *4* you may he open an eternal spring which [does not dry up.] From the heavens may [...] *5* in your hand [...] May he bestow upon you all the bless[ings ...] in the congregation of the holy ones. *6* [...] eternal spring, and not [withhold living waters] from the thirsty. And you, [...] *7* [...] May he save you from all [...] his hate, with no survivor. *8* [...] every foe [...] of holiness [...] *9* [...] ... [...] his holiness will remain [...] *10* ... [...]

Col. II   *1* [...] your fathers *2* [...] of you. May he lift *3* [...] May he bestow upon you and lift *4* [...] your work *5* [...] the gods. *6–21* [...] *22* [...] May the Lord bestow upon you [...] *23* May he delight you with his rewards, may he bestow upon you [...] *24* May he bestow upon you a spirit of holiness and of favour [...] *25* May he bestow upon you the eternal covenant and may you rej[oice ...] *26* May he bestow upon a just judgment [...] *27* May he show favour to you in all your works [...] *28* in everlasting truth [...]

Col. III   *1* May the Lord lift his face towards you and the ple[asant] aroma [... and be pleased] with all the inhabitants of [...] *2* May he choose and visit all his holy ones and in [...] all their descendants. May he lift *3* his face towards all your community. May he raise [...] above your head ... *4* in [perpetual] glory [and] make your descendants holy with eternal glory. May he lift [his face upon ...] *5* May he bestow up[on you ...] May he give you eternal [...] and the royalty [...] *6* [...] of the flesh. And with the holy ang[els ...] *7* May he wage war [in front of] the thousands [against] the corrupt generation [...] *8* [...] of them all [...] *9–16* [...] *17* [...] ... [...] *18* [...] for you [...] and not [...] *19* [...] all the wealth of the world, so that [...] of the spring *20* [...] he will seek it, because God has established all its foundations *21* [...] (he) has established its peace for all the everlasting centuries. *22 Blank* Words of Blessing. Of the Ins[tructor. To bless] the sons of Zadok, the priests whom *23* God has chosen to strengthen the covenant, for [ever, to dis]tribute all his judgments in the midst of his people, to teach them *24* in accordance with his commandment. They have established [his covenant] in truth and have examined all his precepts in justice, and they have walked in accordance with what *25* he chooses. May the Lord bless you from [his] holy [residence]. May he set you as a glorious ornament in the midst of *26* the holy ones. For you may he renew the covenant of [eternal] priesthood.

May he grant you a place [in the] holy [residence]. *27* May [he judge] all the nobles by your works and by what issues from your lips, all the [princes of] *28* the peoples. As inheritance may he give you the first fruits of [all de]lights. And by your hand may he bless the designs of all flesh.

Col. IV   *1* He will be pleased with the tread of your feet [...] of man and of the holy ones [...] *2* [...] and has been mingled with him [...] ... [...] *3* May everlasting blessings be the crown of your head. [...] *5-19* [...] *20* [...] to control [...] *21* [...] around him over [...] *22* [...] and has justified you from all [...] he has chosen you [...] *23* [...] to raise above the heads of the holy ones, and with you to [...] by your hand *24* the men of the council of God and not by the hand of the prince of [...] one to his fellow. You shall be *25* like an angel of the face in the holy residence for the glory of the God of the Hosts [...] You shall be around, serving in the temple of the *26* kingdom, sharing the lot with the angels of the face and the Council of the Community [...] for eternal time and for all the perpetual periods. For *27* [all] your judgments [are truth.] They have made you holy among your people, like a luminary [which lights up] the world with knowledge, and shines on the face of the Many *28* [...] consecrated for the holy of holies. because [you shall be made holy] for him and give glory to his name and his holy things.

Col. V   *2* you have separated them from [...] *3* ... [...] *4* those who see you[...] *5* and renew for you [...] *6* his strength upon you [...] *7* [...] ... [...] *8* [...] and Lord [...] *9-16* [...] *17* [...] may he fill your hand [...] *18* with everlasting time and with all the perpetual periods. And your glory [...] not [...] *19* God [will put] your dread upon all who hear speak of you, and your renown [...] *20 Blank* Of the Instructor. To bless the prince of the congregation, who [...] *21* [...] And he will renew the covenant of the Community for him, to establish the kingdom of his people for ever, [to judge the poor with justice] *22* to reproach the humble of the earth with uprightness, to walk in perfection before him on al his paths [...] *23* to establish the [holy] covenant [during] the anguish of those seeking it. May the Lord raise you to an everlasting height, like a fortified tower upon the raised rampart. *24* May [you strike the peoples] with the power of your mouth. With your sceptre may you lay waste *Blank* the earth. With the breath of your lips *25* may you kill the wicked. [May he send upon you a spirit of] counsel and of everlasting fortitude, a spirit *Blank* of knowledge and of fear of God. May *26* your justice be the belt of [your loins, and loyalty] the belt of your hips. May he place upon you horns of iron and horseshoes of bronze. You will gore like a bull [... you will trample the peo]ples like mud of wheels. For God has established you as a sceptre. *28* Those who rule [... all the na]tions will serve you. He will make you strong by his holy Name. *29* He will be like a li[on ...] the prey from you, with no-one to hunt it. Your steeds will scatter over

4QBlessings^f (4Q280 [4QBerakot^f])

1 [...May God keep him apart] for evil from the amongst the sons of light, [for they turn away from following him ...] *2* [and they will say: Accur]sed are you, Melki-resha^c, in all the pla[ns of your guilty inclination. May] God [make you] *3* an object of dread at the hand of those exacting vengeance. May God not favour you when you call on him. [May he lift his angry face] *4* upon you for a curse. May there be no peace for you in the mouth of those who intercede. [Be cursed,] without a remnant; and be damned, without salvation. And accursed be those who put into operation [their wicked plans] *6* and those who have implanted wickedness in their hearts to plot against the covenant of God [... and against] *7* [the wo]rds of those seeing his tru[th. And all those who refuse to enter [his covenant ...]

4QPurification Rules B^a (4Q275 [4QTohorot B^a])

Frag. 3   *1* and the elders with him up to [...] *2* and he will record in the list [...] *3* The Inspector [will curse ... and there will be no] *4* mercy. Curs[ed be ...] *5* of his inheritance forever [...] *6* in his destruc[tive] visitation [...]

4QBlessings^a (4Q286 [4QBerakot^a])

Frag. 1 *col.* II   *1* the residence of your honour, and the footstool of the feet of your glory in the heights of your position, and the step of *2* your holiness, and the chariots of your glory with their multitudes and their wheels and all their secrets, *3* foundations of fire, flames of your lamp and brilliance of honour, luminous rays and wonderful gleams, *4* honour and majesty and sublime glory, holy secret and place of splendour and sublime crown [...] *5* [...] store of forces, honour of praises and greatness of fears [...] *6* and wonderful deeds, secret of wisdom and image of knowledge and source of understanding [...] *7* holy counsel and secret of truth, store of intelligence of the sons of justice and residence of the upright [...] *8* mercies and humility of goodness, and true mercies and eternal kindnesses, and won[derful] mysteries [...] *9* [...] and the holy weeks in their measures, and the signs of the months [...] *10* [...] in their stations, and the glorious festivals in their testimonies [...] *11* [...] and the sabbaths of the earth in their divi[sions and the fes]tivals of rel[ease ...] *12* [... and the] perpetual [re]lease ...] *13* [... l]ight and darkn]ess ...

Frag. 2   *1* [...] and all the spirits who support the temple [...] *2* [... and in] their dominion the divine brave ones with strength *3* [...] the zeal of judgment in the time of *4* ...] ... the name of your holiness *5-6* [...] ...

Frag. 5   *1* [...] the land and all [...] that dwells in it, the earth and all its plans *2* [... and a]ll its substance [... and a]ll its heights, the valleys and all the torrents, one earth [...] *3* [...] the precipices and the forests and all the deserts of Hor[eb (?) ...] *4* [...] and its abysses, and the foundations of its mountains, the islands [...] *5* [...] its fruits, tall trees and all the cedars of Leba[non ...] *6* [... wine]-juice and oil and all the produce [...] *7* [...] and all the offerings of the globe in the months [...] *8* [...] your word. Amen. Amen. *Blank* [...] *9* [...] and waters from the springs of the abyss [...] *10* [...] all the torrents, the streams of the precipices [...] *11* [...] ... [...] *12* [...] all its secrets [...] *13* [...] ... [...]

Frag. 7 *col.* I   *1* [...] the lands *2* [...] its chosen ones *3* [...] and all its companions with hymns of *4* [...] and blessings of truth in the epochs of [...] *5* [...] and he who bears your kingdom in the midst of [...] *6* [... the se]cret of the gods of purity with all those who know for ever to pr[aise ...] *7* [... to bl]ess the name of your glory for all [the centuries.] Amen. Amen. *8* [...] they will continue blessing God [... a]ll his truth

Frag. 7 *col.* II   [the men of the] *1* Community Council shall say, all together, Amen. Amen. *Blank* And afterwards they shall damn Belial *2* and all his guilty lot. Starting to speak, they shall say: Accursed be Belial in his plan of hostility, *3* and may he be damned in his guilty service. And cursed be all the spirits of his lot in their wicked plans, *4* and may they be damned in their plans of foul impurity. For (they are the lot) of darkness, and his visitation will be *5* for the everlasting pit. Amen. Amen, *Blank* And cursed be the wicked [...] of his rule, and damned be *6* all the sons of Belial in all the sins of their functions until their annihilation [for ever. Amen. Amen.] *Blank* *7* And [cursed be ... an]gel of the pit and the sp[irit of des]truction in all the designs of your [guilty] inclination *8* [...] and in your wicked counsel. And damned be you in the ru[le of] *9* [...] with all the hu[miliations of She]ol and with [...] *10* [...] destruction [...] by the destructive wrath of [God ...] Amen. Amen. *11* [And cursed be] all who carry out [their ev]il [designs,] and those who implant wickedness [in their hearts, to plot] *12* [against the covenant of] God and to [...] and to alter the precepts [of the law] *13* [...] ... [...]

4QBlessings*ᵇ* (4Q287 [4QBerakot*ᵇ*])

Frag. 2   *1* [...] ... [...] its interwoven [...] *2* [...] ... [...] his honour [...] *3* [...] of his glory, the gates of his wonders [...] *4* [... the ea]rth, the angels of fire and the spirits of the clouds [...] *5* [... the sp]lendour, embroidery of the spirits of the holy of ho[lies ...] *6* [...] the holy firmaments [...] *7* [...] the holy ones in all the festivals [...] *8* [...] the holy name of your God [...] *9* [...] and all the ho[ly] servants [...] *10* [...] in the perfection of his deeds [...] *11* [... ho[ly in the

palaces of his king[ship ...] *12* [...] all his servants [...] of his honour. The angels of *13* [...] his holiness in the resi[dence ...] the angels of justice

Frag. 3   *1* [...] ... And they will bless the name of his holiness with bless[ings ...]
2 [...] all the creatures of flesh, all those whom you cre[ated ...] *3* [...] the animals, the birds, the reptiles and the fish of the seas and all [...] *4* [...] you have
created all of them again [...]

Frag. 5   *8-9* [...] ... [...] *10* [...] justice in he who be[ars ...] *11* [...] all the centuries. Amen. *Blank* [...] *12* [... che]rubim for you and the se[ed ...] *13* [...] the
families of the earth to be [...]

4QBless, Oh my Soul*a* (4Q434 [4QBar*e*ki Napshi*a*])

Frag. 1 col. I   *1* Bless, my soul, the Lord for all his marvels, for ever. And blessed
be his name, because he has saved the soul of the poor. And *2* the needy he has
not despised and he has not forgotten those oppressed. He has opened his eyes
upon the oppressed and has heard the cry of the orphans and has paid attention
to *3* their entreaties. In the abundance of his mercy he has favoured the needy
and has opened their eyes so that they see his paths, and their ears so that they
hear *4* his teaching. He has circumcised their hearts and has saved them by his
grace and has set their feet firm on the path. In their many sorrows he did not
forsake them, *5* and did not deliver them into the hands of violent men, nor did
he judge them with the wicked; he did not kindle his anger against them, nor
did he destroy them *6* in his wrath, although all the wrath of his anger does not
lessen, he did not judge them with the fire of his zeal. *Blank* *7* He judged them
with much mercy. The judgments of his eyes are to test them. And the abundance of [...] he caused to return from among the peoples [...] *8* from the man
he saved them. He did not judge the multitude of the peoples, and in the midst
of the nations did not [...]. He hid them in [...] *9* and transformed in front of
them their darkness to light, their twisted places into straight ones. He revealed
to them abundance of peace and of truth. [...] *10* their spirits to the measure,
established his words on the scales and his uprightness like flutes. He will give
them a heart, for ... his spirit and arose [...] commanded a plague against [...]
12 *Blank* And he positioned his angel in the vicinity of the children of [Isra]el so
that they would not be destroyed [...] *13* from their enemies [...] his fury for
[...] his wrath [...] with them [...] *14* He hates [...] his glory [...] *15* [...] *Blank*
Blank *16-18* [...] ... [...]

Frag. 1 col. II   *1* in evil [...] the distress [...] *2* his deeds [...] to them against the
sons of man, and you saved them for your sake [...] *3* And they worsened their
sin and the sin of their fathers, but they atoned for [...] *4* the judgments, and
for your path which [...] *5* again, for ... [...]

4QBless, Oh my Soul^c (4Q436 [4QBar^cki Napshi^c])

Frag. 1   *1* knowledge to strengthen the downcast heart, and to triumph in him over the spirit; to console those oppressed in the epoch of their anguish; and his hand *2* will lift the fallen to make them receptacles of knowledge; and to give knowledge to the wise and increase the instruction of the upright; to understand *3* your marvels which you did in the years preceding the years, generation after generation, eternal knowledge which *4* [...] before me. You preserve your law before me, and your covenant is confirmed for me, and you strengthen upon my heart *5* [...] to walk in your paths. You govern my heart and you sharpen my kidneys so that I do not forget your laws. *6* [...] your law, and you will open my kidneys and you will strengthen me so that I will follow your paths *7* [...] You will place my mouth like a sharpened sword; you have opened my tongue to the words of holiness; and you will place *8* [...] instruction, so that they do not meditate on the actions of the man whose lips are in the well. You have strengthened my feet *9* [...] and by your hand you have fortified me with days and you will send me. *Blank* In [...] *10* [...] you have removed from me, and in its place you will put a pure heart. The evil inclination [...]

6QBenediction (6Q16)

Frag. 1   *1* [...] like a sweet aroma [...] *2* [...] all the men of [...] *3* [...] penalties to all [...] *4* [...] all [...]

Frag. 3   *1* [...] the covenant [...] *2* [...] the commandments [...] *3* [...] of jus[tice ...] *4* [...] blessings [...]

6 Other Texts

1QLiturgical Text ? (1Q30)

Frag. 1   *1* [...] ... [...] *2* [...] the holy messiah [...] *3* [...] in the third, all [...]
4 [...] ... divided into five [...] *5* [...] and the remainder over four [...] *6* [...]
and its interpretation according to [...]

1QLiturgical Text ? (1Q31)

Frag. 1   *1* [Al]l the men of the Community, the volunteers [...] *2* from his mouth
all the [...] shall drink *3* ... [...]

1QHymnic Compositions ? (1Q37)

Frag. 1   *1* [...] in him. Israel [...] *2* [...] who have rewarded their souls with evil
[...] *3* [...] the chosen of Israel [...]

1QHymnic Compositions ? (1Q38)

Frag. 4   *1* [...] ... [...] *2* [...] and those made holy [...] *3* [...] you have humiliated
me [...] *4* [...] you did all this [...] *5* [...] among those sa[ved...]

1QHymnic Compositions ? (1Q39)

Frag. 1   *1–2* [...] ... [...] *3* [...] before you all the days [...] *4* [...] and he will be
honoured [...] *5* [...] when he has searched among [...] [...] by your holy spirit
[...]

4QLiturgical Work (4Q392)

Frag. 1   *1* [...] and of the kingdom [...] *2* [...] God to man, and not to turn away
from [...] *3* and their soul adheres to his covenant and [they keep] the words of
his mo[uth ...] God [...] the heavens *4* above and to examine the paths of the
sons of man, for whom there is no hiding-place. He created for himself darkness and light; *5* and in his dwelling the light shines, and all the shades rest
before him; and he does not need to separate light *6* from darkness, for (only)
for men are light and the sun separated during the day, the moon and the stars
at night. *7* With him there is a light which cannot be inspected nor can it be
known [...] for it doubles all the deeds of God. We *8* are flesh, which does not
understand these things. With us [...] and dead without number *9* [... wi]nds
and lightning [...] ...

4QGrace after Meals (4Q434a)

Frag. 1 *1* [...] to be consoled in the sorrow of the poor [...] *2* to destroy the peoples and tear apart the nations and the wicked [...] renew *3* the deeds of the heavens and of the earth, and may they rejoice and may his glory fill [all the earth ...] ... *4* he will atone and the great in goodness will console them. Good is the [...] to eat *5* its fruit and its goodness. *Blank* [...] *Blank* *6* As a man consoles his mother, so will he console Jerusa[lem ... Like a fiancé] with his fiancée *7* he will live for e[ver ... f]or his throne is for ever and ever and his glory [...] and all the peoples *8* [...] and he went with him [...] desirable *9* [...] splendour [...] *10* [...] Blessed be the name of the Most High [...] *Blank* *11* Blessed be [...] his mercy upon me *12* [...] for the Law which you established *13* [...] the book of your laws

4QBaptismal Liturgy (4Q414)

Frag. 2 *col.* I *1* [... he will reply] and will say: Blessed are you *2* [...] the pure ones of the epoch of *3* your light [...] to atone for us *4* according to your will [...] the pure ones in your presence *5* ... [...] in every word *6* [...] to purify before *7* [...] You have made us

Frag. 2 *col.* II *1* and you will purify him for your ho[ly] laws [...] *2* for the first, the third and the six[th ...] *3* in the truth of your covenant [...] *4* to purify from impurity [...] *5* And afterwards he will enter the water [...] *6* And he will reply and say: Blessed are you [...] *7* because what issues from your mouth [...] *8* men ... [...]

Frag. 7 *col.* II *1* his cloth[es] and in the water [...] *2* [...] he will bless [...] *3* Israel which [...] *4* before from all [...] *5* you have forsaken [...]

Frag. 10 *1* the soul [...] *2* he is [...] *3* for you as a pu[re] people [...] *4* And I, too, ... [...] *5* today, when [...] *6* in the periods of purification [...] *7* of the community. *Blank* [...] *8* During the purifications of Israel not [...] *9* And it will happen on the day of [...] *10* a woman, and she will give thanks [...] *11* [...] ... [...]

Frag. 12 *1* for you made the [...] *2* your [w]ill, to purify in your presence [...] *3* and he established for him a glorious regulation [...] *4* to be in purity [...] *5* and he will wash in water and he will be [pure ...] *6* [...] And afterwards he will come out of the [water ...] *7* purifying his people with the water which washes [...] *8* [And he will be] the second in his position, and he will re[ply and will say: Blessed are you ...] *9* [...] your purification in the glory of [...] *10* [...] ... [...]

4QRitual of Marriage (4Q502)

Frags. 1–3   *1* [...] the man who acknowledges [...] when you add [...] *2* [...] the law of God [...] who lacks [...] *3* [...the man] and his wife for [...] ... [...] *4* [...] to procreate offspring [...] these [...] *5* [...] which [...] holy ones praising God [...] *6* [...] to be be holy [...] for him, daughter of truth and who walks [...] *7* [...] her (female) friend who [...] for her, intelligence and knowledge in the midst of [...] *8* [...] ... [...] together, to be [...] *9* [...] sufferings [...] and atoning [...] *10* [...] for the sons of justice [...] on this day [...] *11* [...] ... [...] Aaron [...]

Frags. 7–10   *1* [...] ...[...] *2* [...] praise [...] *3* [...] together [...] *4* [...They shall bless the] God of Israel, and starting to speak, they shall [say:] *5* [Blessed is the God of Israel who ...] the time of happiness to praise his name *6* [...] adults and youths *7* [...] rams and he-goats [...] in our flocks, and reptiles *8* [...who cree]p in our shadow, birds [who fly in our sky,] our land and all its produce, *9* [and al]l the fruits of the trees. And or waters [...] the waters of the abyss. We all *10* [ble]ss the name of the God of Israel who[has given us] a feast for our happiness and also *11* [...] the witness of [...] among just adults *12* [...] in peace for [...] I give thanks to God and celebrate *13* [...] brothers for me. The adults *14* [...] those who bless in our midst *15* [...] holy [...] adults of perfect holiness *16* [...] Today I [...bless] the God of Israel [...] *17* [...] adults of know[ledge ...] ... [...] *18* [... he has made us hap]py in the tes[timony ...] to be *19–20* [...] ... [...]

Frag. 14   *1–2* [...] ... [...] *3* [...] the stipulations and also [...] *4* [...] the God of Israel who has required the sons of [...] *5* [...] your glory ... and the love of your favour [...] *6* [...] sons and daughters [...] *7* [...] also [...] *8* [...] Israel [...]

Frag. 16 (= 1QS IV, 4–6 ?)   *1* [... a spirit of knowledge in all their plans of] action, [of zeal for the precepts of justice,] *2* [of holy plans with firm purpose, of abundant] compassion with [all the sons of truth, of glorious purity] *3* [which loathes all the impure idols] of modest behaviour with prudence [in everything, of discretion about the truth of the mysteries of knowledge. These are the counsels of the spirit] *4* [to the sons of truth] in the world. And the visitation of all [those who walk in it will be for cure]

Frag. 19   *1* and he will sit with him in the assembly of the holy on[es ...] *2* seed of blessing, old men and old w[omen ...] *3* and virgins, boys and gi[rls ...] *4* together with all of us. And I, I [...] *5* And afterwards the men of [...] will start speaking *6* [...] their errors [...] *7* [...] ... [...]

Frag. 24　*1* [...] all the feasts [...] *2* [...] /the man of praises./ Blessed be the God of Israel who has helped [...] *3* [...he will exte]nd your life in the midst of an everlasting people [...] *4* [...] and she will take a place in the assembly of old men and old wom[en...] *5* [...] your days in peace [...] *6* [...] in the midst of the el[ders ...]

4QRitual of Purification (4Q512)

Frag. 39 col. II　*1* expiations. And I, I will praise your na[me ...] *2* because you have purified me and brought me into [...]

Frags. 36–38 *col.* III　*1* [...] his clothes [...] *2* [...] all the tongues [...] *3* [...] to you the counsel of me[n ...] *4* [...] *Blank* [...] *5* [...] ... [...] *6* [...] of all the impurity of our flesh [...]

Frags. 33 and 35 *col.* IV　*1* [...] for the feast of the sabbath, on the sabbaths of all the weeks of [...] *2* [...] ... [...] and four feasts of *3* [...] the feast of the harvest /and of summer/ and the feast of the s[tart of the] month [...] *4* [...] *Blank* [...] *5* [...] in water [...] to make holy *6* [...] ... [He will bless.] He will start speaking [and say: May you be blessed ...] *7* [...] by your compass[ion ...] ... *8* [...] and I [...] ... *9* [...] in the impur[ity ...] ... *10* [...] the purification [...] *11* [...] ...[...]

Frag. 34 *col.* V　*1* [...] ... [...] *2* [...] in the midst of his people [...] *3* [...] to ask mercy for all my hidden fault [...] *4* [...] who are just in all your works [...] *5* [...] from the impure disease [...] because [...]

Frags. 29–32 *col.* VII　*1* [...] Blessed be you, [God of Israel] *2* [...] holy people [...] *3* [...] the mistake [...] *4* [...] in water [...] *5* [...] And there he will bless [...] *6* [...] before you in the feast of [...] *7* [...] for purity [...] *8* [...] and his burnt offering. And he will bless. He will start speaking and say: May you be blessed, [God of Israel, who] *9* [forgave me all] my faults and purified me from impure immodesty /and atoned/ so that I can enter *10* [...] the purification. And the blood of the burnt offering of your approval and the pleasant memory [...] *11* [...] the holy incense and the pleasant aroma and your approval [...] *12–17* [...] ... [...] *18* [...] my sin [...] *19* [...] justice [...] *20* [...] leave without punishment until the judgment [...] Israel who [...] *21* [...Blessed] may you be, God of Is[rael ...] for the expiations [...]

Frags. 10–11 *col.* X　*1* [...] his impure flux [...] *2–4* [...] ... [...] *5* [And when] the seven days of his pur[ification have been completed...] *6* [...] he will purify his clothes with water [and wash his body...] *7* And he will cover himself with his clothes and bless on [...] *5* God of Israel [...]

Frags. 7–9 *col.* XI   *1* All these thin[gs ...] *2* in the purification of her fl[ux ...] purity of flesh [...] *3* to eat and to dr[ink ...in their cities of residence, *4* and to be a [holy] people [...] *Blank 5 Blank* [...]

Frags. 1–6 *col.* XII   *1* On the third day [...] He will start speaking and sa[y: Blessed] *2* be you, God of Israel, [who commanded the tempo]rarily impure to purify themselves from the impurity of] *3* [...] the soul with the atonement [...] holy ash [...] *4* [...] in the water of [...] in constant streams *5* and the lustral water for temporary purification [...] his clothes and afterwards [they will sprinkle over him] *6* the waters of sprinkling to purify him, and all [...] *7* After [having been sprin]kled with the waters [of sprinkling he will bless. He will start speaking and say: Blessed be you] *8* [God of Is]rael, you give [...] *9* from the defilements of impurity. Today [...] *10* contamination, to make you holy [...]

Frags. 42–44 *col.* II   *1* ... [...] *2* And afterwards he will enter [...] *3* And he will say: Blessed are you, God of Is[rael, ...] *4* by your mouth the purification of all [...] has been required *5* they are not purified in water of purification. And today I [...] *6* [...] ... [...]

Astronomical Texts, Calendars and Horoscopes

This chapter assembles a sample of a whole series of compositions which are of an astronomical character from calendars which determine synchronisms among the movements of heavenly bodies or which establish feasts in accordance with the different rosters of the priestly families, and one text which can be identified as a horoscope. Unfortunately, these texts have reached us in an extremely fragmentary condition, and most of them have not yet been published.

In the first section are three of the four exemplars of a composition known as *Astronomical Enoch*, an Aramaic work of which the astronomical chapters of *Ethiopic Enoch* or *1 Enoch* (chapters 72-82) are a muddled and very abbreviated summary. The work comprised an extensive calendar in which the movements of the sun and of the moon were correlated (of which nothing remains in the Ethiopic text) as well as other material which refers to various heavenly phenomena. Out of the four copies recovered from Cave 4, the oldest (4Q208) preserves only remnants of the synchronic calendar; there are no traces of the calendar in the few fragments of the two later manuscripts (4Q210 and 4Q211); but in the longest and best preserved copy (4Q209), both sections are represented.

In the second section are some of the seven manuscripts which include different types of calendar. In these calendars the festivals of the year are determined, usually in terms of the priestly rosters; these manuscripts are, therefore, also labelled as *Mishmarot*. The longest document of this type is to be found in the translation of one of the copies of the *Community Rule* (4Q259) to which it belonged. The extremely bad condition of the other manuscripts of the same type, and the impression that several fragments, bundled together as part of a single work, actually include the remains of calendars of different kinds, prevent their inclusion here. This same section includes the longest fragment of a work in Hebrew, but copied in code, which describes the various phases of the moon in a style similar to the synchronic calendar of *Astronomical Enoch* and the two fragments of a brontologion.

The third section contains astrological compositions. The first one has been copied in code, with Greek and Palaeo-Hebrew letters alternating with letters in the square script and the whole text written from left to right, but the language is Hebrew. The second one is in Aramaic. Both of them can be termed horoscopes.

1 Astronomical Enoch

4QAstronomical Enoch*b* (4Q209 [4QEnastr*b* ar])

Frags. 1 + 2   *1* [and shines during the sixth night of this month for three sevenths.] Next, it sets [and enters and it is four sevenths covered] *2* [the rest of
that night. And during that day it grows up to three and a half sevenths; its
light is equivalent] to three and a half sevenths. *3* [Then it rises and keeps
watch the rest of that day for three and a half sevenths. And it shines during
the seventh night of that month with three and a half sevenths. *4* [Next, it sets
and enters and is three and a half sevenths dark the rest of that night. And it
gr]ows during that day up to four sevenths; its light is equivalent *5* [to four
sevenths. Then it rises and keeps watch during the rest of that day for three
sevenths.] And it shines during the eighth night of that month with *6* [four]
sevenths. Next, it sets and enters and it is dark for the rest [of that night for
three sevenths. And it grows during that day] up to four and a half sevenths;
its light is equivalent *7* [to four sevenths. Then it rises and keeps watch the rest
of that day for two and a half sevenths.] And it shines during the ninth night
of that month *8* [with four and a half sevenths. Next, it sets and enters and is
[two and a half sevenths] covered the rest [of that night . And it grows during
that day] up to five sevenths; *9* [its light is equivalent to five sevenths.] Then
[it rises and keeps watch during the rest of that day two sevenths. And it shines
during the tenth night] *10* [of this month with five sevenths. Next, it sets and
enters and is two sevenths covered the rest of that night. And it grows during
that day up to five and a half sevenths;] *11* [its light is equivalent to five and a
half sevenths. Then it rises and keeps watch during the rest of that day one and
a half sevenths.] *12* [And it shines during the eleventh night] of this month
[with five and a half sevenths. Then it sets and enters and is one and a half
sevenths covered the rest of that night. And it grows] *13* [during that day] up
to six sevenths; its light is equivalent [to six sevenths.] Then it rises and keeps
watch during the rest of that day one seventh.

Frag. 3   *1* [And it shines during the twelfth night] of this month [with six sevenths. Next it sets and enters and is one seventh covered the rest of that night.]
2 [And it grows during] that day up to six and a half sevenths; its light is equivalent [to six and a half sevenths. Then it rises and keeps watch during the rest
of that day] half a seventh. And it shines during the [thirteenth] night [of that
month with six and a half sevenths. Next, it sets and enters and is half a seventh covered *4* [the rest of that night.] And it grows during all that whole day
[...] *5* [...] And it shines during the fourteenth night of that month, during all
that night [...] *6* [And during the] fifteenth [night] of that month it is half a
seventh covered; it lacks [half a seventh of its light. Then it rises and shines]

7 [during the rest of that night] with six and a half sevenths. And it grows during that day [...] *8* [...] six and a half sevenths. And during the [sixteenth night of that month it is half a seventh (?) covered. Of its light it lacks] *9* [half a seventh (?)]. Then it rises and shines the rest of that night [six and half sevenths (?). And it grows during that day up to a seventh. Next] *10* [it sets and enters and is covered] the rest of that day [six sevenths...]

Frags. 4 + 5   *1* Fi[ve and a half [sevenths...] *2* two sevenths. Then [...] *3* that day up to two sevenths. Next it sets [and enters and is covered] the re[st of that day up to five sevenths.] *4* And during the nineteenth night of that month it is two sevenths co[vered; it lacks two sevenths of its light. Then *5* it rises and shines the rest of that night with five sevenths. [And it grows during] that day [up to two and a half sevenths. Next] *6* it sets and enters and is four and a half sevenths covered] the rest of that day. [And during the twentieth night of that month it is] *7* [two and a half sevenths covered; it lacks two] and a half sevenths of its light.

Frag. 6   *1* [Then it rises through the gate ... and shines during the rest of that night with one and a half sevenths; it grows during that day up to six sevenths. *2* [Next it sets and enters and is one seventh covered the rest of that day. During the twenty-seventh night] of that month it is six sevenths covered; it lacks [six sevenths] of its light. *3* [Then it rises and shines during the rest of that night with a seventh, and grows during] that day up to six and a half sevenths. Next it sets *4* [and enters and is covered during the rest of that day up to a half of a seventh. During the twenty-eighth night of that month it is six and half sevenths covered; it lacks *5* [six and a half sevenths of its light. It rises and shines] the rest of that night with half of a seventh and grows during that day to completeness. Next it sets and enters *6* [through the gate ... and is completely covered the rest of that day. It lacks] all the rest of its light, and its disc rises deprived of all light, occluded by the sun. *7* [...] ... [...]

Frag. 7 *col.* II   *1* [During that day it grows up to four and a half sevenths. Next it sets and enters and is two and a half sevenths covered the rest] of that day. *2* [*Blank* During the twenty-fourth day] of that months it is covered up to four and a half sevenths]. Then it rises and shines during the rest of that night with two and a half sevenths. And it grows *4* [during] that day up to five sevenths. Next it sets and enters and is two sevenths covered the rest of that day. *5* During the twenty-fifth night of that month its is covered up to five sevenths; it lacks five sevenths of its light. *6* Then it rises and shines during the rest of that night with two sevenths and grows during that day up to five and a half sevenths. *7* Next it sets and enters through the second gate and is covered the rest of that day with one a half sevenths *Blank* 8 During the twenty-sixth night of that month it is five and half sevenths covered; it lacks five and a half sevenths of its light. *9* Then it rises from the second gate and shines during the rest of that night with one and a half sevenths; and it grows during that day *10* up to six sevenths. Next it sets and enters and is one seventh covered the rest of that day. *Blank* During the twenty-seventh *11* night of that month it is six sevenths covered; it lacks [six sevenths] of its light. [Then it rises and shines] *12* [during the rest] of that night with one and a half sevenths; and it grows during that day [up to six and a half sevenths.] Next it sets and enters

Frag. 7 col. III   *1* [...And shines during the eighth night of that month] with four sevenths. Next it sets and enters. During that night *2* the sun completes its passage through all the sections of the first gate and again begins to enter and rise through the sections. Then the moon *3* sets and enters and is three sevenths dark the rest of that night. And during that day it grows up to four [and a half] sevenths. [Next] it rises and keeps watch the rest of that day two and a half sevenths. *Blank* During the ninth night of that month it shines with *5* four and a half sevenths. Next it sets and enters. During that night the sun again begins to pass through its sections [and to set] *6* through them. Then the moon sets and enters through the fifth gate, and is [two] and a half [seven]ths dark the rest of that night. *7* And during that day it grows up to five [sevenths;] its light is equivalent to five complete sevenths. [Next it rises] *8* through the fifth gate [and keeps watch during the rest of that day, two sevenths. During the tenth night of that month, it shines with] [five sevenths. Next it sets and enters and is two sevenths dark the rest of that night. And it grows during that day] *10* [up to five and a half seve]nths [...]

Frag. 8   *1* [and it shines the rest of] that night [with three sevenths. And it grows up to four and a half sevenths during that day. Next it sets and enters] *2* [and is] two and a half sevenths [covered the rest of that] day. [And during the twentieth night...] *3* [of that month it is] four and a half sevenths [covered.] [It lacks four and a half sevenths of its light. Then it rises and shines] *4* [during the rest of that night with] two and a half sevenths. [And it grows during that day up to five sevenths. Next it sets and enters and is covered]

Frag. 9   *1* [Then it sets and enters through the] third gate [and is ..... sevenths covered the rest of that day.] *2* [And during the] twentieth [night [...] of that month it is [.... sevenths] covered; it lacks .... sevenths of its light. *3* [Next it rises from the] third gate and shines [during the rest of that night...]

Frag. 23 (〉 1 *Enoch* 76 : 13–77 : 4)   *1* [... drought and] destruction and death and [violence and desolation.] *2* [The twelve gates of the four cardinal points] of the sky [ceased.] I have shown you their full explanation, [Methuselah, my son.]

3 [The East they call the East, because it is the] first. The South they call the South, because the Great One lives there, and in him *4* [...] lives [bles]sed for ever. The great cardinal point [they call the West, because] *5* the stars of the sky [go there;] through there all the stars set and through there they rise; that is why they call it the West. *6* [The North they call the North] because all the stars of the sky hide and gather in it and return to it and head towards the East of the skies. *7* [And the East they call] the East, because the heavenly bodies ascend from there; also they call it the Levant because they 'levitate' through there. *8* [And I saw three sections] of the earth: one so that the sons of men could live in it; another for all [the seas] *9* [and the rivers, and another] for the deserts, for «The Seven», [and for the Paradise] of Justice. *10* [And I saw seven mountains higher] that all the mountains [which there are upon the earth; snow covers them...]

Frag. 25 (⟩ 1 *Enoch* 79 : 9–12 ?)   *1* [...] years for [...] *2* [...] *Blank* [...] *3* [And Uriel taught me] another computation, having shown me that ... [...] *4* [its light is in the sky. The first days they call] new moons, because [...]

Frag. 26 (⟩ 1 *Enoch* 79 : 2–5)   *1* [...] ... [...] *2* [...] through the sixth gate, for it [its light is completed...] *3* [...twenty-five weeks and] two days. And it lags behind in relation to the sun [...] *4* [...] it is corrected in it. It seems like the image of a vision. When its light lags behind in it [...] *5* [In the night] that vision seems to be in part the image of a man, and in the night [seems in part the image of the sun in the sky; and there is nothing in it,] *6* [except only its light.] And now, my son, I will show you [...] *7* [...] another computation

Frag. 28 (⟩ 1 *Enoch* 82 : 9–13)   *1* [in relation to] its constellations, its new moons, its signs. [These are the names] *2* [... and according to] his authority in relation to all their stations. Four [...] *3* [...] chiefs of a thousand [...] *4* [... dividing up the days [...] *5* [...and these] are the names [...]

4QAstronomic Enoch^c (4Q210 [4QEnastr^c ar])

Frag. 1 col. II (⟩ 1 *Enoch* 76 : 3–10)   *1* and the following three, to the North. [And the following three, to the West. Out through four of them go the winds which] *2* are for the healing of the earth and its revitalization. And [out through eight go the harmful winds; when they are sent they destroy all the earth] *3* and the waters and all there is in them, what grows and flowers and creeps, [both in the waters as on dry land and all that lives in it. First,] *4* the wind from the East goes out through the first gate which is in the [East and veers to the South. Out through it go destruction, drought, heat and desolation.] *5* Out through the second gate, (the middle one), goes the wind from the East-by-Ea[st: rain, fruits, renewal of life and dew. Out through the third goes the wind] *6* from the North-east, which is close to the wind from the North: [cold and aridity. Behind them,] *7* out goes, first, through the first gate, [a wind from the South, which is to the South and the East: [a hot (?) wind. Out through the second gate goes a wind from the South] *8* which they call the South: dew, [rain, well-being and renewal of life. Out through the third gate goes a wind from the South-east: dew, rain, locust and destruction.] *9* Behind it a wind from the [North] goes out [...] *10–13* [...] *14* and desolation. The twelve gates of the four cardinal points of the sky came to an end. [I have shown you their complete explanation, Methuselah, my son. The East they call the East] *15* because it is the first; the South they call the South because the [Great One lives there, and in it he lives since eternity. The great cardinal point they call the West because the stars] *16* of the sky [go there;] all the stars set through there and rise through there; that is why [they call it the West. The North they call the North, because] *17* all the stars [of the skies hide,] gather together and turn back in it, [and head] towards the East of the skies. [The East they call the East because from there the heavenly bodies rise. They also call it the Levant because] *18* the moons 'levitate' through there [becoming fuller day by day] to appear above the earth...] *19* [I saw three sections] of the earth: one for the sons of men to live in;] another [...] *20* [And I see sev]en moun[tains...]

Frag. 1 *col.* III (◊ *Enoch* 78 : 6–8)   *1–2* [...] *3* [When the moon rises, half of a seventh of its light] shines in the skies to appear [above the earth] *4* [... and it becomes com]plete from day to day until day fourteen, [when...] *5* [all its light is complete. Its light grows by fifteenths and becomes complete, day by day, until day] fifteen, on which all its light is complete. *6* [...] and achieves its phases in half-sevenths. *7* [In its waning (?) phase the moon decreases its light. The first day, a fourteenth;] the second day, a thirteenth; *8* [the third day, a twelfth; the fou]rth day an eleventh

4QAstronomic Enoch*d* (4Q211 [4QEnastr*d* ar])

Frag. 1 *col.* I   *1* [...] ... *2* [...dew] and rain falling upon the earth, and the seed *3* [...] grass of the earth and wood. The sun] rises and sets *4* [...]and it is winter; the leaves of the trees *5* [turn white and fall, except for the fo]urteen trees in which [...] does not appear *6* ... [... their] leaves remain.

Frag. 1 *col.* II   *1* [...] *2* that one, of its measure [...] *3* a tenth of its ninth [part...] *4* of a ninth [part]. The stars move through the first gate of the skies. [Next] they go out *5* in the first days, a tenth through a sixth; in the second, a fifteenth *6* through a sixth; in the third, a thirteenth through a sixth.

Frag. 1 *col.* III   *1-3* [...] *4* On [day fif]teen [...] and on the same day [...] *5* only in that night, of [...a thi]rd of a ninth [part] and five [...] *6* and a tenth of a ninth part. *Blank* [...] *7* [...] ... [...]

2 Calendars and Priestly Rosters

4QPhases of the Moon (4Q317 [4QAstrCrypt])

1 [...] ... [...] *2* [On the] fifth (day) of it (the month) [it is covered for] *3* twelve (fourteenths,) and thus [enters the day. On the sixth of it,] *4* it is covered for thir[teen, and thus it enters the day.] *5* On the seventh of it, it is co[vered for fourteen, and thus] *6* enters the day. *Blank* [...] *7* On the eighth of it, [its light dominates the day in the centre of the] *8* high vault, [/fourteen and a half (?)/ and at the arrival of the sun] *9* its light is obscured [and thus it starts to be visible] *10* on the first (day) of the week. *Blank* [On the ninth of it, it is visible] *11* by one part [and thus enters the night.] *12* On the tenth of it it is vi[sible by two, and thus enters] *13* the night. *Blank* On the ele[venth in it, it is visible by three] *14* and thus it enters the night. *Blank* [...]

4QBrontologion (4Q318 [4QBr ar])

Frag. 1   *1* [on the 7th (day), Sagittarius. On the 8th and on the 9th, Capricorn. On the 10th and on the 11th, Acquarius. On the 12th and on the] 13th and on the 1[4th,]

2 [Pisces. On the 15th and on the 16th, Aries. On the 17th and on the 18th, Taurus. On the 1]9th, on the 20th and on the 2[1st]

3 [Gemini. On the 22nd and on the 23rd, Cancer. On the 24th and on the 25th, Leo. On the 26th,] on the 27th and on the 28th,

4 [Virgo. On the 29th, on the 30th and on the 31st, Libra.] *Blank*

5 [(Month of) Tishri: On the 1st and on the 2nd, Scorpio. On the 3rd and on the 4th, Sagittarius. On the 5th, on the 6th and on the] 7th, Capricorn. On the 8th

Frag. 2 col. I   *1* and on the 13th and on the 14th, Cancer. On the 15th and on the 16th, Leo. On the 17th and on the 18th,

2 Virgo. On the 19th, on the 20th and on the 21st, Libra. On the 22nd and on the 23rd, Scorpio. On the 24th

3 and on the 25th, Sagittarius. On the 26th, on the 27 and on the 28th, Capricorn. On the 29th

4 And on the 30th, Acquarius. *Blank* (Month of) Shebat: On the 1st and on the 2nd, Pisces. On the 3rd and on the 4th,

5 Aries. On the 5th, on the 6th and on the 7th, Taurus. On the 8th on the 9th, Gemini. On the 10th

6 And on the 11th, Cancer. On the 12th, on the 13th and on the 14th, Leo. On the 15th and on the 16, Virgo.

7 On the 17th and on the 18th, Libra. On the 19th, on the 20th and on the 21st, Scorpio. On the 22nd

8 and on the 23rd, Sagittarius. On the 24th and on the 25th, Capricorn. On the 26th, on the 27th and on the 28th,

9 Acquarius. On the 29th and on the 30th, Pisces. *Blank*

Frag. 2 col. II   *1* (Month of) Adar: On the 1st and on the 2nd, Aries. On the 3rd and on the 4th, Taurus. On the 5th, on the 6th and on the 7th, Gemini.

2 On the 8th, on the 9th, Cancer. On the 10th and on the 11th, Leo. On the 12th, on the 13th and on the 14th,

3 Virgo. On the 15th and on the 16th, Libra. On the 17th, on the 18th, Scorpio.

4 On the 19th, on the 20th and on the 21st, Sagittarius. On the 22nd and on the 23rd, Capricorn. On the 24th and on the 25th,

5 Acquarius. On the 26th, on the 27th on the 28th, Pisces. On the 29th, on the 30th and on the 31st,

6 Aries. *Blank* If it thunders in the sign of Taurus, revolutions (in) the wor[ld...]

7 problems for the cities and destru[ction in the cour]t of the King and in the province of [...]

8 there will be, and for the Arabs [...] famine. And some will plunder others [...]

9 *Blank* If it thunders in the sign of Gemini, fear and distress of the foreigners and of [...]

4QCalendrical Document A (4Q320 [4QCalendrical Doc A])

Frag. 1 *col.* I   *1* [...] to display itself from the East *2* [and] shine [in] the centre of the sky, at the base of the *3* [va]ult, from evening to morning, on the *4*th (Wednesday) of Shebat *4* [son of Ga]mul, in the first month of the *5* [fir]st year. *Blank* *6* [The 5th (Thursday) of (the week of) Yeda^cy]ah (corresponds) to the 29th (and falls) on the 30th of the first (month). *7* [The sabbath of Ha]qoz, (corresponds) to the 30th, on the 30th of the second. *8* [The 1st (Sunday) of Elya]shib, the 29th, on the 29th of the third. *9* [The 3rd (Tuesday) of Bil]gah to the 30th, on the 28th of the fourth. *10* [The 4th (Wednesday) of Petay]yah, to the 29th, on the 27th of the fifth. *11* [The 6th (Friday) of Delayah,] to the 30th on the 27th of the sixth. *12* [The sabbath of She^co]rim, to the 29th on the 25th of the seventh. *13* [The 2nd (Monday) of Abiyah, to the 3]oth, [on the] 25th of the eighth. *14* [The 3rd of Yaqim, to the 2]9th, on the 24th of the ninth.

Frag. 1 *col.* II   *1* The 5th (Thursday) /of Immer/, to the 30th, on the 22nd of the tenth. *2* The 6th (Friday) of Yehezkiel, to the 29th, on the 22nd of the eleventh. *3* The 1st (Sunday) of Yoyarib, to the 30th, on the 22nd of the twelfth month *4* of the second year. *Blank* *5* The 2nd of Malkiyah, to the 29th, on the 20th of the first. *6* The 4th (Wednesday) of Yeshu^ca, to the 30th, on the 20th of the second. *7* The 5th (Thursday) of Juppa, to the 29th, on the 19th [of the third]. *8* The sabbath of Hapizez, to the 30th, on the 18th of the fo[urth.] *9* The

1st (Sunday) of Gamul, to the [29th, on the 17th of the fifth.] *10* The 3rd
(Tuesday) of Yeda^cyah, to the 30th, [on the 17th of the sixth.] *11* The 4th
(Wednesday) of Miyyamim, to the 2[9th, on the 15th of the seventh.] *12* The
6th (Friday) of Shekanyah, to the 3[0th, on the 15th of the eighth.] *13* The
sabbath of Bil[gah, to the 29th, on the 14th of the ninth.] *14* [The 2nd of
Petayyah, to the 30th, on the 13th of the tenth.]

Frag. 1 *col.* III   *1* [The 3rd (Tuesday) of Delayah, to the 29th, on the 12th of the
eleventh.] *2* [The 5th (Thursday) of Yarim, to the 30th, on the 12th of the eleventh month.] *3* [The 6th (Friday) of Haqoz, to the 29th, on the 10th of the
first.] *4* [The 1st (Sunday) of Yaqim, to the 30th, on the 10th of the second.]
5 [The 2nd (Monday) of Immer, to the 20th, on the 9th of the third.] *6* [The
4th (Wednesday) of Yehezkiel, to the 30th, on the 8th of the fourth.] *7* [The 5th
(Thursday) of Ma^caziyah, to the 29th, on the 7th of the fifth.] *8* [The sabbath
of Malkiyah, to the 30th, on the 7th of the sixth.] *9* The 1st (Sunday) of
Ye[shu^ca, to the 29th, on the 5th of the seventh.] *10* The 3rd (Tuesday) of
Juppa, to the 30th, on the 5th of the eighth. *11* The 4th (Wednesday) of Yazir,
to the 29th, on the 4th of the ninth. *12* The 6th (Friday) of Yaqim, to the 30th,
on the 3rd of the tenth. *13* The sabbath of Yeda^cyah, to the 29th, on the 2nd of
the twelfth month. *14* The 2nd (Monday) [of Miyya]mim, to the 30th, on the
second day of the twelfth month.

Frag. 2 *col.* I   *1* [...] *2* [...] second. The holy *3* [...] holy creation *4* [...] the 4th of
Shebat *5* [...] beginning of all the years. *6* [... of the] year of the second jubilee.
7 [...] ...

Frag. 2 *col.* II   *1* ... [...] *2* in the sacrifices [...] *3* holy [...] *4* The second, 30 [...]
5 The third, 3[1 ...] *6* The fourth, 30 [...]

Frag. 4 *col.* I   *11* [...] Yoyarib *12* [...] Malkiyah *13* [...] Yeshu^ca *14* [...] Yeshabeb

Frag. 4 *col.* II   *10* the days, the weeks, *11* and the months, *Blank* *12* the years, the
Releases *13* and the jubilees. The 4th of *14* Shebat, son of Gamul.

Frag. 4 *col.* III   *1* The first year. Its festivals: *2* The 3rd, on the sabbath of
Me^cozayah, the passover. *3* The 1st [of] Yeda^c[yah, the waving of the sh[eaf.]
4 The 5th of She^corim, the [second] passover. *5* The 1st of Yeshu^ca, the feast
of weeks. *6* The 4th of Me^cozayah, the day of remembrance. *7* The 6th of
Yeoyarib, the day of atonement *8* [in the seventh mo]nth. *Blank* *9* The 4th of
Yeda^cyah, the feast of tents. *10* *Blank* *11* The second. Its feasts: *12* [The 3rd] of
She^corim, the passover. *13* [The 1st of Miy]yamim, the waving of the [sheaf.]
14 [The 5th of A]biyah, [the second passover.]

Frag. 4 *col.* IV   *1* The 1st [of Jup]pa, [the feast of w]eeks. *2* The 4th of She^corim, the day /of remembrance/. *3* The 6th of Malkiyah, the day of atonement. *4* The [4th of] Miyyamim, the feast of tents. *5 Blank 6* The third. Its festivals: *7* The 3rd of Abiyah, the passover. *8* The 1st of Shekanyah, the waving of the sheaf. *9* The 5th of Yaqim, the se[cond] passover. *10* [The 1st] of Chazir, [the feast of weeks.] *11* [The 4th of Abiyah, the day of remembrance.] *12* [The 6th of Yeshu^ca, the day of atonement.] *13* [The 4th of Shekanyah, the feast of tents.] *14* [The fourth. Its festivals:]

Frag. 4 *col.* V   *1* [The 3rd of Ya]qim, the passover. *2* The 1st [of Yesha]beb, the waving of the sheaf. *3* The [5th of Im]mer, the second passover. *4* [The 1st of Hapi]zez, [the feast of] weeks. *5* [The] 4th of Yaqim, the day of remembrance. *6* [The] 6th of Juppa, the day of atonement. *7* [The 4th] of Yeshabeb, the feast of tents. *8* [...] *Blank 9* [The fifth.] Its festivals: *10* The 3rd of Immer, the passover. *11* The 1st of Hapizez, the waving of the sheaf. *12* [The] 5th of Yehezkiel, the second passover. *13* [The 1st of Yeo]arib, the feast of [weeks.] *14* [The 4th of Immer, the day of remembrance.

Frag. 4 *col.* VI   *1* The 6th of Jazir, the day of atonement. *2* The 4th of Hapizez, the feast of tents. *3 Blank 4* The sixth. Its festivals: *5* The 3rd of Yehezkiel, the passover. *6* The 1st of Gamul, the waving of the sheaf. *7* [The 3rd] of Ma^caziyah, the se[cond] passover. *8* The 1st of Malkiyah, the feast of w[eeks.] *9* [The] 4th of Yehez[kiel, the day of remembrance. *10* [The] 6th of Yaqim, [the day of atonement.] *11* [The 4th of Gamul, the feast of tents.]

4QCalendrical Document B^a (4Q321 [4QCalendrical Doc B^a])

Frag. 1 *col.* I   *1* [And the new moon enters the first (Sunday) of (the week of) Yedayah of the twel]fth (month), (which is) the second (Monday) of (the week of) Abiyah, the twenty-[fifth of the eighth (month). And the new moon enters] *2* [the third (Tuesday) of Miyyamim of the twelfth,] the third of Yaqim, the twenty-[fourth of the ninth. And the new moon enters the fourth (Wednesday)] *3* [of Shekanyah of the twe]lfth, the fifth (Thursday) of Immer, the twenty-third of the te[nth. And the new moon enters the sixth (Friday) of Ye]shabeb *4* [of the tenth,] the sixth of Ezekiel, the twenty-second of the eleventh month. And [the new moon enters the sabbath of] Petayyah *5* of the ninth,] the first (Monday) of Yoyarib, the twenty-second of the twelfth month. [And the new moon enters the second (Monday) of Delayah *6* [of the ninth. *Blank* The] second (Monday) of the first, the second of Malkiyah, the twentie[th of the first. And] the new moon enters *7* [the third (Tuesday) of Yarim of the sev]enth, the fourth (Wednesday) of Yeshu^ca, the twentieth of the second. And [the new moon enters the fifth (Thursday) of Ha]qoz of the ninth, *8* [the fifth (Thurs-

day) of Juppa, the nine]teenth of the third. And the new moon enters the sixth
(Friday) of El[iashib of the six[th, the sa]bbath of Hapizez,

Frag. 1 col. II   *1* [the eighteenth of the fourth. And the new moon enters the first
(Sunday) of Immer of the fifth,] the first of Ga[mul, the seventeenth of the
fifth.] *2* [And the new moon enters the second (Monday) of Ez]eki[el of the
fourth, the third (Tuesday) of Ye]dayah, the [seventeenth of the sixth. And the
new moon enters the fourth (Wednesday)] *3* of Ma^caziyah of the fourth, the
fourth [of Miyyamim of the fifth, the fifteenth] of the seventh. And the new
moon enters the fifth (Thursday) of She^corim of the second, *4* the sixth (Friday) of Shekanyah, the fifteen[th of the eighth. And the new] moon enters the
sabbath of Abiyah of the second, [the sabbath of Bilgah,] *5* the fourteenth of
the ninth. And (there is) a new moon [the first (Sunday)] of the ninth, and (a)
second new moon enters the third (Tuesday) of [Chazir, the thirty]*6*-first, the
seond of Petayyah, the thir[teenth of the tenth.] And the new moon enters the
fourth (Wednesday) of Yaqim, the twenty-[ninth,] *7* the [third (Tuesday) of
Delayah,] the second of the eleven[th. And the new] moon enters the sixth
(Friday) of Yeyarib, the twenty-eighth. The third (year). The first *8* [of the
sixth of Haqoz, of the

4QCalendrical Document E^b (4Q327 [4QCalendrical Doc E^b])

Frag. 1 col. I   *3* The sixteenth *4* falls on a sabbath. *5* The twenty-*6*third *7* falls on
a sabbath. *8* The thirty

Frag. 1 col. II   *1* falls on a sabbath. *2* On the twenty-*3*second *4* falls the feast *5* of
oil. *6* Af[ter the sabbath *7* [...] *8* the offering of

Frag. 2 col. I   *4* The twenty-*5*third *6* falls on a sabbath. *7* The thirtieth *8* falls on
a sabbath.

Frag. 2 col. II   *2* falls on a sabbath. *3* On the twenty-*4* eighth *5* a sabbath falls *6* on
it. After *7* the sabbath *8* the [fe]stival of [...]

Frag. 2 col. III   *1* falls [on a sabbath.] *2* The eleven[th] *3* falls on a sabbath. *4* The
eight*5*eenth falls on a sabbath. *6* The twenty-*7*fifth *8* falls on a sabbath. *9* The
second *10* of the month

3 Horoscopes

4QHoroscope (4Q186)

Frag. 1 *col.* I   *1-2* ... [...] *3 Blank* [...] *4* And the man who will be [...] *5* wide, circular [...] *6* pleasant and not the flesh of ... [...]

Frag. 1 *col.* II   *1* [...] impure *2* [...] a granite stone *3* [...] a man of [...] *4* [...]
secrets. *5* And his thighs are long and slender, and the toes of his feet are
6 slender and long. And he is in the second position. *7* His spirit has six (parts)
in the house of light and three in the pit of *8* darkness. And this is the sign in
which he was born: the foot of Taurus. He will be poor. And his animal is the
bull.

Frag. 1 *col.* III   *1* and ... [...] *2* and his head [...] *3* terrifying [...]. And his teeth
are of differing lengths (?). The fingers of *4* his hand are stumpy. His thighs are
fat and each one covered in hair. His spirit has *6* eight (parts) in the house [of
darkness] and one in the house of light.

Frag. 1 *col.* IV   *1* [...] there. These *2* [...] (he) will be in the middle of *5* [...] ...

Frag. 2 *col.* I   *1* rule. His eyes are of a colour between black and stripy. His beard
is *2* ... [...] and frizzy. The sound of his voice is simple. His teeth *3* are sharp
and well aligned. He is neither tall *4* nor short, and like that from his birth.
Then the fingers of his hands are slender *5* and long. His thighs are smooth and
the soles of his feet *6* [...] are even. His spirit *7* has eight (parts) [in the house
of light] in second position, and one *8* [in the house of darkness ...] And the
sign in which he was born is *9* [...] And his animal is [...] *10* [...] this [...]
11 [...] ... [...]

4QAramaic Horoscope (4Q561 [4QHor ar])

Frag. 1 *col.* I   *1* [...] and they will be mixed and will not be numerous. His eyes
(will be) *2* between clear and dark. His nose (will be) long *3* [and] handsome.
And his teeth (will be) well aligned. And his beard *4* will be thin and not abundant. His limbs (will be) *5* smooth and be[tween ma]imed and fat. *6* ... [...]
7 from the elbows (will be) prominent [...] *8* wide. And his thighs (will be) [be-
tween ...] *9* and fat. [And] the sole of his feet [:..] *10* lo[ng ...] His foot (will be)
[...] *11* [...] ... [...] *12* [...] ... [...]

Frag. 1 *col.* II   *1* The voice will be [...] *2* it will be full (?) [...] *3* it will not stretch
[...] *4* The hair of his beard (will be) abun[dant ...] *5* he will be between fat and

[...] 6 And they will be short [...] 7 as fat. His nails (will be) [...] 8 for his height [...] 9 ... [...] 10 And the foot (will be) [...] 11 ... [...]

Frag. 2   1 [...] will be reddish [...] 2 [...] will be clear and circular [...] 3 [...] for him. The hair of his head [...]

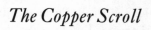

The Copper Scroll

Possibly the most mystifying of all the documents found in the caves of the Qumran region is the one known as *The Copper Scroll*. It was made of two separate sheets of copper, rolled up and oxidised right through. Its contents could only be determined after it had been carefully cut into parallel strips. The composition was the cause of fierce debate in the seventies and its precise meaning has still not been established.

Is it a legend from folklore about fictitious treasures or a catalogue of hiding-places for real treasures? If it is just folklore, how is it possible to account for the medium chosen for writing it down and the terse and apparently authentic nature of the formulas used? If it is a historical document, how are the vast amounts it mentions to be understood? What connection does it have with the other manuscripts found in the same cave? Is it a composition by the Qumran group or a document which was stored there later on?

There are difficulties in reading the text and the transcriptions are uncertain. It is impossibe to differentiate between some letters and others almost like them. The text is couched in uncouth Hebrew and there are the numerous mistakes of the copyist, and so on. All this confuses even more the task of understanding the document and of offering an intelligible translation.

In spite of all these problems, the text itself is very interesting and provides us with an endless mine of topographic and linguistic information since it is written in colloquial Hebrew which is definitely pre-Mishnaic.

The translation follows, in part, the transcription from the official edition by J. T. Milik in the series *Discoveries in the Judaean Desert of Jordan III*, pp. 211-302, and in part alternative readings suggested in other studies of the document. The question marks indicate places where the reading or the meaning seems particularly difficult.

The upper case Greek letters which the reader will find at the end of some lines of the first four columns appear just like that in the original. Their meaning still remains as mysterious as the remainder of the document.

3QCopper Scroll (3Q15)

Col. I *1* In the ruin which is in the valley, pass under *2* the steps leading to the East *3* forty cubits {...}: (there is) a chest of money and its total: *4* the weight of seventeen talents. *KEN* *5* In the sepulchral monument, in the third course: *6* one hundred gold ingots. In the great cistern of the courtyard *7* of the peristyle, in a hollow in the floor covered with sediment, *8* in front of the upper opening: nine hundred talents. *9* In the hill of Kochlit, tithe-vessels of the lord of the peoples and sacred vestments; *10* total of the tithes and of the treasure: a seventh of the *11* second tithe made unclean(?). Its opening lies on the edges of the Northern channel, *12* six cubits in the direction of the cave of the ablutions, *XAΓ* *13* In the plastered cistern of Manos, going down to the left, *14* at a height of three cubits from the bottom: silver, forty *15* *Blank* talents. *Blank*

Col. II *1* In the filled tank which is underneath the steps: *2* forty-two talents. *Blank* *HN* *3* In the cavity of the carpeted house of Yeshu(?), in the *4* third platform sixty-five gold ingots. *θE* *5* In the cellar which is in Matia's courtyard there is wood and in the middle of it *6* a cistern; in it there are containers with seventy talents of silver. *7* In the cistern which is in front of the Eastern Gate, *8* at a distance of fifteen cubits, there are vessels. *9* And in the gutter which is in it: ten talents. *ΔI* *10* In the cistern which is underneath the East wall, *11* in a spur of the rock: six silver bars *12* in the entrance, underneath the large threshold. *13* In the pool to the East of Kochlit, in the *14* North corner dig for four cubits: *15* twenty-two talents. *Blank*

Col. III *1* In the courtyard of [...], underneath the South corner, *2* at nine cubits: gold and silver *3* tithe-vessels, goblets, cups, jars, *4* vases; total: six hundred and nine. *5* Beneath the other, eastern corner, *6* dig for sixteen cubits: *7* forty talents of silver. *TP* *Blank* *8* In the tunnel which is in Milcham, to the North: *9* tithe-vessels and my garments. Its entrance is *10* beneath the western corner. *11* In the tomb which is in Milcham, to the North-*12*east, three cubits below the trap: *13* thirteen talents.

Col. IV *1* In the large cistern which is in [...,] in the pillar *2* of the North [...] fourteen talents. *ΣK* *3* In the channel which goes [up to ...,] when you go forward *4* fort[y-]one cubits: *5* fifty-five talents of silver. *Blank* *6* Between the two buildings which are in the valley of Akon, *7* at their midpoint, dig for three cubits: *8* there are there two jugs filled with silver. *9* In the earth tunnel which is on the edge of the Asla: *10* two hundred talents of silver. *11* In the eastern tunnel which is to the North of Kochlit: *13* seventy talents of silver. *14* In the (burial-)mound of the valley of Sekaka, dig *15* for a cubit: twelve talents of silver.

Col. v   *1* At the start of the water conduit [which is in] *2* Sekaka, to the North, bene[ath the] *3* large [stone,] dig for [three] cubits: *4* seven talents of silver. *5* In the fissure which is in Sekaka, to the East of *6* Solomon's cistern: tithe-vessels. *7* Close by, *8* above Solomon's trench, *9* sixty cubits up to the large rim, *10* dig for three cubits: *11* twenty-three talents of silver. *12* In the tomb which is in the ha-Kippa stream, *13* in the approach from Jericho to Sekaka, *14* dig for seven cubits: thirty-two talents.

Col. vi   *1* In the cave of the column with two *2* entrances, facing East, *3* in the North entrance, dig for *4* three cubits: there is an amphora there, *5* in it a book, under it *6 Blank* forty-two talents. *Blank 7* In the cavity at the base of *8* the rock, facing *9* East, dig in the entrance *10* for nine cubits: twenty-one talents. *11* In the queen's residence, on the *12* West side dig for twelve *13* cubits: twenty-seven talents. *14* In the burial-mound of the ford of the High

Col. vii   *1* Priest, dig *2* for nine [cubits]: twenty-two talents. In the channel of Qi[...] *4* in the North cistern [which is lar]ge *5* with four si[des ...] *6* measure twenty-four cubits: *7* four hundred talents. *Blank 8* In the cavity next to it, in the vicinity of *9* Beth-Chagosh, dig for six cubits: *10* six silver bars. *Blank 11* In Doq, under the East corner of the citadel, *12* dig for seven cubits: *13 Blank* twenty-two talents *Blank 14* Above the mouth of the water outlet of Koziba *15* dig for three cubits towards the parapet: *16* sixty talents (of silver), two talents of gold.

Col. viii   *1* In the channel which is on the road to the East of Beth-*2*Achsar, to the East of Achzar: *3* tithe-vessels and books and a bar of silver. *4* In the outer valley, in the middle of the pen, *5* in the stone, dig for seven-*6*teen cubits under it: silver *7* and gold, seventeen talents. *Blank 8* In the burial-mound which is at the entrance to the narrow pass of the potter, *9* dig for three cubits: four talents. *10* In the ploughed land which is in ha-Shave', facing the *11* West, in the southern part, in the cellar *12* facing North, dig *13* for twenty-four cubits: sixty-six talents. *14* In the irrigated land which is in ha-Shave', in the landmark which is there, dig for *15* eleven cubits: *Blank 16 Blank* seventy talents of silver.

Col. ix   *1* In the dovecote which is on the edge of Nataf, measure from the edge *2* thirteen cubits, dig for two, and under seven slabs: *3* four bars of two minas. *Blank 4* In the second estate, under the cellar facing *5* to the East, dig for eight cubits: *6 Blank* the tithe of Chasa, twenty-two and a half talents. *7* In the cellars of Choron, in the cellar facing the sea, *8* in the basin dig for sixteen cubits: *9 Blank* twenty-two talents. *Blank 10* In Qob^cah: a mina of silver, a sacred offering. *11* In the waterfalls near the edge of the conduit, *12* to the East of its outlet, dig *13 Blank* for seven cubits: nine talents. *14* In the cistern which is to the North of the mouth of narrow pass of Beth-*15*Tamar, in the rocky ground of Ger

Pela, *16* everything which is there is a sacred offering. *17* In the dovecote of the fortress of Nabata [...]

Col. X   *1* to the South of the second, on the second floor when going down *2* from above: nine talents. *Blank 3* In the waterwheel (?) of the irrigation ditches fed by the *4* great stream, at its foot: twelve talents. *5* In the cistern which is in Beth ha-Keren, going *6* to the left for ten paces: *Blank 7 Blank* sixty-two talents of silver. *Blank 8* In the water tank of the valley of Zok (?) on the West side, *9* there is a stone held in place by two supports (?); *10* it is the entrance: three hundred talents *11 Blank* of gold and twenty atonement vessels. *12* Under Absalom's memorial, on the *13* West side dig for twelve paces: *14 Blank* eighty talents. *Blank 15* In the basin of the latrines of Siloam, beneath the *16* water outlet: seventeen talents. *17* [In its pool,] at its four

Col. XI   *1* corners, tithe-vessels. Very near there, *2* underneath the South corner of the Portico, *3* in Zadok's tomb, underneath the column of the exedra *4* tithe-vessels of pine (?) resin and of the tithe of cassia (?) resin. Very near there, *5* in the concession at the tip of the rock, towards the West, *6* opposite Zadok's garden, under the large *7* slab which covers the water outlet: (a) sacred offering. *8* In the grave which is underneath the colonnades: forty talents. *9* in the grave of the sons of Ha'amata of Jericho (?), *10* there are vessels of myrtle (?) there, and of the tithe of pine (?) (resin). *11 Blank* Very close by, *12* in Beth Esdatain, in the cistern *13* at the entrance to the smallest water basin, *14* vessels of the tithe of aloes and of the tithe of white pine. *15* Very close by, *Blank 16* at the West entrance of the sepulchre room *17* there is a platform for the stove (?) above [...] nine-hundred [talents of silver,]

Col. XII   *1* five talents of gold. Sixty talents in its West entrance, *2* under the black stone. At its side, underneath the *3 Blank* threshold of the burial-chamber: forty-two talents. *4* On Mount Garizim, underneath the staircase of the upper tunnel: *5* a chest and all its contents and sixty talents of silver. *6* In the mouth of the spring of Beth-Sham: silver vessels and gold vessels *7* for the tithes; in total: six hundred talents. *8* In the large conduit of the burial-chamber up to Beth-Hakuk: *9* the total of its weight: seventy-two talents, twenty minas. *10* In the tunnel which is in Sechab, to the North of Kochlit, which opens towards the North *11* and has graves in its entrance: a copy of this text *12* and its explanation and its measurements and the inventory of everything, *13 Blank* item by item.

List of the Manuscripts from Qumran

This list contains all the manuscripts which come from the various caves of Qumran and about which information is at present available, both those published in full (with an indication of the work in which the *editio princeps* is to be found) as well as those published in part (with an indication of the work in which the reference occurs). This list extends and completes the «Lista de MSS procedentes de Qumrán (List of MSS which come from Qumran)» which I published in the periodical *Henoch* 11 (1989) 149-132. The complete catalogue of verses preserved in each biblical manuscript included in the *Henoch* list has been omitted here, whereas the non-biblical manuscripts, the subject of this book, are presented in a much more complete form.

This list fulfils a twofold purpose. It enables the reader to locate the editions of the non-biblical manuscripts which, together with the photographs, have formed the basis for the translations given. And it also provides a comprehensive view of all the material recovered from the various caves of Qumrân.

After the series number, the official abbreviation (in brackets) and the title given in the present book to each composition, the list indicates the *editio princeps*, or the partial edition, of each text, to which is added a very short description or identification of its contents. For the non-biblical texts, the pages in this book where the translation can be found are added [in square brackets]. Other, later editions are not included, nor are other studies (monographs or articles), even when these new editions or studies provide different readings or different restorations of the fragments. For this information the reader can refer to the corresponding sections in the *Introducción al estudio de los manuscritos de Qumrân*.

In this list, the manuscripts of the different Caves have been divided into biblical manuscripts and non-biblical manuscripts. The biblical manuscripts are catalogued in the sequence of the Hebrew bible. The non-biblical manuscripts have been arranged according to the official number of the series. An asterisk (*) marks those manuscripts of which a translation has been provided in this book. The other sign (o) denotes all those manuscripts of which so little has been preserved that there is no sense in translating them and for this reason they have not been included.

In the first reference to a book or article we give the complete bibliographical details; for later references, only the title in abbreviated form.

CAVE 1 Biblical Manuscripts

1Q1 (1QGen) *1QGenesis* D. Barthélemy, *Discoveries in the Judaean Desert* I (DJD I) (Oxford 1955), 49-50, pl. VIII. Fragmentary remains of Genesis.

1Q2 (1QExod) *1QExodus* D. Barthélemy DJD I, 50-51, pl. VIII. Fragmentary remains of Exodus.

1Q3 (1QpaleoLev) *1QLeviticus* D. Barthélemy, DJD I, 51-54, pls. VIII-IX. Barthélemy accepts that possibly they are three or four separate MSS, to which fragments 1-15, 16-21, 22-23 and 24 respectively belonged. M. D. McLean, *The Use and Development of Paleo-Hebrew in the Hellenistic and Roman Period* (Thesis, Harvard 1982), 41-42, distinguishes three different MSS: 1QpaleoLev^a: fragments 1-8.10-15; 1QpaleoLev^b: fragments 22-23; 1QpaleoNum: fragments 16-21. Fragmentary remains of Leviticus in palaeo-Hebrew script.

1Q4 (1QDeut^a) *1QDeuteronomy^a* D. Barthélemy, DJD I, 54-57, pl. IX. Fragmentary remains of Deuteronomy.

1Q5 (1QDeut^b) *1QDeuteronomy^b* D. Barthélemy, DJD I, 57-62, pl. X. Another fragmentary copy of Deuteronomy, with chap. 32 arranged stichometrically.

1Q6 (1QJud) *1QJudges* D. Barthélemy, DJD I, 62-64, pl. XI. Fragmentary remains of Judges.

1Q7 (1QSam) *1QSamuel* D. Barthélemy, DJD I, 64-65, pl. XI. Fragmentary remains of 1 and 2 Samuel.

1QIs^a *1QIsaiah^a* M. Burrows (ed.) with the assistance of J. C. Trever and W. H. Brownlee, *The Dead Sea Scrolls of St Mark's Monastery* (The American Schools of Oriental Research, New Haven 1950), vol. 1, pls. I-LIV. Complete text of Isaiah with a few small lacunae, mainly in the bottom edges.

1QIs^b *1QIsaiah^b* E. L. Sukenik, *'Osar ham-megillôt hag-genúzôt she-bîdê ha-'únibersitah ha-ʿibrit* (Bialik Foundation-The Hebrew University, Jerusalem 1954 4Q The Dead Sea Scrolls of the Hebrew University [The Magnes Press-The Hebrew University, Jerusalem 1955]); pls. 1-15. E. Puech, JJS 39 (1988) 55, n. 40, transcribes an as yet unpublished fragment which completes Is 44:23-25. Remains of another lengthy but fragmentary copy of Isaiah.

1Q8 (1QIs^b) *1QIsaiah^b* D. Barthélemy, DJD I, 66-68, pl. XII. Part of the foregoing manuscript of Isaiah, published by Sukenik.

1Q9 (1QEzek) *1QEzekiel* D. Barthélemy, DJD I, 68-69, pl. XII. One identified fragment of Ez and another, unidentified.

1Q10 (1QPs^a) *1QPsalms^a* D. Barthélemy, DJD I, 69-70, pl. XIII. Fragmentary copy of Pss, with the divine name written in palaeo-Hebrew characters.

1Q11 (1QPs^b) *1QPsalms^b* D. Barthélemy, DJD I, 71, pl. XIII. Another fragmentary copy of Pss, with the divine name written in palaeo-Hebrew characters.

1Q12 (1QPs^c) *1QPsalms^c* D. Barthélemy, DJD I, 71-72, pl. XIII. Remains of Ps 44.

1Q71 (1QDan^a) *1QDaniel^a* D. Barthélemy, DJD I, 150-151; J. C. Trever, 'Completion of the Publication of Some Fragments from Qumran Cave I', RQ 5/18

(1965) 323-336, pls. I-VII, esp. p. 330, pl. V. A single fragment, with remains of two columns, of Daniel.

1Q72 (1QDan^b) *1QDaniel^a*   D. Barthélemy, DJD I, 150-151; J. C. Trever, RQ 5/18 (1965) 330, pl. VI. Another fragmentary copy of Daniel.

1Q13 (1QPhyl) *1QPhylactery*   D. Barthélemy, DJD I, 72-76, fig. 10, pl. XIV. Remains of a phylactery which includes the text of the decalogue.

CAVE 1 Non-biblical manuscripts

* 1QpHab *1QHabakkuk Pesher*   M. Burrows (ed), *The Dead Sea Scrolls of St Mark's Monastery*, vol. 1, pls. LV-LXI. Commentary on Habakkuk 1:2-17; 2:1-20. [197-202]

* 1Q14 (1QpMic) *1QMicah Pesher*   J. T. Milik, DJD I, 77-80, pl. XV. Materials, 264-265. Remains of a commentary on Mic 1:2-5.5-7.8-9; 4:13(?); 6:14-16; 7:6(?).8-9(?).17. [193-194]

* 1Q15 (1QpZeph) *1QZephaniah Pesher*   J. T. Milik, DJD I, 80, pl. XV. Remains of a commentary on Zeph 1:18-2:2. [202]

* 1Q16 (1QpPs) *1QPsalms Pesher*   J. T. Milik, DJD I, 81-82, pl. XV. Remains of a commentary on Ps 57:1.4; Ps 68:12-13.36-27.30-31. [206]

* 1Q17 (1QJub^a) *1QJubilees^a*   J. T. Milik, DJD I, 82-83, pl. XVI. Copy of the Book of Jubilees. Remains of Jub 27:19-21. [245]

* 1Q18 (1QJub^b) *1QJubilees^b*   J. T. Milik, DJD I, 83-84, pl. XVI. Copy of the Book of Jubilees. Remains of Jub 35:8-10 and unidentified fragments. [245].

* 1Q19 (1QNoah) *1QNoah*   J. T. Milik, DJD I, 84-86, pl. XVI. Possibly a copy of the lost Book of Noah, related to the Book of Enoch. [263]

* 1Q19bis *1QNoah*   J. T. Milik, DJD I, 152; J. C. Trever, RQ 5/18 (1965) 334, pl. VII. Fragment 2 of the preceding MS. [263]

* 1QapGen ar (1Q20) *1QGenesis Apocryphon*   N. Avigad and Y. Yadin, *A Genesis Apocryphon. A Scroll from the Wilderness of Judaea* (Magnes Press-Heikhal hasefer, Jerusalem 1956). J. Greenfield – E. Qimron, 'The Genesis Apocryphon Col. XII', in: T. Muraoka (ed.), *Studies in Qumran Aramaic* (Abr-Nahrain Supplement 3) (Peeters, Louvain 1992), 70-77. Aramaic paraphrase of Genesis. Only cols. II, XIX-XXII have been published. [230-237]

* 1Q20 (1QapGen ar) *1QGenesis Apocryphon*   J. T. Milik, DJD I, 86-87, pl. XVII. 8 fragments of the foregoing MS, published as 'Apocalypse de Lamech'. [230]

* 1Q21 (1QTLevi ar) *1QAramaic Levi*   J. T. Milik, 'Le Testament de Lévi en araméen. Fragment de la grotte 4 de Qumrân', RB 62 (1955) 398-399; . –DJD I, 87-91, pl. XVII. Remains of an Aramaic work related to the Aramaic Testament of Levi from the Genizah, and to the Greek Testament of Levi, which forms part of the Testaments of the Twelve Patriarchs. [266]

* 1Q22 (1QDM) *1QWords of Moses*   J. T. Milik, DJD I, 91-97, pls. XVIII-XIX. E. Schuller, '4Q372 1: A Text about Joseph', in F. García Martínez (ed.), *The Texts*

of Qumran and the History of the Community. Vol. II (Paris 1990), 349-376. Remains of a Hebrew work, referred to as 'Words of Moses' (Dibrê Mosheh). It should be identical to 4Q373. [276-277]

* 1Q23 (1QEnGiants*ᵃ* ar) *1QBook of Giantsᵃ* J. T. Milik, DJD I, 97-98, Pl. XIX. Published as remains of an Aramaic apocryphon, they were later identified by Milik as a copy of the Book of Giants in *The Books of Enoch*, 301-302. [260]

o 1Q24 (1QEnGiants*ᵇ* ar) *1QBook of Giantsᵇ* J. T. Milik, DJD I, 99, pl. XX. Aramaic apocryphon; according to Milik, *The Books of Enoch*, 309, possibly another copy of the Book of Giants.

o 1Q25 (1QApocryphal Prophecy) J. T. Milik, DJD I, 100-101, pl. XX. Remains of 'an apocryphal prophecy' (?) in Hebrew.

o 1Q26 (Wisdom Apocryphon) J. T. Milik, DJD I, 101-102, pl. XX. Remains of an apocryphal work, of sapiential character, in Hebrew. According to P. W. Skehan, 'The Biblical Scrolls from Qumran and the Text of the Old Testament', BA 28 (1965) 90, there are another four copies of the same work in 4Q. (See *Sapiential Work Aᶠ*).

* 1Q27 (1QMyst) *1QMysteries* J. T. Milik, DJD I, 102-107, pls. XXI-XXII. 'Book of the Mysteries', a pseudepigraphical prophecy. [399-400]

* 1QS (1QS) *1QRule of the Community* M. Burrows (ed.), *The Dead Sea Scrolls of St Mark's Monastery*, vol. 2, fasc. 2: *The Manual of Discipline* (American Schools of Oriental Research, New Haven, 1951). Community Rule, cols. I-XI. [3-19]

* 1Q28a (1QSa) *1QRule of the Congregation* D. Barthélemy, DJD I, 108-118, pls. XXIII-XXIV. Appendix to the Community Rule, eschatological in content. [126-128]

* 1Q28b (1QSb) *1QRule of the Blessings.* J. T. Milik DJD I, 118-130, pls. XXV-XXIX. Collection of various blessings preserved as an appendix to the Community Rule and the Rule of the Congregation. [432-433]

* 1Q29 *1QLiturgy of the Three Tongues of Fire* J. T. Milik, DJD I, 130-132, pl. XXX. J. Strugnell, 'Moses-Pseudepigrapha at Qumran, 4Q375, 4Q376, and similar works', in: L. H. Schiffman (ed.), *Archaeology and History in the Dead Sea Scrolls* (JSP 8) (Sheffield 1990), 221-234. Remains of a work, liturgical in character, called Liturgy of the 'three tongues of fire'. It should be identical to the apocryphal composition (pseudo-Moses) preserved in 4Q376. [277-278]

* 1Q30 *1QLiturgical Text (?)* J. T. Milik, DJD I, 132-133, pl. XXX. Fragment of indeterminate character. [438]

* 1Q31 *1QLiturgical Text (?)* J. T. Milik, DJD I, 132-133, pl. XXX. Fragment of indeterminate character. [438]

o 1Q32 (1QJN ar) *1QNew Jerusalem* J. T. Milik, DJD I, 134-135, pl. XXXI. Minute remains of the Aramaic work: 'Description of the New Jerusalem'.

* 1QM (1QM) *1QWar Scroll* E. L. Sukenik, *The Dead Sea Scrolls of the Hebrew University*, pp. 1-19, pls. 16-34.47. Rule of the War of the sons of light against the sons of darkness. [95-115]

* 1Q33 (1QM) *1QWar Scroll*   J. T. Milik, DJD I, 135-136, pl. XXXI. Two fragments of the foregoing MS of the War Scroll. [113-115]

* 1Q34 (1QPrFêtes) *1QFestival Prayers*   J. T. Milik, DJD I, 136, pl. XXXI. Collection of prayers for the various feasts of the liturgical year. Two (4Q508-509) or three (4Q507) other copies of this work have been preserved. [411]

* 1Q34bis *1QFestival Prayers*   J. T. Milik, DJD I, 152-155; J. C. Trever, RQ 5/18 (1965) 328-329, pls. II-IV. Fragments of the foregoing MS, with remains of the prayers for the feasts of the New Year, Yom Kippur and Tabernacles (?). [411]

* 1QH (1QH^a) *1QHymns^a*   E. L. Sukenik, *The Dead Sea Scrolls of the Hebrew University*, cols. 1-18, frags. 1-66, pls. 35-58. Three additional fragments have been published by E. Puech, 'Un hymne essénien en partie retrouvé et les Béatitudes', RQ 13 (1988) 59-88, pl. III. E. Puech has also suggested a new arrangement and numbering of the fragments, 'Quelques aspects de la Restauration du Rouleau des Hymnes (1QH)', JJS 39 (1988) 38-55. The Hymns scroll, or *Hodayot*. [317-361]

* 1Q35 (1QH^b)*1QHymns^b*   J. T. Milik, DJD I, 136-138, pl. XXI. Remains of a second copy of the *Hodayot*; see E. Puech, 'Quelques aspects de la Restauration du Rouleau des Hymnes (1QH)', JJS 39 (1988) 39-40. [361-362]

o 1Q36 *1Qhymnic compositions (?)*   J. T. Milik, DJD I, 138-141, pl. XXXII. Remains of an unspecified hymn.

o 1Q37 *1Qhymnic compositions (?)*   J. T. Milik, DJD I, 141, pl. XXXIII. Remains of an unspecified hymn.

* 1Q38 *1QHymnic Compositions (?)*   J. T. Milik, DJD I, 142, pl. XXXIII. Remains of an unspecified hymn. [438]

* 1Q39 *1QHymnic Compositions (?)*   J. T. Milik, DJD I, 143, pl. XXXIII. Remains of an unspecified hymn. [438]

o 1Q40-69 *1Qunclassified fragments*   J. T. Milik, DJD I, 144-148, pls. XXXIII-XXXIV. Unidentified Hebrew and Aramaic fragments.

o 1Q70 *1Qunclassified fragments*   J. T. Milik, DJD I, 148-149, pl. XXXVII. J. C. Trever, RQ 5 (1964-1966) pl. VII. Unidentified fragments of papyri.

CAVE 2 Biblical manuscripts

2Q1 (2QGen) *2QGenesis*   M. Baillet, *Discoveries in the Judaean Desert of Jordan* III (Oxford 1962) (DJD III), 48-49, pl. X. Remains of a copy of Genesis.

2Q2 (2QExod^a) *2QExodus^a*   M. Baillet, DJD III, 49-52, pl. X. Remains of a copy of Exodus.

2Q3 (2QExod^b) *2QExodus^b*   M. Baillet, DJD III, 52-55, pl. XI. Remains of another copy of Exodus, with the divine name written in palaeo-Hebrew characters and in which Ex 34:10 comes immediately after Ex 19:9.

2Q4 (2QExod^c) *2QExodus^c*   M. Baillet, DJD III, 56, pl. XII. A single fragment of possibly another copy of Exodus.

2Q5 (2QpalaeoLev) *2QLeviticus* M. Baillet, DJD III, 56-57, pl. XII. A single fragment of Leviticus, written in palaeo-Hebrew characters.

2Q6 (2QNum*ᵃ*) *2QNumbersᵃ* M. Baillet, DJD III, 57-58, pl. XII. Two fragments with remains of a copy of Numbers.

2Q7 (2QNum*ᵇ*) *2QNumbersᵇ* M. Baillet, DJD III, 58-59, pl. XII. A fragment of another copy of Numbers.

2Q8 (2QNum*ᵇ*) *2QNumbersᶜ* M. Baillet, DJD III, 59, pl. XII. A fragment with remains of possibly another copy of Numbers.

2Q9 (2QNum*ᶜ*) *2QNumbersᵈ* (?)M. Baillet DJD III, 59-60, pl. XII. A fragment with remains of possibly another copy of Numbers.

2Q10 (2QDeut*ᵃ*) *2QDeuteronomyᵃ* M. Baillet, DJD III, 60-61, pl. XII. A fragment with remains of Dt 1.

2Q11 (2QDeut*ᵇ*) *2QDeuteronomyᵇ* M. Baillet, DJD III, 60-61, pl. XII. A fragment with remains of possibly another copy of Deuteronomy.

2Q12 (2QDeut*ᶜ*) *2QDeuteronomyᶜ* M. Baillet, DJD III, 61-62, pl. XII. A fragment with remains of Dt 10.

2Q13 (2QJer) *2QJeremiah* M. Baillet, DJD III, 62-69, pl. XIII. Remains of a copy of Jer related to MT.

2Q14 (2QPs) *2QPsalms* M. Baillet, DJD III, 69-71, pl. XIII. Remains of Pss 103 and 104, written partly in red ink.

2Q15 (2QJob) *2QJob* M. Baillet, DJD III, 71, pl. XIII. A fragment with remains of Job 3.

2Q16 (2QRuth*ᵃ*) *2QRuthᵃ* M. Baillet, DJD III, 71-74, pl. XIV. Remains of a copy of Ruth.

2Q17 (2QRuth*ᵇ*) *2QRuthᵇ* M. Baillet, DJD III, 74-75, pl. XV. Two fragments, one unidentified, of another copy of Ruth.

2Q18 (2QSir) *2QBen Sira* M. Baillet, DJD III, 75-77, pl. XV. Remains of chap. 6 of Ecclesiasticus (or Ben Sira) in Hebrew.

CAVE 2 Non-biblical manuscripts

* 2Q19 (2QJub*ᵃ*) *2QJubileesᵃ* M. Baillet, DJD III, 77-78, pl. X. A single fragment of the Book of Jubilees, with remains of Jub 23:7-8. [244]

* 2Q20 (2QJub*ᵇ*) *2QJubileesᵇ* M. Baillet, DJD III, 78-79, pl. XV. Three fragments of another copy of the Book of Jubilees. Only one has been identified. [245]

* 2Q21 (2QapMoses?) *2QApocryphon of Moses* M. Baillet, DJD III, 79-81, pl. XV. Remains of a dialogue of Moses with God. [281]

* 2Q22 (2QapDavid?) *2QApocryphon of David?* M. Baillet, DJD III, 81-82, pl. XV. Remains of an 'Apocryphon of David' (?) or of another 'Apocryphon of Moses', which Baillet completes with another copy from Cave 4, 4Q373, still unpublished. [224]

o 2Q23 (2QapProph) M. Baillet DJD III, 82-84, pl. XV. Remains of an 'Apocryphal prophecy'.

* 2Q24 (2QJN ar) *2QNew Jerusalem*   M. Baillet, 'Fragments araméens de Qumrân 2. Description de la Jérusalem Nouvelle', RB 62 (1955) 225-245, pls. II-III; . – DJD III, 84-89, pl. XV. Remains of an Aramaic work, 'Description of the New Jerusalem'. [129]

* 2Q25 *2Qjuridical text*   M. Baillet, DJD III, 90, pl. XVI. Remains of a halakhic work. [86]

o 2Q26 (2QEnGiants ar) *2QBook of Giants*   M. Baillet, DJD III, 90-91. A single fragment in Aramaic, published as a fragment of a ritual (?) and later identified by J. T. Milik, *The Books of Enoch*, 334, as another copy of the Book of the Giants.

o 2Q27-33 *2Qunclassified fragments*   M. Baillet, DJD III, 91-93, pl. XVII. Fragments of unidentified works.

CAVE 3 Biblical manuscripts

3Q1 (3QEz) *3QEzekiel*   M. Baillet, DJD III, 94, pl. XVIII. Fragments with remains of Ez 16.

3Q2 (3QPs) *3QPsalms*   M. Baillet, DJD III, 94, pl. XVIII. Fragments with remains of Ps 2.

3Q3 (3QLam) *3QLamentations*   M. Baillet, DJD III, 95, pl. XVIII. Remains of a copy of Lamentations with the divine name written in palaeo-Hebrew characters.

CAVE 3 Non-biblical manuscripts

* 3Q4 (3QpIsa) *3QIsaiah Pesher*   M. Baillet, DJD III, 95-96, pl. XVIII. Remains of a pesher on Isaiah. [185]

* 3Q5 (3QJub) *3QJubilees*   M. Baillet, DJD III, 96-98, pl. XVIII. Published as an 'Apocryphal prophecy'; identified as a copy of the Book of Jubilees, by A. Rofé, 'Further Manuscript Fragments of the Jubilees in the Third Cave of Qumran', Tarbiz 34 (1965) 333-336 and R. Deichgräber, 'Fragmente einer Jubiläen-Handschrift aus Höhle 3 von Qumran', RQ 5 (1964-65) 415-422. Three of the seven fragments have been identified as a copy of Jubilees. [244]

* 3Q6 *3QHymn*   M. Baillet, DJD III, 98, pl. XVIII. Hymn of praise. [401]

* 3Q7 (3QTJuda?) *3QTestament of Judah* (?)   M. Baillet, DJD III, 99, pl. XVIII. Published as 'Apocryphon which mentions the angel of the presence'; identified by J. T. Milik, 'Écrits préesséniens de Qumrân', 98, as a Hebrew version of the Aramaic Testament of Judah. [265]

o 3Q8 *3Qunclassified fragments*   M. Baillet, DJD III, 100, pl. XIX. 'Text which mentions an angel of peace'.

o 3Q9 *3Qsectarian text* (?)   M. Baillet, DJD III, 100-101, pl. XIX.

o 3Q10-14 *3Qunclassified fragments*   M. Baillet, DJD III, 101-105, pl. XIX. Unidentified texts.

* 3Q15 *3QCopper Scroll* J. M. Allegro, *The Treasure of the Copper Scroll* (London 1960); J. T. Milik, DJD III, 211-302, pls. XLVIII–LXXI. Copper Scroll. [461-463]

CAVE 4 Biblical manuscripts

4Q1 (4QGen-Exod*ᵃ*) *4QGenesis-Exodusᵃ* J. R. Davila, *Unpublished Pentateuchal manuscripts from Cave IV, Qumran: 4QGenExodᵃ, 4QGenᵇ⁻ʰʲ⁻ᵏ*, Diss. Harvard 1988, 11-61. Copy which contains combined remains of Genesis and Exodus.

4Q2 (4QGenᵇ) *4QGenesisᵇ* J. R. Davila, *Unpublished Pentateuchal manuscripts*, 62-74. Copy of Gn, text identical to MT. Origin uncertain.

4Q3 (4QGenᶜ) *4QGenesisᶜ* J. R. Davila, *Unpublished Pentateuchal manuscripts*, 75-89. Remains of Gn 40-41.

4Q4 (4QGenᵈ) *4QGenesisᵈ* J. R. Davila, *Unpublished Pentateuchal manuscripts*, 90-98. A single fragment with remains of Gn 1.

4Q5 (4QGenᵉ) *4QGenesisᵉ* J. R. Davila, *Unpublished Pentateuchal manuscripts*, 99-116. Copy of Gn from a textual type similar to MT and the Samaritan text.

4Q6 (4QGenᶠ) *4QGenesisᶠ* J. R. Davila, *Unpublished Pentateuchal manuscripts*, 117-127. Remains of one column with part of Gn 48.

4Q7 (4QGenᵍ) *4QGenesisᵍ* J. R. Davila, *Unpublished Pentateuchal manuscripts*, 128-137. Two fragments of Gn 1-2

4Q8 (4QGenʰ) *4QGenesisʰ* J. R. Davila, *Unpublished Pentateuchal manuscripts*, 138-142. Minute fragment of Gn 1, 2 and 12.

4Q9 (4QGenʲ) *4QGenesisʲ* J. R. Davila, *Unpublished Pentateuchal manuscripts*, 143-183. Copy of Gn of a textual type close to the Samaritan text.

4Q10 (4QGenᵏ) *4QGenesisʲ* J. R. Davila, *Unpublished Pentateuchal manuscripts*, 164-173. Small fragments with remains of Gn 1-3.

4Q11 (4QpaleoGen-Exodˡ) *4QGenesis-Exodusˡ* P. W. Skehan, E. Ulrich, J. E. Sanderson, *Discoveries in the Judaean Desert IX* (= DJD IX), Oxford 1992, 17-50, pl. I–VI. A manuscript in palaeo-Hebrew script with remains of de Gn 50:26 and Exod 1-36.

4Q12 (4QpaleoGenᵐ) *4QGenesisᵐ* DJD IX, 51-52, pl. VI. A fragment with remains of Gn 26 in palaeo-Hebrew script.

4Q13 (4QExodᵇ) *4QExodusᵇ* F. M. Cross, 'Le travail d'édition', 56; . – The Ancient Library of Qumran, 137, pl. 18; P. W. Skehan, SDB, 809. Fragments with remains of Ex 1-5.

4Q14 (4QExodᶜ) *4QExodusᶜ* F. M. Cross, 'The Song of the Sea and Canaanite Myth', Journal for Theology and the Church 5 (1968) 1-25. Large fragments with remains of Ex 9-18.

4Q15 (4QExodᵈ) *4QExodusᵈ* F. M. Cross, 'The Song of the Sea'. Fragments with remains of Ex 1-5.

4Q16 (4QExodᵉ) *4QExodusᵉ* A single fragment of five lines with remains of Ex 13.

4Q17 (4QExod-Lev*f*) *4QExodus-Leviticus*f F. M. Cross, *The Ancient Library of Qumran*, 33.121; . – Scrolls from the Wilderness of the Dead Sea, 12.21. It might be most ancient of the biblical manuscripts to come from Qumran, copied towards 250 BC. Its contents are practically identical to MT. Remains of Ex 38–Lev 2.

4Q18 (4QExod*g*) Part of a column of eight lines with remains of Ex 13.

4Q19 (4QExod*h*) Minute fragment with remains of three lines fom Ex 6:3-5.

4Q20 (4QExod*j*) Fragment with remains of Ex 7-8.

4Q21 (4QExod*k*) Minute fragment with remains of Ex 36:9-10.

4Q22 (4QpaleoExod*m*) P. W. Skehan 'Exodus in the Samaritan Recension from Qumran', JBL 74 (1955) 182-187; photographs in BA 28 (1965) 98; *Scrolls from the Wilderness of the Dead Sea*, 26; SDB 51, 887-890. J. E. Sanderson, *An Exodus Scroll from Qumran* (HSS 30) (Atlanta 1986). DJD IX, 51-130, pl. VII-XXXIII. Another lengthy copy of Exodus in palaeo-Hebrew characters, Samaritan in type.

4Q23 (4QLev-Num*a*) *4QLeviticus-Numbers*a Very many fragments of a MS which contains remains of Lev and of Num.

4Q24 (4QLev*b*) *4QLeviticus*c Another copy of Lev, with remains of Lev 1-3 and 22-25.

4Q25 (4QLev*c*) *4QLeviticus*c E. Tov, *Festschrift Milgrom*. Fragments with remains of Lev 3-4, one of them written by two different hands.

4Q26 (4QLev*d*) *4QLeviticus*d E. Tov, '4QLev*d* (4Q26)', in F. García Martínez et al. (eds.), *The Scriptures and The Scrolls. Studies in Honour of A. S. van der Woude on the Occasion of his 65th Birthday* (VTsup 49) (Brill, Leiden 1992), 1-5. Four small fragments of another copy of Lev. Numerous fragments, small in size and in a bad state of preservation, of another copy of Lev, with remains of Lev 14-15.

4Q27 (4QNum*b*) *4QNumbers*b N. R. Jastram, *The Book of Numbers from Qumran Cave IV (4QNum*b*)*, Diss. Harvard 1990. Lengthy copy, of an expansionist type, of Nm, of which remains of 38 columns have been preserved.

4Q28 (4QDeut*a*) *4QDeuteronomy*a S. A. White, *A Critical Edition of Seven Deuteronomy Manuscripts*, Diss. Harvard 1988, 8-18; . – 'Three Deuteronomy Manuscripts from Cave 4, Qumran', JBL 112 (1993) 23-28. A fragment with remains of Dt 23-24.

4Q29 (4QDeut*b*) *4QDeuteronomy*b J. A. Duncan, *A Critical Edition of Deuteronomy Manuscripts from Qumran Cave IV: 4QDt*b*, 4QDt*e*, 4QDt*h*, 4QDt*j*, 4QDt*k*, 4QDt*l**, Diss. Harvard 1989, 9-31. Four fragments with remains of Dt 29-32.

4Q30 (4QDeut*c*) *4QDeuteronomy*c S. A. White, *A Critical Edition*, 19-132. Lengthy copy of Dt, of a textual type related to LXX.

4Q31 (4QDeut*d*) *4QDeuteronomy*d S. A. White, *A Critical Edition*, 133-154. A fragment with remains of Dt 2-3.

4Q32 (4QDeut*e*) *4QDeuteronomy*e J. A. Duncan, *A Critical Edition of Deuteronomy*

Manuscripts, 32-49; . – 'Three Deuteronomy Manuscripts from Cave 4, Qumran', JBL 112 (1993) 28-34. The three main fragments contain remains of Dt 7-8.

4Q33 (4QDeut*f*) *4QDeuteronomy*f   S. A. White, *A Critical Edition*, 155-214. 'Proto-rabbinic' copy of Dt.

4Q34 (4QDeut*g*) *4QDeuteronomy*g   S. A. White, *A Critical Edition*, 215-240. . – 'Three Deuteronomy Manuscripts from Cave 4, Qumran', JBL 112 (1993) 35-42. Copy of Dt of a masoretic type.

4Q35 (4QDeut*h*) *4QDeuteronomy*h   J. A. Duncan, *A Critical Edition of Deuteronomy Manuscripts*, 50-77. E. Eshel and M. Stone, 'A New-fragment of 4QDeut*h*', JBL 112 (1993), 487-489. Copy of Dt of a septuagintal type, with remains of Dt 1-2, 31 and 33.

4Q36 (4QDeut*i*) *4QDeuteronomy*i   S. A. White, *A Critical Edition*, 241-262. Another copy of Dt.

4Q37 (4QDeut*j*) *4QDeuteronomy*j   J. A. Duncan, *A Critical Edition of Deuteronomy Manuscripts*, 78-114. The manuscript contains various passages from Dt and Ex 12:43-13:5, which follows Dt 11:21, and because of that the editor is inclined to consider it as a kind of catena rather than as a biblical text, see 'Considerations of 4QDt*j* in Light of the "All Souls Deuteronomy" and Cave 4 Phylactery Texts', in *The Madrid Qumran Congress*, 199-215 and 356-361 (plates).

4Q38 (4QDeut*k*) *4QDeuteronomy*k   J. A. Duncan, *A Critical Edition of Deuteronomy Manuscripts*, 115-154. Eleven fragments which may could belong to two different copies of Dt. The preserved remains come from Dt 5, 11, 19, 20, 23, 25, 26 and 32.

4Q39 (4QDeut*l*) *4QDeuteronomy*l   J. A. Duncan, *A Critical Edition of Deuteronomy Manuscripts*, 155-168. Eight tiny-sized fragments of another copy of Dt.

4Q40 (4QDeut*m*) *4QDeuteronomy*m   F. García Martínez, 'Les manuscrits du désert de Juda et le Deutéronome', in F. García Martínez et al. (eds.), *Studies in Deuteronomy* (SVT 53) (Leiden 1994), 66-69. Three fragments with remains of Dt 3 and 7, written with plene spelling.

4Q41 (4QDeut*n*) *4QDeuteronomy*n   F. M. Cross, *Scrolls from the Wilderness of the Dead Sea*, 20.31-32; H. Stegemann, 'Weitere Stücke von 4QpPsalm 37, von 4QPatriarchal Blessings, und Hinweis auf eine unededierte Handschrift aus Höhle 4Q mit Exzerpten aus dem Deuteronomium', RQ 6/22 (1967) 217-227; S. A. White, *A Critical Edition*, 263-299; . – 'The All Souls Deuteronomy and the Decalogue', JBL 109 (1990), 193-206. The famous 'All Souls Deuteronomy', possibly a text with excerpts from Dt, see S. A. White, '4QDt*n*: Biblical Manuscript or Excerpted Text?', in H. Attridge et al. (eds.), *Of Scribes and Scrolls* (Lanham 1990), 13-20; E. Eshel, '4QDeut*n* – A Text That Has Undergone Harmonistic Editing', HUCA 62 (1991), 117-154.

4Q42 (4QDt*o*) *4QDeuteronomy*o   F. García Martínez, 'Les manuscrits du désert de

Juda et le Deutéronome', 69-72. Fifteen tiny-sized fragments of another copy of Dt.

4Q43 (4QDt*^{b}*) *4QDeuteronomy*^{b} F. García Martínez, 'Les manuscrits du désert de Juda et le Deutéronome', 72-75. Four small fragments of another copy of Dt, with remains of Dt 5 and 14.

4Q44 (4QDeut^Q) *4QDeuteronomy*^{b} P. W. Skehan, 'A Fragment of the 'Song of Moses' (Deut 32) from Qumran' BASOR 136 (1954) 12-15; – 'Qumran Manuscripts and Textual Criticism' in *Volume du congrès, Strasbourg 1956* (VTSup 4) (Leiden 1957), 150. Remains of the 'Song of Moses'.

4Q45 (4QpaleoDt^r) *4QpaleoDeuteronomy*^{r} DJD IX, 131-152, pl. XXXIV-XXXVI. Abundant fragments of another copy of Deuteronomy written in palaeo-Hebrew characters.

4Q46 (4QpaleoDeut^s) *4QpaleoDeuteronomy*^{s} DJD IX, 153-154, pl. XXXVII. A single fragment in palaeo-Hebrew of Dt 26.

4Q47 (4QJosh^a) *4QJoshua*^{b} E. Ulrich, '4QJoshua^a and Joshua's First Altar in the Promised Land', in G. J. Brooke (ed.), *New Qumran Texts and Studies. Proceedings of the First Meeting of the International Organization, Paris 1992* (STDJ 15) (Leiden 1994), 89-104, Pl. 4-6. Fragments of a copy of Joshua with remains of Josh 2-10.

4Q48 (4QJos^b) *4QJoshua*^{b} E. Tov, '4QJosh^b', in Z. J. Kapera, *Intertestamental Essays in Honour of Józef Tadeusz Milik* (Qumranica Mogilanensia 6) (Kraków 1992), 205-212. Five fragments of another copy of Joshua with remains of Jos 2-4 and 17.

4Q49 (4QJud^a) *4QJudges*^{a} J. Trebolle, 'Textual variants in 4QJudg^a and the textual and editorial history of the book of Judges', in *The Texts of Qumran and the History of the Community*. Vol. I, 229-245. Remains of a copy of Judges.

4Q50 (4QJud^b) *4QJudges*^{b} J. Trebolle, 'Édition préliminaire de 4QJudges^b. Contribution des manuscrits Qumrâniens des Juges à l'étude textuelle et littéraire de ce livre'. In: E. Puech and F. García Martínez (eds.), *Mémorial Jean Starcky* Vol. I (Gabalda, Paris 1991) 79-100. Two fragments of another copy of Judges.

4Q51 (4QSam^a) *4QSamuel*^{a} F. M. Cross, 'A New Qumran Biblical Fragment Related to the Original Hebrew underlying the Septuagint', BASOR 132 (1953) 15-26; . – 'The Oldest Manuscript from Qumran', JBL 74 (1955) 165, n. 40; . – 'The Ammonite Oppression of the Tribes of Gad and Reuben: Missing Verses from 1 Sam 11 Found in 4QSamuel^a', in: E. Tov (ed.), *The Hebrew and Greek Texts of Samuel. 1980 Proceedings IOSCS* (Jerusalem 1980), 105-116. E. Ch. Ulrich, *The Qumran Text of Samuel and Josephus* (HSM 19) (Chico 1978) analyses all the variants and on p. 271 indicates the contents of the whole MS. Copy of 1 and 2 Samuel.

4Q52 (4QSam^b) *4QSamuel*^{b} F. M. Cross, 'The Oldest Manuscript from Qumran', JBL 74 (1955) 147-172, pl. 6; . – The Ancient Library of Qumran, pl. 18. Remains of another copy of Samuel.

4Q53 (4QSam^c) *4QSamuel^c*   E. Ch. Ulrich, '4QSamuel^c: A Fragmentary Manuscript of 2 Samuel 14-15 fom the Scribe of the Serek Hay-yahad (1QS)', BASOR
235 (1979) 1-25, pls. 4-5. Remains of a copy of 1 and 2 Samuel.

4Q54 (4QKgs) *4QKings*   J. Trebolle, '4QKings (4Q54): A Preliminary Edition', in
J. Trebolle–L. Vegas, (eds.), *The Madrid Qumran Congress*, 229-246. Remains
of the only copy of 1 Kings preserved.

4Q55 (4QIsa^a) *4QIsaiah^a*   J. Muilenburg, 'Fragments of Another Qumran Isaiah
Scroll', BASOR 135 (1954) 28-32. P. W. Skehan, SDB 51, 811 provides a list with
detailed contents of all the MSS of Isa found at Qumran; all the variants preserved have been collected in F. J. Morrow, *The Text of Isaiah at Qumran*, Diss.
The Catholic University of America 1973.

4Q56 (4QIsa^b) *4QIsaiah^b*   P. W. Skehan, SDB 51, 810-811. Another copy of Isa.

4Q57 (4QIsa^c) *4QIsaiah^c*   P. W. Skehan, 'The Text of Isaias at Qumran', CBQ 17
(1955) 158-163; SDB 51, 811.

4Q58 (4QIsa^d) *4QIsaiah^d*   P. W. Skehan, SDB 51, 811.

4Q59 (4QIsa^e) *4QIsaiah^e*   P. W. Skehan, SDB 51, 811.

4Q60 (4QIsa^f) *4QIsaiah^f*   P. W. Skehan, SDB 51, 811.

4Q61 (4QIsa^g) *4QIsaiah^g*   P. W. Skehan, SDB 51, 811.

4Q62 (4QIsa^h) *4QIsaiah^h*   P. W. Skehan, SDB 51, 811. Although numbered as a
single MS, this copy of Isa seems, in fact, to comprise small fragments of 5 different manuscripts.

4Q63 (4QIsa^j) *4QIsaiah^j*   P. W. Skehan, SDB 51, 811. A fragment of Isa 1.

4Q64 (4QIsa^k) *4QIsaiah^k*   P. W. Skehan, SDB 51, 811.

4Q65 (4QIsa^l) *4QIsaiah^l*   P. W. Skehan, SDB 51, 811.

4Q66 (4QIsa^m) *4QIsaiah^m*   P. W. Skehan, SDB 51, 811. A fragment of Isa 61.

4Q67 (4QIsa^n) *4QIsaiah^n*   P. W. Skehan, SDB 51, 811. A fragment of Isa 58.

4Q68 (4QIsa^o) *4QIsaiah^o*   P. W. Skehan, SDB 51, 811.

4Q69 (4QpapIsa^p) *4QIsaiah^p*   P. W. Skehan, SDB 51, 811. Papyrus with remains
of Isa 5.

4Q69a (4QIsa^Q) *4QIsaiah^Q*   P. W. Skehan, SDB 51, 811. A fragment of Isa 54.

4Q69b (4QIsa^r) *4QIsaiah^r*   Details unknown.

4Q70 (4QJer^a) *4QJeremiah^a*   F. M. Cross, *The Ancient Library of Qumran*, 33; J. G.
Janzen, *Studies in the Text of Jeremiah* (HSM 6) (Harvard University, Cambridge
1973) 173-184. E. Tov, 'The Jeremiah Scrolls from Cave 4' in *The Texts of
Qumran and the History of the Community*. Vol. I, pp. 189-206, modifies the data
provided by Janzen. Copy of Jer of LXX type.

4Q71 (4QJer^b) *4QJeremiah^b*   F. M. Cross, *The Ancient Library of Qumran*, 139-140;
J. G. Janzen, *Studies in the Text of Jeremiah*. E. Tov, 'The Jeremiah Scrolls',
suggests attributing the three fragments previously attributed to 4QJer^b to three
different MSS; 4Q71 corresponds to the old 4QJer^b 1. A fragment of Jer 9.

4Q71a (4QJer^d) *4QJeremiah^d*   [previously denoted by 4QJer^b 2]. E. Tov, 'Three
Fragments of Jeremiah from Qumran Cave 4', RQ 15/60 (1992), 538-540. A
fragment of Jer 43.

4Q71b (4QJer^e) *4QJeremiah^e* [previously denoted by 4QJer^b 3]. E. Tov, 'Three Fragments of Jeremiah from Qumran Cave 4', RQ 15/60 (1992), 540-541. A fragment of Jer 50.

4Q72 (4QJer^e) *4QJeremiah^e* E. Tov, '4QJer^e (4Q72)', in: G. Norton et al. (eds.), *Tradition of the Text* (Göttingen 1991), 248-276, pl. I-VII. The longest copy of Jer.

4Q73 (4QEz^a) *4QEzekiel^a* J. Lust, 'Ezekiel Manuscripts in Qumran', in: J. Lust (ed.), *Ezekiel and his Book: Textual and Literary Criticism and their Interrelation* (BETL 74) (Leuven 1986) 90-100; photograph in W. Zimmerli, *Ezekiel* (Hermeneia) (Fortress, Phladelphia, vol. I, 1979, vol. II, 1983); corrections of readings in: L. A. Sinclair, 'A Qumran Biblical Fragment: 4QEz^a (Ezek 10,17-11,1)', RQ 14/53 (1989) 99-105 and E. Puech, '4QEz^a: Note additionnelle', RQ 14/53 (1989) 107-108.

4Q74 (4QEz^b) *4QEzekiel^b* J. Lust, 'Ezekiel Manuscripts in Qumran'. Remains of chap. 1 of Ez.

4Q75 (4QEz^c) *4QEzekiel^c* A single minute fragment, with remains of Ez 24:2-3.

4Q76 (4QXII^a) *4QMinor Prophets^a* R. E. Fuller, *The Minor Prophets manuscript from Qumrân, Cave 4*, Diss. Harvard 1988, 5-38. The MSS would have been copied between 150-125 B. C., conatins remains of Zech, Mal and Jon, and would occupy a position midway between MT and the LXX.

4Q77 (4QXII^b) *4QMinor Prophets^b* R. E. Fuller, *The Minor Prophets manuscript from Qumrân*, 39-53. Only six small fragments have been preserved, with remains of Zeph and Hag.

4Q78 (4QXII^c) *4QMinor Prophets^c* M. Testuz, 'Deux fragments inédits des manuscripts de la Mer Morte', Semitica 5 (1955) 37-38. R. E. Fuller, *The Minor Prophets manuscript from Qumrân*, 55-104. Remains of Hosea, Joel, Amos, Zephaniah and Malachi. The manuscript cotains many mistakes, but also very many original readings.

4Q79 (4QXII^d) *4QMinor Prophets^d* R. E. Fuller, *The Minor Prophets manuscript from Qumrân*, 105-115. A single fragment from the beginning of the roll, with remains of Hos 1:7-2:5.

4Q80 (4QXII^e) *4QMinor Prophets^e* R. E. Fuller, *The Minor Prophets manuscript from Qumrân*, 116-140. Remains, almost exclusively from Zechariah. The manuscript is of a textual type related to the LXX.

4Q81 (4QXII^f) *4QMinor Prophets^f* R. E. Fuller, *The Minor Prophets manuscript from Qumrân*, 141-150. A fragment of Jonah and another of Micah.

4Q82 (4QXII^g) *4QMinor Prophets^g* P. W. Skehan, 'Le travail d'édition', RB 63 (1956) 59. Remains of Hosea and Nahum.

4Q83 (4QPs^a) *4QPsalms^a* P. W. Skehan, 'The Qumran Manuscripts and Textual Criticism', 218; .–SDB 51, 813-817; .–'Qumran and Old Testament Criticism' in M. Delcore (ed.), *Qumrân. Sa piété, sa théologie et son milieu* (BETL 46) (Paris-Leuven 1988) 173-182, collation of variants of all the Psalms MSS from 4Q; G. H. Wilson, *The Editing of the Hebrew Psalter* (SBLDS 76) (Chico 1985) 96-98.

4Q84 (4QPs^b) *4QPsalms^b* P. W. Skehan, 'A Psalm Manuscript from Qumran (4QPs^b)', CBQ 26 (1964) 313-322; . – SDB 51, 813-817; . – 'Qumran and Old Testament Criticism', 173-182; G. H. Wilson, *The Editing of the Hebrew Psalter*, 98-101.

4Q85 (4QPs^c) *4QPsalms^c* P. W. Skehan, SDB 51, 813-817; . – 'Qumran and Old Testament Criticism', 173-182; G. H. Wilson, *The Editing of the Hebrew Psalter*, 101-103.

4Q86 (4QPs^d) *4QPsalms^d* P. W. Skehan, SDB 51, 813-817; . – 'Qumran and Old Testament Criticism', 173-182; G. H. Wilson, *The Editing of the Hebrew Psalter*, 103.

4Q87 (4QPs^e) *4QPsalms^e* P. W. Skehan, SDB 51, 813-817; . – 'Qumran and Old Testament Criticism', 173-182; G. H. Wilson, *The Editing of the Hebrew Psalter*, 103-105.

* 4Q88 (4QPs^f) *4QPsalms^f* J. Starcky, 'Psaume apocryphes de la grotte 4 de Qumrân (4QPs^f VII-X)', RB 73 (1966) 350-371, pl. XVIII; P. W. Skehan, SDB 51, 813-817; . – 'Qumran and Old Testament Criticism', 173-182; G. H. Wilson, *The Editing of the Hebrew Psalter*, 105-106. [303-304]

4Q89 (4QPs^g) *4QPsalms^g* P. W. Skehan, SDB 51, 813-817; . – 'Qumran and Old Testament Criticism', 173-182. Remains of Ps 119.

4Q90 (4QPs^h) *4QPsalms^h* P. W. Skehan, SDB 51, 813-817; . – 'Qumran and Old Testament Criticism', 173-182. Remains of Ps 119.

4Q91 (4QPs^j) *4QPsalms^j* P. W. Skehan, SDB 51, 813-817; . – 'Qumran and Old Testament Criticism', 173-182.

4Q92 (4QPs^k) *4QPsalms^k* P. W. Skehan, SDB 51, 813-817; . – 'Qumran and Old Testament Criticism', 173-182.

4Q93 (4QPs^l) *4QPsalms^l* P. W. Skehan, SDB 51, 813-817; . – 'Qumran and Old Testament Criticism', 173-182. Remains of Ps 104.

4Q94 (4QPs^m) *4QPsalms^m* P. W. Skehan, SDB 51, 813-817; . – 'Qumran and Old Testament Criticism', 173-182.

4Q95 (4QPs^n) *4QPsalms^n* P. W. Skehan, SDB 51, 813-817; . – 'Qumran and Old Testament Criticism', 173-182.

4Q96 (4QPs^o) *4QPsalms^o* P. W. Skehan, SDB 51, 813-817; . – 'Qumran and Old Testament Criticism', 173-182.

4Q97 (4QPs^p) *4QPsalms^p* P. W. Skehan, SDB 51, 813-817; . – 'Qumran and Old Testament Criticism', 173-182. Remains of Ps 143.

4Q98 (4QPs^Q) *4QPsalms^Q* J. T. Milik, 'Deux documents inédits du Désert de Juda', Biblica 38 (1957) 245-255, pl. I; P. W. Skehan, SDB 51, 813-817; . – 'Qumran and Old Testament Criticism', 173-182.

4Q98a (4QPs^r) *4QPsalms^r* P. W. Skehan, SDB 51, 813-817; . – 'Qumran and Old Testament Criticism', 173-182.

4Q98b (4QPs^s) *4QPsalms^s* P. W. Skehan, SDB 51, 813-817; . – 'Qumran and Old Testament Criticism', 173-182; . – 'Gleanings from Psalm Texts from Qumran' in: A. Caquot and M. Delcor (eds.), *Mélanges bibliques et orientaux en l'honneur de M. Henri Cazelles* (AOAT 212) (Kevelaer/Neukirchen-Vluyn 1981) 445-448.

4Q98c (4QPs. frg. 1) *4QPsalms fragment 1*   E. Ulrich, 'The Biblical Manuscripts from Cave 4', 226.

4Q98d (4QPs. frg. 2) *4QPsalms Fragment 2*   E. Ulrich, 'The Biblical Manuscripts from Cave 4', 226.

4QPs89 (4Q236) *4QPsalm 89*   J. T. Milik, 'Fragment d'une source du psautier (4QPs89) et fragments de Jubilés, du Document de Damas, d'un phylactère dans la grotte 4 de Qumrân', RB 73 (1966) 95-98, pl. I; P. W. Skehan, SDB 51, 813-817; . – 'Qumran and Old Testament Criticism', 173-182; . – 'Gleanings from Psalm Texts from Qumran' in: *Mélanges bibliques et orientaux en l'honneur de M. Henri Cazelles*, 439-445. Remains of Ps 89.

4QPs 122 (4Q522) *4QPsalm 122*   E. Puech, 'Fragments du Psaume 122 dans un manuscrit hébreu de la Grotte IV', RQ 9/36 (1978) 547-554. Part of a non-biblical MS of Starcky's lot, with remains of Ps 122.

4Q99 (4QJob^a) *4QJob^a*   F. M. Cross, 'Le travail d'édition', RB 63 (1956) 57; . – *The Ancient Library*, 121. Remains of Job 36.

4Q100 (4QJob^b) *4QJob^b*   Minute remains of another copy of Job.

4Q101 (4QpaleoJob^c) *4QpaleoJob^c*   DJD IX, 155-157, pl. XXXVII. Remains of Job 13-14 in palaeo-Hebrew script.

4Q102 (4QProv^a) *4QProverbs^a*   P. W. Skehan, 'Le travail d'édition', RB 63 (1956) 59.

4Q103 (4QProv^b) *4QProverbs^b*   A single fragment of a stichometric copy of Proverbs.

4Q104 (4QRuth^a) *4QRuth^a*   Three fragments of a copy of Ruth, including the beginning of the book.

4Q105 (4QRuth^b) *4QRuth^b*   Three minute fragments of another copy of Ruth.

4Q106 (4QCant^a) 4QCanticles^a A single fragment with remains of two columns of Cant.

4Q107 (4QCant^b) *4QCanticles^b*   Two fragments of another copy of Cant. The longest has remains of Cant 2:9-3:1.

4Q108 (4QCant^c) *4QCanticles^c*   Three minute fragments of possibly another copy of Cant.

4Q109 (4QQoh^a) *4QQohelet^a*   J. Muilenburg, 'A Qohelet Scroll from Qumran', BASOR 135 (1954), 20-28; E. Ulrich, 'Ezra and Qohelet Manuscripts from Qumran', in E. Ulrich et al., *Priest, Prophets and Scribes. Essays on the Formation and Heritage of Second Temple Judaism in Honour of Joseph Blenkinsopp* (JSOTS 149) (Sheffield 1992), 142-147. pl. 2.

4Q110 (4QQoh^b) *4QQohelet^b*   E. Ulrich, 'Ezra and Qohelet Manuscripts from Qumran', 148, pl. 1. Two fragments of another copy of Qoh with remains of Qoh 1:101-14.

4Q111 (4QLam^a) *4QLamentations*   F. M. Cross, 'Studies in the Structure of Hebrew Verse: The Prosody of Lamentations 1:1-22', in: C. L. Meyers and M. O'Connor, *The Word of the Lord Shall Go Forth* (Winona Lake 1983) 129-155 [photograph p. 131; description of MSS, transcription and reconstruction, 133-135].

4Q112 (4QDan*ᵃ*) *4QDanielᵃ* E. Ulrich, 'Daniel Manuscripts from Qumran. Part 1: A Preliminary Edition of 4QDan*ᵃ*', BASOR 268 (1987) 17-37.

4Q113 (4QDan*ᵇ*) *4QDanielᵇ* E. Ulrich, 'Daniel Manuscripts from Qumran. Part 2: Preliminary Editions of 4QDan*ᵇ* and 4QDan*ᵇ*', BASOR 274 (1989) 3-26.

4Q114 (4QDan*ᶜ*) *4QDanielᶜ* E. Ulrich, 'Daniel Manuscripts from Qumran. Part 2', 3-26.

4Q115 (4QDan*ᵈ*) *4QDanielᵈ* E. Ulrich, 'Daniel Manuscripts from Qumran', 17-18.

4Q116 (4QDan*ᵉ*) *4QDanielᵉ* E. Ulrich, 'Daniel Manuscripts from Qumran', 17-18. Remains of Dn 9.

4Q117 (4QEzra) *4QEzra* F. M. Cross, 'Le travail d'édition', RB 63 (1956) 58. Three snall fragments with remains of Ezr 4-5.

4Q118 (4QChr) *4QChronicles* J. Trebolle, 'Édition préliminaire de 4QChroniques', RQ 15/60 (1992) 523-529. A single fragment with remains of five lines.

4Q119 (4QLXXLev*ᵃ*) *4QSeptuagint Leviticusᵃ* DJD IX, 161-165, pl. XXXVIII. A column of Lev in Greek, with remains of Lev 16.

4Q120 (4QpapLXXLev*ᵇ*) *4QSeptuagint Leviticusᵇ* DJD IX, 167-186, pl. XXXIX-XLI. Papyrus fragments of the first thirteen columns of a copy of Lev in Greek, with remains of Lev 1-5. E. Ulrich, 'The Greek Manuscripts of the Pentateuch from Qumrân, including newly-identified fragments of Deuteronomy (4QLXXDeut)' in: A. Pietersma and C. Cox (eds.), *De Septuagint. Studies in Honour of John William Wevers on his sixty-fifth birthday* (Mississauga 1984) 71-72.79-80, provides a study of all the variants.

4Q121 (4QLXXNum) *4QSeptuagint Numbers* DJD IX, 187-194, pl. XLII-XLIII. P. W. Skehan, 'The Qumran Manuscripts and Textual Criticism', 155-157; . – '4QLXXNum: A Pre-Christian Reworking of the Septuagint', HTR 70 (1977) 39-50.

4Q122 (4QLXXDeut) *4QSeptuagint Deuteronomy* DJD IX, 195-197. pl. XLIII. E. Ulrich, 'The Greek Manuscripts of the Pentateuch from Qumrân', 72-77. Remains of Dt 11 in Greek.

4Q123 (4QpaleoParaJosh) *4QParaphrase of Joshua* DJD IX, 201-202, pl. XLVI. E. Ulrich, 'The Biblical Manuscripts from Cave 4', 211. Pseudo-Joshua, a non-biblical text in palaeo-Hebrew characters.

4Q124 (4QpaleoUnid[1]) *4Qunidentified paleo-Hebrew text 1* DJD IX, 205-214, pl. XLIV-XLV. E. Ulrich, 'The Biblical Manuscripts from Cave 4', 211. Unidentified MS in palaeo-Hebrew script.

4Q125 (4QpaleoUnid[2]) *4Qunidentified paleo-Hebrew text 2* DJD IX, 215, pl. XLVI. E. Ulrich, 'The Biblical Manuscripts from Cave 4', 211. Unidentified MS in palaeo-Hebrew script.

4Q126 (4QUnid gr) *4Qunclassified text*   DJD IX, 219-221, pl. XLVI. E. Ulrich, 'The Biblical Manuscripts from Cave 4', 211. Unidentified Greek fragments.

4Q127 (4QpapParaExod) *4QParaphrase of Exodus*   DJD IX, 223-242, pl. XLVII. E. Ulrich, 'The Biblical Manuscripts from Cave 4', 211. Unidentified Greek fragments related to Exodus.

4Q128 (4QPhyl*ᵃ*) *4QPhylactery A*   K. G. Kuhn, *Phylakterien aus Höhle 4 von Qumran* (Heidelberg 1957) 15-16, pls. 9-10; J. T. Milik, *Discoveries in the Judaean Desert* VI (Oxford 1977 = DJD VI), 47-51, pls. VII-VIII. Obverse: remains of Dt 5:5-14; 5:27-6:3; 10:12-11:17; reverse: remains of Dt 11:18-21; Ex 12:43-13:7.

4Q129 (4QPhyl*ᵇ*) *4QPhylactery B*   K. G. Kuhn, *Phylakterien aus Höhle 4 von Qumran*, 11-15, pls. 1-4; J. T. Milik, DJD VI, 51-53, pl. IX. Obverse: remains of Dt 5:1-6:2; reverse: remains of Ex 13:9-16.

4Q130 (4QPhyl*ᶜ*) *4QPhylactery C*   J. T. Milik, DJD VI, 53-55, pls. X-XI. Remains of Ex 13:1-16; Dt 6:4-9; 11:13-21.

4Q131 (4QPhyl*ᵈ*) *4QPhylactery D*   J. T. Milik, DJD VI, 55-56, pl. XII. Remains of Dt 11:13-21.

4Q132 (4QPhyl*ᵉ*) *4QPhylactery E*   J. T. Milik, DJD VI, 56-57, pl. XIII. Remains of Ex 13:1-10.

4Q133 (4QPhyl*ᶠ*) *4QPhylactery F*   J. T. Milik, DJD VI, 57, pl. XIV. Remains of Ex 13:11-16.

4Q134 (4QPhyl*ᵍ*) *4QPhylactery G*   J. T. Milik, DJD VI, 58-60, pl. XV. Obverse: remains of Dt 5:1-21; reverse: remains of Ex 13:11-12.

4Q135 (4QPhyl*ʰ*) *4QPhylactery H*   K. G. Kuhn, *Phylakterien aus Höhle 4 von Qumran*, 16-20, pls. 11.14; J. T. Milik, DJD VI, 60-62, pl. XVI. Obverse: remains of Dt 5:22-2:5; obverse: remains of Ex 13:14-16.

4Q136 (4QPhyl*ⁱ*) *4QPhylactery I*   J. T. Milik, 'Fragment d'une source du Psautier', RB 73 (1966) 105-106, pl. IIb; . - DJD VI, 62-63, pl. XVII. Obverse: remains of Dt 11:13-21; Ex 12:43-13:10; reverse: remains of Dt 6:6-7 (?).

4Q137 (4QPhyl*ʲ*) *4QPhylactery J*   K. G. Kuhn, *Phylakterien aus Höhle 4 von Qumran*, 5-11, pls. 5-8; J. T. Milik, DJD VI, 64-67, pls. XVIII-XIX. Obverse: remains of Dt 5:1-24; reverse: remains of Dt 5:24-32; 6:2-3.

4Q138 (4QPhyl*ᵏ*) *4QPhylactery K*   J. T. Milik, DJD VI, 67-69, pl. XX. Obverse: remains of Dt 10:12-11:7; reverse: remains of Dt 11:7-12.

4Q139 (4QPhyl*ˡ*) *4QPhylactery L*   J. T. Milik, DJD VI, 70, pl. XXII. Remains of Dt 5:7-24.

4Q140 (4QPhyl*ᵐ*) *4QPhylactery M*   J. T. Milik, DJD VI, 71-72, pl. XXI. Obverse: remains of Ex 12:44-13:10; reverse: remains of Dt 5:33-6:5.

4Q141 (4QPhyl*ⁿ*) *4QPhylactery N*   J. T. Milik, DJD VI, 72-74, pl. XXII. Remains of Dt 32:14-20.32-33.

4Q142 (4QPhyl*ᵒ*) *4QPhylactery O*   J. T. Milik, DJD VI, 74-75, pl. XXII. Obverse: remains of Dt 5:1-16; reverse: remains of Dt 6:7-9.

4Q143 (4QPhyl*ᵖ*) *4QPhylactery P*   J. T. Milik, DJD VI, 75-76, pl. XXIII. Obverse: remains of Dt 10:22-11:3; reverse: remains of Dt 11:18-21.

4Q144 (4QPhyl^Q) *4QPhylactery Q* J. T. Milik, DJD VI, 76, pl. XXIII. Obverse: remains of Dt 11:4-8; reverse: remains of Ex 13:4-9.

4Q145 (4QPhyl^r) *4QPhylactery R* J. T. Milik, DJD VI, 77-78, pl. XXIII. Obverse: remains of Ex 13:1-7; reverse: remains of Ex 13:7-10.

4Q146 (4QPhyl^s) *4QPhylactery S* J. T. Milik, DJD VI, 78, pl. XIII. Remains of Dt 11:19-21.

4Q147-148 (4QPhyl^t,u) *4QPhylactery T, U* J. T. Milik, DJD VI, 79, pls. XXIV-XXV. Undeciphered phylacteries.

4Q149 (4QMez^a) *4QMezuzah A* J. T. Milik, DJD VI, 80-81, pl. XXVI. Remains of Ex 20:7-12.

4Q150 (4QMez^b) *4QMezuzah B* J. T. Milik, DJD VI, 81, pl. XXVI. Remains of Dt 6:5-6; 10:14-11:2.

4Q151 (4QMez^c) *4QMezuzah C* J. T. Milik, DJD VI, 82-83, pl. XVII. Remains of Dt 5:27-6:99; 10:12-20.

4Q152 (4QMez^d) *4QMezuzah D* J. T. Milik, DJD VI, 83, pl. XXVI. Remains of Dt 6:5-7.

4Q153 (4QMez^e) *4QMezuzah E* J. T. Milik, DJD VI, 83, pl. XXVI. Remains of Dt 11:17-18.

4Q154 (4QMez^f) *4QMezuzah F* J. T. Milik, DJD VI, 83-84, pl. XXVI. Remains of Ex 13:1-4.

4Q155 (4QMez^g) *4QMezuzah G* J. T. Milik, DJD VI, 84-85, pl. XXV. Remains of Ex 13:11-18.

CAVE 4 Non-biblical manuscripts

* 4Q156 (4QtgLev) *4QTargum of Leviticus* DJD VI, 86-89, pl. XXVII. Minute remains of an Aramaic Targum of Leviticus. [143]

* 4Q157 (4QtgJob)*4QTargum of Job* J. T. Milik, DJD VI, 90, pl. XXVIII. Minute remains of an Aramaic Targum on Job. [143]

* 4Q158 (4QRP^a) *4QReworked Pentateuch^a* J. M. Allegro, *Discoveries in the Judaean Desert of Jordan V* (Oxford 1968) (= DJD V), 1-6, pl. I. J. Strugnell, 'Notes', 168-175. Paraphrase of Gn 32:25-32; Ex 24:27-28. Gn 32:31 (?). Ex 3:12; 24:4-6; 19:17-23; 20:19-22; Dt 5:29; 15:18-20.22; Ex 20:12.16.17; Dt 5:30-31; Ex 20:22-26; 21:1.3.4.6.8.10; 21:15.16.18.20.22.25; 21:32.34.35-37; 22:1-11.13; 30:32.34. [219-222]

* 4Q159 (4QOrd^a) *4QOrdinances^a* J. M. Allegro, 'An Unpublished Fragment of Essene Halakah (4QOrdinances)', JSS 6 (1961) 71-73; . – DJD V, 6-9, p. II. J. Strugnell, 'Notes', 175-179. Halakhic text which rephrases biblical precepts: Dt 23:25-26; Ex 30:12; Lv 25:42; Dt 22:5; 22:13-14; see 4Q513 and 4Q514. [86-87]

* 4Q160 (4QVisSam) *4QVision of Samuel* J. M. Allegro, DJD V, 9-11, pl. III. J. Strugnell, 'Notes', 179-183. Apocryphon focused on the figure of Samuel. Fragment 1 is a paraphrase of 1 Sam 3:14-17. [284]

* 4Q161 (4QpIsaᵃ) *4QIsaiah Pesherᵃ*   J. M. Allegro, 'Further Messianic Reflections in Qumran Literature', JBL 75 (1956) 177-182, pls. II-III; . –DJD V, 11-15, pls. IV-V. J. Strugnell, 'Notes', 183-186. Commentary on Isa 10:20-21.22.24-27.28-32.33-34; 11:1-5. [185-186]

* 4Q162 (4QpIsaᵇ) *4QIsaiah Pesherᵇ*   J. M. Allegro, 'More Isaiah Commentaries from Qumran's Fourth Cave', JBL 77 (1958) 215-218, pl. 1; . –DJD V, 15-17, pl. VI. J. Strugnell, 'Notes', 186-188.199-204. Commentary on Isa 5:5-6.11-14.24-25.29-30; 6:9 (?). [186-187]

* 4Q163 (4QpIsaᶜ) *4QIsaiah Pesherᶜ*   J. M. Allegro, 'More Isaiah Commentaries', 218-220, pl. 2; . –DJD V, 17-27, pls. VII-VIII. J. Strugnell, 'Notes', 188-195. Commentary on Isa 8:7.8.9(?); 9:11(?).14-20; 10:12.13.19(?).20-24; 14:8.26-30; 19:9-12; 29:10-11.15-16.19-23; Zech 11:11; Isa 30:1-5.15-18; Hos 6:9; Isa 30:19-21; 31:1; 32:5-6. Other unidentified fragments can be found in 4Q515. [187-190]

* 4Q164 (4QpIsaᵈ) *4QIsaiah Pesherᵈ*   J. M. Allegro, 'More Isaiah Commentaries', 220-221, pl. 3; . –DJD V, 27-28, pl. IX. J. Strugnell, 'Notes', 195-196. Commentary on Isa 54:11-12. [190-191]

* 4Q165 (4QpIsaᵉ) *4QIsaiah Pesherᵉ*   J. M. Allegro, DJD V, 28-30, pl. IX. J. Strugnell, 'Notes', 197 ⟨HHP⟩ 199. Commentary on Isa 1:1(?); 40:12; 14:19; 15:4-6; 21:2(?).11-15; 32:5-7. [191]

* 4Q166 (4QpHosᵃ) *4QHosea Pesherᵃ*   J. M. Allegro, 'A Recently Discovered Fragment of a Commentary on Hosea from Qumran's Fourth Cave', JBL 78 (1959) 142-147; DJD V, 31-32, pl. X. J. Strugnell, 'Notes', 199-201. Commentary on Hos 2:8-9.10-14. [191-192]

* 4Q167 (4QpHosᵇ) *4QHosea Pesherᵇ*   J. M. Allegro, 'Further Light on the History of the Qumran Sect', JBL 75 (1956) 93, pl. 2; . –DJD V, 32-36, pls. X-XI. J. Strugnell, 'Notes', 201-203. Commentary on Hos 5:13-15; 6:4.7.9-10; 8:6-7.13-14. [192-193]

* 4Q168 (4QpMic) (?) *4QMicah Pesher* (?)   J. M. Allegro, DJD V, 36, pl. XII. J. Strugnell, 'Notes', 204. Commentary on Mic 4:8-12. [194-195]

* 4Q169 (4QpNah) *4QNahum Pesher*   J. M. Allegro, 'Further Light on the History of the Qumran Sect', 90-93, pl. 1; . –'More Unpublished Pieces of a Qumran Commentary on Nahum (4QpNah)', JSS 7 (1962) 304-308; . –DJD V, 37-42, pls. XII-XIV. J. Strugnell, 'Notes', 204-210. Commentary on Nah 1:3-6; 2:12-14; 3:1-5.6-9.10-12.14. [195-197]

* 4Q170 (4QpZeph) *4QZephaniah Pesher.* J. M. Allegro DJD V, 42, pl. XIV. J. Strugnell, 'Notes', 210-211. Commentary on Zeph 1:12-13. [203]

* 4Q171 (4QpPsᵃ) *4QPsalms Pesherᵃ*   J. M. Allegro, 'A Newly Discovered Fragment of a Commentary on Psalms XXXVII', PEQ 86 (1954) 69-75; . –'Further Light on the History of the Qumran Sect', 94-95, pl. 4. H. Stegemann, 'Weitere Stücke von 4QpPsalm 37', RQ 6/22 (1967) 193-210, pl. 1; J. M. Allegro, DJD V, 42-51, pls. XIV-XVII. J. Strugnell, 'Notes', 211-218. Commentary on Ps 37:7-8-19a.19b-26.28c-40; Ps 45:1-2; Ps 60:8-9 (Ps 108:8-9). [203-206]

o 4Q172 (4QpUnid) *Unidentified Pesher*   J. M. Allegro, DJD V, 5051, pl. XVIII. J. Strugnell, 'Notes', 218-219. Unidentified pesher. Possibly part of 4Q161, 4Q167 or 4Q171.

* 4Q173 (4QpPs*b*) *4QPsalms Pesher*b   J. M. Allegro, DJD V, 51-53, pl. XVIII. J. Strugnell, 'Notes', 219-220. Commentary on Ps 127:2-3.5; Ps 129:7-8; Ps 118:26-27 (?). [206-207]

* 4Q174 (4QFlor) *4QFlorilegium*   J.M. Allegro, 'Further Messianic References', JBL 75 (1956) 176-177, pl. 1; . - 'Fragments of a Qumran Scroll of Eschatological Midrashim', JBL 77 (1958) 350-354; . - DJD V, 53-57, pls. XIX-XX. J. Strugnell, 'Notes', 220-225. Florilegium made up quotations from: 2 Sam 7:10-14 (1 Chr 17:9-13); Ex 15:17-18; Am 9:11; Ps 1:1; Isa 8:11; Ez 37:23 (?); Ps 2:1 with pesher; Dn 12:10 and 11:32 with pesher; Dt 33:8-11 with pesher; Dt 33:12(?) with pesher; Dt 33:19-21 with pesher and unidentified fragments. The whole is presented as a commentary on Psalms 1-2. A. Steudel, *Der Midrasch zur Eschatologie aus der Qumrangemeinde (4QMidrEschat*a-b*)* (STDJ 13) (Leiden 1994), 5-53. [136-137]

* 4Q175 (4QTest) *4QTestimonia*   J. M. Allegro, 'Further Messianic References', 182-187, pl. 4; . - DJD V, 57-60, pl. XXI. J. Strugnell, 'Notes', 225-229. Collection of quotations from Dt 5:28-29; 18:18-19 (Samaritan form of Ex 20:21); Num 24:15-17; Dt 33:8-11; Jos 6:26 and from the apocryphal work 'Psalms of Joshua' (4Q378-4Q379). [137-138]

* 4Q176 (4QTanh) *4QTanhumim*   J. M. Allegro, DJD V, 60-67, pls. XXII-XXIII. J. Strugnell, 'Notes', 229-236. Anthology of biblical passages of consolation, principally from Deutero-Isaiah. quotations of and commentaries on Ps 79:2-3; Isa 40:1-5; 41:8-9; 49:7.13-17; 43:1-2.4-6; 51:22-23; 52:1-3; 54:4-10; 52:1-2; Zech 13:9. [208-209]

* 4Q176   fragments 19-21 (*4QJub*f) *4QJubilees*f, M. Kister, 'Newly-identified Fragments of the Book of Jubilees: Jub 23,21-23. 30-31', RQ 12/48 (1987) 529-536. He identifies fragments 19-20 of 4Q176 as Jub 23:21-23, and fragment 21 as Jub 23:30-31. The fragments would come from 4QJub*f*. [244]

* 4Q177 (4QCatena*a*) *4QCatena*a   J. M. Allegro, DJD V, 67-74, pls. XXIV-XXV. J. Strugnell, 'Notes', 236-248. Exegesis of eschatalogical character in the form of a commentary on Pss 6-17, with the use of other quotations and biblical allusions. [209-211]

o 4Q178 *unclassified fragments*   J. M. Allegro, DJD V, 74-75, pl. XXV. J. Strugnell, 'Notes', 248-249. Unidentified fragments.

* 4Q179 (4QapocrLam A) *4QApocryphal Lamentations A*   J.M. Allegro, DJD V, 75-77, pl. XXVI. J. Strugnell, 'Notes', 250-252. Lamentation in verse on the destruction of Jerusalem. [401-402]

* 4Q180 (4QAgesCreat) *4QAges of Creation*   J. M. Allegro, 'Some Unpublished Fragments of Pseudepigraphical Literature from Qumran's Fourth Cave', ALUOS 4 (1962-63) 3-4; . - DJD V, 77-79, pl. XXVII. J. Strugnell, 'Notes', 252-

254. Commentary on salvation history and on the periods of sin, starting from the fall of the angels. J. T. Milik, 'Milkî-sedeq et Milkî-resaᶜ dans les anciens écrits juifs et chrétiens', JJS 23 (1972) 109-126 and *The Books of Enoch*, 248-252, suggests considering this MS and 4Q181 as parts of a single work: 'Pesher on (the book of) the Periods', of which 11QMelch would be another copy; but see D. Dimant, 'The 'Pesher on the Periods' (4Q180) and 4Q181', Israel Oriental Studies 9 (1979) 77-102. [211-212]

* 4Q181 (4QAgesCreat) *4QAges of Creation*   J. M. Allegro, 'Some Unpublished Fragments', 4-5; .–DJD V, 79-80, pl. XVIII. J. Strugnell, 'Notes', 254-255. Document which describes the destiny of the chosen and the damned. See the studies cited in the previous number. [212-213]

* 4Q182 (4QCatenaᵇ) *4QCatenaᵇ*   J. M. Allegro, DJD V, 80-81, pl. XXVII. J. Strugnell, 'Notes', 256. Document similar to 4Q177, with a possible quotation of Jer 5:7. [213]

* 4Q183 *4QHistorical Work*   J. M. Allegro, DJD V, 81-82, pl. XXVI. J. Strugnell, 'Notes', 256-257. Document of historical-exegetical character, although it is not possible to specify which biblical text it comments on. [213]

* 4Q184 *4QWiles of the Wicked Woman*   J. M. Allegro, 'The Wiles of the Wicked Woman: A Sapiential Work from Qumran's Fourth Cave', PEQ (1964) 53-55; .–DJD V, 82-85, pl. XXVIII. J. Strugnell, 'Notes', 263-268. Allegorical wisdom poem on Need, personified as a woman, inspired by Prov 7 and with obvious magical connotations. [379-380]

* 4Q185 *4QSapiential Work*   J. M. Allegro, DJD V, 85-87, pls. XXIX-XXX. J. Strugnell, 'Notes', 269-273. Wisdom discourse in which the author urges the seeking of wisdom or the Law. [380-382]

* 4Q186 *4QHoroscope*   J. M. Allegro, 'An Astrological Cryptic Document from Qumran', JSS 9 (1964) 291-294; .–DJD V, 88-91, pl. XXXI. XXXI. J. Strugnell, 'Notes', 274-276. Physiognomical and astrological text which determines the parts of light and darkness each person possesses. [456]

[The numbers 4Q187-195 of the series do not seem to have been assigned to any manuscript].

* 4Q196 (4QTob arᵃ) *4QTobitᵃ*   J. T. Milik, 'La patrie de Tobie', RB 73 (1956) 522, where Milik lists the contents of the preserved fragments; .–*Dédicaces faites par des dieux (Palmyre, Hatra, Tyr) et des thiases sémitiques à l'époque romaine* (Paris 1972) 149, 199, 210, 384 and *The Books of Enoch*, 163, 186, where he cites 4QTobaramᵃ 2 II 5; 2 III 2 and 4. Aramaic original of the biblical book of Tobias. Copy written out on papyrus. Plenty of fragments although only one is a good size. [293-294]

* 4Q197 (4QTob arᵇ) *4QTobitᵇ*   J. T. Milik, 'La patrie de Tobie', 522; *Dédicaces*, 210, 379 and *The Books of Enoch*, 191 with quotations of 4QTob arᵇ 1 XX 2.8 and 2 III 2. K. Beyer, *Die aramäischen Texte vom Toten Meer. Ergänzungsband* (Göttingen 1994), 134-147. Aramaic original of Tobias. It is the copy with most text preserved. [295-297]

* 4Q198 (4QTob ar^c) *4QTobit^c* J. T. Milik, 'La patrie de Tobie', 522. K. Beyer, *Ergänzungsband*, 134-147. Only two fragments, with remains of Tob 14. [297]

* 4Q199 (4QTob ar^d) *4QTobit^d* J. T. Milik, 'La patrie de Tobie', 522. K. Beyer, *Ergänzungsband*, 134-147. A single fragment with a few words. [297]

* 4Q200 (4QTob hebr) *4QTobit^e* J. T. Milik, 'La patrie de Tobie', 522. K. Beyer, *Ergänzungsband*, 134-147. Remains of a Hebrew version or of the original of Tobias. Only a few fragments are good-sized. [297-299]

* 4Q201 (4QEn^a ar) *4QEnoch^a* J. T. Milik, *The Books of Enoch. Aramaic Fragments from Qumrân Cave 4* (Oxford 1976) 139-163, 340-343, pls. I-V. Copy of the Book of the Watchers from 1 Enoch. Remains of 1 En 1:1-6; 2:1-5.6; 6:4-8:1; 8:3-9:3; 9:6-8; 10:3-4.21-11:1; 12:4-6; 14:4-6. [246-248]

* 4Q202 (4QEn^b ar) *4QEnoch^b* J. T. Milik, *The Books of Enoch*, 164-178, 344-346, pls. VI-IX. Another copy of the Book of Watchers from 1 Enoch. Remains of 1 En 5:9-6:4; 6:7-8:1; 8:2-9:4; 10:8-12. [248-250]

* 4Q203 (4QEnGiants^a ar) *4QBook of Giants^a* J. T. Milik, *The Books of Enoch*, 310-317, pls. XXX-XXXII. Copy of the Book of Giants. [260-261]

* 4Q204 (4QEn^c ar) *4QEnoch^c* J. T. Milik, 'Hénoch au pays des aromates (ch. XXVII à XXXII): Fragments araméens de la grotte 4 de Qumrân', RB 65 (1958) 70-77, pl. I; . – *The Books of Enoch*, 178-217, 346-353, pls. IX-XV. Copy of the Book of Watchers, the Book of Giants (4QEnGiants^a), the Book of Dreams and the Letter of Enoch, from 1 Enoch. Remains of 1 En 1:9-5:1; 6:7; 10:13-19; 12:3; 13:6-14:16; 14:18-20; 15:11 (?); 18:8-12; 30:1-32:1; 35; 36:1-4; 89:31-37; 104:13-106:2; 106:13-107:2. [250-254]

* 4Q205 (4QEn^d ar) *4QEnoch^d* J. T. Milik, *The Books of Enoch*, 217-225, 353-355, pls. XVI-XVII. Copy of the Book of Watchers and the of the Book of Dreams, from 1 Enoch. Remains of 1 En 22:13-24:1; 25:7-27:1; 89:11-14; 89:29-31; 89:43-44. [254-255]

* 4Q206 (4QEn^e ar) *4QEnoch^e* J. T. Milik, 'Hénoch au pays des aromates', 70-77, pl. I; . – *The Books of Enoch*, 225-244, 355-359, pls. XVIII-XXI. Copy of the Book of Watchers, the Book of Giants (4QEnGiants^e ?) and the Book of Dreams, from 1 Enoch. Remains of 1 En 18:15 (?); 21:2-4; 22:3-7; 28:3-29:2; 31:2-32:3; 32:3.6; 33:3-34:1; 88:3-89:6; 89:7-16; 89:26-30. [256-257]

* 4Q207 (4QEn^f ar) *4QEnoch^f* J. T. Milik, *The Books of Enoch*, 244-245, 359, pl. XXI. Copy of the Book of Dreams from 1 Enoch. Remains of 1 En 86:1-3. [258]

4Q208 (4QEnastr^a ar) *4QAstronomical Enoch^a* J. T. Milik, *The Books of Enoch*, 273. Description of the MS. Its 36 fragments are still unpublished. A copy of the Astronomical Book of 1 Enoch. Contains only remains of a synchronous calendar.

* 4Q209 (4QEnastr^b ar) *4QAstronomical Enoch^b* J. T. Milik, 'Hénoch au pays des aromates', 76; . – 'Problèmes de la littérature hénochique à la lumière des fragments araméens de Qumrân', HTR 64 (1971) 338-343; *The Books of Enoch*, 278-284, 288-296, pls. XXV-XXVII, XXX. Another copy of the Astronomical Book.

Remains of a synchronous calendar and of other passages corresponding to: 1 En 76:13-77:4; 78:9-12; 79:3-5 + 78:17-79:2; 82: 9-13. [445-448]

* 4Q210 (4QEnastr*c* ar) *4QAstronomical Enoch*c*   J. T. Milik, 'Hénoch au pays des aromates', 76; . - *The Books of Enoch*, 284-288, pls. XXVIII, XXX. Another copy of the Astronomical Book of 1 Enoch. Remains of 1 En 76:3-10; 76:13-77:4; 78:6-8. [448-449]

* 4Q211 (4QEnastr*d* ar) *4QAstronomical Enoch*d*   J. T. Milik, *The Books of Enoch*, 296-297, pl. XXIX. Another copy of the Astronomical Book of 1 Enoch. Remains of three cols. which would follow 1 En 82:20. [449-450]

* 4Q212 (4QEn*g* ar) *4QEnoch*g*   J. T. Milik, *The Books of Enoch*, 245-272, 360-362, pls. XXI-XXIV. Copy of the Letter of Enoch from 1 Enoch, remains of 1 En 91:10 (?); 91:18-19; 92:1-2; 92:5-93:4; 93:9-10; 91:11-17; 93:11-94:2. [258-259]

* 4Q213 (4QTLevi*a* ar) *4QAramaic Levi*a*   J. T. Milik, 'Le Testament de Lévi en araméen: Fragment de la grotte 4 de Qumrân', RB 62 (1955) 398-406, pl. IV; . -RB 73 (1966) 95, n.2; . - 'Problèmes de la littérature hénochique', 344-345; . - *The Books of Enoch*, 23-24, 263. M. E. Stone and J. C. Greenfield, 'The Prayer of Levi', JBL 112 (1993), 247-266. R. Eisenman and M. Wise, *The Dead Sea Scrolls Uncovered* (Shaftesbury 1992) 136-141. K. Beyer, *Ergänzungsband*, 71-78. Remains of an Aramaic work related to the Aramaic Testament of Levi from the Geniza and the Greek Testament of Levi which forms part of the Testaments of the XII Patriarchs. [266-268]

* 4Q214 (4QTLevi*b* ar) *4QAramaic Levi*b*   J. T. Milik, RB 73 (1966) 95, n.2; . - *The Books of Enoch*, 214, 244, 188-209. R. Eisenman and M. Wise, *The Dead Sea Scrolls Uncovered*, 136-141. K. Beyer, *Ergänzungsband*, 71-78. Another copy of the same work. [268-269]

* 4Q215 (4QTNaph) *4QTestament of Naphtali*   R. Eisenman and M. Wise, *The Dead Sea Scrolls Uncovered*, 156-160. Hebrew Testament of Nephtali, not related to Testament of Nephtali which forms part of Testaments of the XII Patriarchs. [270-271]

* 4Q216 (4QJub*a*) *4QJubilees*a*   J. C. VanderKam and J. T. Milik, 'The First Jubilees Manuscript from Qumran Cave 4: A Preliminary Publication', JBL 110 (1991) 243-270. It is the oldest copy of Jubilees. Copied by two different scribes. [238-240]

o 4Q217 (4QJub*b*) *4QJubilees*b*   Possibly a copy of the Book of Jubilees on papyrus.

o 4Q218 (4QJub*c*) *4QJubilees*c*   A single fragment with remains of four lines, corresponding to Jubilees 2:26-27.

* 4Q219 (4QJub*d*) *4QJubilees*d*   J. C. VanderKam and J. T. Milik, 'A Preliminary Publication of a Jubilees Manuscript from Qumran Cave 4: 4QJub*d* (4Q219)', Biblica 73 (1992), 62-83. Copy of the Book of Jubilees, with remains of ch. 21. [242-243]

* 4Q220 (4QJub*e*) *4QJubilees*e*   A single fragment, with remains of Jubilees 21:5-10. [242]

* 4Q221 (4QJub^f) *4QJubilees^f* J. T. Milik, 'Fragment d'une source du Psautier (4QPs89) et fragments de Jubilés, du Document de Damas, d'un phylactère dans la grotte 4 de Qumrân', RB 73 (1966) 104, pl. II. Copy of the Book of Jubilees. Remains of Jubilees 21-23. 33 and 37-39. [243-244]

o 4Q222 (4QJub^g) *4QJubilees^g* J. C. VanderKam and J. T. Milik, '4QJubilees^g (4Q222), *New Qumran Texts and Studies, 105-114*, Pl. 7. Six fragments with meagre remains of Jubilees 25 and 27.

o 4Q223-224 (4QJub^b) *4QJubilees^b* Copy of Jubilees on papyrus. In spite of the double number it is a single manuscript. Remains of the last chapters of the Book of Jubilees.

o 4Q225 (4QpsJub^a) *4QPseudo-Jubilees^a* B. Z. Wacholder and M. G. Abegg, *A Preliminary Edition of the Unpublished Dead Sea Scrolls. Fascicle Two* (Washington 1992), 204-206. Composition related to the Book of Jubilees.

o 4Q226 (4QpsJub^b). *4QPseudo-Jubilees^b* B. Z. Wacholder and M. G. Abegg, *Fascicle Two*, 207-210. Composition related to the Book of Jubilees.

* 4Q227 (4QpsJub^c) *4QPseudo-Jubilees^c* J. T. Milik, *The Books of Enoch*, 12, 14, 25, 60. B. Z. Wacholder and M. G. Abegg, *Fascicle Two*, 211. Hebrew apocryphon related to Jubilees and 1 Enoch. Only one fragment of this MS has been preserved. [245]

o 4Q228 *Work with citation of Jubilees* Remains of work which cites the Book of Jubilees (?). The biggest fragment, with remains of two columns, seems to contain the ending of the work.

4Q229 *Pseudepigraphic work in Mishnaic Hebrew* Remains of a pseudepigraphic work in Mishnaic Hebrew (?). Details unknown.

o 4Q230-231 *Catalogue of Spirits^{a,b}* Catalogues of the names of the spirits (?). Details unknown.

4Q232 (4QNJ ?) *4QNew Jerusalem (?)* J. T. Milik, *The Books of Enoch*, 59. Hebrew version (?) of the Aramaic work: Description of the New Jerusalem. Only one fragment of this MS has been preserved.

o 4Q233 *Fragments with place names* Fragments with geographical names. Details unknown.

o 4Q234 *Writing exercise* Fragments with writing exercises. Contains Gn 27:20.

o 4Q235 *Fragments in Nabataean writing* Three fragments in the Nabataean script with remains of the Book of Kings.

4Q236 (= 4QPs89) *(supra)*

4Q237 *Psalter* (?) Details unknown.

4Q238 *Habakkuk 3 and songs* Details unknown.

o 4Q239 *Pesher on the True Israel* Details unknown.

o 4Q240 *Commentary on Canticles* (?) Details unknown.

o 4Q241 *Fragments citing Lamentations* Details unknown.

* 4Q242 (4QPrNab ar) *4QPrayer of Nabonidus* J. T. Milik, 'Prière de Nabonide', 407-411, pl. I. Remains of an Aramaic apocryphon related to the Daniel cycle: 'Prayer of Nabonidus'. [289]

* 4Q243 (4QpsDan*ᵃ* ar) *4QPseudo-Danielᵃ*   J. T. Milik, 'Prière de Nabonide et autres écrits d'un cycle de Daniel', 411-415. R. Eisenman – M. Wise, *The Dead Sea Scrolls Uncovered*, 64-68. K. Beyer, *Ergänzungsband*, 105-107. Aramaic apocalyptic work related to Dn. [288]

* 4Q244 (4QpsDan*ᵇ* ar) *4QPseudo-Danielᵇ*   J. T. Milik, 'Prière de Nabonide et autres écrits d'un cycle de Daniel', 411-415. R. Eisenman – M. Wise, *The Dead Sea Scrolls Uncovered*, 64-68. K. Beyer, *Ergänzungsband*, 105-107. Fragments of another copy of the same work. [288-289]

* 4Q245 (4QpsDan*ᶜ* ar) *4QPseudo-Danielᶜ*   J. T. Milik, 'Prière de Nabonide et autres écrits d'un cycle de Daniel', 411-415. R. Eisenman – M. Wise, *The Dead Sea Scrolls Uncovered*, 64-68. K. Beyer, *Ergänzungsband*, 105-107. Third copy of the same composition. [289]

* 4Q246 *4QAramaic Apocalypse*   E. Puech, 'Fragment d'une apocalypse en araméen (4Q246 = pseudo-Dan*ᵈ*) et le "Royaume de Dieu"', RB 99 (1992), 98-131. Fragment of an apocalyptic work in Aramaic which uses the titles 'son of God' and 'son of the Most High', previously known as 4QPsDan A*ᵃ*, 4Q243 and 4QSon of God. [138]

o 4Q247 *Apocalypse of Weeks* (?)   J. T. Milik, The Books of Enoch, 256. Hebrew commentary on the Apocalypse of Weeks from 1 Enoch (?). A single fragment has been preserved, with remains of six lines.

o 4Q248 *Acts of a Greek King*   Fragments with allusions to Hellenistic history (?). Only one fragment with remains of nine lines has been preserved.

4Q249 (4QMSM) *4QCryptic A: Midrash Sefer Moshe*   J. T. Milik, 'Milkî-sedeq et Milkî-resaᶜ', 138. Commentary on Genesis in cryptic script, copied on papyrus. Many fragments have been preserved, but small in size. The title of the work, 'Commentary on the Book of Moses', is located on the back, not in the cryptic but in the square script.

o 4Q250   Part of the fragments of the preceding work contains, on the reverse, an unidentified composition in cryptic script.

* 4Q251 (4QHalakhah*ᵃ*) *4QHalakhah*   Halakhic fragments concerning dietary and sexual regulations. [87-88]

* 4Q252 (4QpGen*ᵃ*) *4QGenesis Pesherᵃ*   J. M. Allegro, 'Further Messianic References in Qumran Literature', JBL 75 (1956) 174-176, pl. 1; H. Stegemann, 'Weitere Stücke von 4QpPs37', 211-217; J. T. Milik, 'Milkî-sedeq et Milkî-resaᶜ', 138. T. H. Lim, 'The Chronology of the Flood Story in a Qumran Text (4Q252), JJS 43 (1992), 288-298. B. Z. Wacholder and M. G. Abegg, *Fascicle Two*, 212-215. The fragment published by Allegro as 'Patriarchal Blessings' contains a commentary on Gn 49:10. the first columns of the manuscript are a paraphase on Gn 6. [213-215]

* 4Q253 (4QpGen*ᵇ*) *4QGenesis Pesherᵇ*   B. Z. Wacholder and M. G. Abegg, *Fascicle Two*, 216-217. Another copy of the same commentary on Genesis. [215]

* 4Q254 (4QpGen*ᶜ*) *4QGenesis Pesherᶜ*   B. Z. Wacholder and M. G. Abegg, *Fascicle Two*, 218-222. Another copy of the same commentary on Genesis. [215-216]

* 4Q255 (4QS*ᵃ*) *4QRule of the Community*ᵃ J. T. Milik, review of P. Wernberg-Möller, *The Manual of Discipline*, in RB 67 (1960) 412-416. Copy of the Community Rule on papyrus. Four fragments have been preserved, two of them very small. [20]

* 4Q256 (4QS*ᵇ*) *4QRule of the Community*ᵇ J. T. Milik, 'Numérotation des feuilles des rouleaux dans le scriptorium de Qumrân', Semitica 27 (1977) 75-81, pl. X. Copy of the Rule of the Comunity. The published column contains a shorter form of 1QS V 1-20. The other four fragments preserved correspond to cols. I-II and have the same text. [20-21]

* 4Q257 (4QS*ᶜ*) *4QRule of the Community*ᶜ Copy of the Rule of the Community on papyrus. A single fragment has been preserved, with part of two columns corresponding to 1QS I-III. [21-22]

* 4Q258 (4QS*ᵈ*) *4QRule of the Community*ᵈ J. T. Milik, review of P. Wernberg-Möller, *The Manual of Discipline*, in RB 67 (1960) 412-416. G. Vermes, 'Preliminary Remarks on Unpublished Fragments of the Community Rule from Qumran Cave 4', JJS 42 (1991) 250-255. The best preserved copy of the Rule of the Community from Cave 4. In my opinion, the beginning of the manuscript has been preserved, which proves that this copy began with a shortened form of 1QS V. [22-25]

* 4Q259 (4QS*ᵉ*) *4QRule of the Community*ᵉ [Sometimes referred to as 4QS*ᵇ* or 4Q260B]. According to J. T. Milik, 'Le travail d'édition des manuscrits du désert de Juda' in: *Volume du Congrès de Strasbourg* (SVT 4) (Brill, Leiden 1957) 25, it is a copy of 1QS from the second half of the 2nd century which includes a calendar of the cycle of seven jubilees. It contains remains of 1QS VII 10 – X 4 in the first four cols. and calendrical material in the rest. [26-29]

* 4Q260 (4QS*ᶠ*) *4QRule of the Community*ᶠ J. T. Milik, review of P. Wernberg-Möller, *The Manual of Discipline*, in RB 67 (1960) 412-416. Another copy of the Rule of the Community with remains of five columns. [29-30]

* 4Q261 (4QS*ᵍ*) *4QRule of the Community*ᵍ J. T. Milik, review of P. Wernberg-Möller, *The Manual of Discipline*, in RB 67 (1960) 412-416. Another copy of the Rule of the Community. 18 fragments have been preserved, but so tiny that only four can be identified with relative certainty. [30-31]

* 4Q262 (4QS*ʰ*) *4QRule of the Community*ʰ J. T. Milik, review of P. Wernberg-Möller, *The Manual of Discipline*, in RB 67 (1960) 412-416. Another copy of the Rule of the Community of which two fragments have been preserved with remains of three lines on each. I have only been able to identify one of them. [31]

* 4Q263 (4QS*ⁱ*) *4QRule of the Community*ⁱ J. T. Milik, review of P. Wernberg-Möller, *The Manual of Discipline*, in RB 67 (1960) 412-416. Another copy of the Rule of the Community of which only one fragment has been preserved. [31]

* 4Q264 (4QS*ʲ*) *4QRule of the Community*ʲ J. T. Milik, review of P. Wernberg-Möller, *The Manual of Discipline*, in RB 67 (1960) 412-416. Another copy of the

Rule of the Community. Only one fragment has been preserved, with the end of the work. [31-32]

* 4Q265 (4QSD) *4QSerek Damascus Document*   J.M.Baumgarten, 'Purification after Childbirth and the Sacred Garden in 4Q265 and Jubilees', *New Qumran Texts and Studies*, 3-10, Pl. 1. Rule which seems to combine elements from the Rule of the Community and the Damascus Document. [72]

* CD-A *Damascus Document^a*   First copy of the *Damascus Document* [= D] which comes from the Cairo Genizah, published by S. Schechter, *Documents of Jewish Sectaries. Vol. 1: Fragments of a Zadokite Work* (Cambridge 1910) and S. Zeitlin, *The Zadokite Fragments. Facsimile of the Manuscripts in the Cairo Genizah Collection in the Possession of the University Library, Cambridge, England* (Jewish Quarterly Review, Monograph Series 1) (Philadelphia 1952) as columns I-XVI of CD. A facsimile of much better quality and a new transcription of the fragments, made by E. Qimron, has been published by M. Broshi (ed.), *The Damascus Document Reconsidered* (Jerusalem 1992). [33-44]

* CD-B *Damascus Document^b*   Second copy of the Damascus Document which comes fom the Genizah, published by Schechter as columns XIX-XX of CD-A. [45-47]

* 4Q266 (4QD^a) *4QDamascus Document^a*   B.Z. Wacholder and M.G. Abegg, *A Preliminary Edition of the Unpublished Dead Sea Scrolls. Fascicule One* (Washington 1991), 1-2. J.M.Baumgarten, 'A "Scriptural" Citation in 4Q Fragments of the Damascus Document', JJS 43 (1992), 95-98. R. Eisenman and M. Wise, *The Dead Sea Scrolls Uncovered*, 212-219. Copy of the Damascus Document, of which three fragments have been preserved, one of them quite long and belonging to the beginning of the work. [47-48]

* 4Q267 (4QD^b) *4QDamascus Document^b*   J. T. Milik, 'Fragment d'une source du Psautier', 103, 105, pl. III. J. M. Baumgarten, 'The 4Q Zadokite Fragments on Skin Disease', JJS 41 (1990) 153-154. A photo with remains of the first and last columns was published in DJD VI, pl. IV to illustrate the method of unrolling the MSS. A much clearer photo and its transcription is also to be found in J. T. Milik, 'Numérotation', 78-79, pl. XI, with material which precedes that preserved in CD-A. B. Z. Wacholder and M. G. Abegg, *Fascicule One*, 3-22. A long copy of the Damascus Document, with a great deal of new material, including the end of the work. [48-57]

* 4Q268 (4QD^c) *4QDamascus Document^c*   B.Z.Wacholder and M.G. Abegg, *Fascicule One*, 23-27. Another copy of the Damascus Document with material not found present in CD-A, which enables reconstruction of the original sequence of certain columns in the copy from the Gemizah. Large framents with remains of four columns. [57-60]

* 4Q269 (4QD^d) *4QDamascus Document^d*   J.M.Baumgarten, 'The 4Q Zadokite Fragments on Skin Disease', JJS 41 (1990) 157-158. B. Z. Wacholder and M. G. Abegg, *Fascicule One*, 28-35. Another long copy of the Damascus Document. [60-62]

* 4Q270 (4QD^e) *4QDamascus Document^e*   B. Z. Wacholder and M. G. Abegg, *Fasci-cule One*, 36-47. Another copy of the Damascus Document, with new material, which has preserved the end of the work. [62-67]

* 4Q271 (4QD^f) *4QDamascus Document^f*   B. Z. Wacholder and M. G. Abegg, *Fasci-cule One*, 48-53. Small fragments of another copy of the Damascus Document. [67-69]

* 4Q272 (4QD^g) *4QDamascus Document^g*   J. M. Baumgarten, 'The 4Q Zadokite Frag-ments on Skin Disease', JJS 41 (1990) 157-158. B. Z. Wacholder and M. G. Abegg, *Fascicule One*, 54-56. Another copy of the Damascus Document which does not match the text of the Cairo Geniza. Only remains of two columns have been preserved in the four fragments published. [69-70]

* 4Q273 (4QD^h) *4QDamascus Document^h*   B. Z. Wacholder and M. G. Abegg, *Fasci-cule One*, 57-59. Small fragments of another copy of the Damascus Document. [70]

* 4Q274 (4QTohorot A) *4QPurification Rules A*   J. T. Milik, 'Milkî-sedeq et Milkî-resa^c', 129. J. M. Baumgarten, 'The Laws about Fluxes in 4QTohora^a', in D. Dimant and L. H. Schiffman, *Time to Prepare the Way in the Wilderness* (STDJ 14) (Leiden 1994), 1-8. R. Eisenman and M. Wise, *The Dead Sea Scrolls Uncov-ered*, 205-210. A 'Rule of purity' related to 1QS and CD. First written version. [88-89]

* 4Q275 (4QTohorot B^a) *4QPurification Rules B^a*   J. T. Milik, 'Milkî-sedeq et Milkî-resa^c', 129-130. Another 'Rule of purity'; second written version. Milik has published fragment 3:1-6 with curses. [89]

* 4Q276 (4QTohorot B^b) *4QPurification Rules B^b*   J. T. Milik, 'Milkî-sedeq et Milkî-resa^c', 129. R. Eisenman and M. Wise, *The Dead Sea Scrolls Uncovered*, 210-212. Other copies of the second written version of a 'Rule of purity'. [89]

* 4Q277 (4QTohorot B^c) *4QPurification Rules B^c*   J. T. Milik, 'Milkî-sedeq et Milkî-resa^c', 129. R. Eisenman and M. Wise, *The Dead Sea Scrolls Uncovered*, 210-212. Another copy of the same text. [89-90]

* 4Q278 (4QTohorot C ?) *4QPurification Rules C*   J. T. Milik, 'Milkî-sedeq et Milkî-resa^c', 129. Another 'Rule of purity'; third written version. [90]

* 4Q279 (4QTohorot D ?) *4QPurification Rules D (?)*   J. T. Milik, 'Milkî-sedeq et Milkî-resa^c', 129. Another 'Rule of purity'. The preserved fragments deal with gleaning. [90]

* 4Q280 (4QBer^f) *4QBlessings^f*   J. T. Milik, 'Milkî-sedeq et Milkî-resa^c', 126-130, pl. I. According to Milik, another copy of the 'Rule of purity'. Recently it has been classified as one of the written texts with 'Blessings and Curses'. Only three fragments seem to have been preserved, of which Milik publishes two; fragment 2:1-7 provides a written version parallel to 1QS II (?). [434]

4Q281-282 (4QTohorot E^{a,b}) *4QPurification Rules E^{a,b}*   J. T. Milik, 'Milkî-sedeq et Milkî-resa^c', 129. Two copies of the fifth written version of a 'Rule of puri-ty'. Details unknown.

4Q283 (4QTohorot F ?) *4QPurification Rules F*   J. T. Milik, 'Milkî-sedeq et Milkî-resaᶜ', 129. Possible a sixth written version of a 'Rule of purity'. Details unknown.

4Q284 (4QSerek ha-niddot) *4QRule for a Menstruating Women*   Fragment of a rule concerning sexual impurities.

* 4Q285 (4QMᵍ ?) *4QWar Scrollᵍ*   J. T. Milik, 'Milkî-sedeq et Milkî-resaᶜ', 143. Possible copy of the lost final part of 1QM (?) which partly overlaps 11QBerakhot. R. Eisenman and M. Wise, *The Dead Sea Scrolls Uncovered*, 24-29; G. Vermes, 'The Oxford Forum for Qumran Research Seminar of the Rule of War from Cave 4 (4Q285)', JJS 32 (1992), 86-90; B. Nitzan, 'Benedictions and Instructions for the Eschatological Community (11QBer; 4Q285)', RQ 16/61 (1993), 77-90. [123-124]

* 4Q286 (4QBerᵃ) *4QBlessingsᵃ*   J. T. Milik, 'Milkî-sedeq et Milkî-resaᶜ', 130-134, pl. II, 287. B. Nitzan, '4QBerakhot (4Q286-290): A Preliminary Report', *New Qumran Texts and Studies*, 53-71, Pl. 3. R. Eisenman and M. Wise, *The Dead Sea Scrolls Uncovered*, 222-230. Liturgical collection given the provisional title 'Blessings (and Curses)', preserved in five copies. Only fragment 10 ii 1-13 has been published and some disconnected phrases from other fragments. Late Herodian MS, fom the beginnings of the 1st century CE. [434-435]

* 4Q287 (4QBerᵇ) *4QBlessingsᵇ*   J. T. Milik, 'Milkî-sedeq et Milkî-resaᶜ', 130-131. R. Eisenman and M. Wise, *The Dead Sea Scrolls Uncovered*, 222-230. Another copy of Berakhot. Script slightly earlier than that of 4Q286. [434-435]

o 4Q288-290 (4QBerᶜ,ᵈ,ᵉ) *4QBlessingsᶜ⁻ᵉ*   minute fragments pf other three copies of the same (?) liturgical collection.

o 4Q291-293 *4Qwork containing prayers*   J. T. Milik, 'Milkî-sedeq et Milkî-resaᶜ', 134. Possibly copies of the same liturgical collection of Blessings and Curses (?). Minute fragments of compositions of liturgical character.

o 4Q294-297 *4Qfragments of rules and euchologies* (?)   Details unknown.

* 4Q298 *4QCryptic A: Words of the Sage to the Sons of Dawn*   Work copied in cryptic writing, apart from the beginning: 'The Sage who speaks to the sons of dawn'. [382]

* 4Q299 (4QMystᵃ) *4QMysteriesᵃ*   B. Z. Wacholder and M. G. Abegg, *Fascicle Two*, 1-28. The longest copy of the 'Book of mysteries' [See 1Q27]. [400]

* 4Q300 (4QMystᵇ) *4QMysteriesᵇ*   B. Z. Wacholder and M. G. Abegg, *Fascicle Two*, 29-34. L. H. Schiffman, '4QMysteriesᵇ: A Preliminary Edition', RQ 16/62 (1993), 203-223. Another copy of the same composition, very fragmentary. [400-401]

* 4Q301 (4QMystᶜ) *4QMysteriesᶜ*   B. Z. Wacholder and M. G. Abegg, *Fascicle Two*, 35-57. Minute fragments of the same composition. [401]

4Q302 *4QPraise of God*   Two sizable fragments and other minute remains, on papyrus, of a composition sapiential in character.

o 4Q303-308   Small fragments of various sapiential works.

○ 4Q309-316   Unidentified Hebrew and Aramaic fragments, on skin and on papyrus, several uninscribed.

* 4Q317 (4QAstrCrypt) *4QPhases of the Moon*   J. T. Milik, *The Books of Enoch*, 68-69. Calendar in Hebrew similar to the Aramaic calendars of 4QEnastr*ᵃ*, but copied in a cryptic script. A dozen large-sized fragments have been preserved and many others of a smaller size. [451]

* 4Q318 (4QBr ar) *4QBrontologion*   J. T. Milik, *Ten Years of Discovery*, 42; J. C. Greenfield and M. Sokoloff, 'Astrological and Related Omen Texts in Jewish Palestinian Aramaic', JNES 48 (1989) 202. R. Eisenman and M. Wise, *The Dead Sea Scrolls Uncovered*, 258-263; K. Beyer, *Ergänzungsband*, 128-129. A large fragment with remains of two columns, and four others of very minute size. [451-452]

* 4Q319 (4QOtot) *4QOtot*   B. Z. Wacholder and M. G. Abegg, Fascicle One, 96-101; R. Eisenman and M. Wise, *The Dead Sea Scrolls Uncovered*, 128-133. The calendrical part of 4QSᵉ [see 4Q259]. [27-29]

* 4Q320 (4QCalendrical Doc A) *4QCalendrical Document A*   J. T. Milik, 'Le travail d'édition des manuscrits du désert de Juda', in: *Volume du Congrès Strasbourg 1956* (VTSup 4) (Brill, Leiden 1957), 25. B. Z. Wacholder and M. G. Abegg, *Fascicle One*, 60-67; R. Eisenman and M. Wise, *The Dead Sea Scrolls Uncovered*, 116-119. Calendar with synchronisms of the phases of the moon, of the priestly rosters and of the feasts, known as 4QMishmarot A. [452-454]

* 4Q321 (4QCalendrical Doc Bᵃ) *4QCalendrical Document Bᵃ*   B. Z. Wacholder and M. G. Abegg, *Fascicle One*, 68-73; R. Eisenman and M. Wise, *The Dead Sea Scrolls Uncovered*, 109-116. Calendar with synchronisms of the phases of the moon and the priestly rosters, known as 4QMishmarot Bᵃ. [454-455]

○ 4Q322-324 (4QCalendrical Doc Cᵃ⁻ᵉ) *4QCalendrical Document Cᵃ⁻ᵉ*   B. Z. Wacholder and M. G. Abegg, *Fascicle One*, 77-85; R. Eisenman and M. Wise, *The Dead Sea Scrolls Uncovered*, 119-127. Minute remains of several copies of a calendar based on the priestly rosters, with allusions to historical events.

○ 4Q325 (4QCalendrical Doc D) *4QCalendrical Document D*   B. Z. Wacholder and M. G. Abegg, *Fascicle One*, 86-87; R. Eisenman and M. Wise, *The Dead Sea Scrolls Uncovered*, 127-128. Two fragments of a calendar of the sabbaths and feasts.

○ 4Q326 (4QCalendrical Doc Eᵃ) *4QCalendrical Document Eᵃ*   B. Z. Wacholder and M. G. Abegg, *Fascicle One*, 88. A small fragment with remains of a calendar of the sabbaths and feasts.

* 4Q327 (Calendrical Doc Eᵇ) *4QCalendrical Document Eᵇ*   B. Z. Wacholder and M. G. Abegg, *Fascicle One*, 89-91. Calendar of feasts. R. Eisenman and M. Wise, *The Dead Sea Scrolls Uncovered*, 182-193, consider it part of one of the copies of 4QMMT [see 4Q394], but see F. García Martínez, 'Dos Notas sobre 4QMMT', RQ 16/62 (1993), 293-297. [455]

○ 4Q328-330 (4QCalendrical Doc F-G-H) *4QCalendrical Document F-G-H*   B. Z.

Wacholder and M. G. Abegg, *Fascicle One*, 92–95. Minute remains of several calendars based on the priestly rosters.

o 4Q331–334 *4QHistorical Works*   Fragmentary remains of works with allusions to historical events (?).

o 4Q335–337 *4QAstronomical fragments*   Fragments of astronomical content or of calendars.

o 4Q338–341 *4QLists of proper names*   Lists of names of persons. 4Q339 and 4Q340 were published by M. Broshi and A. Yardeni, 'On Netinim and False Prophets', *Tarbiz* 62 (1993), 45–54. 4Q341 was published by J. M. Allegro, *The Dead Sea Scrolls and the Christian Myth* (Newton Abbot 1979) 235–2443, pls. 16–17, as a medical document. However, later it was identified as a writing exercise, cf. J. Naveh, 'A Medical Document or a Writing Exercise? The So-called 4QTherapeia', IEJ 36 (1986) 52–55, pl. 11.

o 4Q342–358 *4QLegal documents*   Remains of contracts, deeds of sale, accounts, letters, etc.

o 4Q359–361   Minute remains, with and without writing.

o 4Q362–363   Fragments in cryptic writing. Undeciphered.

* 4Q364 (4QRP^b) *4QReworked Pentateuch^b*   Paraphrase of the Pentateuch, described by its editor, J. Strugnell as: 'A wildly aberrant text of the whole Pentateuch containing several non-Biblical additions, some identical with the Samaritan Pentateuchal pluses, others unattested elsewhere (e.g. a song of Miriam at the Red Sea)', in: *Salvación en la Palabra*, 563–564. Photograph of two of the fragments of 4Q364 in Y. Yadin, *The Temple Scroll*, Suppl. pls. 38, 40. E. Tov, 'The textual Status of 4Q354-367', in: *The Madrid Qumran Congress*, 43–82; S. A. White, '4Q364 & 365: A Preliminary Report', in: *The Madrid Qumran Congress*, 217–228. [222–224]

* 4Q365 (4QRP^c) *4QReworked Pentateuch^c*   Another copy of the same (?) work with remains of the five books of the Pentateuch. [222–224]

4Q366 (4QRP^d) *4QReworked Pentateuch^d*   Another copy with remains of Ex 21–22, Num 29 and Dt 14 and 16.

4Q367 (4QRP^e) *4QReworked Pentateuch^e*   Another copy with remains only of various chs. of Leviticus.

4Q368 (4QapocrPent) *4QApocryphon Pentateuch*   Fifteen fragments, of which three are a good size, of a narrative worked related to the Pentateuch.

4Q369 (4QPEnosh ?) *4QPrayer of Enosh* (?)   A good fragment with remains of two columns and other lesser fragments of an apocryphal composition related to the generations before the Flood.

* 4Q370 *4QExhortation based on the Flood*   C. Newsom, '4Q370: An Admonition based on the Flood', RQ 13 (1988) 23–43, pl. I. Exhortation based on the story of the flood, of which only two cols. have been preserved. [224–225]

4Q371 (4QapocrJoseph^a) *4QApocryphon of Joseph^a*   E. M. Schuller, *Non-Canonical Psalms from Qumran*, 2. Narrative work with apocryphal psalms.

* 4Q372 (4QapocrJoseph*b*) *4QApocryphon of Joseph*b* E.M.Schuler, 'A Preliminary Study of 4Q372 1', in: F. García Martínez (ed.), *The Texts of Qumran and the History of the Community*. Vol. II (Paris 1990) 349-376. Text with narrative and psalms. Fragment 1 contains a psalm about the character of Joseph. [225-226]

* 4Q373 (4QapocrJoseph*c*) *4QApocryphon of Joseph*c* E. Schuller, 'A Preliminary Study of 4Q373 and Some Related (?) Fragments', in: *The Madrid Qumran Congress*, 515-530. Another copy of 2Q22. In addition the text matches fragment 19 of 4Q372. [226]

* 4Q374 (4QapocrMoses A) *4QApocryphon of Moses A* C. A. Newsom '4Q374: A Discourse on the Exodus/Conquest Tradition', in E. Dimant and U. Rappaport (eds.), *The Dead Sea Scrolls. Forty Years of Research* (STDJ 10) (Leiden-Jerusalem 1992), 40-52. Moses and Joshua apocryphon. [278]

* 4Q375 (4QapocrMoses B) *4QApocryphon of Moses B* J. Strugnell, 'Moses-Pseudepigrapha at Qumran. 4Q375, 4Q376, and similar works', in L. Schiffman (ed.), *Archaeology and History in the Dead Sea Scrolls* (JSP 8) (Sheffield 1990) 221-234. Moses-pseudepigraph, distinct from the preceding composition. [278]

* 4Q376 *4QLiturgy of the Three Tongues of Fire* J. Strugnell, 'Moses-Pseudepigrapha at Qumran', 234-247. Moses-pseudepigraph identical with 1Q29. [279]

o 4Q377 (4QapocrMoses C) *4QApocrypohon of Moses C* Moses and Joshua apocryphon, copied onto the reverse of 4Q375 and very badly preserved.

* 4Q378 (4QPsJosua*a*) *4QPsalms of Joshua*a*, C. Newsom, 'The "Psalms of Joshua" from Qumran Cave 4', JJS 39 (1988) 56-73, pl. 1. The editor describes the work and published fragments 3:, 6 I; 14 and 22 I (pp. 61-65). [282]

* 4Q379 (4QPsJosua*b*) *4QPsalms of Joshua*b* P. A. Spijkerman, 'Chronique du Musée de la Flagellation', Studii Biblici Franciscani Liber Annuus 12 (1991-62) 324-325 (photograph of fragment 1); C. Newsom, 'The "Psalms of Joshua" from Qumran Cave 4', 65-70. Publication of fragments 1, 12, 15-17 and 22 II. [283]

* 4Q380 *4QNoncanonical Psalms A* E. M. Schuller, *Non-Canonical Psalms from Qumran. A Pseudepigraphical Collection* (HSS 28) (Atlanta 1986) 241-165, pl. VIII. Pseudepigraphical collection of apocryphal psalms. [311-312]

* 4Q381 *4QNoncanonical Psalms A* E. M. Schuller, *Non-Canonical Psalms from Qumran*, 61-240, pls. I-VII. IX. Another (or the same?) pseudepigraphical collection of apocryphal psalms. [312-316]

4Q382 *4QParaphrase of Kings* abundant fragments in papyrus with narratives and psalms related to Samuel-Kings.

o 4Q383-384 *4QApocryphon of Jeremiah A-B* (?) Minute remains of two compositions related to Jeremiah

* 4Q385 (4QpsEz*a*) *4QPseudo-Ezekiel* J. Strugnell and D. Dimant, '4QSecond Ezekiel', RQ 3 (1988) 54-58, pl. II. D. Dimant, 'The Merkaba Vision in Second Ezekiel (4Q385 4)' in: *The Text of Qumran and the History of the Community*, Vol. II, 331-348. Pseudepigraphical apocalypse attributed to the prophet Ezekiel. [286]

○ 4Q385a (4QpsMoses^a) *4QPseudo-Moses^a*   D. Dimant, the editor of the group of fragments previously attributed to 4QPseudo-Ezekiel, considers them to represent at least three separate compositions: Pseudo-Ezekiel, Pseudo-Moses and Pseudo-Jeremiah. Hence the subdivision of the numbers and their allocation to separate compositions. D. Dimant, 'New Light From Qumran in the Jewish Pseudepigrapha – 4Q390', *The Madrid Qumran Congress*, 405-448.

* 4Q385b (4QapocrJer C) *4QApocryphon of Jeremiah C*   D. Dimant, 'An Apocryphon of Jeremiah from Cave 4 (4Q385^b = (4Q385 16)', *New Qumran Texts and Studies*, 11-30, Pl. 2. Scant remains of the third pseudepigraphic work attributed to Jeremiah. [285]

* 4Q386 (4QpsEz^b) *4QPseudo-Ezekiel^b*   Scant remains of a second copy of Pseudo-Ezekiel. [287]

* 4Q387 (4QpsEz^c) *4QPseudo-Ezekiel^c*   Scant remains of a third copy of the same composition.

* 4Q387a (4QpsMoses^b) *4QPseudo-Moses^b*   Scant remains of a second copy of the Mosaic pseudepigraph. [279]

* 4Q387b (4QapocrJer D) *4QApocryphon of Jeremiah D*   Scant remains of a fourth pseudepigraphic composition attributed to Jeremiah. [285]

* 4Q388 (4QpsEz^d) *4QPseudo-Ezekiel^d*   Scant remains of a fourth copy of Pseudo-Ezekiel.

* 4Q388a (4QpsMoses^c) *4QPseudo-Moses^c*   Scant remains of a third copy of the Mosaic pseudepigraph. [279-280]

* 4Q389 (4QpsMoses^d) *4QPseudo-Moses^d*   Scant remains of a fourth copy of the same composition. [280]

* 4Q390 (4QpsMoses^e) *4QPseudo-Moses Apocalypse^e*   D. Dimant, 'New Light From Qumran in the Jewish Pseudepigrapha – 4Q390'. Another (?) Moses pseudepigraph or a fifth copy of the preceding composition. [280-281]

○ 4Q391 (4QpsEz^g) *4QPseudo-Ezekiel^g (?)*   Pseudepigraphical work copied on papyrus, related to the preceding compositions.

* 4Q392 *4QLiturgical Work*   B. Z. Wacholder and M. G. Abegg, Fascicle Two, 38-39. Wisdom-type composition of which only one fragment is sizable. [438]

4Q393 *4QLiturgical Work (?)*   Three good fragments, and others of smaller sizes. One of the fragments preserves remains of two sheets with different writing but sewn together. The content appears to be sapiential although mention of Moses could connect it with the preceding compositions.

* 4Q394 (4QMMT^a) *4QHalakhic Letter^a*   E. Qimron and J. Strugnell, 'An Unpublished Halakhic Letter from Qumran', in: *Biblical Archaeology Today. Proceedings of the International Congress on Biblical Archaeology, Jerusalem, April 1984* (Jerusalem 1985) 400-407. E. Qimron and J. Strugnell, *Discoveries in the Judean Desert X* (= DJD X) (Oxford 1994), 3-13, pl. i-iii. First copy of the 'Halakhic Letter'. With remains of a calendar at the beginning. [79-81]

* 4Q395 (4QMMT^b) *4QHalakhic Letter^b*   DJD X, 14-15, pl. III. Copy of which only one fragment has been preserved. [81]

* 4Q396 (4QMMT^c) *4QHalakhic Letter^c* DJD X, 15-21, pl. IV. Copy of the central part of the work. [81-82]

* 4Q397 (4QMMT^d) *4QHalakhic Letter^d* DJD X, 21-28, pl. V-VI. Copy with relatively abundant material from the different sections of the letter. [83-84]

* 4Q398 (4QMMT^e) *4QHalakhic Letter^e* DJD X, 28-38, pl. VII-VIII. Copy on papyrus which preserves the end of the composition. A photograph of this manuscript is to be found in: E. Qimron and J. Strugnell, 'An Unpublished Halakhic Letter from Qumran', Israel Museum Journal 4 (1985) 9-12, pl. 1. [84-85]

* 4Q399 (4QMMT^f) *4QHalakhic Letter^f* DJD X, 38-40, pl. VIII. A single fragment, with remains of two columns, from the end of the work. [85]

* 4Q400 (4QShirShabb^a) *4QSongs of the Sabbath Sacrifice^a* C. Newsom, *Songs of the Sabbath Sacrifice: A Critical Edition* (HSS 27) (Atlanta 1985) 85-123, pl. I. Copy of the work 'Songs of the sabbath sacrifice', with remains of the songs of the first two sabbaths. Of this work a copy has been preserved which comes from Cave 11 (11Q17 *infra*) and another found during the excavations of Masada (4Q MasShirShab, see Y. Yadin, 'The Excavations of Masada', IEJ 15 (1965) 105-108; C. Newsom and Y. Yadin, 'The Masada Fragment of the Qumran Songs of the Sabbath Sacrifice', IEJ 34 (1984) 77-88; C. Newsom, *Songs of the Sabbath Sacrifice*, 167-184, pl. XVI. E. Puech, 'Notes sur les manuscrits des Cantiques du Sacrifice du Sabbat trouvé à Masada', RQ 12/48 (1987) 575-583. [419-420]

* 4Q401 (4QShirShabb^b) *4QSongs of the Sabbath Sacrifice^b* C. Newsom, *Songs of the Sabbath Sacrifice*, 125-146, pls. II-III. Another copy of the same work, with remains, possibly, of the songs for the first, third and sixth sabbath. [420]

* 4Q402 (4QShirShabb^c) *4QSongs of the Sabbath Sacrifice^c* C. Newsom, *Songs of the Sabbath Sacrifice*, 147-166, pl. III. Another copy of the same work with remains of the song for the fifth sabbath. [420-421]

* 4Q403 (4QShirShabb^d) *4QSongs of the Sabbath Sacrifice^d* J. Strugnell, 'The Angelic Liturgy at Qumrân. 4QSerek Shirot ʿOlat hashshabbat', *Congress Volume, Oxford 1959* (SVT 7) (Brill Leiden 1960) 322-327, pl. Ia. C. Newsom, *Songs of the Sabbath Sacrifice*, 185-247, p. IV. Another copy of the same work with remains of the songs for the sixth, seventh and eighth sabbaths. [421-424]

* 4Q404 (4QShirShabb^e) *4QSongs of the Sabbath Sacrifice^e* C. Newsom, *Songs of the Sabbath Sacrifice*, 249-255, pl. V. Another copy of the same work with remains of the songs for the sixth, seventh and eighth sabbaths. [424-425]

* 4Q405 (4QShirShabb^f) *4QSongs of the Sabbath Sacrifice^f* J. Strugnell, 'The Angelic Liturgy at Qumrân', 336-342, pl. Ib. C. Newsom, *Songs of the Sabbath Sacrifice*, 257-354, pls. VI-XIV. Another copy of the same work with remains of the songs for the last seven sabbaths. [426-430]

o 4Q406 (4QShirShabb^g) *4QSongs of the Sabbath Sacrifice^g* C. Newsom, *Songs of the Sabbath Sacrifice*, 355-357, pl. XV. Another copy of the same work with remains of the beginning of an unidentified song.

o 4Q407 (4QShirShabb*h*) *4QSongs of the Sabbath Sacrifice*h   C. Newsom, *Songs of the Sabbath Sacrifice*, 259-260, pl. XV. Possibly another copy of the same work. Remains of two small fragments.

o 4Q408 *4QSapiential Work*   Minute fragments of a wisdom-type composition.

* 4Q409 *4QLiturgy*   E. Qimron, 'Time for Praising God: A Fragment of a Scroll from Qumran (4Q409)', JQR 80 (1990) 341-347. Remains of a hymnic composition. [402]

o 4Q410 *4QSapiential Work*   B. Z. Wacholder and M. G. Abegg, *Fascicle Two*, 40. Minute remains of a wisdom composition.

o 4Q411 *4QSapiential Work*   A single fragment, with the first words of a 17-line column.

o 4Q412 *4QSapiential Work*   B. Z. Wacholder and M. G. Abegg, *Fascicle Two*, 41-42. Minute remains of a wisdom composition.

* 4Q413 *4QSapiential Work*   B. Z. Wacholder and M. G. Abegg, *Fascicle Two*, 43. A single fragment with the beginning of a wisdom composition. [382-383]

* 4Q414 *4QBaptismal Liturgy*   R. Eisenman and M. Wise, *The Dead Sea Scrolls Uncovered*, 230-233. Remains of a hymnic composition. [439]

4Q415 (4QSap. Work A*d*) *4QSapiential Work A*d (?)   B. Z. Wacholder and M. G. Abegg, *Fascicle Two*, 44-53. Numerous fragments of a wisdom composition, possibly part of the next work, although the preserved fragments provide no matches.

* 4Q416 (4QSap. Work A*b*) *4QSapiential Work A*b   B. Z. Wacholder and M. G. Abegg, *Fascicle Two*, 54-62. R. Eisenman and M. Wise, *The Dead Sea Scrolls Uncovered*, 241-254. Wisdom composition. [383-385]

* 4Q417 (4QSap. Work A*c*) *4QSapiential Work A*c   B. Z. Wacholder and M. G. Abegg, *Fascicle Two*, 63-76. Another copy of the same wisdom composition. [385-387]

* 4Q418 (4QSap. Work A*a*) *4QSapiential Work A*a   B. Z. Wacholder and M. G. Abegg, *Fascicle Two*, 77-154. R. Eisenman – M. Wise, *The Dead Sea Scrolls Uncovered*, 241-254. The longest copy of this wisdom composition. Nearly 300 fragments have been preserved although only a few are a good size. [388-393]

* 4Q419 (4QSap. Work B) *4QSapiential Work B*   B. Z. Wacholder and M. G. Abegg, *Fascicle Two*, 155-158. Another wisdom composition, of which only the first fragment is of some length. [393]

o 4Q420-421 *Ways of Righteousness*a-b   B. Z. Wacholder and M. G. Abegg, *Fascicle Two*, 159-165. Minute remains of two copies of another wisdom composition.

o 4Q422 *4QParaphrase of Genesis-Exodus*   Minute remains of a biblical paraphrase.

o 4Q423 (4QSap. Work A*e*) *4QSapiential Work A*e   B. Z. Wacholder and M. G. Abegg, *Fascicle Two*, 166-173.

* 4Q424 (4QSap. Work C) *4QSapiential Work C*   B. Z. Wacholder and M. G. Abegg, *Fascicle Two*, 174-176. R. Eisenman – M. Wise, *The Dead Sea Scrolls Uncovered*, 166-168. Another wisdom composition. [393-394]

o 4Q425-426 *4Qsapiential works* B. Z. Wacholder and M. G. Abegg, *Fascicle Two*, 174-184. Minute remains of wisdom compositions.

* 4Q427 (4QH*ᵃ*) *4QHymnsᵃ* E. Schuller, 'A Hymn from a Cave Four *Hodayot* Manuscript: 4Q427 7 I+II', JBL 112 (1993), 605-628. B. Z. Wacholder and M. G. Abegg, *Fascicle Two*, 254-261. [362-366]

* 4Q428 (4QH*ᵇ*) *4QHymnsᵇ* B. Z. Wacholder and M. G. Abegg, *Fascicle Two*, 262-274. [367]

* 4Q429 (4QH*ᶜ*) *4QHymnsᶜ* B. Z. Wacholder and M. G. Abegg, *Fascicle Two*, 275-278. [367-369]

* 4Q430 (4QH*ᵈ*) *4QHymnsᵈ* B. Z. Wacholder and M. G. Abegg, *Fascicle Two*, 279. [369]

* 4Q431 (4QH*ᵉ*) *4QHymnsᵉ* B. Z. Wacholder and M. G. Abegg, *Fascicle Two*, 280. [270]

o 4Q432 (4QH*ᶠ*) *4QHymnsᶠc* B. Z. Wacholder and M. G. Abegg, *Fascicle Two*, 281-184. Minute remains of a copy on papyrus of the *Hodayot*.

o 4Q433 *4QHodayot-like text* Three minute fragments of a composition similar to the Hymns.

* 4Q434 (4QBarᵉki Napshiᵃ) *4QBless, Oh my Soulᵃ* R. Eisenman and M. Wise, *The Dead Sea Scrolls Uncovered*, 233-241. First copy of a composition with hymns of praise which usually begin with the sentence: Bless, Oh my soul. A good fragment with remains of two columns, and other lesser fragments. [436]

* 4Q434a *4QGrace after Meals*, M. Wienfeld, 'Grace after Meals at the Mourners' House in a Text from Qumran', Tarbiz 41 (1992), 15-23 [English version, JBL 111 (1992) 427-440]. Two fragments of thanksgiving after a meal in the house of a person in mourning. [439]

o 4Q435 (4QBarᵉki Napshiᵇ) *4QBless, Oh my Soulᵇ* Minute fragments of a second copy of the blessings of praise.

* 4Q436 (4QBarᵉki Napshiᶜ) *4QBless, Oh my Soulᶜ* R. Eisenman and M. Wise, *The Dead Sea Scrolls Uncovered*, 233-241. A single fragment with one column almost complete from another copy of the same composition. [437]

  4Q437 (4QBarᵉki Napshiᵈ) *4QBless, Oh my Soulᵈ* Various fragments of another copy of the same composition.

o 4Q438 (4QBarᵉki Napshiᵉ) *4QBless, Oh my Soulᵉ* Minute fragments of another copy of the same composition.

o 4Q439 *4QWork similar to Barᵉki Napshi* Three tiny fragments of a composition similar to the preceding.

  4Q440 *4QHodayot-like text* Two fragments from the end of a hymnic composition similar to the Hymns.

o 4Q441-447 Minute fragments of prayers or hymns.

o 4Q448 *4QApocryphal Psalm and Prayer* E. Eshel, H. Eshel and A. Yardeni, 'A Qumran Composition Containing Part of Ps. 154 and a Prayer for the Welfare of King Jonathan and his Kingdom', Tarbiz 60 (1991), 295-324 [English version, IEJ 42 (1992), 199-229] o 4Q449-57 *4QPrayers*   Minute remains of liturgical compositions.

* 4Q458 *4QNarrative*   R. Eisenman and M. Wise, *The Dead Sea Scrolls Uncovered*, 47-49. Minute remains of an unspecified composition. [228]

4Q459-60 *4QPseudepigraphic Works*   Remains of narrative works with biblical reminiscences; of the second a good-sized fragment has been preserved.

o 4Q461 *4QNarrative*   five minute fragments of a narrative work.

* 4Q462 *4QNarrative*   M. S. Smith, '4Q462 (Narrative) Fragment 1: A Preliminary Edition', *Mémorial Jean Starcky*. Vol. I, 55-77. [226-227]

o 4Q463   A. Steudel, *Der Midrash zur Eschatologie aus der Qumrangemeinde*. Four fragments of a wisdom-type composition.

o 4Q464   M. S. Stone and E. Eshel, 'An Exposition on the Patriarchs (4Q464) and two Other Documents (4Q464a and 4Q464b)', Le Muséon 105 (1992), 243-264.

o 4Q464a-69 *4QUnclassified fragments*   Fragments of unidentified works.

o 4Q470 *4QFragment mentioning Zedekiah*   E. Larson, L. H. Schiffman and J. Strugnell, '4Q470, With a Fragment Mentioning Zedekiah', RQ 16/62 (1994). Three minute fragments of an unidentified work which mentions Zedekiah and the angel Michael.

* 4Q471 *4QWar Scroll^h*   E. and H. Eshel, '4Q471. Frag. 1 and Ma'amadot in the War Scroll', in: *The Madrid Qumran Congress*, 611-620. Minute remains of a composition which is perhaps related to The War Scroll. [124-125]

* 4Q471a *4QPolemical fragment*   E. Eshel and M. Kister, 'A Polemical Qumran Fragment', JJS 43 (1992), 277-281. Fragment four of the preceding composition. [124-125]

o 4Q472 *4QSapiential work*   Minute remains of a wisdom composition.

o 4Q473 *4QThe Two Ways*   Two minute fragments of a wisdom composition.

o 4Q474-476 *4Qsapiential works*   Minute fragments of three wisdom-type compositions.

* 4Q477 *4QDecrees*   R. Eisenman and M. Wise, *The Dead Sea Scrolls Uncovered*, 269-273; E. Eshel, 'The Rebukes by the Overseer', JJS 45 (1994), 111-232. [90-91]

o 4Q478-81 *4Qunclassified fragments*   Minute remains of unidentified works.

o 4Q482 (4QJub ?), *4QJubilees* (?)   M. Baillet, *Discoveries in the Judaean Desert* VII (Oxford 1982) (= DJD VII), 1-2, pl. I. Possibly a copy of the Book of Jubilees.

o 4Q483 *4QGenesis or Jubilees* (?)   M. Baillet, DJD VII, 2, pl. I. Possibly remains of Gen 1:18 or Jub 2:14 (?).

o 4Q484 (4QTJud) *4QTestament of Judah*   M. Baillet, DJD VII, 3, pl. I. Remains of a work related to the Testament of Judah (?).

o 4Q485 *4QProphecy*   M. Baillet, DJD VII, 4, pl. II. Minute remains of a prophetical or wisdom text on papyrus.

o 4Q486 *4QSapiential Work^a*   M. Baillet, DJD VII, 4-5, pl. II. Minute remains of a sapiential work (?).

o 4Q487 *4QSapiential Work^a*   M. Baillet, DJD VII, 5-10, pls. III-IV. Numerous remains (53 fragments) of a sapiential (?) work copied on papyrus.

o 4Q488-490 *4Qapocrypha* M. Baillet, DJD VII, 10-11, pl. II. Remains of apocryphal works in Aramaic (?).

* 4Q491 (4QMᵃ) *4QWar Scrollᵃ* C. H. Hunzinger, 'Fragmente einer älteren Fassung des Buches Milhama aus Höhle 4 von Qumrân', ZAW 69 (1957) 131-151, pl. 1; M. Baillet, 'Les manuscrits de la règle de la guerre de la grotte 4 de Qumrân', RB 79 (1972) 217-226; .-DJD VII, 12-44, pls. V-VI. Text related to the War Rule. Hunzinger considers the text to be an older form of the War Rule, Baillet considers it to be later and dependent on 1QM. The MS contains elements which seem to correspond to 1QM, others which seem to be a cento of phrases which are also found in 1QM in other contexts, and others which have no parallel in 1QM. One of these new hymnic compositions (the 'song of Michael' of fragment 11 i) also occurs in another MS from 4Q as yet unpublished, 4Q471B [4Q(Sl)86]. [115-119]

* 4Q492 (4QMᵇ) *4QWar Scrollᵇ* M. Baillet, DJD VII, 45-49, pl. VII. Another copy of the War Rule. Fragment 1 corresponds to 1QM xix 1-14 and to fragments 2, 8 and 1Q33 2; fragments 2-3 have not been identified. [120]

* 4Q493 (4QMᵇ) *4QWar Scrollᶜ* M. Baillet, DJD VII, 49-53, pl. VIII. Text related to 1QM; the preserved material has no equivalent in 1QM. [120-121]

* 4Q494 (4QMᵈ) *4QWar Scrollᵈ* M. Baillet, DJD VII, 53-54, pl. VIII. Another copy of the War Rule. The only fragment preserved partly corresponds to 1QM ii 1-2. [121]

* 4Q495 (4QMᵉ) 4Q*War Scrollᵉ* J. T. Milik, 'Milkî-sedeq et Milkî-resaᶜ', 140; M. Baillet, DJD VII, 54-56, pl. VIII. Another copy of the War Rule. Fragment 2 corresponds to 1QM xiii 9-12. [121]

* 4Q496 (4QMᶠ) *4QWar Scrollᶠ* M. Baillet, 'Débris de textes sur papyrus de la grotte 4 de Qumrân', RB 71 (1964) 353-371; .-DJD VII, 57-68; pls. X, XII, XIV, XVIII, XXIV. Another copy of the War Rule. The first 16 fragments (of the 122 preserved) have been grouped into five columns which partly correspond to 1QM i 4-iv 2. [121-123]

o 4Q497 (4QMᵍ ?) M. Baillet, DJD VII, 69-72, pl. XXVI. Text related to the War Rule (?).

o 4Q498 *4QSapiential Hymn* M. Baillet, DJD VII, 73-74, pl. XXVII. Hymnic or sapiential (?) fragments.

o 4Q499 *4QHymnic Prayer* M. Baillet, DJD VII, 74-77, pl. XXV. Fragments of hymns or prayers.

* 4Q500 *4QBenediction* M. Baillet, DJD VII, 78-79, pl. XXVII. Remains of a blessing (?); J. M. Baumgarten, '4Q500 and the Ancient Exegesis of the Lord's Vineyard', JJS 40 (1989) 1-6 interprets it as an exegesis of the canticle of the vine of Isa 5. [402]

* 4Q501 *4QApocryphal Lamentations B* M. Baillet, DJD VII, 79-80, pl. XXVIII. Remains of a 'Lamentation', poetic composition related to 1QH. [403]

* 4Q502 *4QRitual of Marriage* M. Baillet, DJD VII, 81-105, pls. XXIX-XXXIV. Frag-

ments of a ritual for a joyous celebration, interpreted by Baillet as a wedding ritual and by J. M. Baumgarten, '4Q502, Marriage or Golden Age Ritual?', JJS 34 (1983) 125-135, as a celebration (related to the feast of tabernacles?) in which the protagonists are old men and women. [440-441]

* 4Q503 (4QPrQuot) *4QDaily Prayers^a*   M. Baillet, DJD VII, 105-136, pls. XXXV, XXXVII, XXXIX, XLI, XLVIII, XLV, XLVII. Remains of a liturgical composition with prayers for each day of the month. Remains have been preserved of prayers for fifteen days, between the 4th and the 26th. [407-410]

* 4Q504 (4QDibHam^a) *4QWords of the Luminaries^a*   M. Baillet, 'Un receuil liturgique de Qumrân, grotte 4: "Les Paroles des Luminaires"', RB 67 (1961) 195-250, pls. XXIV-XXVIII; . - 'Remarques sur l'édition des Paroles des Luminaires', RQ 5/17 (1964) 23-42; .-DJD VII, 137-168, pls. XLIX-LIII. Copy of a liturgical work, of which the title, 'Words of the luminaries', has been preserved on the back of fragment 8, and contains prayers for every day of the week (the beginning of the prayer of Wednesday and of the sabbath have been preserved). [414-417]

* 4Q505 (4QDibHam^b) *4QWords of the Luminaries^b*   M. Baillet, DJD VII, 168-170, pl. XXIII. Identified by the editor as another copy of the 'Words of the Luminaries' (4QDibHam^b); in fact, the preserved fragments seem to belong to the 'Festival prayers' (4Q509). [418]

* 4Q506 (4QDibHam^c) *4QWords of the Luminaries^c*   M. Baillet, DJD VII, 170-175, pls. XVIII, XX, XXIV. Another copy of the 'Words of the Luminaries'. [418]

* 4Q507 (4QPrFêtes^a ?) *4QFestival Prayers^a*   M. Baillet, DJD VII, 175-177, pl. XXVIII. Another copy (?) of a liturgical work which contained prayers for the different festivals of the liturgical year, known from the remains preserved in 1Q34-34bis. [411-412]

* 4Q508 (4QPrFêtes^b) *4QFestival Prayers^b*   M. Baillet, DJD VII, 177-184, pl. LIV. Another copy of a liturgical work with prayers for the different festivals, with remains, possibly, of the prayers for feasts of the waving of the sheaves, of weeks, of the New Year and of Yom Kippur (?). [412]

* 4Q509 (4QPrFêtes^c) *4QFestival Prayers^c*   M. Baillet, DJD VII, 184-215, pls. IX, XI, XIII, XV, XVII, XIX, XXI, XXII. Another copy of the same work, with remains of the prayers for the feasts of the New Year, Yom Kippur, tabernacles, the second passover and pentecost (?). [412-413]

* 4Q510 (4QShir^a) *4QSongs of the Sage^a*   M. Baillet, DJD VII, 215-219, pl. LV. Collection of songs of the Maskil for praising God and expelling demons. [371]

* 4Q511 (4QShir^b) *4QSongs of the Sage^b*   M. Baillet, DJD VII, 219-262, pls. LVI-LXII. Another copy of the same work of which 224 fragments have been preserved. [371-376]

* 4Q512 *4QRitual of Purification*   M. Baillet, DJD VII, 262-286, pls. XXXVI, XXXVIII, XL, XLII, XLIV, XLVI, XLVIII. Numerous remains (232 fragments) of a purification ritual with directives concerning various purifications and with the prayers to be recited on the occasions of these purifications. [441-442]

* 4Q513 (4QOrd*b* ?) *4QOrdinances*b* M. Baillet, DJD VII, 287-295, pls. LXXII-LXXIII. Halakhic text related to 4QHalaka*a* and 4QMMT, considered by the editor as another copy of the halakhic work represented by 4Q159. [91]

* 4Q514 (4QOrd*c* ?) *4QOrdinances*c* M. Baillet, DJD VII, 295-298, pl. LXXIV. Another halakhic text which deals with the conditions of purity required for participation in the community meals; considered by the editor as possibly another copy of the same halakhic work. [91-92]

o 4Q515-520 *4QUnidentified fragments* M. Baillet, DJD VII, 299-312, pls. LXXV-LXXX. Fragments of unidentified works.

* 4Q521 *4QMessianic Apocalypse* E. Puech, 'Une apocalypse messianique (4Q521)', RQ 15/60 (1992) 475-522. Wisdom text which exhibits belief in the resurrection. [394-395]

* 4Q522 *4QWork with Place Names* E. Puech, 'La pierre de Sion et l'autel des holocaustes d'après un manuscrit hébreu de la grotte 4 (4Q522), RB 99 (1992), 676-696. Work in Hebrew with place-names. A good fragment with remains of two columns and a dozen small fragments. [227-228]

o 4Q523-524 *4QHalakhic texts* Minute Hebrew fragments, halakhic in content.

* 4Q525 (4QBéat) *4QBeatitudes* J. Starcky, 'Le travail d'édition', 67; E. Puech, 'Un hymne essénien en partie retrouvé et les Béatitudes', in: *Mémorial Carmignac*, 84-87; . – '4Q525 et les péricopes des béatitudes en Ben Sira et Matthieu', RB 98 (1991) 80-106. Fragment of a sapiential work which contains a series of blessings. [395-398]

o 4Q526-528 *4QHebrew Fragments C-D-E* Three minute unidentified Hebrew fragments, each in a different hand.

* 4Q529 *4QWords of Michael* R. Eisenman and M. Wise, The Dead Sea Scrolls Uncovered, 37-39. K. Beyer, *Ergängzungsband*, 127-128. J. Starcky, 'Le travail', 66; J. T. Milik, *The Books of Enoch*, 91. Aramaic work with the title 'Words of the book of which Michael spoke to the Angels'. Two further copies have been preserved in 4Q to which belong the fragments from 6Q23. [125]

* 4Q530 (4QGiants*b* ar) *4QGiants*b* J. T. Milik, 'Turfan et Qumrân', 121-125; . – *The Books of Enoch*, 230, 304-307. K. Beyer, *Ergängzungsband*, 119-124. Another copy of the Book of Giants. [261-262]

* 4Q531 (4QGiants*c* ar) *4QGiants*c* J. T. Milik, *The Books of Enoch*, 307-313. K. Beyer, *Ergänzungsband*, 119-124. Another copy of the Book of Giants. [262]

o 4Q532 (4QGiants*d* ar) *4QBook of Giants*d* R. Eisenman and M. Wise, *The Dead Sea Scrolls Uncovered*, 95. K. Beyer, *Ergänzungsband*, 119-124. Small fragments of another copy of the Book of Giants.

o 4Q533 (4QGiants*e* ar?) J. T. Milik, *The Books of Enoch*, 237-238. Another copy of the Aramaic Book of Giants (?) or a pseudo-Enochic composition.

* 4Q534 (4QMess ar) *4QElect of God* J. Starcky, 'Un texte messianique araméen de la grotte 4 de Qumrân', in: *École des langues orientles anciennes de l'Institut Catholique de Paris. Mémorial du cinQuantenaire 1914-1964* (Bloud et Gay, Paris

1964) 51-66. The text refers to the birth of Noah, fragment J. A. Fitzmyer, 'The Aramaic 'Elect of God' Text from Qumrân Cave IV', CBQ 27 (1965) 348-372; J. T. Milik, *The Books of Enoch*, 56. According to E. Puech, it is one of the three manuscripts referred to as 4QNoah*ᵃ⁻ᶜ*. [263]

* 4Q535 *4QAramaic N* R. Eisenman and M. Wise, *The Dead Sea Scrolls Uncovered*, 33-37. K. Beyer, *Ergänzungsband*, 125-127. Tiny Aramaic fragments of a composition connected with Noah. [263-264]

* 4Q536 *4QAramiic C* K. Beyer, *Ergänzungsband*, 125-127. Minute Aramaic fragments of a composition connected with Noah. [264]

* 4Q537 (4QAJa ar) *4QApocryphon of Jacob* J. T. Milik, 'Ecrits préesseniens de Qumrân', 103-104. Remains of an Aramaic work: Visions of Jacob (?). The tyext has been published by E. Puech, 'Fragments d'un apocryphe de Lévi et le personnage eschatologique, 4QTestLévi*ᶜ⁻ᵈ* (?) et 4QAJa', in: *The Madrid Qumran Congress* 449-501. [265]

* 4Q538 (4QAJu ar) *4QApocryphon of Judah* J. T. Milik, 'Ecrits préesseniens de Qumrân', 97-101, pl. I. Remains of an Aramaic Testament of Judah (?). [265-266]

* 4Q539 (4QAJo ar) *4QApocryphon of Joseph* J. T. Milik, 'Ecrits préesseniens de Qumrân', 97-101, pl. I. Remains of an Aramaic Testament of Joseph (?). [266]

* 4Q540 (4QTLevi*ᶜ* ar?) *4QAaronic Text A (bis) = Testament of Levi*ᶜ (?) work described by J. Starcky, 'Les Quatre étapes du messianisme à Qumrân', RB 70 (1963) 492, as an Aramaic work of Aaronite content (4QAhA) and edited by E. Puech as another copy of the Aramaic Testament of Levi, 'Fragments d'un apocryphe de Lévi et le personnage eschatologique, 4QTestLévi*ᶜ⁻ᵈ* (?) et 4QAJa' in: *The Madrid Qumran Congress* 449-501. [269]

* 4Q541 (4QTLevi*ᵈ* ar?) *4QAaroniic Text A = 4QTestament of Levi*ᵈ (?) E. Puech, 'Fragments d'un apocryphe de Lévi et le personnage eschatologique, 4QTest-Lévi*ᶜ⁻ᵈ* (?) et 4QAJa' in: *The Madrid Qumran Congress* 449-501. [269-270]

* 4Q542 (4QTQahat ar) *4QTestament of Qahat* J. T. Milik, '4Q Visions de ᶜAmram', 97. E. Puech, 'Le Testament de Qahat en araméen de la grotte 4 (4QTQah)', Mémorial Jean Starcky Vol. I, 23-54. Remains of an Aramaic Testament of Qahat. Only one fragment of the work has been preserved, with remains of one and a half columns of text. [271-272]

* 4Q543 (4QᶜAmram*ᵃ* ar) *4QVisions of Amram*ᵃ J. T. Milik, '4QVisions de ᶜAmram et une citation d'Origène', RB 79 (1972) 77-99. R. Eisenman and M. Wise, *The Dead Sea Scrolls Uncovered*, 151-156. K. Beyer, *Ergänzungsband*, 85-92. Aramaic work of apocalyptic character, preserved in five copies with the title 'Visions of ᶜAmram'. Milik transcribes a few isolated fragments. [272-273]

* 4Q544 (4QᶜAmram*ᵇ* ar) *4QVisions of Amram*ᵇ J. T. Milik, '4QVisions de ᶜAmram', 77-99, pl. I. K. Beyer, *Ergänzungsband*, 85-92. [273]

* 4Q545 (4Q'Amram*ᶜ* ar) *4QVisions of Amram*ᶜ J. T. Milik. '4QVisions de 'Amram', 77-99; R. Eisenman and M. Wise, *The Dead Sea Scrolls Uncovered*, 151-156. K. Beyer, *Ergänzungsband*, 85-92. [274]

o 4Q546 (4Q'Amram^d ar) *4QVisions of Amram^d* J. T. Milik, '4QVisions de 'Amram', 77-99. R. Eisenman – M. Wise, *The Dead Sea Scrolls Uncovered*, 151-156. K. Beyer, *Ergänzungsband*, 85-92.

* 4Q547 (4Q'Amram^e ar) *4QVisions of Amram^e* R. Eisenman and M. Wise, *The Dead Sea Scrolls Uncovered*, 151-156. K. Beyer, *Ergänzungsband*, 85-92. [274]

* 4Q548 (4Q'Amram^f ar) *4QVisions of Amram^f* J. T. Milik, '4QVisons de 'Amram', 90. R. Eisenman – M. Wise, *The Dead Sea Scrolls Uncovered*, 151-156. K. Beyer, *Ergänzungsband*, 85-92. E. Puech, *La croyance des Esséniens en la vie future* (Gabalda, Paris 1993), 537-540. [275]

* 4Q549 *Work Mentioning Hur and Miriam* R. Eisenman and M. Wise, *The Dead Sea Scrolls Uncovered*, 93-94. K. Beyer, *Ergänzungsband*, 92-93. Aramaic work which mentions Hur and Miriam. A good fragment with remains of two columns and three smaller fragments. [275]

* 4Q550 *4QProto-Ester^{a-f}* J. T. Milik, 'Les modèles araméens du livre d'Esther dans la grotte 4 de Qumrân', in: E. Puech and F. García Martínez (eds.), *Mémorial Jean Starcky*. Vol. II (Paris 1992) 321-406. Five copies of a narrative work which might have been the source of the book of Esther. The sixth copy attributed by Milik to this composition seems to come from a different work, F. García Martínez, 'Las fronteras de lo Bíblico', Scripta Theologica 23 (1991), 774; K. Beyer, *Ergänzungsband*, 133. [291-292]

o 4Q551 *4QDaniel-Suzanna* (?) J. T. Milik, 'Daniel et Susanne à Qumrân?', in: *De la Torah au Messie*, 337-359. Minute fragments which the editor connects with the story of Suzannah. [289-290]

* 4Q552 *4QFour Kingdoms^a* R. Eisenman and M. Wise, *The Dead sea Scrolls Uncovered*, 71-73. K. Beyer, *Ergänzungsband*, 108-109. An Aramaic apocalyptic work about the four kingdoms. [138-139]

* 4Q553 *4QFour Kingsdoms^b* R. Eisenman and M. Wise, *The Dead Sea Scrolls Uncovered*, 71-73. K. Beyer, *Ergänzungsband*, 108-109. Another copy of the same composition. [139]

* 4Q554 (4QNJ^a ar) *4QNew Jerusalem^a* J. Starcky, 'Jérusalem et les manuscrits de la mer Morte', Le Monde de la Bible 1 (1977) 38-40. R. Eisenman and M. Wise, *The Dead Sea Scrolls Uncovered*, 39-46. K. Beyer, *Ergänzungsband*, 95-104. Copy of the Aramaic work. Description of the New Jerusalem. [129-131]

* 4Q555 (4QNJ^b ar) *4QNew Jerusalem^b* K. Beyer, *Ergänzungsband*, 95-104. Another copy of the same work. [131]

o 4Q556-557 *4QVisions* Minute remains of three Aramaic compositions about visions.

o 4Q558 *4QVision* K. Beyer, *Ergänzungsband*, 93-94. Aramic composition on papyrus, similar to the preceding compositions.

* 4Q559 *4QBiblical Chronology* J. Starcky, 'Le travail d'édition', 66. R. Eisenman and M. Wise, *The Dead Sea Scrolls Uncovered*, 92-93. Aramaic work written on papyrus which includes a genealogy which extends to the Judges. [228-229]

* 4Q560 *4Q Against Demons*   R. Eisenman and M. Wise, *The Dead Sea Scrolls Uncovered*, 265-267. K. Beyer, *Ergänzungsband*, 129-130. Remains of an Aramaic composition which apparently contains incantations. [378]

* 4Q561 (4QHor ar)   J. Starcky, 'Les quatre étapes du messianisme', 503, n. 66. R. Eisenman and M. Wise, *The Dead Sea Scrolls Uncovered*, 263-265. K. Beyer, *Ergänzungsband*, 125-127. Copy in Aramaic of the horoscope 4Q186. [456-457]

o 4Q562-575 *4QAramaic D-Z*   Unidentified fragments of remains of Aramaic works.

CAVE 5   Biblical manuscripts

5Q1 (5QDeut) *5QDeuteronomy*   J. T. Milik, DJD III, 169-171, pl. XXXVI. A fragment with remains of two columns of Deuteronomy.

5Q2 (5QKgs) *5QKings*   J. T. Milik, DJD III, 171-172, pl. XXXVI. Remains of 1Kgs 1.

5Q3 (5QIsa) *5QIsaiah*   J. T. Milik, DJD III, 173, pl. XXXVI. A fragment with remains of Is 40.

5Q4 (5QAmos) *5QAmos*   J. T. Milik, DJD III, 173-174, pl. XXXVI. A fragment with remains of Amos 1.

5Q5 (5QPs) *5QPsalms*   J. T. Milik, DJD III, 174, pl. XXXVII. Remains of Ps 119.

5Q6 (5QLam^a) *5QLamentations^a*   J. T. Milik, DJD III, 174-177, pls. XXXVII-XXXVIII. Remains of a copy of Lamentations.

5Q7 (5QLam^b) *5QLamentations^b*   J. T. Milik, DJD III, 177-178, pl. XXXVIII. A fragment with remains of another copy of Lam 4.

5Q8 (5QPhyl) *5Qphylactery*   J. T. Milik, DJD III, 178, pl. XXXVIII. Phylactery in its case. Not unrolled.

CAVE 5   Non-biblical manuscripts

o 5Q9 *5QWork with Place Names* J. T. Milik   DJD III, 179-180, pl. XXXVIII. Unidentified work with toponyms.

o 5Q10 (5QpMal?) *5QMalachi Pesher*   J. T. Milik, DJD III, 180, pl. XXXVIII, 288. Identified as possibly a commentary on Malachi, by J. Carmignac, 'Vestiges d'un pesher de Malachie (?)', RQ 4/13 (1963) 97-100. [203]

* 5Q11 (5QS) *5QRule of the Community*   J. T. Milik, DJD III, 180-181, pl. XXXVIII, 110-124. Possibly a copy of the Rule of the Community, with remains of 1QS ii 4-7 and ii 12-14 (?). [32]

* 5Q12 (5QD) *5QDamascus Document*   J. T. Milik, DJD III, 181, pl. XXXVIII, 189-198. Copy of the Damascus Document, with remains of CD IX 7-10. [70-71]

* 5Q13 *5QRule*   J. T. Milik, DJD III, 181-183, pls. XXXIX-XXXX, 210-211. Sectarian rule (?), inspired by 1QS and CD, which cites 1QS iii 4-5 in fragment 4. [73]

* 5Q14 *5QCurses*   J. T. Milik, DJD III, 183-184, pl. XL, 322. Written text with curses. [403]

* 5Q15 (5QNJ ar) *5QNew Jerusalem*   J. T. Milik, DJD III, 184-193. Remains of an Aramaic work: 'Description of the New Jerusalem', which includes readings from the copy of the same work from 4Q. [131-133]
o 5Q16-25 *5Qunclassified fragments*   Remains of unidentified works or of unclassified fragments, 360-367.

CAVE 6 Biblical manuscripts

6Q1 (1QpaleoGen) *6QGenesis*   M. Baillet, DJD III, 105-106, pl. XX. A fragment with remains of Gn 6.

6Q2 (6QpaleoLev) *6QLeviticus*   M. Baillet, DJD III, 106, pl. XX. A fragment in palaeo-Hebrew, with remains of Lv 8.

6Q3 (6QDeut?) *6QDeuteronomy* (?)   M. Baillet, DJD III, 106-107, pl. XX. A fragment with remains, possibly, of Dt 26.

6Q4 (6QKgs) *6QKings*   M. Baillet, DJD III, 107-112, pls. XX-XXII. Remains of a copy of 1 and 2 Kgs.

6Q6 (6QCant) *6QCanticles*   M. Baillet, DJD III, 112-114, pl. XXIII. A fragment with remains of Cant 1.

6Q7 (6QDan) *6QDaniel*   M. Baillet, DJD III, 114-116, pl. XXIII. Remains of a copy of Daniel.

CAVE 6 Non-biblical manuscripts

* 6Q8 (6QEnGiants ar) *6QGiants*   M. Baillet, DJD III, 116-119, pl. XXIV. Published as a 'Genesis apocryphon', it was identified by J. T. Milik, *The Books of Enoch*, 300.309, as another copy of the Aramaic Book of Giants. [262]
* 6Q9 *6QApocryphon on Samuel-Kings*   M. Baillet, DJD III, 119-123, pls. XXIV-XXV. Apocryphon, related to Sm-Kgs in content. [284]
o 6Q10 *6QProphecy*   M. Baillet, DJD III, 123-125, pl. XXVI. Prophetic text (?).
* 6Q11 *6QAllegory of the Vine*   M. Baillet, DJD III, 125-126, pl. XXVI. 'Allegory of the vine'. [403]
o 6Q12 *6QApocryphal Prophecy*   M. Baillet, DJD III, 126, pl. XXVI. 'Apocryphal prophecy' which uses a calculation in jubilees.
o 6Q13 *6QPriestly Prophecy*   M. Baillet, DJD III, 126-127, pl. XXVI. 'Priestly prophecy' related to Ezra-Nehemiah (?).
o 6Q14 *6QApocalypse*   M. Baillet, DJD III, 127-128, pl. XXVI. Aramaic 'Apocalyptic text'.
* 6Q15 (6QD) *6QDamascus Document*   M. Baillet, DJD III, 128-131, pl. XXVI. Copy of the Damascus Document. With remains of CD IV 19-21; V 13-14; V 18-VI 2; VI 20-VII 1, and a fragment with no equivalent in CD. [71]
* 6Q16 *6QBenediction*   M. Baillet, DJD III, 131-132, pl. XXVII. Blessings. [437]
o 6Q17 *6QCalendrical Document*   M. Baillet, DJD III, 132-133, pl. XXVII. Fragment of a calendar.

* 6Q18 *6QHymn* M. Baillet, DJD III, 133-136, pl. XXVII. Hymnic composition. [404]

* 6Q19 *6QGenesis* (?) M. Baillet, DJD III,, 136, pl. XXVIII. Text related to Gn (?). [227]

* 6Q20 *6QDeuteronomy* (?) M. Baillet, DJD III, 136-137, pl. XXVIII, 357. Text related to Dt (?). [228]

o 6Q21-22 *4Qunclassified fragments* M. Baillet, DJD III, 137, pl. XXVIII. Unidentified texts.

o 6Q23 M. Baillet, DJD III, 138, pl. XXVIII. Aramaic text; identified by J. T. Milik, *The Books of Enoch*, 91 as a copy of 4Q(Words of) Michael (?).

o 6Q24-25 *6Qunclassified fragments* M. Baillet, DJD III, 138, pl. XXVIII. Unidentified texts.

o 6Q26 *6Qfragments of accounts or contracts* M. Baillet, DJD III, 138-139, pl. XXIX. Remains of accounts or of a contract in Aramaic.

o 6Q27-31 *6Qunclassified fragments* M. Baillet, DJD III, 129-141, pl. XXIX. Unidentified texts.

CAVE 7 Biblical manuscripts

7Q1 (7QLxxExod) *7QSeptuagint Exodus* M. Baillet, DJD III, 142-143, pl. XXX. Remains of chap. 28 of Exodus, in Greek.

7Q2 (7QLxxEpJer) *7QEpistle of Jeremiah* M. Baillet, DJD III, 143, pl. XXX. Remains of the Letter of Jeremiah, vv. 43-44.

CAVE 7 Unidentified manuscripts

o 7Q3-19 *7Qunclassified fragments* M. Baillet, DJD III, 143-144, pl. XXX. Unidentified Greek manuscripts. J. O'Callaghan, '¿Papiros neotestamentarios en la cueva 7 de Qumrán?', Biblica 53 (1972) 91-100; . – '¿I Tim 3,16; 4,13 en 7Q4?', Biblica 53 (1972) 362-367; . – *Los papiros griegos de la cueva 7 de Qumrán* (BAC, Madrid 1974) has suggested identifying these remnants of papyrus as I Tim 3:16; 4:1.3 (7Q4); Mk 6:52-53 (7Q5); Mk 4:28 (7Q6,1); Acts 27:38 (7Q6:2); Mk 12:17 (7Q7); Jac 1:23-24 (7Q8); Rom 5:11-12 (7Q9); 2 Pet 1:15 (7Q10); Mc 6:48 (7Q15). Other scholars have suggested identifying them with other biblical texts [G. D. Fee, JBL 92 (1973) 109-112: 7Q4 = Num 14:23-24; P. Garnet, EvQ 45 (1973) 8-9: 7Q5 = Ex 36:10-11; C. H. Roberts, JTS 23 (1972) 446, n.4: 7Q5 = 2Kgs 5:13-14] or with non-biblical texts [G. W. Nebe, RQ 13 (1988) 629-632: 7Q4 = Enoch 103:3-4].

CAVE 8 Biblical manuscripts

8Q1 (8QGen) *8QGenesis* M. Baillet, DJD III, 147-148, pl. XXXI. Two fragments with remains of Gn 17-18.

8Q2 (8QPs) *8QPsalms*   M. Baillet, DJD III, 148-149, pl. XXXI. Remains of Pss 17-18.

8Q3 (8QPhyl) *8QPhylactery*   M. Baillet, DJD III, 149-157, pls. XXXII–XXXIII. Remains of Ex 13:1-10; 13:11-16; Dt 6:4-9; 11:13; 6:1-3; 10:20-22; 10:12-19; Ex 12:43-51; Dt 5:1-14; Ex 20:11; Dt 10:13(?); 11:2; 10:21-22; 11:1.6-12.

8Q4 (8QMez) *8QMezuzah*   M. Baillet, DJD III, 158-161, pl. XXXIV. Remains of Dt 10:12-11:21.

CAVE 8 Non-biblical manuscripts

* 8Q5 *8QHymn*   M. Baillet, DJD III, 161-163, pl. XXXV. Hymnic text. [404]

CAVE 9

Only a small fragment of papyrus, unidentified, was found, M. Baillet, DJD III, 163, pl. XXXV.

CAVE 10

Only an *ostracon* was found, a fragment of a jar with traces of two leters of the owner's name, M. Baillet, DJD III, 164, pl. XXXV.

CAVE 11 Biblical manuscripts

11Q1 (11QpaleoLev^a) *11QLeviticus^a*   D. N. Freedman, 'Variant Readings in the Leviticus Scroll from Qumran Cave 11', CBQ 36 (1974) 525-534; E. Tov, 'The Textual Character of 11QpaleoLev', Shnaton 3 (1978-79) 238-244 [Hebrew]; D. N. Freedman and K. A. Mathews, *The Paleo-Hebrew Leviticus Scroll (11QpaleoLev)* (Winona Lake 1985); F. García Martínez, 'Texts from Cave 11', *'The Dead Sea Scrolls: Forty Years of Research* (STDJ 11) (Leiden 1992). E. Puech, 'Notes en marge de 11QPaléoLévique', RB 96 (1989) 161-183. Copy of Leviticus in palaeo-Hebrew characters.

11Q2 (11QLev^b) *11QLeviticus^a*   J. P. M. van der Ploeg, 'Lév IX,23-X,2 dans un texte de Qumrân', in: S. Wagner (ed.), *Bibel und Qumran*, 153-155; . - 'Les manuscrits de la Grotte XI de Qumrân', RQ 12/45 (1985) 10; F. García Martínez, 'Texts from Cave 11'. Two fragments with remains of another copy of Leviticus.

11Q3 (11QDeut) *11QDeuteronomy*   J. P. M. van der Ploeg, 'Les manuscrits', 10; F. García Martínez, 'Texts from Cave 11'. A fragment with remains of Dt 1.

11Q4 (11QEz) *11QEzekiel*   W. H. Brownlee, 'The Scroll of Ezekiel from the Eleventh Qumran Cave', RQ 14/13 (1963) 11-28, pls. I–II.

* 11Q5 (11QPs^a) *11QPsalms^a*   J. A. Sanders, *The Psalms Scroll of Qumran Cave 11*

(11QPs^a^) *(Discoveries of the Judaean Desert of Jordan IV)* Oxford 1965; Y. Yadin, 'Another Fragment (E) of the Psalms Scroll from Qumran Cave 11 (11QPs^a^)', Textus 5 (1966), 1-10, pls. I-V. Copy of Pss, in a different sequence from MT, with other pseudepigraphical compositions. [304-310]

* 11Q6 (11QPs^b^) *11QPsalms^b^*   J.P.M. van der Ploeg, 'Fragments d'un manuscrit de psaumes de Qumrân (11QPs^b^)', RB 74 (1967), 408-412, pl. XVIII. Another copy of the foregoing MS. With remains of the 'Plea for Deliverance' 1-15 and of Pss 141:10; 133:1-3; 144:1-2; 118:1.15-16. [310-311]

  11Q7 (11QPs^c^) *11QPsalms^c^*   J.P.M. van der Ploeg, 'Fragments d'un Psautier de Qumrân', in: *Symbolae biblicae et mesopotamicae F. M. T. de Liagre Böhl dedicatae* (Brill, Leiden 1973) 308-309, pl. 1; . - 'Les manuscrits', 13; F. García Martínez, 'Texts from Cave 11'. Remains of another copy of Pss.

  11Q8 (11QPs^d^) *11QPsalms^d^*   J.P.M. van der Ploeg, 'Les manuscrits', 13; F. García Martínez, 'Texts from Cave 11'. Remains of another copy of Pss.

  11Q9 (11QPs^e^) *11QPsalms^e^*   J.P.M. van der Ploeg, 'Les manuscrits', 13; F. García Martínez, 'Texts from Cave 11'. Two fragments with remains of Pss 36-37 and 86, possibly another copy of Pss, or part of 11Q7.

CAVE 11   Non-biblical manuscripts

* 11Q10 (11QtgJob) *11QTargum of Job*   J.P.M. van der Ploeg and A.S. van der Woude, *Le targum de Job de la grotte XI de Qumrân* (KNAW-Brill, Leiden 1971). B. Zuckerman, 'A Fragment of an Unstudied Column of 11QtgJob: A Preliminary Report', Newsletter The Comprehensive Aramaic Lexicon 10 (1993), 1-7. For the last column see E. Puech – F. García, 'Remarques sur la Colonne XXXVIII de 11QtgJob', RQ 9/35 (1978) 401-407. Aramaic Targum of Job. [143-153]

* 11Q11 (11QApPs^a^) *11QApocryphal Psalms^a^*   J.P.M. van der Ploeg, 'Le Psaume XCI dans une recension de Qumrân', RB 72 (1965) 210-217, pls. VIII-IX; . - 'Un petit rouleau de psaumes apocryphes (11QPsAp^a^)', in: *Tradition und Glaube*, 128-139, pls. II-VII; E. Puech, 'Les deux derniers psaumes davidiques du rituel d'exorcisme 11QPsAp^a^ IV, 4-V, 14', in: *Forty Years of Research in the Dead Sea Scrolls*. Psalms for expelling demons. The MS ends with Ps 91. [376-378]

* 11Q12 (11QJub) *11QJubilees*   A.S. van der Woude, 'Fragmente des Buches Jubiläen aus Qumran Höhle XI (11QJub)', in: *Tradition und Glaube*, 140-146, pl. VIII; J.T. Milik, 'À propos de 11QJub', Biblica 54 (1973) 77-78; F. García Martínez, 'Texts from Cave 11'. Copy of the Book of Jubilees. [241-242]

* 11Q13 (11QMelch) *11QMechizedec*   A.S. van der Woude, 'Melchisedek als himmlische Erlösergestalt in den neugefundenen eschatologischen Midraschim aus Qumran Höhle XI', Oudtestamentische Studiën 14 (1965) 354-373, pl. 1; J.T. Milik, 'Milkî-reša^c^', 96-109.124-126; E. Puech, 'Notes dur le manuscrit de 11QMelkîsédeQ', RQ 12/48 (1987) 483-513. Eschatological pesher, based on Lv 28, with the angelic form of Melchizedek as the protagonist. [139-140]

* 11Q14 (11QBer) *11QBlessings*   A.S. van der Woude, 'Ein neuer Segensspruch aus Qumran (11QBer)', en: Bibel und Qumran, 253-258, pl.1. J. Strugnell, RB 77 (1970), 268 denotes another copy of the same work from Cave 4 (4Q285); B. Nitzan, 'Benedictions and Instructions from Qumran for the Eschatological Community (11QBer, 4Q285)', RQ 16/61 (1993), 77-90. Collection of Blessings, which come from a copy of the War Scroll. [124]

* 11Q15 (11QHymns^a) *11QHymns^a*   J.P.M. van der Ploeg, 'Les manuscrits', 11-12. Collection of hymns. Only a small fragment has been preserved. [404]

o 11Q16 (11QHymns^b) *11QHymns^b*   J.P.M. van der Ploeg, 'Les manuscrits', 11-12. F. García Martínez, 'Texts from Cave 11'. Another collection of hymns.

* 11Q17 (11QShirShabb) *11QSongs of the Sabbath Sacrifice*   A.S. van der Woude, 'Fragmente einer Rolle der Lieder für das Sabbatopfer aus Höhle XI von Qumran', in: *Von Kanaan bis Kerala* (AOAT 211) (Kevelaer-Neukirchen-Vluyn 1982) 311-332, pls. 1-6; C. Newsom, *Songs of the Sabbath Sacrifice*, 361-387, pls. XVII-XIX; F. García Martínez, 'Texts from Cave 11'. Copy of the work 'Songs of the sabbath sacrifice' which preserves the last part of the composition, with remains of the songs for the tenth, eleventh, twelfth and thirteenth sabbaths. [430-431]

* 11Q18 (11QJN ar) *11QNew Jerusalem*   B. Jongeling, 'Publication provisoire d'un fragment provenant de la grotte 11 de Qumrân (11QJérNouv ar)', JSJ 1 (1970) 58-64; F. García Martínez, 'The Last Surviving Columns of 11QNJ', *The Scriptures and the Scrolls*, 178-192, pl. 3-9. K. Beyer, *Ergänzungsband*, 95-104. Copy of an Aramaic work: 'Description of the New Jerusalem'. [143-153]

* 11Q19 (11QTemple^a) *11QTemple Scroll^a*   Y. Yadin, *Megillat ham-miqdash – The Temple Scroll*, 3 vols. + Suppl. (Jerusalem 1977) (Hebrew edition; English edition with supplements, 1983). Complete edition of the 'Temple Scroll'.

* 11Q20 (11QTemple^b) *11QTemple Scroll^b*   Y. Yadin, *Megillat ham-miqdash*, vol. III. Supplementary Plates, 35-40; A.S. van der Woude, 'Ein bisher unveröffentlichtes Fragment der Tempelrolle', RQ 13 (1988), 89-92; M.O. Wise, 'A New Manuscript Joint in the "Festival of Wood Offering" (Temple Scroll XXIII)', JNES 47 (1988), 113-121. F. García Martínez, '11QTemple^b: A Preliminary Publication', *The Madrid Qumran Congress*, 363-390, pl. 9-15. B.Z. Wacholder, 'The Fragmentary Remains of 11QTorah (Temple Scroll)', HUCA 62 (1991), 1-116. [179-184]

o 11Q21-25 *11Qunclassified fragments*   F. García Martínez, 'Texts from Cave 11'. Remains of unidentified works.

Published by
E. J. Brill, Plantijnstraat 2, PO Box 9000, 2300 PA Leiden, the Netherlands
E. J. Brill (USA) Inc, 24 Hudson Street, Kinderhook, NY 12106, USA

Cover Design: Roland van Helden
Typographical Design: Alje Olthof
This book was set in Ehrhardt typeface by Perfect Service, Schoonhoven,
the Netherlands and printed by the Sigma Press, Zoetermeer, the Netherlands

The paper in this book meets the guidelines for performance and durability of the
Committee on Production Guidelines for Book Longevity of the Council on Library
Resources